MW01232924

# Microsoft® FrontPage

# UNLEASHED

*William Robert Stanek, et al.*

201 West 103rd Street
Indianapolis, IN 46290

# Copyright © 1996 by Sams.net Publishing

FIRST EDITION

International Standard Book Number: 1-57521-140-8

Library of Congress Catalog Card Number: 96-68592

99  98  97  96          4  3  2  1

Interpretation of the printing code: the rightmost double-digit number is the year of the book's printing; the rightmost single-digit, the number of the book's printing. For example, a printing code of 96-1 shows that the first printing of the book occurred in 1996.

*Composed in AGaramond and MCPdigital by Macmillan Computer Publishing*

*Printed in the United States of America*

| | |
|---|---|
| **President, Sams Publishing** | *Richard K. Swadley* |
| **Publishing Manager** | *Mark Taber* |
| **Managing Editor** | *Cindy Morrow* |
| **Director of Marketing** | *John Pierce* |
| **Assistant Marketing Managers** | *Kristina Perry* |
| | *Rachel Wolfe* |

**Acquisitions Editor**
*Beverly M. Eppink*

**Development Editor**
*Kelly Murdock*

**Software Development Specialist**
*Bob Correll*

**Production Editor**
*Ryan Rader*

**Copy Editors**
*Margaret Berson, Anna Huff*
*Howard Jones, Marla Reece*
*Kris Simmons, Beth Spencer*
*Heather Stith, Faithe Wempen*
*Colleen Williams*

**Indexer**
*Chris Barrick*

**Technical Reviewer**
*Bill Vernon*

**Editorial Coordinator**
*Bill Whitmer*

**Technical Edit Coordinator**
*Lorraine Schaffer*

**Resource Coordinator**
*Deborah Frisby*

**Editorial Assistants**
*Carol Ackerman*
*Andi Richter*
*Rhonda Tinch-Mize*

**Cover Designer**
*Tim Amrhein*

**Book Designer**
*Gary Adair*

**Copy Writer**
*Peter Fuller*

**Production Team Supervisor**
*Brad Chinn*

**Production**
*Mike Dietsch, Chris Livengood*
*Paula Lowell, Andrew Stone*

# Overview

# Contents

## Part II  FrontPage Basics

## Part V   Templates, Web Wizards, and WebBots

## Part VIII   Advanced Issues: Multimedia, CGI, and Indexed Databases

## Part IX   Putting It All Together

# Acknowledgments

Beverly Eppink deserves a note of thanks for shepherding my many projects from inception to completion. Thanks for working the extra hours to ensure that we had a truly outstanding book, borrowing time from your weekends to check up on progress when needed, and being there when the inevitable problems arose.

Once again, the team at Sams.net has been terrific to work with! It is wonderful to work with a team of experts who really know their stuff. Mark Taber's wisdom and quick decision making helped in the crucial development stages. Kelly Murdock scoured my chapters in development review. Ryan Rader kept the book on track in editing.

Special thanks to my wife and family who continue to put up with the tappety-tap of my keyboard at all hours of the day and night. Without your support, this book wouldn't have been possible.

—*William R. Stanek*

# About the Authors

## Lead Author

**William R. Stanek** is a leading Internet technology expert and also one of the hottest technology writers today. Stanek (`director@tvp.com`) is a working professional who directs an Internet start-up company called The Virtual Press (`http://tvp.com/` and mirror site `http://www.tvpress.com/`). As a publisher and writer with more than 10 years of experience on networks, Stanek brings a solid voice of experience on the Internet and electronic publishing to his many projects. He has been involved in the commercial Internet community since 1991 and was first introduced to Internet e-mail in 1988 when he worked for the government. His years of practical experience are backed by a solid education: Master of Science in Information Systems and a Bachelor of Science in Computer Science. In addition to authoring best-sellers such as Sams.net's *Web Publishing Unleashed* and *Microsoft FrontPage Unleashed*, Stanek advises corporate clients and develops hot new Web sites.

Stanek served in the Persian Gulf War as a combat crew member on an Electronic Warfare aircraft. During the war, he flew on numerous combat missions into Iraq and was awarded nine medals for his wartime service, including one of our nation's highest flying honors, the Air Force Distinguished Flying Cross. He has written many books, articles, and essays. His book-length projects include nine fiction titles and seven nonfiction titles. When he's not writing or working, he spends time with his family, his favorite time of the day being when he reads to his youngest child.

## Contributing Authors

**Mark L. Chambers** has been a PC software technical writer, bulletin board system operator, and game programmer for more than 10 years. He is the author of Que's *Running a Perfect BBS* and has contributed chapters for Que's *Introduction to PC Communications* and *Using PC Tools 8*. You can reach him on the Internet at `sysop@batboard.org`.

**Rick Darnell** (`darnell@montana.com`) is a midwest native currently living with his wife and two daughters in Missoula, MT. He began his career in print at a small weekly newspaper after graduating from Kansas State University with a degree in broadcasting. While spending time as a freelance journalist and writer, Rick has seen the full gamut of personal computers, since starting out with a Radio Shack Model I in the late 1970s. When not in front of his computer, he serves as a volunteer firefighter and member of a regional hazardous materials response team.

**Sanjaya Hettihewa** is an accomplished Webmaster and a consultant specializing in integrating Windows NT–based information systems on the Internet. He has been living in the Washington DC area for the last six years and is a Computer Science major attending the University of Maryland. For the last two years, Sanjaya has done extensive research in setting up Internet information systems with Windows NT as well as exploring various ways of utilizing Windows NT's unique features to publish information on the Internet. Sanjaya is the author of *Web Site Developer's Guide for Windows NT* and co-author of *Windows NT Unleashed* by Sams Publishing. Sanjaya can be reached at `http://www.NetInnovation.com/` (or, if you prefer the old-fashioned way, `sanjaya@NetInnovation.com`).

**Dick Oliver** has authored and co-authored several graphics programs, articles, and books including *Web Page Wizardry, Netscape Unleashed, Internet Graphics Gallery,* and *Tricks of the Graphics Gurus.* Dick is president of Cedar Software of Wolcott, Vermont, which specializes in new approaches to advanced graphics and 3D modeling. He also publishes the Nonlinear Nonsense netletter (`http://netletter.com/`), an online Web site and paper newsletter covering creative computer graphics. You can contact him at `dicko@netletter.com`.

**Ned Snell** is an award-winning computer journalist and author. Ten years ago, after a brief career as a teacher, Ned entered the software industry as a documentation and training specialist for several of the world's largest software companies. He then moved into the computer trade magazine business, where he served as a staff writer and eventually editor for several national publications.

In 1991, he became a freelancer so that he could pursue his dual professions: computer journalist and actor. Since then, he has written for international publications such as *Datamation* and *Software* magazine, and he has also developed documentation and training materials for diabetes management software. At the same time, he has acted in regional professional theaters, commercials, and industrial films. Ned is the author of the Sams titles *Laura Lemay's Web Workshop: Netscape Navigator Gold 3, Navigating the Microsoft Network, Navigating the Internet with Windows 95* (now in a Deluxe Edition with CD), *Curious About the Internet* and *Souping Up Windows.* He lives with his wife—Nancy Gonzales, a writer and translator—and their two sons in Florida ('cause it's warm there).

# Tell Us What You Think!

As a reader, you are the most important critic and commentator of our books. We value your opinion and want to know what we're doing right, what we could do better, what areas you'd like to see us publish in, and any other words of wisdom you're willing to pass our way. You can help us make strong books that meet your needs and give you the computer guidance you require.

Do you have access to CompuServe or the World Wide Web? Then check out our CompuServe forum by typing **GO SAMS** at any prompt. If you prefer the World Wide Web, check out our site at `http://www.mcp.com`.

> **NOTE**
>
> If you have a technical question about this book, call the technical support line at (800) 571-5840, ext. 3668.

As the team leader of the group that created this book, I welcome your comments. You can fax, e-mail, or write me directly to let me know what you did or didn't like about this book—as well as what we can do to make our books stronger. Here's the information:

FAX:     317-581-4669

E-mail:  `newtech_mgr@sams.mcp.com`

Mail:    Mark Taber
         Comments Department
         Sams Publishing
         201 W. 103rd Street
         Indianapolis, IN  46290

# Introduction

*by William Robert Stanek*

Web technologies are growing at a phenomenal rate. At one time, there was only HTML; now there is HTML 3, HTML extensions for Netscape and Microsoft Explorer, VRML, CGI, Java, and much more. Keeping pace with this ever-growing array of technology is confusing. Enter FrontPage, an integrated WYSIWYG tool for creating and managing Web sites that is years ahead of the competition.

As the first authoring tool created for nonprogrammers that is robust enough for professional Web developers, FrontPage provides everything you need to design, publish, and manage your Internet or intranet Web site. Millions of Microsoft Office users around the world will find that FrontPage uses the very familiar Microsoft interface. In fact, FrontPage is the only Web site creation and management tool that is a member of the Microsoft Office family of applications. All tools included in FrontPage are also part of one complete package. You will find that it is surprisingly easy to become a Web publisher using FrontPage!

Whether your Web publishing plans are large or small, you do not want to wait any longer to get into the action. By the end of 1998, more than 100 million people will have access to the global Internet and to the World Wide Web. What this means is that for a few dollars a month, you can reach a potential audience of millions. If you think this is hype, think again. The World Wide Web has caught the eye of the media, businesses, entrepreneurs, and governments. Media coverage of the Internet and related issues grows every day. Thousands of articles related to the Internet are published every month in books, magazines, newspapers, and newsletters. You will find discussions about the Internet and the Web on TV shows, radio, and the news. You will also find addresses to Web pages in all forms of advertising, from magazine ads to television commercials.

As you read this book, you will learn about the things that the Web has to offer. I have taken great care to provide invaluable tips and pour my expertise into every page of *Microsoft FrontPage Unleashed*. Today's Web publishers have powerful resources at their fingertips, and this book shows how to use every one of them.

## Who Should Read This Book

*Microsoft FrontPage Unleashed* is for anyone who wants to publish on the Web or who has considered publishing on the Web. Although this book is intended for those with a casual to accomplished knowledge of the Internet or the World Wide Web, the plain English approach makes this book perfect for just about anyone. I truly hope you find this book to be invaluable as you plot your course to success in Web publishing.

# How This Book Is Organized

This book is designed to be the most comprehensive resource guide to FrontPage available anywhere. Chapter by chapter, you will learn everything you need to know to create, design, and publish dazzling Web publications with FrontPage.

Part I, "Getting Started in Web Publishing," covers everything you need to know to get started as a Web publisher. Chapter 1 explores the issues you should consider before publishing on the Web. Coverage of these issues is intended to save you time, money, and resources. Chapter 2 answers the questions about why you should publish on the Web, what you can publish on the Web, and who is already publishing on the Web. Chapter 3 helps you design and plan an intranet.

Part II, "FrontPage Basics," introduces you to the FrontPage development environment. In Chapter 4, you get a first glimpse of the Personal Web Server, the FrontPage Explorer, and the FrontPage Editor. You also learn about hot features such as Web Wizards, templates, and WebBots. A quick walkthrough of the FrontPage Explorer and the FrontPage Editor is the subject of Chapter 5. Afterward, in Chapters 6 and 7, you learn the basics of creating pages and Webs with FrontPage.

Part III, "Working with FrontPage," explores the WYSIWYG features of FrontPage and includes extensive coverage of the hottest and latest Web publishing issues. Chapter 8 is a power primer for creating Web documents with FrontPage. You will find useful tips, expert advice, and a strong emphasis on sound design. Chapter 9 covers adding features to your pages, such as hypertext references and lists. The chapter also discusses how to use alternative document transfer protocols. Chapter 10 tells you when, how, and why to use images and image maps in your Web publications. Chapter 11 tells you how to create forms using the Forms Wizard. Chapters 12 and 13 explore two of the hottest elements in Web publishing: tables and frames. Not only do leading browsers such as Netscape and Internet Explorer support tables and frames, but these elements are also a part of the new HTML specification.

Integrating FrontPage with Microsoft Office is a key concept that millions of MS Office users will want to learn all about, and Part IV, "Microsoft Office Web Publishing," provides you with everything you need to know. The first chapter in this part, Chapter 14, introduces the Microsoft Internet Assistant and includes tips for installing and configuring the Internet Assistant on your system. Chapter 15 examines the Internet Assistant for Word and discusses how to use Word with FrontPage. Chapter 16 examines the Internet Assistant for PowerPoint and discusses how to use PowerPoint with FrontPage. Chapter 17 examines the Internet Assistants for Excel, Access, and Schedule+.

Part V, "Templates, Web Wizards, and WebBots," explores three of the hottest features of FrontPage and how they make Web publishing a snap. Chapter 18 looks at the dozens of templates included in FrontPage. Not only will creating Web pages with templates save you time, but the templates themselves are guides that can help you design better pages. In Chapter 19, you learn how to automatically generate content for your Web page with Web Wizards. The final chapter in this section looks at WebBots. At the touch of a button, WebBots enable you to add advanced capabilities to your Web site, including interactive forms, navigation bars, text searches, and discussion forums, with no programming involved at all.

Customizing FrontPage with the FrontPage Developer's Kit is the subject of Part VI, "Using the FrontPage Developer's Kit." Chapter 21 introduces you to the features of the developer's kit, and Chapters 22 and 23 tell you how to create your own templates and wizards. Not only will you be able to use these templates and wizards with FrontPage, but you can also share the templates and wizards with other FrontPage publishers.

Although managing your Web site is the key topic in Part VII, "Managing Your Web," the section covers everything you need to know to set up, configure, manage, and maintain Web sites. In Chapter 24, you learn all about using Web servers with FrontPage. Chapter 25 explores Web server administration. Because server security is an extremely important aspect of server management, Chapter 26 looks at how you can manage server security with built-in FrontPage features. Web publishers who plan to create advanced Web sites with multiple authors will also want to know how to manage these large projects. Chapter 27 tells you how to create and manage discussion groups. Finally, because no section on server management would be complete without a troubleshooting guide, Chapter 28 provides you with expert advice on troubleshooting.

Part VIII, "Advanced Issues: Multimedia, CGI, and Indexed Databases," is a power tour of advanced concepts related to Web publishing. Chapter 29 covers the specifics of adding multimedia (sound and video) to Web publications. The chapter tells you when, how, and why to use sound and video. Chapter 30 provides a top-notch introduction to CGI scripts that will not leave you confused and wondering how it all works. Chapter 31 shows you firsthand how to use the hypertext facilities of the Web to put the world's most powerful search engines at your fingertips. The chapter also provides in-depth coverage on how to build an indexed database. Chapters 32 and 33 tell you how to use the most powerful scripting languages available today: JavaScript and VBScript. Chapter 34 is for anyone who wants to create documents using the hottest Web programming language—Java.

Practical application of this book's many topics is the subject of Part IX, "Putting It All Together." Every success story has a beginning, and in Web publishing, the first step is creating and publishing a Web page following sound design techniques. Chapter 35 tells you how to do this. The chapter covers everything you need to know to build a terrific home page: publishing strategies, page structure, creating the page, adding features, proofing the page, testing the page, and publishing the page. Creating and publishing your first Web page is only a starting point. The next chapter tells you how to build a cool Web site. But the chapter doesn't stop there; it goes on to tell you how to publicize your Web site as well. Chapter 37 tells you how to publish on an intranet. You will definitely find the detailed information in this chapter to be invaluable as you design and publish your corporate intranet site.

The final section of the book puts the reference resources that you need into your hands. Appendix A is an HTML reference. Appendix B is an ActiveX Control Automation Command Reference. Appendix C gives a VBScript reference. Finally, Appendix D gives you a rundown of everything on the book's CD-ROM.

# Getting Started in Web Publishing

**PART**

I

# Web Publishing
# Issues To Consider

1

*by William
Robert Stanek*

**IN THIS CHAPTER**

The World Wide Web is rapidly evolving into a medium that rivals television for information content and entertainment value. Millions of people and thousands of businesses around the world are racing to get connected to the global Internet and the World Wide Web because the Web is the most powerful and least expensive medium to publish in. Whether you are an information provider or simply a creative person who wants to publish your own work, you will find that there is no other medium that empowers the individual like the Web. The Web levels the playing field, allowing a one-person operation to compete head-to-head with corporate conglomerates that employ thousands of people.

To publish successfully on the Web, you do not have to be a genius, a programmer, or a computer guru with insider secrets. What you need are the practical advice, tips, and techniques you will find throughout this book. Many books on Internet and Web publishing discuss theories, cover key subjects, and show basic examples, but rarely follow a practical approach to Web publishing. Books without practical examples and genuinely useful information can leave you wondering where to start, how to start, and what to do when you do finally manage to start. This book's chapters are filled with useful information designed to unleash the topic of Web publishing with FrontPage and help you become one of the thousands of successful Web publishers providing ideas, services, and products to millions of Web users.

This chapter provides an overview of some basic information you need to know and decisions you need to make before you start publishing on the Web.

# What Is FrontPage, and Why Do You Need It?

Web technologies are growing at a phenomenal rate. When once there was only HyperText Markup Language (HTML), now there is HTML 3.2, HTML extensions for Netscape and Microsoft Explorer, VRML, CGI, Java, ActiveX, and much more. Keeping pace with this ever growing array of technology is confusing. Enter FrontPage, an integrated what-you-see-is-what-you-get (WYSIWYG) tool for creating and managing Web sites that is years ahead of the competition.

Microsoft FrontPage is much more than an easy-to-use tool for creating and managing Web sites. It will soon be the authoring and management tool of choice for thousands of current Web publishers, thousands of large and small businesses seeking to set up intranets, and thousands of people around the world who thought they would never be able to establish a presence on the Web due to the complexity of creating and managing a world-class Web site.

Millions of Microsoft Office users around the world will find that FrontPage utilizes the very familiar Microsoft interface. In fact, FrontPage is the only Web site creation and management tool that is a member of the Microsoft Office family of applications. All tools included in FrontPage are also part of one complete package. You will find that it is surprisingly easy to become a Web publisher using FrontPage!

# WYSIWYG Creation of Advanced HTML Documents

FrontPage includes two powerful tools for creating advanced HTML documents using a WYSIWYG authoring environment: The FrontPage Explorer and the FrontPage Editor. Not only does the FrontPage WYSIWYG authoring environment display documents in a style that mirrors the style of the actual published documents, but the FrontPage Explorer and FrontPage Editor are also very easy to use.

The FrontPage Explorer, as shown in Figure 1.1, presents your Web site in a manner similar to the Windows 95 Explorer and simplifies Web site creation and maintenance, particularly for complex sites. The FrontPage Explorer gives you multiple ways to view your site. The two primary views are shown in Figure 1.1.

**FIGURE 1.1.**

*The FrontPage Explorer: a hot graphical display tool.*

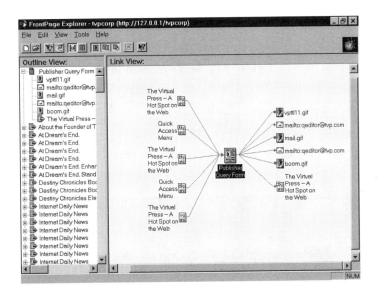

As you can see, Outline View provides a hierarchical representation of your Web site with icons that indicate the different kinds of pages in your Web. You can expand the view to show all links to images and pages, or collapse the view for a higher-level picture. Link View shows a graphical representation of your Web site that includes icons and titles with arrows between pages indicating the direction of each link. The final view, Summary View, displays a list of all pages, images, and other files used in your Web site. You can sort this list by title, author, modification date, creation date, and any comments you've added.

Another FrontPage Explorer feature is the drag-and-drop interface, which lets you create a link by simply dragging a page or image icon to a specific place on a page in the FrontPage Editor. With the FrontPage Editor (shown in Figure 1.2), you can create your Web pages in a fully WYSIWYG environment. Because FrontPage supports all standard file formats and protocols, you can link to any file, such as MPEG or PDF, as well as link to any FTP site, Gopher site, or newsgroup.

**FIGURE 1.2.**

*The FrontPage Editor: WYSIWYG authoring at its best!*

Also, as you can see from Figure 1.2, the FrontPage Editor fully supports image formats and displays images as you will see them in your published Web page. In fact, you can import any of more than a dozen common image formats into your Web page, and based on your selection, FrontPage will automatically convert these image formats to either the Graphical Interchange Format (GIF) or Joint Picture Experts Group (JPEG) format.

> **NOTE**
>
> With over 99 percent of all images on the Web in either GIF or JPEG format, you definitely want your images to be in one of these formats. However, if you don't want to convert the image format, FrontPage will still let you use the image.

# Page Wizards for Tables, Forms, Frames, and More

As the first authoring tool created for nonprogrammers that is robust enough for professional Web developers, FrontPage provides everything you need to design, publish, and manage your Internet or intranet Web site. Responding to the need for powerful, easy-to-use Web creation tools, FrontPage provides Web authoring and editing features that help you create rich, dynamic Web sites. One of the most advanced features is the Page Wizard.

Page Wizards help you automatically generate content for your Web page. If you want to create Netscape frame-enhanced documents, follow the frame wizard's step-by-step advice. If you want to create tables using the advanced layout features of HTML 3.2, use the table wizard and you'll be able to create an advanced table in minutes. If you want to create fill-out forms that use a search engine, use the form wizard and then drop a WebBot into your page, and you're ready to go.

At the touch of a button, WebBots allow you to add advanced capabilities to your Web site, including interactive forms, navigation bars, text searches, and discussion forums. WebBots offer drop-in interactive functionality, which greatly streamlines the development process and eliminates the need to write your own scripts or add complicated HTML commands. No programming is involved at all.

Figure 1.3 shows the Frames Wizard setup page. This page allows you to set the number of columns and rows in the frame-enhanced document. Because you can manipulate the size of any frame using the mouse, there is no more guess work in determining the frame size.

**FIGURE 1.3.**

*The Frames Wizard: frame-enhancing your documents made easy.*

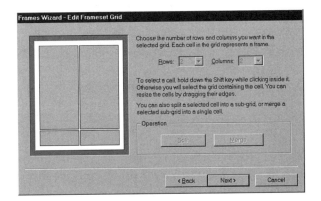

# The Personal Web Server and Administration Tools

Thousands of Web publishers face the complex task of keeping their sites up-to-date. With addresses to Web sites and pages changing every day, it is a frustrating task simply to keep sites current. FrontPage introduces integrated tools that virtually do the job for you. For example, using a feature called backlink, you can tell FrontPage to verify every link in your entire Web site. FrontPage examines onsite and offsite links in the background while you go on to other tasks. When it finishes, you will see a complete report of all invalid and questionable links. Using a single interface, you can then update these links automatically for specific pages or for all pages in your Web site. This means an end to chasing down broken links.

FrontPage also includes a Web server called the Personal Web Server that fully supports the Hypertext Transfer Protocol (HTTP) and the Common Gateway Interface (CGI) standards. If you don't have a Web server, you can use the Personal Web Server to serve one Web site or a dozen Web sites to the Internet community. If you already have a Web site, you can use Microsoft Server Extensions and integrate your Web site with FrontPage. The extensions do much more than simple integration. They let you effortlessly copy or post your Web site between platforms and to other servers while still allowing you to use all FrontPage features.

FrontPage also includes a server administration tool that manages security and access to your server. The FrontPage Server Administrator is shown in Figure 1.4.

**FIGURE 1.4.**

*The FrontPage Server Administrator: point-and-click Web site administration.*

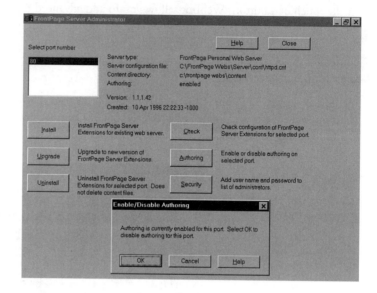

With this tool, access is controlled with password and Internet Protocol (IP) address user-authentication, which keeps unwanted visitors from modifying information. Access controls are divided into categories for administrators, authors, and end users with permissions ranging from unrestricted to content viewing only. You can set and modify these permissions using a simple point-and-click interface. FrontPage also allows you to use firewalls via proxy servers.

# Overview of Web Publishing's Past

The World Wide Web is an open-ended information system designed specifically with ease of use and of document interchange in mind. In early 1989, Tim Berners-Lee of the European Laboratory for Particle Physics (CERN) proposed the Web as a way for scientists around the world to collaborate using a global information system based on hypertext. Work on the World Wide Web project proceeded slowly but amazingly, and near the end of 1990, the pieces started to fall into place.

In the fall of 1990, the first text-only browsers were implemented and CERN scientists could access hypertext files and other information at CERN. However, the structure of hypertext documents and the way they would be transferred to remote sites still had to be further defined. Based on proposals by Berners-Lee, the structure of hypertext documents was defined by a new language called the HyperText Markup Language (HTML). HTML was based on a subset of the Standard Generalized Markup Language (SGML) that was already in wide use at the time. To transfer HTML documents to remote sites, a new protocol was devised. This protocol is called HTTP.

HTTP offers a means of moving from document to document and indexing within documents. The power of hypertext is in its simplicity and transparency. Users can navigate through a global network of resources at the touch of a button. Hypertext documents are linked together through keywords or specified hot areas within the document. These hot areas could be graphical icons or even parts of indexed maps. When a new word or idea is introduced, hypertext makes it possible to jump to another document containing complete information on the new topic. Readers see links as highlighted keywords or images displayed graphically. They can access additional documents or resources by selecting the highlighted keywords or images.

In the fall of 1991, conference-goers around the world started hearing about the promise and ease of hypertext. A few people started talking about hypertext and its potential, but sparks still weren't flying. In early 1993 there were only about 50 Web sites worldwide. Then a wonderful thing happened. A browser enabling users to exploit the graphical capabilities of the Web was developed at the National Center for Supercomputing Applications (NCSA). NCSA called the browser Mosaic. For a time, it seemed the Web and Mosaic were synonymous. Interest in the Web began to grow—at first a trickle of interest, and then a great flood of enthusiasm. Looking back, it seems the Web sprang to life overnight. Today, the Web is the hottest and fastest growing area of the Internet, and Mosaic is only one of the dozens of available browsers.

While you undoubtedly have used a browser before, you might not have thought about the processes that make a browser work the way it does. The purpose of a browser is to request and display information. Another term for a browser is a client. Clients make requests to servers. Servers process requests made by clients based on a set of rules for communicating on the network called a protocol. Protocols specify how the programs talk to each other and what meaning to give to the data they receive. Many protocols are in use on the Internet, and the Web makes use of them all. However, the primary protocol in use on the Web is HTTP.

Generally, HTTP processes are transparent to users. To initiate a request for information from a server, all the user has to do is activate a hypertext reference. The user's browser takes care of interpreting the hypertext transfer commands and communicating requests. The mechanism on the receiving end, which is processing the requests, is a program called the Hypertext Transfer Protocol Daemon (HTTPD). A *daemon* is a UNIX term for a program that processes requests. If you have used a UNIX system, you have probably unknowingly sent requests to the Line-Printer Daemon (LPD) to print material to a printer using the commands lp or lpr. The HTTPD resides on the Web server, which is at the heart of your connection to the Web.

Using the hypertext facilities of the Web, you have the freedom to provide information to readers in powerfully innovative ways. The entrepreneurs who fostered the growth of the Web started by creating small publications that used few of the Web's graphical and multimedia capabilities. This changed dramatically in a few short years, and today's Web publications use many of the graphical, interactive, and multimedia features of the Web. New ways to publish on the

Web are constantly being defined, and the features that tomorrow's publications will have may amaze you.

A recent development in HTML publishing is the specification for HTML 3.2. HTML 3.2 is a subset of the original HTML 3.0 specification and is based on features and extensions used in Web documents before May 1996. The first draft of the HTML 3.2 specification was released in May 1996. Because the developers of FrontPage had the foresight to support many extensions to HTML, FrontPage directly supports nearly all HTML 3.2 elements.

Yet, the Web is not defined by HTML alone. Many Web publishers are going back to the standard language that HTML is based upon. SGML is an advanced markup language that, although complex, offers better control over the layout of documents than HTML. SGML is also the basis for many page definition languages used by publishing production systems such as Adobe Acrobat and Common Ground.

While some Web publishers are looking at the origins of Web publishing, others are taking giant leaps forward. These giant leaps forward are possible in part due to innovators such as Netscape Communications Corporation, Microsoft Corporation, and Sun Microsystems, Inc. In the fall of 1994, Netscape Communications Corporation released the first browser to support unique extensions to HTML. The Netscape Navigator took the Internet community by storm and quickly became the most popular browser on the Net. (Netscape's Web site is featured in Figure 1.5.) FrontPage fully supports Netscape Navigator 1.0 and 2.0 extensions. You will see these extensions highlighted throughout this book.

**FIGURE 1.5.**

*The Netscape Navigator: a hot Web browser.*

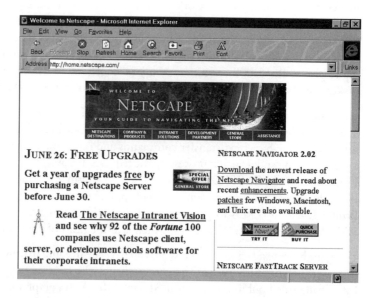

The browser that might replace top-dog Netscape Navigator is Microsoft's Internet Explorer. Microsoft's Web site is featured in Figure 1.6, and as you can imagine, the site showcases the

Internet Explorer browser and FrontPage. Internet Explorer features extensions that enable Web publishers to add soundtracks and live video segments to their Web publications. When a reader accesses a publication with a soundtrack or a live video segment, the sound or video plays automatically if the reader's browser supports these extensions. FrontPage directly supports most Internet Explorer extensions. Extensions that are not directly supported can still be used in your documents. These extensions are highlighted throughout this book.

**FIGURE 1.6.**

*Microsoft's Web site featuring the Internet Explorer.*

Sun Microsystems, Inc. has been a leading supporter of Web innovation. Recently, Sun Microsystems released the HotJava browser, which is written entirely in the Java programming language developed by Sun. The Java language is similar to C and C++, but is unique in that it is platform-independent. Using Java, you can add programs called *applets* to your Web publications. Applets are self-running applications that readers of your Web publications can preview and play automatically. Sun has set up several Web servers to handle requests related to Java. One of those servers is featured in Figure 1.7. FrontPage allows you to use documents with Java applets. (See Chapter 34, "Writing Java Applets," for a discussion of Java.)

Innovations by Netscape, Sun, and Microsoft represent only a small portion of the changes that are revolutionizing the way information is provided to millions of people around the world. These innovations, coupled with the explosive growth and enthusiasm in the Web, make now a more exciting time than ever to be a Web publisher.

As a Web publisher, you can publish information that will be seen by people in dozens of countries around the world, but the best news is that you as an individual can compete solely on the merits of your ideas, products, and services—not the size of your bank account. In Web publishing, you can reach the same audience whether your Web site is based on a $25 basic account from a service provider or a corporate Web server with leased lines costing $5,000 a month.

Web users will judge your publications based on their information content and entertainment value.

**FIGURE 1.7.**

*Sun's Web site featuring Java.*

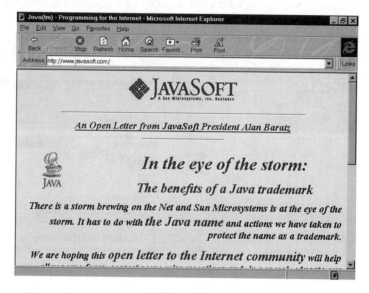

# Internet Standards and Specifications

Many standards are in place on the Web to enable information to be transferred the way it is. Many of these standards relate to specifications for protocols that predate the Web, such as File Transfer Protocol (FTP) and Gopher. FTP provides a way to access files on remote systems. Using FTP, you can log onto an FTP server, search for a file within a directory structure, and download the file. FTP also enables you to upload files to the FTP server. Searching the file structures on FTP servers is a time-consuming process, especially if you do not know the directory of the file you are looking for. The basic functions of FTP have been extended in various ways. The most popular extension is Archie. Using Archie, you can search file archives easily using keywords.

The Gopher protocol is similar to HTTP, but not as powerful or versatile. Using Gopher, you can search and retrieve information that is presented as a series of menus. Menu items are linked to the files containing the actual text. Gopher is most useful as the basis protocol for its more powerful and recent extensions, including Gopher Jewels, Jughead, and Veronica. Gopher Jewels enables you to search catalogs of Gopher resources indexed by category. Jughead lets you search Gopher indexes according to specified information. Veronica enables you to search Gopher menus by keyword.

The major shortcoming of early Internet protocols was the inability to access information through a common interface. Generally, files available via one interface were not available through another interface. To access information on an FTP server, you used FTP. To access information on a Gopher server, you used Gopher. For files that weren't available through either FTP or Gopher, you could try to initiate a remote login to a host using telnet. Sometimes you went from host to host looking for the information you needed.

Even with this simplified scenario, you can probably imagine how time-consuming and frustrating it was to track down the information you needed. Consequently, a major design issue for the Web was how to provide a common easy-to-use interface to access information on the Internet. To ensure that information available through previous protocols is accessible on the Web as well, the Web was built upon existing standards and specifications like those related to FTP and Gopher. You will find that using these other protocols in your Web documents is easy. You simply specify the protocol in a reference to a uniform resource locator (URL). URLs provide a uniform way to access and retrieve files. Without a single way to retrieve files, Internet publishers and users would still be pulling their hair out.

While the specification for URLs is an extremely important specification for finding files on the Web, many other specifications play a major role in defining the Web. Specifications for the hypertext transfer protocol define how hypertext documents are transferred. Specifications for markup languages define the structure of Web documents. Specifications for multipurpose Internet mail extensions define the type of data being transferred and enable you to transfer any type of data on the Web. Finally, specifications for the Common Gateway Interface (CGI) make it possible for you to create dynamic documents. The following sections look briefly at each of these specifications with emphasis on how they affect you as the Web publisher.

## Transferring Files Using HTTP

HTTP is the primary protocol used to distribute information on the Web. It is a powerful and fast protocol that allows for easy exchange of files. It is evolving along with other Web technologies. The original specification for HTTP is HTTP/0.9. HTTP Version 0.9 has many shortcomings. Two major shortcomings are that HTTP/0.9 does not allow for content typing and does not have provisions for providing meta-information in requests and responses.

Content typing enables the computer receiving the data to identify the type of data being transferred. The computer can then use this information to display or process the data. Meta-information is supplemental data, such as environment variables that identify the client's computer. Being able to provide information about the type of data transferred as well as supplemental information about the data is extremely important.

To address the shortcomings of HTTP/0.9, the current version of HTTP, HTTP/1.0, allows for headers with a Content-Type field and other types of meta-information. The type of data being transferred is defined in the Content-Type field. You can also use meta-information to provide additional information about the data, such as the language, encoding of the data, and state information. The Personal Web Server included with FrontPage fully supports HTTP/1.0. (See Chapter 8, "Creating Web Documents with FrontPage," for a preliminary discussion on using meta-information in HTML documents.)

An issue that most Web users and publishers want HTTP to address is security. Web publishers and users want to be able to conduct secure transactions. The key issue in security that needs to be addressed to promote the widespread use of electronic commerce is the ability to authenticate and encrypt transactions. Currently, there are several proposals for secure versions of HTTP. The two most popular secure protocols are Secure HTTP (S-HTTP) and Secure Socket Layer (SSL). When one of these specifications is embraced, secure transaction using HTTP will become a reality for mainstream Web users.

HTTP is a powerful protocol because it is fast and light, yet extremely versatile. To achieve this speed, versatility, and robustness, HTTP is defined as a connectionless and stateless protocol. This means that generally the client and server do not maintain a connection or state information related to the connection.

## Connectionless Versus Connection-Oriented Protocols

HTTP is a connectionless protocol. Connectionless protocols differ from connection-oriented protocols in the way requests and responses to requests are handled. With a connectionless protocol, clients connect to the server, make a request, get a response, and then disconnect. With a connection-oriented protocol, clients connect to the server, make a request, get a response, and then maintain the connection to service future requests.

An example of a connection-oriented protocol is FTP. When you connect to an FTP server, the connection remains open after you download a file. The maintenance of this connection requires system resources. A server with too many open connections quickly gets bogged down. Consequently, many FTP servers are configured to allow only 250 open connections at one time; that is, only 250 users can access the FTP server at once. Additionally, processes that are not disconnected cleanly can cause problems on the server. The worst of these processes run out of control, use system resources, and eventually crash the server. The best of these processes simply eat up system resources.

In contrast, HTTP is a connectionless protocol. When clients connect to the server, they make a request, get a response, and then disconnect. Because a connection is not maintained, no system resources are used after the transaction is completed. Consequently, HTTP servers are only limited by active connections and can generally service thousands of transactions with low system overhead. The drawback to connectionless protocols is that when the same client requests additional data, the connection must be reestablished. To Web users, this means a delay whenever additional data is requested.

## Stateless Versus Stateful Protocols

HTTP is a stateless protocol. Stateless protocols differ from stateful protocols in the way information about requests is maintained. With a stateless protocol, no information about a transaction is maintained after a transaction has been processed. With a stateful protocol, state information is maintained after a transaction has been processed.

Servers using stateful protocols maintain information about transactions and processes, such as the status of the connection, the processes running, the status of the processes running, and so on. Generally, this state information is resident in memory and uses up system resources. When a client breaks a connection with a server running a stateful protocol, the state information has to be cleaned up and is often logged as well.

Stateless protocols are light. Servers using stateless protocols maintain no information about completed transactions and processes. When a client breaks a connection with a server running a stateless protocol, no data has to be cleaned up or logged. By not tracking state information, there is less overhead on the server and the server can generally handle transactions swiftly. The drawback for Web publishers is that if you need to maintain state information for your Web documents, you must include this as meta-information in the document header.

# Determining the Structure of Web Documents

The way you can structure documents is largely determined by the language you use to lay out the document. Some languages are advanced and offer you rich control over document layout. Other languages are basic and offer ease of use and friendliness instead of advanced features. The following sections take a look at commonly used languages, including

- SGML
- Virtual Reality Modeling Language (VRML)
- HTML
- Page definition

## SGML

Most Web documents are structured using a markup language that is based on SGML. SGML defines a way to share complex documents using a generalized markup that is described in terms of standard text. Describing complex structures in terms of plain text ensures the widest distribution to any type of computer and presents the formatting in a human-readable form called markup. Because the markup contains standard characters, this also means anyone can create documents in a markup language without needing special software.

SGML is an advanced language with few limitations. In SGML, you have full control over the positioning of text and images. This means text and images will be displayed by the user's SGML browser in the precise location you designate. Although SGML is a powerful markup language, it is not widely used on the Web. However, this is changing as more publishers become aware of the versatility of SGML.

# VRML

Technology on the Web is growing at an explosive pace, and one of the most recent developments is VRML. VRML enables you to render complex models and multidimensional documents using a standardized markup language. The implications of virtual reality for Web publishers are far reaching.

Using VRML, you can reduce calculations and data points that would have filled 10MB of disk space to a few hundred lines of markup code. Not only does this drastically reduce the download time for VRML files and save network bandwidth, it also presents complex models in a readable and—gasp—understandable format. While VRML is not yet widely used on the Web, it is attracting tremendous interest within the Internet community and the world community as well. Although the current version of VRML is VRML 1.0, the Moving Worlds specification for VRML 2.0 has recently been approved and is gaining widespread support.

# HTML

HTML is the most commonly used markup language. HTML's popularity stems in large part from its ease of use and friendliness. With HTML, you can quickly and easily create Web documents and make them available to a wide audience. HTML enables you to control many of the layout aspects for text and images. You can specify the relative size of headings and text as well as text styles, including bold, underline, and italics. There are extensions to HTML that enable you to specify font type, but standard HTML specifications do not give you that capability.

Although many advanced layout controls for documents are not available using HTML, it is still the publishing language of choice on the vast majority of Web sites. Remember, the limitations are a way to drastically reduce the complexity of HTML. Currently, three specifications are associated with HTML: HTML 1.0, HTML 2.0, and HTML 3.2. Each level of the specification steadily introduces more versatility and functionality.

In addition to these specifications, several Internet developers have created extensions to HTML. While the extensions are nonstandard, many have been embraced by Web publishers. Some extensions, such as Netscape's and Microsoft's, are so popular that they seem to be standard HTML.

# Page Definition Languages

Some Web documents are formatted using page definition languages instead of markup languages. Page definition languages often use formats that are specific to a particular commercial page layout application, such as Adobe Acrobat or Common Ground. Page layout applications are popular because they combine rich control over document layout with user-friendly graphical interfaces. While the formats these applications use are proprietary, most of the formats are based on the standards set forth by SGML.

# Identifying Data Types with MIME

Using HTTP, you can transfer full-motion video sequences, stereo sound tracks, high-resolution images, and any other type of media you can think of. The standard that makes this possible is Multipurpose Internet Mail Extensions (MIME). HTTP utilizes MIME to identify the type of object being transferred across the Internet. Object types are identified in a header field that comes before the actual data for the object. Under HTTP, this header field is the Content-Type header field. By identifying the type of object in a header field, the client receiving the object can appropriately handle it.

For example, if the object is a GIF image, the image will be identified by the MIME type image/gif. When the client receiving the object of type image/gif can handle the object type directly, it will display the object. When the client receiving the object of type image/gif cannot handle the object directly, it will check a configuration table to see whether an application is configured to handle an object of this MIME type. If an application is configured for use with the client and is available, the client will call the application. The application called will then handle the object. Here, the application would display the GIF image.

Not only is MIME typing extremely useful to HTTP, but it is useful to other protocols as well. MIME typing was originally developed to allow e-mail messages to have multiple parts with different types of data in each part. In this way, you can attach any type of file to an e-mail message. The MIME standard is described in detail in Requests for Comments (RFCs) 1521 and 1522. (See Chapter 30, "Writing CGI Scripts," for a complete listing of MIME types and their uses in your Web documents.)

**NOTE**

Many Internet standards and specifications are described in RFCs, which are a collection of documents pertaining to the Internet that cover everything from technical to nontechnical issues.

# Accessing and Retrieving Files Using URLs

To retrieve a file from a server, a client must know three things: the address of the server, where on the server the file is located, and which protocol to use to access and retrieve the file. This information is specified as a URL. URLs can be used to find and retrieve files on the Internet using any valid protocol.

Although you normally use HTTP to transfer your Web documents, you can include references to other protocols in your documents. For example, you can specify the address to a file available via FTP simply by naming the protocol in a URL. Most URLs you will use in your documents look something like this:

```
protocol://server_host:port/path_to_resource
```

The first part of the URL scheme names the protocol that the client will use to access and transfer the file. The protocol name is generally followed by a colon and two forward slashes. The second part of the URL indicates the address of the server and terminates with a single slash. The server host can be followed by a colon and a port address. The third part of the URL indicates where on the server the resource is located and can include a path structure. In a URL, double slash marks indicate that the protocol utilizes the format defined by the Common Internet Scheme Syntax (CISS). Colons are separators. In this example, a colon separates the protocol from the rest of the URL scheme; the second colon separates the host address from the port number.

> **NOTE**
>
> CISS is a common syntax for URL schemes that involve the direct use of IP-based protocols. IP-based protocols specify a particular host on the Internet by a unique numeric identifier called an IP address or by a unique name that can be resolved to the IP address. Non-CISS URL schemes do not name a particular host computer. Therefore, the host is implied to be the computer providing services for the client.

Here's a URL using HTTP to retrieve a file called `index.html` on the Macmillan Computer Publishing Web server:

```
http://www.mcp.com/index.html
```

URLs, which are defined in Request for Comment (RFC) 1738, are powerful because they provide a uniform way to retrieve multiple types of data. The most common protocols you can specify using URLs are

| | |
|---|---|
| FTP | File Transfer Protocol |
| Gopher | Gopher Protocol |
| HTTP | Hypertext Transfer Protocol |
| mailto | Electronic mail address |
| Prospero | Prospero Directory Service |
| news | Usenet news |
| NNTP | Usenet news accessed with Network News Transfer Protocol |
| telnet | Remote login sessions |
| WAIS | Wide Area Information Servers |
| file | Files on local host |

Using these protocols in your Web documents is explored in Chapter 8, "Creating Web Documents with FrontPage."

# Creating Dynamic Documents with CGI

The popularity of the Web stems in large part from interactivity. Web users click on hypertext links to access Web documents, images, and multimedia files. Yet the URLs in your hypertext links can lead to much more than static resources. URLs can also specify programs that process user input and return information to the user's browser. By specifying programs on the Web server, you can make your Web publications highly interactive and extremely dynamic. You can create customized documents on demand based on the user's input and on the type of browser being used.

Programs specified in URLs are called gateway scripts. The term gateway script comes from UNIX environments. Gateways are programs or devices that provide an interface. Here, the gateway or interface is between your browser and the server. Programs written in UNIX shells are called scripts by UNIX programmers. This is because UNIX shells, such as Bourne, Korn, and C-shell, aren't actual programming languages. Because UNIX shells are easy to use and learn, most gateway scripts are written in UNIX shells.

The specification CGI describes how gateway scripts pass information to servers. CGI provides the basis for creating dynamic documents, which can include interactive forms, graphical menus called image maps, and much more. The power of CGI is that it provides Web publishers with a common interface to programs on Web servers. Using this common interface, Web publishers can provide dynamic documents to Web users without regard to the type of system the publisher and user are using.

> **NOTE**
>
> FrontPage features direct support for CGI and allows you to drop CGI-based WebBots directly into your publications with no programming involved. Nearly a dozen WebBots perform advanced functions on most Web publishers' wish lists. However, if there isn't a WebBot for a specific task you want to perform, you can still write your own CGI script that will interact with documents you created using FrontPage. (See Chapter 30, "Writing CGI Scripts," for more information on writing scripts and using FrontPage with scripts.)

# The Evolution of Standards and Specifications

The standards and specifications you read about in the previous section are the result of coordinated efforts by standards organizations and the working groups associated with these organizations. Generally, these organizations approve changes to existing standards and specifications and develop new standards and specifications. Three primary standards groups develop standards and specifications that pertain to the Internet and to networked computing in general. These groups are

- ISO: The International Organization for Standardization
- IETF: The Internet Engineering Task Force
- W3C: The World Wide Web Consortium

# The International Organization for Standardization

The International Organization for Standardization is one of the most important standards-making bodies in the world. The ISO doesn't generally develop standards specifically for the Internet; rather, the organization develops standards for networked computing in general. One of the most important developments by the organization is the internationally recognized seven-layer network model. The seven-layer model is commonly referred to as the Open Systems Interconnection (OSI) Reference Model.

Most Internet specifications and protocols incorporate standards developed by the ISO. For example, ISO standard 8859 is used by all Web browsers to define the standard character set. ISO 8859-1 defines the standard character set called ISO-Latin-1. The ISO-Latin-1 character set has been added to and the addition is called the ISO-Added-Latin-1 character set. You will refer to these character sets whenever you want to add special characters—such as &, ©, or ®—to your Web documents.

## The Internet Engineering Task Force

The Internet Engineering Task Force (IETF) is the primary organization developing Internet standards. All changes to existing Internet standards and proposals for new standards are approved by the IETF. The IETF meets three times a year to set directions for the Internet.

Changes to existing specifications and proposals for new ones are approved by formal committees that meet to discuss and propose changes. These formal committees are called working groups. The IETF has dozens of working groups. Each group generally focuses on a specific topic within an area of development. Some areas of development include

- Applications
- IP: Next generation
- Internet
- Network management
- Operational requirements
- Routing
- Security
- Transport
- User services

RFCs are permanently archived and are valid until they are superseded by a later RFC. As their name implies, RFCs are made available to the general Internet community for discussion and suggestions for improvements.

Many RFCs eventually become Internet Standards, but the process isn't a swift one. For example, URLs were introduced by the World Wide Web global information initiative in 1990. While URLs have been in use ever since, the URL specification did not become an RFC until December 1994 and was only recently approved as an Internet standard.

Figure 1.8 shows IETF's site on the Web. At the IETF, you can find information on current IETF initiatives, which include the latest standards and specifications pertaining to the Internet.

**FIGURE 1.8.**

*The Internet Engineering Task Force Web site.*

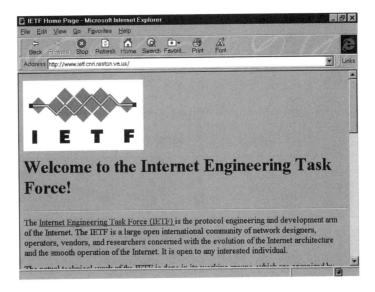

Membership in the IETF is open to anyone. The directors of the working group areas handle the internal management of the IETF. These directors, along with the chairperson of the IETF, form the Internet Engineering Steering Group (IESG). The IESG, under the direction of the Internet Society, handles the operational management of the IETF.

You can find more information on the Internet Society and membership in the Internet Society at the following Web site:

```
http://www.isoc.org/
```

# The World Wide Web Consortium

The World Wide Web Consortium (W3C) is managed by the Laboratory for Computer Science at the Massachusetts Institute of Technology. The W3C exists to develop common standards for the evolution of the World Wide Web. It is a joint initiative between MIT, CERN, and INRIA. The U.S. W3C center is based at and run by MIT. The European W3C center is at the French National Institute for Research in Computing and Automation (INRIA). CERN and INRIA cooperate to manage the European W3C center.

The W3C was formed in part to help develop common standards for the development of Web technologies. One of the W3C's major goals is to provide Web developers and users with a repository of information concerning the Web. Toward that end, the W3C has sites available where you can find the most current information related to Web development. At the W3C Web site shown in Figure 1.9, you can find the most recent drafts of specifications, including those for HTML 3.2 and HTTP 1.0.

**FIGURE 1.9.**

*The World Wide Web Consortium Web site.*

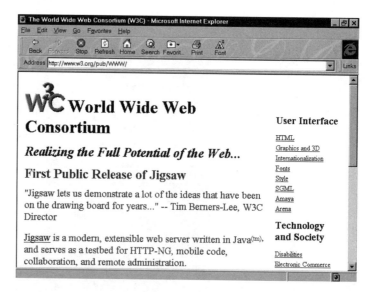

Another goal of the W3C is to provide prototype applications that use new technologies proposed in Internet Drafts. The W3C works with its member organizations to propose specifications and standards to the IETF. Member organizations pay a fee based on their membership status. Full members pay $50,000 and affiliate members pay $5,000 for a one-year membership.

# Evaluating Your Access Needs

Before you start publishing on the Web, you must evaluate your access needs so that you can determine what type of account will meet your needs as a Web publisher and obtain the level of access to the Web that is right for you. If you plan to provide Internet-related services or products specifically for Internet-smart consumers, you will want your own domain. A domain address is a unique address that only you will have. Web users can use programs, such as Whois, to obtain information about your domain.

> **NOTE**
>
> Whois is a basic protocol to find information on Internet users and domains. If you have an account with an Internet Service Provider (ISP) with access to a UNIX shell, you can type whois at the shell prompt. For example, to find more information on my domain, tvp.com, you would type the following at the shell prompt:
>
> ```
> whois tvp.com
> ```

Having your own domain plays a key role in establishing a presence on the Web. Many users make specific judgments about you based on the address URL to your Web pages. Most people believe that you must set up a Web server to obtain your own domain. This is not true. Web publishers who want their own domain have several options to make this possible.

Most people do not need to set up their own Web server. If you plan to go through an ISP to obtain an account with Web publishing privileges, you do not need to set up your own Web server. You will use your ISP's Web server to publish your Web documents. If you already have an account with an ISP, you might already have all you need to publish on the Web.

Your access options are the following:

- Installing your own Web server
- Using an ISP's Web Server with a standard account
- Using a commercial online service's Web server with a standard account
- Getting a phantom domain

## Installing Your Own Web Server

Installing your own Web server is the most expensive option for Web publishing, yet with this expense comes significant advantages. With a dedicated connection, you can provide 24-hour Web services to users worldwide. You will have complete control over your Web server and can publish whatever you wish. You can configure the server to handle other services as well, such as FTP, Gopher, telnet, and CGI scripts. You will also have your own domain, which will establish a clear presence on the Web for you or your company. Your URL will look something like the following:

```
http://www.your_company.com/
```

## Server Software and Platform Options

FrontPage includes a Web server software package called the Personal Web Server. This server runs on Windows NT and Windows 95 platforms, yet has extensions for the most popular Windows 95, Windows NT, and UNIX-based servers. This means you can create and manage documents on a Windows 95 or Windows NT computer and publish your documents on a Windows 95, Windows NT, or UNIX platform.

> **NOTE**
>
> A Macintosh version of FrontPage, which was scheduled for release in Summer 1996, might already be available. This addition will mean that you can use FrontPage to create, manage, and publish your documents on virtually any operating system.

You might be amazed at how easy it is to install server software, especially if you plan to use the Personal Web Server. Like most commercial server software, the Personal Web Server is nearly trouble-free and includes an automatic installation process. If you don't have a Web server, you will probably want to use the Personal Web Server, which can be installed in about five minutes.

For an individual or small company wanting to set up a Web server, the best server software to use is most likely the software that will run on the computer system you are most familiar with. For a company with an installed computer network, you might want to use one of the computers already available as your Web server. Before you install the Web server, you will want to carefully consider security options such as a firewall to shield your internal network from illegal activities.

If you do not have a computer capable of providing Web services, you will need to purchase one at a cost of $3,000 to $25,000 or lease one at a cost of $75 to $500 per month. Before buying or leasing a computer, you must determine what platform the Web server runs on. Again, the best server software for you is most likely the software that runs on a platform familiar to you or your support staff. However, before you make any decision, examine carefully how and for what purpose the company plans to use the Web server.

Commercial options are usually the easiest to install, support, and maintain; however, the primary reason for using commercial Web server software is support. If you believe you will need outside software support to keep the server alive, commercial software is the best choice.

Most shareware servers run on UNIX systems. UNIX servers are typically the best maintained and supported. As a result, UNIX servers are some of the most reliable and secure servers available. If you have a strong need for reliability and security, you should look at UNIX Web server software. However, you might need an experienced team to compile the source code and configure the server parameters.

## Internet Connection Options

You will also need to obtain an Internet connection. Generally, you will obtain an Internet connection for a fee from an Internet Service Provider or a commercial online service. The speed of the connection will drive the monthly fees. To determine the best connection speed for you, you will need to estimate the volume of traffic for the site. A good way to estimate traffic is to visit a site similar in content and structure to your intended site. Because most popular sites provide some historical information on the usage of the site, you can use the data to make a better estimate of traffic for your site.

Although the Internet is a global structure, usage of your site probably will not be at a constant pace throughout the day. For example, a site with 25,000 hits a day might experience peak usage periods within fluctuating time-windows. These peak periods present a problem when assessing your Internet connection needs. For this reason, for a Web site with an anticipated high volume of traffic, such as daily network traffic of more than 25,000 hits per day, you might want to consider using a high-speed T1 connection to the Internet. Leasing a T1 line will cost you $2,500 to $5,000 per month, plus an installation fee of $2,500 to $5,000.

Most Web sites do not need a T1 connection to the Internet. In fact, the average site needs only a 56 Kbps line. A 56 Kbps connection can adequately handle daily network traffic of 2,000 hits per day, and the really good news is that the cost of a 56 Kbps connection to the Internet is only $300 to $500 per month, plus a startup fee of up to $500.

## Using an Internet Service Provider's Web Server with a Standard Account

Obtaining an Internet account with Web publishing privileges is an inexpensive option. Typical costs for such an account are $20 to $50 per month, plus a start-up fee of up to $50. The account should include at least 2 to 3MB of storage space on the service provider's computer. Most ISPs offer unlimited access time to the Internet, meaning whether you log on for 40 or 400 hours a month, you will generally pay the same monthly fee. While your e-mail, standard files, and Web-published files will use this space, 2 to 3MB is usually adequate to maintain a modest-sized site. If you currently have an account with an ISP that allows Serial Line Internet Protocol (SLIP) or Point-to-Point Protocol (PPP) access to the Web, you might already have Web publishing privileges!

Your account with an ISP is available on a dial-up basis. A dial-up connection requires a computer, which may or may not be dedicated to networking, with communications software and a modem. The good news about a dial-up connection is that it utilizes a regular phone line with speeds ranging from 9.6 Kbps to 28.8 Kbps. Your computer is used to establish a connection over the modem and phone line for a temporary period, and at the end of use, the connection to the Internet is broken. You will use the connection to browse the Web, navigate around the Net, or check on your site published on the ISP's Web server.

Before you set up an account, check with your ISP for specifics on storage space, additional fees for storage space that should not be more than $2 per megabyte, and possible additional fees if you have a popular site. You will also want to check on the availability of other services such as FTP, Gopher, telnet, and CGI scripts, which should be available for free use if they are available at all.

While an account with an ISP is an inexpensive option, it is also a very basic one. You do not have control over the Web server. You will be at the mercy of the ISP for additional services, including CGI scripts. You will not have your own domain, and people will know this immediately because your URL will look something like this:

```
http://www.your_service_provider.com/~you
```

# Using a Commercial Online Service's Web Server with a Standard Account

America Online, CompuServe, GEnie, and Prodigy all offer or plan to offer Web publishing privileges to their customers. Publishing on the Web through a commercial online service is your least expensive alternative if you use your account wisely. Typical costs for such an account are $10 to $20 per month, plus a small additional fee for maintaining your Web pages on the online service's Web server. Most commercial online services provide only a few hours of free connection time each month. After you use your free connection time, you will have to pay additional connection charges. If you currently have an account with a commercial online service, you might already be able to publish on the Web!

Your account with a commercial online service is available on a dial-up basis. You will use the connection to browse the Web, navigate around the Net, or check on your site published on the online service's Web server. Before you set up an account, check with the commercial online service for specifics on storage space and possible additional fees if you have a popular site.

Although an account with a commercial online service is the least expensive option, it is also the most basic option. Many online services are fairly new to Web publishing themselves and do not offer the access to essential additional services. While this, of course, will change in time and probably quickly, you should ask your online service about additional services, such as FTP,

Gopher, and CGI, to find out when they will be available. You will not have your own domain, and people will know this immediately because your URL will look something like this:

```
http://www.commercial_online_service.com/~you
```

---

**TIP**

If you are interested in Web publishing with a commercial online service, visit these Web sites where you will find current rates and publishing options:

| America Online | `http://www.aol.com/` |
| CompuServe | `http://www.compuserve.com/` |
| GEnie | `http://www.genie.com/` |
| Prodigy | `http://www.prodigy.com/` |

---

# Getting a Phantom Domain

Getting a phantom domain is often the best option available for anyone wanting to Web publish. With a phantom domain, you get most of the benefits of having your own Web server and affordability. When you have your own domain, Web users can use programs, such as Whois, to learn additional information about you.

Typical costs for a phantom domain are only slightly more than a basic account with an ISP and range from $25 to $75. The primary advantage of a phantom domain is that you will have your own domain and your URL will look something like this:

```
http://www.your_company.com/
```

The preceding address URL is easier to type and remember than an address URL containing the tilde. Instead of telling people your URL is www.yourserviceprovider.com/~yourcompany, you can tell them your URL is www.yourcompany.com. You might be surprised to learn that many users try to find sites based on the company name. For example, when I look for a site associated with a major company, I usually type http://www.companyname.com in my browser's URL window. If the URL is valid, I am at the company's Web site without having to look up the URL in a Web database that may or may not have the site's URL.

Some ISPs call this service Web server hosting. This generally means that by hosting, the ISP is creating a phantom domain for you on its system. Maintaining a phantom domain is no more taxing on the ISP's server than your standard account and is, in fact, little more than clever linking to make the outside world think you have your own domain. With a phantom domain, you still have no control over the Web server or additional services. However, most ISPs that offer phantom domains include additional services as part of the deal, and these additional services are the only real justification for higher fees.

## PHANTOM DOMAINS

Phantom domains are the wave of the future in Web publishing. If you already have an account with an ISP, check to see if they offer phantom domains. Many ISPs provide phantom domains to their users because it is an easy way to generate extra revenues.

You can obtain a phantom domain from an ISP, a commercial service provider, or an Internet presence provider. Internet presence providers specialize in setting up Web sites. Most of the sites that presence providers set up are phantom domains. A typical presence provider will service hundreds of phantom domains off one or more Web servers. While servicing hundreds of businesses off one server might sound like a lot, the power and capacity of the server and the speed of its connection to the Internet are more important than anything else.

Because Internet presence providers specialize in servicing businesses instead of individual users, business-oriented sites might do better than these providers. Dozens of presence providers are available. For more information on service providers, visit

```
http://www.isoc.org/~bgreene/nsp1-5c.html
```

To find a comprehensive list of Internet Service Providers, visit The List. This site maintains one of the best ISP listings:

```
http://www.thelist.com/
```

or

```
http://www.cybertoday.com/ISPs/ISPinfo.html
```

# Summary

The Web was built upon existing protocols and intended to provide a common interface to other protocols. Because of this design, you can use any valid protocol to transfer files. While you will primarily use HTTP to access your Web documents, you can use other protocols, such as Gopher and FTP, to enhance the usability of your documents. The face of Web publishing is changing rapidly and the way you can specify the structure of Web documents is changing just as rapidly. The most common way to structure Web documents is with HTML. You can also use the SGML, VRML, and page layout applications to structure documents you provide on the Web.

The mechanism that enables you to provide access to any type of document on the Web is the MIME standard. Using multipurpose Internet mail extensions, you can provide information about documents in the Content-Type header field. Browsers will use the content type to take appropriate action on the document, such as displaying an image or calling another application. The mechanism that enables you to access and retrieve files on the Web is the URL standard. With URLs, you can locate and retrieve files using the appropriate protocol. The final specification of interest to Web publishers is CGI. Using CGI, you can create dynamic documents.

To stay current with the latest developments on the Web, you should follow the Internet standards and specifications proposed by Internet standards groups, such as the IETF and the W3C. While you should consider all these issues before you start Web publishing, you should also evaluate your own access needs. This is true even if you already have an Internet account. By evaluating your access needs, you can determine what type of account will meet your needs as a Web publisher.

# Navigating and Publishing on the Web

**2**

*by William Robert Stanek*

**IN THIS CHAPTER**

An entire universe is growing in cyberspace, and you might not even know it. The Internet connects 50,000 computer networks and 6 million host computers worldwide. Almost every country in the world has computers that access the Internet, and by the end of 1996, 50 million people will have access to the Internet. What is even more incredible is that in two years, the number of users is expected to double, which means more than 100 million people will have access to the global Internet by the end of 1998. The segment of the Internet driving this tremendous growth is the World Wide Web. Not only can you reach these millions of consumers on the Web, you can do so in mind-blowing proportions and in ways that are limited only by your imagination.

In 1995 alone, more than 8 million people gained access to the Web. The source of this great influx of new users was primarily commercial online services such as CompuServe, Prodigy, and America Online, which provide their users with full access to the Internet. When these figures are added to a conservative growth rate of 10 percent per month for new users accessing the Web, this means that 25 to 50 million people will have access to the Web by the end of 1996.

# Navigating the Web

If you have browsed the Web before, you know that navigating the Web can be as easy as activating a hypertext link. You activate the link by moving your mouse pointer to the area of the link and clicking the left mouse button. Text containing a hypertext link is underlined and generally displayed in a different color from other text on the page. By default, most browsers display links that you have not visited in blue and links that you have visited in purple or light red.

When you move your mouse pointer over a link, most browsers display the URL path to the file or object that will be retrieved if you activate the link. This is useful to identify the type of file referenced by the link.

> **NOTE**
>
> Some browsers let you select the color of text on the page. The four basic color definitions that you can assign to text pertain to the color of ordinary text, unvisited links, active links, and visited links. Under HTML 3.2, you, as the Web publisher, can define the color of text on the page. These color definitions generally override color definitions defined in the user's HTML 3.2-compliant browser. FrontPage fully supports the color definitions set forth in HTML 3.2.

Although following text-based links on Web pages is easy, following links embedded in graphic objects is not always easy. Some clickable images are displayed on the page with a distinctive blue border. This type of clickable image is easy to identify. Other clickable images have no borders around them at all, primarily because of extensions to HTML that enable Web publishers to suppress the border around images. Yet there are other extensions to HTML that enable Web publishers to place borders around nonclickable images. So, how do you know when an image is clickable if it has no distinctive border?

One way to tell whether the image is clickable is to move your mouse pointer over the image. If your browser shows that a URL path is associated with the image, you can click on it.

As you point and click your way through the Web, you probably don't stop to think about the URLs you are using to access Web resources. However, as a Web publisher, you should stop and think about the URLs you use. For example, the URL `http://www.microsoft.com/frontpage/pricing.htm` tells a browser to use the hypertext transfer protocol (HTTP) to obtain a file called `pricing.htm` in the `frontpage` directory on the `www.microsoft.com` Web server. URLs are much more powerful and complex than this simple example. The next section takes a closer look at the structure of URLs and how they are used on the Web.

# Using URLs

URLs provide a uniform way of identifying resources that are available using Internet protocols (IP). To better understand URLs, you need to know about URL schemes and formats, how URLs are defined, and how to use escape codes in URLs.

## URL Schemes and Formats

The basic mechanism that makes URLs so versatile is the standard naming scheme. URL schemes name the protocol that the client will use to access and transfer the file. Web clients use the name of the protocol to determine the format for the information that follows the protocol name. The protocol name is generally followed by a colon and two forward slashes. The colon is a separator. The double slash marks indicate that the protocol uses the format defined by the Common Internet Scheme Syntax.

The Common Internet Scheme Syntax is a common syntax for URL schemes that involve the direct use of IP-based protocols. These protocols specify a particular host on the Internet by a unique numeric identifier called an IP address or by a unique name that can be resolved to the IP address. The information after the double slashes follows a format that is dependent on the protocol type referenced in the URL. Here are two general formats:

```
protocol://hostname:port/path_to_resource
protocol://username:password@hostname:port/path_to_resource
```

> **NOTE**
>
> If you use a DOS/Windows-based system, you normally type a backslash to change directories and maneuver around the system. Consequently, you might have to remind yourself that the Web follows the UNIX syntax for slashes, and the slashes you type for URLs should be forward slashes.

## Defining Host Information in URLs

Hostname information used in URLs identifies the address to a host and is broken down into two or more parts separated by periods. The periods are used to separate domain information from the hostname. Common domain names for Web servers begin with www, such as www.tvp.com, which identifies the Web server called tvp in the commercial domain. Domains you can specify in your URLs include

| | |
|---|---|
| COM | Commercial sites |
| EDU | Education sites |
| GOV | Nonmilitary government sites |
| MIL | Military sites |
| NET | Network sites (developers, Internet Service Providers, and so on) |
| ORG | Organizational sites |

## Defining Port Information in URLs

Ports are rather like telephone jacks on the Web server. The server has certain ports allocated for certain things, such as port 80 for your incoming requests for hypertext documents. The server listens on a particular port. When it hears something, in essence it picks up the phone and connects the particular port.

Port information used in URLs identifies the port number to be used for the connection. If you don't specify a port number, a default value is assumed as necessary. Generally, you don't have to specify port numbers in your URLs unless the connection will be made to a port other than the default. Default values for ports are defined in the URL specification as follows:

| | |
|---|---|
| File Transfer Protocol (FTP) | Port 21 |
| Gopher | Port 70 |
| HTTP | Port 80 |
| Network News Transfer Protocol (NNTP) | Port 119 |
| Telnet | Port 23 |
| Wide Area Information Server (WAIS) | Port 210 |

# Defining Username and Password Information in URLs

By specifying the username and password information in a URL, you allow users to log in to a system automatically. The two protocols that use both username and password information are FTP and telnet. In an FTP session, the username and password information are often utilized to allow users to log in to FTP servers anonymously. When a connection is made to an FTP server and username and password information is not specified, the following default values are assumed: anonymous for username and the user's e-mail address as the password.

In telnet, there are no default values. If you do not supply the username and password, the user will be prompted for this information. To avoid this, you could allow users to log in automatically by specifying a user and password in your URL. However, you generally do not want to specify a personal password in a URL. Therefore, if you want users to be able to log in automatically using telnet, you should create a guest account with a generic password.

# Defining Path Information in URLs

The final part of a URL is the path to the resource. This path generally follows the directory structure from the root or slash directory to the resource specified in the URL. A completely specified path to a resource is called an absolute path. You can also specify a path to a resource relative to the current directory. You will learn more about specifying paths to resources in Chapter 9, "Adding Features to the Page."

# Protocol Schemes Defined

Most protocol schemes follow the two general forms of URLs discussed earlier. Protocol schemes conforming to the CISS standard use the double slashes. CISS-compliant protocols are FTP, Gopher, HTTP, NNTP, WAIS, and File. Protocols that do not conform to the CISS standard omit the double slashes. Noncompliant protocols include Mailto and News. Table 2.1 shows the URL schemes associated with each protocol.

FrontPage allows you to create documents that reference any of the protocols shown in Table 2.1. In Chapter 9, you will learn how to reference alternative protocols in your Web documents.

## Table 2.1. URL schemes and formats.

| Scheme | Description/Protocol | URL Format |
|--------|----------------------|------------|
| FTP | File Transfer Protocol | `ftp://username:password@hostname:port/path_to_resource` |
| Gopher | Gopher protocol | `gopher://hostname:port/path_to_resource` |

*continues*

**Table 2.1. continued**

| Scheme | Description/ Protocol | URL Format |
|---|---|---|
| HTTP | Hypertext transfer protocol | `http://hostname:port/path_to_resource` |
| Mailto | Electronic mail address | `mailto:username@host` |
| News | Usenet news | `news:newsgroup-name` |
|  |  | `news:message-number` |
| NNTP | Usenet news accessed with Network News Transfer Protocol | `nntp://hostname/newsgroup-name` |
| telnet | Remote login sessions | `telnet://username:password@hostname:port` |
| WAIS | Wide area information servers | `wais://hostname:port/database` |
| File | Files on local host | `file://hostname/path_to_resource` |

# How URLs Are Defined

URLs consist of characters defined by the ASCII character set. The URL specification allows for the use of uppercase and lowercase letters. Because URLs typed in uppercase are generally treated the same as URLs typed in lowercase, most Web publishers use only lowercase letters in their URLs. A result of this is that most Web documents and object files are named in lowercase letters as well. If you are on a system that has case-sensitive file naming, such as UNIX, you will find naming your files in lowercase is extremely useful in avoiding possible conflicts.

Although URLs consist of characters defined by the ASCII character set, you cannot use all ASCII characters in your URLs. You can use the letters a–z, the numerals 0–9, and a few special characters including

- Asterisks
- Dollar signs
- Exclamation points
- Hyphens
- Parentheses (left and right)
- Periods
- Plus signs

- Single quotation marks
- Underscores

You are limited to these characters because other characters used in URLs have specific meanings, as shown in Table 2.2.

## Table 2.2. The meaning of characters used in URLs.

| Character | Meaning | Example |
|---|---|---|
| : | The colon is a separator. | |
| | Separates protocol from the rest of the URL scheme. | `http://tvp.com/vpfound.html` |
| | Separates host name from the port number. | `http://www.tvp.com:80/` |
| | Separates username from the password. | `ftp://anonymous:william@tvp.com/vpinfo.txt` |
| // | The double slash marks indicate that the protocol uses the format defined by the Common Internet Scheme Syntax. | |
| | This protocol follows the CISS format. | `ftp://tvp.com/vpinfo.txt` |
| | This protocol does not follow the CISS format. | `news:newsgroup-name` |
| / | The slash is a separator and is used to separate the path from host name and port. | `http://tvp.com/vphp.html` |
| | The slash is also used to denote the directory path to the resource named in the URL. | `/usr/cgi-bin/useit.pl` |
| ~ | The tilde is generally used at the beginning of the path to indicate that the resource is in the specified user's public html directory. | `http://www.aloha.com/~william` |

*continues*

## Table 2.2. continued

| Character | Meaning | Example |
|-----------|---------|---------|
| % | Identifies an escape code. Escape codes are used to specify special characters in URLs that otherwise have a special meaning or are not allowed. | `gopher://unm.edu/books/english/`<br>`Book%20Table%20of%20Contents` |
| @ | The at symbol is used to separate username and/or password information from the host name in the URL. | `mailto:william@tvp.com` |
| ? | The question mark is used in the URL path to specify the beginning of a query string. Query strings are passed to CGI scripts. All the information following the question mark is data the user submitted and is not interpreted as part of the file path. | `/usr/cgi-bin/useit.pl?keyword` |
| + | The plus sign is used in query strings as a place-holder between words. Instead of using spaces to separate words the user has entered in the query, the browser substitutes the plus sign. | `/usr/cgi-bin/`<br>`useit.pl?word1+word2+word3` |
| = | The equal sign is used in query strings to separate the key assigned by the publisher from the value entered by the user. In the sample URL, `username` is the key assigned by the publisher and the value entered by the user is `william`. | `/usr/cgi-bin/`<br>`useit.pl?username=william` |

| Character | Meaning | Example |
|---|---|---|
| & | The ampersand is used in query strings to separate sets of keys and values. In the sample URL, `name` is the first key assigned by the publisher and the value entered by the user is `william`. The second key assigned by the publisher is question, and the value entered by the user is `why+not`. | `/usr/cgi-bin/`<br>`query.pl?name=william&question`<br>`➥=why+not` |
| ^ | Reserved for future use. | |
| {} | Reserved for future use. | |
| [] | Reserved for future use. | |

# Using Escape Codes in URLs

To make URLs even more versatile, the specification enables you to use escape codes in URLs. Escape codes are used to specify special characters in URLs that are either reserved or not otherwise allowed. This is particularly useful for protocols (such as Gopher) that allow resources to be defined with spaces between words. For example, to use the Gopher resource `Book Table of Contents`, you would have to rewrite the resource name using the escape code for spaces. The percent sign identifies an escape code. The number following the percent sign identifies the character being escaped. The escape code for a space is a percent sign followed by the number 20. To use the preceding resource name in a URL, you would rewrite it as follows:

`Book%20Table%20of%20Contents`

Using the ISO Latin 1 character set, you can determine the values for characters you need to escape. To do this, you convert the decimal value defined in the character set to a hexadecimal value. The decimal value for a space is 32. When you convert this decimal value to hexadecimal, the resulting value is 20. Table 2.3 shows common character values from the ISO Latin 1 character set and the associated escape codes.

**Table 2.3. Common character values and their associated escape codes.**

| Numeric Value | Character Description | Escape Code |
|---|---|---|
| 09 | Tab | %09 |
| 32 | Space | %20 |
| 35 | Number sign (#) | %23 |
| 37 | Percent sign (%) | %25 |
| 38 | Ampersand (&) | %26 |
| 39 | Apostrophe (') | %27 |
| 63 | Question mark (?) | %3f |
| 64 | At symbol (@) | %40 |
| 95 | Caret symbol (^) | %5f |

**TIP**

When you use escape codes such as %09 for a tab, be sure to include the zero. The computer will interpret the hexadecimal value 09 as a tab.

# Who's Publishing on the Web?

The Web is a powerful interface to everything the Internet has to offer. Today when most people think of the Internet, they think of the dynamic environment that enables them to search through and access complex webs of text, graphics, sound, and video. In short, they equate the Web with the Internet—and that's because the Web has swallowed the Net.

The Web was born at the European Laboratory for Particle Physics (CERN), and it should be no surprise that universities, colleges, and research institutes represent some of the largest segments of Web publishers. Some of the most wonderful Web sites are created by college students and research scientists. These same students and researchers also represent most of the innovators creating new technologies for the Web.

Although Web sites created by research and educational organizations are plentiful, their presence has been dwarfed in recent months by commercial sites. Thousands of businesses are already plugged in to the Internet. These businesses have built some of the hottest sites on the Web and are attracting thousands of visitors every day.

Not all the companies running commercial sites are multibillion dollar conglomerates with thousands of employees. Many commercial sites are run by startup companies who represent small groups of entrepreneurs with big dreams. Many more commercial sites are mom and pop businesses from down the street and home businesses run from the kitchen table.

Behind the massive wave of companies and entrepreneurs carving their niche in cyberspace, the governments of the world watch. They know what commerce without national borders, tariffs, and taxes means to global markets and aren't sure how to regulate it—or even if they can regulate it. Many governments are doing much more than watching; they are taking active roles in the development of the Internet and fostering its growth with funding. Government agencies are publishing their own Web sites loaded with useful information and are among the first organizations to publish on the Web. U.S. government agencies publishing on the Web include the Environmental Protection Agency, the Central Intelligence Agency, the National Security Agency, the Census Bureau, and a very humorous site from the IRS.

Although many Web publishers represent organizations, this is not always the case. A growing number of Web publishers are individuals who want to share their ideas and interests with the world. These individuals aren't publishing on the Web to make a profit. They are publishing on the Web because it's fun to create something that people around the world will see, it's challenging to test new publishing techniques, and it's exciting to build something dozens, hundreds, and often thousands of people will talk about.

# Conducting Business

On the Web, your business is never closed. Consumers have access to your site 24 hours a day, 7 days a week, 365 days a year. They don't have to worry about fighting traffic to get to the mall. They don't have to race to the store after work and hope that it's not closed. They don't have to talk to a sales representative who's having a bad day and doesn't want to answer their questions. They can access information related to your products and services at their own pace and when it's most convenient for them, even if it's 3 a.m. on Christmas morning.

Businesses are striving to establish a presence on the Web for many different reasons. Some businesses are experimenting and trying to discover the benefits of Web publishing. They are promoting their company's product and service online. Often, they try to gauge consumer interest areas and figure out the directions the Web site should grow in to best serve customers.

Other businesses focus strictly on profits from Web publishing. They expect to make direct sales to customers and are interested in little else. These businesses are often disappointed when their Web publishing operation does not generate thousands of new sales. What these businesses fail to realize is that benefits of Web publishing are not always tangible.

Although advertising agencies would undoubtedly argue to the contrary, you cannot precisely gauge the sales generated from a $100,000 television commercial. You can estimate the potential sales based on the estimated size of the viewing audience, but you cannot directly relate sales to a particular 30-second television commercial. The same is true in Web publishing. If your consumers aren't purchasing your product at your online order center, that does not mean they aren't reading about the product online and purchasing the product locally.

Although increasing the bottom line because of Web publishing can be a goal, it should not be the only goal. Internet savvy businesses have many goals for their Web publishing operations and know the Web is best used for

- Providing enhanced customer service
- Public relations
- Marketing to global audiences
- Direct sales

# Enhanced Customer Service

What do you do when the customer has questions and wants answers at 3 a.m.? Most customer service departments are not open 24 hours a day, primarily because of the tremendous expense of providing around-the-clock service. The best time to reach customers is at their leisure, and when they have questions about your products or services.

One of the biggest customer complaints is the wait to get service. Nothing frustrates customers more than waiting on the phone or in a line to get service. Some companies solve this problem by hiring additional customer services representatives during peak periods. Other companies simply cannot afford the additional expense of hiring extra personnel, and the result is poor customer service and long waits for service.

On the Web, there is no wait to get customer support. Customers access the Web site, follow your links to your customer support area, and find the information they need. Ideally, the customer service area would have search facilities so that customers could search for specific information quickly.

The Web dramatically reduces the cost of publishing product information. Not only can you provide product information to customers, but you can do so on a scale that would be prohibitively expensive through traditional mediums. You can turn your one-page ad for a leading magazine into a 20-page exposé on your product for a fraction of the cost of publishing in the magazine. In fact, for the same cost as publishing a one-page ad in a leading magazine, you can probably publish detailed information on your entire product line.

Quick access to information is often critical to the success of your products and services. The Web dramatically reduces the lag time for access to new product information. Instead of having to wait days for product information to arrive in the mail, customers can access new product information at your Web site within seconds after you publish it.

Documentation for products is a key area customers focus on. Manuals delivered with products aren't always detailed enough for customers. Poorly written manuals are sometimes the result of a rush to get the product to market or publishing constraints that limit the size of the manual to reduce costs. Many manuals also contain typos and inconsistencies. Correcting these inconsistencies is costly and impractical when products have already been shipped to wholesalers, retailers, and customers. You can correct the deficiencies of your printed manual by providing a deluxe version of the manual online.

The Web dramatically reduces the costs of distributing upgrades to customers. Not only can you provide information on patches for software products, you can make the patches available for downloading online. Providing customers with free upgrades to your products is good business, especially because most minor upgrades fix bugs in the original product. The company saves money because disks and documentation do not have to be published and shipped to the customer.

To provide quality service and to ensure you are meeting the needs of the customer, you need feedback from customers. Your Web pages can have forms that customers fill out and submit online via e-mail. In this way, you can keep in touch with the needs of your customers. Fill-out forms can also be used to obtain customer opinions on your latest products and services. You can compile these opinion surveys and use the statistics to identify areas for improvement in future product releases.

## Public Relations

Building the image of your business is extremely important. One of the best ways to build your company's image is through press coverage. Savvy businesses with Web sites have the Web equivalent of neon signs leading the press to special areas set up for them.

Often these areas contain lists of contacts for key personnel in the company, such as the marketing director, the public relations manager for hardware issues, or the public relations manager for new product releases. On the Web you can do much more than simply list names; you can include color photos of the company representatives and executive officers. You can include their phone numbers, fax numbers, and e-mail addresses. You can even include online forms for quick submission of public relations questions.

Along with contact information, these areas often contain press releases. Press releases on your business's products and services are free advertising. Many Web sites publish current and past press releases as well as information to be freely distributed by the press. Coverage in the press shows interested parties what your company has done in the past and what it is doing now. Press releases aren't only for the press, however. You should also provide access to press releases in areas frequented by your customers. In this way, customers can also see what the company has done in the past and is doing now.

You can also provide demos and screen shots of your products for downloading. In this way, people who are interested in your products can see them firsthand. If they are interested, they can test the demo. If they need screen shots for publication in a book, magazine, or newspaper, they can download and use the material you provide.

# Marketing to Global Audiences

Selling your products and services to consumers is accomplished through marketing. The interactive and dynamic nature of the Web makes it a powerful tool for marketing. If you don't market your products, they won't sell. If you don't tell people about your services, no one is going to hire you. Large corporations spend millions of dollars on marketing every year. Traditional direct advertising mediums include television and radio commercials, display advertising in magazines and newspapers, and mass marketing campaigns through direct mail.

The problem with direct marketing is that there is no guarantee your product will sell based on the advertisement, or that you will actually make sales to the consumers you reach. For example, the typical response rate for direct mailings is 3 to 4 percent. This means if you distribute 10,000 flyers to a targeted mailing list, you will generally make 300 to 400 sales.

In recent years, many companies have been turning to marketing mediums that are more interactive than direct advertising and less expensive than personal sales visits. Companies are using telemarketing to reach potential customers by phone. Companies are also using the long, documentary-style commercials called infomercials to provide customers with information about products in a setting that seems interactive. Although telemarketing and infomercials are more interactive than traditional forms of marketing, they also have drawbacks.

Many people view telemarketing as an invasion of their privacy and when telemarketers get through to a person willing to listen, they only have a few minutes to make a sale. Infomercials, like personal sales visits, are not always practical. Infomercials are produced television programs that cost hundreds of thousands of dollars to produce and televise. To produce a successful infomercial, you need the right type of product.

The wonderful thing about Web marketing is that it is right for all types of products and provides a level of interaction with customers that is on a par with personal sales visits. You don't have to spend $100,000 or even $10,000 to reach a global audience. You can publish on the Web for $100 a month or less.

Your Web pages can help you establish connections with new customers and build relationships with your current customers. Web users reach businesses in the world market at the click of a button. One click can take them to a business in London, England. Another click can take them to a business in Albuquerque, New Mexico. The image you present through your Web site is often all the potential customer will know about your business; thus, you can gain a substantial competitive advantage in a global market simply by projecting a strong image.

Web marketing is not a replacement for traditional marketing and is best used in combination with other types of marketing. However, Web marketing can certainly help companies of any size meet their marketing needs. The following sidebars show some comparisons that you might want to consider.

---

### TELEVISION ADVERTISING COMPARED TO SETTING UP AND MAINTAINING A COMMERCIAL WEB SITE

**Option A: Television commercial**
Audience: One million television viewers
Cost: $125,000
Breakdown of costs:
Development and production: $50,000
Broadcast expense: $75,000
Duration: 30 seconds
Recurring costs for broadcasting same commercial to similar-sized audience: $75,000

**Option B: Web site with hundreds of megabytes of data available**
Audience: 10,000 hits per day for 365 days (3.65 million hits)
Cost: $120,000
Breakdown of costs:
Purchase high-capacity Web server: $20,000
One-year salary for server administrator: $50,000
Professional site design: $20,000
One-year T1 connection to Internet: $25,000
Installation fees for T1: $5,000
Average duration of exposure to advertising: 3–5 minutes/hit
Recurring costs for maintaining Web site: $75,000

---

### MAGAZINE ADVERTISING COMPARED TO RUNNING A WEB SITE FROM AN INTERNET SERVICE PROVIDER'S (ISP) WEB SERVER

**Option A: One-page magazine advertisement**
Audience: 100,000 readers
Cost: $18,000
Breakdown of costs:
Development and design: $8,000
Publication expense: $10,000
Average duration of exposure to advertising: 30–60 seconds
Recurring costs for running same advertisement in other magazines: $10,000

**Option B: Web site on ISP's Web server with 10 to 20 megabytes of available data**
Audience: 2,500 hits per day for 365 days (912,500 hits)
Cost: $11,300
Breakdown of costs:
Professional site design: $10,000
One-year account fee: $1,200
Phantom domain set up and registration: $100 (includes $50 annual fee for domain registration)
Average duration of exposure to advertising: 3–5 minutes/hit
Recurring annual costs: $1,250 minimum, additional $2,000–5,000 for site maintenance

## DIRECT MAIL ADVERTISING COMPARED TO PRODUCING A WEB PUBLICATION

**Option A: Mass marketing campaign through direct mailings**
Audience: 10,000 consumers
Cost: $2,000
Breakdown of costs:
10,000 sheets paper: $75
10,000 envelopes: $125
10,000 envelope labels: $50
Printer supplies for laser printer: $100
Mail expense (bulk rate): $1,400
Targeted mailing list: $250
Average duration of exposure to advertising: 0–60 seconds
Recurring costs for subsequent mailings: $1,750–2,000

**Option B: Web publication with 23 megabytes of data**
Audience: 500 hits per day for 365 days (182,500 hits)
Cost: $650
Breakdown of costs:
One-year account fee: $600
Set up: $50
Average duration of exposure to advertising: 3–5 minutes/hit
Recurring annual costs: $600

# Electronic Commerce

Making direct sales on the Web is not only a possibility, it is a reality, and the interactive nature of the Web is largely responsible for making these sales. Businesses all over the world have online order centers. Primarily, their customers use fill-out forms to directly submit orders for processing.

---

**CAUTION**

Online ordering has tremendous potential. Dozens of Internet-savvy businesses have increased revenues 200 to 300 percent through online ordering. However, for every success story there are several companies that fail miserably. The primary reason companies don't generate sales online is that they don't take the time to learn about the market. Traditional advertising and marketing schemes simply do not work on the Web.

The company I founded, The Virtual Press, Inc., offers many services to businesses wanting to establish a presence on the Web. When I wear my Internet consulting hat, the advice I often offer new businesses is this: Don't measure the success of your Web site by the revenues generated from online orders.

The Web is best viewed as an extremely powerful advertising medium and marketing tool. Television commercials don't generate sales that can be specifically correlated to a single commercial either. You wouldn't pull the plug on your television commercials when 10,000 viewers fail to run out and buy your latest gizmo immediately after the commercial. So why would you pull the plug on your Web site?

---

Because electronic commerce is in its infancy on the Internet, the mechanism behind direct ordering differs greatly from site to site. A growing number of businesses have set up ways for customers to make secure transfers. In this way, sensitive information, such as credit card numbers, is protected by encryption. More businesses will adopt secure transfer methods when true security standards are implemented.

Currently, businesses with online order centers use a variety of methods to secure transfers. Many businesses have customers set up an account with the business before ordering online. Customers are assigned an account number that can be used for online ordering at the customer's convenience. Normally, any orders placed using the account number can only be shipped to the address the customer specified when the account was set up.

Some businesses allow customers to place orders online and then ask them to confirm the order by phone or fax. Customers would typically get an order reference number that they could provide to a sales representative or automated voice mail system along with their credit card number. Because the customer would have already provided all the essential information online, the whole confirmation process by phone or fax would typically take less than a minute.

# Spreading the Word About Your Ideas

Often the focus of Web publishing is on the business benefits, yet the Web is much more than a place to conduct marketing and advertising. You don't have to publish on the Web for profit. For every business publishing on the Web to increase the bottom line, someone somewhere is publishing on the Web simply to spread the word about his or her ideas.

The Web is an open repository for information. Research institutes, universities, colleges, non-profit organizations, and individual Web publishers freely publish information. One of the primary reasons to Web publish is to gain recognition for your ideas, research findings, and projects. Yet, you can Web publish simply because you want to share information and ideas with others. Knowledge is power and is the key to freedom for all people of the world.

Spreading the word about ideas you have published on the Web is easy and, more importantly, free. Dozens of Web sites specialize in indexing and cataloging information that is available on the Web. Some of these sites maintain specialized lists of popular, new, and cool documents. Other sites maintain comprehensive lists.

Web users rely on these databases to find resources on the Web. To add your documents to a list, all you have to do is register your documents. This generally means filling out a form and submitting it online, which takes only a few minutes. The key information you enter into a fill-out form includes your name, business address, e-mail address, uniform resource locator (URL), and a brief description of your document. You can find a comprehensive list of catalog sites in Chapter 36, "Designing and Publishing a Web Site."

# Features of the Web

The Web is the most dynamic medium you will ever publish in. Using the rich features of the Web, you have virtually limitless possibilities for publishing your ideas.

Much has changed since the early days of the Web. Although the first Web publications were largely textual in nature and limited in multimedia features, today's Web publications are highly graphical and rich in multimedia features. Using the facilities of the Web, you can easily incorporate images into your publication.

Web publishers use images to convey their messages in ways more powerful than text alone. FrontPage features support for over a dozen image formats. Because FrontPage is a WYSIWYG authoring tool, all images you use in your publications can be viewed directly in the FrontPage Editor.

Interactivity is a key ingredient for making connections with readers. Highly interactive documents invite readers to become participants. When your readers are actively involved, they are no longer simply watching as you unfold ideas in page after page. They are deciding how they want to unfold the story and are choosing their own path through it. Although the Web is not the only medium you can use to create interactive publications, it is the most versatile and least expensive publishing medium available.

Creating multimedia documents for use on the Web is easier than you might think. In fact, the Web is the easiest publishing medium to create multimedia documents in. At the Web publisher's fingertips is the world's greatest multimedia library—the Internet and all its archives. Not only does this library have thousands of multimedia clips that you can obtain for free or for a small fee; it is complete with a multimedia developer's toolkit that you can obtain for free or for a small fee as well.

As if free clips and tools weren't enough to persuade you that Web publishing is your best choice for creating multimedia publications, the wonderful thing about Web technology is that it is advancing at an explosive pace. Already you can create publications with animation, soundtracks, and video without needing any special tools at all.

# Summary

Navigating the Web is easy if you understand the principles of hypertext linking and URLs. Although hypertext references can be text- or graphics-based, they are all defined by URLs that specify the path to the resources to be accessed and retrieved.

The most exciting time to publish on the Web is right now. You have a ground floor opportunity to be a part of something truly wonderful and for once, it isn't going to cost you a bundle to join. People all around the world are publishing on the Web for fun and profit—and because they can.

The Web is the most versatile medium you will ever publish in. Web publishers have proven time and time again that there are no real limits to what can be published on the Web. Not only are they publishing every imaginable type of document that has ever been created, but they are doing it successfully, and they are helping to build the most powerful information system in the world: the World Wide Web. Best of all, with FrontPage, publishing on the Web has never been easier. So, what are you waiting for?

# Publishing on a Corporate Intranet

**3**

*by William Robert Stanek*

**IN THIS CHAPTER**

Intranet publishing is the practical application of Web publishing to a real-world business problem—publishing on the corporate network. Networks situated in a small geographic area, such as an office building, are called local area networks (LANs). A typical LAN may have 100 computers attached to it. Networks that spread across large geographic areas, such as states and countries, are called wide area networks (WAN).

While a typical WAN may be a network of hundreds of computers and is composed of any number of LAN segments or nodes, the key distinction between a LAN and a WAN is not size; rather it is geographic area. WANs generally span geographic boundaries and are connected using phone lines, satellite links, or cables. Yet when it comes to intranet publishing, the size of the network and the area it spans do not matter as long as the computers are linked in some form of network. The network could be 10 or 10,000 computers. The network could span the globe. The type of computer doesn't matter either. The computers on the network can be a mix of Sun Sparcs, Macintoshs, IBM compatibles, or any other platform you can think of.

Although many types of intranet publishing operations are possible with today's technology, the focus in this chapter is on using the hypermedia capabilities of the World Wide Web to set up an intranet publishing operation. As you've seen in previous chapters, the power of the Web is in its diversity. Its handling of hypertext objects enables cross-platform solutions. With intranet publishing, you easily can set up a mini-Internet within your company. Your mini-Internet can be accessible by the outside world or exclusive to the company. No matter how you decide to set up your intranet, the purchase of FrontPage and *Microsoft FrontPage Unleashed* is your first step toward success in intranet publishing.

# What Is Intranet Publishing?

A reality in the business world is that company-wide databases tax resources in both labor costs and real-money terms. Even the best conventional database tools have high learning curves. Another reality is that sometimes you just don't have two to four weeks to train new personnel on the use of the database. And, company-wide databases are growing in size and complexity.

Databases aren't the only part of the company that grows as the company grows. The paper trail of documents—brochures, information packets, and policies—also grows with the company. Maintaining an ever-growing paper trail is costly and personnel-intensive. Every time there is a product release, product update, or press release, documents must be distributed to support personnel and other key personnel within the company. This costs money.

Other problems stem from this paper trail. For example, the customer support department could be misinforming customers based on data that is days or weeks old. To better serve customers, employees need access to the most current information. What employees really need to stay current is a metaindex of company resources and documents in a searchable form so that information can be retrieved in an instant. A company-wide metaindex of resources and documents would be astronomically expensive using conventional means. Publishing these documents electronically on a LAN or WAN is a nonconventional solution to this problem that will drastically reduce costs and save countless hours.

Extending the functionality of the World Wide Web to LAN and WAN environments is a cost- and time-effective business solution. The facilities of the World Wide Web don't have high learning curves. In fact, there isn't much of a learning curve at all if the facilities and tools are a part of the company's infrastructure.

Intranet publishing requires only that you install and configure two things:

> Web server communications
> Web browser communications

Although FrontPage includes the Personal Web Server, the package does not include a browser. Many browsers are available as shareware and as commercial software. The two hottest browsers are Internet Explorer and Netscape Navigator.

## MANAGING BROWSER LICENSES ON YOUR INTRANET

If you choose a commercial browser such as Netscape Navigator, you must pay a licensing fee for each copy of the browser used at your site. There are several ways you can determine the number of licenses you need to purchase.

You could purchase a license for each computer on your network. In this case, if you had 500 computers on the network, you would purchase 500 licenses. Although the software companies love this model, few network administrators follow it. Under most circumstances, all 500 computers will not be running the browser.

The trick is to determine what percentage of the users on the network will be running the browser at the same time. In a typical network environment where the intranet documents are not critical to the corporate mission, probably only 20 to 25 percent of users will use the browser at any one time. Thus, on a 500-node network, you might want to start with 100 to 120 licenses for the browser of your choice.

To ensure that only the number of browsers for which you've purchased licenses are running at any one time, you should set up a license server. The job of the license server is to track the number of licenses in use and deny access to the browser software as necessary. When users try to exceed the license count, your license server should display a message stating that no licenses are currently available and that the user should try again in a few minutes. The license server should also log the number of disallowed accesses with a time stamp. Using the server logs, you can periodically re-evaluate your license needs.

Setting up and managing a license server might seem like a hassle, but it can save you and your company thousands of dollars. If the browser software you chose costs $35 per license, a 500-node network using 120 licenses will save over $13,000.

Through intranet publishing, you can provide a metaindex of documents, access to company databases, and much more. Using FrontPage, you can directly publish existing documents or convert document formats to the Hypertext Markup Language (HTML) format. The great thing about HTML documents is that they are dynamic. Personnel don't have to rummage through a paper trail or learn the commands to interface with the company database. To find a related reference with HTML, all they have to do is click on links. To perform a database search, they just need to enter a word or two at a prompt. Some of the types of documents you can network publish include

  Policies
  Standards
  On-the-job training documentation
  Online help manuals
  User manuals
  Department/company-wide memos
  Project descriptions, goals, and contacts
  News releases
  Trip reports
  Employee recognition awards
  Company mission, goals, and objectives
  Company background and history
  Company forms
  Company product and sales information
  Company telephone directory
  Office and key personnel rosters

# Why You Don't Have To Be on the Internet

A common misconception about the Web is that to set up a Web server you must be on the Internet. This simply is not true. The company does not have to be connected to the Internet to take advantage of Web tools. The Web server doesn't have to be linked to the Internet, and company personnel don't have to be able to access the Internet to make intranet publishing a reality within the company.

Several books concerning the Web and the Internet specifically—and mistakenly—state that a Transmission Control Protocol/Internet Protocol (TCP/IP) connection to the Internet is an absolute requirement for setting up a Web server. It's true that an Internet connection would help in obtaining Web server software because server software is widely available on the Internet. However, this software, the installation instructions, and manuals can be downloaded from any Internet account and subsequently loaded onto the company network. You can also use the Personal Web Server included with FrontPage as your company's server software.

Therefore, a more correct statement is that if the company wants to use the Internet and take advantage of the World Wide Web that is a part of the Internet, there must be some kind of connection to the Internet. The company does not have to be connected to the Internet or any part of the Internet to set up a Web server for use within the company.

The Federal government has *private Internets*. Some large corporations have private Internets. You could call these mini-Internets simply *intranets*. An intranet is a network within an organization that takes advantage of Internet and Web technologies. What these private intranets allow on their networks is their business. What you provide on your network is your business.

When you set up a Web server, you tell it the domain—structure—you want it to operate within. You can include or exclude links to the outside world as you see fit. You can even include or exclude divisions within the company. It all depends on how you set up the Web server and the permissions you grant or deny.

# Intranet Publishing Versus Paper Publishing

You have probably heard the term *paperless office* before. Don't cringe. Although this eventuality isn't outside the realm of possibility, this isn't a lecture on how Web publishing can help make the office paperless. The truth is that Web publishing company documents won't eliminate the paper trail, but it can help to dramatically reduce the paper trail. It can help to streamline the update and correction process. It can also help to distribute large amounts of up-to-date information throughout the organization. The decision to intranet publish or not to intranet publish ultimately comes down to simple economics:

- Is intranet publishing affordable?
- Is intranet publishing cost-saving?
- Is intranet publishing cost-effective?

## Intranet Publishing Is Affordable

Costs for incorporating Web publishing into an existing network are negligible. Often a network will already have a workstation capable of carrying the additional load as the Web server. The Web server doesn't have to be a dedicated machine. This is especially true for small networks or networks where a limited number of personnel have access to the Web server.

Usually, you won't need a full-time Web server administrator. Existing networks already have, or should have, a system administrator who can handle the additional duties as the Web server administrator. Web servers are easy to administer once they are set up and running.

Although using an existing workstation is not always a possibility, the good news is that the Web server doesn't have to be a power machine. Web servers serving thousands of users are running on network-configured computers with Intel Pentium processors.

# Intranet Publishing Saves Money

Intranet publishing the company documents can reduce print costs and other associated costs dramatically. Printed documents quickly become outdated. Technical manuals, company policies, and other important documents are expensive to maintain and reprint. With intranet publishing, there aren't any print costs, and you'll find that maintaining Web documents is easier than maintaining printed documents.

There simply aren't high learning curves in a point-and-click interface environment. There are even ways to automate the updating of documents. Time savings for easy maintenance and use add up to big money savings over traditional alternatives. The savings also extend to personnel. Your company can realize these savings in personnel in the fewer hours spent building, searching, and maintaining company documents. Ease of use means finding information is less frustrating for workers, and a less stressful environment is good for the company and its workers.

Ease of use might also mean that new employees can become productive company assets sooner. Using a Web browser, such as Mosaic, a new employee with little training could make retrievals from the company's Oracle database on the first day of the job. To do this, the employee would access a Web page with a fill out form or query box like those discussed in Chapter 11, "Using Forms and the Form Page Wizard." After typing in the information he or she wants to retrieve, the user would simply click on the submit button and soon afterward, the retrieval would display on the screen.

# Intranet Publishing Is Cost-Effective

Intranet publishing is a highly efficient way to ensure that company information is distributed throughout the organization. Putting a document on the company Web can provide instant access for all personnel, several departments, or an individual department. You'll discover that Web documents are easier to maintain, produce, index, and use—which translates directly to cost efficiency.

If cost efficiency is a big consideration for the company (and it should be), consider the case of the company with global offices. These offices are probably already connected via a WAN or have some kind of dial-up access to the Internet. Despite the ease of use of electronic mail, company documents flow back and forth through conventional mail every day. This is because some types of documents aren't suited for posting to e-mail. Posting a 500-page policy manual via e-mail to all company personnel would probably bring the network to a screeching halt. Even if it didn't, the people who should be reading the policy manual wouldn't because of the form of the message.

With intranet publishing, the policy manual would be an interactive, indexed document that personnel could easily search for references important to the operations of their respective departments. More importantly, the entire huge manual wouldn't have to be mailed and re-mailed to a dozen global or regional offices.

# Platforms for Your Corporate Web Server

Before setting up or installing software, you must determine what platform the Web server will run on and select server software for your platform of choice. The FrontPage Personal Web server runs on Windows 95 and Windows NT platforms, yet has extensions for the most popular Windows 95, Windows NT, and UNIX-based servers. This means you can create and manage documents on a Windows 95 or Windows NT computer, and publish your documents on a Windows 95, Windows NT, or UNIX platform.

> **NOTE**
>
> A Macintosh version of FrontPage is scheduled for release in Summer 1996 and may already be available. This addition will mean that you can use FrontPage to create, manage, and publish your documents on virtually any operating system.

Currently, there are FrontPage server extensions for the servers shown in Table 3.1. These extensions are free from Microsoft.

**Table 3.1. Server software for use with FrontPage extensions.**

| Server Software | UNIX Solaris | SunOS | HP/UX | IRIX | Other | Windows NT | Windows 95 |
|---|---|---|---|---|---|---|---|
| Apache | X | X | X | X | X | | |
| CERN | X | X | X | X | X | | |
| Microsoft IIS | | | | | | X | |
| NCSA | X | X | X | X | X | | |
| Netscape Communications | X | X | X | X | X | X | |
| Commerce | X | X | X | X | X | X | |
| Open Market | X | X | X | X | X | | |
| O'Reilly Website | | | | | | X | X |

The best server software for you is most likely the software that will run on the workstation you plan to use as the network's Web server, but several factors come into play that could change your mind. The four primary factors are

- Expertise of the installation team
- Reliability of the Web server

- Necessity of support
- Security

## The Expertise of the Installation Team

The level of expertise of the installation team will be a major determining factor in your choice of server. To configure for specific types of platforms, and primarily UNIX platforms, some Web server software must be compiled from source code. This is a good thing if you have an experienced team capable of setting parameters within the code to optimize for the intended system. Having the source code also means you can easily trace down and correct bugs and create enhancements to the existing code.

However, having the source code will do you no good if you cannot optimize and compile it. Therefore, if you do not have an experienced team or are looking for an easy solution for your intranet publishing operation, you will want to look at server software that does not need to be compiled or optimized. Fortunately, the easiest server software to install is included with FrontPage—Personal Web Server.

## Reliability of the Web Server

The necessary reliability of the Web server is the second major determining factor in choosing a server. Examine carefully how the company plans to use the Web server. The projected nature of the use will help drive your decision. Some server software is being continually updated and improved. Some platforms have a variety of support tools. Both are especially true for UNIX platforms, but not necessarily true for other platforms.

UNIX systems are the lifeblood of the Internet, and naturally some of the best server software is for UNIX systems. Because UNIX server software has been around longer, most of the bugs have been worked out, and the software is generally being continually improved.

The Personal Web Server included with FrontPage is very reliable. Still, the server has its limits and is best used with medium to low traffic sites.

## The Necessity of Support

The type of support needed to maintain the Web server is the third major determining factor in choosing your server. The primary reason for opting to use commercial Web server software is software support. If you believe the organization will need software support to keep the operation alive, commercial software is the best choice. Freeware software is generally provided on an as is basis. The creators ask that if you improve the software or fix bugs, you send them the updates.

**NOTE**

Because software support might play a major role in your decision to purchase Web server software, you should also know about other options such as hiring a software support firm to provide your company with technical support. Software support firms are a $100 million-a-year niche of the computer industry and are growing in number. Software support firms specialize in providing technical support for a wide range of products and are positioned well to replace many traditional help desk centers. Several of the early software support companies have been tremendously successful because of the strong need in the business community for prompt, reliable, and accurate technical support. As the Internet and the World Wide Web grow, these companies will undoubtedly start to support key Internet and Web software applications.

## Security Concerns

Security is the fourth major determining factor in choosing your server. Web server software that lacks adequate security constraints can put the company's network in jeopardy. This is critically important when the company plans to connect to the Internet.

All Web server software has some security features. Permissions granted or denied to users when the server software is being configured play an important role in security. Some of the most secure server software is available for UNIX. Again, this is primarily because Web server software for UNIX platforms has been around longer and has had more developers working on it.

# Web Server Software

This section examines server software supported by FrontPage server extensions. If you plan to use the Personal Web Server on a Windows 95/NT system, you do not need to obtain additional software.

**NOTE**

For detailed information on the Personal Web Server, see Part VII, "Managing Your Web." Part VII also covers server management and security.

The central process running on a Web server is the Hypertext Transfer Protocol Daemon (HTTPD). A daemon is a program that runs in the background and handles requests. Similarly the HTTP Daemon, or HTTPD, is the process that handles requests for a Web server. Although the daemon is only a part of server software, the term HTTPD is often used to refer to the server itself. For example, the Web server from the European Laboratory for Particle Physics (CERN) is referred to as CERN HTTPD. When people refer to CERN HTTPD, they are generally referring to the entire Web server software package from CERN.

Some servers have the capability to proxy serve documents. This means company personnel could access the Web past an existing firewall, and the outside world could get Web documents on the firewall but should not be able to get past the firewall. A *firewall* is a workstation that shields the internal network from the outside network—the Internet. It is the only machine that is directly connected to the Internet. This a great way to minimize unauthorized access to the company network.

## Apache HTTPD

The Apache HTTPD server runs on UNIX platforms and is free. Because Apache is a plug-in replacement for NCSA's Web Server versions 1.3 and 1.4, it is extremely popular. Apache is designed for speed and reliability. It also fixes security problems found in NCSA HTTPD.

Some of Apache's features include

- Access authorization mechanisms
- Content negotiation in which the server can serve clients with documents that offer the best representation of information that the client is capable of accepting
- Customized responses to errors and problems
- Directory indexing
- Multihomed servers where requests made to different IP addresses can be mapped to the same machine
- The capability to include the output of commands or other files in HTML documents
- The capability to process CGI scripts
- Unlimited numbers of Alias and Redirect directives
- User Authentication on a database model

You can learn more about Apache HTTPD and obtain the source at

```
http://www.apache.org/
```

## CERN HTTPD

CERN HTTPD runs on UNIX platforms. This is one of the most popular pieces of server software. It is well-maintained freeware with excellent documentation. One of CERN Web server's greatest selling points is that it can also be run as a caching proxy server. The server will cache recently or frequently retrieved documents to improve response time.

This server's features include

- Access to authorization mechanisms
- Automatic generation of directory tree for browsers
- The capability to process CGI scripts
- Content negotiation in which the server can serve clients with documents that offer the best representation of information that the client is capable of accepting
- Directory indexing
- Document name to filename mapping for longer-lived document names

You can learn more about CERN HTTPD and obtain the source at

```
http://www.w3.org/hypertext/WWW/Daemon/Status.html
```

# Microsoft Internet Information Server

Microsoft Internet Information Server (IIS) is a power option for intranets using Windows NT servers. The main server is an integrated HTTPD, File Transfer Protocol (FTP), and Gopher server with a graphical installation utility that allows you to completely install the product in less than 10 minutes. IIS is optimized for performance, speed, and reliability. Currently, you can also get free trial versions of IIS from Microsoft's Web site at

```
http://www.microsoft.com/
```

Some of the features include

- Advanced fault tolerance with disk mirroring, drive duplexing, and Raid 5
- The capability to process CGI scripts
- Graphical server management and performance monitor
- Integration with existing databases using the Internet Database Connector
- Multihomed servers where requests made to different IP addresses can be mapped to the same machine
- Support for the Secure Sockets Layer, which provides strict user and access authentication
- Support for the Internet Server Application Programming Interface (ISAPI)

You can learn more about Microsoft IIS at

```
http://www.microsoft.com/BackOffice/InfoServ/default.htm
```

# NCSA HTTPD

NCSA HTTPD runs on UNIX platforms. NCSA's server was designed to be fast and have a low overhead, which means it's not taxing on the system. It is freeware and rich in features. The current version is 1.5.X.

This server's features include

- Access to authorization mechanisms
- The capability to include the output of commands or other files in HTML documents
- The capability to process CGI scripts
- Directory indexing
- Multihomed servers where requests made to different IP addresses can be mapped to the same machine

With NCSA HTTPD, you can make the server more secure by limiting access to server directories. You can learn more about NCSA HTTPD and obtain the source at

`http://hoohoo.ncsa.uiuc.edu/docs/Overview.html`

## Netscape Servers

Netscape offers several commercial server software packages for UNIX and Windows NT platforms. FrontPage currently supports the two most widely used Netscape servers. These include the following:

| | |
|---|---|
| Netscape Commerce Server | Designed to enable secure commerce on the Internet |
| Netscape Communications Server | Designed to handle heavy loads and multimedia |

Netscape claims that its server software offers increased performance over the competition and can easily be integrated with commercial or custom applications. The software tends to have higher overhead than other HTTP servers, but it definitely makes up for this by reducing response times and making better use of the communications bandwidth. Netscape servers are also some of the most secure in the world.

You can learn more about Netscape servers at

`http://home.mcom.com/comprod/server_central/index.html`

## Open Market

The Open Market WebServer is a commercial server for UNIX platforms and comes in two versions: standard and secure. The Open Market Secure WebServer offers simultaneous support for both the Secure Hypertext Transfer Protocol (S-HTTP) and the Secure Sockets Layer (SSL).

Some of the features of Open Market include

- Advanced tools for server administration and performance monitoring
- The capability to process CGI scripts

- Directory indexing
- Enhanced logging of statistics
- Flexible access control with the Tool Command Language (Tcl)
- A multithreaded design

You can learn more about Open Market servers at

```
http://www.openmarket.com/segments/servers/
```

# O'Reilly Website

O'Reilly Website is an award-winning commercial server that runs on Windows 95 and Windows NT platforms. This server features many advanced utilities for Windows 95/NT environments and was designed for ease of use. Website is an integrated server package that includes an HTML browser, HTML editor, and comprehensive book.

Some of the features include

- The capability to process CGI scripts
- Directory indexing
- Enhanced logging of statistics
- Graphical server management and performance monitor
- A multithreaded design
- Strict access control

You can learn more about O'Reilly Website at

```
http://website.ora.com/
```

# Selecting a Domain Name

After you've selected a platform and server software, you should decide on a domain name for the Web server. During the installation process, you'll have to enter a domain name for the Web server. Common domain names for Web servers begin with www, such as

```
www.yourhostname.com
```

If the company has decided to connect the server to the Internet, the network must have a unique identifier and domain name. You must register with the Internet Address Naming Authority (IANA), also called the InterNIC. Your company can select any domain name as long as it is unique. The InterNIC charges for domain name registration. If you plan to register a domain, check with the InterNIC for the current price for registration.

Each computer connecting to the Internet must have a unique IP address. The necessity of a unique IP address might mean changing the IP address on computers you plan to connect to the Internet. Obtaining IP addresses from the InterNIC is a three-part process:

1. Obtain the InterNIC Internet number registration form from

   `ftp://rs.internic.net/templates/internet-number-template.txt`

2. Follow the comprehensive instructions included with the form you received using the FTP address to fill out the form.

3. E-mail the completed form to

   `hostmaster@internic.net`

Domain name registration for ROOT, EDU, GOV, COM, NET, and ORG domains is also a three-part process:

1. Obtain the InterNIC domain name registration form from

   `ftp://rs.internic.net/templates/domain-template.txt`

2. Follow the comprehensive instructions included with the form you received to fill out the form.

3. E-mail the completed form to

   `hostmaster@internic.net`

**CAUTION**

Beware of people trying to sell registration services on the Internet. Ultimately, these individuals must go through the InterNIC to register your domain. These individuals provide easy-to-use fill-out forms for processing your registration and charge fees ranging from $100-$500. As you have seen, the submission process is not difficult and is certainly not worth $500.

**NOTE**

The InterNIC is a very busy organization. Not only does it provide detailed explanations with registration forms, but it also includes multiple sources to find additional information with each of its forms. Refer to these sources of additional information before sending inquiries to the InterNIC. If you have a unique situation that is not covered in either the IP or domain registration forms, such as registering as an Internet Service Provider, you can find a list of registration forms provided by the InterNIC here:

`http://rs0.internic.net/templates.html`

# The Basics of Installing Your Corporate Web Server

Now that you've selected your platform and software, you're ready to begin the installation process. After following the tips you'll find throughout the rest of this chapter, you should have your server up and running before the day is through.

You might be amazed at how easy it is to get the server up and running now that the major decisions as to the platform and software are behind you. Although commercial server software is nearly trouble-free and includes automatic installation processes, freeware server software is not a bad way to go either. As you have seen, for most freeware server software there are precompiled versions of the software available. This makes installation very easy.

The server installation process includes six basic steps:

1. Purchase or download the software.
2. Begin the installation process by compiling the software or selecting installation options after initiating the automatic installation process.
3. Configure the server or select automatic configuration options.
4. Ensure that all the files are in the locations specified in the documentation and that permissions are set correctly. This is usually an automatic process for commercial and freeware software, but it doesn't hurt to be safe.
5. Start the server.
6. Test the server.

Each of these steps is described in more detail in the following sections.

> **NOTE**
>
> The section titled "Quick Setup and Installation" in Chapter 4, "Introducing FrontPage," details how you can set up and test the Personal Web Server. If you have decided to use the Personal Web Server and are eager to get started with FrontPage, you might want to jump ahead to that chapter. After you set up the Personal Web Server and FrontPage, you should read the remainder of this chapter to gain more insight on intranet publishing.

## Purchasing or Downloading the Server Software

Most server software packages are available for downloading on the Internet. If you have access to the Web, visit the site that has the software you would like to obtain. There, you will find information about the most current version of the software and instructions on downloading the software. Many of these sites have installation instructions available at the Web site and complete operating manuals that also might be viewed as HTML documents or downloaded.

Some commercial server software packages must be purchased directly from the creators and are not available for downloading. Before paying big money for a product you are unsure of, visit the company on the Web and check the available documentation carefully to ensure that the software will meet the needs of your organization. It might also be possible to obtain a test version (Alpha/Beta versions) of the software for trial and evaluation.

# Beginning the Installation Process

Most of the server software packages you'll find on the Internet are compressed. Although the type of compression really depends on the platform for which the software was designed, the installation instructions will usually explain how to uncompress the software. Before uncompressing the software, you should create a new directory and move the file to that directory for unpacking. Uncompress the software, if necessary, and then start the installation process. You might be prompted to enter the domain name you selected earlier or be directed to add the domain name to a system file.

# Configuring the Server

Each type of server software has different configuration steps. The best source for configuration information is the server documentation. Read the documentation thoroughly. If the documentation isn't clear on an area that involves security, you should follow the strictest security option.

Configuring commercial server software is a simple process. After starting the installation process, you either select configuration options or make simple adjustments to your system. At some point during this process, you'll be asked to input the domain name you have selected.

For shareware server software there are some special considerations. After you've unpacked the files and compiled the software, if necessary, you will need to edit configuration files and create logs as necessary. Configuring these servers is an involved process that could fill a chapter for each software package. This is primarily because of the numerous options and features available. Read the manuals and go through the configuration files line by line. After carefully considering the options, enable or disable the server parameters.

# Double-Checking for Security

This is a last check for security. Always make sure that all the server files are where they are supposed to be and that file permissions are set as appropriate. This is normally done for you during the installation process. However, if you updated files or moved files around the system, you might have changed file permissions.

Server and network security is critically important. Even if you don't plan to connect to the Internet, it is best to test the server internally for a trial period before opening the floodgates. Let your Tiger Team discover possible security problems and not hackers that might be after company secrets.

> **NOTE**
>
> A *Tiger Team* is a group of people assigned to find security problems. They try to break into the system to find its weaknesses. If you don't have a special team assigned, or you are a one-person operation, test the server's security yourself. You probably will be glad you did.

## Start the Server

After setup, configuration, and final checks for security, you're ready to begin. Start the server and enter the world of intranet publishing! If you haven't already created your documents and moved them into place, follow the procedures in this book.

## Test the Server

Now that the server is up and running, you should test it out. If the server isn't running, check the next section for some helpful troubleshooting tips. The best way to test the server's operational status is with a Web browser. Load your favorite browser software and access the Web server with either of the following uniform resource locators (URLs):

```
http://www.yourcompany.com/
http://www.yourcompany.com:portnumber/
```

The name between the slashes is the name you gave to the server—its domain name—during the setup process. If you set up the Web server's ports in a location other than the default port, you must enter the port number parameter. If all went well, this should be the last step in the setup and configuration process. Congratulations!

# Troubleshooting Problems

Even the best of plans can go awry. If you know the type of problems you might experience and their symptoms, there is a better chance that you'll be able to correct the problem quickly. In this early stage of trying to get the server running and testing your document, you might experience the following:

- Problems with server processes—the server simply won't run the HTTPD.
- Problems accessing documents—you can't load a page into the browser or you're denied permission to do so.
- Problems within documents—the pages just don't look right.

# Problems with Server Processes

Don't fret if something goes wrong and the server software doesn't start. If this happens, review the server documentation step by step. Ensure that you've performed every step and that things on the server are as they should be. Chances are you skipped an important step or forgot to change the mode on a file. Some good indicators of problems with setup are

- Server processes start and then die.
- Server processes start, and many errors are written to the screen.
- Server processes start but won't execute properly.
- Other erratic behavior occurs, such as the server freezing up.

As you re-examine the installation procedures, pay close attention to syntax. Syntax is critically important, particularly on UNIX systems. Syntax includes punctuation marks such as periods or dashes that are included in filenames. Syntax problems could also come from files being in the wrong case. UNIX is case sensitive, meaning WSERVER, WServer, and wserver are three different filenames. Additionally on a UNIX system, type in the lines exactly as they are shown, including all spaces between assignment operators.

# Problems Accessing HTML Documents

Sometimes the server processes and other associated processes might seem to be running fine, but you can't access your documents. The first thing you should do is to make sure all files are where they should be. Most of the time, HTML documents and associated files must be in specific directories in order for the files to be accessed. If they are in the correct place, there are several key things on the server you should check next. Problems accessing HTML documents stem from three main sources:

- Incorrect file or directory permissions
- Incorrect file extensions
- Lack of an index file

## Incorrect File or Directory Permissions

Restrictions on files and directories are another key area to examine when you are having problems accessing files. During setup and configuration, you might have restricted access to files or directories inadvertently or purposefully but forgot the parameters you set. Check the configuration files to see what features you turned on or off, and then check permissions.

The permissions on the HTML documents and directories are important. This is especially true on UNIX systems where the default file permissions are set according to an involved permission set. All operating systems flag documents with permissions. Here are a few examples of flags on DOS/Windows systems:

Is this a system file?
Is this a hidden file?
Is this a read-only file?
Is this file executable?

UNIX systems add to this simple set of permissions by an order of magnitude. Files and directories have owners and group membership. Additionally, these files and directories have associated privileges: read, write, and execute permissions for the owner, the group, and others with access to the system. On UNIX systems, a directory must be executable to be accessible.

## Incorrect File Extensions

The file extension of HTML documents and other file formats is also critically important. Web servers can use the extension to determine what type of file you are trying to access. Web browsers can use the extension to determine what type of file you are retrieving and the action to take on the file. The proper extension for HTML documents is `.html` or `.htm`.

Without additional server configuration steps, most software will not recognize the extension of `.htm` as being a valid HTML document. The primary exception to this rule is on Windows systems where file extensions are limited to three characters.

## Lack of an Index File

If you are having problems accessing documents, you should check for a lack of an index file. Most Web server software wants directories with HTML documents to have an index file. If you don't include these index files, you might experience problems. The server will generally display this default document when a user specifies a directory name instead of a filename. This file is sometimes called `index.html` but not always. For example, MacHTTP, NCSA HTTPD, and CERN HTTPD each have different conventions for this index file:

| | |
|---|---|
| MacHTTP | Each folder should have a filename: `default.html`. |
| NCSA HTTPD | Although an `index.html` file isn't required for each directory, `srm.conf` should be set up properly to deal with this. |
| CERN HTTPD | Although this server will let you use alternate filenames for `index.html` (`Welcome.html`, `welcome.html`, `index.html`), these files should exist in the appropriate directories. |

# Problems Within HTML Documents

If you are having problems displaying documents, the appearance of objects and text in documents, or with hypertext links, the first place to check for problems should be the HTML structure in the documents. Syntax is critically important in HTML. Two of the most common syntax problem areas revolve around two sets of characters:

> The tag enclosure set: < >
>
> The double quotation mark set: " "

These two sets of characters will cause more problems than you can imagine. If the HTML document has an <, the closing > must be present. Consider the following example:

```
<STRONG>This is standard text./STRONG>
<STRONG>This is standard text.</STRONG>
```

The first line has a syntax problem that will cause problems in the HTML document. The missing closure on the STRONG tag will cause all text in the document up to the next properly closed STRONG tag to be in bold or emphasized type.

If the HTML document has a " inside a tag, the closing " must be present. Consider this example:

```
<A HREF="the_linked_document.html>Visit the new link.</A>
<A HREF="the_linked_document.html">Visit the new link.</A>
```

The syntax problem in the first line will cause problems in the HTML document. Not only will the missing quotation mark cause the link to fail, but the browser will think that everything up to the next quotation mark is a part of the link. This means that part of your document will not be displayed. The quotes must also be the standard American Standard Code of Information Interchange (ASCII) double quotes. Some word processors have so-called *smart* quotes, where the opening quotes look different from closing quotes. If your word processor has this feature, disable it. Smart quotes are not standard ASCII and will not work in your HTML documents.

# Administering an Intranet

Someone should be assigned to administer the new server. Although the network administrator or system administrator could easily take over the additional responsibilities, administrative duties do not have to be the responsibility of one person. As you'll see, it is sometimes a good idea to share these responsibilities.

The four general administrative duties include

- Answering technical questions
- Checking logs

■ Keeping the server running

■ Adding updates to the server

# Answering Technical Questions

The server should have a point of contact for technical questions. This is normally the Webmaster, an electronic mail alias providing a point of contact for the site. Web users can direct queries or comments to the Webmaster. A mail alias is a generic mail address that can be assigned to a single user or group of users.

On UNIX systems, common administrative mail aliases are `root` and `postmaster`. When you assign the `root` mail alias to your system administrator, she can receive feedback concerning system problems. When you assign the `postmaster` alias to your e-mail administrator, she can receive feedback for e-mail problems.

Similarly, the Webmaster can be a single person, your system administrator, or many people who answer specific types of questions. The mail address for the Webmaster is typically

`webmaster@yourcompany.com`

# Checking Logs

Checking system logs should be the responsibility of one person. Although there are different types of logs, the most important log is the server's error log. The error log keeps track of system problems. Another important log is the access log. The access log tracks who accessed what documents.

If the system seems sluggish or is experiencing problems, the first place the administrator should look is in the error log. The error log will tell the administrator what has been going wrong, and the repeated entries will provide an excellent time-picture of the problem. The error log also tracks bad links and bad HTML documents. If you search through the log for these problems, you will be able to identify problem documents and erroneous links.

The access log is another good log for the administrator to check periodically. This log tracks who accessed what documents. The accesses to documents can be critically important in tracking down security violators and suspicious system activity. The access log will also come in handy when you want to count the number of accesses to your site or accesses to particular pages at your site. For example, you might want to count all accesses to the site for the first week of the month.

A single access is usually referred to as a hit. A hit count is completely different from a visitor count, which is especially true for large sites that might have hundreds of pages. For example, one visitor to your site accesses 25 pages. If you look only at the number of hits, it looks like 25 visitors came to the site. Keep this example in mind when you try to determine the number of visitors to your site.

Server logs tend to grow rapidly, and the contents of these files are erased on a periodic basis. A better method is to periodically copy the old logs to backup files and save old files for the longest time that seems practical. The logs might be your only proof that someone has been violating system security.

## Keeping the Server Running

The most critical administrative duty is keeping the server running. Just as someone is responsible for the operational status of other networked workstations, someone must be responsible for the operational status of the Web server. The best choice for this duty is at the system administrative level. Let your system administrators tack a new title onto their old one as the Web server administrator.

## Updates to the Server

The Web server administrator should ensure that the server software and tools are kept up-to-date. Most server software is under constant development. The most recent version will probably run more efficiently and include new features.

The responsibility of publishing, maintaining, and ensuring the accuracy of Web documents should not rest on the shoulders of the Web server administrator. Although intranet publishing is understandably a cooperative process between the administrator and department personnel, the administrator should be responsible for technical problems and not content. The administrator is there to answer questions and to help with the general intranet publishing process if need be. He is not there to create documents for every department within the organization.

Large organizations should assign the additional duty of creating and maintaining Web documents to appropriate personnel in each major department that will network publish. Often, the logical choice for this additional duty will be the person who was responsible for creating and disseminating these documents under the old mechanism for distribution.

# Intranet Publishing on Your New Server

Intranet publishing on your new server might be frustrating at times. This is especially true when you are first trying to install and configure the server. The important thing to remember is that intranet publishing can pay off in huge dividends. The time and money savings for intranet publishing company user and technical manuals alone make intranet publishing worthwhile. Not only could the documentation be maintained so that it is always up-to-date at a cost less than the original publishing and distribution of the manuals, but employees will be able to search the entire text of manuals in an instant and at the touch of a button.

While intranet publishing can bring dramatic improvements in the accessibility of information within the company, part of the problem with any project is that people often have unrealistic expectations or mismatched perceptions. The process of setting up your intranet publishing operation is no exception. The best thing you can do is to remember the following:

- Intranet publishing is a learning process.
- Take it one step at a time.
- Set realistic goals.
- Adopt a company-wide policy for use and publishing of information on the company Web.

# A Learning Process

This is your first intranet publishing operation. It should be a learning process. Do not expect all the pieces to fall into place in a day. It simply will not happen. Give yourself and the project a fighting chance. Manage your expectations to help the project become a success. Remember, your expectations might not match the expectations of your superiors.

Before you start to set up the Web server, complete these tasks:

- Make sure that your expectations and the expectations of your supervisors mesh.
- Make sure that the communication channels between you and your supervisors are open.
- Discuss expectations at the start and manage them properly.

# One Step at a Time

Never let your thoughts about the complexity of the project overwhelm you. Your perceptions about the project play a decisive role in whether you will ever finish the project. Convince yourself you can do this.

Often, people forget that sometimes you need to take a breather. You cannot possibly try to do everything all at once. Set up your intranet publishing operation one step at a time. Begin by planning your course of action, and slowly progress from platform selection to server installation.

# Set Realistic Goals

One of the first things you should do is make sure that your goals are realistic. Your goals should take into account both the complexities of the project and the possible setbacks. Your goals should be clear and relevant to the problem at hand—setting up the Web server and a net-working publishing operation. As you set goals and milestones for each stage of the project, remember to provide flexibility. Never give yourself deadlines you cannot meet. If possible, give yourself a window for project completion.

## Adopt a Company-Wide Policy

When you complete the project, remember to adopt a company-wide policy pertaining to the use and publishing of information on the network. The key is to not only adopt a policy, but to communicate it throughout the organization. Be sure that company personnel know the following information:

- Who to contact for technical problems
- Who to contact for setup
- Who to contact for training
- What documents or services are available
- How to access Web documents
- The responsibilities of departments and individuals
- The acceptable uses of the company's intranet publishing operations

# Summary

Intranet publishing is an extremely cost-effective and time-saving way to publish company documents. To set up an intranet publishing operation, you need to install and configure a Web server. Although you must be on the Internet to take advantage of the information resources of the Web, you do not have to be on the Internet to take advantage of the features offered by Web servers and browsers.

The Web server could be one of your existing network workstations or a new workstation you purchase specifically for the task. After you have selected a platform for the server, you need to select server software. Server software is often freely available or available for a reasonable fee. After the server is set up, you are free to publish the company's documents.

PART

# II

# FrontPage Basics

# Introducing FrontPage

**4**

*by William Robert Stanek*

**IN THIS CHAPTER**

Whether you plan to set up a corporate intranet or create a site on the World Wide Web, FrontPage should be your application of choice. With this easy-to-use toolkit, anyone can create and manage a world-class Web site. This chapter introduces the applications that are a part of the FrontPage toolkit and provides a quick tour that should help you get started.

# Quick Setup and Installation

Before installing FrontPage, you should quit all other applications running on your desktop. This ensures that there are no conflicts for files FrontPage must update on your system.

Installing FrontPage from CD-ROM or floppy disk is easy. The first step is to select Run from the Windows 95/NT Start menu. Then, as shown in Figure 4.1, enter the directory path to the FrontPage setup program on your CD or floppy drive, such as

```
E:\Setup.exe
```

In the example, E: is the location of the CD-ROM drive and Setup.exe is the name of the file you want to run. If your CD-ROM is on the D drive, you would type the following to run the setup program:

```
D:\Setup.exe
```

**FIGURE 4.1.**

*Running the setup program.*

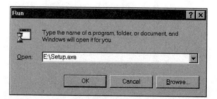

FrontPage should soon be available for Windows 95, Windows NT, and Macintosh systems. The installation shown is for Windows 95. Installation on Windows NT and Macintosh systems should be similar.

When you start the FrontPage setup program, you will see the Welcome dialog box (see Figure 4.2). Most dialog boxes used in FrontPage contain buttons you can use to obtain help, make selections, or exit the program. The Help button accesses the online help. The Cancel button exits the program. To move to the previous or next phase of the setup process, use the Back or Next buttons. When you have completed the setup process, you can press the Finish button, and the setup program will start installing FrontPage on your system. You should click on the Next button to continue.

**FIGURE 4.2.**

*The first step in the setup program.*

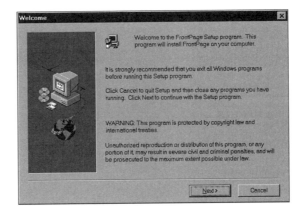

You will need about 9MB of free space to install FrontPage and the FrontPage server extensions. By default, the Setup Program installs FrontPage on the C drive in a folder called Microsoft FrontPage under the `Program Files` directory. To change the default, click on the Browse button, shown in Figure 4.3. This opens a dialog box that lets you specify a new folder and path for the base installation. When you are satisfied with the path, click on the Next button.

**FIGURE 4.3.**

*Determining the location of FrontPage on your file system.*

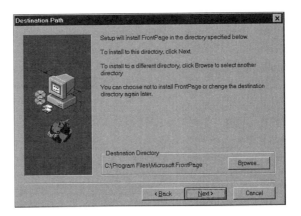

As shown in Figure 4.4, FrontPage allows you to select one of two types of installation: typical and custom. The typical installation installs everything most users will need including the Client Software, the Personal Web Server, and the FrontPage Server Extensions. The custom installation allows you to select the components you would like to install. The client software includes the FrontPage Explorer and the FrontPage Editor. The Personal Web Server is the server you will use to provide services for just about everything you do in FrontPage. The FrontPage server extensions are used with external Web servers, such as your Internet Service Provider's (ISP) UNIX-based Web server.

**FIGURE 4.4.**

*Selecting the type of installation.*

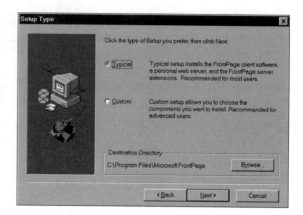

Because most users will need all the components, you will probably want to use the typical installation option. However, the typical installation assumes that you have enough space on your hard drive for the installation. If you want to check the space on your hard drive, you should select the custom installation option and possibly change the destination directory.

When you select custom installation and click on the Next button, you will see the setup page shown in Figure 4.5. Not only can you select the FrontPage components you would like to install from this page, you can also see the disk space you need and the amount of free space on your hard drive.

**FIGURE 4.5.**

*Custom installation lets you see all the components and disk space.*

If you choose to install the Personal Web Server, the next setup page lets you specify a directory for the server executables (see Figure 4.6). Keep in mind, the same directory is used to store all the files and documents you create or import into FrontPage. By default, the server directory is

C:\FrontPage Webs

**FIGURE 4.6.**

*Determining the location of the Personal Web Server and content.*

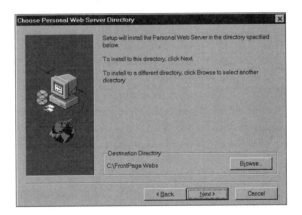

After you select a server directory or decide to accept the default, click on the Next button (see Figure 4.7). You can now choose a name for the folder that will hold the program icons.

your computer exclusively or mostly for Web publishing, you can also move the FrontPage Editor, the FrontPage Explorer, and the Personal Web Server to the Startup folder, which ensures the applications are started every time you turn on your computer.

**FIGURE 4.7.**

*Selecting a folder name for the FrontPage installation.*

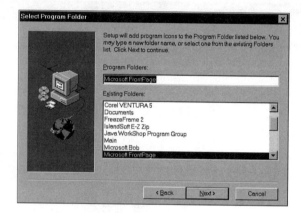

After you enter a folder name, the Setup program is ready to begin the installation process. When you click on the Next button, you will be able to review the current settings for the installation (see Figure 4.8). If you are not satisfied with any settings, click on the Back button. Otherwise, click on the Next button, and the setup program will begin copying files to your hard drive.

**FIGURE 4.8.**

*Reviewing the installation settings before starting to copy files.*

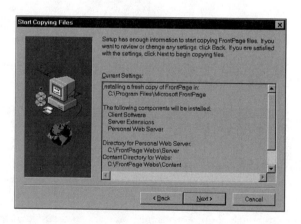

Before setup completes, you need to set up an account for the server administrator. FrontPage prompts you for this information automatically.

Another name for the server administrator is the Webmaster. The Webmaster is the person who controls access to the server and also is responsible for administering the server. As shown in Figure 4.9, you need to enter a user name and password for the server administrator. You also need to re-enter the password in the Password Confirmation field. Remember the user name and password you enter. You need it to verify your user name and password each time you restart the FrontPage Explorer.

**TIP**

To protect the security of your Web, you should use a secure password. I recommend using a password that is at least 6 characters long that includes numbers and wild card characters, such as !, @, #, $, and ?.

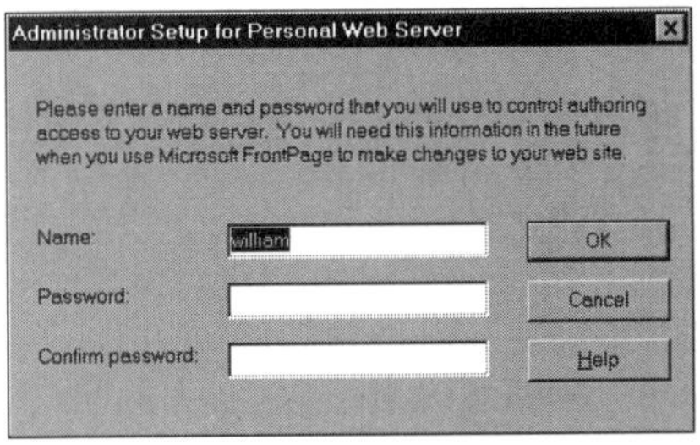

**FIGURE 4.9.**

*Setting a user name and password for the server administrator.*

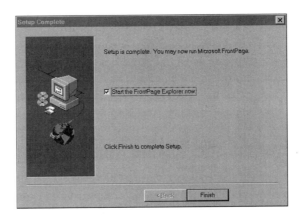

When setup completes successfully, you have the option of starting the FrontPage Explorer (see Figure 4.10). The explorer lets you create new Webs. Usually, you want to start the FrontPage Explorer immediately. You can click on the Finish button to complete the setup process.

**FIGURE 4.10.**

*A successful installation.*

After the Explorer starts, FrontPage tries to determine the IP address and host name of your system, and you see the dialog box shown in Figure 4.11. FrontPage uses a tool that checks for a Transmission Control Protocol/Internet Protocol (TCP/IP) connection to a network.

**FIGURE 4.11.**

*FrontPage checks your IP address and host name automatically.*

If you are connected to a network and your system has an IP address and host name, FrontPage should return accurate results. If you are not connected to a network but use a TCP/IP dialer to access the Internet, as most Web publishers do, FrontPage might return inaccurate results. For example, on my system FrontPage returned my login name with my ISP instead of a valid server name. Don't worry, the next section looks briefly at configuring your new Web server.

# Configuring Your New Web Server

If you have browsed the Web, you know how Hypertext Markup Language (HTML) documents are served to your browser. The browser is a client application. When you access a file with a client, the client contacts a server and requests a uniform resource locator (URL), such as http://www.mcp.com/. The Web server gets the referenced file and passes it to the client. The client displays the file in its viewing window.

In FrontPage, there are two client applications: the FrontPage Explorer and the FrontPage Viewer. Both applications depend on a server to retrieve files for them. The server included in FrontPage is the Personal Web Server. FrontPage also includes two tools for configuring and testing the server: the Server Administrator and the FrontPage TCP/IP Test.

Although Part VII, "Managing Your Web," covers server administration and testing in detail, this section is designed to get you started so that you can use FrontPage. You can use one of two basic setups to do this. The first basic setup is for anyone using a computer physically connected to the corporate network or to the Internet and who does not want to test FrontPage locally before publishing documents. The second setup is for anyone using a computer not physically connected to a network. If you will use the second setup, jump forward to the section, "Configuring and Testing Your Non-Networked System."

## Configuring and Testing Your Networked System

To configure and test your server using the networking techniques discussed in this section, you must be using a computer physically connected to the corporate network or to the Internet. This means your computer has a numeric IP address and a host name. If your system is connected or you plan to connect to the Internet, you must also have registered your IP address and host name with the InterNIC as discussed in Chapter 3, "Publishing on a Corporate Intranet."

> **NOTE**
>
> When you are done reading this section, you can skip the section "Configuring and Testing Your Non-Networked System."

When you installed FrontPage, the TCP/IP Test probably returned valid results. You can test the results using the TCP/IP Test tool included with FrontPage. After you start the test tool, you will see a dialog box similar to the one shown in Figure 4.12.

**FIGURE 4.12.**

*The TCP/IP Test tool at startup.*

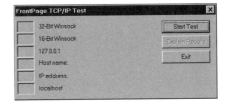

To have FrontPage automatically test your TCP/IP connection, click on the Start Test button. It takes a few minutes for the test tool to check your connection. When the test finishes, you will see information similar to that shown in Figure 4.13. To see a detailed explanation that relates to your system, click on the Explain Results button.

> **NOTE**
>
> When you click on the Start Test button, the test tool might launch your Internet dialer, and you will see a dialog box prompting you for user name and password information. If this happens, you are not on a network or do not have a dedicated connection to the Internet. You should skip this section and read the next section in this chapter. Although you can enter the login name and password you use to connect to your Internet or commercial service provider's Web server and follow the steps you would normally take to log in, you probably will not be able to use the results returned by the TCP/IP Test tool.

**FIGURE 4.13.**

*The TCP/IP Test tool returns results.*

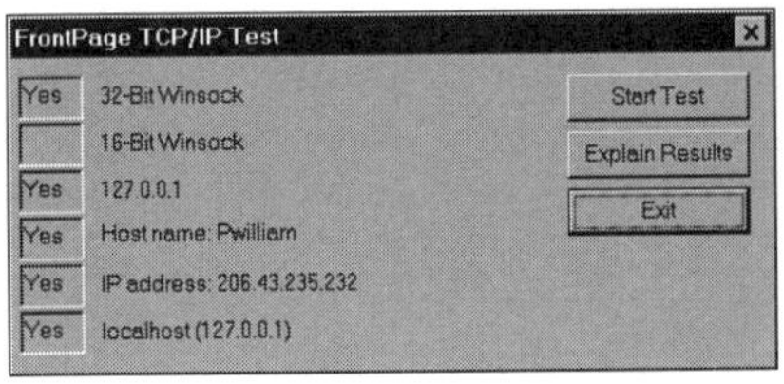

As you can see from the figure, FrontPage tests to see whether your system uses a 16-bit or 32-bit Winsock. The Winsock is used in network communications. Next, FrontPage checks to see whether the local loopback host 127.0.0.1 is usable on your system. On most networked systems, 127.0.0.1 is the IP address listed in the /etc/hosts file for the local host. You will use the local host when you want to test your Web or publish documents for testing purposes.

The next three tests determine your system's host name, IP address, and local loopback address. The final test ensures that if your local host is different from the standard 127.0.0.1, you will know about it. You should write down this information if you do not already know it.

Now that you know key server information, you can start the Personal Web Server and the FrontPage Explorer. In the FrontPage Explorer, select New Web from the File menu. This opens the New Web dialog box, shown in Figure 4.14. You will use this dialog box to create new Webs.

**FIGURE 4.14.**

*Selecting a New Web template.*

For now, create a Web based on the Normal Web by double-clicking on the words Normal Web. The Explorer will prompt you with the dialog box shown in Figure 4.15. You should verify the server name or IP address in the Web Server field, and then select a name for your Web and enter it in the Web Name field.

**CAUTION**

If you use your system's host name or IP address, anything you publish in FrontPage will be available to anyone accessing your Web server. To start, you might want to publish files only locally, which means only someone logged into the Web server will be able to access the files. To publish files locally, enter the IP address of the local host, such as 127.0.0.1. Because FrontPage allows you to use multiple host names and IP addresses, you can enter the valid host name or IP address when you decide to publish materials for others to access.

**FIGURE 4.15.**

*Creating a New Web for testing purposes.*

After you enter this information, FrontPage creates your Web and loads the related pages into the FrontPage Explorer. If you have not identified yourself to FrontPage by entering your user name and password, the FrontPage Explorer displays a dialog box that asks you to enter that information. Whenever you create Webs, you will probably want to use the account you created for the system administrator.

In the FrontPage Explorer, double-click on the Normal Page icon in the Link View window. If your Web is working normally, the FrontPage Explorer should contact the Personal Web Server, which in turn starts the FrontPage Editor with the normal page loaded for editing. If the FrontPage Editor does not start, re-read this section and ensure you have followed the instructions. Remember, both the FrontPage Explorer and the Personal Web Server should have been running on your system before you tried to access the normal page in your new Web.

# Configuring and Testing Your Non-Networked System

If your system is not physically connected to a network and you do not have a dedicated connection to the Internet, FrontPage can create a pseudonetworked environment for you. This pseudonetworked environment works only on your local system.

When you installed FrontPage, the TCP/IP test probably returned results you will not want to use. Primarily this is because FrontPage thinks you have a dedicated connection to the Internet and you do not. The first step in testing the server is to start the Personal Web Server and the FrontPage Explorer. In the FrontPage Explorer, select New Web from the File menu. This opens the New Web dialog box shown in Figure 4.16. You will use this dialog box to create new Webs.

For now, create a Web based on the Normal Web by double-clicking on the words Normal Web. The explorer will prompt you with the dialog box shown in Figure 4.17. The server name entered in the Web Server field is probably the user name you used to log into your Internet or commercial service provider's Web server. Delete the server name and enter the IP address 127.0.0.1. This IP address is for the local loopback, and it allows you to set up a pseudonetwork on your system. All requests to the local loopback are served directly by the Personal Web Server.

**FIGURE 4.16.**

*Selecting a New Web template.*

---

**CAUTION**

If you do not change the server name, it is possible that the only time you have access to your server is when you are connected to the Internet. Although it might seem that you are publishing files on the Internet or commercial service provider's Web server, you are actually using the local loopback. Because of this, it is better to use the local loopback directly. You can do this by specifying the IP address of 127.0.0.1, as shown in Figure 4.17. Keep in mind that when you use the local host, your files are only available on the local system, and you must transfer the files to a public server for the files to be available for others to access.

---

**FIGURE 4.17.**

*Change the IP address so that it points to the local host.*

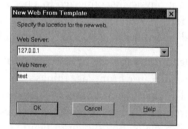

The next field you need to fill in is the name of your Web. After you enter the server and Web information, FrontPage creates your Web and loads the related pages into the FrontPage Explorer. If you have not identified yourself to FrontPage by entering your user name and password, the FrontPage Explorer will display a dialog box that asks you to enter your user name and password. Whenever you create Webs, you will probably want to use the account you created for the system administrator.

In the FrontPage Explorer, double-click on the Normal Page icon shown in the Link View window. If your Web is working normally, the FrontPage Explorer should contact the Personal Web Server, which in turn starts the FrontPage Editor with the normal page loaded for editing. If the FrontPage Editor does not start, re-read this section and ensure you have followed the instructions. Remember, both the FrontPage Explorer and the Personal Web Server should have been running on your system before you tried to access the normal page in your new Web.

# FrontPage Quick Tour

FrontPage publishing relies on three tools: the FrontPage Explorer, the FrontPage Editor, and the Personal Web Server. This section looks at these tools as they relate to the two most basic FrontPage Publishing concepts: pages and Webs.

## Creating and Manipulating Pages with the FrontPage Editor

Pages are HTML documents that can contain references to images, sound, and even video files. You view pages in the FrontPage Editor. Because the FrontPage Editor is a what-you-see-is-what-you-get (WYSIWYG) editor, your HTML documents look the same in the FrontPage Editor as they do in most Web browsers, which means all document formatting and inline images are displayed just as they should be. Most pages are a part of a specific Web. For detailed information on using pages, see Chapter 6, "Working with Pages and Files."

Figure 4.18 shows the FrontPage Editor with a page for editing. Just as you can open multiple documents in most word processors, you can open multiple documents in the FrontPage Editor. In fact, for all practical purposes there is no limit on the number of documents you can have open at one time. You can find detailed information on the FrontPage Editor in Chapter 5, "The FrontPage Explorer and Editor Step by Step."

**FIGURE 4.18.**

*Viewing a page in the FrontPage Editor.*

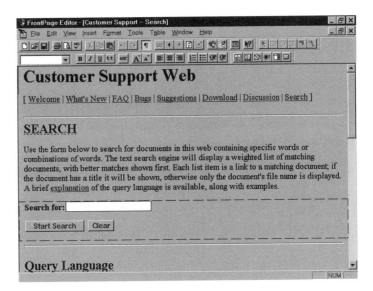

# Creating and Manipulating Webs with the FrontPage Explorer

Webs are collections of pages and their related image, sound, and video files. You will use the FrontPage Explorer to create new Webs, to access existing Webs, and to set the current Web for editing. Setting the current Web is important.

When you save a new page, it generally becomes part of the current Web. When you open pages in the FrontPage Editor, you generally open them from the current Web. At any given time, you can only have one open Web, which is always considered to be the current Web. For detailed information on using pages, see Chapter 7, "Working with Webs."

Figure 4.19 shows the FrontPage Explorer with a sample Web. As you can see from the figure, the explorer provides an overview of your Web. You can use this information to quickly examine the layout of any Web and to access any pages for editing. You can find detailed information on the FrontPage Explorer in Chapter 5.

**FIGURE 4.19.**

*Viewing a Web in the FrontPage Explorer.*

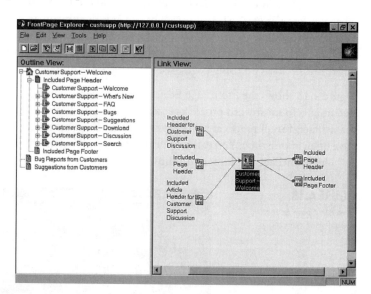

# Personal Web Server

Without the Personal Web Server running, you cannot manipulate or access Webs because the Personal Web Server is the mechanism that retrieves pages from the current Web and saves pages to the current Web. Whenever you use FrontPage, you should start the Personal Web Server along with the FrontPage Explorer and the FrontPage Editor. Otherwise, when you use a FrontPage function that uses the Personal Web Server, you might see an error dialog box similar to the one shown in Figure 4.20. For detailed information on the Personal Web Server, see Part VII, "Managing Your Web."

> **NOTE**
>
> Port 80 is the port normally used for the Hypertext Transfer Protocol (HTTP). You will see the error depicted in Figure 4.20 if you incorrectly set up the server, if you changed the port setting to a port that cannot be used, or if the server is not running. Thus, if the server is running and you get this error, check your server configuration.

**FIGURE 4.20.**

*This error indicates that the server cannot be accessed.*

# FrontPage Features

Beyond pages and Webs, you should learn about three additional FrontPage publishing concepts: templates, wizards, and WebBots. These are important concepts to understand, especially because you will find references to them throughout this book.

## What Are Templates?

When you create a page or a Web in FrontPage, you will usually base the page or Web on a template. FrontPage includes dozens of templates designed to make content creation a snap. You will find two types of templates in FrontPage: page templates and Web templates.

A page template is an outline for a specific type of page, such as a home page or a customer survey page. A Web template contains outlines for a specific set of pages, such as all the pages that relate to a business-oriented Web site. Usually, templates for Webs and pages contain guidelines that make development easier. Just as there are very basic templates, such as the normal page template, there are also very advanced templates, such as the template for a customer support Web. See Chapter 22, "Creating Your Own Templates," for more information on templates.

## What Are Wizards?

Some pages and Webs you create in FrontPage are very complex. To ensure that anyone can create these complex pages and Webs without any problems, FrontPage includes powerful tools called wizards. Wizards help you automatically generate content. All you have to do is start the wizard and follow the prompts. As with templates, FrontPage includes two types of wizards: page wizards and Web wizards.

You can use page wizards to create documents with fill-out forms and frames. Forms allow you to collect information from the reader. Frames allow you to display documents with multiple windows displayed in a single viewing area. A page wizard will also help you create a home page.

You can use Web wizards to create entire Webs with dozens of pages. FrontPage includes two powerful Web wizards: the Corporate Presence Wizard and the Discussion Web Wizard. Using the Corporate Presence Wizard, you can create a site that is designed to help you establish a presence on the Web. Using the Discussion Web Wizard, you can create a Web with multiple discussion groups that company employees and customers alike can use to discuss topics of interest. To learn more about wizards, see Chapter 19, "Instant Web Sites with FrontPage's Web Wizards."

## What Are WebBots?

In FrontPage, you will find more than a dozen WebBots. Another name for a WebBot is simply a bot. Each bot can be thought of as a program that runs when needed. Bots automate complex administration processes and eliminate the need to write your own scripts or add complicated HTML commands. For detailed information on using WebBots, see Chapter 20, "Automation with FrontPage's WebBots."

Before FrontPage introduced WebBots, administration of world-class Web sites was the realm of those who earned the name Webmaster by being the best at what they did. Great Webmasters know how to create scripts that process the input of forms; can insert headers, footers, and images into documents at any time using programs they created; can change colors used in backgrounds, links, and text using UNIX tools such as Sed and Auk; and much more. With a WebBot you can collect the results from forms, automatically add navigation bars, create pages with full text searches, allow registered users to access key areas of your Web, and do just about anything else that once only a skilled Webmaster could do.

WebBots are great for most publishing tasks. However, they cannot do advanced follow-on processing of input from forms, and they cannot help you generate content based on the type of the user's browser. Therefore, in some instances, you might have to use a custom script. For more information on using scripts, see Chapter 30, "Writing CGI Scripts."

## Summary

After reading this chapter, FrontPage should be installed successfully on your system. This chapter teaches you about key FrontPage publishing tools and concepts. You will use the FrontPage Explorer, the FrontPage Editor, and the Personal Web Server whenever you create and edit files in FrontPage.

# The FrontPage Explorer and Editor Step by Step

**5**

*by William Robert Stanek*

**IN THIS CHAPTER**

The FrontPage tools you will use the most are the Explorer and the Editor. Both tools feature powerful and friendly interfaces that make Web content development and management easy. You should use this chapter as a starting point because it takes a step-by-step look at using these tools.

# A Look at the FrontPage Explorer

You can use the FrontPage Explorer to create and manage Webs. Webs are collections of pages organized within a common directory structure.

## A Starting Point: The Base Web

The base Web is called the Root Web. When you install FrontPage, the Root Web contains several files including an index page for your site. Most servers display this default document when a user specifies a directory name instead of a filename. This file is sometimes called `index.html` or `index.htm`.

If you are using the Personal Web Server only on the local host, meaning you are using the Internet Protocol (IP) address for a local loopback host, you can view this page in a browser with the uniform resource locator (URL):

`http://127.0.0.1/`

Similarly, when you publish your Web on your Internet Service Provider's Web server or if you are on a networked system, you can view this document in your browser using one of these URLs:

`http://www.yourcompany.com/`

or

`http://www.your_service_provider.com/~you`

> **CAUTION**
>
> Before you make your Web accessible to others, you will want to replace the default index page with the home page to your site.

The Root Web is a starting point for content on your new Web server. All the Webs you create based on templates and wizards will be placed in subdirectories under the main directory for the Root Web. These Webs can and usually do have index files. If you create a customer support Web called `custsupport`, users will be able to access this Web using the following URL:

`http://www.`*`yourcompany`*`.com/custsupport/`

or

`http://www.`*`your_service_provider`*`.com/~you/custsupport/`

# Examining Webs in the FrontPage Explorer

While it is a good idea to test documents in your browser, you get a much better picture of what is in the Root Web by using the FrontPage Explorer. A Web loaded into the Explorer reveals a great deal about itself (see Figure 5.1).

> **NOTE**
>
> Figure 5.1 shows the FrontPage Explorer with the Link View and Links to Images options of the View menu selected. You can use these special options to depict the hypertext references and images used in your documents.

**FIGURE 5.1.**

*Initial view of the Root Web in the FrontPage Explorer.*

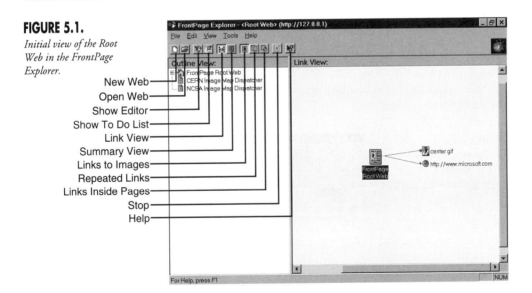

The line at the very top of the figure tells you the name and URL of your Web within FrontPage. In this case, the Web name is Root Web and the URL is `http://127.0.0.1`.

> **NOTE**
>
> When you enter the URL without the final slash, the browser adds the slash if it is needed. Thus, browsers interpret `http://127.0.0.1` and `http://127.0.0.1/` as the same thing, and in both cases, the index document for the directory will be retrieved.

The main part of the window shows the two primary views for the Explorer. The Outline View provides a textual picture of all the files and links in your Web. Web documents are listed by title. Images are listed by filename, and links are listed with their URL path. The Link View provides a graphical picture of how documents are linked to each other and to other resources. Together, these views provide an at-a-glance picture of everything in your Web.

In the Outline View in Figure 5.1, there is a plus sign next to the document titled FrontPage Root Web. Whenever you see a plus sign, it means the document contains references or objects. You can double-click on the document's title in the Outline View to see the images and objects it contains.

When you double-click on the title FrontPage Root Web, you find that it contains an image called `center.gif` and a hypertext reference to `http://www.microsoft.com`. This is not new information because the Outline View already displayed the image and link. However, now that these additional references are displayed in the Image view, you can select them to see how they are referenced and linked throughout the Web.

Figure 5.2 shows the change in the FrontPage Explorer when you click on the filename for the image called `center.gif`. In a complex Web with images and links referenced in multiple documents, you can use this technique to get an instant picture of every document in the Web that utilizes the image or link.

**FIGURE 5.2.**

*Another view of the Root Web in the FrontPage Explorer.*

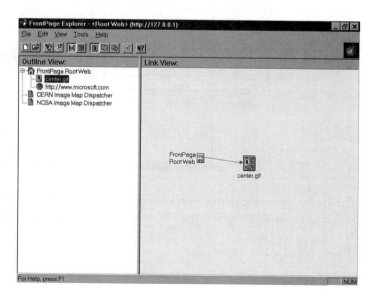

# Opening and Closing the FrontPage Explorer

Starting the FrontPage Explorer is as easy as double-clicking on the Explorer icon in the FrontPage folder. However, if you don't have the FrontPage folder on your desktop, you might have to go through a system of menus to start the FrontPage Explorer. For example, in Windows 95, you can access the FrontPage Explorer through the taskbar's Start menu and follow the submenus to the location where you installed the FrontPage Explorer. To close the Explorer, select Exit from the File menu.

> **NOTE**
>
> You can also start the FrontPage Explorer from the FrontPage Editor. To do this, click on the Explorer's icon, which depicts a green ball with a red arrow and a scroll.

# Using the Menu

All applications have pull-down menus. The more complex the application, the more menus and selections for those menus. FrontPage Explorer has five pull-down menus: File, Edit, View, Tools, and Help.

> **NOTE**
>
> Menu items that are grayed out currently cannot be selected. These grayed out options will become available when you perform an action that makes them usable. For example, most of the options in the Explorer's menus are grayed out until you open a Web or create a new Web.

# Using the File Menu

You will use the File menu whenever you want to manipulate Webs. This menu also lets you import files to the current Web or export files from the current Web. Figure 5.3 shows the available options for this menu.

As you can see from Figure 5.3, most selections are for manipulating Webs. You can create a Web in a snap by selecting the New Web option; then when you want to work on your killer Web site again, you can select the Open Web option. Other options on the menu allow you to close, copy, or delete the current Web. You will learn all about Webs in Chapter 7, "Working with Webs."

**FIGURE 5.3.**

*Options on the FrontPage Explorer's File menu.*

You can use the Import option to bring existing documents, images, and other resources into the current Web. This is how you let FrontPage know you have existing resources that you want to work with. FrontPage also allows you to export any selected document from the current Web. Generally, you will export documents from FrontPage when you want to save them in an alternate location. You will learn all about files in Chapter 6, "Working with Pages and Files."

The numbered options at the bottom of the menu allow you to quickly access Webs you previously opened in FrontPage. The Explorer tracks the last four Webs you opened. You can reopen these Webs by clicking on the Web name in this menu.

The final menu option lets you exit the Explorer and close the current Web.

## Using the Edit Menu

You will use the FrontPage Explorer's Edit menu when you want to manipulate files. However, because manipulating files is really the job of the Editor, the actions you can do are limited. Figure 5.4 shows the options available for this menu.

**FIGURE 5.4.**

*Options on the FrontPage Explorer's Edit menu.*

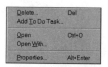

The Delete option lets you delete a file that is selected in any of the Explorer's views. Whenever you try to delete a file, the Explorer warns you that the document will be deleted permanently and asks you to confirm that you want to delete the file.

The Add To Do Task option adds a task related to the currently selected document to the To Do list. When you select this option, the Explorer opens the Add To Do Task dialog box, shown in Figure 5.5. A To Do list helps you manage the tasks related to creating and running a Web.

The Open option allows you to open a selected document for editing in the FrontPage Editor. Another way to open files in the Explorer is with the Open With option, which lets you select an Editor you've configured for use with FrontPage. The Open With option is very useful when you want to open files that are not in Hypertext Markup Language (HTML) format. For example, you can use it to edit a Graphical Interchange Format (GIF) image used in your Web. Instead of starting your image Editor, searching for the image file, and then opening the file for editing, you simply select the image and use the Open With option.

**FIGURE 5.5.**

*The To Do list helps you manage tasks.*

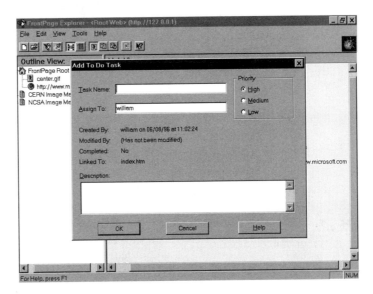

The dialog box associated with the Open With option is shown in Figure 5.6. When you install FrontPage on most systems, three editors are available: the FrontPage Editor, the Frames Wizard, and the Windows Notepad text editor. As you can see, I configured an editor for GIF and Joint Picture Experts Group (JPEG) image files. You will use the Configure Editors option in the Tools menu to configure your own editors.

The final option on the Edit menu is Properties. When you use this option, the Explorer opens the Properties dialog box. This dialog box has two properties pages that you can access by clicking on tabs labeled General and Summary. The Property values you can examine with the General tab are shown in Figure 5.7. Property values you can examine with the Summary tab are shown in Figure 5.8.

*FrontPage Basics*

**Part II**

**FIGURE 5.6.**

*Open documents with a specific Editor using the Open With option.*

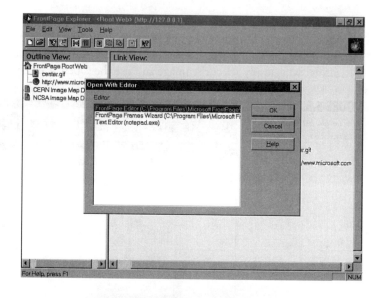

**FIGURE 5.7.**

*Examining property values with the General tab.*

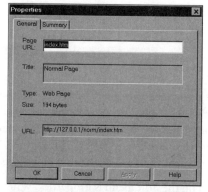

**FIGURE 5.8.**

*Examining property values with the Summary tab.*

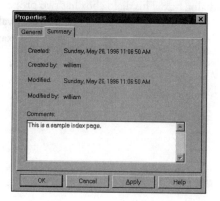

# Using the View Menu

The View menu lets you customize the type of information available in the Explorer. The options available for this menu are shown in Figure 5.9.

**FIGURE 5.9.**

*Options on the FrontPage*
*Explorer's View menu.*

The Toolbar option lets you add or remove the toolbar from the display window. The most commonly used Explorer commands are available by clicking on an icon in the toolbar. Using the Status Bar option, you can add or remove the status area at the bottom of the Explorer's display window. The status area is used to display command summaries and other key information. Usually, you will want to display both the toolbar and the status area.

In the Explorer, you can view the resources in your Web in three ways: Outline View, Summary View, and Link View. The Outline View always appears on the left side of the Explorer's display. On the right side of the display, you can switch between the Summary View and Link View using the Link View and Summary View menu options.

To adjust the size allocated to the views displayed in the Explorer, you can use the Split option, which highlights the bar dividing the views. You can then move the mouse pointer to adjust the size of the views. When the views are sized appropriately, click the left mouse button.

**NOTE**

Another way to resize the views is to move the mouse pointer over the dividing bar, and then click and hold the left mouse button. Now you can drag the dividing bar to resize the views. When the views are sized appropriately, release the left mouse button.

The next three options allow you to add detail to the views. To see images used in the Web, select the Links to Images option. To see links every time they appear in the Web, select the Repeated Links option. To see links within pages called bookmarks, select the Links Inside Page option.

The final option lets you refresh the views. Sometimes, when you are accessing Webs on another server, you will find that the Web did not completely display in the Explorer views. If this happens, use the Refresh option.

# Using the Tools Menu

The Tools menu lets you perform Web management functions. Figure 5.10 shows the options available for this menu. Management of Webs is an advanced and very detailed concept. You will find references to the Tools menu throughout this book. In fact, Part VI, "Using the FrontPage Developer's Kit," is devoted to managing Webs. So for now, I will just provide an overview of what the options in this menu are used for.

**FIGURE 5.10.**

*Options on the FrontPage Explorer's Tools menu.*

The Web Settings option opens the Web Settings dialog box, which contains three server configuration pages that you can access with tabs labeled Parameters, Configuration, and Advanced. The Parameters tab lets you add keywords and values that you can insert into documents in any Web using the Substitution WebBot. Using the Configuration tab shown in Figure 5.11, you can check server information and change the name and title for a Web. The Advanced tab lets you configure the type of image maps you want to use with your Webs. (To learn all about image maps, see Chapter 10, "Enhancing Your Web Publication with Images—the Easy Way.")

To set permissions for your Webs, you will use the Web Permissions option. As you can see from Figure 5.12, this Web Permissions dialog box has four tabs. The Settings tab lets you set access permissions for the current Web. The Administrators tab lets you add and remove accounts for those who manage Webs. The Authors tab lets you add and remove accounts for those who can create documents for the current Web. The End Users tab lets you add and remove accounts for users of a restricted access Web.

**FIGURE 5.11.**

*Checking the server configuration.*

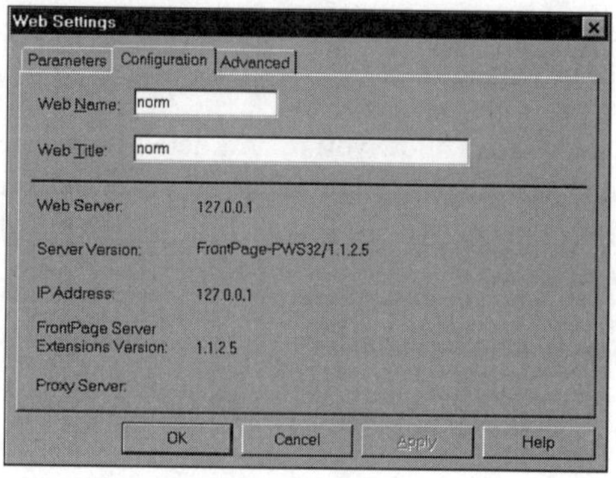

> **NOTE**
>
> The Settings tab of the Web permissions dialog box is not available if the Root Web is the current Web. Primarily, this is because the Settings tab allows you to base permissions on the Root Web settings, which is only valid in Webs other than the Root Web.

**FIGURE 5.12.**

*The Web Permissions dialog box is used to set access permissions.*

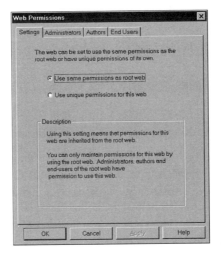

You can configure Editors for use with FrontPage using the Configure Editor option. As discussed earlier, you will probably want to configure an editor for images. (See the section, "Associating Files with Editors," in Chapter 6 to learn how to configure editors.)

The Change Password option opens the dialog box shown in Figure 5.13. Using this dialog box, you can change the password for the user you are currently logged in as. As a security precaution, to change the password you must first enter the password you originally logged in with.

**FIGURE 5.13.**

*Use the Change Password option to enter a new password.*

Using the Proxies option, you can set up a firewall between your network and the Internet. The purpose of the firewall server is to shield your network.

With the Verify Links option, you can check the validity of all the links in your Web. This includes links to resources on the Internet. A similar command is the Recalculate Links option. This option searches the current Web for links and dependencies and then updates the links and text index related to the Web. You will use this option to update the Explorer views when you are adding or changing the content of a Web in the Editor.

The Stop option tells the Explorer to stop trying to load a Web. If FrontPage is trying to access a Web on another server and the server is not responding, use this option to tell FrontPage to stop trying to load the Web.

The final two options in this menu are used to display FrontPage tools. The Show FrontPage Editor option starts the Editor, if it is not already started, and displays it. The Show To Do List option starts the To Do List manager, if it is not already started, and displays it.

## Using the Help Menu

The Help menu is used to display information about the FrontPage Explorer and to access the online help system. Figure 5.14 shows the options available on this menu.

To access FrontPage's very comprehensive help documentation, you will use the Microsoft FrontPage Help Topics option. This option opens the dialog box shown in Figure 5.15. This dialog box has three tabs labeled Contents, Index, and Find. The Contents tab lets you browse a table of contents for the help system. The Index tab lets you find topics using an index of key terms. Using the Find tab, you can search on key words and phrases.

**FIGURE 5.14.**

*Options on the FrontPage Explorer's Help menu.*

**FIGURE 5.15.**

*FrontPage features extensive online help.*

The About Microsoft FrontPage Explorer option displays information on your version of FrontPage.

# Using the Toolbar

Compared to the FrontPage Editor, the 12 icons on the Explorer's toolbar are very basic. If you are familiar with Microsoft Office, you will probably recognize most of the icons. The following is a summary of the icons and their uses:

| Icon | FrontPage Menu Option | Description |
| --- | --- | --- |
| | New Web | Used to create a new Web |
| | Open Web | Used to open an existing Web |
| | Show FrontPage Editor | Displays the FrontPage Editor |
| | Show To Do list | Displays the To Do List |
| | Link View | Shows view of page links |
| | Summary View | Shows summary information for Web documents |
| | Links to images | Shows links to images |
| | Repeated links | Shows repeated links |
| | Links inside pages | Shows links inside pages |
| | Stop | Tells the Explorer to stop trying to load a Web or page |
| | Help | Displays online help documentation when you click on a button, menu, or window after selecting this icon |

# Views Explained

The FrontPage Explorer provides you with three ways of viewing the files in your Webs. Generally, the Outline View is always displayed, and you can switch between the Link View and the Summary View. Let's look at each of these views to give you an understanding of what they are used for.

# Examining the Outline View

The Outline View displays your Web in a hierarchical form, starting with the home page. You can tell that a document is the home page for the Web because the icon shaped like a house replaces the document icon. Two other types of document icons are used in the Outline View. When you see the normal document icon without the arrow, it means the document has not linked to other resources. When you see the linked page document icon with the arrow, it means the document is linked to other documents.

As with any outline, there are various levels of information. Sometimes you want to see only the highest levels of the outline—the top-level pages used in the Web. Other times, you want to get a detailed picture of every resource used in the Web—every document, image, and link.

> **NOTE**
>
> Images used in the Web are only displayed if the Links to Images option is selected.

Figure 5.16 shows a sample Web. In the Outline View section of the Explorer window, I've expanded some of the outline items to the lowest level. You can tell that an item in the Outline View has been expanded because the minus sign precedes it. If you click on the minus sign, you unexpand the view for that item. Items whose outline levels are not expanded are preceded with a plus sign. Just as you can click on the minus sign to unexpand the view for an item, you can click on the plus sign to expand the view for an item.

**FIGURE 5.16.**

*You can expand and unexpand the Outline View to fit your needs.*

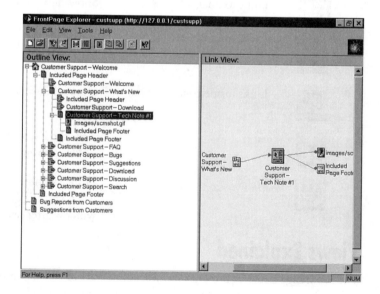

# Examining the Link View

The Link View depicts the organization of your Web graphically. When you select a page in the Outline View, the Link View associated with the document is displayed in the Link View area. Links to and from the selected document are shown with a line. The line ends with an arrow that symbolizes the relationship between the linked documents.

Just as you can expand and unexpand the levels within the Outline View, you can also expand the levels of linking in the Link View. Figure 5.17 shows an expanded view of links related to a document titled Customer Support—Search. You can click on the plus sign to expand the Link View and the minus sign to unexpand the Link View.

You can easily edit any file shown in the Link View. All you have to do is double-click on the file's icon, and it will be opened for editing using the Editor you have configured for the file type. Thus, you can double-click on an HTML document to open it for editing in the FrontPage Editor. You can also click on an image to open it for editing using the image editor you've configured for use with FrontPage.

**FIGURE 5.17.**

*The Link View lets you see a graphical depiction of links to and from a document.*

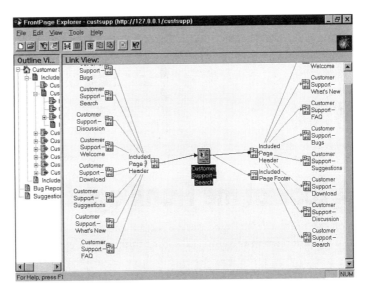

# Examining the Summary View

The Summary View is used to display summary information of all the files used in the current Web. As you can see from Figure 5.18, the information summarized is quite extensive and is organized into a table with many columns.

The column title bars are more than decoration. You can click on any of the column title bars to alphabetize your files based on the information in the column. By default, your files are organized alphabetically by title. You can, for example, click on the File name title bar to alphabetize by filename.

All the columns can be resized as well. To resize a column, move the mouse pointer over the title bar area so that it is between the column you want to resize and the column that follows it. When you do this, the mouse pointer changes to a pointer with arrows on both ends. Now click and hold the left mouse button and drag the dividing bar to resize the column. When the column is sized appropriately, release the left mouse button.

Files in the Summary View can be easily edited. Just move the mouse pointer over an item summarizing information for the file and double-click the left mouse button. The FrontPage Explorer will open the file for editing using the Editor you have configured for the file type.

**FIGURE 5.18.**

*The Summary View displays lots of information about the files in your Web.*

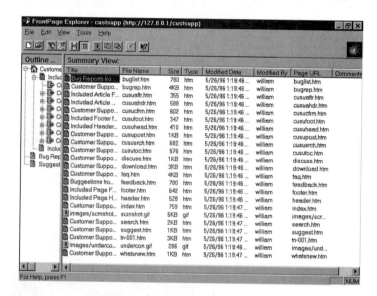

# A Look at the FrontPage Editor

You can use the FrontPage Editor to create and edit pages. Pages are HTML documents that can contain references to images, sound, and even video files.

## Opening and Closing the FrontPage Editor

You can start the FrontPage Editor by double-clicking on the Editor icon in the FrontPage folder. However, if you don't have the FrontPage folder on your desktop, you might have to go through a menuing system to start the FrontPage Editor. For example, in Windows 95, you access the FrontPage Editor through the taskbar's Start menu and follow the submenus to the location where you installed the FrontPage Editor. To close the Editor, select Exit from the File menu.

**NOTE**

You can also start the FrontPage Editor from the FrontPage Explorer. To do this, click on the Editor's icon, which depicts a red feather quill and a scroll.

## Using the Menu

If you've used the FrontPage Editor, you probably know the menu is quite extensive. The menu bar includes nine pull-down menus that lead to over 60 menu options. Because there are so many options, this section does not examine the options in detail. Instead, it examines the basic menus that are not discussed in other chapters and provides an overview of other menus.

**NOTE**

Most menus in the FrontPage Editor are not available when you first open the editor. To activate these menus, you will need to open a file or create a new file. Even when pages are loaded into the editor you will find that some of the options are grayed out. These grayed out options are not available until you perform a specific action. For example, the Paste option is not available until you place an object on the clipboard using the Cut or Copy options.

## Using the File Menu

You can use the File menu whenever you want to manipulate files. The menu also lets you view file properties and printer settings. Figure 5.19 shows the available options for this menu.

**FIGURE 5.19.**
*Options on the FrontPage Editor's File menu.*

The first section of the File menu is for creating, opening, and closing files. To create a new page, select the New option. To open a file on your hard drive, select the Open File option. Files you open can be in HTML, rich text format (RTF), or text format. To open a file from the current Web, select the Open from Web option. To open a file from an external location on the Internet, you select the Open Location option. To close the current page, you select the Close option.

The File menu allows you to save pages in one of three ways. You can save the page to its current filename and location using the Save option. This means if you opened the document from the current Web, the document will be saved to the current Web. If you opened the document from a file on your hard drive, the file will be saved to its location on the hard drive and not to the current Web. If you want to save a file to the current Web that you opened from a file on your hard drive or an external location on the Internet, you should use the Save As option. You can also use the Save As option to save a file opened from the current Web to a new location on your hard drive. To save all the files currently open in the FrontPage Editor, select the Save All option. You will learn all about files in Chapter 6.

To examine properties associated with a page, you can use the Page Properties option. Page properties relate to the color of text, backgrounds, and links and are different from the page settings used for printing the document that you will see if you select the Page Setup option. Before you print a document, you might want to preview it. You can use the Print Preview option to do this.

The numbered options at the bottom of the menu allow you to quickly access files you previously opened. The Editor tracks the last four files you opened. You can reopen these files by clicking on the filename in this menu.

The final menu option lets you exit the Editor and closes all open files. If you've made changes to files, the Editor displays a prompt asking if you want to save the files.

## Using the Edit Menu

You will use the Edit menu when you want to perform editing functions such as cut, copy, or paste. Figure 5.20 shows the options available for this menu.

**FIGURE 5.20.**

*Options on the FrontPage Editor's Edit menu.*

A terrific feature of the FrontPage Editor is multilevel undo and redo. What this means is that the Editor tracks when you use any options that affect the content of the current page and allows you to undo them one by one. Then if you undo something by mistake, you can select the redo option to put the Editor back in its previous state. Sometimes the undo or redo options are not available (see Figure 5.20). Usually this happens when there is nothing to undo or redo. However, there are some actions that can't be recovered, and if you try to undo or redo them, the Editor will not let you.

Many of the other options in the Edit menu are used just as you would use them in your favorite word processor. You use the Cut option to remove selected text, images, and resource references from the page and copy them to the clipboard. The Copy option copies selected items to the clipboard. When they are on the clipboard, you can use the Paste option to insert the items into the page at the current insertion point.

The Clear option is a simple delete function that erases selected text, images, and resource references. Because these items are not placed on the clipboard, you need to be careful when using this option.

> **NOTE**
>
> An easier way to delete selected items is to press the Delete key or Backspace key.

To find text referenced in the current page, you can use the Find option. When you select this option, the Editor opens the dialog box shown in Figure 5.21. In the `Find what` field of the Find dialog box, enter the word or phrase you want to search for. To restrict the search, you can check the `Match whole word only` and `Match case` fields. By default, the Editor searches down from the current insertion point for the word or phrase you are looking for. You can change the direction by clicking on the field labeled `Up`.

**FIGURE 5.21.**

*Finding text used in the
current page.*

To search for and replace text referenced in the current page, you can use the Replace option. The Replace dialog box is shown in Figure 5.22. In the `Find what` field, enter the word or phrase you want to search for. In the `Replace with` field, enter the word or phrase you want to replace the search text with. To restrict the search, you can check the `Match whole word only` and `Match case` fields. To find an occurrence of the search text before replacing it, click on the Find Next button. After the search text is highlighted, you can click on the Replace button to replace it with the text you've entered in the `Replace with` field. You can replace all occurrences of the search text by clicking on the Replace All button.

The Add To Do List option adds a task related to the currently selected document to the To Do list. When you select this option, the Editor opens the Add To Do Task dialog box. The To Do list helps you manage the tasks related to creating and running a Web.

**FIGURE 5.22.**

*Replacing text used in the current page.*

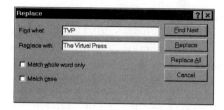

The Bookmark, Link, and Unlink options are used to add hypertext references to your pages. Links and bookmarks are explained in Chapter 9, "Adding Features to the Page."

Finally, the Properties option lets you specify properties for a selected HTML element, such as a table.

## Using the View Menu

The options available for the View menu are shown in Figure 5.23. You will use the View menu to add and remove toolbars from the command area. The toolbars are examined later in this chapter.

**FIGURE 5.23.**

*Options on the FrontPage Editor's View menu.*

Using the Status Bar option, you can add or remove the status area at the bottom of the Editor's display window. The status area is used to display command summaries and other key information.

The Format Marks option is similar to the show/hide formatting option in Microsoft Word. Using this option, you can see line breaks and other formatting that are not normally displayed. By default, this option is always turned on when you open a new page.

The final option in the View menu lets you view the HTML source for the current page. When you view the source, you will see HTML markup tags such as <H1> and </H1>.

## Using the Insert Menu

The Insert menu is used to add HTML elements to the current page. Figure 5.24 shows the options available for this menu. You will learn all about these elements in Part III, "Working with FrontPage."

**FIGURE 5.24.**

*Options on the FrontPage
Editor's Insert menu.*

## Using the Format Menu

You will use the Format menu to add character and paragraph formatting to your pages. Figure 5.25 shows the options available for this menu. In Part III, you will learn how to use character and paragraph formatting.

**FIGURE 5.25.**

*Options on the FrontPage
Editor's Format menu.*

## Using the Tools Menu

The Tools menu includes many miscellaneous functions, such as the spelling checker. The options available for this menu are shown in Figure 5.26.

**FIGURE 5.26.**

*Options on the FrontPage
Editor's Tools menu.*

The FrontPage Editor utilizes a spell checker similar to the one used in other Microsoft Office products. You start the spell checker by clicking on the Spelling option. When a misspelled word is found, you'll see the dialog box shown in Figure 5.27. If possible, the Editor will suggest words to replace the misspelled word with. You can select any of the suggested words by clicking on it.

**FIGURE 5.27.**

*The spell checker used in
FrontPage is similar to the
one used in other Microsoft
Office products.*

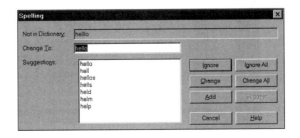

The FrontPage Editor maintains a list of all open pages. You can use the Forward option to display the next page in the list and the Back option to display the previous page in the list.

**NOTE**

The Forward option is only available if you used the Back option at least once.

Sometimes when you are accessing pages on external files, you will find that the file did not completely display in the Editor. If this happens, use the Reload option. Another option you might want to use is the Stop option to stop loading a file. You will use this option if the server you are trying to access is not responding.

The final two options in this menu are used to display FrontPage tools. The Show FrontPage Explorer option starts the Explorer, if it is not already started, and displays it. The Show To Do List option starts the To Do List manager, if it is not already started, and displays it.

## Using the Table Menu

The Table menu is used to add tables to the current page. Figure 5.28 shows the options available for this menu. Chapter 12, "Creating Tables with FrontPage," explores the table creation and design process. Most of the options in the table menu are grayed out if you haven't started a table in the current document.

**FIGURE 5.28.**

*Options on the FrontPage Editor's Table menu.*

## Using the Window Menu

The Window menu is used to change the way pages are organized in the FrontPage Editor and to access any open pages. The options available for this menu are shown in Figure 5.29.

Using the Cascade option, you can arrange all open pages in overlapping windows for easy access. This option is especially useful when you have three or more pages open, and you are switching back and forth between them. For example, in Figure 5.30, five pages are cascaded. I can access any page and bring it to the front by clicking anywhere on its window.

**FIGURE 5.29.**

*Options on the FrontPage Editor's Window menu.*

**FIGURE 5.30.**

*Cascading multiple pages for easy access.*

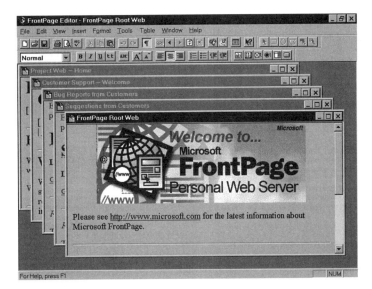

With the Tile option, you can resize all open pages in windows that are completely visible in the FrontPage Editor's main viewing area. Figure 5.31 shows how five pages are tiled. As you can see, when you have a lot of open pages, the tile option is not as useful as the cascade option. For this reason, you should use the file option when you have four pages or fewer open, and you want to be able to easily move back and forth between them.

The numbered options at the bottom of the menu allow you to quickly access any files currently open. Although the Editor will only list the first nine open pages, you can use the More Windows option to open the dialog box shown in Figure 5.32. With this dialog box, you can open any of the currently open pages.

**FIGURE 5.31.**

*Tiling multiple pages for easy access.*

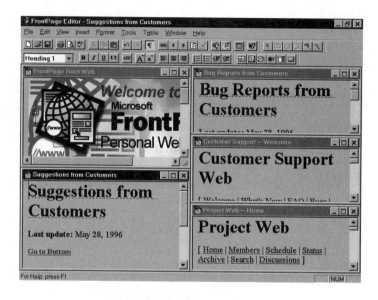

**FIGURE 5.32.**

*You can select a page to view with this dialog box.*

## Using the Help Menu

The Help menu is used to display information about the FrontPage Editor and to access the online help system. Figure 5.33 shows the options available on this menu.

**FIGURE 5.33.**

*Options on the FrontPage Editor's Help menu.*

To access FrontPage's very comprehensive help documentation, use the Microsoft FrontPage Help Topics option. The About Microsoft FrontPage Editor option displays information on your version of FrontPage.

## Using the Toolbar

The FrontPage Editor has one of the most extensive toolbars you will find in any application. In all, there are four toolbars: Standard, Format, Image, and Forms. You can add and remove any of the toolbars by selecting the appropriate options in the View menu. Because the toolbars are independent elements, you can move them to any area of your screen.

To change the location of a toolbar, move the mouse pointer over the toolbar, but not on top of any of the toolbar's icons, and then click and hold the left mouse button. Now you can drag the toolbar to a new location on the screen. When the toolbar is where you want it, release the left mouse button. From then on, the toolbar will be displayed in the new location.

The most versatile toolbar is the Standard toolbar (see Figure 5.34). This toolbar has icons for over 20 of the most commonly used FrontPage Editor menu options. From this toolbar you can open, save, and print pages. You can also perform editing functions such as cut, copy, paste, undo, and redo.

**FIGURE 5.34.**

*The FrontPage Editor's Standard toolbar.*

The Format toolbar, shown in Figure 5.35, includes most of the options you will use to manipulate the layout of your pages. You can use the icons on this toolbar to add text highlights, alignment, and indentation.

**FIGURE 5.35.**

*The FrontPage Editor's Format toolbar.*

When you add images to your pages, you will use the Image toolbar shown in Figure 5.36. You will want to use this toolbar when you create image maps or transparent GIFs.

**FIGURE 5.36.**

*The FrontPage Editor's Image toolbar.*

When you add fill-out forms to your pages, you will use the Form Fields toolbar, shown in Figure 5.37. The icons in this toolbar let you add input fields to your forms at the click of a button.

**FIGURE 5.37.**

*The FrontPage Editor's Form Fields toolbar.*

# Summary

FrontPage publishing is easy with the FrontPage Explorer and the FrontPage Editor. Both are powerful tools with specific uses. Use the Explorer to create and manage Webs and the Editor to create and edit pages.

# Working with Pages and Files

**6**

*by William Robert Stanek*

**IN THIS CHAPTER**

The most basic contents of your FrontPage Webs are the individual files that make up the Web. These files can be pages, images, and even multimedia objects. Working with pages and files is easy if you take the time to learn how FrontPage works. Although this chapter focuses primarily on working with pages, you can use the concepts covered in this chapter to manipulate other types of files as well. Because this chapter covers basic concepts, advanced users might want to skim the chapter for key points.

# Editing Pages

Before you can edit a page, you must first create it. The easiest way to create a page is to select New from the File menu in the FrontPage Editor, which opens the New Page dialog box shown in Figure 6.1. Now you can choose a template or wizard to base your page on by double-clicking when the pointer is over the template or wizard title. Alternatively, you can use the arrow keys on your keyboard to highlight a template or wizard, and then press the Enter key to make a selection.

**FIGURE 6.1.**

*Selecting a template or wizard for your new page.*

For now, you probably want to base your pages on the normal page template. All this template does is create a blank page for you. To learn all about the other templates available in FrontPage, see Chapter 18, "Creating Web Pages with FrontPage's Templates."

To edit pages, you use the FrontPage Editor. You enter text just as you would in any word processor. Because the editor is a WYSIWYG tool for creating HTML documents, behind the scenes it is generating HTML markup for your document as you enter text, formatting, and images. There are dozens of HTML elements you can add to your pages with the FrontPage Editor. You will learn how to add these elements to pages in Part III, "Working with FrontPage."

# Opening Existing Pages

The FrontPage Editor's File menu provides three ways to open existing pages: Open from Web, Open File, and Open Location. Normally, the option you use depends on the location of the page.

# Opening Pages from the Current Web

The Open from Web option enables you to open pages from the current Web without having to know where the files are stored on your hard drive. You use this option when you want to open files that are part of the current Web. The dialog box opened when you select this option is the Current Web dialog box. As you can see from Figure 6.2, all pages in the current Web are listed by page title and page URL.

**FIGURE 6.2.**

*Using the Current Web dialog box to open files from the current Web.*

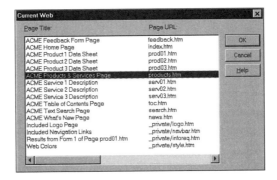

# Opening Files from Your Hard Drive

With the Open File option, you can open a file that exists anywhere on your hard drive. As you can see from Figure 6.3, the dialog box associated with this option is the same dialog box you see when you open files in most Windows applications. Although you might be tempted to use the Open File option often, you should use this option only to open pages that are not available in a Web you created with FrontPage.

**FIGURE 6.3.**

*Using the Open File dialog box to open local files that are not part of the current Web.*

Files can be in HTML, RTF, or ASCII text format. When you open files in a format other than HTML, the FrontPage Editor converts the page to HTML format.

Pages in Rich Text Format (RTF) are automatically converted to HTML format. You will find that the converted page is usually formatted exactly as it should be. However, pages in ASCII text format are not automatically converted. Before the editor converts the page, you must specify how you want the page to be formatted using the dialog box shown in Figure 6.4.

Usually you'll want to use the default option, which will import the page with most paragraph returns intact. Here is a summary of each of the options:

| | |
|---|---|
| One formatted paragraph | Your page will be imported as formatted text and paragraph returns will not always be preserved. |
| Formatted paragraphs | Your page will be imported as formatted text with paragraph returns preserved. |
| Normal paragraphs | Your page will be imported as text using the normal text style, and paragraph returns will not always be preserved. |
| Normal paragraphs with line breaks | Your page will be imported as text using the normal text style, and paragraph returns will be preserved. |

**NOTE**

The difference between normal text and formatted text is the font the browser uses. Normal text is displayed with the standard proportional font used by the browser, such as Times Roman. Formatted text is displayed with a non-proportional font like the one most typewriters use, such as Courier.

**FIGURE 6.4.**

*Selecting a style for ASCII text pages.*

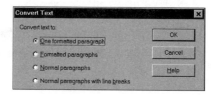

## Opening Pages from the Internet

The Editor enables you to open pages located on external Web servers with the Open Location option of the File menu. Figure 6.5 shows the dialog box associated with this option. In the Location field, enter the fully qualified URL to the external resource, such as the following:

```
http://www.mcp.com/index.html
```

**FIGURE 6.5.**

*Using the Open Location
dialog box to open resources
from external sources.*

# Saving Pages

After editing a page, you will want to save it. Generally, all pages are saved to the current Web. This means that before you create a page, you should create a Web in the FrontPage Explorer. (See Chapter 7, "Working with Webs," to learn more about creating Webs.)

To save a page, select either Save or Save As from the File menu. All pages are saved to the location you opened them from, which is usually the current Web. For new pages, the Save As dialog box will open when you select Save. The reason for this is that a new page must specify a title and filename for your page, and this is done with the Save As dialog box. Figure 6.6 shows the Save As dialog box.

All pages you create in the Editor are given a default title and filename. Usually, you will want to enter a new title and filename. Enter the title in the Page Title field. The title should describe the contents of the page. Enter the filename in the Page URL field. The filename should end with a .htm or .html extension, which identifies the page as an HTML document. When you are finished, click on the OK button to save the page to the current Web.

**FIGURE 6.6.**

*The Save As dialog box.*

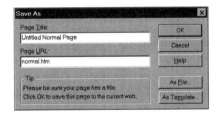

If you do not have a Web open in the FrontPage Explorer when you try to save a page and you have already started the FrontPage Explorer, you will see the error message shown in Figure 6.7. This error message tells you to open a Web in the FrontPage Explorer so that you can save the page. When you click on the OK button, the Explorer is displayed with the Open Web dialog box ready so that you can select a Web to open.

> **NOTE**
>
> If you have not created a Web, the only Web available is the Root Web. Generally, you should not save pages to the Root Web. Instead, create a test Web as discussed in Chapter 7.

**FIGURE 6.7.**

*When no Web is open and
you try to save a page, you
will see this error message.*

If you have not started the FrontPage Explorer and you try to save a page, the OK button is grayed out so you cannot click on it. When this happens, you can click on the Cancel button to cancel the save. You should then start the FrontPage Explorer, open a Web, and save the page.

The Save As dialog box enables you to save pages as files and as templates. To save the page as a file, click on the As File button. When you save the page as a file, the page is saved on your hard drive, which means that the file is not saved to the current Web. To save the page as a template, click on the As Template button. This creates a new page template based on the contents of your page. You can now create pages based on this template using the New Page dialog box.

> **NOTE**
>
> If a page you save as a file on your hard drive contains images or other objects, the Editor will display a dialog box asking if you want to save the images and objects with the page. Saving these objects with the page ensures that you have everything you need to publish the page in one place.

Another error message you might see when saving pages is shown in Figure 6.8. You will see this message when you are saving a page from a Web that is not the current Web. If you click on the Yes button, the page will be saved to the current Web. Because this is usually not where you want to save the page, click on the No button, and then do the following:

1. In the FrontPage Explorer, make the Web that the page came from the current Web.
2. In the FrontPage Editor, save the page.

**FIGURE 6.8.**

*When saving a page from a
Web that is not the current
Web, you will see this error
message.*

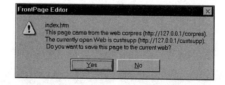

# Renaming and Moving Pages

You can use the Save As option on the FrontPage Editor's File menu to create a new file. However, the old file the page is based on still exists at its original location. To make sure that there is only one copy of the file in a Web, you need to use the Properties option on the FrontPage Explorer's Edit menu.

When you use the Properties option, the Explorer opens the Properties dialog box, shown in Figure 6.9. You can rename the file by entering a new filename in the Page URL field of the General tab. Because the file is moved to this new location, you can use the same dialog box to move the page to a new directory. All you have to do is enter the directory structure as part of the page URL. For example, if you want to move a page called `bookdemo.htm` to a subdirectory called `demo` in the current Web, you enter the following in the Page URL field:

```
demo/bookdemo.htm
```

> **NOTE**
>
> If the directory you are moving the file to does not exist, the FrontPage Explorer will automatically create the directory for you.

**FIGURE 6.9.**

*Use this dialog box to rename files.*

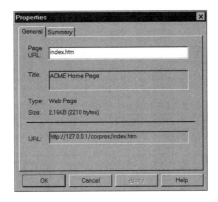

Files you move around a Web often affect other pages in the Web, especially if there are links pointing to the file you are moving. Fortunately, the Explorer automatically tracks all links to files in your Webs, and if moving the file will invalidate links in other files, the Explorer gives you the option of automatically updating links to the file. The dialog box you will see when this happens is shown in Figure 6.10. By clicking on the Yes button in the Confirm Updating Links dialog box, you can confirm that you want to update links throughout the Web.

**FIGURE 6.10.**

*FrontPage can update links in your Web when you move files.*

# Hiding Files from Browsers

In FrontPage, all directories beginning with the underscore character are hidden from users. Often when you create a Web, you will have files that users should not access or view directly. For example, if the headers and footers for pages in your Web are in separate HTML documents, you usually do not want users to be able to access the header or footer documents directly. In this case, you move the files to a directory users cannot access, such as `_private`.

# Deleting Files from the Current Web

Deleting files from the current Web is easy but not necessarily intuitive, especially because you can only delete files in the FrontPage Explorer. To delete a file, select the file in any of the views, and then use the Delete option on the Edit menu. Alternatively, you can select the file in any view and press the Delete key. Whenever you try to delete files, the FrontPage Explorer asks you to confirm that you want to delete the files. If you do, click on the Yes button in the confirmation dialog box.

> **TIP**
>
> Using the Summary view, you can select multiple files for deletion. After selecting the first file by clicking on it, hold down the Ctrl key to select additional files. You can select a group of consecutively listed files by clicking on the first file you want to select and then moving the mouse pointer to the last item and holding the Shift key as you click the left mouse button.

# Associating Files with Editors

Most files end with a 3- or 4-letter extension that identifies the file type or the formatting of the file, such as HTML documents that end with the `.htm` or `.html` extension. The FrontPage Explorer uses the file extension to determine the editor to use with the file you are trying to open for editing.

Using the FrontPage Explorer, you can configure additional editors for use with FrontPage by selecting Configure Editors from the Tools menu. This opens the dialog box shown in Figure 6.11, which lists all currently configured editors.

When you install FrontPage, three editors are configured for your use. The FrontPage Editor is configured as the editor for files ending with the `.htm` or `.html` extension, which are treated as HTML pages. To handle frame-enhanced documents, the Frames Wizard is configured as the editor for documents ending with the `.frm` extension, which is the extension FrontPage uses to identify the source file for frame-enhanced pages. Although the Windows Notepad is configured as the editor of choice for other file types, it is used only if FrontPage cannot resolve which editor to use for a file.

---

**TIP**

If you have default editors set on your desktop, you might not have to configure editors at all. In Windows 95/NT, editors are configured for most file types automatically when you install software and can be manually configured using the Windows Explorer. When the FrontPage Explorer tries to determine the editor to open, it will look first at the editors you configured locally and then at the editors configured for the Windows desktop.

---

**FIGURE 6.11.**

*The Configure Editors dialog box shows the editors configured for use with FrontPage.*

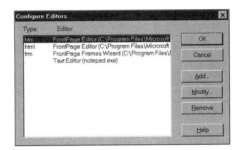

To add an editor to the list, click on the Add button in the Configure Editors dialog box. As you can see from Figure 6.12, the Explorer then displays a dialog box in which you can configure the editor. In the File Type field of the Add Editor Association dialog box, enter the 3- or 4-letter extension that identifies the type of file you will use the editor with. In Figure 6.12, you can see that the user is configuring an editor for use with GIF images, so the file type is GIF.

In the Editor Name field, enter a name for the editor. The name does not have to be the actual name of the program; rather, it is the name with which you want to identify the editor. In the Command field, enter the full path to the editor's binary executable file. If you do not know the path, click on the Browse button and the Explorer will display a dialog box that enables you to browse your file system.

Although most editors can be used with multiple file types, the Explorer allows you to configure only one file type at a time. Therefore, you should go through the configuration process one time for each file type you plan to use with the editor.

**FIGURE 6.12.**

*To add editors, you must specify the file type.*

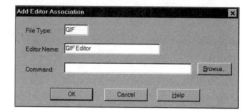

For editors that you configure, you can make changes to editor definitions or remove them from the editor list. After selecting an editor you want to change, click on the Modify button in the Configure Editors dialog box. This will open a dialog box labeled Modify Editor Association, which has the same fields as the dialog box shown in Figure 6.12. To remove an editor from the list, select it, and then click on the Remove button.

# Summary

Creating, editing, and deleting files is easy if you take the time to learn how FrontPage works. After reading this chapter, you should be able to work with just about any type of file in FrontPage. You are now ready to learn about working with Webs.

# Working with Webs

**7**

*by William Robert Stanek*

**IN THIS CHAPTER**

The previous chapter looked at pages. This chapter focuses on Webs and the directory structure associated with Webs. *Webs* contain sets of pages and resource files for the pages, such as images, sound files, and video files. All the pages and resource files in Webs are organized into easy-to-manage directory structures. Because this chapter contains basic concepts, advanced users might want to skim the chapter for key points.

# Creating Webs

You create, edit, and manage Webs in the FrontPage Explorer. When you installed FrontPage, a base Web called the RootWeb was created on your server. As long as you work with the same server, all Webs you create in the Explorer are organized in subdirectories under the same RootWeb.

To create a Web, select New Web from the File menu or press Ctrl+N in the FrontPage Explorer. This opens the New Web dialog box, shown in Figure 7.1. Now you can choose a template or wizard to base your Web on by double-clicking the left mouse button when the pointer is over the template or wizard title. Alternatively, you can use the arrow keys on your keyboard to highlight a template or wizard, and then press the Enter key to make a selection.

**FIGURE 7.1.**

*Selecting a template or wizard for your new Web.*

For now, you probably want to base your Web on the normal Web template. All this template does is create a new Web with a single page. This page is based on the normal template and hence the name of the Web. To learn all about creating Webs with wizards and templates, see Chapter 19, "Instant Web Sites with FrontPage's Web Wizards."

If you create a new Web in the Explorer and another Web is already open, you can select the Add to the current Web field to merge the contents of the new Web with the current Web. However, if any of the pages added by the new Web have the same filename as a file in the current Web, you will see the dialog box shown in Figure 7.2. This dialog box asks you to confirm that you want to replace the existing file with the new file. Although you usually do not want to overwrite existing files, you can click on the Yes button to confirm that you want the new file to replace the old file.

## FIGURE 7.2.

*The Confirm Save dialog box asks you to confirm that you want to replace old files with new files.*

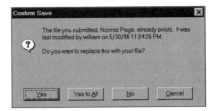

### CAUTION

As you can see from the figure, the Confirm Save dialog box also has a button labeled Yes to All. Use this button only when you know for sure what files the Explorer plans to overwrite. You could accidentally replace all the files in your Web with a template outline.

After you select the Web template, click on the OK button and the FrontPage Explorer will open the dialog box shown in Figure 7.3. In this dialog box, you need to enter a valid designator for the server and a name for the Web. The server designator should be an Internet Protocol Address or a valid host name for a Web server. The IP address is a series of numbers separated by periods that is used to determine the machine's location on a network. An example IP address is 198.5.16.29. The host name is a string of characters that usually forms a word with periods used to separate key parts of the naming structure. An example host name is tvpress.com.

Generally speaking, host names are used because words are easier to remember than numbers. Thus, the host name is for users like you and me, and IP addresses are for the computers that do the work for us.

Because FrontPage supports publishing on multiple servers, the Web server field has a drop-down list that provides quick access to IP addresses and host names you have used before. To activate the drop-down list, click on the down arrow on the right side of the Web server input field. With the drop-down list activated, move the mouse pointer up or down and click the left mouse button to make a selection.

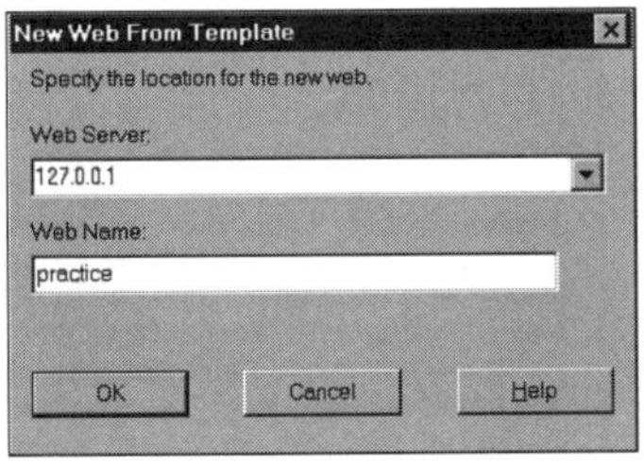

## FIGURE 7.3.

*Before you can create a Web, you must specify where to place the Web.*

---

> **TIP**
>
> If you are not on a network or do not want to access the network, use the local host IP address of 127.0.0.1 as the server designator. In this way, you can set up a Web without having to connect to the Internet or the corporate intranet.

After you enter the server designator, you should name the Web. Web names can contain numbers, letters, and punctuation characters, but they cannot contain spaces. The best Web names are short but descriptive. This is primarily because visitors to your Web might have to type the complete URL path to your Web documents in their browser to reach your Web site. If you use long names, visitors have to type more and might become irritated.

When you are finished specifying the information for the new Web, click on the OK button. If this is the first time you have manipulated Webs during this session with the FrontPage Explorer, you will be prompted with the dialog box shown in Figure 7.4. As the dialog box instructs, you must enter the user name and password for the FrontPage administrator before the Web can be created.

**FIGURE 7.4.**

*Only FrontPage administrators can create Webs.*

After the Explorer authenticates your user name and password, it will create your new Web as a child of the RootWeb. This means that the new Web is located in a subdirectory under the main directory for the RootWeb, and because of this, actions you take in the RootWeb might affect the new Web.

Because FrontPage creates a subdirectory named after the Web, all Web names must be unique. If you try to create a Web with the same name as an existing Web, you will see the error message shown in Figure 7.5. Unfortunately, when you click on the OK button in this situation, the FrontPage Explorer kicks you back to the New Web dialog box, and you must select the type of Web you want to create again.

**FIGURE 7.5.**

*All Web names must be unique, or you will get this error message.*

# Opening Existing Webs

FrontPage can access any Web you created on any server. To open a Web, select Open Web from the File menu in the FrontPage Explorer. Then in the Open Web dialog box, shown in Figure 7.6, select the server that the Web is stored on from the Web server field's drop-down list. Next, click on the List Webs button to see a listing of available Webs for the server you have chosen.

**FIGURE 7.6.**

*Opening a Web in the FrontPage Explorer.*

Sometimes when you try to open a Web, you will not be able to establish a connection to the Web's server. If this happens, you will see an error similar to the one shown in Figure 7.7. After you click on the OK button, you should check the following:

1. Make sure that the Personal Web Server is started.

2. If you are trying to access a remote server, be sure you have a connection to the network or to the Internet.

**FIGURE 7.7.**

*A server connection error message.*

# Editing Webs

Because Webs represent complex structures of pages and files, editing Webs is very different from editing pages. Generally, when you edit a Web, you manipulate the Web's attributes. Attributes for a Web include its title, name, and location.

# Changing a Web's Title and Name

The two primary attributes for a Web are its title and name. The only use for the Web title is as an identifier in the FrontPage Explorer. Otherwise, the Web title is not used anywhere else. For this reason, when you create a Web, the Web title is set the same as the Web name.

The Web name, on the other hand, identifies part of the URL path to the files in the Web. When you change a Web's name, you are actually moving the Web to a new subdirectory.

You can change a Web's title and name using the Configuration tab of the Web Settings dialog box. To open this dialog box, select Web Settings from the Tools menu in the FrontPage Explorer.

# Creating a New Directory in a Web

Sometimes, you want to create subdirectories for files and pages within a Web. To create a new directory in a Web, move a page to the directory by entering the directory structure as part of a new URL for the page. If the directory to which you are moving the page does not exist, the FrontPage Explorer will automatically create the directory for you. The section titled "Renaming and Moving Pages" in Chapter 6 discusses moving pages to new directories.

# Displaying Hidden Documents in a Web

In the previous chapter, you learned that you could create directories hidden from users. These directories use the underscore as the first character of a directory name, which means that they are private. As a Web administrator, you might need to view and edit files in private directories. To show these directories in the FrontPage Explorer views, you will use the Advanced tab of the Web settings dialog box. As shown in Figure 7.8, select the Show documents in hidden directories field, then click on the OK button.

When you make changes in the Advanced tab, the Explorer displays the dialog box shown in Figure 7.9. This dialog box asks if you want to refresh the Web. Generally, you will want to click on the Yes button to tell FrontPage to refresh the Web. When you refresh a Web, the FrontPage Explorer instructs the server to retrieve the Web with the new settings, make updates as necessary, and build a new text index for the Web.

**FIGURE 7.8.**

*Using the Advanced Tab in the Web Settings dialog box to display hidden directories.*

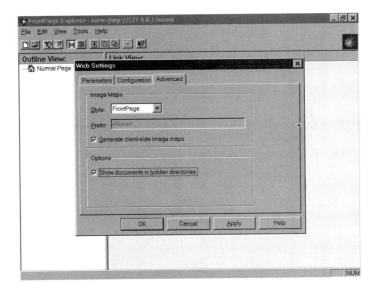

**FIGURE 7.9.**

*Refreshing the Web updates the views.*

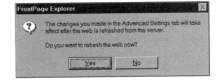

# Importing Files to the Current Web

If you have already published on the Web, you probably have Web documents and images on your hard drive. When you want to use these files in FrontPage, you should import them for use in a specific Web. This makes the files easier to manage and makes it possible for you to get all the benefits of FrontPage.

You can import files of any type in the Explorer. When you import text-based documents that are in a format other than HTML, the Explorer does not convert the page to HTML format. Thus, another reason you might want to import files is to preserve the original formatting of the file.

> **NOTE**
>
> Be sure to configure an editor for all files you import that are not in an HTML or standard image format. To learn how to configure editors for use in FrontPage, see the section titled, "Associating Files with Editors."

Before you import files, start the FrontPage Explorer and make the Web to which you want to add the files the current Web. Then from the Explorer's File menu, select Import to open the Import dialog box shown in Figure 7.10. Initially, almost all the dialog box's buttons are grayed out. The reason for this is that you need to add files to the import list before you can use the other options. Thus your first step is to select the files you want to import.

**FIGURE 7.10.**

*Using the Import dialog box to import files.*

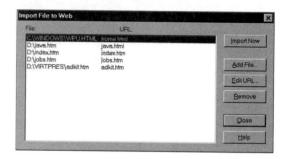

Start by clicking on the Add File button, which opens the Add File to Import List dialog box shown in Figure 7.11. As you can see, this dialog box has all the features of the normal open file dialog box. After you select files for importing, they will be displayed in the import list until they are removed from the list with the Remove button or imported into the current Web with the Import Now button. Because of this, you can click on the Close button to close the dialog box. Exit the Explorer and then restart the Explorer, and the files will still be on the import list.

**FIGURE 7.11.**

*Adding files to the import list.*

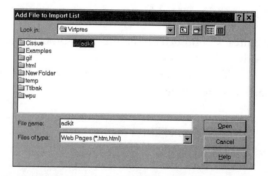

**TIP**

Your import list can contain dozens of files. Sometimes you do not want to import them all at the same time. You can select individual files from the import list by moving the mouse pointer to the filename in the list and clicking the left mouse button. You can add files to the selection list by holding down the Ctrl key as you select the additional files. You can select a group of consecutively listed files by clicking on the first file you want to select and then moving the mouse pointer to the last item and holding the Shift key as you click the left mouse button.

Another useful button on the Import dialog box is the Edit URL button, which opens the Edit URL dialog box shown in Figure 7.12. Using the Edit URL dialog box, you can change the URL associated with a file you are importing.

**FIGURE 7.12.**

*Editing the URL of a file you plan to import.*

An error you might see when adding files to the import list is shown in Figure 7.13. Be careful when you see this error message. The file you are trying to import already exists on the current Web, and if you click on the Yes button, you will overwrite a file in the current Web. Unless you are quite sure you want to replace the file, click on the No button.

**FIGURE 7.13.**

*Be careful when you see this error message.*

# Exporting Files

Just as you might need to import files for use with FrontPage, sometimes you want to export files from FrontPage. When you export files from FrontPage, you are really only saving the files to a location other than the Web they are stored in. Although you could use the Save As function of the FrontPage Editor to perform the same task, the reason you will want to use the Explorer to export files is that you export files without having to open them.

The dialog box associated with the Export Selected option is shown in Figure 7.14. You use this dialog box as you would the Save As dialog box.

**FIGURE 7.14.**

*Exporting files from the current Web.*

> **NOTE**
>
> If a page you are exporting contains images or other objects, the Explorer will display a dialog box asking whether you want to save the images and objects with the page. Saving these objects with your pages ensures that you have everything you need to publish the pages in one place.

# Deleting, Copying, and Moving Webs

Occasionally, you will need to delete a Web and all the files associated with the Web. To delete a Web, select Delete Web from the File menu in the FrontPage Explorer. After you delete the Web, there is no way to get the Web back, and the Explorer displays a warning to tell you this.

Part of the Web administration process involves protecting your investment of time, resources, and money. One way to do this is to make backup copies of the pages and resource files used in the Web.

You can copy an entire Web using the Copy Web option in the File menu, which opens the dialog box shown in Figure 7.15. In the Destination Web Server field, enter the host name or IP address of the host to which you want to copy the Web. In the Destination Web Name field, enter the name for the Web. Although the Web name is used to build the directory path to the Web, you cannot enter a directory path that includes subdirectories, such as `/samples/ docs`.

The Copy Web dialog box has two optional fields. If you check the Add to Existing Web field, the FrontPage Explorer allows you to merge the Web you are copying into an existing Web. When you insert files into a Web, you might find that some files have duplicate names. Usually, you do not want the new files to overwrite the old files. The second optional field, Copy Child Webs, is available only when you are copying the RootWeb. If you check the Copy Child Webs field, all Webs listed when you access the RootWeb's server will be copied to the new destination.

As you can see, copying a Web is essentially the same as moving the Web to a new location. Thus, when you want to move a Web from one server to another, you use the File menu's Copy Web option. Interestingly enough, when you copy a Web from a local server to a server on the World Wide Web or even on the corporate intranet, you are actually publishing the Web.

**FIGURE 7.15.**

*Copying your Webs.*

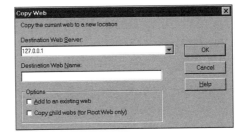

# Summary

Although Webs are more complex than pages, FrontPage has great features that make creating, editing, and deleting Webs easy. After reading this chapter, you should be able to work with Webs in FrontPage. You are now ready to learn how to create powerful Web documents.

**PART**

## IN THIS PART

# Working with FrontPage

# Creating Web Documents with FrontPage

**8**

*by William Robert Stanek*

**IN THIS CHAPTER**

Although you can easily create boring, run-of-the-mill documents with FrontPage, it is your design that will help sell your ideas, products, or services to a global audience. You do not have to be a programmer or a computer wizard to design dazzling HTML documents. What you need is a firm understanding of HTML design concepts and the pointers you will find in this book.

# What Is HTML?

When Tim Berners-Lee envisioned the World Wide Web, he envisioned it having a common and easy-to-use interface that would allow anyone to Web publish. To accomplish this, he and others at the European Laboratory for Particle Physics (CERN) developed the Hypertext Markup Language (HTML), which is based on a subset of the Standard Generalized Markup Language (SGML). Using SGML as the basis of HTML ensured that the new markup language for the Web was rooted in a solid standard that was already proven to be a cross-platform solution.

Only the essential elements of SGML were adopted to form the original specification for HTML. This drastically reduced the complexity of the original HTML specification and reduced the overhead for transferring hypertext documents over the network. Another advantage of using SGML as the basis for HTML was that SGML document type definitions (DTDs) provided an easy way to extend the HTML standard. Thus, it was the intent of the developers of HTML to create a language for Web documents that was initially simple, yet could grow more complex over time.

## BROWSERS: WINDOWS TO THE WEB

You will see references to HTML and the format of markup code throughout this book, and you might wonder why. Although FrontPage automatically puts your documents in HTML format, you should know the basic structure of HTML and the level of HTML being used in your document at any particular time. This will help you understand what is going on behind the scenes and why your document might not look the way you want it to in a particular browser.

A *browser* is a software application that enables you to access the Web. You can think of a browser as your window to the Web. Change your browser and you get a whole new view of the Web. When you use Lynx, your window to the Web has only text. Text-only browsers are the original browsers for the Web. Although it might be hard to believe, several text-only browsers are still being developed.

When you use NCSA Mosaic, your window to the Web has text and graphics. Browsers that enable you to view Web documents containing text and graphics are the second generation of browsers. These browsers are largely responsible for the phenomenal success of the Web.

When you use HotJava, your window has text, graphics, and live animation. Browsers that enable you to view Web documents containing text, graphics, and inline multimedia are the third generation of browsers. These browsers are driving the Web's transition to an extremely visual medium that rivals television for information content and entertainment value.

# What Are the Features of HTML?

The HTML specification has come a long way since the early days. Presently, three specifications for HTML are defined. Each new specification is fully backward-compatible with previous specifications and includes many enhancements to the HTML standard. In addition to these specifications, many Web publishers are using extensions to the standard. These extensions offer Web publishing solutions that current HTML specifications do not support.

The following sections take a look at the HTML standard and extensions to the standard, including

- HTML 1.0
- HTML 2.0
- HTML 3.0/3.2
- Netscape extensions
- Internet Explorer extensions
- Java extensions
- ActiveX extensions

## HTML 1.0

HTML version 1 is the original specification for HTML. Because of the limited capabilities of the specification, documents created with HTML 1.0 have very basic designs. The primary features of HTML 1.0 documents include

- Multiple levels of headings
- Paragraphs
- Hypertext references
- Special formatting for lists of items

FrontPage is fully compliant with HTML 1.0. While all HTML browsers can display HTML 1.0 documents, few Web publishers produce documents written exclusively in HTML 1.0.

This is primarily because of the significant improvements offered by later HTML specifications. Consequently, if you plan to publish HTML documents, you should look to the later specifications described in the following sections.

# HTML 2.0

HTML version 2 offers better control over the layout and highlighting of text within Web documents and is based on the features and extensions Web publishers were using in their documents before June 1994. The primary enhancements HTML 2.0 provides to the HTML standard are

- Inline images
- Fill-out forms

FrontPage is fully compliant with HTML 2.0. Being able to display images with the text on the page finally enabled Web publishers to tap into the multimedia capabilities of the Web. Fill-out forms provided Web publishers with a quick and easy way to get participation from users.

When the final draft of HTML 2.0 was ratified recently, the HTML 2.0 specification became a Request for Comment (RFC). Most HTML documents on the Web meet the specification for HTML 2.0. You will find dozens of HTML browsers that are HTML 2.0 compliant. If you plan to publish HTML documents on the Web, HTML 2.0 should be your basic publishing solution.

# HTML 3.0/3.2

Even before the HTML 2.0 draft was ratified, Web publishers, eager to create better and more powerful documents, started looking to the advanced features offered by HTML version 3. HTML version 3 is the next level in HTML publishing and offers powerful features such as

- Advanced layout control
- Banners
- Client-side handling of hot spots in images
- Customized lists
- Dynamic documents with client-push/server-pull
- Mathematical equations
- Style sheets
- Tables
- Tables within forms

The original specification for HTML version 3 was called HTML 3.0. Although HTML 3.0 was widely written about, the specification was never fully implemented in client browsers, which was largely because of the complexities involved with implementing the advanced features found in HTML 3.0. Instead of fully implementing HTML 3.0, many browsers—including the Netscape Navigator, Internet Explorer, and NCSA Mosaic—only supported key enhancements of the HTML 3.0 specification.

As you might expect, the supported enhancements are those that are high on most Web publishers' wish lists but are not extremely difficult to implement. The supported enhancements include the following:

- Advanced layout control
- Client-side handling of hot spots in images
- Customized lists
- Dynamic documents with client-push/server-pull
- Tables
- Tables within forms

This subset of the original HTML 3.0 specification was reworked into a new specification called HTML 3.2. Just as HTML 2.0 is based on the features and extensions used in documents before June 1994, HTML 3.2 is based on features and extensions used in documents before May 1996. HTML 3.2 is designed as a replacement for HTML 2.0 and, as such, is fully backward-compatible with HTML 2.0 features.

> **NOTE**
>
> The subset of enhancements supported by HTML 3.2 does not include all the extensions proposed in HTML 3.0. For example, HTML 3.2 does not implement the full HTML 3 table model. Instead, HTML 3.2 implements the tables as supported by browsers such as Netscape and Internet Explorer.

The features that HTML 3.0 promised to bring to Web publishing are not gone with the death of HTML 3.0. Instead, many advanced features are being developed as separate specifications. For example, a complete specification is in development for style sheets. There is also a specification for the HTML 3 table model.

FrontPage directly supports most of the elements defined in HTML 3.2 and allows you to easily add elements not directly supported. A growing number of HTML documents have features defined in the HTML 3.2 specification. You will find thousands of documents featuring tables, client-side image maps, and client-pull/server-push. If you plan to publish HTML documents on the Web, you should strongly consider using HTML 3.2 enhancements.

> **NOTE**
>
> The next version of HTML after HTML 3.2 will add support for embedded multimedia objects, client-side scripting, style sheets, and extensions to fill-out forms. The draft specification for this future version of HTML, code-named Cougar, is expected to be released in the Fall of 1996.
>
> The next version of FrontPage should be released in early 1997 and is currently dubbed FrontPage 97. It is expected that FrontPage 97 will directly support all HTML 3.2 elements and will also directly support hot features such as Java programming, JavaScript, ActiveX, and VBScript.

## HTML Extensions for Netscape

Netscape Communications Corporation developed the most popular extensions to the HTML standard. Netscape has many unique extensions. These extensions, like the HTML specification itself, are changing. Many Web users confuse Netscape extensions and HTML 3.2 enhancements. While it is true Netscape created extensions to HTML that are being incorporated into current draft specifications for HTML 3.2, Netscape adopted key features, such as tables, from early drafts of the HTML 3.0 standard.

Netscape implemented the following unique extensions with the release of Netscape Navigator 1.0:

- Layout extras such as center and blink
- Horizontal rule extensions for width, length, and shading
- Control over relative font sizes
- Control over font color
- Use of images or colors to form a background for a document

Although these extensions were once unique to the Netscape Navigator Version 1.0, other companies are adopting these extensions for use in their browsers as well. For example, when Microsoft released the Internet Explorer browser for the Web, the browser featured full support for most Netscape Navigator 1.0 extensions. The development team at Netscape didn't stop with the original extensions. Netscape introduced the following extensions with the release of Netscape Navigator 2.0:

- Additional control over font sizes
- Support for multiple windows in a document called frames
- Netscape scripting language for client-side scripts
- The capability to embed multimedia objects and use an add-on module for the browser called a plug-in

The latest version of the Netscape Navigator is 3.0. New extensions introduced by Navigator 3.0 Beta 5 and later include support for the following:

- Internet Explorer's font face extension
- Multicolumn text layout
- Spacers that provide total control over the vertical and hortizontal whitespace on a page
- Enhancements for frames, which are subwindows within the browser's viewing space

The frame enhancements enable you to specify a color for frame borders and also to remove frame borders. Although Navigator 3.0 does not introduce as many new extensions as previous versions, it is bundled with many client applications including CoolTalk—an Internet phone software package—and features broader support for new Internet technologies such as JavaScript and Java.

> **NOTE**
>
> Throughout the book, I discuss HTML elements used by browsers that support Netscape extensions. Although I usually refer to these extensions as Netscape extensions, keep in mind that many browsers support these extensions. For example, the Internet Explorer 2.0 and later versions support all Netscape Navigator 1.0 and 2.0 extensions.

FrontPage directly supports all Netscape 1.0 extensions and most of the Netscape 2.0 and 3.0 extensions. Netscape extensions offer terrific solutions for your advanced Web publishing needs. Keep in mind that if you use Netscape extensions, only browsers capable of handling Netscape extensions will display your document as you intended. Because approximately 50 percent of Web users have at least a Netscape Version 1.0–capable browser, using Netscape extensions in your publications is something you should seriously consider.

> **NOTE**
>
> Although FrontPage does not directly support embedded multimedia objects and client-side scripts, you can still use FrontPage to create documents with these HTML extensions. You use the HTML Markup WebBot to add HTML elements not directly supported by FrontPage. See Chapter 20, "Automation with FrontPage's WebBots," to learn more about the HTML Markup WebBot.

# HTML Extensions for Internet Explorer

Until recently, if you used video or sound in your Web publications, users had to select and download the files to preview them. But before they could play the sound or video, they needed to have a helper application configured and available for use with their browser. This required an extra step that not all Web users are willing to take. Yet even the countless millions of users who want to play sound and video files have to install a video or audio player on their system, which isn't always easy.

To solve this problem, Web programmers and developers looked at ways to play multimedia files directly in a user's browser. The first result of this effort came from the computer industry giant, Microsoft. Microsoft's Internet Explorer is the premier browser that directly supports internal multimedia. With direct support for internal multimedia, users are freed from the hassles of installing and configuring helper applications to view the multimedia, and Web publishers have greater freedom to include multimedia in their publications.

Like the Netscape Navigator, the Internet Explorer supports unique extensions. Although Microsoft is the current developer of FrontPage, FrontPage version 1.1 does not directly support most of the unique Internet Explorer extensions. Extensions unique to Internet Explorer 2.0 include the following:

- Specify font types and colors
- Use scrolling marquees
- Use dynamic sources to create inline motion video
- Create documents with sound tracks

Internet Explorer extensions are powerful multimedia solutions for your advanced Web publishing needs. However, only browsers capable of handling Internet Explorer extensions can use these features. Currently, Internet Explorer extensions support video in Microsoft AVI format and sound in WAV, AU, and MIDI formats. If you plan to incorporate sound and video into your Web publications, you should seriously consider using Internet Explorer extensions in addition to hypertext references to the multimedia files.

> **NOTE**
>
> Sound and video formats are fully explained later in the book. See Chapter 29, "Adding Sound and Video to Web Pages," for complete details on multimedia formats.

Internet Explorer version 3.0 was released in early 1996. This version of Internet Explorer features complete support for HTML 3.2 and has the broadest support for the latest Internet technologies and standards. When IE 3.0 was introduced, it was the only browser to fully support the HTML table model standard first proposed in HTML 3.0 and the only browser to fully support the cascading style sheets standard. IE 3.0 also supports TrueType fonts, ActiveX, client-side scripting, Java, VRML, Active VRML, and features enhancements for frames.

> **TIP**
>
> With IE 3.0, you can view documents with borderless frames and floating frames. Internet Explorer 3.0 implements borderless frames automatically when you do not set a border width value. Floating frames are implemented by placing frames that do not fill the browser's window within the document. See Chapter 13, "Using Frames and the Frames Wizard," for more information on frames. For more cool frame enhancements, look for the upcoming release of Internet Explorer 4.0 in early 1997.

# HTML Extensions for Java

Java is Sun Microsystem's contribution to Web publishing. With Java you can create extremely dynamic documents that feature inline applications called applets. Not only are Java applets displayed on the page, they are self-running, interactive programs that can be previewed on any Java-capable browser. The Java language is simple and easy to learn, and like HTML, Java provides a common language that can be used on any computer platform. The implications of a common language for creating applications had such a far-reaching effect that Java became an instant hit with Web publishers and users.

Java introduces only a single extension to HTML: the applet tag. However, the applications you can create with Java are limitless. Already hundreds—perhaps thousands—of Web sites feature Java applets. You can use Java to create games, product demos, utilities, and business applications. Because of the tremendous demand for Java-enhanced publications, many browsers already support or plan to support Java applets. However, keep in mind that only users with a Java-capable browser can view or use an applet. Several browsers currently support applets. The HotJava browser, created by Sun to showcase Java, directly supports applets. The Netscape Navigator 2.0 and Internet Explorer 3.0 can use Java applets as embedded applications. Oracle PowerBrowser versions after 1.5 also support Java. You should use Java applets as feature attractions, but not as the only attractions at your Web site.

> **NOTE**
>
> Throughout most of 1995, the Java programming language was evolving and the latest version of Java is not compatible with the original alpha release. Because of this, older versions of popular browsers such as HotJava will not work with the current version of Java. For this reason, if you want to use Java, you should ensure that you use the following versions:

HotJava version Beta 1 or later

Netscape Navigator version 2.02 or later

Internet Explorer version 3.0 Beta 2 or later

Oracle PowerBrowser versions after 1.5

# HTML Extensions for ActiveX

ActiveX is a technology for creating live documents with powerful and easy-to-use interfaces. Although Microsoft has been developing ActiveX for some time, it is only recently that ActiveX technology has come to the forefront as the hottest Internet innovation. ActiveX is so hot that it is stealing the Java programming language's spotlight. This is primarily because ActiveX technology is the key to fulfilling all the needs of Web publishers and users for years to come.

Although FrontPage 1.1 does not directly support ActiveX, your documents can certainly benefit from using ActiveX technology. At the heart of ActiveX is a base concept for merging technologies using an enhanced object linking and embedding interface. Following the broad guidelines of the core ActiveX specification, developers can create add-on modules, which provide additional functionality. Add-on modules currently available include ActiveX Controls, ActiveX Scripting, ActiveX Documents, and ActiveX Conferencing.

ActiveX Controls are the key to adding live and interactive multimedia to your Web documents. Using ActiveX Controls, you can embed and execute software applications in a Web page. These applications allow users to view and interact with movies, animation, and audio.

**NOTE**

ActiveX Controls are similar to Netscape plug-ins. Both ActiveX Controls and Netscape plug-ins enable you to embed applications in your documents. Just as Netscape allows third party developers to create plug-ins for the Navigator, Microsoft allows third party developers to create new ActiveX Controls. In the coming months, you should see an avalanche of cool ActiveX Controls from third party developers.

Recently, client-side scripting languages have gained popularity. Two of the most popular scripting languages are JavaScript and VBScript. With ActiveX Scripting, you can use any client-side scripting language in your documents. You can also link your client-side scripts to Java applets, embedded applications, and ActiveX Controls. (See Chapter 32, "Using JavaScript in Your Web Pages," and Chapter 33, "Using VBScript in Your Web Pages," for more information on client-side scripting.)

The ActiveX Documents module is really very similar to FrontPage's support for Microsoft Office applications. You can use ActiveX Documents to import documents formatted for MS Word, Excel, Powerpoint, Schedule, and Access into your Web pages. These documents are imported using a special viewer that is inserted into the browser's viewing windows. This viewer has its own toolbars, menus, and interface.

Another giant step forward for Internet technology integration is Microsoft's ActiveX Conferencing, which enables real-time, multiparty communications over the Internet. Other specifications that use ActiveX technology include Active VRML and ActiveMovie Stream.

# FrontPage Support for HTML Specifications and Extensions

Through its terrific support for HTML specifications and extensions, FrontPage once again proves it is well ahead of the competition. However, even the most advanced tool has its limitations, and this section outlines some of those limitations.

## FrontPage Support for HTML Specifications

Although FrontPage is fully HTML 1.0 and HTML 2.0 compliant, it is not fully compliant with HTML 3. This is primarily because the HTML 3 specification is still evolving, and the developers of any product that supports the specification must determine which features are stable enough to support and which features may change in future revisions. For this reason, FrontPage supports all major features of the specification, but does not support features that are not fully defined.

FrontPage 1.X directly supports the following HTML 3 features:

- Advanced layout control
- Client-side handling of hot spots in images
- Customized lists
- Dynamic documents with client-push/server-pull
- Tables
- Tables within forms

FrontPage 1.X has limited support for the following HTML 3 feature:

- Style sheets

FrontPage 1.X does not directly support the following HTML 3 features:

- Banners
- Mathematical equations

All features that FrontPage directly supports are available at the press of a button. Although FrontPage does not directly support a few HTML 3 features, you can include these features in your HTML pages if you so desire. To do this, all you need to know is the markup code for the feature you want to add.

> **TIP**
>
> Because there are varying degrees of support for HTML 3, this book points out FrontPage features that use HTML 3. Hopefully, this will serve as a reminder to you that a few visitors to your Web site might not be able to see your page as you see it with an HTML 3–compliant browser. Keep in mind that at the present time, most HTML 3–compliant browsers conform to the document type definition specified in the HTML 3.2 specification.

# FrontPage Support for HTML Extensions

Many companies have created extensions to the HTML standard. FrontPage supports only those extensions to HTML that have become fairly standardized and are in wide acceptance. For this reason, FrontPage directly supports all extensions for Netscape 1.0 and Internet Explorer 1.0, but does not support all extensions for Netscape 2.0+ and Internet Explorer 2.0+.

The key features of Netscape versions 2.0 and higher that FrontPage does not directly support include

- Embedded client-side scripts
- Embedded multimedia objects
- Multicolumn text layout
- Enhanced frames

The key features of Internet Explorer versions 2.0 and higher that FrontPage does not directly support include

- Scrolling marquees
- Dynamic sources to create inline motion video
- Documents with sound tracks
- Borderless and floating frames

FrontPage also does not directly support the markup used to add Java applets or ActiveX components to documents. Although FrontPage does not directly support a few popular extensions, you can include these features in your HTML pages if you desire. To do this, all you need to know is the markup code for the feature you want to add. (See Chapter 34, "Writing Java Applets," for a discussion on using FrontPage to add Java applets to your documents.)

**NOTE**

The next version of FrontPage will include direct support for all HTML extensions for Netscape 2.0 to 3.0, Internet Explorer 2.0 to 3.0, Java, and ActiveX. Because this upcoming version of FrontPage is due to be released in early 1997, the version is being called FrontPage 97.

# The Basic Structure of HTML and HTML Documents

To help you understand how HTML works, let's briefly look at the basic structure of HTML and HTML documents. The formatting of HTML documents depends on markup codes called tags. Tags define the structure of the document and include an element name enclosed by brackets, such as <H1>, which indicates the start of a level one heading. HTML is not case-sensitive. This means <h1> and <H1> both denote the same thing.

As you read this section, keep in mind that FrontPage automatically adds markup tags for you whenever you create a new document. Most tags are used in pairs. A tag called the begin tag tells the browser a document element is beginning. Another tag called the end tag tells the browser an element is ending. The only difference between a begin tag and an end tag is that the end tag contains a forward slash before the element name. For example, the begin heading tag <H1> is paired with the end heading tag </H1>. The initial <H1> tag tells the browser a level one heading is starting, and the end tag </H1> tells the browser the heading is ending.

Typically when you create documents in a word processor or text editor, the documents contain text formatting such as tabs, spacing, paragraph markings, or page breaks. A key concept to keep in mind as you create your first Web page is that American Standard Code of Information Interchange (ASCII) text formatting is normally ignored. When your browser sees any of these text formatting techniques, no matter how many times you repeat them, the browser interprets them as a single space.

Because FrontPage knows that this type of text formatting is ignored, the FrontPage editor does not allow you to unintentionally add multiple spaces, tabs, or page breaks. However, because the developers knew that sometimes publishers want to add empty paragraphs for spacing, FrontPage allows you to create empty paragraphs and adds special markup instructions so that the empty paragraphs will be displayed properly. The developers also knew that sometimes you would want to intentionally add extra spaces. For this reason, FrontPage allows you to add hard spaces using Ctrl+Shift+Space.

In HTML, you can also define a special character to display. Special characters are described by an element name preceded by an ampersand and ending with a semicolon, such as &amp; for the ampersand symbol. When a browser sees a special character, the browser interprets the special character and displays the corresponding symbol if possible.

Every HTML document should begin with the markup tag <HTML> and end with the markup tag </HTML>. The begin tag <HTML> tells the browser the document is an HTML-formatted document and marks the beginning of the document. The end tag </HTML> marks the end of the document and is always the last item in any HTML document.

Every HTML document should also have a header and a body. The header immediately follows the first <HTML> tag. The header is used to specify key aspects of the document, such as the title of the document. The beginning of the header is specified with the begin header tag <HEAD>, and the end of the header is specified with the end tag </HEAD>.

Following the header is the main section of the document called the body. The body contains the text and objects you want to display in the reader's browser. Like the header, the body has a begin tag <BODY> and an end tag </BODY>.

Most markup tags have attributes that assign default formats for text or graphics associated with the tag, such as the attribute ALIGN=CENTER. This attribute is used to center a text or graphic element on the page. Most markup tags have one or more attributes.

Using the three markup tags discussed in this section, you can create the framework for an HTML document as follows:

```
<HTML>
<HEAD>
. . .
</HEAD>
<BODY>
. . .
</BODY>
</HTML>
```

**NOTE**

In the example, the ellipses are used to show where additional information would go in an actual document.

Well, that's enough on markup tags for a while. Amazingly, this section showed only a small part of what FrontPage does for you in the background, but that's the wonderful thing about FrontPage. FrontPage takes care of inserting the necessary markup and you only have to learn about markup tags if you want to.

# Creating the Page

Before you create your first Web page, you should create a new Web. Let's create a new Web called test. To do this, start the FrontPage Explorer, use the mouse to open the File menu and select New Web or simply press Ctrl+N. Because you want to base this new Web on the Normal Web, select Normal Web and then press return or click on the OK button.

Next, as shown in Figure 8.1, enter a designator for the server and a name for the Web. If you use the Internet Protocol address of 127.0.0.1 as the server designator, you will be able to set up the test Web without having to connect to the Internet or corporate intranet.

**FIGURE 8.1.**

*Creating a test Web.*

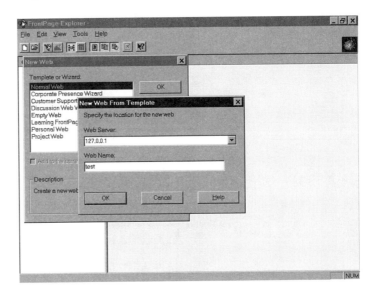

---

### NOTE

The local address 127.0.0.1 should allow you to isolate the test Web to the computer you are currently using. In this way, you can experiment with the features of FrontPage without interfering with current network operations.

---

Your first Web document will be based on the Normal template. You can access this document by double-clicking on the document labeled Normal Page in the Link View of the FrontPage Explorer. If the FrontPage Editor is not running, double-clicking on any document icon automatically starts the FrontPage editor and loads the document into the current frame. If the FrontPage Editor is running, double-clicking on any document icon loads the document into the editor's current frame.

Alternatively, you can access the Normal Page by starting the FrontPage Editor, selecting Open from Web from the File menu, and double-clicking on Normal Page in the Current Web pop-up window.

# Setting Page Properties

Now that you have a new page, let's look at its default properties. All pages, even new pages, have default attributes. Figure 8.2 shows the default properties for most new pages. Each input area lets you define attributes for markup tags used in the HEAD element of your documents.

**FIGURE 8.2.**

*Setting page properties.*

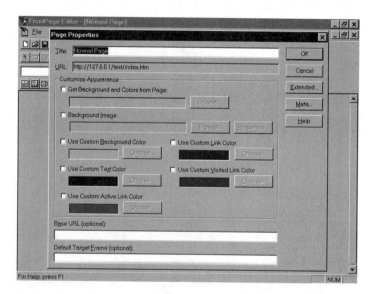

To set page properties, select Page Properties from the File menu. Alternatively, you can click on the right mouse button and then select Page Properties on the submenu that appears.

FrontPage allows you to define attributes for the HEAD element tags without having to learn the specifics of each tag. Not only does the point and click interface save you frustration, but it also saves you time. Most of the input fields pertain to setting base attributes for the document, such as the background color. If you've played the color guessing game with your HTML pages before, you know how cool it is to be able to see a color palette and select a color from this palette at the touch of a button.

The following sections teach you how these properties are used. Admittedly, setting page properties by pointing and clicking is easy. What is not so easy is knowing why and when to use these page properties.

# Document Titles

By default, FrontPage bases the document title on the name of the template used to create the document. If you refer back to Figure 8.2, you will see that the default title for Normal Page is Normal Page. The rules for titles are simple. Each document can only have one title. Your title should be short but descriptive. A general rule to follow for the length of the title is 65 characters or less. If your title is over 65 characters in length, it might get truncated when the document is displayed. Additionally, the title can contain no extra formatting or markup. This means it should only contain plain ASCII characters.

> **NOTE**
>
> Carefully think about the title for your document and the information it provides to readers. The title is the most referenced component of any document. It will appear on a user's bookmark or hot list, which contains a list of a user's favorite online places saved for future reference. The title will appear on the user's history list, which is a list of places visited during the current session. Most search engines list the page title in the query results. Furthermore, most Web browsers prominently display the document title in a special location. Browsers such as NCSA Mosaic display the title in a clear window appropriately called Document Title. Browsers such as Netscape Navigator display the title at the top of the browser's viewing area. Other browsers, such as Lynx, do not display the title unless the user enters a set of keystrokes that tell the browser to display the title.

Because the title might be referenced separately from your document by the user, it should provide insight into the contents or topic of the document. A good title for an extreme sports service in Australia could be

```
Extreme Sports Australia
```

Depending on the focus of the document, a better title might be

```
Extreme Sports in Australia and New Zealand
```

or

```
Extreme Sport Experiences in Australia and New Zealand
```

# Document URLs

By default, FrontPage bases the document uniform resource locator (URL) on the name of the template used to create the document, on the path to the current Web, and sometimes on the purpose of the page. If you refer back to Figure 8.2, you will see that the URL for the page is

```
http://127.0.0.1/test/index.htm
```

From the discussion on URLs, you might remember that http specifies the document will be transferred using the Hypertext Transfer Protocol. The Internet Protocol (IP) address 127.0.0.1 is the numeric equivalent of the host name for the local machine. This is just as easy for the computer to interpret as an actual host name, such as mcp.com. In fact, all host names are actually equated to numeric addresses by networked computers anyway. Because we created a new Web called test, test is the name of the primary directory on the local host that will contain our files for this Web. The final part of the page URL is the name of the file. When you publish the test Web or if you look in the test directory in the FrontPage Webs folder, you'll see the file index.htm.

> **NOTE**
>
> Most server software, including the Personal Web Server, allows you to specify a base document in a directory that is displayed whenever the user doesn't fully specify the URL path to a directory rather than a document. This base document is typically called index.html and can be accessed by adding a forward slash to the directory name in the URL path. Using the slash, you can reference shorter URLs and provide shorter URLs to those who might want to visit your Web site.
>
> For example, if you want to access the index.htm document in the newly created test Web, you could point your browser at
>
> http://127.0.0.1/test/

Because the URL property is grayed out in the properties window, you cannot update this field directly. If you want to change the filename, you must select Save As from the File menu and make the changes in the popup window, shown in Figure 8.3.

**FIGURE 8.3.**

*Changing the filename.*

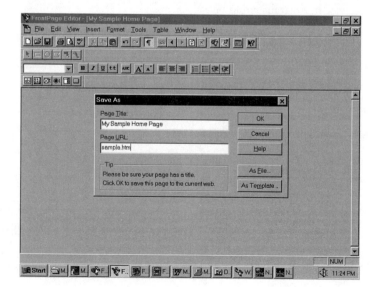

# Customizing the Appearance of Your Page

Most browsers display all text on a slate gray background. Netscape Navigator 1.0 introduced extensions that let you add images and color to the background. Other Netscape extensions let you specify the color of normal text and links. These extensions are so popular that they have been worked into the HTML 3 specification. FrontPage introduces a powerful what-you-see-is-what-you-get (WYSIWYG) interface for selecting the background images and colors to be used in your documents. Let's examine each of these properties.

## Getting Background and Colors from Another Page

One page property you might be tempted to use often is Get Background and Colors from Page. This property lets you set background images, background colors, and color definitions for text and links based on another page. To use this property, enable the Get Background and Colors property on the Property Page by clicking on the checkbox beside the property label, as shown in Figure 8.4. Next, specify the name of the file you want to use as the source for these settings. If you don't know the name of a file, you can use the Browse button to view a list of all HTML documents in the current Web.

**FIGURE 8.4.**

*Getting background and colors from another page.*

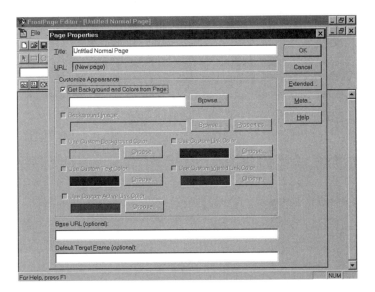

> **NOTE**
>
> Notice that when you enable the Get Background and Colors property, the properties for background images, background colors, text colors, and link colors are grayed out. This tells you these properties cannot be set at the present time and any current settings for these properties will not be used.

Although the process of basing color and background definitions on another document seems fairly straightforward, this is a good example of FrontPage shielding the publisher from the complexities of what's actually taking place. If you use this feature, the file you name is used as the style sheet for the current document. Style sheets are a very complex feature of HTML 3. In fact, the specification for style sheets in HTML 3 runs more than 50 pages.

## ALL ABOUT STYLE SHEETS AND WHY YOU MIGHT NOT WANT TO USE THEM YET

The developers of HTML 3 reached a compromise that allowed additional features to be used in documents but ensured that the standard remained simple, easy-to-use, and widely portable. The design compromise was to allow for the use of style sheets that provide rich control over document layout to both the user and publisher. Style sheets allow you to separate the presentation from the content, and the style sheet assignments are used instead of the browser's standard defaults. This provides you with additional control over the rendering of the document. Style sheets will be implemented in the HTML specification code-named Cougar, which is the follow-up to HTML 3.2.

Style sheets you create will probably be based on the Document Style Semantics and Specification Language (DSSSL), but will be written in DSSSL Lite. DSSSL Lite is a subset of DSSSL created by James Clark that reduces the complexity of DSSSL and makes it suitable for use on the Web. Using DSSSL or DSSSL Lite, you can map the content tags in the body of your document to style tags that will give you better control over the formatting and style of text. You can control the font style, color, and size associated with any tag. You can also control the indentation of lists, paragraphs, and headings.

Style sheets are fairly new to Web publishing, but they are powerful enough to warrant close attention. As browsers start to support them, you should start to see dramatic changes in the way textual information is published on the Web. One way to keep pace with changes in Web publishing that might be associated with style sheets is to add the following address to your browser's hot list:

```
http://www.w3.org/hypertext/WWW/Style/
```

However, at the present time, there are inherent problems with using style sheets as implemented in FrontPage. FrontPage attaches the style sheet as an attribute of the BODY tag, which is nonstandard and not well supported. What this means to you is this: If you use the Get Background and Colors from Page property, many browsers will not display the page as you want it to be displayed.

Keep in mind that in your corporate intranet environment you have control over the servers and browsers used. Therefore, you can test the environment to see if it supports style sheets as implemented by FrontPage. If it does, you might want to consider using this feature as long as you do not plan to introduce new server or browser software into the environment in the short term.

# Using Background Images

With the Background Image property, you can specify an image to be used as the background for the document. The image is tiled or repeated to fill the background area. You can use tiling to create design effects using small images. The best image formats to use for background images are Graphical Interchange Format (GIF) and Joint Picture Experts Group (JPEG), which are fully supported by all graphics-capable browsers.

You enable this property for editing by clicking on the checkbox beside the property label. Then, to specify a background image in FrontPage, enter the filename of the image you want to use. If you don't know the name of a file, you can use the Browse button to view a list of all images in the current Web.

> **TIP**
>
> The image you plan to use as the background image must be available for use in the current Web. If it is not, you will have to import the image to the Web so that FrontPage knows the image exists. Although using images in your documents will be discussed in depth in Chapter 10, "Enhancing Your Web Publication with Images—the Easy Way," you can import an image into the Web using the FrontPage Explorer. To do this, select Import from the File menu; then in the Import File to Web dialog box, click on the Add File button to browse files on your system. Be sure to select the appropriate file type.

# Using Background Colors

The Use Custom Background Color property allows you to specify a color for the background. To select a background color, enable the property, and then click on the Choose button. When you do this, a pop-up window, similar to the one shown in Figure 8.5, is displayed. You can now select a color.

By default, FrontPage lets you select from a palette of 48 basic colors. The currently selected color is highlighted by a thin black border. To select a different background color, move the mouse pointer to the color you want to use, click the left mouse button, and then click on the OK button.

**FIGURE 8.5.**

*Using background colors.*

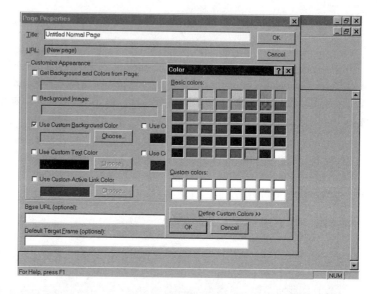

---

FrontPage allows you to set a background color and a background image for the same document. I highly recommend you use this feature when you want to ensure that your pages are displayed in a unique way. If the background image cannot be displayed for any reason, such as the user has turned off the auto load image feature of the browser, the background color you specified will be displayed. Additionally, if you do not specify a background color and the background you specified cannot be displayed, the browser will not use your color assignments for text and links. This is a failsafe way that ensures you didn't specify text and link colors that would conflict with the standard gray background.

## Using Text and Link Colors

Until recently, the color of the font used in your documents was either black by default or set by the users to a specific color if their browser supported a color option. However, black text on a black background is unreadable. Thus, when you use background images or colors, you will normally need to specify the color for text and links to ensure the text and links are readable. To ensure text and links on the page are readable no matter which background color or type of image you use, FrontPage allows you to set the colors:

| | |
|---|---|
| `Use Custom Text Color` | Specifies the color for normal text |
| `Use Custom Active Link Color` | Specifies the color for active links |

| Use Custom Link Color | Specifies the color for links that are unvisited |
|---|---|
| Use Custom Visited Link Color | Specifies the color for visited links |

To select a color for text or links, enable the property and then click on the Choose button. When you do this, a pop-up window will display. You can now select a color.

By default, FrontPage lets you select from a palette of 48 basic colors. The currently selected color is highlighted by a thin black border. To select a different background color, move the mouse pointer to the color you want to use, click the left mouse button, and click on the OK button.

## Customizing Your Colors

If the 48 colors in the basic palette aren't enough, you can create custom colors for text, links, and backgrounds. FrontPage will also let you store values for up to 16 custom colors for use in your other pages.

To create a custom color, enable the property you want to associate the color with, and then click on the Choose button. Next, click on the Define Custom Colors button. As you can see from Figure 8.6, this adds a new area to the Color window.

**FIGURE 8.6.**

*Customizing your colors.*

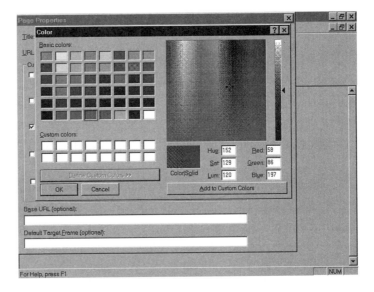

You define custom colors using one of the following methods:

1. Specify the red, green, and blue values associated with the custom color using the Red, Green, and Blue edit fields. Valid values are between 0 and 255.

2. Specify the hue, saturation, and luminosity values using the Hue, Saturation, and Luminosity edit fields. Valid values are between 0 and 255.

3. To set hue and saturation values using the color cube, click and drag the mouse across the color spectrum field. To set the luminosity value, move the triangle pointer up or down in the vertical color bar to the right of the color spectrum field.

The Color/Solid field displays the dithered and solid colors that correspond to your current color selection. When the custom color is set to your liking, click on the OK button to use the value for the current property.

> **TIP**
>
> If you want to save the custom color, select a rectangle in the Custom Colors grid, create your custom color, and then click on the Add to Custom Colors button.

# Defining Font Colors

The Internet Explorer 1.0 introduced a way for Web publishers to control font color anywhere in the text of the document. When you set a font color, you override the default text color you set with the Use Custom Text Color property. Although you set the font color using the same dialog box you use to set custom colors for the page, the way you access this color window is different.

To access the color window, you must do one of these two things:

1. Select the Text Color button on the Format toolbar. This button is labeled ABC.

2. Open the Format menu and select Characters. On the Character Style window, enable the Set Color property, and click on the Choose button.

> **NOTE**
>
> While the capability to assign font colors is extremely useful, the use of color in publications has always caused problems. Some color combinations just don't go together—for example, purple, green, and hot pink text all on the same Web page would be unattractive. Don't use color in your publication because you can; instead, use color as a design technique to enhance your page.
>
> When using colorful text in Web publications, you should follow three general rules:
>
> 1. Use basic colors for text whenever possible, such as black, gray, red, yellow, green, blue, and white.

2. Ensure your font colors are readable on the background you have chosen.

3. Limit the number of colors you use on any single page, and if practical, follow the same color scheme throughout your publication. Four colors are usually sufficient.

# Using Base URLs

The Base URL property on the Property Page allows you to set a base URL for your page. Normally, you access files on a local Web server using a relative file path. When you use a relative path to locate a file, you are locating the file in relation to the current file. Although this is the normal way to use relative paths, you can define a base path for all relative links in your document. Using the Base URL property, you can tell the browser to locate files in relation to a specific path that could actually point to a remote server.

You could define a base path as follows:

```
http://tvp.com/
```

The base path example tells the browser to add `http://tvp.com/` to all relative links in the document. You will find that defining a base path is most useful when your document is available at two different locations and you want to relate them to documents at a specific location. For example, you could publish your home page at a free Web mall without changing relative addresses to absolute addresses.

Whenever a user accessed the example document, no matter where the document was actually located on the Web, any links the user followed would lead to pages at the `tvp.com` Web site. The base path also ensures that other relative paths on the page are valid at the new site, including the path to the images on your page.

Using the previously defined base path, the relative references `vpbg.html`, `vpttl11.gif`, `bboard.gif`, and `vphp.htm` would be interpreted as

```
http://tvp.com/vpbg.html
```

```
http://tvp.com/vpttl11.gif
```

```
http://tvp.com/bboard.gif
```

```
http://tvp.com/vphp.html
```

# Setting a Default Target Frame

The Default Target Frame property on the Property Page is used with frame-enhanced pages. Because frames are featured in Chapter 13, "Using Frames and the Frames Wizard," a better place to discuss this property is in that chapter.

# Using the Meta Property

On the right side of the Property Page, there is a set of push buttons. One of these buttons is labeled Meta. Pushing the Meta button brings up a dialog box called Meta Information. As shown in Figure 8.7, this window shows all currently defined meta information and lets you add new meta information using a button labeled Add.

**FIGURE 8.7.**

*The* Meta *property.*

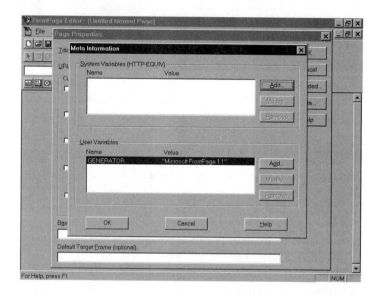

When you press the Add button, the dialog box shown in Figure 8.8 is displayed. You can now enter the meta information and an associated value.

When a client application requests an HTML document, a Web server normally passes the document with a response header prepended. This header is separate from the HTML HEAD element and contains information that the client needs to interpret the document. Sometimes you will want to modify the standard header or create your own header for special situations. Other times, you will want to provide information to the client that you could not pass using standard HTML elements.

Using the META property, you could pass this extra or specialized information in the HEAD element of a document. The server retrieving the document would include this information in the response header for the client's use.

Two types of variables are associated with the META property:

- System variables
- User variables

**FIGURE 8.8.**

*Adding meta information.*

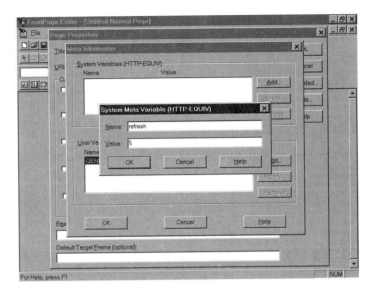

System variables allow you to specify information to be included in the response header using the HTTP-EQUIV attribute. When you use system variables, you should use a valid HTTP header name and supply a value for it.

If you do not know the valid HTTP header name or do not want to supply a header name using HTTP-EQUIV, you should use a user variable instead. User variables allow you to reference meta information. FrontPage uses the standard user variable generator and sets an associated value that tells anyone viewing the HTML markup for the page that it was generated using Microsoft FrontPage.

In general, you would use the META property only when there wasn't a more standard HTML tag you could use to provide the information. Using the Expires system variable, you could specify an expiration date for your document. A Web server would add this meta information to the document's response header as

```
Expires: Mon, 31 Dec 1998 10:00:00 HST
```

Using the Keywords system variable, you could set keywords for the document, such as publishing, books, and magazines. A Web server would add this meta information to the document's response header as

```
Keywords: Publishing, Books, Magazines
```

Using the Refresh system variable, you could specify a time interval that the client should re-request the file, such as every thirty seconds. A Web server would add this meta information to the document's response header as

```
Refresh: 30
```

If you use user variables, the server will not generate a response header. Some information you might want to pass in this way includes an e-mail address for the document's author, the date the document was published, and other information not specifically addressed by other HTML tags. You could specify the e-mail address of the document's author with a user variable called author and the document's publication date with a user variable called published.

## Using the Extended Property

On the Property Page, the pushbutton labeled Extended allows you to define new attributes for the current HTML tag. Generally, you will use this feature to add HTML extensions that FrontPage does not directly support. Pushing the Extended button brings up the Extended Attributes dialog box. This window shows all currently defined extended attributes and lets you add new attributes using a button labeled Add (see Figure 8.9).

**FIGURE 8.9.**

*Using the* Extended
*property.*

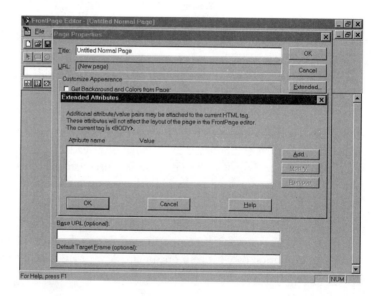

When you press the Add button, the dialog box shown in Figure 8.10 is displayed. You can now enter the new attribute and the associated value.

**FIGURE 8.10.**

*Adding an attribute.*

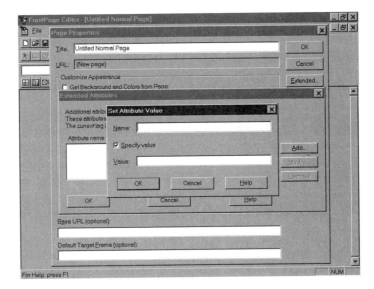

# Designing the Page

Well-designed documents look effortless and achieve their impact from simplicity of design. They are organized in a way that is coherent and flowing. Yet designs that seem simple and natural to the reader are often the result of intense efforts to make them seem this way. You can use many techniques to structure the document in powerful yet uncomplicated ways.

Sometimes it is not what you have on the page that helps convey your message, but what you do not have. Empty space on the page makes material easier to read and helps focus the reader's attention on your ideas. Interestingly enough, it is the separation of the material that creates the emphasis and draws the reader's attention. Two key components of the page that can help you create whitespace are paragraphs and headings.

Browsers typically display an empty space between paragraphs, so a page with many paragraphs will have more whitespace. You should use short paragraphs the most and long paragraphs the least. A short paragraph has fewer than six lines. A long paragraph has 10 or more lines. Varying the length of paragraphs is a key technique to keep the reader's attention. If you use the same paragraph length repeatedly, even the most lively material seems monotonous.

Browsers also display an empty space between headings. Using headings, you can divide the document into sections or topics. A document broken into topics looks more manageable and interesting. Headings help the reader identify the main points of the document at a glance. They also help the reader quickly find topics of interest.

Color is another key feature you can add to the document. Most browsers display your document on a gray background. Netscape introduced an extension that enables you to add images and color to the background. Other Netscape extensions enable you to specify the color of text and links. If you plan to enhance your documents specifically for users with a browser that uses Netscape extensions, the background color element can be a good extension to take advantage of.

Often the best way to add color to the page is through graphic images. A few pictures placed strategically on the page can dramatically increase the impact of the page. Your pictures do not have to be sophisticated or high resolution. Simplicity is usually best. You should place the images so that they focus the reader's attention on the key aspects of the page. For example, place a small eye-catching graphic at the beginning of a key paragraph. Adding pictures to your documents is featured in Chapter 10.

The key components of a basic HTML document are headings and paragraphs. Most basic documents also use comments and special characters, and text elements such as preformatted text or addresses. The next sections discuss the five basic document components:

- Headings
- Paragraphs
- Comments
- Special characters
- Additional text elements

# Creating Headings

By using headings, you can better organize your ideas. The chapters of most nonfiction books use many levels of headings. You will usually find chapter headings, section headings that pertain to each major topic, and subheadings pertaining to subtopics. Usually, headings are in a bold type and larger than the normal font size. The size of the font is often related to the level of the heading. Chapter headings use the largest font size, section headings use a slightly smaller font size, and so on. The boldfaced text at the top of this section is an example of a subtopic heading level.

HTML enables you to create up to six levels of headings. HTML headings are displayed in bold type. In general, a level one heading uses the largest font of heading sizes, and a level six heading uses the smallest font of heading sizes. Browsers typically insert a space before and after the heading. This whitespace is proportional to the size of the heading.

Setting the heading level in FrontPage is done using a pulldown menu on the Format toolbar. To make selections from the pulldown menu, click and hold your mouse button, and then move the mouse pointer up or down. Figure 8.11 shows how the FrontPage editor displays the six heading levels. Note that the pulldown menu that allows you to set text properties is in the left corner of the active toolbar.

**FIGURE 8.11.**

*Using headings in your pages.*

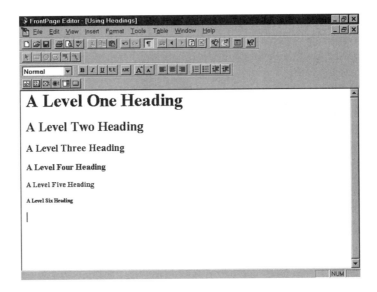

To add a heading to your document, move the cursor to the point where you want to insert the heading or select the text you want to format in a particular heading; then select a heading level from the Format toolbar's pulldown menu. You can also set the heading level by selecting Heading in the Insert menu.

Yet another way to set heading levels is to open the Format menu and select Paragraph. This brings up the Paragraph Format window, which can be used to set the heading level at the current insertion point.

> **NOTE**
>
> As the Web publisher, you only have direct control over font size using style sheets. Because style sheets are not supported in HTML up to version 3.2, the majority of Web publishers can only control the relative size of a font. With relatively sized fonts, the size of the font is determined by configurations set up in the browser displaying the document, and font sizes will be consistent relative to each other and the main text. Most browsers display visible differences only in heading levels one to four. Consequently, a level four heading is often displayed in the same font size as level five and six headings.

# Creating Paragraphs

After years of casual or professional writing, some processes of writing seem automatic. You probably don't think about the need to place a period at the end of a sentence, or why we use apostrophes in contractions. Similarly, when you start a new paragraph, you probably add a blank line, indentation, or both to separate the new paragraph from the previous one without giving much thought about why. You add the blank line or indentation because it makes sense and because it is what your grammar teacher told you to do. Blank lines and indentation serve to visually separate the paragraphs and break up the document.

In HTML, the way to visually break up the document into paragraphs is to use the paragraph tag <P>. When a browser sees the paragraph tag, it ends the current line and inserts a blank space before inserting the text or object following the paragraph tag.

FrontPage eliminates the need to insert tags and allows you to add paragraphs just as you would with any word processor—by using the normal format. If you change text formats, you can use the Format toolbar's pulldown menu to set the format back to normal.

> **NOTE**
>
> Keep in mind that when you add empty paragraphs to your document, FrontPage adds special markup that ensures your document will be displayed with the spacing you select.

## Aligning the Text

FrontPage offers push-button ease for changing the alignment of all text elements. To align a paragraph, heading, or other text element on the page, just move the insertion point to the text element you want to align, and then select the alignment you want to use from the Format toolbar. Alternatively, you can select any portion of the text element, and then select the alignment you want to use from the Format toolbar. Three alignment options are currently available: Center, Align Right, and Align Left.

You can also indent text by using the Format toolbar's Increase Indent Button. Each time you press this button, the FrontPage Editor indents the text element about an inch. To decrease the indentation, use the Decrease Indent button.

> **AN INSIDE LOOK AT TEXT ALIGNMENT**
>
> Behind the scenes, FrontPage is hard at work ensuring that the text alignment works with the widest range of browsers. Text alignment is a feature of HTML 3 that was originally introduced by Netscape Navigator 1.0. Originally, the Navigator only allowed you to center text using a unique tag. Unique tags present problems to Web publishers because they aren't supported by some browsers. When the designers of HTML 3 implemented text alignment, they did not adopt the Netscape tag for

centering text. For this reason, when FrontPage centers text, it inserts both the HTML 3 and Netscape tags for centering. This ensures your text is centered in nearly all current browsers.

To achieve text indentation, FrontPage adopts a favorite trick of the Web publishing gurus, which is to bend the rules to meet your needs. Here, the developers of FrontPage needed a way to indent text. They knew that if they inserted an HTML BLOCKQUOTE element, browsers would indent the text without altering the style of the text. Thus, to indent multiple levels, FrontPage actually inserts multiple BLOCKQUOTE elements. An unfortunate side effect of using the BLOCKQUOTE element to create indentation is that it can cause strange results with some HTML elements. Although this problem is more a function of how FrontPage terminates HTML elements when starting a new element, it is a problem you should be aware of.

## Using Superscripts and Subscripts

By using superscript and subscript text, you can add more variety to the textual portions of your page and create more advanced documents. Superscript text is displayed by raising the vertical alignment of the associated text. Similarly, subscript text is displayed by lowering the vertical alignment of the associated text. FrontPage allows you to specify the number of points the alignment is offset. In this way, you can create multiple levels of superscript or subscript text.

FrontPage allows you to add superscripts and subscripts using the Character Styles dialogue box, which is shown in Figure 8.12. To access this dialog box, select Characters from the Format menu, or click the right mouse button and then select Characters on the submenu that appears.

## Defining Font Size

The original HTML specification had no way to define a specific font size to use. This is primarily because the font size is traditionally controlled by configurations in the user's browser, and the user is the one who selects the font size she would like to use for viewing Web documents. Using various heading levels, Web publishers had some control over font size. Generally, a level one heading could be used to create text with an approximate font size of 36, a level two heading could be used to create text with an approximate font size of 24, and so on. However, this still didn't give Web publishers accurate control over font sizes, especially if the publisher wanted to change font size in the middle of a line of text.

**FIGURE 8.12.**

*Setting superscript and
subscript values.*

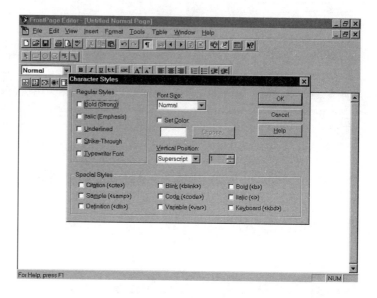

Netscape corrected this shortcoming by allowing Web publishers to define the font size relative to a base font size. You can define the size for the font using values between 1 and 7. A value of 1 is used for the smallest text. A value of 7 is used for the largest text. The default value of 3 usually corresponds to the size of standard text on the page.

EDITING
TECHNIQUE

FrontPage allows you to quickly decrease or increase the size of selected text using the Decrease Text Size and Increase Text Size buttons, respectively. You can also use the Character Styles dialog box to set the size of selected text. To access this dialog box, select Characters from the Format menu. Or, you can click the right mouse button and then select Characters on the submenu that appears.

Being able to adjust the font size is very handy. A small font size is useful for disclaimers or copyright notices you want to place on the page but do not want to eat up page space. A large font size is useful when you want to draw attention to specific keywords or paragraphs of text. You can adjust the font size to create a large first letter for keywords or the first word in a paragraph. You can also create word art by adjusting the font size within words or sentences, as shown in Figure 8.13.

**FIGURE 8.13.**

*Creating word art with relative fonts.*

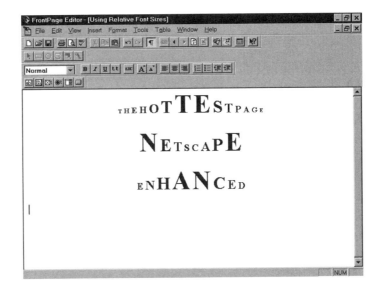

**FIGURE 8.13.**

*Creating word art with relative fonts.*

# Adding Comments to Your Documents

If you are a programmer or have looked at the printout of a computer program, odds are you have seen comments inserted into the code. Comments are used in computer code to make notes or explanations to anyone who might see the code. Even the original programmer finds the comments useful when changes or additions to the code are necessary, especially if they come up months or years after writing the program. Programmers use comments because having to work through the logic of code every time it has to be changed is a waste of time and resources.

Web publishers can similarly use comments to save time and resources when making changes and additions to HTML documents. You can use comments to track the update history of the document, to make notes about text, links, or objects in the document, or to pass information to anyone who might be reading the source code. Comments are not displayed by the browser with the text and objects on the page and are only viewable if you look at the source code for the document.

In FrontPage, you add comments using the annotation bot. The annotation bot allows you to automate the process of creating and maintaining annotations. To invoke the annotation bot, open the Insert menu and select Bot. On the Insert Bot window, select the annotation bot by double-clicking on the word Annotation. Alternatively, you can select Annotation and then click on the OK button or press Enter on the keyboard. Next, enter the comment in the Annotation Bot Properties window. Because your comments can only be one paragraph long, you can press Enter on your keyboard or choose the OK button to accept your edits.

**EDITING TECHNIQUE**

The annotation bot will then insert your comments on the page. While this text can be viewed from the FrontPage Editor, it is not displayed by a Web browser unless the reader views the HTML markup for the page. Annotation text is displayed in purple and retains the character size and other attributes of the current paragraph style. Figure 8.14 shows the Annotation Bot Properties window in the FrontPage Editor.

**FIGURE 8.14.**

*Making annotations.*

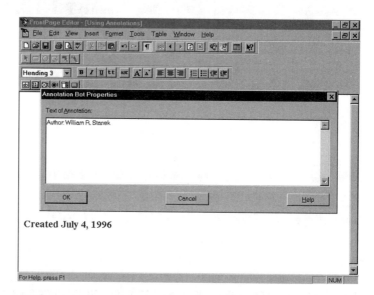

---

**TIP**

When you move your pointer over the annotation text, you will see a robot icon. This icon indicates that a WebBot is embedded in the page. You access an edit window associated with the bot by double-clicking when the robot icon is visible.

## Using Special Characters

In HTML, special characters are also called entities. There are two types of entities: character entities and numeric entities. Character entities use actual text characters to define the special character, such as &quot; for the double quotation mark symbol. Numeric entities use numbers to define the special character and add a hash mark before the number, such as &#124; for the vertical bar (¦) symbol. The numbers used with numeric entities correspond to character positions in the ISO Latin I character set.

With FrontPage, using special characters in your Web document is easy, and you don't have to memorize symbols. Wherever the special character should appear in the text of your document, you simply open the Insert menu, select Special Character, and choose a character to insert.

When a browser sees that special character, the browser interprets the character and displays the corresponding symbol, if possible. For example, when a browser reads the entity value &#124;, it will display the vertical bar symbol.

> **NOTE**
>
> In HTML, you must use entity values for any characters used in markup tags, which include the following symbols: #, <, >, and &. Fortunately, FrontPage automatically inserts these special characters for you.

# More Text Elements

In addition to headings, paragraphs, and special characters, many Web documents contain other text elements, such as

- Addresses
- Preformatted text

# Using Addresses

In HTML, addresses get special attention. Browsers typically display address text in italics with a paragraph break before and after the address. No other special formatting is associated with addresses.

To add an address to your document, move the cursor to the point where you want to insert the address or select the text you want to format as an address, and then select address from the Format toolbar's pulldown menu.

Another way to add an address is to open the Format menu and select Paragraph. This brings up the Paragraph Format window, which can be used to add address formatting at the current insertion point.

> **TIP**
>
> An address entered in multiple lines using the Enter key will have lots of empty space. This is a function of HTML formatting and not a fault of FrontPage. To avoid extra spacing, use Shift+Enter, which inserts a line break.

# Using Formatted Text

Defining a section of text as formatted is extremely useful and enables you to use standard ASCII text formatting techniques to format text in your documents. In a section of text declared as formatted, you can use any of your favorite ASCII spacing tricks, including tabs, multiple tabs, multiple spaces, and multiple blank lines without fear that a browser will discard them. Normally, formatted text is displayed in a monospaced font such as Courier.

When you use formatted text, the FrontPage Editor is really working overtime. Not only is the editor adding HTML tags, it is also inserting ASCII formatting that will be saved with your document. Figure 8.15 shows a sample document with formatted text.

**FIGURE 8.15.**

*A document with formatted text.*

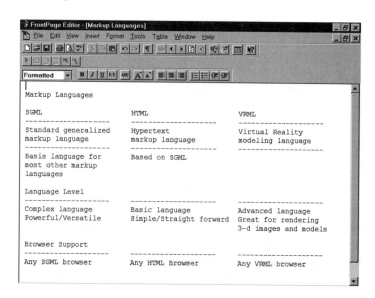

To add formatted text to your document, move the cursor to the point where you want to insert the formatted text or select the text you want to be in this format; then select Formatted from the Format toolbar's pulldown menu.

Another way to add formatted text is to open the Format menu and select Paragraph. This brings up the Paragraph Format window, which can be used to add formatted text at the current insertion point.

> **CAUTION**
>
> When using preformatted text, keep in mind that monospaced fonts appear much wider than proportional fonts. Proportional fonts use the amount of screen space proportional to their size, which means that an *i* uses less screen space than a *w*. In a monospaced or nonproportional font, each letter uses the same amount of screen space.

# Summary

FrontPage makes Web publishing easy. Using the techniques discussed in this chapter, you can create simple yet effective Web documents. Although dozens of HTML tags are used to create the features discussed in this chapter, FrontPage allows you to create pages without having to worry about tags and their attributes. Not only does this save you time, but it also allows you to concentrate on building the visual impact of your documents.

# Adding Features to the Page

**9**

*by William
Robert Stanek*

**IN THIS CHAPTER**

A key ingredient for success in Web publishing is the ability to create documents with high visual impact and a high level of interactivity. Basic techniques that add to the visual impact of the document include using line breaks to create a column of text and horizontal lines to visually divide the document into sections. To increase the interactive nature of your document, you can create links to other documents on the Web. You can also create internal links in your document that help guide readers to key parts of your publication. You can also add any of several types of lists to your document, which add to the visual impact of the document by clearly organizing material.

# Using Line Breaks and Horizontal Lines

Sometimes the features that seem very basic aren't. Line breaks enable you to break a line without adding a space between the lines. Horizontal lines are graphical lines drawn across the width of the document. Although line breaks and horizontal lines might seem straightforward, they both have many advanced features.

## All About Line Breaks

You can use the simple facility of a line break to format text on your document in many creative ways. Sometimes you don't want a space between lines of text, or you want to highlight an example by breaking the line and starting a new line showing the example.

Here is how this could be done:

```
This section will contain:
An introduction to the document
```

You can also use line breaks to format your text into a column or simple list. Not only does text formatted in a column add to the visual impact of the document, but it also gets the reader's attention. The following example shows how you could create a simple list:

```
Our on-line publications include:

Books
Magazines
Newspapers
Newsletters
```

To add a line break with FrontPage, press Shift+Enter. Behind the scenes, FrontPage adds the appropriate markup for the line break.

You can use line breaks inside other text formatting without affecting the font or style of the previously declared formatting. If you insert a line break into a heading, the text before and after the break will be formatted in the style and font of a heading. All that the line break does is start a new line, like the carriage return on a typewriter.

Netscape 1.0 introduced an extension to line breaks that enables you to clear the margins after a line break. This enhancement is extremely useful when you want to clear the left, right, or both margins after placing an image on the page. If you do not clear the margin, the text might be aligned in a column to the left or right of the image. In FrontPage, you specify the clear margin attribute after you insert the line break.

To specify margin breaks, move the cursor to the place where you inserted the line break and press Alt+Enter. This brings up the Line Break properties window, which has a series of radio buttons that enable you to set line break properties.

In addition to creating more useful ways to break up text and images, Netscape 1.0 added a way to ensure that text stays together. A *non-breaking space tag* ensures that two words appear on the same line with no line breaks. A non-breaking space is useful to ensure that text is formatted as you want it to be, but keep in mind that users might have to scroll their browser window to finish reading the line of text.

To insert a non-breaking space, press Shift+Space.

# All About Horizontal Lines

Another way to easily add to the visual impact of the document is to use a horizontal line. The two basic styles of horizontal lines are *shaded* and *unshaded*. Because shaded lines appear to be engraved into the document and add a special touch, unshaded lines aren't used very often.

Wherever the horizontal line should appear in the text of your document, open the Insert menu and select Horizontal Line. After you insert a horizontal line, select it by double-clicking on it, and then press Ctrl+Enter to set properties for a horizontal line.

The great thing about horizontal lines is that you can use them to divide your document visually into sections. However, you should use horizontal lines sparingly. Too many horizontal lines in the document can spoil the effect. Therefore, use them to highlight or to help the reader better identify the major sections of the document.

Figure 9.1 depicts a combined example using line breaks and horizontal lines. Although the figure shows only the outline of the document, you can see how horizontal lines could be used to divide the document into four major sections.

Horizontal lines become helpful design tools with Netscape extensions. With these extensions, you can size the horizontal rule to make the separation of topics and subtopics on your pages more distinct. The size of a horizontal line is defined in terms of pixels.

To separate topics and subtopics visually, you could use one size value for main topics and another size value for each level of subtopics. You should experiment with line sizes in your publications. A size of five pixels is usually sufficient to separate main topics, and a size of two pixels is usually sufficient for subtopics. To set horizontal line properties, select a horizontal line you've added to the document and press Alt+Enter. This will open the dialog box shown in Figure 9.2.

**FIGURE 9.1.**

*You can break up the document using horizontal lines and line breaks.*

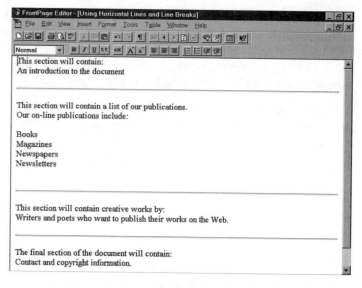

**FIGURE 9.2.**

*Setting horizontal line properties.*

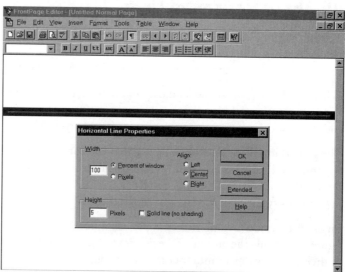

You can align a horizontal line with the left margin, right margin, or center of the page and define the length of the horizontal line in pixels or as the percentage of the browser's window width. By combining the two attributes, you can create powerful effects, such as the one shown in Figure 9.3.

**FIGURE 9.3.**

*Using fancy horizontal lines.*

Keep in mind that some browsers might ignore the Netscape sizing and alignment values for horizontal lines. These browsers will also display the multiple horizontal lines in the example as ordinary horizontal lines. Therefore, it is best to use multiple horizontal lines only on pages that will be displayed by a Netscape-capable browser.

Some Web publishers want to make their documents stand out from other documents on the Web and use graphical lines based on GIF images instead of the standard horizontal line. These graphical lines, although visually appealing, have a major drawback in that readers with text-only browsers see no line break at all. To a reader with a text-only browser, documents with graphical lines based on images have no subdivisions, which is a problem.

To clear up this problem, HTML 3 enables you to specify images to be used with the horizontal line. Because the image is specified as a part of the horizontal line element, a user with a graphical browser sees a graphical line and a reader with a text-only browser sees a standard horizontal line.

You specify an image to use instead of the standard horizontal line using an attribute called SRC. To add this attribute, you will need to bring up the Horizontal Line Properties window, and then access the Extended Attributes dialog box by clicking on the button labeled Extended. In the Extended Attributes dialog box shown in Figure 9.4, select the Add button. This will bring up the Set Attribute Value window shown in Figure 9.5.

**FIGURE 9.4.**

*Extending horizontal line properties.*

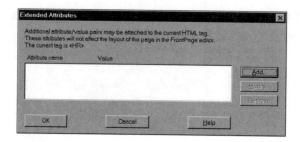

In the Set Attribute Value dialog box, enter the name of the attribute you want to add to the currently selected element and the value associated with the attribute. As shown in Figure 9.5, you should enter the attribute name SRC and the name of the image you want to use as a graphical line.

**FIGURE 9.5.**

*Setting a source for a rule.*

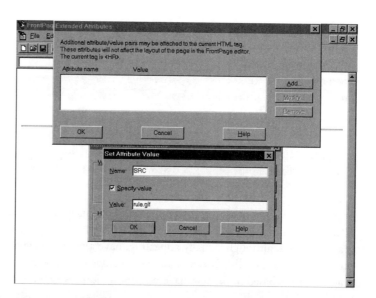

**NOTE**

The image name can include the full path to the image. (Paths are covered later in this chapter.) Although you can use any image as the source for the horizontal line tag, you should use an image that creates a graphical line. By doing this, you follow the spirit of what the creators of HTML 3 intended and also ensure that readers see your image as a section divider.

# Adding Visual Variety to Your Documents

A Web document that contained only paragraphs and headings would be boring. Often you will want to highlight and emphasize key sections of the text. To do this, you can use a special set of HTML tags called *character style tags*. Character style tags highlight your text using techniques such as boldface and italics. Unlike heading and paragraph tags that insert white space into the document, character style tags do not insert white space, which makes it possible to use character style tags within other tags to highlight a single word or a group of words.

FrontPage enables you to add physical and logical styles using the Character Styles dialog box, which is shown in Figure 9.6. To set character styles, select Characters from the Format menu. Or, you can click the right mouse button, and then select Characters on the popup menu that appears.

**FIGURE 9.6.**

*Setting text styles.*

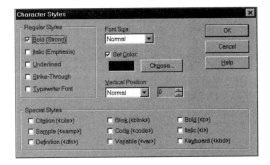

In HTML, there are two subsets of character style tags: *physical styles* and *logical styles*. Physical styles tell the browser the precise format to display. HTML defines physical styles for bold, italics, underlined, strikethrough, and monospace type.

A browser accessing documents containing physical styles will try to display the text using the strict format you have specified. If it is unable to, it might substitute another style for the one you are using or, worse, it might ignore the tag and display the text in the standard style. Consequently, when you want to make sure text will be highlighted, use logical styles. Logical styles are the preferred method of adding highlights to Web documents.

Unlike physical style tags, logical style tags do not specify a strict format. They tell your browser how the text should be used and let the browser display the text according to a set of configurations specific to the browser. The logical assignment of the style to the browser ensures that your text will be highlighted in the document in some way. HTML defines logical styles for citations, samples, definitions, code, variables, keyboard input, emphasized text, and strongly emphasized text.

FrontPage does not organize styles as specified by the standard. Styles are grouped into regular styles and special styles. These generic style groupings include both physical and logical styles, which might lead to confusion if a browser doesn't support what FrontPage calls a regular style.

Just as in your favorite word processor, all regular style formats are directly accessible from the Format toolbar. Regular styles include emphasized, strongly emphasized, underlined, strikethrough, and monospace type. Browsers usually display emphasized text in italics and strongly emphasized text in bold type. However, because these are defined as purely physical styles in HTML, the exact style is ultimately determined by the browser.

Because the purely physical styles are preferred to the logical styles, the actual markup for bold and italics text is placed in the special style section. Thus, despite what the Format toolbar indicates, when you select the I or B button, you are using emphasized text and strongly emphasized text.

Netscape 1.0 introduced blinking text, which has been a subject of controversy ever since. Imagine an entire paragraph or, worse, an entire page blinking on and off while you are trying to read it. Text blinking on and off is like a tiny neon sign on your page that attracts the reader's eyes. Sometimes blinking text is good. You draw the reader's attention temporarily to a key area of the page. At other times, blinking text is bad. It distracts the readers while they are trying to read the text on the page. The controversy surrounding the blinking text might be the reason the Internet Explorer does not support this feature.

> **TIP**
>
> The key to using blinking text is to confine it to a small area of your page and to be sure that it only affects a few key words.

Other styles in the special style section are not uniquely supported by browsers and duplicate styles you can create using other means. Consequently, these styles are rarely used. These styles are as follows:

| | |
|---|---|
| Citation | Indicates the text is a citation. Most browsers display this style in italics. |
| Code | Indicates that text is computer code or a program sample. Most browsers display this style in a monospace font such as Courier. |
| Definition | Indicates that you are defining the highlighted word. Most browsers display this style in italics. |
| Keyboard | Indicates text that a user would type in on the keyboard. Most browsers display this style in a monospace font such as Courier. |
| Sample | Indicates a sample of literal characters. Most browsers display this style in a monospace font such as Courier. |
| Variable | Indicates that text is a variable name such as those used in computer programs. Most browsers display this style in italics. |

Figure 9.7 shows an example of how these styles are displayed in FrontPage and in most browsers.

**FIGURE 9.7.**

*Using styles.*

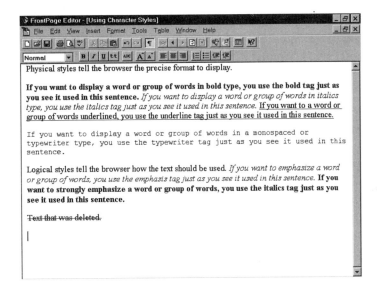

## Using Links

The Web without links would not be interactive, so now it is time to put the "hyper" into hypertext. Most Web documents contain hypertext *links*. Links act as pointers to other resources or files on the Web. Using links, you can connect text, graphic images, and multimedia objects to your documents. The great thing about hypertext linking is that linked text, images, or objects can be located anywhere on the Web. You can add images to your document that don't even reside on your Web server and then link them back to the source. For example, if you are a fan of the Dilbert comic strip, you could (with United Media's permission) display the latest Dilbert comic every day by accessing the image on United Media's Web site. You could then make the image a hypertext link to the Dilbert home page.

Such links might look like a tangled mess of code, but you can easily untangle the mess. Links tell the browser where to send a request for a particular file. Initially, the browser does not care what type of file it is supposed to retrieve; it just tries to retrieve the file. To get to a file, browsers need to know the location of the resource. The resource's location is specified as a Uniform Resource Locator, commonly called a URL.

For this example, you need to know the URL of the image and the URL of the Dilbert home page. These URLs are

```
http://www.unitedmedia.com/comics/dilbert/
```

and

```
http://www.unitedmedia.com/comics/dilbert/todays_dilbert.gif
```

The first URL tells the browser to use the hypertext transfer protocol to access a file on the `www.unitedmedia.com` Web server. Here, the file is the base document in the `/comics/dilbert` directory. The base document is typically called `index.html` and can be accessed using the forward slash. Using the slash, you can reference shorter URLs and provide shorter URLs to those who might want to visit your document.

The second URL tells the browser to use the hypertext transfer protocol to access a file called `todays_dilbert.gif` on the `www.unitedmedia.com` Web server. Here, the file is a graphic image in the `/comics/dilbert` directory. URLs with complete address information such as these enable you to link your documents to files on other Web servers.

The address in a link is not visible unless the mouse pointer is over the anchor text or graphic. The anchor is the portion of the link that is visible when a browser displays the document. To activate a link, you move your mouse pointer over the anchor and click the left mouse button. If a line of text is the anchor, the reader can click on the text to activate the link. If an image is the anchor, the reader can click on the image to activate the link. You can also create an anchor that uses both text and an image. More information on using images and linking to images can be found in Chapter 10, "Enhancing Your Web Publication with Images—the Easy Way."

As Figure 9.8 shows, generally text links will be shown in blue letters, and images with links will have a blue border around them. The first link uses text to anchor the link in the document. The reader would click on `The Writer's Gallery` to activate the link. The second link uses an image to anchor the link in the document. The reader would click on the image to activate the link. The third link combines a text and image anchor. The reader could click on either the text or the image to activate the link.

**FIGURE 9.8.**

*Using text and images to create links.*

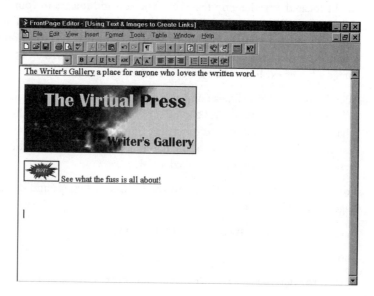

As you can see, hypertext links to text and objects can be the most powerful features on your document. Adding links to your document can be accomplished in three key ways:

- Using relative paths to files in links
- Using direct paths to files in links
- Using links within your documents called bookmarks

# Using Relative Paths in Links

You can access *local files*—files on your local Web server—using a relative file path. URLs with relative file paths generally do not name a protocol or a Web server in the link. This is because when you use a relative path to locate a file, you are locating the file in relation to the current file. Being able to access a file in relation to the current file implies that you have already accessed a file on a particular Web server.

You can use relative file paths in three key ways:

1. A file in the current directory.

   When you click on a link with the following URL path, your browser will expect to find the file `orders.html` in the current directory:

   `orders.html`

2. A file in a parent directory of the current directory.

   This file is located in the directory above the current directory:

   `../orders.html`

   This file is located two directories above the current directory:

   `../../orders.html`

3. A file in a subdirectory of the current directory.

   This file is in the subdirectory called `info`:

   `info/orders.html`

---

**TIP**

Good links do not say `Click here`. A `click here` link disrupts the flow of the text and the natural thought processes. The interactive nature of the Web is such that you should never have to say `click here`. Build hypertext links into the text, and by doing so, you'll create documents that flow.

When using links, keep in mind that links are highlighted in the document. Typically, links are shown in underlined blue letters, which makes them stand out from surrounding text.

# Using Direct Paths in Links

Another way to access files is directly. You do this by specifying the complete path to the file you want to access. Although you must specify the protocol to be used for files directly accessed on a nonlocal Web server, you do not have to specify the protocol for files directly accessed on a local Web server.

This means that there are two key ways to access files directly:

1. Specify the full path to the file including the transfer protocol.

   The following file could reside on a nonlocal server:

   ```
   http://www.unitedmedia.com/comics/dilbert/index.html
   ```

2. Specify the full path to the file excluding the transfer protocol.

   The following file must reside on a local server:

   ```
   /comics/dilbert/index.html
   ```

> **TIP**
>
> Designing good links is easy once you know the basics of using relative and direct paths. The key is to keep the anchor text for the link short but descriptive. Usually this text should be three to five words describing the link in a way that is clear to the user. Anchor text can be the key words of a sentence, but sometimes you might want the anchor text to include an entire short-but-descriptive sentence. Later sections of this chapter show how you can better organize links using lists and menus.

# Using Links within Documents

Internal document links are called *bookmarks*. Bookmarks can provide powerful navigation mechanisms for your readers and are especially useful in long documents. Using bookmarks, you can provide ways to quickly jump to key sections of any document.

Creating links within documents is a two-part process. First, you specify a link with a keyword in a form similar to other links you have seen. The next step is to label the location within the document to which you want the reader to jump.

The keyword used in the link and anchor name must match exactly. When a user activates a bookmark, the section you've labeled will be displayed. If the bookmark is within the current document, the browser will quickly search the document for the label containing a keyword that matches the keyword in the link. When the browser finds the matching keyword label, the browser will display the corresponding section of the document. If the internal link is within a different document, the browser will load the document and then search for the label that matches the keyword in the link. The location of the label relative to the link in the document does not matter. As long as the label is within the body of the document, the browser will find it.

Using bookmarks, you could create an index for your document such as the one shown in Figure 9.9. If you clicked on the overview link, your browser would search for the keyword overview. When your browser found the keyword, the section associated with the keyword would be displayed. In the example, the browser would scroll forward and display the overview section of the document. The ellipses show where actual document content would go.

**FIGURE 9.9.**

*After activating a link, your browser would jump to a section associated with the keyword.*

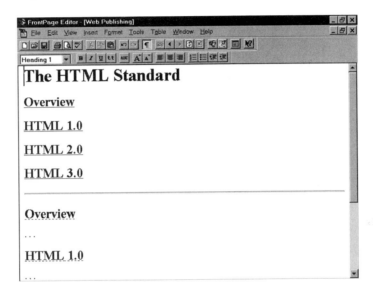

You can specify bookmarks to other documents in many ways. Using relative paths and keywords, you can access specific locations in documents on the local Web server. Using direct paths and keywords, you can access specific locations in documents located anywhere on the global Web.

Relative paths can be used with bookmarks in three key ways:

1. A bookmark to a file in the current directory
2. A bookmark to a file in a parent directory of the current directory
3. A bookmark to a file in a subdirectory of the current directory

Direct paths can be used with internal links as well. The two key ways you will use internal links with direct paths are as follows:

1. Append the bookmark to the full file path that includes the transfer protocol.
2. Append the bookmark to the full file path that excludes the transfer protocol.

> **CAUTION**
>
> Be careful when specifying internal links to someone else's document. Web documents tend to change frequently, and a keyword label that is specified today might not be there tomorrow.

# Creating Links with FrontPage

FrontPage offers a very friendly interface for creating links and bookmarks. This section takes you step by step through these processes.

## Creating a Link to an Open Page

You can easily create a link to an open page in the FrontPage Editor. In the editor, select the text that will identify the link; then either choose Link from the Edit menu or click the Link button. This opens the Create Link dialog box shown in Figure 9.10.

**FIGURE 9.10.**

*Creating a link to an open page.*

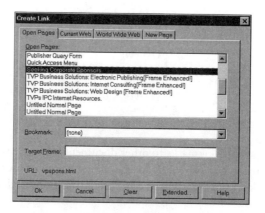

In the Create Link dialog box, click on the Open Pages tab, and then select the page to which you want to link by double-clicking on the title text for the page. Alternately, you can use the cursor keys to move up or down the list of open pages and press the Enter key to make your selection.

As you make your selection, the URL field displays the URL to which you will link. If you want to link to a bookmark on the page you selected, locate the bookmark in the drop-down list in the Bookmark field.

# Creating a Link to a Resource in the Current Web

You can create a text link to a page or file in the current Web. In the FrontPage Editor, select the text that will identify the link, and then either choose Link from the Edit menu or click the Link button. In the Create Link dialog box, select the Current Web tab. As shown in Figure 9.11, this brings up a new view for the dialog box. If you know the URL of the page or file you want to link to, enter it in the Page field.

**FIGURE 9.11.**

*Creating a link to a resource in the current Web.*

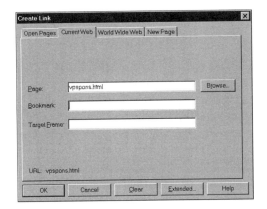

If you do not know the URL, click on the Browse button. From the Current Web dialog box, select the page or file you want to link to, and then click on the OK button. If you want to link to a bookmark on the page you selected, locate the bookmark in the drop-down list in the Bookmark field, and click on the OK button.

# Creating a Link to a Web Resource

When creating a link to a Web resource, you have to specify the protocol that will be used to transfer the file. FrontPage enables you to easily specify the following protocols: file, FTP, Gopher, telnet, http, mailto, News, and WAIS.

In the FrontPage Editor, select the text that will identify the link, and then either chose Link from the Edit menu or click the Link button. In the Create Link dialog box, select the World Wide Web tab. As shown in Figure 9.12, this brings up a new view for the dialog box.

**NOTE**

See the section called "Using Alternate Protocols in Web Documents" at the end of this chapter for more information on protocols used in Web documents.

**FIGURE 9.12.**

*Creating a link to a Web resource.*

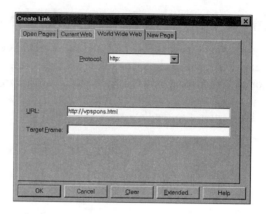

After you select the transfer protocol from the list of supported protocols, the editor will create the protocol portion of the URL in the URL field. In the URL field, enter the absolute URL of the Web page or resource to which you want to link. When you are done, click the OK button.

> **NOTE**
>
> If you want to use a protocol that is not on the list, select Other from the Protocol pull-down menu.

## Creating a Link to a New Page

When you create a link to a new page, FrontPage creates the page and then creates a link to it from the selected text. In the FrontPage Editor, select the text that will identify the link; then either select Link from the Edit menu or click on the Link button. In the Create Link dialog box, select the New Page tab. As shown in Figure 9.13, this brings up a new view for the dialog box.

In the Page URL field, enter the URL for the new page. In the Page Title field, enter a title for the new page. If you enter a title first, the FrontPage Editor fills in a URL based on the title. To edit the page as soon as the link is created, select the Edit New Page Immediately radio button. To create the new page and add a task to finish the page to the current Web's To Do List, select the Add New Page to To Do List radio button. When you are finished creating the link, click the OK button.

**FIGURE 9.13.**

*Creating a new page.*

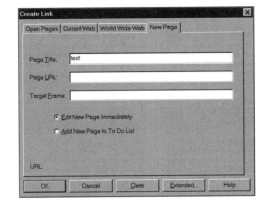

# Creating a Link from the FrontPage Explorer

FrontPage will also let you create a link from any open page to another page in the current Web using the FrontPage Explorer. In the FrontPage Explorer, select the page to which you want to link by clicking and holding the left mouse button; then drag the mouse pointer from the FrontPage Explorer to the line in the FrontPage editor at which you want to create the link, and release the mouse button.

FrontPage creates the link to the page on the line you chose. The anchor text for the link is the name of the page you linked from. As shown in Figure 9.14, the best way to create a link from the FrontPage Explorer to the FrontPage Editor is to resize them so that they can be displayed side by side.

**FIGURE 9.14.**

*Creating a Link from the FrontPage Explorer.*

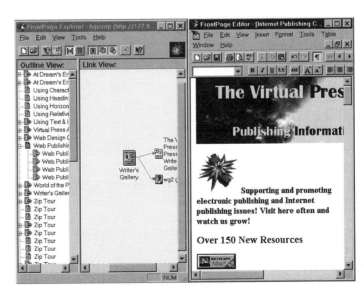

# Editing Links with FrontPage

Any link you create can be updated, changed, or deleted as necessary. This section guides you through the link editing process.

## Changing a Link

FrontPage enables you to easily change a link. In the FrontPage Editor, place the pointer anywhere in the text containing the link, or select any part of the link; then either choose Link from the Edit menu, or click the Edit Link button. This opens the Create Link dialog box.

To change the link to an open page, select the Open Pages tab, and then edit the Open Pages and Bookmark fields. To change the link to a page in the current Web, select the Current Web tab, and edit the Page and Bookmark fields. To change the link to a page in the World Wide Web, select the World Wide Web tab, and edit the URL field. To change the link to a new page, select the New Page tab, and then edit the Page URL and Page Title fields. When you are done editing the link, click the OK button.

## Deleting a Link

The FrontPage Editor enables you to delete links in one of two ways. You either delete the link entirely or delete part of the link text. As you will see, deleting a link is not the same as cutting the link and its associated text using the cut feature of the editor.

To delete an entire link in the FrontPage Editor, place the insertion point on the link, and then choose Unlink from the Edit menu. The FrontPage Editor will delete the link, but not the text associated with the link.

To delete part of a link in the FrontPage Editor, select the text from which you want to delete the link, and then choose Unlink from the Edit menu. The FrontPage Editor deletes the link from the text you selected, but not the text associated with the link.

## Following a Text Link

Sometimes before you edit a link, you will want to see where the link leads to. FrontPage enables you to follow a link from an open page to the targeted page or bookmark. If the page is not already opened in another window, the FrontPage Editor will open the target page for editing and make it the active page. If the link is to a bookmark, the FrontPage Editor displays the section of the page containing the bookmark. If the target page is not in the current Web, FrontPage opens a copy of the page that you can save to the current Web.

To follow a link in the FrontPage Editor, place the pointer anywhere in the text containing the link or select any part of the link; then either choose Follow from the Tools menu or click the Follow Link button. While FrontPage is fetching the page, the Follow Link pointer is displayed. After following a link, you can follow the link back to its source by clicking the Follow Back button. When you do this, the FrontPage Editor opens the source page and displays the section of the page containing the source of the link.

> **NOTE**
>
> Following a link from the FrontPage Editor to a page or resource on the World Wide Web might take a long time. The FrontPage Editor will not time out because it assumes that the page link is valid and that the server on which the resource resides is valid. Thus if FrontPage doesn't display your page after a suitable amount of time, you might have to stop following the link by choosing Stop from the Tools menu or clicking the Stop button.

# Creating and Editing Bookmarks with FrontPage

Because bookmarks are links within documents, you create and edit them using a slightly different technique than for other links. Creating a bookmark is a two-part process that involves labeling the bookmark and creating a link to the bookmark.

## Labeling a Bookmark

When you label a bookmark, you give the bookmark a name. To create a bookmark in the FrontPage Editor, select one or more characters of text, and then select Bookmark from the Edit menu. This opens the Bookmark dialog box shown in Figure 9.15.

In the Bookmark Name field, enter the name of the bookmark. The bookmark name can include spaces but must be unique within the document. Because the name must be unique in the current document, the Bookmark dialog box shows you a listing of bookmark names you've already defined. When you are done, click the OK button.

**FIGURE 9.15.**

*Labeling a bookmark.*

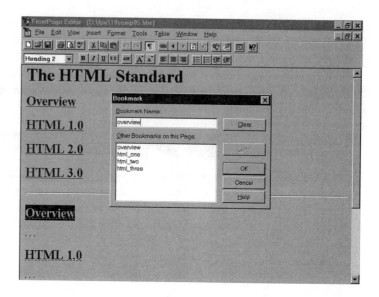

## Creating a Link to a Bookmark

After a bookmark is labeled, you can create a link to it. To create a link to the page containing the bookmark in the FrontPage Editor, select Link from the Edit menu. This opens the Create Link dialog box. You can now link to a bookmark in an open page, a page in the current Web, or a page on the World Wide Web.

To link to a bookmark on an open page or in the current Web, select the appropriate tab, and choose the bookmark name from the Bookmark drop-down list. To link to a bookmark on the World Wide Web, select the World Wide Web tag, and then enter the bookmark name in the URL field. Be sure to place a pound-sign character (#) before the bookmark name to the URL, such as

```
http://tvp.com/fiction.html#Mystery
```

or

```
http://www.tvpress.com/toc.html#orders
```

When you are done, click the OK button.

## Changing or Deleting a Bookmark

Changing or deleting a bookmark in the FrontPage Editor is easy. To do so, either place the pointer anywhere in the text containing the bookmark, or select any part of the bookmark, and then select Bookmark from the Edit menu. This opens the Bookmark dialog box.

To change the name of the bookmark's label, simply enter the new name. To delete the bookmark, click the Clear button. When you are done editing the bookmark, click on the OK button.

## Visiting a Bookmark

You can visit a bookmark on the current page or on another page using the FrontPage editor. When you visit a bookmark on the current page, the corresponding link does not have to exist. However, when you visit a bookmark on another page, there must be a link to that page and the page must have a label that corresponds to the keyword in the link.

To visit a bookmark on the current page, select any text, and then choose Bookmark from the Edit menu. In the Other Bookmarks on this Page field, select the bookmark that you want to visit, and click the Goto button. The FrontPage Editor displays the section of the page containing the bookmark you selected. You can close the Bookmark dialog box by clicking the OK or Cancel button.

To visit a bookmark on another page, place the pointer anywhere in the link; then select Follow Link from the Tools menu or click on the Follow Link button. The FrontPage Editor opens the new page and displays the section of the page containing the bookmark you selected.

# Using Lists

Lists are one of the most useful tools in your writing and publishing tool kit. Lists can give a clear order to your ideas and add to the visual impact of your document. You can use lists to grab the attention of readers, especially those readers who might be simply browsing or Web surfing your site in their quest to find new and interesting places to visit.

The best lists are designed for a specific purpose. For example, the steps for creating a Web document discussed in this chapter would make a great list:

- Develop a strategy.
- Define the document structure.
- Create the document.
- Add features to the document.
- Proof the document.
- Test the document.
- Publish the finished document.

This type of list is called a *bulleted list*. Bulleted lists are often used to outline goals, objectives, or tasks that have no specific order. Bulleted lists are also called unordered lists. This list, however, is in a specific order, so a bulleted list is not the best way to present it.

A better way to present the list of steps for creating a Web document would be to number the list:

1. Develop a strategy.
2. Define the document structure.
3. Create the document.
4. Add features to the document.
5. Proof the document.
6. Test the document.
7. Publish the finished document.

This type of list is called a *numbered list.* Numbered lists are used when tasks must be performed in a specific order. Numbered lists are also called ordered lists.

Lists are also used in the glossary section found in many nonfiction books. A glossary contains a list of keywords and their definitions. You can use definition lists whenever you want to associate a keyword with a concept or definition. Many definition lists look something like this:

*HTML*

HyperText Markup Language

The HyperText Markup Language is a markup language based on the Standard Generalized Markup Language that enables you to format information in visually appealing ways without sacrificing ease of use and the potential for wide distribution.

*SGML*

Standard Generalized Markup Language

The Standard Generalized Markup Language forms the basis for most markup languages and is an advanced language with few limitations.

*VRML*

Virtual Reality Modeling Language

Virtual Reality Modeling Language is an advanced markup language based on the standard markup language that enables you to create multidimensional documents.

Although the three fundamental types of lists are strongly supported by the HTML standard, the standard defines two additional types of lists designed primarily for programmers. Menu lists can be used to list the contents of program menus. Directory lists can be used to list the contents of directories. Menu lists and directory lists have fallen into disuse and are poorly supported by browsers. If you use a menu or directory list, the chances are very high that your browser will display the list following the rules for another list type. Therefore, it is generally not a good idea to use menu or directory lists.

# Creating Lists

The FrontPage editor enables you to create the five list types defined in the HTML standard. However, like Web browsers, the editor only uniquely supports the three primary types—bulleted lists, numbered lists, and definition lists. For this reason, the sections that follow focus only on the primary list types.

## Bulleted Lists

Bulleted lists are used to outline goals, objectives, or tasks with no specific order. When your browser sees the beginning of a bulleted list, it does two things:

- Starts a new line.
- Inserts a character called a bullet before the listed item.

As Figure 9.16 shows, bulleted lists are generally single-spaced. Although most browsers display the bullet as a large solid dot, the actual size and shape of the bullet might be different in your browser. Text browsers, such as Lynx, display the bullet as an asterisk. Other browsers use a different symbol for the bullets at each level of nested lists.

**FIGURE 9.16.**

*Using a bulleted list.*

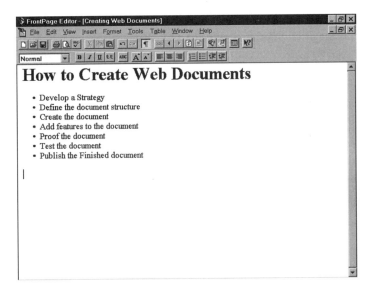

Creating bulleted lists with the FrontPage editor is a three-step process. The first step is to begin the list. To begin a bulleted list on a line below the insertion point, choose List from the Insert menu, and then select Bulleted from the List submenu. To begin a bulleted list on the same line as the insertion point, click the Bulleted List button or select Bulleted from the Format toolbar's drop-down list.

The second step is to enter your list items. FrontPage automatically continues the list for you. Therefore, to begin a new list item, simply press the Enter key. When you want to end the list, press the Enter key twice, or press Ctrl+Enter.

FrontPage also enables you to reformat existing text as a bulleted list. To do this, select one or more paragraphs; then click the Bulleted List button or select Bulleted from the Format toolbar's pull-down menu.

# Definition Lists

A definition list is generally for words and their definitions, but that does not mean you must use glossary lists for this strict purpose. You can use glossary lists whenever you want to associate a keyword, phrase, or sentence with a concept. Each item in a definition list contains two elements:

- A keyword called the *definition title*
- The definition called the *definition data*

As the example in Figure 9.17 shows, glossary lists are normally formatted with the terms and definitions on separate lines. The terms are aligned with the left margin, and the definitions are indented. Additionally, all aspects of glossary lists are generally single-spaced.

Creating definition lists with the FrontPage editor is a four-step process. The first step is to begin the list. To begin a definition list on a line below the insertion point, choose Definition from the Insert menu, and select either List or Term from Definition submenu. After entering the keyword or phrase you want to define, do not advance to the next line unless you want to enter another term.

To insert a definition for the current term, choose Definition from the Insert menu, and then select Definition. To add more definitions for the same term, simply press the Enter key. When you are done adding definitions, you can add a new term. To end the list, press Ctrl+Enter or select a new format from the pull-down menu on the Format toolbar.

**FIGURE 9.17.**
*Using a glossary list.*

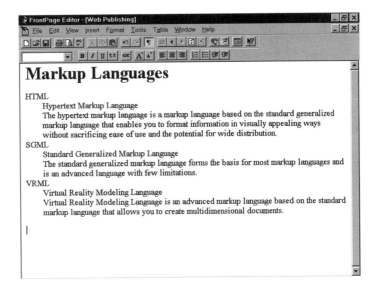

# Numbered Lists

Numbered lists are also called ordered lists. Each item in an ordered list is consecutively numbered or lettered. Letters are used only when you nest lists. When a browser sees the beginning of an ordered list, it does three things:

1. Starts a new line.
2. Indents the text of the list item.
3. Puts the appropriate number or letter in front of the list item.

As you can see from the example shown in Figure 9.18, numbered lists are single-spaced like other types of lists discussed earlier. You should use numbered lists when tasks must be performed in a particular order or when you want to add specificity to the list. When you number and add a label to a list of resources such as those shown in Figure 9.18, you add specificity to the list. Instead of the list being just another list of resources, the list represents *the* 12 reference works you wish were on your bookshelf.

Creating numbered lists with the FrontPage editor is a three-step process. The first step is to begin the list. To begin a numbered list on a line below the insertion point, choose List from the Insert menu, and then select Numbered from the List submenu. To begin a numbered list on the same line as the insertion point, click the Numbered List button, or select Numbered from the Format toolbar's pull-down menu.

EDITING
TECHNIQUE

**FIGURE 9.18.**

*Using a numbered list.*

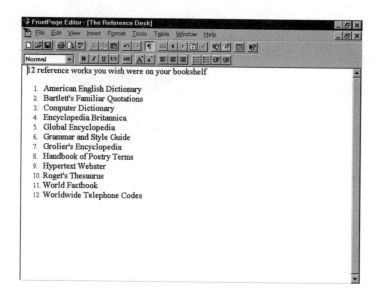

The second step is to enter your list items. FrontPage automatically continues the list for you. Therefore, to begin a new list item, simply press the Enter key. When you want to end the list, press the Enter key twice, or press Ctrl+Enter.

FrontPage also enables you to reformat existing text as a numbered list. To do this, select one or more paragraphs; then click the Numbered List button or select Numbered from the Format toolbar's pull-down menu.

## Nesting Lists

A nested list is a list inside another list. In HTML, you nest a list by including the entire structure for a list within your current list. For example, you could put bulleted lists within your numbered list structure.

To create a nested list, move the insertion point to where you want the nested list to begin. Next, select the list you want to insert from the Insert menu and enter the new list items. When you are finished, press the Enter key twice to end the nested list. You might have to press the Enter key a third time to get back to the previous list type. If you press the Enter key a fourth time, you will end the previous list type as well.

## Changing a List Type

FrontPage enables you to quickly change one list type to another list type. For example, you can change a bulleted list to a numbered list or a numbered list to a bulleted list.

To change a list type, select the entire list you want to change by moving the mouse cursor to the area where the list begins and double-clicking. You will know you've selected the list because the FrontPage Editor highlights the entire section containing the list.

After the list is selected, open the List Properties dialog box by selecting Properties from the Edit menu or pressing Alt+Enter. In the List Format field, select the new list format, and click the OK button.

> **NOTE**
>
> Because FrontPage changes only the formatting of the outermost select list, the formatting of any nested lists is retained. Also, when you change a list to a Definition list, all list items are changed to the format for definitions, not terms.

# Using Alternate Protocols in Web Documents

The Web was designed to be an open-ended multimedia system based on hypertext. However, the hypertext transfer protocol is not the only protocol you can reference in your Web publications. You can reference files using any valid protocol in the hypertext links used by your documents. The format of URLs in hypertext links should follow the URL scheme.

The next sections explain how to use these protocols in your Web documents:

- FTP
- Gopher
- mailto
- NNTP and News
- telnet
- WAIS

## Using FTP

Thousands of files are available on FTP sites around the world. Your Web documents can contain links to files that will be retrieved using the File Transfer Protocol. The general form for using a hypertext reference to an FTP file is

```
ftp://host/path
```

If you specify a directory path instead of the full path to a file, the reader's browser will display a listing of the directory's contents. The following hypertext reference will retrieve a listing of the MS-DOS directory from an FTP server at the University of Florida:

```
ftp://ftp.eng.ufl.edu/pub/msdos
```

## Using Gopher

Gopher information is presented to readers as easy-to-navigate menus. You can enable readers to access gopher files using a hypertext reference, such as this:

```
gopher://host/path
```

The following hypertext reference will retrieve information on the DILS Project from a Gopher server at the University of Toronto:

```
gopher://gopher.epas.utoronto.ca/11/cch/disciplines/medieval_studies/keefer
```

## Using Mailto

You could use a special type of link that starts a create mail session in the reader's browser:

```
mailto:william@tvp.com
```

This mailto reference tells the reader's browser to open a create mail session that will be sent to william@tvp.com. This type of link enhances the interactivity of the page and provides a mechanism for getting feedback from readers. Don't forget to anchor the link to the page with text or graphics that readers can click on.

## Using NNTP and News

In your Web documents, you can reference any of the thousands of newsgroups on the Internet in two key ways: using the reader's local news server or through NNTP. Referencing newsgroups on a local news server is easy—you just specify the name of the newsgroup in the following form:

```
news:newsgroup.name
```

Here you could include a link to the alt.books.reviews newsgroup as follows:

```
news:alt.books.reviews
```

The network news transfer protocol is used to transfer postings to and from a news server. Here's how NNTP could be used to link to the alt.books.reviews newsgroup:

```
nntp://news.aloha.com/alt.books.reviews
```

**CAUTION**

Generally, to access the news server, the reader must be a known client. Although this protocol could be useful to an exclusive group of known users, most readers will be accessing your pages from a remote site and will be unable to use the named news server. Consequently, you should use reference newsgroups available on the reader's local news server using news whenever you want to ensure broader accessibility.

## Using telnet

Using telnet, you can enable readers to access an interactive service on a remote host. In the telnet session, readers can input commands at a command prompt as if they were logged on to the remote host. You can reference telnet in your Web documents as follows:

```
telnet://tvp.com
```

## Using WAIS

You can reference indexed databases on wide area information systems using a WAIS URL. To use WAIS, the reader's browser must either be configured to invoke a WAIS client that the reader has installed on his system or be able to act as a WAIS client. You can reference WAIS in your Web documents as follows:

```
wais://tvp.com/wwwdata
```

# Summary

The ability to create documents with high visual impact and a high level of interactivity is essential to your success as a Web publisher. Basic techniques that add to the visual impact and interactivity of the document include line breaks, horizontal lines, lists, hypertext links, and bookmarks. Line breaks can create a column of text. Horizontal lines can visually divide the document into sections. Lists add to the visual impact of the document by clearly organizing material. Hypertext links increase the interactive nature of your document. Bookmarks guide readers to key parts of your publication.

# Enhancing Your Web Publication with Images—the Easy Way

by William
Robert Stanek

**10**

**IN THIS CHAPTER**

By adding graphics, you can create visually stunning pages that will entice readers to visit your page time after time. This chapter is filled with insider tips and techniques for incorporating images and image maps into your publications. Image maps are graphical menus that contain *hotspots*. Each hotspot is an area the user can click on to go to an associated page. Image maps are as simple or complex as you make them. A single image map could be a menu for 5 or 25 Web pages. The choice is yours.

# Using Images in Your Web Pages

Images are the key to unleashing the power of your Web publications. Everywhere you look on the Web, you will find images. Web publishers use images to enhance their pages and get the reader's attention. You can use thumbnail icons to create highlights and navigation mechanisms. You can use computer-designed images as logos, page titles, illustrations, and maps to the hot features at your site. You can use digitized photos to convey your message in a way more powerful than text alone. These photos can help sell your products and services and can even show the rest of the world what your part of the world looks like.

Adding images to your Web pages is easy and can be accomplished using either external images or inline images. Readers access external images by activating a hypertext link to the image, such as a link that says 67 Chevy fire-engine red.

When a reader clicks on the link, the image is downloaded to his computer. If an image viewer is available and configured for use in the reader's browser, the image is displayed. If an image viewer is not available, the image is stored on the reader's hard disk for later viewing.

Although adding external images to your Web publications is as easy as providing a link to the image, it does require forethought and a fundamental understanding of image formats and related concepts. Browsers know which image viewer to launch based on the file type extension (.jpeg, .gif, and so forth) of the external image referenced in your document. When a reader accesses a link to a GIF image, the browser checks a configuration table to see which application should display the image, which is why your Web files should always be named with the appropriate extension. If the file is in GIF format, name it with a .gif extension. If the file is in JPEG format, name it with a .jpeg or .jpg extension.

Unlike external images that are not displayed directly, inline images can be viewed directly. When a reader with a graphics-capable browser accesses your page, the images can be automatically loaded with the text on the page. When you add an image to a page, you specify the location of the image by using a URL. The URL can be a relative path such as

```
67chevy.gif
```

Or it can be a full path such as

```
http://tvp.com/usr/images/gifs/67chevy.gif
```

All image files are in a specific format. The two most popular image formats on the Web are GIF and JPEG. All graphics-capable browsers support both the GIF and JPEG formats. Beyond support for GIF and JPEG, FrontPage supports images in the following formats: BMP (Windows and OS/2), EPS, MAC, MSP, PCD, PCX, RAS, TIFF, WMF, and WPG. These additional formats are popular formats for graphic design tools, image packages, and shareware image libraries.

Whenever you use any of these additional image formats, FrontPage converts the image to either the GIF or JPEG format depending on the number of colors in the image. FrontPage converts images with 256 or fewer colors to GIF and images with more than 256 colors to JPEG. Image formats are discussed in more detail later in this chapter.

When you specify an image, you can also specify alternate text to display in place of the image. Readers with a text-only browser will see the alternate text instead of the image. If you do not specify alternate text, readers with a text-only browser will see a note that marks the location of the image on the page, such as [IMAGE].

Browsers handle inline images in many different ways. Some browsers load all text and associated images before displaying any part of your document. Some browsers display text and graphics as they read in your document. Other browsers load and display the textual portions of the page, leaving placeholders where the images will go, and then retrieve the images one by one. A few advanced browsers let the reader select options for displaying the components of the page.

Individual browsers handle inline images in many different ways, but all graphics-capable browsers provide readers with a mechanism for turning off the automatic image-loading feature of the browser. This nice feature for readers means more work for Web publishers.

Before you add inline images, there are many concepts you should consider. The most important matters you should think about are when and how to use images in your publications.

# Working with Images in FrontPage

FrontPage provides terrific control over images and enables you to see all the images your page contains as you edit it. You can use images in two key ways: insert them directly into a page or import them into your Web for future use. All images come from one of three sources: the current Web; an external source, such as the World Wide Web; or a local file.

## Inserting Images from the Current Web

Using the FrontPage Editor, you can easily insert images from the current Web. The first step is to move the insertion point where you want the image inserted, and then choose Image from the Insert menu. This opens the dialog box shown in Figure 10.1. When you open the Image dialog box, a listing of all images imported to the current Web is displayed by image title and image URL. To insert one of these images, all you have to do is select the image you want to insert by image title or image URL, and then click on the OK button.

**FIGURE 10.1.**

*The Insert Image dialog box.*

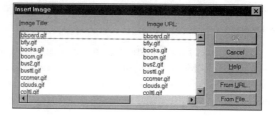

## Inserting Images from a File

Inserting an image from a file involves a little more work. To start, move the insertion point where you want the image inserted, and then choose Image from the Insert menu, which opens the Image dialog box. When you click on the From File button, the FrontPage Editor displays the Insert dialog box, shown in Figure 10.2. As you can see, the Insert dialog box is the standard Windows dialog box for opening files. Using the Look In drop-down list, you can select the folder you want to browse. FrontPage displays a list of files that match the current file type selected in the Files of Type field.

**FIGURE 10.2.**

*Inserting images from a file.*

If you know the name of the image you want to insert, you can enter the name in the File Name field. If you do not know the name of the image, you can browse folders until you find the image you are looking for. When you find the image, you can insert it into your page by double-clicking on the filename; selecting the filename, and then clicking on the Open button; or typing the filename, and then clicking on the Open button.

> **NOTE**
>
> When you insert an image from a file, you can import it to your Web when you save the page. Because FrontPage tracks all images you've imported or changed and will give

you the option of saving each new or changed image before closing or saving the page, you don't have to worry about tracking the images yourself.

# Inserting Images from an External Web

When you insert an image from the World Wide Web, FrontPage displays the image but does not allow you to import it to your Web. The primary reason for this is that you are referencing an external image source and specifying the full URL path to the image, which eliminates the necessity of having the image file physically located on your Web site.

> **TIP**
>
> If you want to access the image remotely, inserting an image from the Web is the way to do it. However, if you want the image to be located on your Web server and accessed from your Web server, you should import the image to your Web and then insert it from the current Web.

To insert an image from a site on the World Wide Web, move the insertion point where you want the image inserted, and then choose Image from the Insert menu, which opens the Image dialog box. When you click on the From URL button, the FrontPage Editor displays the Open Location dialog box shown in Figure 10.3. Now, enter the full URL path to the image you want to insert. Like the sample URL shown in Figure 10.3, the URL path should use the HyperText Transfer Protocol.

**FIGURE 10.3.**

*Inserting images from the Web.*

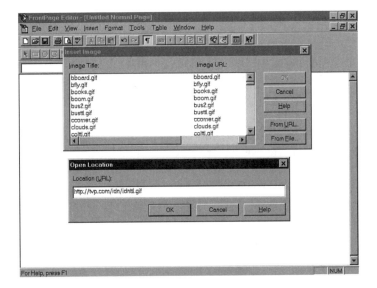

# Importing Images

Using the FrontPage Explorer, you import images for future use. When you insert an image that is not in the GIF or JPEG format, FrontPage converts the image to either GIF or JPEG format. Because FrontPage stores all files by Web on your file system, you generally should not edit the original image file. However, if you do edit the file in its original location, you must import the image again so that FrontPage can store the updated image.

In the FrontPage Explorer, choose Import from the File menu. This opens the Import File to Web dialog box, which is shown in Figure 10.4. Before you specify files to import, only two options are available in this dialog box: Add File and Close.

**FIGURE 10.4.**

*Importing files.*

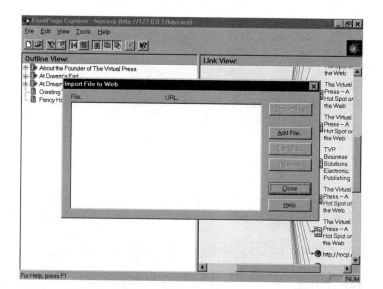

The Add File button enables you to add to the list of files you want to import. Clicking on this button opens the Add File to Import List dialog box, which is shown in Figure 10.5. Using the Look In pull-down, you can select the folder you want to browse. FrontPage displays a list of files that match the current file type selected in the Files of Type field.

If you know the name of the image you want to import, you can enter the name in the File Name field. If you do not know the name of the image, you can browse folders until you find the image you are looking for. When you find the image, you can add it to the list of files to import by double-clicking on the filename; selecting the filename, and then clicking on the Open button; or typing the filename, and then clicking on the Open button.

**FIGURE 10.5.**

*Adding files to the import list.*

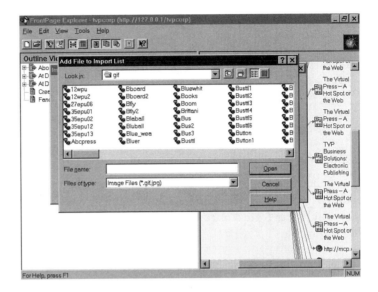

---

**TIP**

FrontPage enables you to select multiple files for importing. By holding down the Ctrl key and clicking the left mouse button on a filename, you can add files to your import list. Using the Shift key and the mouse, you can select a group of files listed consecutively. To do this, click the left mouse button on the first file you want to select, move the mouse pointer to the last file you want to select, and hold down the Shift key as you press the left mouse button.

---

When there are files in the import list, the FrontPage Explorer displays them in the Import File to Web dialog box as shown in Figure 10.6. FrontPage adds the filenames and their locations to a file for safekeeping. This enables you to close the dialog box and import some or all of the files at a later date. To remove a file that you added to the import list by mistake or otherwise do not want to import, select the image's filename from the import list, and then click on the Remove button.

You should note that all the buttons in the dialog box are active when there are files to import. By default, the Explorer selects all the files for importing. By clicking on the Import Now button with all the files selected, you can import all the files at once. Using the techniques for selecting multiple files, you can select a group of files to import. When you start importing files, the Import Now button changes to a Stop button. The Stop button enables you to stop importing files to the current Web at any time.

**FIGURE 10.6.**

*A list of files to import.*

If a conflict occurs when you are importing files, FrontPage displays a warning, such as the one shown in Figure 10.7. To continue importing files, you must make a selection. In this case, you would select Yes to replace the existing file with the one you are importing and No to keep the existing file.

**FIGURE 10.7.**

*FrontPage displays warnings when conflicts occur.*

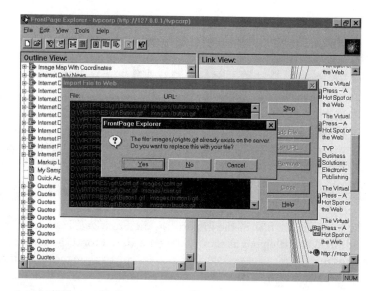

In the Import File to Web dialog box, clicking on the Edit URL button opens the dialog box shown in Figure 10.8. By default, the FrontPage Explorer imports all images to a subdirectory called images within the current Web's main directory. To change this default, you need to edit the image's URL path using the Edit URL dialog box. Unfortunately, you will have to set a new path individually for each image you are importing.

If you put the image in a new subdirectory, FrontPage will move the image to the new folder. If you enter a subdirectory that is not currently in the Web, FrontPage will create the subdirectory and move the image to it. Any links or WebBots in documents within the current Web are updated to use the new path to the image.

**FIGURE 10.8.**

*Changing an image's URL before importing it.*

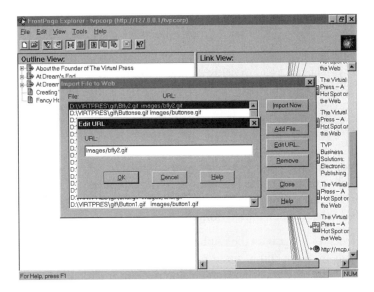

# Cutting, Copying, and Pasting Images

When you edit your documents in the FrontPage editor, you will often want to manipulate images just as you would text, which FrontPage enables you to do using the familiar cut, copy, and paste mechanisms you'll find in most word processors. Before you can cut, copy, or paste an image, you need to select it.

You can select an image by doing any of the following:

1. Click on the image.
2. Move the pointer to the left or right side of the image, and then click the left mouse button and drag the pointer over the image.
3. Move the insertion point to the left or right side of the image, and press Shift+left-arrow key or Shift+right-arrow key.

When you click on an image, the FrontPage Editor assumes that you want to manipulate but not permanently delete the image. Thus, the FrontPage Editor activates the Image toolbar and won't let you inadvertently delete the image by pressing the Delete key.

On the other hand, when you use method 2 or 3 to select an image, the FrontPage Editor assumes that you want to manipulate and possibly delete the image. As a warning, the Editor displays the image in reverse video, and the Image Toolbar does not activate. If you press the Delete key when the image is displayed in reverse video, the editor will remove it from the page and the only way to get the image back is to use the undo function.

> **TIP**
>
> When you delete an image, it is removed from the page but is not copied to the Clipboard. You can delete an image without selecting it first. One way to delete an image without selecting it first is to move the insertion point after the image and press the Backspace key. Alternatively, you can place the insertion point before the image and press the Delete key.

Now that the image is selected, you can use the cut, copy, or paste buttons on the Standard toolbar or access these functions from the Edit menu. When you cut an image, it is removed from the page and copied to the Clipboard. When you copy an image, it is copied to the Clipboard but is not removed from the page.

When an image is on the Clipboard, you can insert it by using the Paste button or by selecting Paste from the Edit menu. Because Windows shares the Clipboard among programs, you can cut an image from your favorite paint program and paste it directly into your document. If the image is not in the GIF or JPEG format, the FrontPage editor automatically converts the image to either GIF or JPEG format. Images with 256 or fewer colors are converted to GIF. Images with more than 256 colors are converted to JPEG. When these formats are discussed in detail later in the chapter, you will understand why FrontPage handles images in this way.

## Saving an Image to the Current Web

FrontPage tracks all changes to images for you. Any images you've inserted into your document from a file, pasted from the Clipboard, or altered in the current document can be imported to the current Web when you save the document. However, the FrontPage Editor does not automatically import the images. The Save Image to Web dialog box is displayed for each image that was inserted or updated since the page was last saved to the Web.

When you are saving a new image to the Web, the editor displays the dialog box shown in Figure 10.9. By default, the editor saves all images to a subdirectory called images within the current Web's main directory. To change this default, you need to edit the image's URL path in the Save to URL field.

**FIGURE 10.9.**

*Saving a new image.*

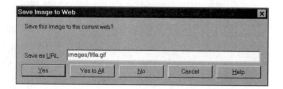

The dialog box gives you four options. You can save the image to the current Web by pressing the Yes button. If you have added or updated several images and you want to save them all without further prompts, you can click the Yes to All button. If you don't want to save the image to the current Web, click the No button. If you want to cancel all further actions, click the Cancel button.

When you are saving an updated image to the Web, the editor displays the dialog box shown in Figure 10.10. You can overwrite the existing image file using the Replace button. If you have added or updated several images and you want to save them all without further prompts, you can click the Yes to All button. If you don't want to save the updated image, click the Use Existing button. If you want to cancel all further actions, press the Cancel button.

**FIGURE 10.10.**

*Updating an existing image.*

> **CAUTION**
>
> Think carefully before overwriting an image that might be used in other documents. Overwriting existing images with a new or updated image will affect all other pages in your Web that use the image.

# When and How To Use Images

As you've seen, adding images to your publications is easy, yet this ease of use makes for easy abuse as well. Your inline images should supplement text and enhance the document, but rarely replace text on the page. One of the most important choices you as the Web publisher have to make is to determine when and how to use images. You can use images in your publications in dozens of ways. Before you add an image to the publication, however, you should ask yourself three questions:

- ▪ Why are you using the image?
- ▪ Will the image add to the impact of the page?
- ▪ Will the image help the reader?

Creating images, even simple images, for use in Web documents is an art form that is largely misunderstood even by professionals. You will find many Web documents with images that are horribly designed and actually lessen the impact of the documents they are in. Many more Web documents have images designed by the skilled hands of graphic designers that fail to create the desired impact because they are over-designed. A common and mistaken philosophy for many of these poorly designed documents is that bigger and more is better. Bigger and more is not better.

When you create images, use a design and style that fit the purpose of the document. Often simple low-resolution images will work just as well as advanced high-resolution images. Nothing gets the reader's attention faster than well-designed and well-placed images. You should use images in your Web documents when they do the following:

- Accent the page
- Highlight key ideas
- Serve a specific purpose

Images can highlight the textual portions of the page. Graphic titles and logos can be eye-opening introductions for your publications. Small images can accent key ideas or concepts. Illustrations, figures, and pictures can support key points discussed in the publication.

Images that serve a specific purpose are the most useful. By putting an image tag inside a hypertext link, you can create images that act as links to other documents. If you use a series of images, you can create a simple menu to key pages at your site. Sometimes images can even be the only element on the page. If the image contains hot areas that are mapped to specific pages at your site, a single image can act as your site's menu. In this way, the image could act as the doorway to key areas at the site.

Other questions you should ask yourself when adding images to your page include

- How large is the image file and how long will it take the average user to download?
- How many images are already on the page, and does the image fit in with the images on the page?

These questions have more consequence than you might think. The more features you add to the page, the longer it will take for the page to load into the reader's browser. If you add too many features, the reader might get impatient and choose another site to visit. Consequently, for large images, you might want to consider using a small image called a *thumbnail* that links to the large image, or even a simple text link to the image. Also, as you will see later in the discussion of color maps, some images just aren't compatible with each other and cause conflicts that can dramatically affect the way readers see your page.

The best Web publications are user-friendly and highly interactive. You can add images to your pages to make them more friendly and more interactive.

# Image Tips for Text-Only Browsers

Providing ways for readers who cannot or choose not to view images to enjoy your site is a key concept in the design of your documents. Users with text-only browsers and users who have turned off the automatic image-loading feature of their browser will not be able to see your images. Consequently, for these users, you will want to provide alternative features in addition to your images.

Sometimes you will want to include alternative text that the reader can see in place of your images. You do this in the Image Properties dialog box, which is shown in Figure 10.11. To display this dialog box, double-click on the image; select the image and then press Alt+Enter; or select Properties from the Edit menu. In the Alternative Representations area of the dialog box, enter the text you want the reader to see when the image is not displayed. For your fire-engine red '67 Chevy, you could specify the alternative text of "Car."

**FIGURE 10.11.**

*Specifying alternative text for an image.*

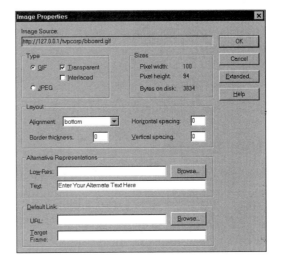

If you specify alternative text, readers see the text instead of the [IMAGE] note telling them an image is on the page. Browsers typically display alternative text for images in brackets. However, telling the reader that a picture of a car is on the page might not enhance the reader's perception of the page. Again, you should add features to increase the impact of the page. A better way to provide information about images is to use several descriptive words that help readers see the image in their mind's eye. Here's a better use of alternative text:

My fire-engine red 67 Chevy

If telling the reader what the image contains doesn't enhance the page, you can remove the reference to the image. Normally, you would use an empty alternative text assignment to do this. However, FrontPage does not allow this. Therefore, you could insert a space as the Text, which effectively replaces [IMAGE] with [ ].

Often images are essential to the understanding of concepts explored in your documents. Although readers with text-only browsers cannot view your inline images, you might want to make key images available both as inline and external images. For example, if you are comparing the hot new design of your latest product to a competitor's product, a digitized photo can support your claims and help you sell the product. While users with text-only browsers cannot display inline images, they probably can display external images using an image viewer to display the picture.

# Image Tips for Graphics-Capable Browsers

As you have seen, there are lots of uses for images in your publications, and readers with graphics-capable browsers will want to see them all. However, you should not add all the features discussed earlier to a single page. Share the wealth, and sprinkle these features throughout your site. Before you add images to your documents, you will want to consider four things:

- Sizing your images
- Placing images in your documents
- Design concepts for images
- Additional image enhancements

## Sizing Your Images

The physical size of your images in terms of bytes is extremely important. Every inline image you include must be loaded when the page is accessed, and a 15KB image will take a lot longer to download than a 3KB image. However, slow-loading graphics aren't necessarily large graphics; they are high-resolution graphics or graphics with many colors. A very large four-color image at low resolution will download faster than a small 256-color image at high resolution.

A good rule to follow when adding images to your Web pages is the 14-second rule. The 14-second rule has the average user in mind. Currently, the average user accessing the Web has a 14,400-bps modem. If you analyze this statistically, use the median so that extremes won't have a large effect on the outcome. The current trend is toward 14,400 bps, with many Web users accessing at 9600 bps and an increasing number accessing at 28,800 bps. The philosophy at the heart of the rule is that if it takes longer than 14 seconds under the best of conditions to download all objects in your document, you might want to restructure your document so that it downloads in 14 seconds or less.

Fourteen seconds is really the average (median) value in a frustration window that weighs poor performance and slow access speeds at one end and the top performance and access speeds at the other end. Don't use the rule as an absolute. Use it as a reality check to help you develop user-friendly pages. This is the basic precept of the rule—make sure your pages are user-friendly by valuing the user's time. After you have browsed the Web for awhile, you will discover that there is nothing more frustrating than waiting for thousands of bytes of graphics to load. Undoubtedly, you will wish that more Web publishers followed this rule.

**NOTE**

To test this rule, make sure that the automatic image-loading feature of your Web browser is turned on; then try loading one of your Web documents. Use a modem speed of 14,400 bps. If, under optimal conditions, it takes more than 14 seconds to fully load all text and graphics—assuming no other time-delaying features are adversely affecting the download—look at the document and see what is slowing the load time. Consider modifying the offending element. Note that your Web documents will load faster for you because of your proximity to the site. If it takes you 14 seconds to download the document, it will probably take users at disparate sites a lot longer.

One way to avoid putting byte-hogging graphics on a page is to use thumbnail images. Thumbnail images are a great way to link to large images and other resources. The notion of a thumbnail describes how these resources are included in your documents. You use a small image to lead to something bigger, such as a large image or another resource. To avoid using an external viewer, you could link the thumbnail image to an HTML document that features the large version of the image.

To make an image clickable, you have to insert the image into a link. You can do this in the FrontPage Editor by selecting the image and then creating a link as discussed in Chapter 9, "Adding Features to the Page." You can verify or update the link using the Image Properties dialog box. The current link is displayed in the URL field of the Default Link area. At any time, you can specify a new link in the URL field. To browse documents you might want to link to, you can use the Browse button that is beside the URL field. This button opens the Edit Link dialog box.

**EDITING TECHNIQUE**

**TIP**

If you know the URL path to the resource you want to link to, you can enter it directly into the URL field. The URL field is located in the Default Link area of the Image Properties dialog box. When you close the dialog box, FrontPage will automatically create the link for you without having to go through the steps discussed in Chapter 9.

# Placing Images in Your Documents

The way you place objects on the page is as important as the colors and sizes you choose for your images, especially when you are aligning text and images. All images in HTML are placed on the page using a specific alignment. By default, FrontPage aligns the bottom of the image with the bottom of any text element that might be associated with the image.

In the Layout area of the Image Properties dialog box, you can specify a more precise alignment for your images. Figure 10.12 shows the Image Properties dialog box with the Alignment field's drop-down list active. As you can see, there are nine alignments you can choose from.

**FIGURE 10.12.**

*Specifying the alignment of images.*

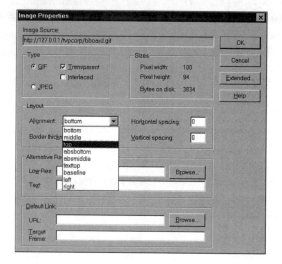

These values align text and images in ways contrary to what you might think when you see the values. For example, the MIDDLE value does not align the middle of the image with the middle of the text. The MIDDLE value aligns the middle of the image with the bottom of the text, which produces a slightly off-center effect. The TOP value does not precisely align the top of the image with the tallest elements in the associated text. The TOP value generally aligns the text and the image along an imaginary line slightly above the text. Similarly, the BOTTOM value does not align the bottom of the image with the lowest element in the text. The BOTTOM value generally aligns the image and text along a baseline such as the ones used on lined paper. Text elements such as an *h* are aligned along the baseline, and text elements such as a *g* extend below the baseline.

One reason the BOTTOM value is the default alignment is that text does not wrap around images. This means that if you align a long line of text with the top of the image, part of your text will be aligned with the top of the image and the remainder of the text will be displayed below the image. Consequently, you should only use the TOP and MIDDLE alignment values to align a single short line of text with an image.

However, using the default value for the ALIGN attribute, you can use this formatting method to your advantage to align an image with a paragraph of text. To do this, the image must appear at the beginning in the paragraph. In this way, the first line of text will be aligned with the bottom of the image, and the next line of text will start on a new line immediately below the image. One way to use this technique is for fancy first letters of a story.

Many of the remaining alignment values were introduced by Netscape to correct the short-comings of the standard HTML alignments. These alignment values behave exactly as their names imply they should. The value of TEXTTOP aligns the top of the image with the top of the tallest element in the line of text associated with the image. The value of ABSMIDDLE aligns the center of the image with the center of the line of text associated with the image. The value of ABSBOTTOM aligns the bottom of the image with the bottom of the line of text associated with the image. The value of BASELINE aligns the base of the image with the baseline of the text associated with the image, which is exactly how the value of BOTTOM handles text and image alignment.

---

**NOTE**

Keep in mind that some browsers might ignore the Netscape-unique alignment values and display your images with the default alignment value of BOTTOM. Consequently, you should use the Netscape alignment values only on pages that will be displayed by the Netscape-capable browser or when the alignment of the image and text is not critical. Netscape-capable browsers include Netscape Navigator 1.0 to 3.0, Aficionado Web Surfer, Enhanced Spyglass Mosaic, IBrowse for the Amiga, Netshark, Netsurfer, Pythia, WebExplorer, and Microsoft Internet Explorer 2.0 to 4.0.

---

HTML 3 enables you to use two additional alignment values, which can be used to align an image and a paragraph of associated text into columns. The LEFT value puts the image in the left margin and wraps the text around the right side of the image. The RIGHT value puts the image in the right margin and wraps the text around the left side of the image.

By aligning text and images into columns using these alignments, you can create documents with rich layout and styles that merge the image into the text of the document in ways more powerful than previously possible. To get the text to wrap around only the left or right side of the image, you would make the image the first element in a short paragraph of text.

As you can see in Figure 10.13, the image is in the left column and the paragraph text is in the right column. Keep in mind that any subsequent text will be aligned with the image until the left margin is clear.

Images and text are aligned with minimal spacing. This spacing sometimes makes the text difficult to read. One way to increase the spacing and make the image more useful is to include the image in a hypertext reference, as shown in Figure 10.14. The image shown has a border around it that clearly separates it from the associated text and is also clickable.

As Figure 10.14 shows, you can get the text to wrap around two or three sides of the image using alignment values of LEFT or RIGHT. To do this, you insert a line of text before the image tag. Your browser should display complete lines of text before inserting the image. However, if you follow this approach, you would want to preview the document using a standard (13-inch) screen size on a Macintosh system or a standard (640×480) video mode on a DOS/Windows system.

**FIGURE 10.13.**

*Aligning text and images into columns.*

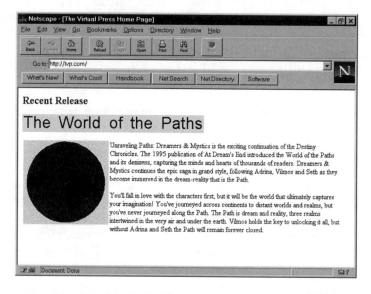

**FIGURE 10.14.**

*Merging the image into the text.*

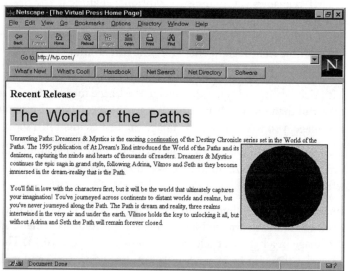

Another useful HTML feature you can use when aligning images and text is the line break. Using the clear attribute of line breaks, you can insert a clean break into the column of text associated with the image. The text before the line break will be aligned with the image in a column. The text after the line break will be inserted when the margin is clear. If the image is aligned with the left margin, you should select a value of Clear Left in the Line Break Properties dialog box. If the image is aligned with the right margin, you should select a value of Clear Right in the Line Break Properties dialog box.

By default, FrontPage inserts HTML markup that tells your browser the width and height of the image. This is useful for advanced browsers that load the text of a document first and leave an appropriately sized space where the images will be located when the document finishes loading. These attributes are also useful for precisely sizing your images to fit the needs of the document.

---

### SIZING IMAGES TO FIT YOUR NEEDS

The ability to shrink or enlarge images on the fly is extremely useful. You can create a menu of images that are consistently sized without having to create new files containing the resized images. You can then reuse the same images later in the document at their original size or sized to suit your needs without having to load new image files. This is convenient for you and reduces the download time of your document.

Unfortunately, the developers of FrontPage chose not to allow you to edit the attributes associated with the width and height of an image. The only way to get around this is to load your document into a standard text editor or word processor that is not capable of WYSIWYG HTML editing. When your document is in this document, you need to update the values associated with the image's width and height.

For example, if the original size of the image is 200×190, you can shrink the image by defining a new width and height:

```
<IMG SRC="title2.gif" ALT="" WIDTH=150 HEIGHT=140>
```

Or you can enlarge it:

```
<IMG SRC="title2.gif" ALT="" WIDTH=275 HEIGHT=190>
```

---

# Designing Highlights with Images

Add images to highlight your page and to showcase your ideas. Most pages on the Web use images to introduce the page. These images range from simple text on a colorful background to eye-popping 3-D images. Both types of images are fine when used for the right reasons. The image you use to introduce your documents should fit in with your publishing style, the subject matter you discuss in the document, and the content of related documents. When starting out, simple is usually best.

Although your style of publishing will be different from that of other Web publishers, you should generally follow a unified design within pages of the same publication. One of the key areas you will want to focus on is the color scheme for images used in your documents, which is an area of Web publishing that is all too often overlooked. As you look at the colors you plan to use in your images, key in on the colors used in backgrounds and in text. These are the colors you will want to limit.

You could follow a similar color scheme for all the images at your site. In this way, your pages will have a familiar look to readers. You could also follow a color scheme for pages associated with a certain publication or key areas at your site. In this way, each publication at your site will have a familiar look to readers, and they will have a visual cue when they enter a new area. The key concept here is to look at the colors you plan to use in a particular document's images and ask yourself if they work well together and if the colors help the reader. Here is an example of colors that don't work well together: a title page that features a logo with a green background and blue text, header titles with a white background and red text, and other images on the page with gray backgrounds and yellow text.

You might also want to use consistent sizing of key images from page to page. This concept goes back to giving your pages a familiar feel and look. For example, you could make the graphical titles for your pages 150×350 pixels and the graphical subtitles for your pages 75×350 pixels. In this way, your titles and subtitles will be positioned in the same location on the screen. Figure 10.15 shows how the concepts of introducing your document with an image, using a color scheme, and using consistent sizing could be used in your Web documents.

**FIGURE 10.15.**

*Introducing your
documents with images.*

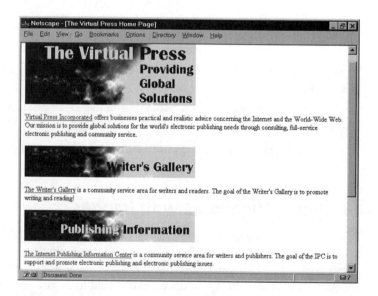

Another way to design highlights for the same document would be to use the images as a graphical menu. Figure 10.16 shows the graphical menu for the redesigned document. This technique provides quick access to the key areas at your Web site.

**FIGURE 10.16.**

*Designing a graphical menu.*

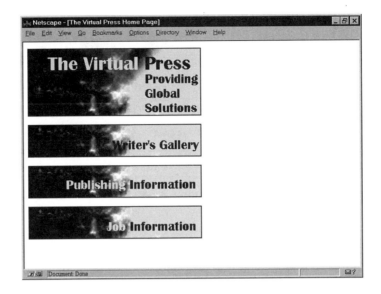

If you use graphical menus in your publications, provide a text-based way for readers to access the menu. You might be surprised to find that text-based alternatives to graphical menus will help all the readers who visit your site, especially those who are impatient and don't want to wait for your images to load. An interesting outcome of placing an image inside a hypertext reference is that whenever the associated alternative text is displayed, it will be clickable anchor text. This provides readers using text-only browsers with a way to access other pages at your site. It also helps readers with graphics-capable browsers who might have switched off automatic image loading, as well as those readers with a browser that displays alternative text while the image is downloading.

Figure 10.17 shows how the alternative text used in the previous example is displayed in a browser. As you can see, the alternative text forms a simple menu that readers can use to access key areas at the site. Without the alternative text, the reader using this browser would be lost.

Graphical menus aren't the only way you can provide readers with navigation mechanisms. Many Web publishers use a standard set of small icons to provide readers with access to pages at their site. The most common navigation icons are variations of the left, right, up, and down arrows. The left arrow is generally used to provide quick access to the previous page. The right arrow provides quick access to the next page. The up arrow provides quick access to the home or top-level page. The down arrow provides quick access to the next level page.

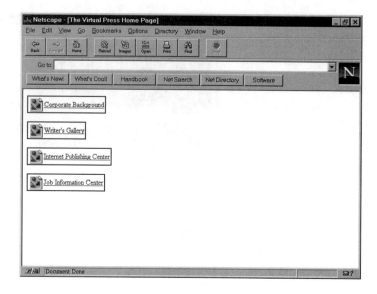

# Additional Enhancements for Images

FrontPage supports additional enhancements for images that enable you to make the following specifications:

- The width of the border surrounding an image that is linked to a resource
- The vertical space around the image
- The horizontal space around the image
- An alternate low-resolution image to load first

These attributes are fully supported by Netscape and Internet Explorer. You can set values for these attributes using the Image Properties dialog box.

Normally, browsers display a border around all images that are linked to another Web resource. Both Web users and publishers alike consider this border to be distracting in most instances. Because of this, FrontPage sets the width of borders around images to zero, which tells the browser not to display a border at all if possible. In recent months, this has become the favorite setting for most Web publishers.

However, sometimes you want the image to have a distinct border. In the Layout area of the Image Properties dialog box, you will find the Border field. You can use this field to set the pixel size of the border to be drawn around an image.

Also in the Layout area of the Image Properties dialog box, you will find the Horizontal spacing field and the Vertical spacing field. You can use the Horizontal spacing field to increase the pixel size of the horizontal margins surrounding the image. Similarly, you can use the Vertical spacing field to increase the pixel size of the vertical margins surrounding the image. Spacing is used to put white space between multiple images or text. If you use these spacing techniques, generally you will not want to use a border around the image.

Finally, specifying a low-resolution image is a timesaver that reduces the wait time and makes it possible for other elements on the page to be displayed before a high-resolution image is displayed. On the first pass through the document, Netscape-capable browsers load the images specified as Low-Res sources. When all other images in the document are loaded, the image specified in the Image Source field is loaded. Browsers that do not support the Low-Res sources load the image specified by the Image Source field.

In the Alternative Representations area of the Image Properties dialog box, you will find the Low-Res field. You can use this field to specify the name of a low-resolution image. The Browse button opens the Insert Image dialog box, which enables you to specify the name of any image imported to the current Web or the absolute path to an external image.

> **TIP**
>
> Try to keep your low-resolution image small in terms of byte size. A 2KB low-resolution image will load many times quicker than your 25KB high-resolution image. Netscape and Internet Explorer-enhanced browsers fade in the high-resolution image over the low-resolution image. The best low-resolution images act as placeholders and are the same size as the high-resolution images. In this way, the text on the page doesn't shift when the high-resolution image is displayed.

# Image Formats

Dozens of image formats are currently in use. Each computer platform has its own format and usually several popular formats. Drawing and design applications have their own proprietary formats. Some formats have become de facto standards because of their tremendous popularity. Other formats are so specialized that only a small group of users benefit from them. Maneuvering through this maze of formats could be a nightmare if you tried to create images for specific groups of users, because just when you think you have the right formats available for the right group of users, another group of users comes along. Fortunately, only two image formats are in wide use on the Web: GIF and JPEG.

## Using GIF

The graphics interchange format developed by CompuServe Information Service is the most widely supported and used image format in the world. All graphics-capable browsers support GIF, as do most drawing, design, and image processing programs. As you might expect, GIF is the favorite format for Web publishers.

Three variations of the GIF format are in use. The original specification, GIF87a, has been around since 1987. Because of its many advantages over other formats, GIF87a quickly became a de facto standard. Creators of drawing programs quickly discovered how easy it is to write a program that decodes and displays GIF images. GIF images are compressed to 20 to 25 percent of their original size with no loss in image quality, using a compression algorithm called LZW. Smaller images require less disk space to store, use less network bandwidth, and download faster. Additionally, because the LZW algorithm can be quickly decoded, images display almost immediately after downloading.

The next update to the format was the GIF89a specification. GIF89a added some useful features, including transparent GIFs. Using transparent GIFs, you can create images that seem to float on the page because they have a transparent background. (See the section on transparent GIFs later in this chapter, "GIFs with Transparent Backgrounds," for more information.)

All browsers support both the GIF87a and GIF89a formats, which is great news for Web publishers. The only drawback is that you can only use 256 colors in a single image. Although this limitation is restricting, it is actually good in most instances. Most images use only a few colors. This is especially true for icons, bullets, or other small features used to accent the page. Most computer systems can only display 256 colors. If you only use 256 colors, the computer will not have to dither the image to create the illusion of additional colors. An image with fewer colors that does not have to be dithered will be displayed faster, will use less disk space, and will also download more quickly.

Recently there has been a lot of controversy over the LZW compression used by GIF images. This compression technology is patented to the Unisys Corporation. In January 1995, Unisys announced that developers using the GIF format in their applications might have to pay a licensing fee. A licensing fee for GIF images could potentially apply to millions of software applications, including your favorite browser. As you might imagine, software developers around the world were in an uproar for months following the announcement. Some developers were so outraged that they removed support for GIF images from their applications. Other developers went in search of alternatives.

One alternative software developers looked to is GIF24. GIF24 has wide support from the Internet user community as well as from CompuServe Information Service. Unlike the original GIF specifications that support only 256 colors, GIF24 supports true 24-bit color, which enables you to use more than 16 million colors. One drawback to using 24-bit color is that most computers currently support only 256 colors. Before a 24-bit image can be displayed on an 8-bit screen, it must be dithered, which requires processing time and might also distort the image.

GIF24 uses a compression technique called PNG, and because there should never be a licensing fee associated with PNG, software developers are gladly turning to GIF24. In the coming months, you should start to see drawing, design, and image processing programs that support GIF24.

After you have inserted a JPEG image into a document, you can convert it to GIF format. To do this, select the image you want to convert, and then open the Image Properties dialog box. In the Type area, there is a field labeled GIF. When you check this field and click the OK button, FrontPage will automatically convert the image from JPEG to GIF. Keep in mind that the number of colors in the image might be reduced, and that the byte-size of the image file might become larger.

# Using JPEG

JPEG is a standard for still image compression that was developed by the Joint Photographic Expert Group. The goal of the JPEG members was to create a standard for storage and transmission of photograph-quality images. JPEG supports true 24-bit color.

True 24-bit color means that each pixel displayed on the screen has 24 bits of information associated with it. There are over 300,000 pixels on an average-size screen, so you can imagine how quickly true-color images can eat up your hard disk space. Fortunately, JPEG is a compression standard that uses powerful compression algorithms to dramatically reduce the disk space requirements for the image. Some images can be reduced to a twentieth of their original size.

Compressing an image into such a small size has its drawbacks. The first drawback is that JPEG compression is *lossy*, meaning that some information in the image is lost in the compression. Depending on how the image is compressed, this loss of information might or might not be perceivable. Another drawback to compressing the image into a small space is that it generally takes longer to decode the image for viewing. However, the actual time period for the decoding depends on the user's system and the amount of compression.

As you consider using JPEG compression for your images, you should consider carefully the types of images that you will compress. While JPEG enables you to use brilliant colors and provides quality support for complex images and digitized photographs, JPEG was not designed to be used for simple images with few colors. JPEG compression might distort simple images, especially if the image has few colors or large areas of the same color. Also, JPEG compression is not as effective as GIF in reducing the size of simple images. A simple image compressed with JPEG compression will be much larger than the same image compressed using GIF.

Because of the drawbacks to JPEG compression, JPEG was not widely supported until recently. One of the issues driving the growth of JPEG use is the controversy surrounding the GIF compression algorithm LZW. The controversy caused many software developers to take another look at JPEG. Most popular browsers, including NCSA Mosaic, Internet Explorer, and Netscape Navigator, will let you use inline JPEG images.

After you have inserted a GIF image into a document, you can convert it to JPEG format. To
do this, select the image you want to convert, and then open the Image Properties dialog box.
In the Type area, there is a field labeled JPEG. When you check this field, an additional field
labeled Quality is displayed. After you select a setting for quality, click the OK button.

Quality settings are often used with compression as a reality check describing the trade-off you
want to make between the resulting file size and the image quality. The range for quality settings in FrontPage is from 1 to 99. The higher the quality setting, the larger the resulting file
will be and the better the image quality. The default quality setting is 75.

Quality settings can be confusing because a quality setting of 75 does not mean that the resulting file will have 75 percent of the information. Compression ratios—which FrontPage sets
automatically—describe how much information to squeeze out of the file. The quality setting
is used to keep the ratio of compression realistic when compared to your need for a usable image.
Generally, your goal should be to select the lowest quality setting that meets your needs.

# Creating Your Own Images

You can create images using drawing, design, and image processing programs. Although commercial drawing tools, such as CorelDRAW! 6, are powerful and fully featured, shareware drawing tools, such as Paint Shop Pro, provide general-purpose image creation solutions.

Using image tools, you can create a simple graphical title or logo in a few minutes. You can use
image tools to alter existing images to meet your publishing needs and to convert these images
from other formats to the GIF or JPEG formats for use as inline images. You can easily create
and modify images, but you can dramatically improve the quality and friendliness of your images
through

- Proper use of color maps
- Interlacing GIFs when necessary
- Using GIFs with transparent backgrounds when necessary

## Using Color Maps

Color maps are one of the biggest problem areas in image design. All images have color palettes
associated with them that define a set of colors for the image. Each color displayed on the screen

is loaded into a color map that tracks colors displayed on the screen at any one time. A computer with an 8-bit display uses a color map that can hold 256 color values. A computer with a 24-bit display uses a color map that can hold 16.7 million color values.

Some computer systems reserve a subset of values in the color map for the standard display. Windows systems reserve 20 values in the color map to display standard colors. In addition to reserved colors, any colors currently displayed on the screen will be allocated in the color map. This means if your browser display takes up only part of the screen and other applications are running, the combined set of colors displayed on the screen by all the applications running will be allocated in the color map.

Although you can create 24-bit images with 16.7 million colors, most computers display only 8-bit images with 256 colors. This means that when you create an image that uses 16 million colors, most computers displaying the image will have to dither the image to create the illusion that there are extra colors in the image when in fact only 256 colors are displayed.

The distortion of the image caused by the dithering is often the least of your problems. Only 256 colors can be displayed at once on an 8-bit color display. This means there will be a conflict in the color map if the first image uses all 256 colors and the next image displayed on the screen at the same time uses additional colors. These additional colors will be mapped to the closest color value in the current color map, which can produce strange results. Your brilliant red will be mapped to orange, or even green, if that is the closest color value available in the current color map.

Some browsers try to solve the color mapping problem by limiting the number of colors any single image can use. This enables you to display more inline images on the screen at once. However, the cost of this trade-off is high. If your images use 256 colors and the browser restricts each image to a maximum of 50 colors, the images will have to be dithered to 50 colors each. The result is often a large reduction in the quality of your image.

The best way to ensure that your documents have no color map problem is to use a common color map for all images in a particular document. If you are creating original images, most drawing programs will let you select a palette of 256 colors to work with. You can add colors or change color definitions in the palette by removing or altering existing color definitions in the palette. After you are done working with the palette, you should save it, if possible, for future reference and use with your images.

Using a single color palette is easy if you are creating original images, but it is not easy if you are incorporating existing images into your documents. One way to overcome this problem is to use an image processing toolkit that can merge the color palettes used in multiple images to a common color palette. A useful image processing toolkit is the UNIX toolkit Netpbm. You can find Netpbm at three places:

```
ftp://ftp.cs.ubc.ca/ftp/archive/netpbm
```

```
ftp://ikaros.fysik4.kth.se/pub/netpbm
```

```
ftp://wuarchive.wustl.edu/graphics/graphics/
```

Unfortunately, mapping multiple images to a single color palette is useful only when the images either contain few colors or already use a similar set of colors. This is because the image processing tool merging the color palettes will generally merge the colors using a best-guess algorithm that tries to analyze how multiple colors that are close in value can best be merged into a single color value. Sometimes the tool guesses right and there is no distortion of your images. Other times the tool guesses wrong and your image is distorted. Ultimately, if your images contain few colors in the first place or use similar maps, there is little reason to merge the color maps. For simple images like these, you might want to preview your document using multiple browsers and worry about a conflict in the color map only when you find one.

Another way to fix the color mapping problem is to reorganize your document so that images with conflicting color maps cannot be displayed on the screen simultaneously. This solution to a color mapping problem is simple and fast.

Finally, a great way to avoid potential color map problems is to limit your use of colors in the images you create. For example, if you use a particular shade of red in one image, use the same shade of red in other images. In a palette of 16.7 million colors, there are probably 50 shades of red that are so close in hue that it is difficult to tell them apart. You can also track the values associated with colors in a table. When you are designing additional images for a particular document and want to use consistent colors, having color values at hand can be invaluable.

# Interlacing GIFs

An advanced feature you can incorporate into your GIF images is *interlacing*. Interlaced GIFs are displayed in four stages. As if you were zooming in on something from far away, during each stage, the image gets progressively more detailed until the image is finished loading. This is accomplished by separating the lines of pixels in the image into four groups of lines that are interlaced and displayed in stages. Your television and possibly your monitor display images in this manner.

Many experienced Web publishers do not understand the value of interlacing images. Interlaced images are timesavers to readers and are especially useful when you use large images in your documents. As the image loads in stages, readers can decide when they have seen enough of the image. Based on what they've seen, they might continue reading the document, they might make another selection, or they might wait to see the image finish loading. Readers value their time, and if you value their time as well, your documents will be friendly and well-perceived.

Older versions of browsers might not display GIFs in stages. Whether the image is a noninterlaced GIF or an interlaced GIF, these browsers wait until the entire image is downloaded and then display the GIF. Although not all browsers display interlaced GIFs in stages, all browsers can display interlaced GIFs.

Creating an interlaced GIF in FrontPage is as easy as selecting Interlaced from the Type area of the Image Properties dialog box. Be sure to save the updated image when you save your page.

# GIFs with Transparent Backgrounds

Using a GIF with a transparent background, you can create an image that appears to float on the page. This is extremely useful when you want to create a fancy title, logo, icon, or image that does not use a solid colored or rectangular background. Creating a GIF with a transparent background is easy. The first step is to assign a color to the image's transparency index.

The color value assigned to the transparency index indicates which color from the image's color map should be transparent. When a browser displays an image with a transparent background, it changes all occurrences of the color value in the transparency index to the color value for the background of the document. The best images to convert to GIF89a format are those with a single background color. This is important because you can only assign one color value to the transparency index, and if your image has several background colors, only one color will be transparent. Figure 10.18 shows the difference between an image with a normal background and one with a transparent background.

**FIGURE 10.18.**

*Images with transparent backgrounds appear to float on the page.*

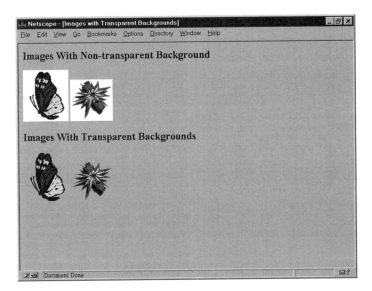

You should also make sure that your background color appears nowhere else in the image. Any part of your image that uses the color value specified in the transparency index will be displayed in the background color for the page. To avoid this problem, you should be sure that your images have a unique background color. When you are creating new images, this is easy. You simply select a color you do not plan to use in the image.

You can easily create an image with a transparent background in the FrontPage Editor. However, the image must be inserted into the current document. To make a color in the image transparent, use the following steps:

1. Select the image that you want to have a transparent background.
2. Click the Make Transparent button on the Image toolbar.
3. Move the tip of the pointer to the color in the image that you want to make transparent, and then click the left mouse button.
4. Now when you view the properties of the image, the Transparent field will be checked.

An image can have only one transparent color. You can change the transparent color at any time by repeating the steps listed in the preceding list and simply selecting a new color. If you select a new transparent color, the previous transparent color is returned to its original color. If you try to set a transparent background on an image that is not in GIF format, the FrontPage Editor prompts you to convert the image to GIF format. Keep in mind that the number of colors in the image might be reduced and that the byte-size of the image file might become larger.

**NOTE**

If you make a mistake when selecting a transparent color and decide you don't want any color to be transparent, you return the transparent color to its original state simply by selecting it again or by opening the Image Properties dialog box and deselecting the Transparent field.

# Finding Image Resources on the Internet

On the Internet, you can find dozens of image archives. Some of the best sites have hundreds of images you can preview and download if you like. Here's a list of some popular image archives:

NASA's image archive:

`http://hypatia.gsfc.nasa.gov/Images`

Smithsonian's image archive:

`gopher://bramble.er.usgs.gov/1ftp%3aphoto1.si.edu%40/`

Sunet's image archive:

`ftp://ftp.sunet.se/pub/pictures`

Sunsite's image archive:

`ftp://sunsite.unc.edu/pub/multimedia/pictures/`

University of Arizona's image archive:

`gopher://dizzy.library.arizona.edu:70/1`

Indiana University's image archive:

`gopher://enif.astro.indiana.edu:70/11/images`

Washington University's image archive:

`http://wuarchive.wustl.edu/multimedia/images/`

or

`http://wuarchive.wustl.edu/graphics/`

Icons come in handy when you need a small image to add a splash of color or to highlight a paragraph of text. You can also find icon archives on the Internet. Here is a list of some popular icon archives:

CERN's icon list:

`http://www.w3.org/hypertext/WWW/Icons`

University of Kansas icon list:

`http://titania.math.ukans.edu:80/icons/`

NCSA and UIUC's icon list:

`http://www.ncsa.uiuc.edu/General/Icons/`

Yahoo's icon list:

`http://www.yahoo.com/Computers/World_Wide_Web/Programming/Icons`

Many Web publishers would say that the Planet Earth home page maintains the definitive page for image resources. From the Planet Earth image page, you can find links to just about every imaginable type of image, including the following:

Space images
NASA images
Earth images and maps
Travel images
Medical images
Image archives
Icon archives
Flag archives

You can find the Planet Earth home page at

```
http://www.nosc.mil/planet_earth/images.html
```

A cool site if you are looking for pictures of animals is the Electronic Zoo. The Electronic Zoo/ NetVet image collection contains links to GIF and JPEG images of just about every animal you can think of. You can find the Electronic Zoo at

```
http://netvet.wustl.edu/pix.htm
```

To stay current with image concepts and resources, you might want to participate or lurk in the newsgroups related to images. Here are some newsgroups you might be interested in:

```
alt.binaries.pictures
alt.binaries.pictures.cartoons
alt.binaries.pictures.fractals
alt.binaries.pictures.misc
alt.binaries.pictures.utilities
```

# What Image Maps Are and Why You Want To Use Them

If you've browsed the Web, you've probably seen image maps. Image maps are high-power graphical menus. There is no better way to create easy, graphic-based ways for users to browse information at your Web site. Using an image map, you can create a graphic image with multiple hotspots. Each hotspot is a specific part of an image that the user can click on to access other documents and objects.

The wonderful thing about images is that you can pack the equivalent of hundreds of words into tiny symbols within your image map. Image maps are friendly and compulsively usable. Besides being friendly and usable, image maps enable you to pack a lot into a relatively small amount of space. Some image maps in use on the Web lead to dozens of pages, so almost everything on the image is a doorway to something new.

Don't worry about having to write a script to interpret image maps. FrontPage handles everything for you and enables you to use either client-side or server-side image maps. Most server-side image map programs follow either the NCSA or the CERN method for defining image maps, or a derivative of these methods. This is true even with Windows and Macintosh Web servers. FrontPage automatically generates the scripts that allow you to use the NCSA and CERN image mapping methods.

# Image Map Design

Under HTML 2.0, gateway scripts are used to process the input from image maps. When a user clicks on the image, the x,y coordinates are sent to the gateway script. The gateway script interprets these coordinates and uses a separately defined map file to determine the action to take. The map file contains a set of coordinates that define the hot areas. The coordinates are the horizontal and vertical locations of hot areas within the image.

The coordinates for image maps are determined in a slightly different way than what you might be used to. The upper-left corner of the image is at coordinate (0,0). As you move outward to the right in a straight line, the x coordinates grow larger. As you move downward in a straight line, the y coordinates grow larger. Figure 10.19 shows an enlarged view of an image that would make a good image map. Coordinates have been placed on the image to show some of the end points you might want to use to create this image map.

**FIGURE 10.19.**

*Enlarged view of an image map.*

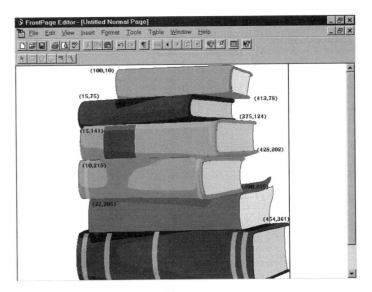

The process of creating an image map with defined hot areas is easier than you think. Hot areas for image maps are defined in terms of three geometric shapes:

- Circle
- Rectangle
- Polygon

Almost any picture can be turned into an image map, but the best images to use for image mapping have sections that include basic geometric patterns. Circular and rectangular areas are the easiest to define within images. When you need to, you can define complex shapes using polygons. The polygon shape allows for an object with three or more sides. For example, you could define the shape of a house with a garage as a polygon.

> **TIP**
>
> The key to using image maps in your documents is to remember the rules about images that were discussed earlier. The usefulness of images is not determined by their size or use of thousands of colors. The best images are simple and serve a specific purpose. Most image maps in use on the Web are between 20KB and 40KB in size. Often you will find that if you limit colors and bit depth and use appropriate compression, you can dramatically reduce the file size of your image map. This is especially true if you create a JPEG image and use a low quality setting to determine the amount of compression.

Until recently, many Web publishers who did not have access to CGI scripts could only dream of using image maps. Now there are two solutions that enable browsers to interpret image maps locally. Locally interpreted image maps are called *client-side image maps*. Although HTML 3.0 introduces what will become the standard for client-side image maps, many browsers have implemented Spyglass Corporation's method for handling image maps.

The HTML 3.0 specification introduces client-side handling of image maps and eliminates problems for Web publishers who don't have access to CGI. With client-side handling of image maps, all processing of the user input is handled by the browser. This means that when a user clicks on an image map, the browser interprets the map locally and performs the appropriate action. Not only is client-side handling of image maps several times faster than relying on a server to process the input, but it makes sense as the Web makes a transition toward an extremely efficient client-server environment.

Creating a client-side image map is easier than creating a server-side image map, especially because you don't have to worry about server support. You merely define the image map to go along with your figure.

Netscape, Internet Explorer, and Spyglass Mosaic browsers support Spyglass Corporation's extensions for the client-side handling of image maps. With this nonstandard extension, you define a client-side image map using the HTML 2.0 image tag. This extension uses several new tags to create client-side image maps.

Spyglass extensions for image maps follow an interesting implementation that enables older browsers to continue to support image maps as they have in the past and new browsers to use the client-side image map definition. To do this, you create a server-side map file and create a client-side map definition.

# Defining the Type of Image Map

FrontPage enables you to define client-side image maps, server-side image maps, or both. You specify image map settings in the FrontPage Explorer. The first step is to select Web Settings from the Tool menu. This opens the Web Settings dialog box. Now click on the Advanced tab.

Figure 10.20 shows the Advanced section for the Web settings dialog box. In the Image Maps area, you can define the type of image maps you want to use. The Style field has a pull-down that lets you specify the type of server-side image maps to use. The options on the Style field's pull-down menu are as follows:

| | |
|---|---|
| NCSA | Use NCSA style for server-side image maps. |
| CERN | Use CERN style for server-side image maps. |
| Netscape | Use Netscape style for server-side image maps. |
| None | Do not use server-side image maps. |

To use client-side image maps, select the Generate client-side image maps check box. If you want FrontPage to generate both client-side and server-side image maps, select a server-side image map style other than None, and check the Generate client-side image maps check box.

---

**TIP**

FrontPage generates all the code necessary to handle the type of image maps you've selected. The Personal Web Server handles server-side image maps using a Web bot. To use server-side image maps on an NCSA, CERN, or Netscape server, you will need to install the FrontPage extensions for your server. After these extensions are installed, you can export documents to your Web site and use server-side image maps. For more information about Web servers, using server extensions, and exporting documents, see Part VII, "Managing Your Web." This part of the book covers everything you need to know to manage Web sites successfully.

**FIGURE 10.20.**
*Setting the image map style.*

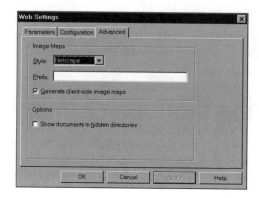

# Creating Image Maps with FrontPage

The FrontPage Editor integrates the best image map tool available. To use this tool, make sure you select Image toolbar from the View menu. The Image toolbar contains four buttons used to make image maps: Rectangle, Circle, Polygon, and Highlight Hotspots.

An image map can contain many hotspots. Hotspots can be rectangular, circular, polygonal, or a combination of the three. Generally, hotspots should not overlap. However, if they do overlap, the hotspot you defined last takes precedence.

## Creating Rectangular Hotspots

To create a rectangular hotspot in the FrontPage Editor, start by selecting the image in which you want to place the hotspot; then select the Rectangle button from the Image toolbar. After you decide what portion of the image you want covered by the rectangular hotspot, position the pointer where you want the first corner of the rectangle to be. Next, click and hold down the left mouse button, drag the rectangle until it encloses the portion of the image you want to be a rectangular hotspot, and then release the left mouse button.

When you release the mouse button, the Create Link dialog box will display on the screen. You can link to resources in an open page, the current Web, the World Wide Web, or a new page as discussed in Chapter 9, "Adding Features to the Page." At any time, you can update the link by double-clicking on the hotspot, which reopens the Create Link dialog box. When you have finished, click the OK button.

## Creating Circular Hotspots

To create a circular hotspot in the FrontPage Editor, start by selecting the image in which you want to place the hotspot; then select the Circle button from the Image toolbar. After you decide what portion of the image you want covered by the circular hotspot, position the pointer where you want the center point of the circle to be located. Next, click and hold down the left mouse button, drag the rectangle until it encloses the portion of the image you want to be a circular hotspot, and then release the left mouse button.

When you release the mouse button, the Create Link dialog box will display on the screen. You can link to resources in an open page, the current Web, the World Wide Web, or a new page as discussed in Chapter 9. At any time, you can update the link by double-clicking on the hotspot, which reopens the Create Link dialog box. When you are done, click the OK button.

# Creating Polygon Hotspots

To create a polygonal hotspot in the FrontPage Editor, start by selecting the image in which you want to place the hotspot, and then select the Rectangle button from the Image toolbar. After you decide what portion of the image you want covered by the polygonal hotspot, position the pointer where you want the first point of the polygon to be located.

Next, click the left mouse button. This creates a pen line that you can move to the next point of the polygon. Move to the next point of the polygon and click the left mouse button. This will create a second end point for the polygon. Keep drawing lines until you complete the polygon.

When you complete the polygon by fully enclosing the specified area, the Create Link dialog box will open automatically. You can link to a resource in an open page, the current Web, the World Wide Web, or a new page as discussed in Chapter 9. At any time, you can update the link by double-clicking on the hotspot, which reopens the Create Link dialog box. When you are done, click the OK button.

> **TIP**
>
> FrontPage can automatically fill in the last end point of the polygon for you. To do this, double-click the left mouse button after you have drawn the next-to-last side of the polygon. FrontPage will complete the polygon and display the Create Link dialog box.

# Highlighting Hotspots

As you create the image map or after you are done, you can check the accuracy of your image map using the Highlight Hotspots button on the Image toolbar. When you click this button, the FrontPage Editor shows only the outlines of the image map you created.

In Figure 10.21, the map definitions are highlighted for the sample image map shown earlier. You can select individual map definitions by clicking on them. A selected image map definition is shown in black. If you double-click on the image map definition, you can edit the related link information.

**FIGURE 10.21.**

*Viewing map definitions.*

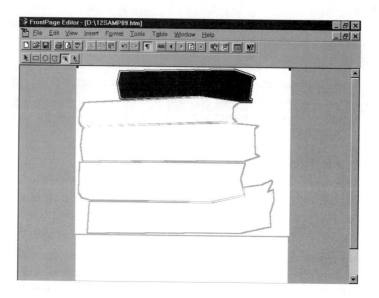

# Editing Hotspots in Images

Often you will want to edit a hotspot, resize it, move it to a new location, or delete it. Before you can edit the hotspot, you must select it by clicking on it. You can tell when a hotspot is selected because the resize handles are displayed on each of its sides and corners. You can delete an unwanted hotspot by pressing the Delete or Backspace key after you've selected it.

---

**TIP**

You can move between selected hotspots, using the Tab key or Shift+Tab. You can also select multiple hotspots. To do this, hold down the Shift button and click on each hotspot.

---

You can move any hotspot to a new location. To move a hotspot, click on it, hold the left mouse button, and then drag the hotspot to its new position. You can also nudge a selected hotspot into place pixel by pixel with the arrow keys.

You can resize any hotspot to make it larger or smaller. When you move the mouse point over the side of a selected hotspot, the pointer changes to the resize pointer—a pointer with arrows on either end. If this pointer is visible, you can resize the hotspot by clicking and holding down the left mouse button and then moving the pointer to resize the hotspot as appropriate. When you are done resizing the hotspot, release the mouse button.

## Setting a Default Link for an Image Map

All image maps can have a default link. The default link is used if the user selects an area of the image that is not defined or has a browser that does not support client-side image maps.

You can set the default link in the URL field of the Image Properties dialog box. To display this dialog box, double-click on the image, select the image and then press Alt+Enter, or select Properties from the Edit menu. If you know the URL to the resource you want to use as the default reference, you can enter this in the URL field. If you do not know the URL, click on the Browse button to open the Edit Link dialog box.

# Summary

Everywhere you look on the Web, you will find Web publications that use images. You can use images to add highlights, navigation mechanisms, logos, page titles, illustrations, and maps to the hot features at your site. Although there are many image formats, the primary image formats in use on the Web are JPEG and GIF.

Images are a basic medium for your publications. Image maps serve as graphical menus that users can click on to access parts of your Web site. Although there is no better way to create easy, graphic-based ways for users to browse your Web site, you should design your image maps carefully so they are useful and aren't byte-hogs.

# Using Forms and the Form Page Wizard

**11**

*by William Robert Stanek*

In the previous chapter, you learned how to create wonderful Web publications that include images and image maps. Yet now that you've created the beginnings of a wonderful publication, how do you get feedback, comments, and praise from visitors that will make all your hard work worthwhile? The answer is easy; add a fill-out form to an appropriate place in your Web publication, and invite the reader to participate.

HTML 2.0 introduced forms, and Web publishing has never been the same. Forms are the primary way to add interactivity and two-way communication to your Web publications. They provide friendly interfaces for inputting data, searching databases, and accessing indexes. To submit a fill-out form, the user only has to click on the Submit button. Your forms can contain pull-down menus, push buttons, text, and graphics.

Before FrontPage, processing input from a form required a CGI script. As anyone who has created a CGI script knows, CGI scripts can range in complexity from a simple 15-line script that processes basic input to a 1,000-line script that performs advanced processing. FrontPage introduces *Web bots* that automatically process the input of forms for you. These Web bots perform the basic to intermediate-level scripting tasks used most frequently by Web publishers. This means that most Web publishers will never have to create a CGI script again.

In this chapter, you will learn all about forms—what they are, how to use them, and much more.

# What Forms Are and Why You Want To Use Them

In our daily lives, we see forms all the time:

- The forms you fill out at the doctor's office
- The credit card bills that require you to fill in the dollar amount in tiny boxes, subtly reminding you to make sure to include all the zeros that go along with the digit
- The surveys and questionnaires you receive in the mail
- The juicy compatibility polls in a magazine that you fill out at the checkout counter

Although you might not think of these items as forms, all of them require you to fill in information or make selections from groups of numbered or lettered items. When you submit a printed form, someone on the receiving end has to file these forms away. In an increasingly computerized world, this usually means entering the information into a database or spreadsheet. Major companies hire dozens of people for the specific task of entering into the company database the thousands of forms that flood the company every day. This is a huge expense and a tremendous burden on the company.

Now imagine a virtual office where thousands of forms are entered into the company database every day without a single worker. The forms are processed efficiently, almost instantly, and the customer can get feedback within seconds of submitting a form. The cost for what otherwise would be a mammoth undertaking is a few hours—the time it takes you to design a fill-out form and add a Web bot or CGI script to process the information.

Using forms, you open a two-way communication channel between you and visitors to your Web publications. Visitors can send comments directly to you. You can add a Web bot or create CGI scripts to process the input automatically. In this way, readers can get immediate results. You can e-mail the input to your e-mail address. This way, you can respond to readers' questions and comments easily and personally. You can also set up a script to process the input, give results to the reader, and send yourself e-mail.

The scripting part of the process runs in the background, and the fill-out form is what the reader sees up close and personal. Readers can interact with forms by entering information in spaces provided, by making selections from pull-down menus, by activating push buttons, and by submitting the data for instant processing. Figure 11.1 shows a simple form with areas for text entry. This form is used to enter product orders online and was created with the Form Page Wizard in less than five minutes.

**FIGURE 11.1.**

*An online order form.*

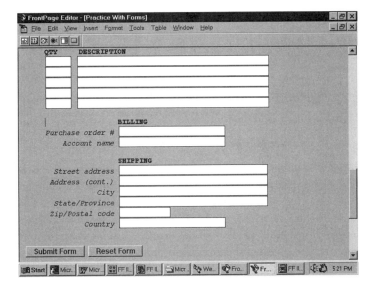

# Form Design

Although creating a form is easy, designing a good form is not always easy. Some publishers use generic all-purpose forms that fail because the form wasn't designed with a specific purpose in mind. The key to designing forms is to use them for a specific purpose. When you want to get feedback from readers, you create a form for reader feedback. When you want to take orders online, you create a form for submitting online orders.

Designing forms that are useful to readers and to you as the publisher should be your primary goal. A form that is useful to readers will be used. A form that is useful to you as the publisher makes your job easier. The key to creating forms that are useful to readers and you as the publisher is also in form design. As you go through the steps for designing forms, keep the following guidelines in mind:

1. A form that is useful to the reader is

   - Friendly
   - Well-organized
   - Sized correctly

2. A form that is useful to you as the publisher does the following:

   - Uses uniquely named and easily identifiable keywords for fields
   - Allows for brevity of processing and quick indexing whenever possible
   - Provides subtle guidance to the reader on the amount of input you are looking for

With these rules in mind, you should always provide descriptions along with form fields. As with print forms, the descriptions for fields should be brief. This makes the form easier to read.

Here is a wordy field description:

> *You should enter your full name in the adjacent text window using your first name, middle initial, and last name as appropriate.*

Here is a better field description:

> *Please enter your name (First, Middle Initial, Last).*

Input fields should be correctly sized to ensure that they are usable. A good field size ensures that all key information entered by the user is visible in the input area. For a telephone number, you could define an input field 12 characters in length. This would allow customers to enter their phone number and area code. If a reader puts parentheses around the area code, the length of the input field should be stretched to 14 characters. If the reader lives in another country, the length of the input field should be stretched to at least 16 characters.

The form itself should be correctly sized and well organized to ensure that readers will take the time to fill it out. A good form balances the number of fields against the length of the fields. This means that a form that requires lengthy input from readers should have few fields, and a form that requires the reader to make many selections but requires limited actual input could have many fields.

# Creating the Form

FrontPage provides both a manual method and an automatic method of creating forms and setting up form elements. Using the manual method, you build the form using FrontPage's WYSIWYG interface. Using the Form Wizard, FrontPage guides you through every step of the form creation process, making the form creation process mostly automated. To give you a solid understanding of how forms work, this chapter focuses first on the manual form building process and then on the automated process.

Within a form, you can use any valid HTML element. Although multiple forms can be on a single Web page, you cannot create subforms within a form. Primarily this is because the form must be submitted to be processed in a specific manner. The way forms are submitted is based on the following criteria:

> The method used to submit the form
>
> The action to be performed when the form is submitted
>
> The optional type of encoding to be performed on the form

FrontPage lets you set these properties for forms using the Form Properties box, which is shown in Figure 11.2. You can access this properties box whenever you add a form element by clicking on the Form button in the element's properties box or by opening the element's properties box and clicking on the Form button. As you can see, this dialog box has two main areas. The Form Handler area is used to define the type of handler that will process the input from the form. The Hidden Fields area is used to define form fields not visible to the user.

**FIGURE 11.2.**

*Setting form properties.*

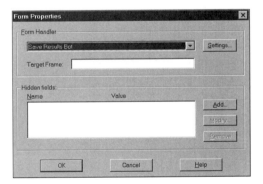

# Defining Form Handlers

You can select a form handler using the Form Properties box. Just as the form creation process in FrontPage is either mostly automated or mostly manual, so is the form handling process. FrontPage enables you to choose one of four form handlers:

Custom CGI script

Discussion bot

Registration bot

Save Results bot

After you choose a form handler from the pull-down menu, click on the Settings button to define settings for the handler. Each handler has its own unique properties and must be set up separately.

CGI scripts are external programs that run on the Web server. You can use CGI scripts to process the input from forms. The standard that defines how external programs are used on Web servers and how they interact with other applications is the common gateway interface. If you want to use CGI scripts to process your form data, you might have to write the script yourself. Using CGI scripts with FrontPage is the subject of Chapter 30, "Writing CGI Scripts."

Discussion groups allow users to interact on the Web, and the Discussion bot automates this process. Creating discussion groups and using the discussion bot handler is the subject of Chapter 27, "Creating and Managing Discussion Groups."

Often you will want to restrict access to an area of your site or require users to register before they can use key areas of your site. You can use the registration bot to do this. For detailed information on using the registration bot, see Chapter 20, "Automation with FrontPage's WebBots." See also Chapter 18, "Creating Web Pages with FrontPage's Templates," for more information on creating a user registration form.

The Save Results bot is the most common type of form handler. This bot lets you save the form data to a file or database. In this chapter, we will take an in-depth look at using this bot to handle form data.

# Hidden Fields in Forms

You can set hidden fields using the Form Properties box. Hidden fields are not displayed and are only useful to provide essential input to a script, database, or file. Hidden elements have two attributes:

Name    The keyword associated with the input field

Value   The value of the field

Use hidden fields as a way to identify the form used to submit an entry or to insert vital information before each entry in a flat file or database. To add a hidden field, click on the Add button in the Form Properties dialog box, which displays the Add Name/Value Pair dialog box. After you've added a hidden value, you can modify or remove it at any time.

# Saving the Results of the Form

Form handlers are set with the Form Properties box. Because the most common type of form handler is the Save Results bot, this section takes an in-depth look at using this bot to handle form data.

Usually it is best to specify how you want the results of the form to be saved when you are defining the first element of the form. However, you can specify this information at any time by accessing a form element's properties box and clicking on the Form button. After you choose the Save Results form handler from the pull-down menu in the Form Handler area of the Form Properties box, click on the Settings button to define settings for the handler.

The Save Results handler has two configuration pages that you can access by clicking on the Results or Advanced tab.

## Setting Up the Results Tab

The Results tab for the Form Properties box is shown in Figure 11.3. Typically the first tab you will set defaults for is the Results tab. As you can see from Figure 11.3, the Results tab has many options.

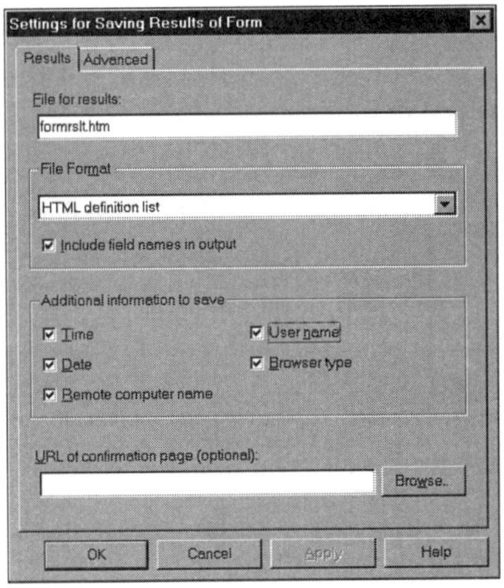

**FIGURE 11.3.**

*Defining the format of results.*

The File For Results field enables you to specify the name of the file to store the results. This field can be a relative or absolute URL path to the file's location on your server. If the results file does not exist, the Save Results bot will create the file the first time the form is submitted.

The File Format field enables you to select the format of the results file from the drop-down list. You should choose the format carefully. If you are unsure of the format you will want your data in, it might be best to experiment with file formats on your local Web. The default format is normal text formatted as HTML paragraphs. The complete list of formats for results includes

- **HTML.** Results are stored in an HTML document and formatted as HTML paragraphs. This is the default format.
- **HTML definition list.** Results are stored in an HTML document and formatted using a definition list. The field names are stored as terms, and values input by the user are indented like definitions.
- **HTML bulleted list.** Results are stored in an HTML document and formatted using a bulleted list.
- **Formatted text within HTML.** Results are stored as formatted text in an HTML document.
- **Formatted text.** Results are stored in ASCII text format without HTML markup.
- **Text database using comma as a separator.** Results are stored in a plain ASCII text file with a comma separating field names and values. This is a good format to use with a database or other application.
- **Text database using tab as a separator.** Results are stored in a plain ASCII text file with a tab separating field names and values. This is a good format to use with a database, spreadsheet, or other application.
- **Text database using space as a separator.** Results are stored in a plain ASCII text file with a space separating field names and values. This is another good format to use with a database or other application.

When the Include field names in output field is checked, both the name and the value of each form field are saved to the results file. When this field is not checked, only values are written to the file.

FrontPage lets you save additional information with the results, which you might find helpful when you process or analyze the results. This information is appended after the form data and includes

- **Browser type.** The type of browser accessing the page as specified by the browser in the HTTP_USER_AGENT variable.
- **Date.** The date the form was submitted.
- **Remote computer name.** The name of the remote computer used to submit the form.

- **Time.** The time the form was submitted.
- **User name.** The name of the user accessing the page.

---

**TIP**

The authors highly recommend tracking most or all of the additional information if you plan to do any analysis of traffic to your Web site. However, this information might not be in a form you will immediately recognize without a little help. For example, if the user submits the form with the Netscape Navigator, the browser type you will see on your results page is Mozilla. See Chapter 30, "Writing CGI Scripts," for complete details on using these and similar variables to identify browser type and users.

---

The final item you can specify in the Results tab is the URL of a confirmation page. Whenever a user submits a form, the confirmation page is displayed to show that the form was submitted successfully. The overwhelming majority of Web publishers use confirmation pages, and you probably will want to as well. To select a confirmation page you've already created in the current Web, click on the Browse button. For this reason, if you do not specify a confirmation page, the Save Results bot creates one automatically.

## Setting Up the Advanced Tab

The Advanced tab for the Form Properties box is shown in Figure 11.4. If you have advanced needs for storing form results, you will use this tab.

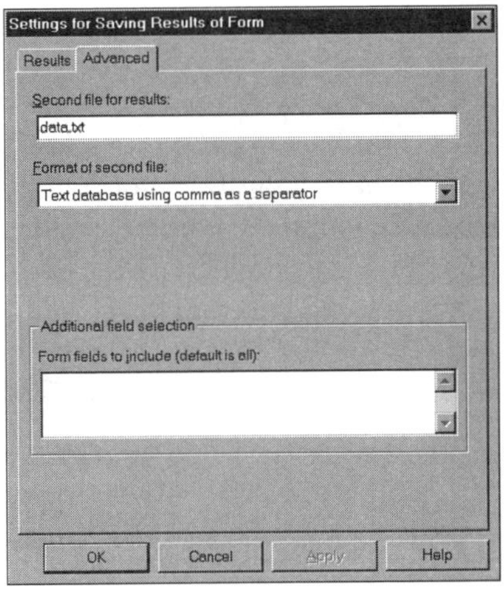

**FIGURE 11.4.**

*Defining settings for advanced needs.*

The primary use for this tab is to allow you to specify a second file for the results. In this way, you can store the results in an easy-to-read format such as HTML and an easily manipulated format such as text with commas for field separators. The Advanced tab also lets you specify the fields you want to store in the second file and the order in which those fields are stored in the file.

# Adding Input Fields to the Form

Before you create your first form in FrontPage, you should activate the Forms toolbar. You can do this by selecting Forms Toolbar from the View menu. The Forms toolbar has six buttons, which are used to add the six key form elements:

- One-line text boxes
- Scrolling text boxes
- Check boxes
- Radio buttons
- Drop-down menus
- Push buttons

These elements designed specifically for use within forms are what make fill-out forms useful and interactive. Associated with each form element is a keyword that describes the type of data the element expects and a value input by the user.

Although the keyword cannot include spaces, the input from the user can. For example, a form element could ask for the user's full name. A keyword describing this element could be called full_name, and a user could submit the value "William R. Stanek". You could then store this input into a database, a flat file, or an HTML document.

## Using One-Line Text Boxes

One-line text boxes are basic input fields for text. To insert this form element, click on the One-line Text Box button on the Forms toolbar. This opens the Text Box Properties dialog box shown in Figure 11.5. After you define the properties for this element and click the OK button, the element is inserted into your document.

**FIGURE 11.5.**

*Defining properties for one-line text boxes.*

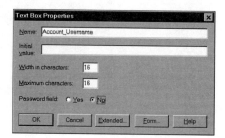

As you can see, the dialog box is used to define settings for the one-line text box you are creating. These values are

| | |
|---|---|
| Name | The keyword associated with the input field. |
| Initial value | An initial value for the field that will be displayed in the text area. The user can add to this information and if necessary delete the information to enter new information. |
| Width in characters | The width of the input field, expressed as the number of characters for the text area. |
| Maximum characters | The maximum allowable length of the field. Beware. If this attribute is not set, there is no limit. |

To allow users to enter password information without revealing the password to onlookers, you can check the Password radio button. All text entered in a password field is seen as asterisks. The asterisks are used only to mask the characters and do not affect how the text is passed to your gateway script. By combining a password input field and an input field for the user's login ID, you can pass this information to a script or Web bot that would validate the user's access to protected areas of your Web site.

---

**TIP**

At any time, you can reopen the properties dialog box associated with an input field by following these steps:

1. Double-clicking on the input field.
2. Selecting the input field and choosing Properties from the Edit menu.
3. Selecting the input field and pressing Alt+Enter.

---

A sample form that uses one-line text boxes is shown in Figure 11.6.

# Using Scrolling Text Boxes

Scrolling text boxes have more functionality than the one-line text boxes because they enable you to define text windows of any size to display on the screen. Text windows can be used to input large amounts of data. Although the size of the window is defined in rows and columns, you have no real control over how much data the user can enter into the window. This is because text windows have vertical and horizontal scroll bars that enable the user to scroll left to right as well as up and down.

Scrolling text boxes can have default text. Default text provided for a text window is displayed exactly as entered. Although the user can erase any default input if necessary, initial input should be used primarily to save the user time.

**FIGURE 11.6.**

*Using one-line text boxes.*

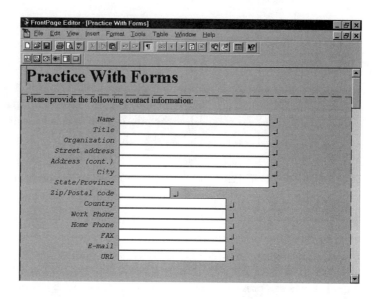

To insert this form element, click on the Scrolling Text Box button on the Forms toolbar. This opens the Scrolling Text Box Properties dialog box shown in Figure 11.7. After you define the properties for this element and click the OK button, the element is inserted into your document.

**FIGURE 11.7.**

*Defining properties for scrolling text boxes.*

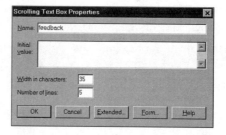

As you can see, the dialog box is used to define settings for the scrolling text box you are creating. These values are

| | |
|---|---|
| Name | The keyword associated with the input field. |
| Initial value | An initial value for the field that will be displayed in the text area. The user can add to this information and, if necessary, delete the information to enter new information. |
| Width in characters | The width of the input field, expressed as the number of characters for the text area. |
| Number of lines | The height of the text window in number of lines. |

A sample form that uses scrolling text boxes is shown in Figure 11.8.

**FIGURE 11.8.**

*Using scrolling text boxes.*

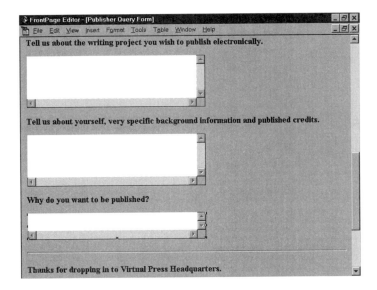

## Using Check Boxes and Radio Buttons

The checkbox input field creates a box that can be checked by a user. The radio button input field creates a circular button that can be checked by a user. Some browsers display selected check boxes and radio buttons using text—an x for a check box and a round bullet for a radio button. Other browsers display check boxes and radio buttons as graphical push buttons with a 3-D flair.

Although the primary difference between a check box and a radio button might seem to be their shape, there is a fundamental difference in the way they behave. Check boxes allow users to make multiple selections. Radio buttons, on the other hand, allow users to make only one selection.

With this in mind, you want to use radio buttons with a single associated keyword value when the user should make only one selection, such as a choice of A, B, or C. You want to use check boxes with multiple associated keyword values when the user can make multiple selections, such as a choice of all or any of A through E.

For each check box or radio button element, you must specify the default properties. The Radio Button Properties box is shown in Figure 11.9. After you define the properties for this element and click the OK button, the element is inserted into your document.

Values you can set in this dialog box are

| | |
|---|---|
| Group Name | The keyword associated with a group of radio button input fields. |
| VALUE | The value to assign if the user activates the check box or radio button. |

| | |
|---|---|
| Selected | The check box or radio button is automatically selected when viewed. The best use of this attribute is for default options that can be unchecked if necessary. |
| Not selected | The check box or radio button is not selected when viewed and can be checked by the user. |

**FIGURE 11.9.**

*Defining properties for radio buttons.*

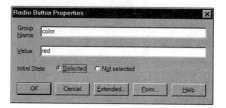

The dialog boxes associated with check boxes and radio buttons are nearly identical. The only difference is that the Check Box Properties box lets you specify a name and the Radio Button Property box lets you specify a group name.

Figure 11.10 depicts how check boxes and radio buttons can be used in a form. The check box groups will accept multiple responses, but the radio button groups will only accept a single response.

**NOTE**

Keep in mind that although the value and label for radio buttons and check boxes are sometimes set with the same key word or phrase, labels and values are not used in the same way. A label is the text that the reader sees. A value is the actual value passed to the form handler.

## Using Drop-Down Menus

Creating drop-down menus for your forms is more difficult than creating other elements. Each element in a drop-down menu is a selection. In some menus, all the selections are completely visible on the screen. In other menus, some or most elements are hidden until the reader activates the menu.

To insert this form element, click on the Drop-Down Menu button on the Forms toolbar. This opens the Drop-Down Menu Properties box shown in Figure 11.11. After you define the properties for this element and click the OK button, the element is inserted into your document.

**FIGURE 11.10.**

*Using radio buttons and check boxes.*

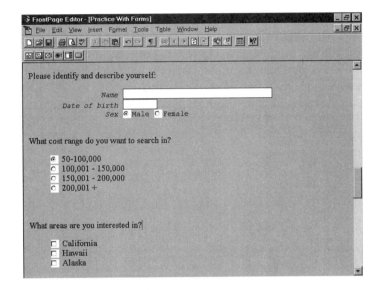

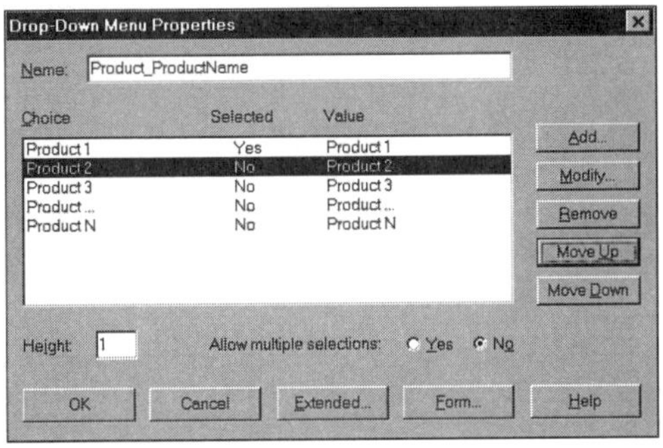

**FIGURE 11.11.**

*Defining properties for drop-down menus.*

As you can see, this dialog box has a lot of options. You use the Name field to specify a key-word for the selection menu. The Add button is used to add selections to the menu. Each selection is identified by a word or phrase the user can select, a value associated with this choice, and the initial state. By default, the value associated with the choice is set to the keyword you have used to identify the choice. The initial state of the choice is either selected or not selected.

The Height field is used to set the number of menu selections displayed on the screen without the user having to activate the drop-down menu. By default, the user can select only one option from the menu. To allow the user to make multiple selections, select the Yes button in the Allow multiple selections field. Most browsers allow you to make multiple selections by holding down the control button on the keyboard and clicking with the left mouse button when the pointer is over the additional item you want to select.

Figure 11.12 shows several types of selection menus. The first example shows a menu with all selections displayed on the screen by default. The second example shows a drop-down menu with the selections hidden. On-screen menus occupy more space. You should consider using on-screen menus when the user can make multiple selections and pull-down menus when the user can only make one selection. The final example shows a menu with part of the selections displayed and part of the selections hidden. The scroll bar can be used to access additional items.

**FIGURE 11.12.**

*Using drop-down menus.*

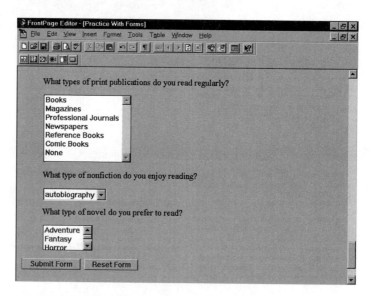

To add selections to your menu, click the Add button on the Drop-Down Menu Properties box. This opens the Add Choice dialog box shown in Figure 11.13.

**FIGURE 11.13.**

*Adding selections to the menu.*

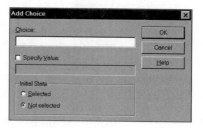

After you've added selections, you can modify those selections, manipulate their order, or remove them using the buttons in the Drop-Down Menu Properties box. To do this, select the item you want to edit, and then click on the appropriate button.

# Using Push Buttons

Push buttons allow you to submit or clear a form. The Push button dialog box is shown in Figure 11.14.

To open this dialog box, select Push button on the Forms toolbar. After you define the properties for this element and click the OK button, the element is inserted into your document.

By default, Reset buttons are labeled with the value of Reset and Submit buttons are labeled with the value Submit. You change the default value in the Push Button Properties box by specifying a new label in the Value/label field such as Clear Form or Submit Form.

**FIGURE 11.14.**

*Defining properties for push buttons.*

Using the Name field, you can track which Submit button a user clicked. This provides another way of tracking the precise form used to submit input. Figure 11.15 shows a sample form with Submit and Reset buttons. As you see, each form only needs one Submit button and one Reset button.

**FIGURE 11.15.**

*Using push buttons.*

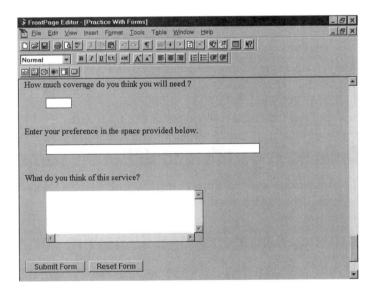

# Using the Form Wizard

Now that you know how to create forms, the next topic is how the form creation process can be automated to perfection. The Form Wizard is optimized for creating forms with common types of inputs. By default, the Form Wizard uses the Save Results bot as the form handler for your form and stores the results to a Web page or file. This section is a walkthrough of everything the Form Wizard has to offer.

You will use the Form Wizard when you want to create a new page that uses a form. To launch the Form Wizard, select New from the File menu or press Ctrl+N; then in the New Page dialog box, click on Form Page Wizard. This displays the Form Page Wizard dialog box shown in Figure 11.16.

**FIGURE 11.16.**

*Using the Form Page Wizard.*

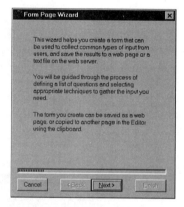

The buttons at the bottom of the dialog box are standard throughout the form creation process. At any time, you can move to the previous or next phase of the creation process using the Back or Next buttons. When you've fully defined the form, you can click the Finish button, and the FrontPage Editor will create the form you've designed.

## Defining Page Title and URL in the Form Wizard

To begin, click the Next button. As you can see from Figure 11.17, the first step is to name the page and define a URL for the page.

## Adding, Modifying, and Removing Form Elements

After you've told FrontPage where to store the page in the current Web, click the Next button again to continue. Figure 11.18 shows the currently defined form elements. From this page, you can add, modify, and remove form elements using the Add, Modify, and Remove buttons respectively. After you've added two or more form elements, you can modify the order of a selected element using the Move Up and Move Down buttons. To completely erase all form elements and start over, you can use the Clear List button.

**FIGURE 11.17.**

*Defining page title and URL.*

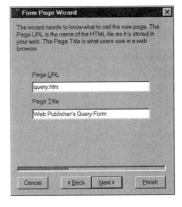

**FIGURE 11.18.**

*Defining and editing form elements.*

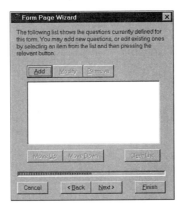

# Selecting the Type of Input

Most forms ask the user a series of questions. The Form Page Wizard enables you to select from a list of common questions used in forms. To access this list, click on the Add button. If the page shown in Figure 11.19 is not visible, use the Back or Next button to get to the page that shows the list of currently defined questions.

When you click on the Add button, you can select the type of input you'd like to collect from the user. As you can see from Figure 11.19, the associated page has three sections: The first section provides a selectable list of common information collected from users; the second area provides a brief description of the input fields the Form Page Wizard will generate based on the information type; and the third section enables you to edit the question associated with the information type.

**FIGURE 11.19.**

*Selecting the type of input.*

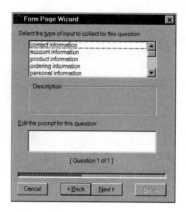

After selecting the type of input you'd like to collect, click on the Next button. This displays a page that you can use to select specific input fields related to the form question, such as name, address, and phone number. Figure 11.20 shows the input fields you can select for contact-related information.

**FIGURE 11.20.**

*Defining input fields for a form question.*

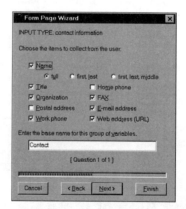

To define another question or set of input fields for the form, click on the Next button and follow the procedure for adding form elements.

## Presentation Options

When you have finished defining element sets for the form, proceed to the Presentation Options page using the Next button. As you can see from Figure 11.21, this page enables you to specify the overall format for form questions and will also generate a table of contents for the page. Usually, form questions are formatted as a numbered list and you might want to use this format as well.

**FIGURE 11.21.**

*Setting presentation options.*

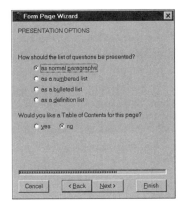

## Output Options

After specifying the presentation options, click on the Next button to select the output options. The Output Options page is shown in Figure 11.22. By default, the Form Page Wizard saves the results from a form in a Web page called `formrslt.htm`. You can change the default setting to save the results to a file or specify a CGI script that will process the form results. You can also change the default filename for the results, by entering the name of the file without the HTML extension in the appropriate field.

**FIGURE 11.22.**

*Setting output options.*

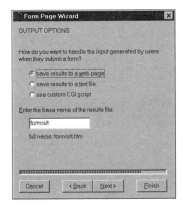

## Finishing the Page and Closing the Form Wizard

To finish the Page and close the Form Wizard, click on the Finish button. You can do this from any page within the Form Wizard. FrontPage will now create your form.

# Summary

Forms add interactivity and provide friendly interfaces for inputting data, searching databases, and accessing indexes. Designing forms that are useful to readers and to you as the publisher should be your primary goal. Using the FrontPage Editor, you can quickly add form elements using the Forms toolbar. With the Form Page Wizard, you can create advanced forms in under five minutes.

# Creating Tables with FrontPage

# 12

*by William Robert Stanek*

**IN THIS CHAPTER**

Tables are one of the most sought-after features in the HTML specification, and until recently, the Netscape Navigator was the only mainstream browser to support this feature. Yet the Netscape Navigator did much more than merely support HTML tables; it helped pioneer the use of tables in Web publishing. In recognition of this, the current table model used in HTML 3.2 is fully compatible with Netscape's table definition.

# Table Design

No doubt you've seen tables in publications, like those used throughout *Microsoft FrontPage Unleashed*, and you might have used tables in your own documents as well. In general, tables have a caption and one or more rows of data organized into columns. The columns of data contain individual cells. Each individual cell is either a header or a data set. A table can have several levels of headings, and all headings serve to identify the data sets contained in the body of the table.

After breaking tables into their component parts, the developers of the table model looked at how the data within a table should be displayed by browsers. This was a major area of concern. Web publishers have no direct control over the size of the window used to display a table, which means that table data defined in absolute terms, such as pixels or characters, could easily get obscured or clipped. To avoid this, the developers made it possible to define column width in relative terms as well as absolute terms.

Defining a table in relative terms enables you to specify a size that is a percentage of the current window size. The browser displaying the table will size the table accordingly, using the currently defined font. The default size for a table is the current window size. Thus, if you do not specify a width for your table, the width is set to 100 percent.

The table model is dynamic in other ways as well. You can do any of the following:

- Add images to your table by defining the image within a cell of your current table.
- Add lists to your table by defining the list within a cell of your current table.
- Build forms within your table by defining the form within a cell of your current table.
- Create tables within your table by defining the new table within a cell of your current table.

The table model has advanced significantly since the first draft of HTML 3.0 and is now a separate specification that has been ratified as a Request For Comments. In many ways, the current model is more flexible and more powerful. This flexibility and power stems largely from the control you have over the way tables are used in your documents. Figure 12.1 shows a sample table.

**NOTE**

Like most current authoring tools, FrontPage supports the table model set forth in the HTML 3.2 specification, which is a subset of the HTML 3 table model standard. As of July 1996, Internet Explorer 3.0 is the only browser to fully support the HTML table model standard. The full table model allows you to add many extras to your tables, including individual colors for cells and precise alignment of text.

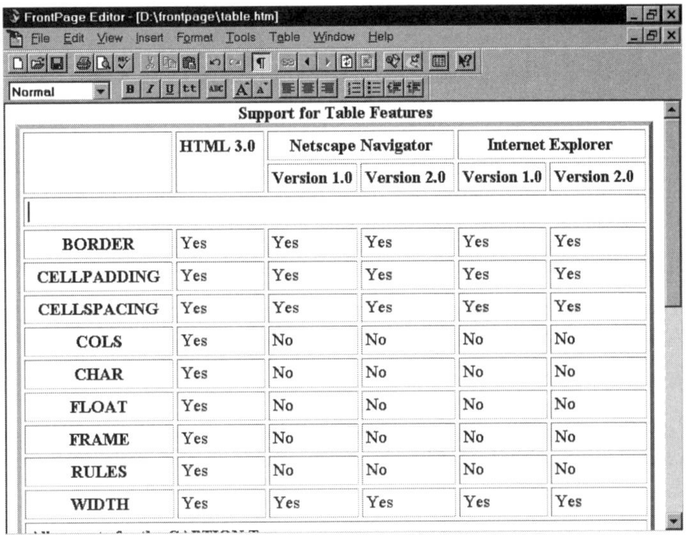

**FIGURE 12.1.**

*Tables are powerful additions to your documents.*

## Creating a Table

To insert a table using the FrontPage Editor, select Insert Table from the Table menu. The editor will display the Insert Table dialog box shown in Figure 12.2. Using this dialog box, you can define the basic layout of your table. In the Size area, you specify the number of rows and columns for the table, and FrontPage determines the number of cells needed to fill the table.

Text in your documents can flow around tables. By default, tables are aligned with the left margin, and text will flow around the right side of the table. You can also align tables with the right margin, which will cause text to flow around the left side of the table. Or you can place the table in the center of the page, in which case no text will flow around the table. To set the alignment of the table, use the Alignment field in the Layout area of the Insert Table dialog box.

Most tables have a border. To set the pixel width of the border, use the Border field. You can use the value zero as a design technique to remove extra white space around the table.

**FIGURE 12.2.**

*Creating the table.*

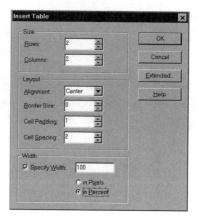

In terms of the readability of your table, cell padding and cell spacing are the most important attributes you will define for the table. Cell padding is used to specify the spacing within data cells. Cell spacing is used to specify the spacing between data cells. You specify padding and spacing in pixels as well.

The Width area of the Insert Table dialog box is used to specify the relative or absolute width of a table. The default width is the current window size. You can specify the width in pixels or as a percentage of the current window size.

Figure 12.3 shows the beginnings of an advanced table. The table includes a caption centered over the body of the table, cells that span multiple cells, and smaller tables within the larger table.

**FIGURE 12.3.**

*Creating an advanced table.*

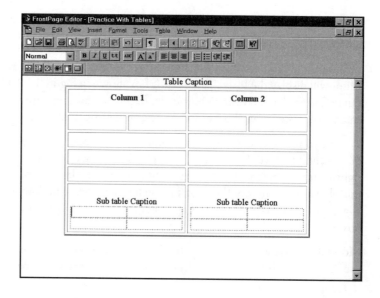

To get beyond the basic table structure that you can create with the Insert Table dialog box, you need to use the Table menu and the individual property boxes for table elements. For easy reference, the Table menu is shown in Figure 12.4.

**FIGURE 12.4.**

*The Table menu.*

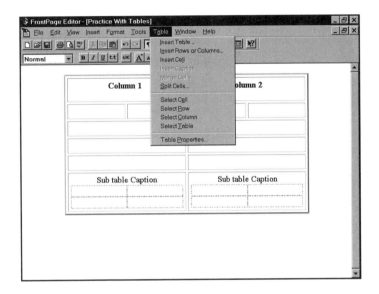

The sections that follow examine how each new menu item is used.

## Inserting Rows or Columns

You can always add rows or columns to a table after you've created it. To do this, move the insertion point to the cell in the table where you want to add a new row or column; then select Insert Rows or Columns from the Table menu. This opens the Insert Rows or Columns dialog box.

By default, the dialog box appears as shown in Figure 12.5. With the Rows field checked, you can insert one or more rows either above or below the current insertion point. With the Columns field checked, you can insert one or more columns either to the left or right of the current insertion point.

**FIGURE 12.5.**

*Inserting rows.*

# Inserting a Table Caption

After you specify how you want the basic components of the table to look, you might want to add a *caption* to the table. Captions provide an explanation or description of the data sets contained in a table. To insert a caption, select Insert Caption from the Table menu.

By default, the FrontPage Editor moves the insertion point above the table so that you can add the caption. You can also place the caption below the table. To do this, you must first select the caption, and then open the Table Caption dialog box. You can select it by double-clicking in the area of the caption. You will know when the caption is selected because the editor will place a highlight for the caption across the width of the page.

While the caption is selected, you can open the Table Caption dialog box by pressing Alt+Enter or selecting Properties from the Edit menu. This dialog box is shown in Figure 12.6. As you can see, table captions have two basic properties that set their alignment either above or below the table.

**FIGURE 12.6.**

*Setting caption properties.*

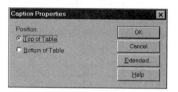

When adding a table caption, keep in mind that the best captions are short and descriptive. One way to make the caption more readable is to use bold type.

# Selecting and Deleting Table Elements

FrontPage enables you to manipulate all of the table elements in whole or in part, but you must first select the element you want to manipulate. To do this, move the insertion point to the cell, row, column, or table you want to manipulate; then choose the appropriate item from the Table menu. To select an individual data cell, choose Select Cell. To select a row of cells, choose Select Row. To select a column of cells, choose Select Column. To select the entire table, choose Select Table.

Now that the table element is selected, you can delete it or edit its properties. To delete the table element, press the Delete or Backspace key. You can copy the selected element to the buffer or cut the element out of the table. After the element is on the buffer, you can paste it anywhere in the page, and the FrontPage Editor will create a new table based on that element.

# Splitting Cells, Rows, and Columns

After you select a cell, row, or column, you can split it into additional cells, rows, or columns. To do this, choose Split Cells from the Table menu while the table element is selected. This opens the dialog box shown in Figure 12.7. When you are done splitting the table element, click on the OK button. Any data in the table element when it is split generally stays in the original cell it was in.

**FIGURE 12.7.**

*Splitting cells into additional columns and rows.*

To add rows to the selected area, choose Split into Rows and select the total number of rows you want in each selected element. For example, if you selected one cell and want to add another cell row, enter 2 in the Number of Rows field.

To add columns to the selected area, choose Split into Columns and select the total number of columns you want in each selected element. For example, if you selected one cell and want to add another cell column, enter 2 in the Number of Columns field.

Figure 12.8 shows an example of using a split on rows and columns. The first table has two columns and two rows. In the second table, the original first row is split into four columns. This was done by selecting the first row and entering 2 in the Number of Columns field in the Split Cell dialog box. In the third table, the original first column is split into two columns. This was done by selecting the first column and entering 2 in the Number of Columns field in the Split Cell dialog box.

**FIGURE 12.8.**

*An example of splitting cells.*

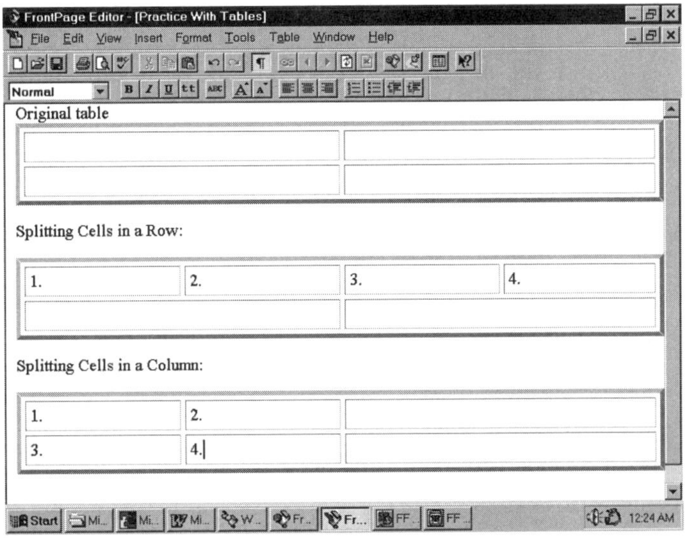

# Merging Rows and Columns

After you select two or more rows or columns, you can merge them into a single row or column. To do this, choose Merge Cells from the Table menu while the table element is selected. Now the data that was once split between two or more rows or columns is merged into one row or column.

# Resetting Table Properties

After you create a table, you can reset most of its default characteristics at any time. To do this, move the insertion point anywhere in the table and select Table Properties from the Table menu. This opens the dialog box shown in Figure 12.9.

**FIGURE 12.9.**

*Resetting table properties.*

The Table Properties dialog box has many of the same elements as the Insert Table dialog box. However, as you can see from Figure 12.10, you cannot change the number of columns or rows from this dialog box. One reason for this is to protect the data cells in the table from accidental deletion.

To set the alignment of the table, use the Alignment field. To set the pixel width of the border, use the Border field. To specify the spacing within data cells, use the Cellpadding field. To specify the spacing between data cells, use the Cellspacing field. You can also specify a relative or absolute width of a table. The default width is the current window size. You can specify the width in pixels or as a percentage of the current window size.

You can check to see what effect individual layout changes make by using the Apply button. Then, when you are sure you like the new layout for the table, click on the OK button.

# Advanced Property Settings for Cells

In general, two types of cells are used in tables: *data cells* and *heading cells*. Data cells contain the numbers, facts, and statements to display in the table. Heading cells contain headings for sections, columns, and rows. When you create a table in the FrontPage Editor, all cells are defined as data cells by default.

Other defaults are assigned to the cells when they are created as well. These settings pertain to the layout, width, and span of each cell. To set new properties for a cell, select the cell, and then open the Cell Properties dialog box by pressing Alt+Enter or choosing Properties from the Edit menu. This dialog box is shown in Figure 12.10. The great thing about this dialog box is that as you make changes, you can see how they affect the table by using the Apply button. Because this does not close the dialog box, you can then make further changes and test those as well.

**FIGURE 12.10.**

*Setting cell properties.*

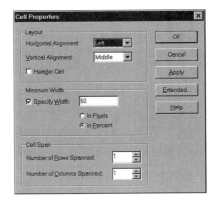

In the Layout area of the Cell Properties dialog box, you can specify the alignment of data within a cell and whether a cell is a header or data cell. Header cells have different properties from data cells. For example, heading cells are displayed in bold type and data cells are displayed in normal type. Other differences have to do with the alignment within cells. The default horizontal alignment for heading cells in a table is center. The default horizontal alignment for data sets in a table is the left margin. The default vertical alignment for both heading cells and data cells is middle.

To change the alignment settings, you will use the Horizontal Alignment and Vertical Alignment fields in the Cell Properties dialog box. Three vertical and three horizontal alignment settings are available. The vertical alignments are top, middle, and bottom. The horizontal alignments are left, center, and right.

Usually, column width is determined by the number of characters in the first heading or data set in the column. FrontPage overrides this function by specifying a relative width for each column that depends on the number of columns in the table. For example, in a table with two columns, FrontPage generally assigns the relative width of 50 percent of the table size to each column; in a table with three columns, FrontPage generally assigns the relative width of 33 percent of the table size to each column; and so on.

You can override this default with either a relative or absolute value. Relative values are expressed as a percentage of the table size. Absolute values are expressed in pixels. Using relative widths is normally better than using a width based on pixels. It saves you the trouble of trying to ensure that your table will be readable and usable regardless of the screen size. It enables you to manipulate an individual column size to fit the user's needs. It also enables you to remove or add columns without recomputing the pixel width. You can set the width of a cell in the Width area of the Cell Properties dialog box.

FrontPage gives you advanced control over the placement of cells within your tables. Normally, cells span only one row and one column, but by specifying the span of a cell, you can create cells that span several columns or rows. You can set the row span and column span of a selected cell in the Cell Span area of the Cell Properties dialog box.

Both header cells and data cells can span multiple columns and rows. You can use header cells that span multiple columns to create major headings for sections of a table. If a heading spans several columns and you define subheadings for those columns, you will need cells that span multiple rows for any columns with only one level of heading. This will ensure that the headings and cells line up appropriately.

# Advanced Property Settings for Groups of Cells

After you define the individual cells that make up a table, you might want to specify general rules for groups of cells within the table. However, usually the attributes assigned to a particular cell apply only to that cell. Thus, if your table has 30 cells, you would have to define the properties for each cell, and setting properties for 30 cells one at a time would be tedious.

To set properties for multiple cells, move the insertion point to the column or row with cells that you want to set with like properties. Next, use either Select Column or Select Row from the Table menu, and then press Alt+Enter or choose Properties from the Edit menu. Now when you set cell properties, those properties will be applied to all selected cells. When you are done setting cell properties, click on the Apply or OK button.

Using this technique, you can easily add row and column heading cells to your table. To add a column of header cells, select the column of cells that you want to place headings in, and then in the Cell Properties dialog box, activate the Header Cell field. To add a row of header cells, select the row of cells that you want to place headings in, and then in the Cell Properties dialog box, activate the Header Cell field. When you are done setting cell properties, click on the Apply or OK button.

# Combined Table Example

Combining the various table creation and design techniques discussed throughout this chapter is easy. Figure 12.11 shows how the first section of a table created to show how browser support for table tags and attributes could be turned into an HTML table. The key concepts of using column and row headers, setting alignments for columns and rows, and column and row spanning are used in the example.

**FIGURE 12.11.**
*A well-designed table.*

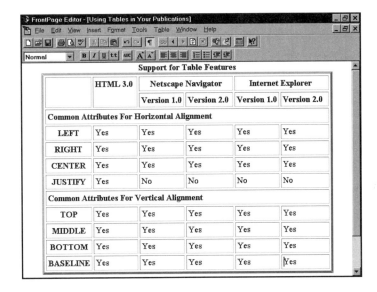

Tables can be a powerful addition to your documents. Use the example as a guideline for creating well-designed tables. The design concepts that went into making the table were simple, but when combined, they created a more powerful table. Cell padding and spacing were used to increase the white space in the table and to ensure that the data did not touch the cell walls.

Headers and subheaders were used for columns. Headers were used for rows. The first letter of the table data was capitalized to enhance the readability of the table. Key table entries were left-aligned, and their associated attributes were centered.

# Summary

Tables are one of the most dynamic elements ever added to the HTML standard. With FrontPage, you can quickly and easily create powerful tables with precisely controlled layout. Most tables have a caption and one or more rows of data organized into columns. The columns of data contain individual cells. Each individual cell is either a header or a data set. Although a table can have several levels of headings, all headings serve to identify the data sets contained in the body of the table. Use tables to add pizzazz to your Web pages today!

# Using Frames and the Frames Wizard

# 13

*by William Robert Stanek*

**IN THIS CHAPTER**

With frames, Netscape took one of the most powerful features of popular publishing applications and incorporated it into HTML in grand style. Frames enable you to create documents with multiple windows and, in doing so, open the door for an entirely new way to publish for the Web. Each frame is a mini-page within your Web publication. You can add scroll bars to a frame; enable users to manipulate the size of a frame; and add frames for permanent headers, footers, and menu bars. Hypertext references within frames can contain pointers to any window defined on the page or can be used to launch an entirely new full-sized window. You can even create frames within frames.

# Frame-Enhancing Your Documents

Frames enable you to create documents with multiple windows. Although Netscape Navigator 2.0/3.0 and Internet Explorer 3.0 are currently the only browsers that support frames, this will change quickly. There are plans to incorporate frames into the HTML 3.2 specification, and other browsers plan to support frames in their next major releases.

The best thing about frames is that they finally provide a way for Web publishers to easily create unique pages for users with Netscape-enhanced browsers. With frames, you can specify a section of a document that will be used by frame-capable browsers and a section of a document that will be used by browsers that cannot use frames.

Within the framed area of a page, you can nest frames. Each frame is identified by a unique source. The source can be any type of document, but it is typically HTML pages. Thus the contents of each mini-window usually comes from a separately defined HTML document merged into a common window using Netscape frames. Some frames have horizontal and vertical scroll bars. Readers can use these scroll bars to read the additional material contained in the document.

You do not have to frame-enhance all the pages at your Web site. A key concept in designing publications for frames is to define frames only on the main page that readers will use to access the publication. This can be your home page or any top-level page at your site. Using a top-level page reduces the amount of work you must do to frame-enhance your site and enables you to use frames as they were meant to be used.

To create a frame-enhanced page, you will use the FrontPage Editor's Frames Wizard. You will use the Frames Wizard when you want to create a new page that is frame-enhanced. To launch the Frames Wizard, select New from the File menu or press Ctrl+N; then in the New Page dialog box click the Frames Wizard. This displays the Frames Wizard dialog box shown in Figure 13.1.

**FIGURE 13.1.**

*Starting the Frames Wizard.*

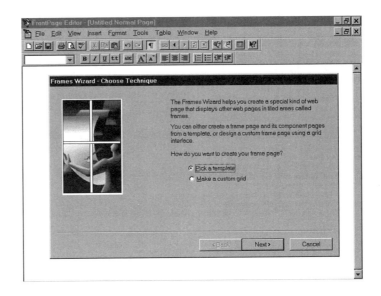

As you can see from Figure 13.1, you can create a frame from a template or design a custom frame using a grid interface. Most Web publishers will find that they want to use a template when creating a new Web site or a new section of an existing Web site. However, if you are frame-enhancing an existing Web site or section of your Web site, you will probably want to design a custom frame.

The buttons at the bottom of the dialog box are standard throughout the frame creation process. At any time you can move to the previous or next phase of the creation process using the Back or Next buttons. When you've fully defined the frame, the Next button will be replaced with a Finish button. You can press the Finish button and the FrontPage Editor will create the frame-enhanced document you've designed.

**TIP**

Usually when you frame-enhance existing pages, you will want to save the old page format to a new location. Then when you create your frame-enhanced page in the Frames Wizard, you can use the old page as the alternate document that will be viewed in browsers not capable of displaying frames. If you are creating a new frame-enhanced page, you should create a page in the current Web that can be used as the alternate document before you start the Frames Wizard.

# Using the Custom Grid Interface

This section looks at how frames are created using the Frames Wizard custom grid interface. Even if you plan to use a template to create your frames, read this section to better understand how frames work. Each frame contains a separately defined document or resource. When you are creating a frame-enhanced document using the custom grid interface, each source document should already be defined.

## Dividing a Browser Window into Frames

With the Frames Wizard dialog box open to the Choose Technique page, select "Make a custom grid" and then click the Next button. This displays the Edit Frameset Grid page shown in Figure 13.2.

**FIGURE 13.2.**

*Creating the frame using the grid interface.*

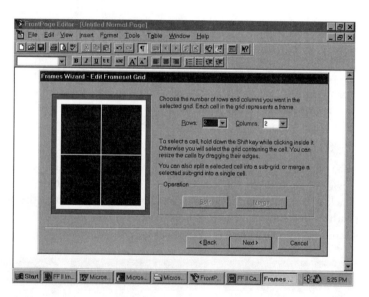

At first glance, the way you divide a browser window into frames can seem confusing. This is because window frames are organized much like a table is, with each window divided into one or more rows and columns. You count the rows for a window as the number of horizontal frame partitions. You count the columns for a window as the number of vertical frame partitions.

Using the Rows field, you can define the number of rows to display in your browser window. The size of a row is expressed as a relative value, meaning it is based on the current window size. You can set the relative size of the row using the grid interface.

Using the Columns field, you can define the number of columns to display in your browser window. The size of a column is expressed as a relative value, meaning it is based on the current window size. You can set the relative size of the column using the grid interface.

The way columns and rows of frames are organized depends on how you make row and column assignments using the grid interface. Each column can have multiple rows, and each row can have multiple columns. To start the frame creation process, you will select the number of columns and rows you want the document to contain.

> **TIP**
>
> By default, the Frames Wizard sets the number of rows and columns to 2. At this point do not worry about the size of the frames. First decide on the number of columns and rows. You will be able to break down each frame into smaller frames.

Next, you can break individual frames into smaller frames. To do this, select the frame by holding down the Shift key and clicking while the pointer is over the frame you want to select. After a frame is selected, you can break it down into smaller sections using the Split button.

Figure 13.3 shows a document being created with the Frames Wizard. This document is initially divided into one column and two rows. To divide the bottom row into two columns, you would select the bottom frame and then click the Split button. By default, the Frames Wizard subdivides the frame into 2 rows and 2 columns.

**FIGURE 13.3.**

*Working with the grid interface.*

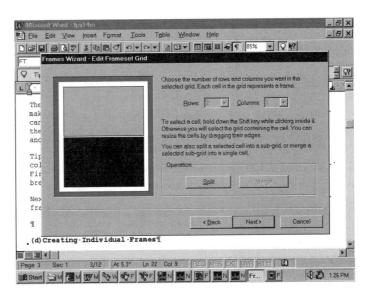

To divide the bottom frame into two columns and only one row, you would change the settings for the Rows and Columns field as shown in Figure 13.4. This activates the Merge button, which allows you to merge all the subframes back into one frame if you've made a mistake.

**FIGURE 13.4.**

*Splitting a selected frame.*

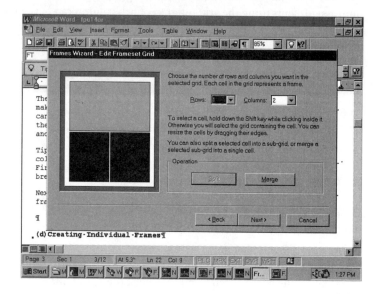

Now that your document is broken down into frames and subframes, you can work on sizing the frames. As you can see from Figure 13.4, each frame is separated by a grid line. These horizontal and vertical grid lines can be moved to resize any frames in your document. To do this, move the pointer to the grid line you want to resize. The arrow pointer changes to the resize pointer—a pointer with arrows on either end. If you press and hold down the left mouse button, you can drag the grid line to resize the frame. When you are done sizing frames, click the Next button to continue.

## Defining Individual Frames

The next page in the Frames Wizard lets you define the source document for individual frames. As you can see from Figure 13.5, you click a frame to define its attributes.

The only field you must define for your frame-enhanced document to display properly is the Source URL field, which specifies the source document or object for the frame. If you do not specify a source URL, the frame appears as an ugly blank space in the window. FrontPage displays a warning if you do not name a source for any of your frames. When you see this warning, you should go back and add a source URL to any frame that does not have one. Because only Netscape-enhanced browsers can use your frames, the source you specify is usually a Netscape-enhanced document.

**FIGURE 13.5.**

*Defining each frame.*

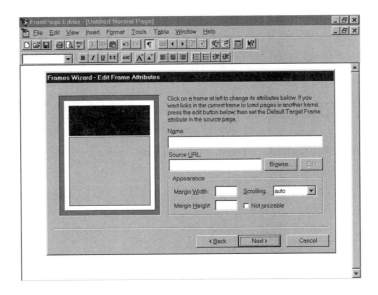

In the Source URL field, you can enter the filename of a document in the current Web or click the Browse button, which opens the dialog box shown in Figure 13.6. As you can see from the figure, the Choose Source URL dialog box has three tabs: HTML Page, Image, and Any Type. The HTML Page tab lets you select a source document from a list of HTML documents in the current Web. The Image tab lets you select a source document from a list of GIF and JPEG images in the current Web. The Any Type tab lets you select a source document from a list of all the files in the current Web.

**FIGURE 13.6.**

*Choosing a source URL.*

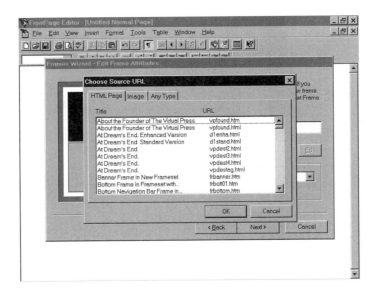

Although the Frames Wizard lets you select document sources that aren't HTML documents, you generally should not do this. Instead, create an HTML document that includes the image or other resource. In this way, you can be sure the user's browser will display the image or resource properly and in a uniform way.

After you've specified a source document for the frame, you can edit the page immediately by clicking the Edit button. Other optional fields for frames include

> Margin Height
> Margin Width
> No Resize
> Scrolling

## Frame Margins

The Margin Height field controls the top and bottom margin sizes for the frame. The minimum margin size is 1. If you assign a margin size of less than 1, your browser displays the frame with a margin to ensure frame edges do not touch. If you do not assign a margin size, the browser uses a default margin size, which can vary. Consequently, you might want to assign a specific margin size for the frame's top and bottom margins.

The Margin Width field controls the frame's left and right margin sizes. The minimum margin size here is also 1. You set margin height and margin width in the Appearance area of the Edit Frame Attributes page shown previously in Figure 13.5.

**TIP**

Internet Explorer 3.0 supports cool enhancements that allow users to view frames without borders. If you are frame enhancing your pages specifically for Internet Explorer 3.0, you might want to set the Margin Height and Margin Width field values to zero for all frames in your document, which is the trick you can use to get borderless frames. Keep in mind that borders and scrollbars are automatically added if the content of the frame is larger than the area dedicated to the frame. Therefore, minimize document content if you want to achieve borderless frames.

# User Adjustment of Frames

Users can adjust frames in two key ways: with scroll bars and by resizing the frame. In general, users will want to be able to manipulate your frames, especially if they are using a screen size other than the one you created the publication for. However, you can turn these features on or off using the Scrolling and Not Resizable fields.

By default, the browser decides whether a window should have scroll bars. If the entire source document is visible in the frame, the browser will automatically display the frame without scroll bars. If the entire source document is not visible in the frame, the browser will automatically display the frame with scroll bars.

Older browsers display both horizontal and vertical scroll bars regardless of whether both are needed. The Frames Wizard lets you set the Scrolling field to either Auto or No. You can override the default Auto value for the Scrolling field by setting the value to No, which ensures scroll bars are never visible.

By default, the size of all frames can be adjusted by the user. Users can adjust frames by moving the pointer over a frame edge, holding down the left mouse button when the resizing icon appears, and dragging the frame edge to a new position. You can turn the resizing feature off by setting the Not Resizable field. Keep in mind, though, that even a single frame that cannot be resized will affect the adjustability of other frames in the window.

# Targeting and Naming Frames

The Name field plays a key role in how your frames interact with other frames and windows. By default, hypertext references within a frame are targeted to the frame itself. This means that when you activate a link within a frame, the new document will normally be loaded into the same frame. By naming a frame, you can target it from other frames on the page. To name a frame, you should use a keyword that begins with an alphanumeric character, such as *Main*.

By default, all frames are unnamed. After you have assigned a name to a frame, that frame can be targeted by other frames. Usually, these frames are on the same page. For example, your page could have a main section named Main and a menu section targeted at the Main frame. In this way, when a user clicks a hypertext reference in the menu, the corresponding document will be loaded into the Main frame.

To target a frame, you must set the Default Target Frame field in the Page Properties dialog box associated with the source page. The value for the Default Target Frame field should be the name of the frame you want to target. This means the Name field for each frame you are defining is very important and should be uniquely specified for all frames in a page.

## Defining an Alternate Document

When you are done defining individual frames, click the Next button. As shown in Figure 13.7, you can then specify a source document that will be displayed by browsers that are not capable of using frames. This source document must be defined in the current Web.

**FIGURE 13.7.**

*Defining an alternate document.*

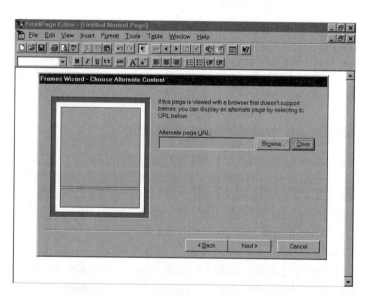

It is always a good idea to define an alternate source document. There is no point in creating a page that arbitrarily excludes a group of Web users. However, if you do not specify an alternate source, the Frames Wizard inserts a warning to users who cannot view the frame-enhanced document that tells them the page uses frames, which is a feature not supported by their browser.

To specify an alternate source document, click the Browse button. The Frames Wizard will then display the Choose Source URL dialog box. Although this dialog box will let you specify source documents that are in HTML format, you should rarely do so.

> **NOTE**
>
> All frame-enhanced pages should contain a fully defined alternate document. This document could simply contain your original page before you frame enhanced it.

## Saving the Page

After defining the alternate document, click the Next button. As shown in Figure 13.8, you can then save the page. Before you click the Finish button, you should specify a title and a page URL for your new frame-enhanced document.

**FIGURE 13.8.**

*Saving the page.*

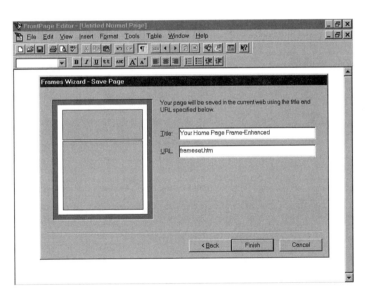

When you click the Finish button, the Frames Wizard creates the document and updates the current Web. Sometimes this process takes longer than you'd expect, so be patient. After the page is created, you can view the page in a frame-enhanced browser such as the Netscape Navigator version 2.0 or higher or the Internet Explorer version 3.0 or higher.

# Using Frame Templates

This section looks at how frames are created using templates defined in the Frames Wizard. Each frame contains a separately defined document or resource. When you are creating a frame-enhanced document using templates, each source document is generated automatically by the Frames Wizard.

With the Frames Wizard dialog box open to the first page, select "Pick a template," and then click the Next button. This displays the template selection page shown in Figure 13.9.

**FIGURE 13.9.**

*Selecting a template.*

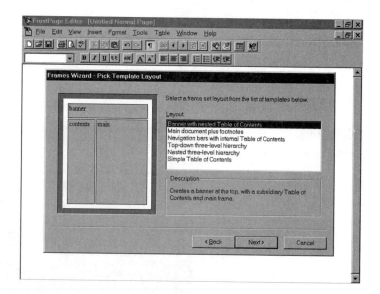

The template currently selected is highlighted. You can select another template using the arrow keys or by clicking the template you want to use. Each template has unique characteristics, which are examined later in this chapter.

After selecting a template that meets your needs, click the Next button. This takes you to the Choose Alternate Content page. Define your alternate content just as you would if you were creating a page using the custom grid. Before you continue, make sure your frames are sized properly. When using templates, this is the only page on which you can resize frames.

After you've defined an alternate document source, click the Next button again. This takes you to the final page in the Frames Wizard. On the Save page, you can specify a title and a page URL for your new frame-enhanced document.

# Template 1: Banner with Nested Table of Contents

The template shown earlier in Figure 13.9 creates a document with a banner at the top, a Table of Contents frame, and a Main frame. The Banner frame targets the Table of Contents frame and should contain the Main navigation links. When users click a link in the Banner frame, their browser will load the referenced document into the Table of Contents frame.

The Table of Contents frame targets the Main frame and should contain links to the main pages in the current section of the Web or to all the bookmarks in Main frame's current page. When users click a link in this frame, their browser will load the referenced document into the Main frame.

The Main frame does not target any other frame and should contain the main information. Thus when users click a link in this frame, their browser will load the referenced document into the Main frame, which overwrites the existing source document. You can change the default target for any frame by editing the page's properties.

Figure 13.10 shows the default contents and appearance of a document created with this template. As you can see, you need to edit the source documents on which the page is based.

**FIGURE 13.10.**

*A frame-enhanced document based on template 1, the banner with nested table of contents.*

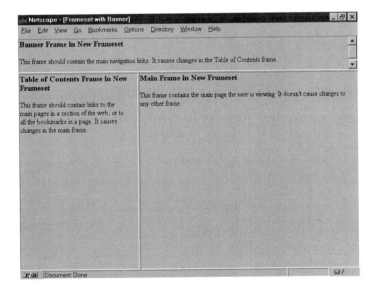

# Template 2: Main Document Plus Footnotes

The template shown in Figure 13.11 creates a document with a Main frame and a scrolling Footnote frame. The Main frame targets the Footnote frame and should contain the main information for the document. When users click a link in the Main frame, the corresponding footnotes are displayed in the Footnote frame.

**FIGURE 13.11.**

*Creating a document with footnotes.*

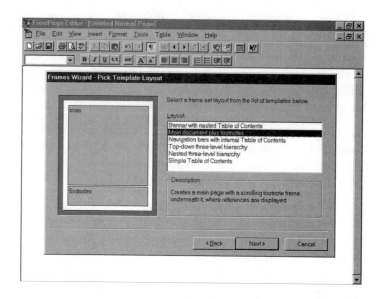

The Footnote frame does not target any other frame and should contain references for the main document. You can change the default target for any frame by editing the page's properties.

A document created with this template is shown in Figure 13.12. As with most frame templates, you will want to edit the source documents for the frames before you publish your page.

**FIGURE 13.12.**

*A frame-enhanced document based on template 2, the main document plus footnotes.*

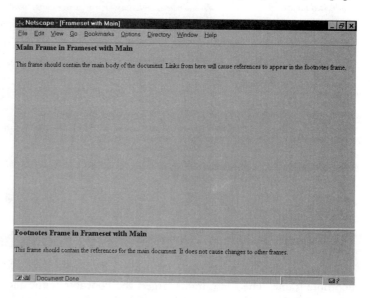

# Template 3: Navigation Bars with Internal Table of Contents

The template shown in Figure 13.13 creates a document with navigation bars at the top and bottom, a Table of Contents frame, and a Main frame. Navigation bars are usually image map banners. Both navigation bars target the Table of Contents frame and should contain the main navigation links. When users click a link in either navigation bar, their browser will load the referenced document into the Table of Contents frame.

**FIGURE 13.13.**

*Creating a document with navigation bars.*

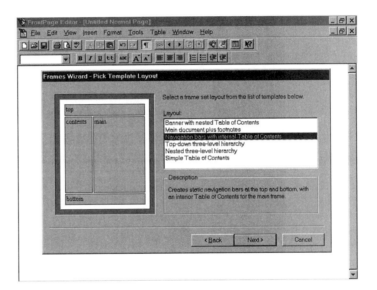

The Table of Contents frame targets the Main frame and should contain links to the main pages in the current section of the Web or to all the bookmarks in the Main frame's current page. When users click a link in this frame, their browser will load the referenced document into the Main frame.

The Main frame does not target any other frame and should contain the main information. Thus when users click a link in this frame, their browser will load the referenced document into the Main frame, which overwrites the existing source document. You can change the default target for any frame by editing the page's properties.

As you can see in Figure 13.14, this template creates one of the most useful frame-enhanced documents. Once again, you need to edit the source documents the page is based on before publishing the page.

**FIGURE 13.14.**

*A frame-enhanced document based on template 3, the navigation bars with internal table of contents.*

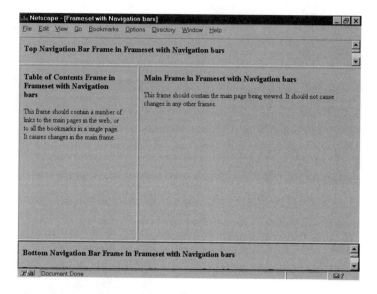

## Template 4: The Top-Down Three-Level Hierarchy

The template shown in Figure 13.15 creates a document with a top-down hierarchy split into three frames. The top frame targets the middle frame and should contain the main sections of your Web. When users click a link in the top frame, their browser will load the referenced document into the middle frame.

**FIGURE 13.15.**

*Creating a document with a top-down hierarchy.*

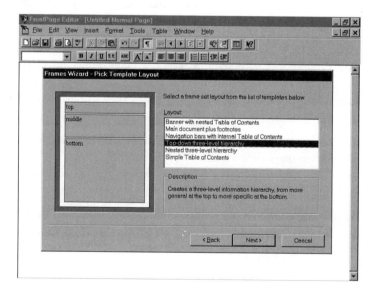

The middle frame targets the bottom frame and should contain links to the main subsections of the Web or to all the bookmarks in the bottom frame's current document. When users click a link in this frame, their browser will load the referenced document into the bottom frame.

The bottom frame does not target any other frame and should contain the detailed information at your site. Thus when users click a link in this frame, their browser will load the referenced document into the bottom frame, which overwrites the existing source document. You can change the default target for any frame by editing the page's properties.

The default document created with this template is shown in Figure 13.16.

**FIGURE 13.16.**

*A frame-enhanced document based on template 4, the top-down three-level hierarchy.*

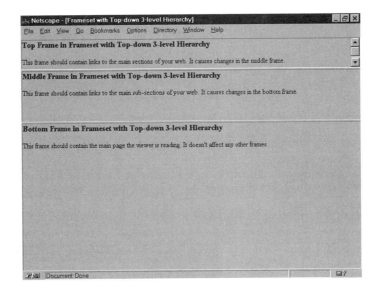

## Template 5: The Nested Three-Level Hierarchy

The template shown in Figure 13.17 creates a document with a nested hierarchy split into three frames. The left frame targets the right top frame and should contain the main sections of your Web. When users click a link in the top frame, their browser will load the referenced document into the right top frame.

The right top frame targets the right bottom frame and should contain links to the main subsections of the Web or to all the bookmarks in the right bottom frame's current document. When users click a link in this frame, their browser will load the referenced document into the right bottom frame.

**FIGURE 13.17.**

*Creating a document with a nested hierarchy.*

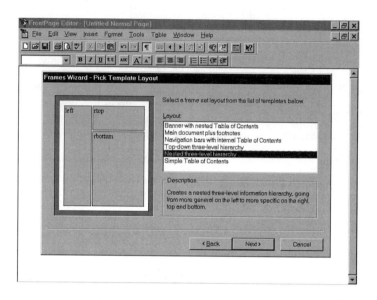

The right bottom frame does not target any other frame and should contain the detailed information at your site. Thus when users click a link in this frame, their browser will load the referenced document into the right bottom frame, which overwrites the existing source document. You can change the default target for any frame by editing the page's properties.

A document using the nested three-level hierarchy is shown in Figure 13.18.

**FIGURE 13.18.**

*A frame-enhanced document based on template 5, the nested three-level hierarchy.*

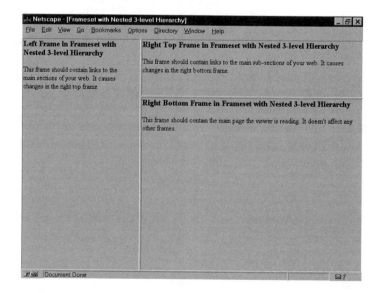

# Template 6: Simple Table of Contents

The template shown in Figure 13.19 creates a document with a Table of Contents frame and a Main frame. The Table of Contents frame targets the Main frame and should contain links to the main pages in the current section of the Web or to all the bookmarks in the Main frame's current page. When users click a link in this frame, their browser will load the referenced document into the Main frame.

**FIGURE 13.19.**

*Creating a document with a table of contents.*

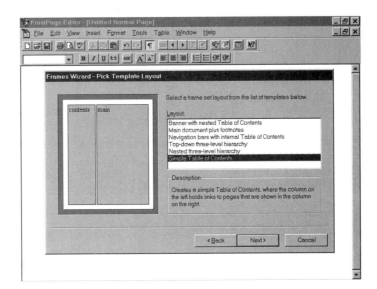

The Main frame does not target any other frame and should contain the main information. Thus when users click a link in this frame, their browser will load the referenced document into the Main frame, which overwrites the existing source document. You can change the default target for any frame by editing the page's properties.

Figure 13.20 shows a document created with this template.

**FIGURE 13.20.**

*A frame-enhanced document based on template 6, the simple table of contents.*

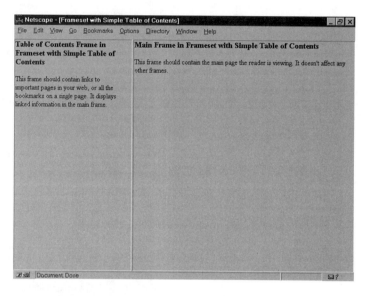

# Targeting Frames and New Windows from Links

To ensure that you have maximum flexibility as a Web publisher, each link in your frame-enhanced document can have its own target frame. This allows you to target any frame in the current window or to open a new window if necessary. You identify a target frame using the name assigned to the frame when you created it.

> **TIP**
>
> To open a new window, you target a frame that does not exist in the current window. When the users click a link targeted to a new window, their browser will open a separate browser window and load the referenced document. If all your links in a particular page target this new window, the user can easily switch back and forth between the two windows.

There are two key ways to define a target for a link. The first way is to define the target frame when you are adding the link to the document. If you remember from Chapter 9, "Adding Features to the Page," you select the text or image that will identify the link and then either choose Link from the Edit menu or click the Link button. This opens the Create Link dialog box. In the Target Frame field, enter the name of the frame you want the link to target. You can also define a target frame for any link you've created by selecting that link and editing its properties.

The NAME and TARGET attributes can also be used to establish the current document's relationship to other documents. Currently, four relationships are defined:

_blank     Load this link into a new, unnamed window.

_self      Load this link over yourself.

_parent    Load this link over yourself and reset the window.

_top       Load this link at the top level.

Although all these relationships are useful, the most useful relationship is _parent. Using the _parent relationship, you can force the browser to reset the window entirely and avoid loading a frame document within the current frame. You will want to use this relationship whenever you have a link that leads to a page containing frame assignments. For example, if lower-level documents reference your home page, you can assign the target of the link as _parent to avoid getting a frame within a frame.

# Editing Frame-Enhanced Pages

For frame-enhanced pages, you should start the editing process from the FrontPage explorer. Figure 13.21 shows the frame-enhanced documents I created as examples for this chapter. As you know, when you select a document in the Outline view, its structure and links are shown in the Link view.

**FIGURE 13.21.**

*To edit frame-enhanced documents, start in the FrontPage Explorer.*

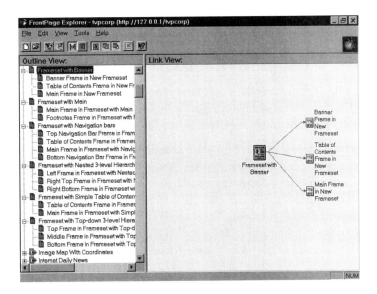

At the top level of the view, you will see the source documents for each frame. To edit any of these source documents, double-click the appropriate document's icon in the Link view. This will start the FrontPage Editor, with the source document loaded so that you can edit it. To edit the properties of the frame-enhanced document, double-click its icon. This will start the Frames Wizard on the Edit Frameset Grid page.

# Combined Frame Example

This section gives you an inside look at how I frame-enhanced the Virtual Press (TVP) Web site. The TVP Web site is organized into seven main areas, or publications:

- TVP Home Page and Corporate Information Pages
- TVP Business Solutions Pages
- TVP Order Center
- The Writer's Gallery
- Internet Job Information Center
- Internet Publishing Center
- Internet Daily News

When I frame-enhanced the TVP Web site, I made a conscious decision to create separate frame-enhanced pages for each of these seven main areas. Primarily, this is because most of the visitors to the site do not start on the TVP home page. They start on one of the other main areas. If I had frame-enhanced only the home page, hundreds of thousands of visitors might have missed out on the powerful features I added for users with frame-capable browsers. Frame-enhancing the seven top-level pages also enables me to give each area a unique look and feel.

In the series of examples that follow, you will see how the Internet Job Information Center (JIC) was frame-enhanced. You will also learn the design concepts that went into frame-enhancing the Internet's JIC. The top-level page is shown in Figure 13.22.

The window shown in Figure 13.22 is divided into three frames. The first row is divided into two columns. The second row has a single frame that occupies the entire width of the window. Each frame has a document associated with it. The source for the small frame on the left side of the window is a document called `vp.html`. The source for the large, Main frame is a document called `vpjic2.html`. The source for the bottom frame is a document called `fmenu.html`. Finally, each frame was named so that it could be targeted from other frames on the page. The side frame is called Vpside. The main frame is called Vpmain. The footer frame is called Vpfooter.

The `vp.html` document is used to display a title graphic. The `vpjic2.html` document contains the source for the Main frame and is a modified version of the original Job Information Center top-level page. The primary modifications were to remove the graphical logo at the top of the page and the links to other top-level pages, because these links are unnecessary.

**FIGURE 13.22.**

*Internet Job Information
Center, frame-enhanced.*

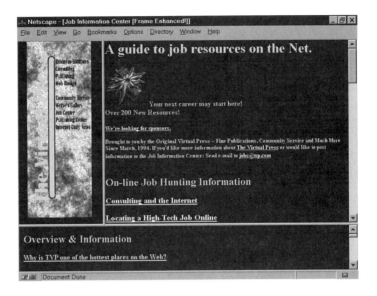

Although the `fmenu.html` document could have used a base target assignment, I did not use one when creating the page. Primarily this is because of the mix of links to top-level pages and supplementary pages. Some links target the Main frame called Vpmain. Activating one of these links will load the associated document into the Main frame. Other links target a parent document. Activating one of these links will cause the parent document to load over the current window. This ensures that a top-level document's frame assignments are not loaded into another frame on the page.

# Summary

Following the frame model specified in Netscape enhancements to HTML, you can frame-enhance your Web publication or site. Frames are more than mini-windows within the larger browser window. In fact, they are the gateway to an entirely new way to publish on the Web. If you've ever wanted to add power features to your Web publications, frames provide definite starting points.

**IV**

**PART**

# Microsoft Office Web Publishing

# Microsoft Internet
# Assistants Overview

# 14

*by Ned Snell*

**IN THIS CHAPTER**

As you know, the FrontPage Editor is an all-inclusive, full-featured, compromise-free Web authoring environment. If you have FrontPage, you need nothing else to produce simple or sophisticated Web documents. So if I tell you that Microsoft, in its infinite wisdom, also supplies free Internet-authoring add-ons ("Internet Assistants") that turn the leading members of its Office applications suite (Word, Excel, PowerPoint, Schedule+, and Access) into Web authoring tools, your natural and completely justifiable reaction might be "If I have FrontPage, why would I need an Internet Assistant's assistance?"

Of course, if everyone ran around willy-nilly asking whether things were necessary before acquiring them, the U.S. economy would quickly collapse, starting with Microsoft and Disney. Who really *needs* Windows, anyway? Who really needed *The Lion King,* or Microsoft Bob, or the Mickey Mouse telephone, or a personal home page? Nevertheless, the Internet Assistants answer the "who needs it" query pretty well, even for the FrontPage-equipped. In effect, the Internet Assistants supplement your FrontPage authoring toolbox with the document creation, editing, and data management tools in the Office application suite. Exactly how they do that varies by application, as you'll see shortly. But the Internet Assistants do their job pretty well, and more importantly, they do it for free. They're not as much fun as the Dumbo ride or a round of Windows Golf, but they're considerably more useful and infinitely cheaper.

If you use Office—or if you use any of the individual Office applications for which an Internet Assistant is available—the chapters in this part of the book show how you can exploit the Internet Assistants within a FrontPage-centered authoring methodology.

**NOTE**

The chapters in this part assume you are familiar with the basics of Web authoring. Before reading this part, you should know what an HTML file and HTML tags are, and you should be familiar with such basic HTML file elements as the title, headings, hyperlinks, horizontal rules, and inline graphics. If you are unfamiliar with these HTML items, you'll benefit by reading Parts I, II, and III before proceeding with Part IV.

# What's an Internet Assistant?

All Internet Assistants start out as a single file freely distributed by Microsoft—you'll find all of the Assistants on the CD-ROM included with this book. You can also easily locate and download the file for each Internet Assistant from the Web, as described in the upcoming chapters. (A great place to learn more about them is the Office Web site, shown in Figure 14.1.) Each file is a self-extracting archive file that, when opened, releases all of the files that make up the Assistant. After the archive files have been extracted, you must make a few extra setup steps to complete installation of the Assistant; the precise steps differ by application and are explained in Chapters 15 through 17.

**FIGURE 14.1.**

*Microsoft's Office Web site.*

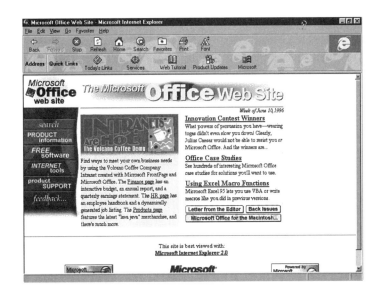

When they are installed, the Internet Assistants differ markedly according to the application to which they apply. Word's Internet Assistant consists mainly of a document template and related files that together tune Word's toolbar and menus for Web authoring. Excel's Internet Assistant is made up of an Excel "add-in" file that opens an Internet Assistant Wizard. The Wizard leads you step-by-step through saving selected cell data as an HTML table. PowerPoint's Internet Assistant adds an Export as an HTML item to the File menu. This item opens an advanced conversion engine for turning PowerPoint slides into Web image maps—clickable online graphics that behave on a Web just as they do in a presentation session on a desktop (the convertor also creates a set of text-only Web pages from your slides to accomodate text-only browsers).

The common elements among these different approaches are as follows:

- You begin with a file in the application's native format.
- You create and edit your document using many of the familiar tools in each application.
- When you finish, you wind up with an HTML file suitable for publishing on a Web or, as is recommended for FrontPage users, for fine-tuning in the FrontPage Editor.

## HOW ELSE DOES OFFICE MAKE WEB CONTENT?

As you well know by now, Web documents are HTML documents. Standardization on HTML, despite variations introduced by Netscape and Microsoft as HTML "extensions," is what allows any Web browser to read almost any Web document.

Microsoft is attempting to expand the document formatting options on the Web by circumventing the standard. By offering free viewers for the three most popular Office file formats—Word, Excel, and PowerPoint—and distributing them widely through the Web, Microsoft is encouraging Web authors to publish Office files, rather than HTML, on the Web when a document requires precise formatting or other capabilities lacking in HTML.

You can build links to Office files in your Web documents, and even offer your guests links to the viewers so that they can download the viewer required to look at your Office-based content.

You can download the viewers from Microsoft's Office Web site (see Figure 14.1, earlier in this chapter).

# How Does FrontPage Interact with an Internet Assistant?

How Does FrontPage Interact with an Internet Assistant? It doesn't, really. (E-mail Microsoft about it, or better yet, fax them.)

That doesn't mean the two can't work together. Whichever Assistant/Application combo you use, you wind up with an HTML file, ready for publishing. You can publish it straight to your FrontPage Web, or better yet, open it first in the FrontPage Editor to test and fine-tune it, adding any desired FrontPage techniques (such as Bots or FrontPage forms) that aren't part of the Assistant's toolset.

For example, if you're an experienced Word user, you might prefer using Word to create your documents, because you can apply editing tools and other capabilities with which you're already familiar. You might also enjoy applying Word's superior spell-checking, thesaurus, or grammar-checking to your Web compositions. After creating and formatting content in Word, you can save the document as an HTML file (a capability added to Word by its Assistant), open the HTML file in the FrontPage Editor (see Figure 14.2), apply any special FrontPage formatting or tools you like, test the page (in the FrontPage Editor and in a browser such as Internet Explorer), and then publish it. This two-tool approach enables you to begin with the application you find most convenient for the type of work you need to do first.

Perhaps more importantly, the Internet Assistants provide an easy-to-use mechanism for using existing content. If your marketing collateral was originally composed in Word, you can turn it into a Web page by opening it in Word, making any desired changes, and then saving it as an HTML file. If you've already got a nicely formatted pricing table in Excel, you can add it to a Web page quickly through Excel's Assistant. Existing PowerPoint sales presentations can be transformed into online presentations in a snap. Similarly, you can conveniently extract Web page content from Access and Schedule+ with their Assistants.

**FIGURE 14.2.**

*Opening an HTML document in the FrontPage Editor.*

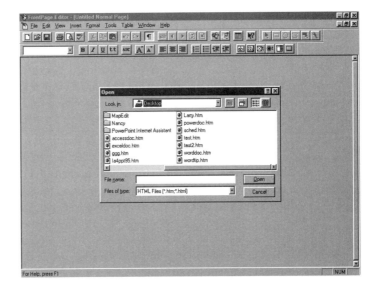

### THE ASSISTANTS SOON TO BE ASSIMILATED

As one small plank in its "Big Internet Strategy," Microsoft has announced that the functionality of the Internet Assistants is soon (in 1997) to become a core part of Office and its applications. In future versions of the Office suite, any Office application can be used to generate Web content without any Assistant or add-on.

# Choosing the Right Assistant for the Job

Having both FrontPage and one or more Internet Assistants, you have multiple doorways into any Web authoring project. How can you decide which application to begin with?

Only the Word Internet Assistant makes an acceptable general-purpose tool for composing a new HTML document. In most cases, new documents begin in FrontPage or in Word. Equipped with its Internet Assistant, PowerPoint is a great tool for building online presentations (such as training sessions) for intranet or, less practically, Internet applications. The remaining Assistants for Excel, Access, and Schedule+ are useful principally as tools for exporting formatted data from these applications to a Web page that will be more fully composed in another application (FrontPage or Word).

Ultimately, choosing a starting point will become a natural decision for you, based on your experiences and comfort level with the authoring tools at your disposal. In the meantime, you might want to consider the questions below before choosing a starting point.

■ **Does the document rely on existing content, and what format is that content saved in?** Using cut and paste and other techniques, you can pull existing content from most Windows applications into the FrontPage Editor. However, you'll usually see much better results (and better preservation of formatting) by working with the existing content first in its original application, and then saving that content (thanks to the Assistant) in HTML format before performing final editing and testing in the FrontPage Editor.

■ **What type of content entry or formatting is required for producing the document, and in which application are those tasks easiest to tackle?** Word is a more mature, sophisticated text entry/editing environment than FrontPage. If your document includes lots of text, you might prefer to enter and develop it in Word first. Similarly, Excel offers better tools for working with tabular material than FrontPage's Tables facilities, and you can produce a slick-looking presentation in PowerPoint much more easily than in FrontPage, thanks to PowerPoint's templates and other presentation-specific features. Not all of the formatting capabilities of these applications carry over into an HTML document, but because each application is designed for a specific type of work, you might be more productive there than in FrontPage during the composition phase of your Web page development.

■ **Does the desired final document rely heavily on elements that must be created in FrontPage?** None of the Internet Assistants supports frames (see Chapter 13, "Using Frames and the Frames Wizard"), and while Word's Internet Assistant enables you to create forms and insert image maps, FrontPage's tools for these elements are not only more powerful, but easier to use as well. (See Chapter 11, "Using Forms and the Form Page Wizard" and Chapter 10, "Enhancing Your Web Publication with Images—the Easy Way.") Also, FrontPage has its own powerful routines for processing forms, and these are not addressed by Word's forms facility. If your document requires frames, forms, or other features that can be applied only by FrontPage (or done better or more easily in FrontPage), FrontPage is your best starting point.

■ **Will the final document be published on a FrontPage Server?** If you intend to publish on a FrontPage server, the precise behavior of your document within the FrontPage environment matters more than anything else. Therefore, you might want to do most or all of your authoring in FrontPage so that you can better predict your progress and the page's final form as you go along, and so that you can take full advantage of FrontPage's features.

# Summary

The FrontPage Editor is your primary Web-authoring application. But it isn't the only Web tool in your toolbox. Under certain scenarios, you might find it more convenient to create Web content in (or export Web content from) another Windows application. The Microsoft Internet Assistants make that possible for Word, PowerPoint, Excel, Access, and Schedule+. You'll learn how to deploy these tools in the next three chapters.

# Using Internet Assistant for Word

**15**

*by Ned Snell*

Among the applications that can be enhanced with an Internet Assistant, Word is by far the most useful. After all, your goal is only to create a document (albeit a Web document), and Word is one of the best document creation, editing, and formatting tools around. As such, Word plus Internet Assistant equals an excellent companion tool to FrontPage, supplementing the FrontPage Editor's capabilities with advanced document creation capabilities such as AutoCorrect, advanced spelling and grammar checking, and more.

# About Internet Assistant for Word 95

What's the difference between Word alone and Word with Internet Assistant? The Internet Assistant adds Web-specific functions and views to Word, and takes away nothing but about 2MB of your hard disk space.

As you'll see shortly, the Assistant adds to Word a number of Web-specific document formatting capabilities. However, because most of these capabilities are also included in FrontPage, the Assistant's real value is that it enables you to apply everyday Word power to your Web authoring tasks. For example, you can apply the following Word tools:

- Spell checking and grammar checking
- AutoFormat
- AutoCorrect
- Find and Replace
- Thesaurus and other integrated reference tools (such as Bookshelf)
- Graphics importing

When applying these and other Word tools, you needn't do anything special—use these as you would when creating any document. However, keep in mind that the Web is the Web, and that your formatting in Word might not look the same to users of various browsers as it does to you in Word (more about that later).

Before beginning to work with HTML files in Word, it's important that I remind you that a Word document is not a Web document, and vice-versa. The HTML specification governing Web document formatting (see Part III) is far more limited than Word's toolset. Some of the formatting you can apply in a Word document has no corollary in the HTML world. For example, as you already know, you can control (in a limited way) the size of the font used for text in your Web document, but you cannot choose the font itself. As a result, Word's font selection capabilities are meaningless when you're working with an HTML document.

Fortunately, when you are working on an HTML document, the Internet Assistant removes from Word's toolbar most of the formatting tools that have no HTML equivalent. And when you convert an existing document from Word format into HTML format, the Internet Assistant discards Word formatting for which it cannot substitute an equivalent HTML tag (you'll learn more about this later in this chapter).

# What the Internet Assistant Does

The Internet Assistant for Word 95 adds to Word five things:

- A WYSIWYG HTML Edit view that includes new toolbar buttons and menu choices specific to Web authoring tasks (such as link creation). Observe the toolbar in Figure 15.1, and notice that the Font selection tools are gone, while several new buttons appear at the right end of the bar. Note that the toolbar appears this way only while you're editing an HTML document; when editing other documents, you'll see your regular Word toolbar.

- A document template, HTML.DOT, for creating new Web pages within the HTML Edit view.

- A new choice in the Save As dialog that enables you to save files in HTML (.HTM) format.

- An HTML source code editor, so you can edit HTML code directly in addition to authoring pages within a WYSIWYG view.

- A Web browser view, for evaluating how your documents may look and behave online.

**FIGURE 15.1.**

*Word's toolbar shows new Web-related buttons after its Internet Assistant has been installed.*

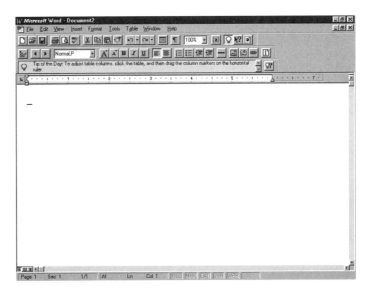

### WHAT'S THE WORD BROWSER FOR?

The browser added to Word by the Word Internet Assistant is a strange animal. It's a bona fide browser, which means it not only accurately interprets and displays local

HTML documents, but it also browses the Web (Internet or intranet) through a Winsock-compliant connection. It has this online capability so that you can test the validity of external links. And if you weren't a FrontPage author, the browser might be valuable to you. But the Word Internet Assistant is just that—an assistant. FrontPage is the boss. Final page evaluation and link testing should always be done from within the FrontPage environment—especially if you move the HTML file location when switching from Word to FrontPage, which might break relative links.

In addition, you can bet that very few of your target guests will be using Word as a browser (unless you've deliberately configured them to do so on your intranet). So although the Word browser displays HTML files in a way roughly similar to that of most graphical browsers, it makes a rather poor evaluation environment. It's better to view your documents in the FrontPage Editor, or through a widely used browser such as Netscape Navigator or Internet Explorer. These browsers give you a better sense than Word does of how your documents will appear to the Web mainstream.

## System Requirements

The Word Internet Assistant described in this chapter requires Microsoft Word for Windows 95 (technically Word version 7.0 or higher). That's it for software requirements, other than the Internet Assistant itself, which you can download as described in the next section.

As for hardware requirements, this book assumes you use FrontPage, or intend to. Given that, there's a very simple way to sum up the requirements for Word's Internet Assistant: If you can run FrontPage, you can run Word's Internet Assistant, provided you have 2MB of disk space in which to store the Internet Assistant's files.

Of course, you might choose not to run Word's Internet Assistant on the same PC you use for the FrontPage Editor. So here's the specific hardware requirements: At a minimum, the PC must be capable of running Windows 95 (and be doing so, in fact), and it must be equipped with at least 8MB of RAM and a pointing device. You have all of that, don't you?

### NOTE

If you intend to use the browser component of Word's Internet Assistant to test your document's external (remote) links online, you must meet a few additional requirements. The PC running the Word Internet Assistant must have a modem and phone line connection (or access to an HTTP intranet, for testing intranet links) and be configured to access the Internet or intranet through a Winsock-compliant TCP/IP stack (such as Windows 95's built-in TCP/IP Winsock).

Note that a modem and Internet setup are not required to view your locally created Web documents through Word Internet Assistant's browser—you can do that offline. You need an Internet connection only for testing external links. And as a rule, you're probably better off testing links from FrontPage or Internet Explorer than from within the Word Internet Assistant browser, as described earlier in this chapter (see the section "What the Internet Assistant Does").

# Finding and Downloading Word's Internet Assistant

Like any freely distributed Microsoft gewgaw, the Word Internet Assistant can be found all over the Web, and on a bunch of FTP sites as well. But to be sure you get the latest, most stable version, you must get your Word Internet Assistant straight from Microsoft.

**NOTE**

All of the Microsoft Internet Assistants are included on the CD-ROM bundled with this book. However, it's important that you know how to get the Assistants straight from Microsoft because they are updated and enhanced regularly.

Microsoft itself makes the Word download available from a variety of links. The best place to start is the Word Internet Tools page (part of the Microsoft Office Web site) at

```
http://www.microsoft.com/msword/it_wd.htm
```

From the Word Internet Tools page (shown in Figure 15.2), you can easily download the Word Internet Assistant file or learn more about the Assistant. By starting at this page (rather than going directly to the file with a Web address or FTP address listed here), you can be assured of picking up the latest version, and you'll also get a chance to read useful announcements (about upcoming versions, for example) along the way.

**NOTE**

The filename of the current version of the Word Internet Assistant is

```
WRDIA20Z.EXE
```

However, updated versions are offered regularly. You should always navigate Microsoft's Web site to find the latest version, which may or may not have the name shown above.

**FIGURE 15.2.**

*The Word Internet Tools page at* http://www.microsoft.com/msword/it_wd.htm.

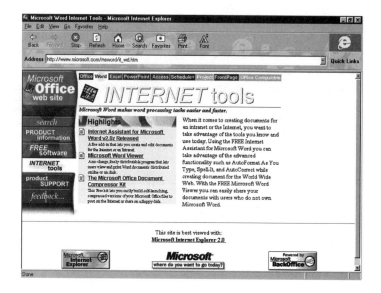

The self-extracting archive file is only about 1.12 MB, so it doesn't take very long to download to your PC, even at 14.4 Kbps. When downloading, you needn't save the file in any special place (your desktop is fine), but be sure not to save it in your WINWORD or WINWORD\INTERNET folder. Also, saving the file on your desktop or in a folder by itself makes deleting the archive file easier after installation is complete.

# Setting Up

To install Word Internet Assistant after downloading the self-extracting archive file, do the following:

---

### CAUTION

Before you begin setting up Word's Internet Assistant, make sure that the following statements are true:

- **All programs are closed**. Check your taskbar for any open programs. If any programs are running, the Setup Wizard might fail because it requires a system file already in use by another program.

- **The self-extracting archive file is not in your WINWORD or WINWORD\INTERNET folder**. If run from within either of these folders, the Setup Wizard might fail.

1. Open the archive file (WRDIA20.EXE) by double-clicking its file icon or right-clicking it and choosing Open from the context menu. After a few moments and a few status messages, a screen appears like the one in Figure 15.3.

**FIGURE 15.3.**
*Starting the Setup Wizard.*

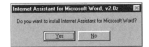

2. Click Yes or press Enter. A Welcome screen appears, reminding you to close any open programs before running setup. Click Continue (or press Enter), and the license agreement appears.
3. On the license agreement screen, click Accept. A dialog appears like the one in Figure 15.4.

**FIGURE 15.4.**
*Running the Setup Wizard.*

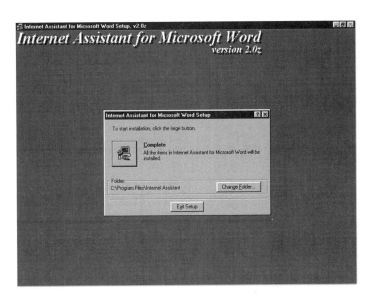

4. From the dialog shown in Figure 15.4, check the default path listed under Folder. The Setup Wizard plans to create the new folder (C:\Program Files\Internet Assistant) and store all of the Internet Assistant files in it. If that's not where you want the files stored, click Change Folder to enter a new path. Otherwise, continue setting up by clicking the big button with the little PC in it (see Figure 15.4).

A progress indicator appears as Setup decompresses the Internet Assistant files and copies them into the new folder. When setup is complete, a dialog appears like the one in Figure 15.5.

> **NOTE**
>
> During the installation process (or, in some cases, the first time you use the Word Internet Assistant), you might be prompted to choose whether you want Word's built-in browser to be your default Windows 95 browser. When prompted, you'll probably want to select No. If you choose Yes, Word will open automatically any time you open an HTML file from a file icon or enter a URL in the Run dialog. Most people prefer to have a more general-purpose browser, such as Internet Explorer or Netscape Navigator, as their default browser.

**FIGURE 15.5.**

*Setup is complete. Internet Assistant is ready to roll.*

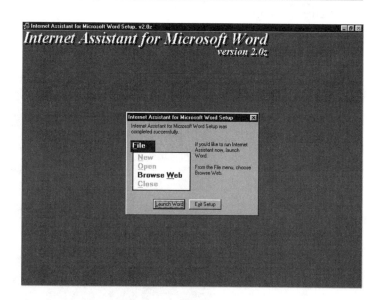

The dialog shown in Figure 15.5 informs you that Setup is complete (you need not restart Windows, as you often must after installing new software). You can click Launch Word to get right to work, or Exit Setup to leave your Internet Assistant authoring for another time.

After installation is complete, you can delete the self-extracting archive file. If you want to uninstall the Internet Assistant in the future, you can do so through the Add/Remove Programs icon in the Control Panel.

> **INSTANT INTERNET ASSISTANCE**
>
> The dialog shown in Figure 15.5 advises you to introduce yourself to the Internet Assistant by opening Word and then choosing File|Browse Web (Browse Web is a new

menu item just added by the Assistant). However, the instruction is a little misleading; choosing Browse Web opens only part of the Internet Assistant, Word's browser view. That view is used for evaluating pages and browsing the Web, not for nuts and bolts authoring. You create a new Web document through a different view, as you'll see in the next section.

Why does Microsoft steer you straight to the browser? It's preconfigured to automatically open an HTML file called DEFAULT.HTM, which is one of the Internet Assistant files the Setup Wizard stored on your hard disk. This file (see Figure 15.6) contains a brief introduction to the Assistant, some answers to common questions, and links for connecting to pages at Microsoft containing more information.

You needn't follow Microsoft's lead, but of course, you're welcome to try File|Browse Web and see what you discover.

**FIGURE 15.6.**

DEFAULT.HTM, *an introduction to Internet Assistant presented in HTML format.*

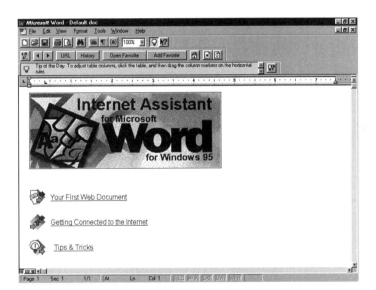

# Using Word's Internet Assistant

As a Word user, you're accustomed to working in a true What-You-See-Is-What-You-Get environment. But when working on Web documents in Word, you must keep in mind the variability among browsers, and that what you see is not always what your guests will get.

---

**TIP**

You can learn more about Word's Internet Assistant in a variety of ways:

- On the Web, Microsoft offers an online tutorial for Word's Internet Assistant. As of this writing, the tutorial has far less information than you get in this chapter, but Microsoft might beef up the tutorial later. You can access the tutorial at

  `http://www.microsoft.com/smallbiz/leverage/nbackgrnd.htm`

- While you edit an HTML document as described in the next section, a new item appears on your Word Help menu for Internet Assistant help.

If you open Word, close all documents (File|Close), and then choose File|Browse Web, Word opens DEFAULT.HTM, a brief introduction to Word's Internet Assistant.

---

## Opening the Document

To begin a new Web document, open a new file in Word by choosing File|New. (Do not use the New button on the toolbar; it won't present the template selection to you.) In the New dialog that opens (see Figure 15.7), click the General tab, and choose the template HTML.DOT, which was added to your templates library by the Internet Assistant.

**FIGURE 15.7.**

*Creating a new HTML document by choosing the HTML.DOT template.*

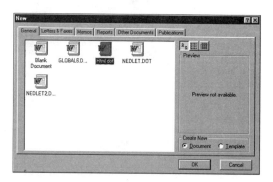

A new, blank document opens on your screen, and the Word toolbar changes. The changes to the toolbar add buttons for HTML-specific page elements such as links and rules. You can begin entering and formatting text and other HTML page elements.

---

**TIP**

You also can create a new HTML document in Word by clicking the Start a New Document button on the Office toolbar, which opens a folder of templates, including the Word template HTML.DOT. Double-clicking HTML.DOT opens Word and opens a new HTML document within Word.

# Saving a Web Document in HTML Format

You might be accustomed to saving documents after doing a good deal of work first. Word's Internet Assistant, however, is a little cranky in this respect. It wants the file named before you do anything that involves phrasing relative links—which includes not only creating hyperlinks to local resources, but also adding pictures to your page. If you attempt to create a link or add a picture without first saving your new document, Word prompts you to do so. As a result, we might as well get saving out of the way right now.

To save your document, choose File|Save. The Save As dialog shown in Figure 15.8 appears. Whenever you use the HTML.DOT template, the selection in Save as type will be HTML Document (*.htm); make sure that's the selection, and if not, choose HTML Document from the Save as type drop-down list. Then type your filename, leaving off the extension (Word supplies the extension .HTM automatically). Click Save or press Enter to save the document and return to your authoring session.

> **CAUTION**
>
> When you save, the Save as type box must say HTML Document for the file to be saved in HTML format, even if you enter an .HTM extension on the filename yourself. The extension alone doesn't do the job.

**FIGURE 15.8.**

*Saving a new HTML document.*

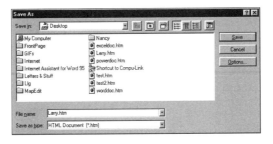

> **TIP**
>
> If you compose many similar Web pages, you might want to save time by creating an HTML document template containing all of the elements and formatting common to the pages you will create. (FrontPage does templates too; see Chapter 18, "Creating Web Pages with FrontPage's Templates.")
>
> To create a new template, compose the HTML document using the HTML.DOT template (you can save the new document as you go along, in HTML format). When finished, choose File|Save As, and choose Document template (*.dot) from the Save as type drop-down list. Word prompts you, asking whether you want a regular Word

Template or an Internet Assistant template. Choose Internet Assistant, name your new template, and finish saving.

When you want to create a new HTML document based on the template, choose File|New, and then choose the template you created.

# Composing and Formatting a New Web Document

In order to better illustrate how a new Web document can be built with Word and Internet Assistant, the examples in this section follow the building of a promotional page for Larry's Luggage.

## Entering <HEAD> Information

Everything you create in the Word document window is treated as part of the body of the HTML file. But as you learned earlier in this book, every HTML file also has a header section that contains important identification information, such as the document title and key words for use by Web search engines.

To enter header information for your document, choose the Title button on the toolbar (a little page with an I on it). A dialog opens like the one in Figure 15.9.

**FIGURE 15.9.**

*Entering header informa-
tion for a Web document.*

In the HTML Document Head Information dialog shown in Figure 15.9, type a brief, descriptive title for your document. The title is the only header information required, so you can simply click OK after typing your title, and return to compose the body of your document. If you want to add to your header such advanced elements as a Base URL or <META> tags, or if you want to designate this document as the Index file for a multipage presentation, click Advanced. (To learn more about advanced header options, see Part III.)

## Composing and Formatting Body Text

To compose the body of your document, enter and edit text as you normally would in any Word document. You can use AutoCorrect, as well as the Spelling, Grammar, and Thesaurus tools on the Tools menu. You can also take advantage of such Edit menu items as Find, Replace, and Undo.

Formatting your document, however, requires a change in your understanding of the word "formatting." Recall from previous chapters that when you edit an HTML document, you don't so much "format" text as assign it attributes that identify what type of page element that text represents: a bold heading, normal body text, a list item, and so on. Each browser used to view the document will display those elements in a different way. Certainly, you'll want to evaluate the appearance of your document in Word, and in practice, the document will appear quite similar when viewed through leading Windows browsers such as Netscape Navigator or Internet Explorer. Still, it helps to adopt a new mindset when formatting an HTML document: You're not really formatting; you're just labeling text with style names, which browsers will use to apply whatever formatting they prefer.

To apply an HTML style, position the edit cursor anywhere within a paragraph, and then choose an appropriate style from the Style drop-down list in the toolbar, as shown in Figure 15.10. (Note that you needn't highlight the text; simply placing the edit cursor anywhere in a paragraph applies the style to the entire paragraph.)

**FIGURE 15.10.**

*Choosing a paragraph style.*

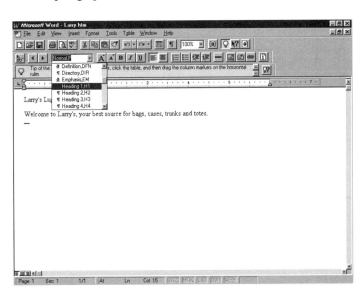

Observe that each choice in the Style drop-down list includes a description, followed by the actual HTML tag the style represents. In the example, I'm making the paragraph "Larry's Luggage" into a level 1 heading, or—as the drop-down menu puts it—Heading 1,H1. "Heading 1" is the description for the style or page element, and "H1" is the actual HTML tag the Assistant applies to my text. Figure 15.11 shows the results of my style selection.

**FIGURE 15.11.**

*The results of the style selection made in Figure 15.10.*

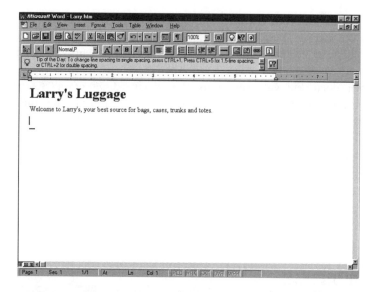

> **NOTE**
>
> Near the bottom of the Style drop-down list, you'll see choices for Bottom of Form and Top of Form. As these choices suggest, you can use Word with Internet Assistant to compose HTML forms designed to interact with server-based CGI scripts to collect and process user input. However, the FrontPage Editor offers a far more sophisticated forms facility, and the forms you can create in Internet Assistant might not work properly with the forms processor of a FrontPage Web, if that is where you intend to publish your Web document.
>
> For these reasons, composing forms in Word is not recommended for FrontPage users. Instead, you can compose the rest of the document in Word, and then switch to the FrontPage editor to add forms.

To the right of the Style drop-down list are five buttons. The first two increase and decrease font size, while the other three apply bold, italic, and underline character formatting, just as they do in Word documents. For each of these tools, you must select the text you want to format, and then click the button.

The six buttons to the right of the Underline button are used just as they are in regular Word documents to control text alignment, make lists, and adjust indenting.

# Adding Rules

To add a standard horizontal rule anywhere in your document, position the edit cursor where you want to insert your rule, and then click the Horizontal Rule button on the toolbar. A rule appears at the insertion point, as shown in Figure 15.12.

**FIGURE 15.12.**

*A horizontal rule added to the document.*

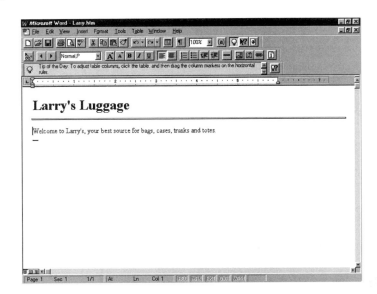

To delete a rule, click the rule and press Delete.

# Adding Pictures

Within Word, you can add inline GIF and JPEG images to your document (for more about GIF and JPEG inline images, see Chapter 10, "Enhancing Your Web Publication with Images—the Easy Way").

To add an inline image to your Web page, follow these steps:

1. Position the edit cursor where you want the picture to appear.

2. Click the Picture button on the toolbar, or choose Insert|Picture. A dialog opens like the one in Figure 15.13.

3. To add a picture, click the Picture tab, and enter in Image Source the full path and filename of a GIF or JPEG image. You also can click Browse to browse for a picture file.

**FIGURE 15.13.**

*Adding a picture to
your document.*

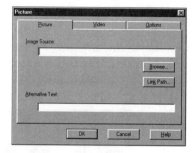

> **NOTE**
>
> In phrasing the path and filename of your GIF or JPEG file, you can use an absolute path, a relative path, or a URL. Which one you must use depends on where both the picture file and your Web document are stored (or rather, where they both will be stored when published).
>
> When you choose a file through Browse, the link is automatically phrased as a relative pathname. To make it an absolute pathname, click Link Path in the Picture tab, click the checkbox next to Use fixed file location, and then click OK.
>
> To learn more about absolute and relative paths, see Chapter 9, "Adding Features to the Page."

After entering the Image Source, you can click OK to insert the image, or you can apply some options. The first option, Alternative Text, appears on the Picture tab along with the Image Source. To use this optional but recommended step, enter in the Alternative Text box some text that carries the same basic meaning as the picture, or text that describes the picture. Whatever text you enter is displayed in place of the image in browsers that don't support inline images. This ensures that your document won't confuse users of non-graphical browsers when a graphic contains important information, such as a company name. (Note that the FrontPage Editor also enables you to supply not only alternative text, but an alternative low-resolution version of a picture. Some browsers can display the low-res version as a pretty placeholder while downloading the final, high-res image.)

The remaining options appear on the Options tab, shown in Figure 15.14.

In the Options tab, you can

- Enter a number of pixels for Height and Width, to scale and shape the picture to a specific dimension.
- Check the Display Border checkbox to draw a black border around the picture. The number you choose in Border Size sets the thickness of the border in pixels.

■ Choose an Alignment setting to determine how the text following the image will align with the image.

■ Check the Image is a sensitive map checkbox to tag the picture as an image map. Note that this alone does not enable image map functions; you also need a map file to tell the client or server how the image map works. (To learn more about image maps, see Chapter 10.)

**FIGURE 15.14.**

*Formatting options for pictures in your document.*

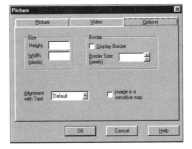

## Adding Hyperlinks

To add a link in your document, follow these steps:

1. Position the edit cursor where you want the link text (the text a guest clicks to activate the link), and then click the Hyperlink button or choose Insert|Hyperlink. The Hyperlink dialog opens, as shown in Figure 15.15.

**FIGURE 15.15.**

*Inserting a link in your document.*

---

**TIP**

In place of step 1, you can type your desired link text directly into your page, highlight the text, and choose the Hyperlink button. The Hyperlink dialog shows the selected text as the Text to Display. You can then skip step 2 and complete your link by performing step 3.

This technique is especially useful for making links out of selected words or phrases within a paragraph.

2. Type the Text to Display. Through a browser, this text is underlined, highlighted, or colored in a unique way to indicate that it is a link.

3. Enter the file or URL. In this box, you can enter a local path and filename, or the URL of a file on the Internet/intranet. You can click Browse to browse for a local file, and you can choose Link Path to open a dialog on which you determine whether the path or URL you've entered is relative or absolute.

4. Click OK. The link text appears in your document, as shown in Figure 15.16.

**FIGURE 15.16.**

*The finished link appears in your page.*

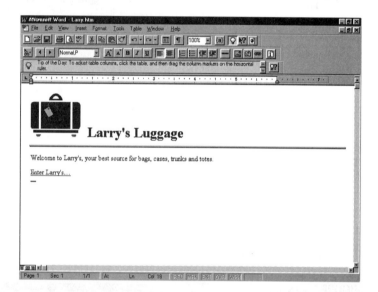

---

**NOTE**

In the Bookmark Location in File box, you can enter the name of a Bookmark within the current document, instead of entering a file or URL. (Bookmarks are more commonly called "anchors" in the Web authoring world.) Activating the link jumps the guest to that spot in the file. You create the Bookmark itself by positioning the edit cursor where you want the bookmark to go, and then clicking the Bookmark button on the toolbar.

Using bookmarks, you can create a table of contents at the top of a long Web page in which each entry is a link to a bookmark later in the page. Such pages are a convenient alternative to multipage Web documents.

# Adding a Background and Text Colors

Using the curiously labeled Background and Links dialog, you can change the color of the background of your page, insert an image in the background, or define custom colors for text and links. Note that all of these page enhancements are supported only by browsers that are compatible with Netscape's enhancements to the HTML specification. They'll show up fine when your page is viewed through Internet Explorer, Netscape Navigator, and several other browsers (which together comprise the overwhelming majority of the Internet), but won't be supported in all browsers.

To customize your background and text colors, follow these steps:

1. Choose Format|Background and Links. A dialog like the one shown in Figure 15.17 opens.

2. In Image, enter the path and filename (or Browse for one) of a GIF or JPEG image to be displayed in the background of your page, behind any text that might appear over it. This feature is used most often for applying a texture of some kind against which overlapping text can be easily read, but it can also be used for splashing a logo or other graphic across the background.

**FIGURE 15.17.**

*Choosing a background
and text colors.*

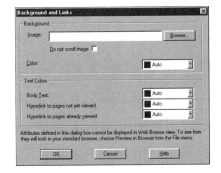

**TIP**

In the Background and Links dialog, click the Do not scroll image checkbox if you want the background image to remain visible on screen no matter where a guest scrolls within the page.

3. To choose a color for your background, select one from the Color drop-down list. As a rule, you shouldn't use both an Image background and a color, unless the image file selected is a transparent GIF image through which the color shows.

4. Under Text Colors, choose colors for your Body Text and Hyperlinks from the drop-down lists provided. Be sure that the three types of text are easy to distinguish from one another, and that all of the types of text stand out well against your selected background.

5. Click OK.

# Adding Inline Video, Scrolling Marquees, and Background Sounds

These three fun and funky page elements are a blessing and a curse. Among popular browsers, only Internet Explorer supports these features. When you use these page elements in a page to be published on the Internet, the majority of your Web guests will not be able to see them. In fact, even Word's Internet Assistant browser cannot show them—you must switch to Internet Explorer to see the results of your work.

With that caveat in mind, here's an overview of how to spruce up your page with these advanced multimedia page enhancements.

■ **Inline Video:** Typically, video clips are added to Web pages *externally*; that is, a link appears on the page, and when the guest clicks the link, the guest's browser downloads a video clip file described by the link and then plays the clip, usually in a helper application. (To learn more about external video, see Chapter 29, "Adding Sound and Video to Web Pages.") To add an external video clip to your Web document, you simply create a link to its file. An inline video clip, on the other hand, appears within the layout of the page itself, just like an inline image. While several different video file formats are supported for external video clips, you must use Video for Windows (AVI) files for inline video clips.

> **NOTE**
>
> If you intend to deploy your page on an intranet populated with users of browsers that support inline video, you might want to try an inline video clip. On the Internet, however, the great majority of Web surfers cannot see inline video clips, so external video clips—which are widely supported—are a better choice.

To add an inline video clip, position the edit cursor in your page where you want the clip to appear, and then click the Picture button on the toolbar (or choose Insert|Picture). In the Picture dialog, click the Video tab. A dialog box like the one in Figure 15.18 appears. In Video Source, enter (or Browse for) the path and filename of the AVI video clip.

**FIGURE 15.18.**

*Adding an inline video clip.*

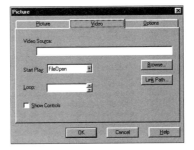

In the Video tab, you can optionally choose the default Start Play setting of FileOpen (video plays as soon as the page appears) to MouseOver (video begins playing when the guest passes the mouse over the clip's position on the page). In Loop, you can choose the number of consecutive times the clip should play, from 1 (clip plays once and then stops) to infinite (clips plays over and over until the guest exits the page). Finally, checking Show Controls displays a small control panel on the guest's screen. The panel enables the guest to start and stop play at will.

- **Scrolling Marquees:** Scrolling marquees are like those scrolling news displays in Times Square, the ones people in movies are always staring up at to discover that Kennedy was shot or to stay abreast of events aboard Apollo 13. Or they're like those weather bulletins your local TV station scrolls across the bottom of *Oprah* when a thunderstorm is on the way.

  To add a scrolling marquee to your page, choose Insert|Marquee. A dialog appears like the one in Figure 15.19. To create a marquee using the default settings, simply type the Text and click OK. You can also select any of the various options for scrolling Direction, Speed, and so on to customize the behavior of your marquee.

**FIGURE 15.19.**

*Adding a scrolling marquee.*

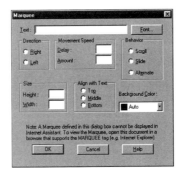

- **Background Sound:** A background sound plays automatically when a guest first displays your page. Your background sound clip must be in the .WAV or .AU file format.

To add a background sound, choose Format|Background Sound. A dialog like the one in Figure 15.20 appears. In Sound, enter the path and filename of your .AU or .WAV sound clip (or Browse for it). In Playback loop, you can select the number of times your sound clip should play after the guest opens your page.

**FIGURE 15.20.**

*Adding a background sound.*

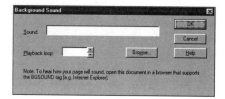

## Viewing Your Document in a Browser

As mentioned earlier in this chapter, the Internet Assistant adds a fully functional Web browser to Word—well, almost. Word's built-in Web browser is handy for quickly evaluating your text layout and other basic page elements, although such elements are displayed WYSIWYG in the regular HTML Edit view. Unfortunately, Word's browser cannot display page elements or formatting based on extensions to HTML. These include font sizing, backgrounds, text colors, and other advanced formatting options.

To better view and test your page, you should open it in a better browser—Microsoft Internet Explorer and Netscape Navigator are excellent choices.

The Preview in Browser button on Word's toolbar opens the current HTML document within your default Windows 95 browser, the browser that opens automatically when you open any HTML file.

# Converting an Existing Word Document to HTML

As you learned earlier in this chapter, not all Word formatting can be carried over into an HTML document. It's impossible to take an existing Word document, convert it to HTML, and expect it to look the same on the Web as it does in Word. Although the Internet Assistant does its best to make a reasonable conversion, you'll almost always want to edit its choices somewhat, either in Word's HTML Edit view or in FrontPage. Still, the conversion usually gives you a good head start.

## How Conversion to HTML Changes Your Word Document

So what do you get when you convert? First, the Internet Assistant does its best to intelligently match your Word formatting to an existing HTML style. For example, a large or bold line of text might be turned into an HTML heading. A Word table becomes an HTML table, and bulleted or numbered lists in Word become HTML bulleted or numbered lists. Inevitably, though, Internet Assistant will find text it doesn't know what to do with. Usually, such text is assigned an HTML <PRE> (preformatted) tag, which preserves as much as possible the general appearance of the text in Word (except for font selection), including preserving tabs, which are omitted by other styles.

The following is a list of Word formatting and page elements that are ignored or deleted when you convert a Word document to HTML:

- Annotations
- Borders and shading (other than table borders and shading)
- Captions
- Fields—only the field result is converted
- Footnotes and endnotes
- Frames (the top and bottom of any frame are converted to horizontal rules, and the sides are lost)
- Headers and footers
- Paragraph indent (except indents used in lists)
- Index entries
- Page breaks and section breaks
- Revision marks
- Tabs (except in the PRE and DL styles)
- Table of contents entries

When converting your document from Word format to HTML, the Internet Assistant automatically converts all pictures in your Word document into .GIF format, and stores the GIF versions in the same directory as the HTML document itself. The Assistant also renames the image files as IMG00001.GIF, IMG00002.GIF (and so on, in the order they appear in the document). These new names are the ones used to phrase the <IMG SRC> links that connect the images to your document.

## Saving a Word Document in HTML Format

Performing the conversion is a simple matter of saving the Word document in HTML format:

1. Open the Word document you want to convert.
2. Choose File|Save As. The Save As dialog opens, as shown in Figure 15.21.
3. In the Save As dialog, type a new name for your document. You need not type an extension (.HTM is added automatically).

342

**FIGURE 15.21.**

*Converting a Word document to HTML.*

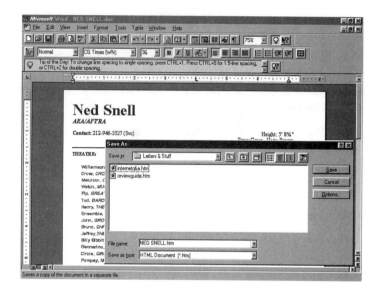

4. In Save as Type, choose HTML Document (*.htm).

5. Click Save.

After conversion, use Word's HTML Edit view or FrontPage to add the header information (such as the title) to your new HTML document, as described earlier in this chapter.

---

## FINE-TUNING WORD'S CONVERSION CHOICES

If you make extensive use of Word styles in documents that will be converted to HTML, you might find it worth the trouble to "map" your Word styles to your selected HTML equivalents. After you do so, whenever you convert a Word document to HTML, each of your Word styles will be converted to the HTML style of your choice.

Note that the following procedure requires editing the Windows 95 registry, which requires an advanced knowledge of Windows 95's innards and is not a job for the squeamish. If you're uncomfortable about attempting the procedure, try some conversions first, and see what you end up with. You might find the default mapping selections adequate to your needs.

1. From the Windows 95 Start menu, choose Run.

2. Enter regedit to open the Windows 95 Registry Editor.

3. In HKEY_CURRENT_USER, select the folder Software\Microsoft\Word, and then select the Internet Assistant\StyleMap folder.

4. On the Edit menu, point to New and then choose String Value from the submenu. A text box with the text New Value #n appears in the Name column of the Registry.

5. Replace New Value #n with the name of the Word style you want to map to an HTML tag. Then select that style name.

6. From the Edit menu, choose Modify.

7. In the Value Data dialog, type the HTML tag to which you want to map the style.

# Moving Your Document to FrontPage

After you've done all you care to in Word's Internet Assistant, it's time to open your Web document in the FrontPage Editor to add any advanced FrontPage formatting or to perform final testing before publishing. All you need to do is open the document in FrontPage, just as you would any other HTML document.

1. Open the FrontPage Editor.

2. Choose File|Open.

3. Enter the path and filename of your document, or browse for it.

The document appears in FrontPage (see Figure 15.22), ready for editing and enhancement.

**FIGURE 15.22.**

*Opening your new document in the FrontPage Editor.*

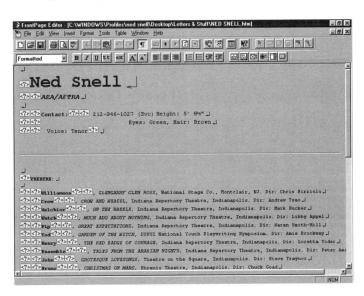

# Learning More About Internet Assistant

If you need further information about Internet Assistant, here are two great starting points:

- Unlike all of the other Internet Assistants, Word's comes with a Help file. A choice for Internet Assistant Help appears in your Word Help menu when—and only when—the open document is an HTML document.

- On its Web site, Microsoft has set up an online tutorial for Word's Internet Assistant (see Figure 15.23) at this address:

  ```
  http://www.microsoft.com/smallbiz/leverage/nbackgrnd.htm
  ```

**FIGURE 15.23.**

*Microsoft's online tutorial for Word's Internet Assistant.*

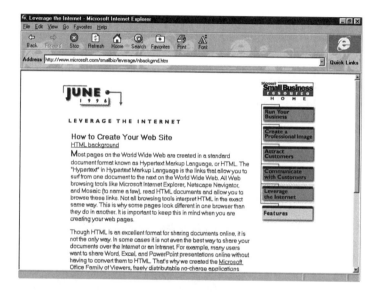

# Summary

Word is by far the most useful of the Office applications that can generate Web content through an Internet Assistant. In particular, you might find Word a great place to start when you want to Web-publish content that already exists in Word format. But don't get the idea that your Word documents can appear on the Web exactly as they appear on your screen. HTML is not a word processing format, and formatting compromises must be made in the translation from Word to Web.

If you want your guests to see your Word document exactly as it was originally formatted, you might consider forgoing any conversion to HTML and instead offer the original Word file for downloading. You can also provide your visitors with Microsoft's free Word viewer (see Chapter 14), so even those who don't have Word can still see your document after downloading it.

# Using Internet Assistant for PowerPoint

# 16

*by Ned Snell*

Unlike Word, which is a general-purpose document maker, PowerPoint is utterly and completely useless for any purpose whatsoever—except for making presentations, of course. (Interestingly, the same can be said of the British Royal Family… but I digress.) By logical extension, PowerPoint plus its Internet Assistant are useless for creating any type of Web page except one that resembles a presentation.

That's more valuable than it sounds. If you use PowerPoint, you know that it does more than just help you create your slides. It has convenient tools for brainstorming, outlining, and otherwise developing your ideas before slide creation ever begins. Such tools are a boon to Web authors; if you've spent much time on the Web, you've seen many documents for which you wished the author had spent more time organizing his or her thoughts, and less time splashing pictures and links everywhere to mask a poorly structured document.

PowerPoint helps you express yourself in a clear, persuasive way. Its handy templates and AutoContent Wizard will help you build a great-looking sales pitch, training session, or orientation with ease.

When all of that's done, PowerPoint's Internet Assistant will convert your finished presentation into a Web document in a snap, enabling you to sell, train, or orient right through the Net. That's power worth having.

# About Internet Assistant for PowerPoint

Installing the PowerPoint Internet Assistant as described later in this chapter adds a single item to PowerPoint's File menu: Export as HTML. PowerPoint's Internet Assistant does not turn PowerPoint into any kind of Web document editing tool—it simply adds a conversion mechanism to turn finished PowerPoint presentations into HTML documents.

## What It Does

After you run a presentation through the Export as HTML routine (as described later in this chapter), you wind up with not one HTML version of your presentation, but two:

- A completely graphical version of your presentation (see Figure 16.1) in which each Web page includes an image of a slide and a set of graphical control buttons for moving among slides. The graphics version is made up of HTML files that open the graphics files containing the slide images (the slide images can be in GIF or JPEG format—you get to choose).

- A text-only HTML version (see Figure 16.2) of your presentation, with added text-only links for moving forward and backward through the presentation.

- In both versions, the rightmost link is used for switching between versions. Guests can enjoy the graphical version, but if the speed with which the graphics download and display taxes their patience, they can switch to the text version.

#### Chapter 16

**FIGURE 16.1.**

*A PowerPoint slide, converted to HTML and displayed on the Web.*

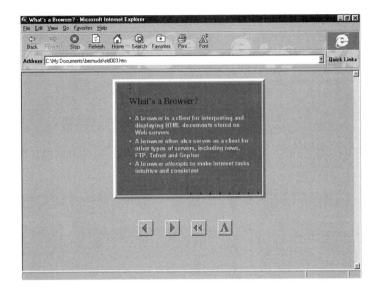

**FIGURE 16.2.**

*The text-only version of the slide shown in Figure 16.1.*

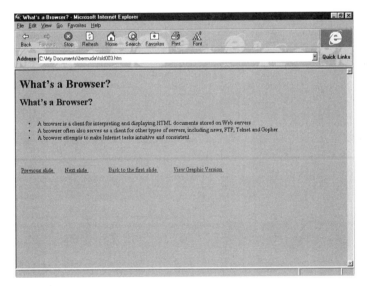

For each presentation, the conversion process churns out the following files and stores them all in a folder together:

- A group of HTML files (extension .HTM) whose names begin with the letters SLD (slide), one file for each slide in the presentation. These files are the HTML files for the graphical version, and they do little more than open the graphics files of each slide.

- A group of GIF or JPEG image files (extension .GIF or .JPG) whose names begin with the letters SLD (slide), one file for each slide in the presentation. These are the slide image graphics files that are opened by the HTML files described earlier. For example, HTML file `SLD001.HTM` opens image `SLD001.GIF`; `SLD003.HTM` opens `SLD003.GIF`; and so on.

■ A group of HTML files whose names begin the letters `TSLD` (text slide), one file for each slide in the presentation. Each of these HTML files contains the full text of one slide, and opens no image file.

■ `INDEX.HTM`, a new HTML page (not a slide) generated automatically by the conversion (see Figure 16.3). This HTML file shows the title of your presentation and your name and company name. It also provides a list of links, one for each slide. Guests can jump from `INDEX.HTM` to the first slide and move in order through the presentation, or they can jump straight to any slide by clicking its name in `INDEX.HTM`.

**FIGURE 16.3.**

*An* `INDEX.HTM` *file, the "top" page for the presentation.*

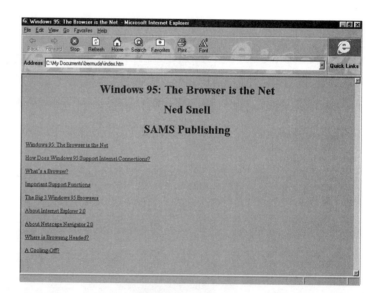

---

**TIP**

When your presentation is published, guide your visitors to `INDEX.HTM`. That's the starting point for viewing your presentation online.

---

In addition to all of the slide image and HTML files, a small collection of GIF files is added to the folder. These are the image files for the control buttons that appear on the pages of the graphics version. (See Figure 16.4.)

**FIGURE 16.4.**

*The files produced for a single Web presentation.*

## System Requirements

The PowerPoint Internet Assistant described in this chapter requires Microsoft PowerPoint for Windows 95 (PowerPoint version 7.0 or higher). If you have the hardware to run PowerPoint 7.0, you can run its Internet Assistant, too.

# Downloading PowerPoint's Internet Assistant

Like all of the Internet Assistants, PowerPoint's can be found all over the Web and on many FTP sites. But as always, to be sure you get the latest, most stable version, get your PowerPoint Internet Assistant straight from Microsoft.

> **NOTE**
>
> All of the Microsoft Internet Assistants are included on the CD-ROM bundled with this book. However, it's important that you know how to get the Assistants straight from Microsoft because they are updated and enhanced regularly.

Microsoft makes the PowerPoint download available from a variety of links on its home page. The simplest place to start is the PowerPoint Internet Tools page (part of the Microsoft Office Web site) at

```
http://www.microsoft.com/mspowerpoint/it_ppt.htm
```

From the PowerPoint Internet Tools page (shown in Figure 16.5), you can download the PowerPoint Internet Assistant file or learn more about the Assistant. By starting at this page (rather than going directly to the file with a Web address or FTP address listed here), you can be assured of picking up the latest version, and you'll also get a chance to read useful announcements along the way.

> **NOTE**
>
> The filename of the current version of the PowerPoint Internet Assistant is
>
> `PPTIA.EXE`
>
> However, updated versions are offered regularly. You should always navigate
> Microsoft's Web site to find the latest version, which may or may not have the
> previously mentioned name.

**FIGURE 16.5.**

*The PowerPoint Internet Tools page at* http://www.microsoft.com/mspowerpoint/it_ppt.htm.

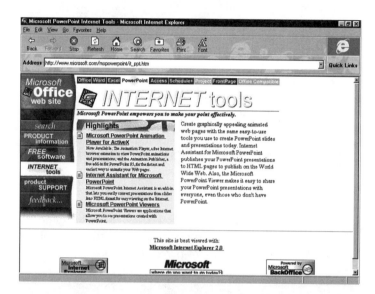

The self-extracting archive file is about 233KB. When downloading, you needn't save the file in any special place, but be sure to move the archive file into its own folder before installation. The archive releases files you'll want to be able to find easily, such as a documentation file.

> **ANIMATE YOUR WEB**
>
> In addition to the PowerPoint Internet Assistant, Microsoft makes two other free,
> Internet-and-PowerPoint-related programs available from the PowerPoint Internet
> Tools page of the Office Web site (see Figure 16.5). As with the Internet Assistants, the
> following two programs also are included on the CD-ROM bundled with this book.
>
> ■ The PowerPoint Animation Publisher is an add-in to PowerPoint that packages
> your PowerPoint presentation as a PPZ (PowerPoint Animation) file for play
> through a Web browser. The PPZ file is compressed for quick transfer through a
> network and decompresses automatically when played.

■ The PowerPoint Animation player is a helper application that gives Windows Web browsers the capability to play your PowerPoint animations. The Player gives plug-in compatible browsers, such as Internet Explorer 3.0 (and higher) and Netscape Navigator 2.0 (and higher), the capability to play the PPZ files inline. The player also functions as a helper application, to play the animation in a separate window in Windows browsers that don't support plug-ins. Note that a 16-bit version of the player is available for Windows 3.1 users. Note, too, that the specially compressed PPZ files created by the Animation Publisher can be viewed only through the player; they cannot be viewed in PowerPoint itself.

Installing and using these programs is very similar to using the Internet Assistant. You first create your PowerPoint presentation, using any of PowerPoint's animation capabilities you choose. You then select an Export to Internet item from PowerPoint's file menu, follow the prompts, and wind up with the PPZ file and a simple HTML file that includes a link to the PPZ file. (The HTML file also includes a link to the Animation Player at Microsoft's home page, so visitors who don't yet have the player can download it to play your animation.) You can then publish the HTML and PPZ files on your FrontPage Web.

It's important to understand the distinctions between PowerPoint's Animation Publisher and its Internet Assistant. The output from the Internet Assistant is standard HTML files, viewable through any Web browser on any platform. The PPZ file output from the Animation Publisher can be played only through a browser equipped with the Animation player, which is available only for Windows 95/NT and Windows 3.1. The Internet Assistant strips animations from your presentation, but makes your presentation accessible to anyone on the Internet. The Animation Publisher preserves your animations, but the presentation can be seen only by Windows users. That makes the Animation Publisher a great tool for publishing animated presentations on a Windows-based intranet, but a little restrictive for wide Web use.

The Animation Publisher can be used in addition to the Internet Assistant. When both are installed, an Export for Internet option appears on PowerPoint's File menu. After you choose that option, a dialog offers you a choice between exporting the current presentation as a PowerPoint animation (through the Animation Publisher) or as an HTML presentation (through the Assistant). You also get an Export as Both option to simultaneously output the same presentation as HTML (stripped of animations) through the Internet Assistant and as a PPZ file and its HTML front-end.

You can quickly add your finished PowerPoint animation to a FrontPage Web by choosing File|Import in FrontPage Explorer and then importing the HTML file (not the PPZ file) output by the Animation Publisher.

# Setting Up

To install PowerPoint Internet Assistant after downloading the self-extracting archive file, follow these steps:

> **CAUTION**
>
> Before you begin setting up PowerPoint's Internet Assistant, make sure that PowerPoint is closed.

1. Open the archive file (PPTIA.EXE) by double-clicking its file icon or right-clicking it and choosing Open from the context menu. In a DOS window (see Figure 16.6), the four files making up the Assistant are decompressed and copied into the same directory as the archive file.

**FIGURE 16.6.**

*Starting the Setup Wizard.*

2. When the title bar on the DOS window reads "Finished," close the DOS window by clicking the X in its upper-right corner.

   Figure 16.7 shows the four files decompressed from the archive (in addition to the archive itself, PPTIA.EXE, which you can now delete). They are as follows:

   - ■ IA4PPT95.EXE: The Setup Wizard that installs the Assistant.

   - ■ IA4PPT95.DOC, IA4PPT95.HTM: A very brief user's manual in two files containing the same text. The .DOC file can be viewed and printed through Word, while the .HTM file can be viewed and printed through any Web browser. Your choice.

   - ■ README.TXT: Notes and asides Microsoft forgot to include in the manual.

**FIGURE 16.7.**

*The Internet Assistant archive files.*

3. Open the Setup Wizard (IA4PPT95.EXE) by double-clicking its file icon or right-clicking it and choosing Open from the context menu. A dialog pops up to ask if you want to install Internet Assistant. Click Yes or press Enter.

   Another DOS window opens to report that files are being copied to the PowerPoint directory and that the registry is being updated. When the process is finished, a message appears to report that installation is complete.

After installation is complete, you can delete the self-extracting archive file, as well as the other files in its folder—although you might want to keep one of the manual files and README.TXT for reference.

# Using PowerPoint's Internet Assistant

In a nutshell, using PowerPoint's Internet Assistant is a simple matter of opening (or creating) a presentation, choosing File|Export as HTML, and following a few prompts. To be sure you end up with the HTML presentation you want, you must first check and prepare some elements of the presentation, make a few choices about how you want the presentation to be presented, and take advantage of a few powerful PowerPoint features that translate into powerful HTML.

## Preparing Your Presentation

Unlike Word, PowerPoint does not limit what you can do in your presentation. You can create your presentation through any means—the AutoContent Wizard, a template, or a blank presentation—or you can use any existing presentation. You also can apply any of PowerPoint's decorative features—such as its drawing tools and clip art—to spruce up a presentation intended for Web display.

Still, the Assistant exhibits a few quirks that you must account for before you export. Of course, if you export the file and don't like the results, you can always edit the original PowerPoint presentation and then repeat the export procedure and overwrite your previously created Web files. But considering the following points before exporting will save you the time and effort that trial and error always demands.

■ **Animations:** The Internet Assistant automatically strips your presentation of any animation or video content. If these features are important to you, and your expected audience comprises only Windows users (as on a Windows-based intranet), consider forgoing the Internet Assistant and instead using the PowerPoint Animation Publisher, described earlier in this chapter. (Like the Internet Assistant, the Animation Publisher is included on the CD-ROM with this book.)

■ **Notes and Hidden Slides:** When you present your presentation on your PC, any speaker notes you've created are hidden from the viewer. However, each page of the HTML version includes any speaker notes for that page, under the heading "Notes" at the bottom of the page. Also, if you've used "hidden" slides in your presentation, they are exported as regular slides. If you don't want the speaker notes or hidden slides to appear to Web visitors, delete them before exporting the presentation. (If you want to keep the notes or hidden slides for future PC presentations, use File|Save As to make a copy of your presentation under a different name; then delete the notes or hidden slides from the copy and export the copy to HTML).

■ **Text Slides:** Consider whether the text versions of your slides are important to you (or your intended guests). If they are important, review all of the text on all of your slides, and consider whether they effectively carry their meaning without any color or graphics. If you've embedded meaningful information (as opposed to mere decoration) in the graphical and color content of your slides, you'll want to rewrite the text so that it can do the job alone.

■ **Font Sizes:** In the graphics versions of your slides, the text appears smaller than it would be in a PowerPoint presentation, because the slide image is smaller than full-screen. Before exporting, consider increasing font size to help your text remain readable after export.

■ **Slide Image Size versus Resolution:** In the graphics versions of your slides, each page displays the slide image as a graphic centered on the page. The size of that graphic is determined by the resolution settings of your display at the time you perform the export. The HTML slides shown in this chapter (refer to Figure 16.1) were exported when the display was set at 800×600 dpi. Changing display resolution (before exporting) to 1024×768, for example, produces larger slide images, while switching to 640×480 produces smaller slide images. When choosing a resolution, keep in mind that bigger images mean bigger graphics files and slower transfers to the guest's desktop.

**TIP**

To change your display resolution, right-click an empty area of the Windows 95 desktop and choose Properties from the context menu. Click the Settings tab, and then use the slider control under Desktop area to choose the display resolution. Click OK. (Windows might prompt you to restart Windows before your changes will take effect, depending on your hardware.)

■ **Grayscale Contrast:** When exporting, you'll have the opportunity to create color images of your slides or grayscale conversions. The grayscale versions will tend to be smaller (and thus faster on the Web) than the color versions. If you choose to use grayscale, make sure that your slides use colors and backgrounds that contrast strongly with one another, for readability. Some combinations that contrast well in color blend together when converted to grayscale.

## ADDING HYPERLINKS TO YOUR WEB PRESENTATION

From within PowerPoint and before exporting, you can add links to your PowerPoint presentation. You select any object in the slide, and attach to it a link that can lead anywhere on your intranet or the Internet. When a guest clicks that object in the image of the slide that appears in the graphics version, the link is activated.

One word of caution, though: This capability relies on a *client-side image map*. Client-side image maps are not supported by all browsers; fortunately, they are supported by Netscape Navigator and Internet Explorer. (For more about image maps, see Chapter 10, "Enhancing Your Web Publication with Images—the Easy Way.")

To create a link, follow these steps:

1. In a slide, select the object you want guests to click to activate the link. (Note that you can create multiple links in a slide, but only one link per object.)

2. Choose Tools|Interactive Settings. A dialog like the one in Figure 16.8 appears.

3. Click the radio button next to Run Program.

4. In the box beneath Run Program, enter the full URL of the resource to which you intend to link. (For more about URLs, see Chapter 9, "Adding Features to the Page.")

5. Click OK.

6. Export your presentation to HTML as described in the next section.

**FIGURE 16.8.**

*Creating a link and image map in a slide.*

# Converting Your Presentation to HTML

After you've considered the issues described earlier under "Preparing Your Presentation" and properly prepared for exporting, exporting is a cakewalk.

To export your PowerPoint presentation to HTML, follow these steps:

1. Open the presentation in PowerPoint.
2. Choose File|Export as HTML. A dialog like the one in Figure 16.9 appears.

**FIGURE 16.9.**

*Exporting your presentation as HTML.*

3. Under Output style, choose Grayscale or Color slides. Color slides retain your presentation's original colors, while grayscale slides take up less disk space and transfer more quickly to a guest's display.

4. Under Output format, choose JPEG or GIF. As a rule, GIF is the better choice, because inline GIF files are supported by more browsers and they tend to better survive scaling to different sizes. Inline JPEG images are supported by fewer browsers (though Internet Explorer and Netscape Navigator both support inline JPEG), but JPEG images can take up less disk space than GIF images, depending upon the JPEG image quality selected.

   If you do choose JPEG, use the slider control to choose image quality. Lower image quality means a fuzzier image, but a smaller, quicker file. Higher quality means sharper images, but fatter, slower files.

5. In the Folder for HTML Export box, enter a path for a folder in which to store the converted presentation files.

**CAUTION**

The Internet Assistant uses the same filenames (SLD001.*, and so on) for every presentation you create. It's crucial, therefore, that you store each presentation you create in a folder by itself, to avoid overwriting old presentations with new ones, and to keep files together and well organized.

6. Click OK, and then immediately release the mouse button. (Do not touch the mouse or keyboard again until the conversion is complete; an errant mouse move or keystroke could display a pop-up menu in the slide window, which would then become part of your presentation.)

A progress indicator appears, informing you that conversion is underway. Shortly thereafter, a small window opens and moves through all of your slides in a mini slideshow. After the slide show finishes, a message reporting "Presentation successfully saved..." appears. You may now open and edit your presentation in the FrontPage Editor, or publish the files.

To review your finished presentation, open INDEX.HTM in a browser.

# Summary

PowerPoint is a presentation maker. If your prospective Web page is a presentation or is presentation-like, PowerPoint's Internet Assistant is a quick way to produce a result that's both effective and polished.

Keep in mind, however, that PowerPoint slides typically contain only a small amount of information per slide—less actual information than the typical Web page. When viewing the graphical version of your online presentation, visitors might have to wait a little while for each slide to appear. If each slide has only a few lines of text, visitors could lose patience and quit the presentation before finishing.

If you intend to deploy your presentation on an intranet, consider using the PowerPoint Animation Publisher instead of the Internet Assistant. The Animation Publisher enables you to retain sound, video, and animation in your online presentation, all of which are stripped out by the Internet Assistant. If your intranet is populated with Windows PCs and relatively speedy modems, the Publisher is your best choice for putting the full power of PowerPoint online.

# Internet Assistants for Excel, Access, and Schedule+

**17**

*by Ned Snell*

**IN THIS CHAPTER**

The Internet Assistants for Word and PowerPoint both crank out complete, fully fleshed-out HTML documents. None of the other Assistants are really practical for that purpose, which makes perfect sense, because none of the other Office applications for which an Assistant is available—Excel, Access, or Schedule+—is really a document-maker by design. Instead, the Assistants for these applications—which one might group together as "data managers"—help you conveniently export formatted data from an application into an HTML document that you'll otherwise compose and edit in another environment, such as the FrontPage Editor or Word.

Of course, the fact that they're not real document makers doesn't prevent them from trying to be. Each of the Assistants has the capability to produce a self-contained HTML document. But to what end? What good is a Web page full of data without more explanatory—or even conversational—material around it? Excel's Internet Assistant recognizes this, enabling you to export a table of data to an existing HTML document as well as a complete Web page. The others produce entire HTML files populated with their data. But you'll create an HTML file in the Assistants for Access or Schedule+ not because either produces a truly finished Web document, but because doing so gives you a way to channel existing application data into the document. You'll then open that document in the FrontPage Editor and add all of the other material and formatting that turns a mere datasheet into a *page*.

> **NOTE**
>
> All of the Microsoft Internet Assistants are included on the CD-ROM bundled with this book. However, it's important that you know how to get the Assistants straight from Microsoft (as described in the following section) because they are updated and enhanced regularly.

# Finding and Downloading the Assistants

The latest version of the archive file for each of the Internet Assistants covered in this chapter can be found on each application's Internet Tools page in the Microsoft Office Web Site. To reach the Internet Tools (see Figure 17.1), point your browser to the Office Internet Tools page at

```
http://www.microsoft.com/MSOffice/MSOfc/it_ofc.htm
```

From the Internet Tools page shown in Figure 17.1, choose the product name (Excel, Access, or Schedule+) from the bar at the top of the page. For example, click Access to see Access's Internet Tools page, shown in Figure 17.2. The Internet Tools page for each product offers a link to a page about its Internet Assistant. Clicking the link shown in Figure 17.2 displays a page describing Access's Internet Assistant (see Figure 17.3) and offers a link that downloads the Assistant.

**NOTE**

After installation, any of the Internet Assistants described in this chapter can be uninstalled through the Add/Remove programs icon in the Control Panel.

**FIGURE 17.1.**

*Finding the Internet Assistants from the Office page.*

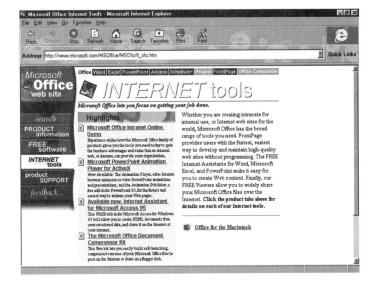

**FIGURE 17.2.**

*The Access Internet Tools page, which features a link to a page about Access's Internet Assistant.*

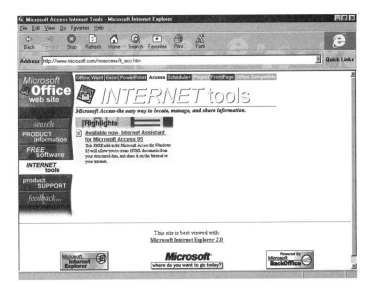

**FIGURE 17.3.**

*The Access Internet Assistant page, which includes installation instructions and a link that downloads the Assistant file.*

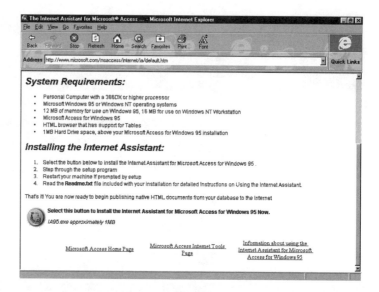

With many browsers, you must first download the file, and then open it after downloading to extract the archived files and run the Setup Wizard. Some browsers, including Internet Explorer and Netscape Navigator, have the capability to automatically open a file immediately after downloading it, saving you a step (see Figure 17.4).

You can take advantage of this feature to quickly install the Access and Schedule+ Assistants. The Excel Internet Assistant, on the other hand, requires a different setup procedure. You should download the Excel Internet Assistant file and save it to disk; then install it as described in the next section.

**FIGURE 17.4.**

*Instructing Internet Explorer to open a file immediately after downloading it.*

# Working with Excel's Internet Assistant

Unlike the other Internet Assistants, Excel's is compatible with several different versions of Excel, thanks to the cross-platform and backwards compatibility of Excel's .XLA add-ins. The Internet Assistant add-in, HTML.XLA, works with the following programs:

- Excel 7.0 (Excel for Windows 95)
- Excel 5.0 for Windows NT (32-bit Excel)
- Excel 5.0 for Windows 3.1 (16-bit Excel)
- Excel 5.0 for Macintosh/Power Macintosh

When using the Assistant, you'll have the option to save data as a complete, new HTML file—including a title, header, and footer you can enter from within the Assistant. Alternatively, you can export an Excel table to an existing HTML file you have prepared with the insertion of a single line of HTML code.

> **NOTE**
>
> The Internet Assistant for Excel does not output equations or other functions—it publishes their results. The finished HTML file shows worksheet output and cannot be dynamically updated as a real worksheet can. To update your Excel-derived Web page, you must first update the worksheet in Excel (or check that it has been updated automatically through OLE), and then re-create the Web page through the Assistant.

## Setting Up

To properly set up the Excel add-in after downloading it, you must first copy it into your system's Excel library folder. If you use a Windows version of Excel and did not install Excel as part of the Office suite, your library folder is probably

*d*:\EXCEL\LIBRARY

where *d*: represents the disk drive where Excel is installed. If you have Office, your Excel library folder is

*d*:\MSOFFICE\EXCEL\LIBRARY

After HTML.XLA is in the library folder, set up the add-in:

Open Excel and choose Tools|Add-Ins. The Add-Ins dialog appears, as shown in Figure 17.5.

**FIGURE 17.5.**

*Setting up the Excel Internet Assistant Add-Ins.*

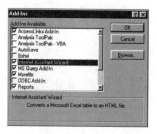

In the Add-Ins dialog, click the checkbox next to Internet Assistant Wizard to place a checkmark there, and then click OK. The Add-In is installed, and a new selection, Internet Assistant Wizard, appears under the Tools menu.

# Selecting Cells to Turn into a Table

Whether you intend to use the Excel Internet Assistant to produce a full page or insert a table into an existing page, your first step is to select the table cells you intend to use.

1. Begin by opening (or creating) the Excel worksheet and cell data. Perform any text formatting you choose, but keep in mind that your font selections will be ignored. Bold, italic, and underlining are supported.

2. Select the cells you want included in your HTML table (see Figure 17.6).

**FIGURE 17.6.**

*Selecting cells to turn into an HTML table.*

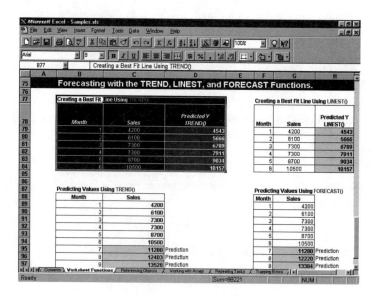

3. Choose Tools|Internet Assistant Wizard. A dialog opens like the one shown in Figure 17.7. The cell range shown is the range you highlighted.

**FIGURE 17.7.**

*Verifying the selected cell range.*

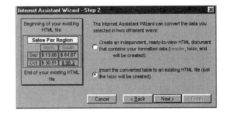

4. Click Next. A dialog like the one in Figure 17.8 is displayed. From this dialog, you must choose whether to insert the table in an existing HTML document, or to create a new HTML document out of the table data. Both approaches are explained in the next two sections.

**FIGURE 17.8.**

*Choosing whether to create a new HTML file or export the table to an existing HTML file.*

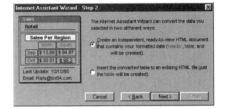

# Making a New HTML Document Out of Selected Cells

To create a new complete HTML document, follow these steps:

1. Click the top radio button in the Step 2 dialog (see Figure 17.8), and then click Next. The Step 3 dialog screen appears (see Figure 17.9).

**FIGURE 17.9.**

*Entering the page content that surrounds the table.*

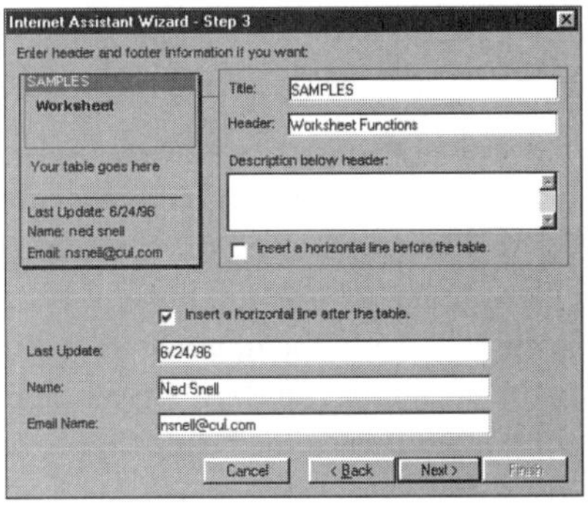

In the Step 3 dialog, you can enter the following:

- The document title (the title that appears in the HTML header, not in the text of the page itself; see Part III).

- A level 1 heading to appear at the top of the page (which the Assistant confusingly labels a "header" even though it's just a big heading at the top of the page).

- A descriptive paragraph to appear between the header and the table.

- Your name and e-mail address, to appear beneath the table.

The sample page that appears on the left side of the dialog illustrates how these elements will be arranged in the finished HTML file.

Note that all of the entries in the Step 3 dialog are optional. Also, some elements are filled in automatically by the Assistant:

- The Title is automatically filled in with the name of the worksheet from which the cells were selected.

- The Header is automatically filled in with the section title from the worksheet.

- Last update is the date you created the HTML page.

- Name is the name of the current Windows 95 user.

You can accept these default choices by leaving them alone, deleting them, or replacing them with your own entries. Note that you can enter or edit any or all of this information later in the FrontPage Editor.

2. When finished entering information in the Step 3 dialog, click Next. The Step 4 dialog appears, as shown in Figure 17.10.

**FIGURE 17.10.**

*Choosing the level of formatting to export.*

In the Step 4 dialog, you choose whether to convert all formatting, including text formatting and cell alignment, into equivalent HTML tags, or whether to export a "bare bones" table that includes only the table and data, but no other formatting. In general, it's best to choose the top button, because browsers that can recognize the formatting tags will apply them, while browsers that can't will simply ignore the tags and display the bare bones anyway. (If you're not sure which way to go, experiment with both options and view the results in browsers you expect your guests to be using.)

3. Click a radio button in the Step 4 dialog, and click Next. The Step 5 dialog is displayed, requesting a path and filename for the HTML file that will be created.

By default, the file is saved in the same directory as the worksheet from which the cells were selected, and the filename is the same as the worksheet, except that the filename extension is changed from .XLS to .HTM. You can change to any path and filename you choose, provided you use the extension .HTM or .HTML on the filename.

4. When the correct path and filename appear in the Step 5 dialog, click Finish.

The file is saved. You can now open it, just as you would any HTML file, in the FrontPage Editor for further editing, or in a browser to view it. Figure 17.11 shows the results of the file created in this example, unedited, as seen through Internet Explorer 3.0.

**FIGURE 17.11.**

*The finished document in Internet Explorer 3.0.*

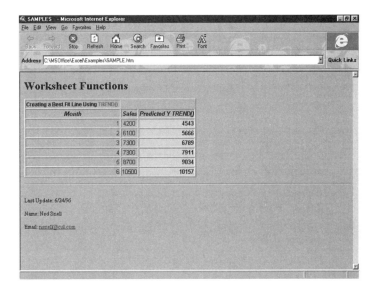

# Inserting Selected Cells into an Existing HTML Document

To insert a table of Excel data into an existing HTML document, you begin not in Excel, but in the FrontPage Editor.

Before selecting cells in Excel and starting the Assistant, you must create and save the document into which the Excel table will be inserted. You can compose as much or as little of that document as you choose (you can always continue working on it after you export the table to it from Excel), but you must at least create and save it to disk, and you must insert the following line into the HTML file.

```
<!--##Table##-->
```

This line is read as a comment by any browser, and is thus ignored. But the Excel Internet Assistant needs this line to determine where to insert the table.

It's important to understand that you can't simply type the line `<!--##Table##-->` into the body of a document in either the FrontPage Editor or the Word Internet Assistant. If you do, the line is simply considered part of the text of your page. You must enter the line as an HTML tag.

To add an HTML tag in the FrontPage Editor, position the cursor in the document at the spot where you want to insert the tag, and then choose Insert|Bot|HTML Markup. Then enter the tag `<!--##Table##-->` and click OK.

Alternatively, you can enter the tag using Word's Internet Assistant (see Chapter 15, "Using Internet Assistant for Word"). Open or create the HTML document in Word, and make sure it appears in HTML Edit View. Click the point in your document where you want the Excel table inserted, and choose Insert|HTML Markup. In the dialog that appears, type `<!--##Table##-->`, and click OK.

After preparing your HTML file, follow these steps:

1. Open Excel, select the table cells, and start the Internet Assistant Wizard as described earlier in this chapter (see "Selecting Cells to Turn into a Table").

2. In the Step 2 dialog (see Figure 17.8, earlier in this chapter), click the bottom radio button, and then click Next. The Step 3 dialog is displayed (see Figure 17.12) to remind you to prepare your HTML file first and to collect the filename of the target HTML file.

**FIGURE 17.12.**

*Identifying the target HTML document into which the table will be inserted.*

3. In the Step 3 dialog, enter the path and filename of the HTML document that contains the `<!--##Table##-->` comment line, and then click Next. The Step 4 dialog appears (see Figure 17.10, earlier in this chapter).

4. In the Step 4 dialog, you choose whether to convert all formatting, including text formatting and cell alignment, into equivalent HTML tags, or whether to export a "bare bones" table that includes only the table and data, but no other formatting. In general, it's best to choose the top button, because browsers that can recognize the formatting tags apply them, while browsers that can't simply ignore the tags and

display the bare bones anyway. (If you're not sure which way to go, experiment with both options and view the results in browsers you expect your guests to use.)

5. Click a radio button in the Step 4 dialog, and then click Next. The table is exported to the target HTML file.

# Working with Access's Internet Assistant

Access, as you know, can manage truckloads of data—as many as 65,000 records per datasheet. A Web page, by comparison, is a smaller, simpler data vehicle—nobody wants to see a 65,000-record Web page. So the most important thing to keep in mind when considering building a Web page from Access data is to carve the data into manageable chunks—each fit for a Web page—before running the Internet Assistant. You can phrase queries to extract just the data you want, and then base a page on each query. Or you can write reports first, and then channel the reports into the Assistant, which creates a separate Web page for each report page.

Note that the Access Internet Assistant exports only formatted data, not any of the decorative or graphical elements that can be included in an Access report. These include any lines or control borders, and also objects created by other applications and imported into Access, such as bitmaps and graphs. As a rule, all you want from Access is its data; you'll provide the decoration yourself, in FrontPage.

Access's Internet Assistant does have a saving grace, though. It includes a collection of templates, HTML files with prebuilt headings, rules, backgrounds, and so on, to dress up your data. Even if you use a template, you'll want to hop over to FrontPage afterward and fine-tune your document. The templates, however, can give you a healthy head-start. You also can create your own custom templates for Access data; you'll learn how later in this chapter.

## Installing Access's Internet Assistant

After you download the file IA95.EXE, open the file by double-clicking its icon or by right-clicking it and choosing Open from the context menu. Then step through the Setup Wizard; no input is required, other than that you click whatever you're told to click. When finished, the Wizard either instructs you to restart Windows (after which setup is complete), or it simply reports that setup was completed successfully (in which case you need not restart Windows).

**NOTE**

After you install Access's Internet Assistant, a README.TXT file appears in the folder where the Assistant's files are stored (/ACCESS/IA95). This file contains a brief but helpful user's manual for the Assistant, plus the most recent notes, tips, and problem-solvers from Microsoft.

# Using Access's Internet Assistant

To create an HTML table from an Access database, follow these steps:

1. Open the database in Access.
2. Choose Tools|Add-ins|Internet Assistant. A Welcome screen opens.
3. On the Welcome screen, click Next. A dialog like the one shown in Figure 17.13 opens.

**FIGURE 17.13.**

*Choosing objects to export to an HTML document.*

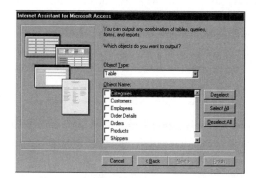

4. In the dialog shown in Figure 17.13, click the checkboxes next to any desired Object Type, and then click the checkboxes next to any desired Object Names. You can choose any combination of tables, queries, forms, or reports, and any combination of objects within each. The datasheet of each selected table, query, or form is output as a single HTML document, including only the data objects selected for that Object Type. For reports, a separate HTML file is produced for each page of the report; links to the other pages are added automatically to each page.

   When finished selecting objects, click Next. A dialog like the one shown in Figure 17.14 opens.

**FIGURE 17.14.**

*Choosing a template.*

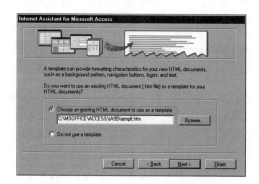

5. In the dialog shown in Figure 17.14, you can choose a template to dress up your Access data. To choose a template, click the radio button next to Choose an existing HTML document, and enter the path and filename of the template or Browse for one. To forego a template, click the radio button next to Do not use a template.

---

**NOTE**

The Access Internet Assistant supports two types of templates: one for datasheets and one for reports. The report templates are identified by the characters _r preceding the .HTM extension. For example, among the templates included with the Access Internet Assistant, the template file STONES.HTM is a datasheet template, while the file STONES_R.HTM is a report template.

The important difference between the types is that the report version includes built-in links for navigating among the pages of the report. When outputting reports to HTML through the Internet Assistant, choose a report template; when outputting datasheets, use a datasheet template. When outputting both at once, choose a datasheet template—the Assistant automatically switches to the report template when outputting reports, if a report version of the selected datasheet template is available.

For more about templates, see "Creating and Editing HTML Templates for Access," later in this chapter.

---

When finished choosing (or not choosing) a template, click Next. A dialog like the one shown in Figure 17.15 is displayed.

6. Enter the path of the folder in which you want your HTML files stored (the default is the folder where the Access Internet Assistant is stored). Click Finish.

**FIGURE 17.15.**

*Choosing a folder for finished HTML documents.*

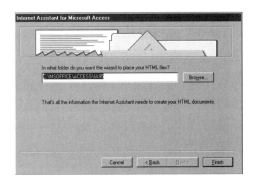

The Internet Assistant generates HTML files from your Access data, and saves the files in the selected folder. The name of each HTML file is automatically derived from the table, query, form, or report on which it is based, followed by the extension .HTM (for example, Customers.HTM).

You can now open the files in the FrontPage Editor for further editing, or view them in a browser.

# Creating and Editing HTML Templates for Access

In the procedure for using the Access Internet Assistant (described in the preceding section), you have the opportunity to plug your Access data into a prebuilt HTML template. The Assistant includes a number of useful templates, but you should be aware that you can easily create your own customized templates to serve as receptacles for Access data. All you need to do is build HTML files with special tags coded as placeholders for Access data. When you run the Assistant and choose your template, the Access data is copied into the Web page exactly where you want it.

To create a template, begin by creating a Web page, using any text, images, backgrounds, or other content you desire. Then add the placeholders for the Access data.

> **NOTE**
>
> As mentioned earlier in this chapter, you cannot insert HTML tags into a document in the FrontPage Editor merely by typing them in the document window. To add an HTML tag in the FrontPage Editor, position the cursor in the document at the spot where you want to insert the tag, and choose Insert|Bot|HTML Markup. Then enter the tag.
>
> Alternatively, you can enter the tag using Word's Internet Assistant (see Chapter 15). Open or create the HTML document in Word, and make sure it appears in HTML Edit View. Click the point in your document where you want to insert the tag, choose Insert|HTML Markup, and then enter your tag.

The following placeholder sets up your template to create an HTML file in which the title is the name of the datasheet object used to create the page. You apply this placeholder in the <TITLE> tag in the header of your HTML file (see the sample HTML file later in this section). If you don't add this placeholder, the name of the template file becomes the title. (You can easily change the title in the FrontPage Editor later, if you choose.)

```
<!ACCESSTEMPLATE_TITLE>
```

The following placeholder sets up your template to receive Access data in the body of the HTML file, in the same spot where you put the placeholder:

```
<!ACCESSTEMPLATE_BODY>
```

Using the <!ACCESSTEMPLATE_BODY> tag is extremely important. If you have included text, images, or other content in the body of your template file, and you fail to insert the preceding tag, the entire body of the HTML file—including any preexisting content—will be replaced by the Access data. If you include the tag, all preexisting content is left alone, and the Access data is simply added to the body in the spot occupied by the placeholder tag.

Note that you create datasheet templates and report templates the same way, except that you must make two adjustments for report templates. First, a report template must feature the characters _r at the end of its filename (right before the .htm extension). Second, the report template must have additional placeholders that the Assistant needs in order to produce the links between the pages of the report. These placeholders, shown next, must appear within the body of the HTML file anywhere after the <!ACCESSTEMPLATE_BODY> placeholder.

```
<A HREF="ACCESSTEMPLATE_FIRSTPAGE>">First</A>

<A HREF="ACCESSTEMPLATE_PREVIOUSPAGE>">Previous</A>

<A HREF="ACCESSTEMPLATE_NEXTPAGE>">Next</A>

<A HREF="ACCESSTEMPLATE_LASTPAGE>">Last</A>
```

The following is a complete Access Template File (for reports) demonstrating where and how the placeholders can be applied.

```
<HTML>
<HEAD>
<TITLE><!ACCESSTEMPLATE_TITLE></TITLE>
</HEAD>
<BODY>
<H1>See My Data</H1>
<BR>
Below appears data culled straight from an Access datasheet and
plugged into this page by the Access Internet Assistant.
<BR>
<HR>
<BR>
<!ACCESSTEMPLATE_BODY>
<BR>
Choose a link to move to another page of my report:
<BR>
<A HREF="ACCESSTEMPLATE_FIRSTPAGE>">First</A>
<A HREF="ACCESSTEMPLATE_PREVIOUSPAGE>">Previous</A>
<A HREF="ACCESSTEMPLATE_NEXTPAGE>">Next</A>
<A HREF="ACCESSTEMPLATE_LASTPAGE>">Last</A>
</BODY>
</HTML>
```

To use your finished template, run the Internet Assistant as described earlier in this chapter. When prompted to choose a template, select your template file.

# Working with the Schedule+ Internet Assistant

I'll be honest—I can't imagine a scenario under which someone would want to make his or her daily schedule accessible to the Internet masses, or even to intranet mini-masses. But Microsoft thinks that you might want to publish your schedule on your intranet; and in fact, in certain settings, intranet access to the schedules of bosses and/or co-workers could be a big help with planning meetings or assigning tasks. Microsoft offers the Internet Assistant for Schedule+ to make that possible.

## Installing Schedule's Internet Assistant

After downloading the file SCHIA.EXE, open the file by double-clicking its icon or by right-clicking it and choosing Open from the context menu. Installation is completed automatically, with no further input from you. When setup is complete, the file Schpost.txt opens automatically in Notepad; this is a readme-type file offering a brief manual to the care and feeding of Schedule+'s Internet Assistant.

## Using Schedule's Internet Assistant

To create a Web page based on Schedule+ data, follow these steps:

1. Open the desired schedule file in Schedule+.
2. Choose File|Internet Assistant. A dialog like the one shown in Figure 17.16 is displayed.

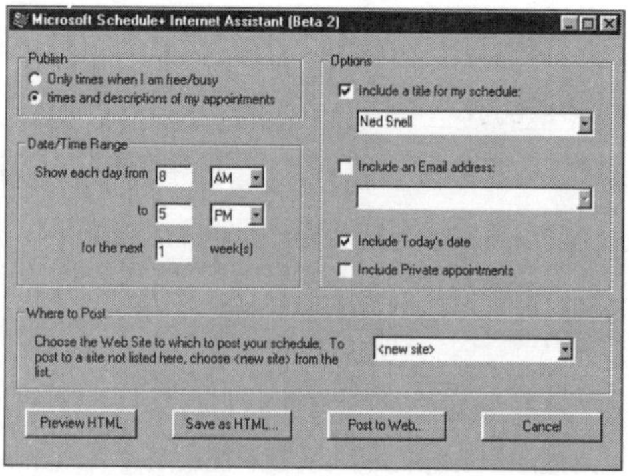

**FIGURE 17.16**

*Choosing which parts of your schedule to publish.*

3. Under Publish, click a radio button to choose whether to restrict the page to showing simply when you're free and when you're busy or to show *why* you're free or busy by including schedule detail.

4. Under Date/Time Range, pick the hours of the day to include in the page, and the number of weeks to include. The hour range enables you to show your schedule during business hours, for example, but keep your after-hours schedule to yourself.

5. Under Options, you can enter the HTML title and an e-mail address guests can click to contact you. (Note that you can just as easily add these items in the FrontPage Editor later.) You also can click checkboxes to Include Today's date or Include Private appointments.

**NOTE**

The dialog box shown in Figure 17.16 has a final section, Post to Web, that enables you to post your schedule page directly from the dialog to a Web server. If you're managing your Web with FrontPage Explorer, however, you'll want to ignore this option so that you can properly locate and manage your schedule page through FrontPage, as you do with your other Web documents.

6. When you are finished, click Save as HTML.

# Summary

The Internet Assistants for Excel, Access, and Schedule+ are minor conveniences; you could call them "utilities" if you want. But given that they're free and pretty easy to use, you should keep them in mind as a quick and dirty way to get existing data out of Office applications and into a FrontPage Web.

**V**

**PART**

# Templates, Web Wizards, and WebBots

# Creating Web Pages with FrontPage's Templates

**18**

*by William Robert Stanek*

FrontPage includes two dozen templates to help you create powerful Web pages. Not only will creating Web pages with templates save you time, but also the templates themselves are guides that can help you design better pages. This chapter discusses each of the major templates, with emphasis on how to use them as the basis for Web pages both within your corporate intranet and on the World Wide Web. Even if you do not plan to use templates, you should read this chapter to gain an understanding of the types of pages used on corporate intranets and Web sites.

# Saving Time with Templates

A template is an outline for a specific type of page that often contains guidelines to make development of the page easier. Although these guidelines do not ask specific questions concerning design and layout of the page, they do cover the major issues you should consider when developing a specific type of page. Because these templates were designed by a team of experts, you gain valuable insight into the specific areas your page should cover.

As you know, you create pages in the FrontPage Editor. To base a new page on a template, select New from the File menu and then choose the template you want to base your page on. Alternatively, you can press Ctrl+N.

Using a template, you can cut an hour or more off the development time of a single page. Webmasters who maintain their own site or a corporate intranet site will find the time savings invaluable, especially when they complete complex projects ahead of schedule and under budget. In the fast-paced profession of Web site design, where cost is usually the deal maker or breaker, the savings you can pass on to your customers by starting with a template could make all the difference in landing the contract.

Generally, all templates include default headings and text that you usually have to replace with headings and text specific to your document. To better understand how templates can save you time and money, let's look at the templates used in FrontPage. By examining each of the templates, you will gain a thorough understanding of what types of pages are used at Web sites and how those pages are designed.

**NOTE**

When you create documents with templates, FrontPage automatically adds comments that guide you through the process of designing the page. To allow you to see the page as it will appear in the reader's browser, these preset comments do not appear in the figures in this chapter.

# Basic Templates

FrontPage includes a set of five basic templates. You will find that these templates are the ones you will use most often.

## Normal Page

If you have been following the examples in this book, you have probably already used the Normal Page template. All this template does is create a blank page for you. By default, the Normal Page template is selected when you open the New Page dialog box. To use this page, you simply press the Enter key or click the OK button without making a selection.

> **NOTE**
>
> Here is a tip to save you some time: After you know how your Web site will be organized, you might want to redefine the properties for the Normal Page template. For example, if your standard background color is white, redefine the template to set the page properties appropriately. Obviously, the more properties that are standardized across your Web site, the more time you will save by redefining this template.

To redefine the Normal Page template, select Save As from the File menu. In the Save As dialog box, click the As Template button. This opens the dialog box shown in Figure 18.1. By default, the template name is that of the template you are using currently. If you want to redefine the template, click the OK button. When FrontPage displays a warning dialog box that asks whether you really want to overwrite the template, select Yes.

> **TIP**
>
> Not only can you redefine templates in FrontPage, but you can also create entirely new templates. Webmasters who maintain multiple sites might want to define variations of the Normal Page template for use with each of their sites. In this way, you can start with a base page for each of your Webs.

**FIGURE 18.1.**

*Redefining a template.*

# HyperDocument Page

The HyperDocument Page template is meant to give you a starting point for large hypertext documents, such as technical manuals or reports. As you can see from Figure 18.2, the template can be used to create links to the major sections of your document.

**FIGURE 18.2.**

*The HyperDocument Page template.*

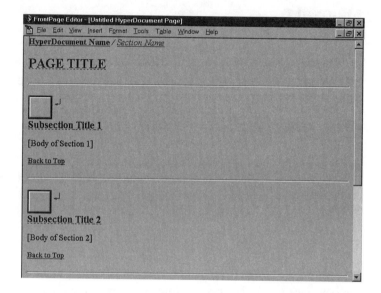

The page titles and subtitles contain links and bookmarks. The easiest way to update the bookmark text is to place the insertion point within the bookmark text, type in your title, and then delete the text before and after the title. If you do not insert your title in this way, you might accidentally delete the bookmark.

Two important links in the page are the document name and section links, which should link to the document's home page and table of contents page, respectively. The document also contains sample images. These gray buttons are placeholders for the icons you will use in your document. Throughout the document, you will find links labeled "Back to Top." Readers can use these links to jump to the top of the Page Title bookmark.

# What's New Page

Most sites use a What's New page to provide readers with an update history for a Web site. Repeat visitors to your Web site will appreciate the effort. You will help them find new information faster, and, ultimately, they will return the favor by revisiting your friendly Web site.

To start a What's New page, you can use the template shown in Figure 18.3. Replace the sample text with your own categories, links, and descriptions. You should make an entry on this page every time you make a significant change to your Web site. The average site tracks about six months of changes. Many small sites track the entire change history of the site. Many large sites use the page to track only the hottest topics and changes to the site.

**FIGURE 18.3.**

*The What's New page template.*

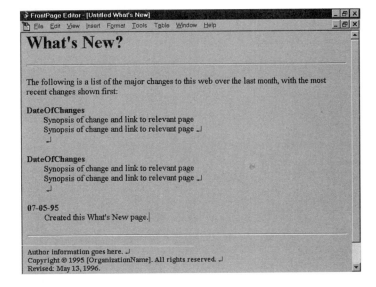

## Frequently Asked Questions

Frequently Asked Questions (FAQ) pages are very common on the Web. Generally, a FAQ is a list of frequently asked questions and their answers. Although a FAQ can cover a broad range of loosely related topics, usually a FAQ exhaustively explores a single topic, such as how to make an MPEG movie or what the options are in digital sound. Many companies that sell commercial software products develop FAQs that explore the uses and benefits of the product.

Figure 18.4 shows the Frequently Asked Questions template. The easiest way to use this template is as a starting point. Again, you should carefully replace the title text so that you do not accidentally delete links and bookmarks. You should add new questions to the end of the Table of Contents section, and then add a new section in the body of the document that answers each question.

To save time when entering a new question, you can copy the entire text of a previous question and then update the associated link properties. To save time when creating a new section, you can copy one of the existing sections and then update the associated bookmark information. Be sure that the link name in the Table of Contents section and the bookmark name in the new section match.

Throughout the document, you will find links labeled "Back to Top." Readers can use these links to jump to the top of the Page Title bookmark.

**FIGURE 18.4.**

*The Frequently Asked Questions template.*

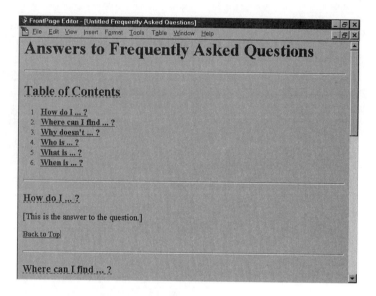

## Hot List

Another common area for most Web sites is a list of links to popular sites. The Hot List Page template shown in Figure 18.5 is organized by topic categories. The best hot lists are for a specific subject category that relates to the features, products, or services at your Web site. You will want to include a brief description of each link featured in your hot list.

**FIGURE 18.5.**

*The Hot List template.*

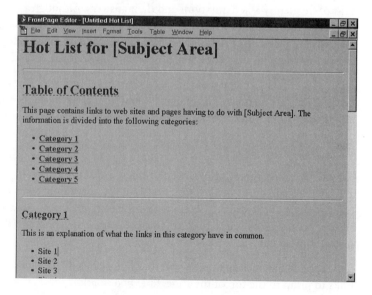

Generally, your hot list page is a community service to those visiting your Web site. Of course, it takes time and resources to maintain. However, it is good business to create an area of your site that serves Internet community interests. For example, Virtual Press, Incorporated, has three main groups: Internet Consulting, Web Design, and Electronic Publishing. We maintain several sites that relate to these subjects. The Writer's Gallery (`http://tvp.com/vpwg.html`) is a community service for anyone interested in writing and literature. The Internet Publishing Information Center (`http://tvp.com/vpjic.html`) is a community service for anyone interested in Web design and Internet consulting.

# Templates for Business Pages

Business pages can serve the corporate intranet and the World Wide Web. If you plan to conduct business on the Web or maintain a Web site for a business, you will probably want to use these templates.

## Employee Directory

The Employee Directory template can be used to create a very complete alphabetized list of employees. The directory page is organized into two main sections. The first section, shown in Figure 18.6, contains an index of employee names that is linked to the detailed list shown in Figure 18.7. As shown, the second section can contain photos and contact information for each employee. Large corporations will probably want separate directory pages for each division.

**FIGURE 18.6.**

*The index to the employee directory.*

**FIGURE 18.7.**

*The listing section of the employee directory.*

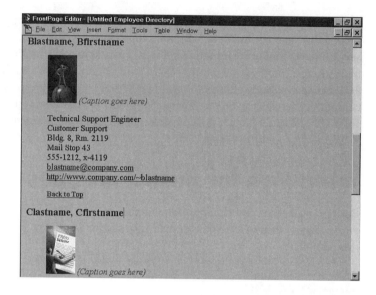

Just as an intranet site could have a hypertext-linked employee directory, so could a site on the Web. However, the goals and scope of pages for internal and external use are usually very different. Within the safety of the corporate firewall, your intranet site could have a division-by-division listing of all employees. This page could be complete with résumés, phone numbers, work hours, and so on. Your corporate directory on the company's Web site, however, would not be a detailed list of all employees. It would probably include only key contacts within specific offices, such as PR, marketing, advertising, and technical support.

Replace the sample text with your own employee information and descriptions. The employee index and contact information contain links and bookmarks. The easiest way to update the bookmark or link text is to place the insertion point within the bookmark or link text, type the new text, and then delete the unneeded text. If you do not insert your text in this way, you might accidentally delete the hypertext reference.

# Employment Opportunities

Most businesses have recurring employment opportunities. When companies spend thousands of dollars placing ads in newspapers and $25,000-$50,000 for each executive recruited through head-hunters and retainers, a low-cost alternative to filling these positions makes sense. The tremendous savings companies can realize from posting their own job openings is surely one of the reasons the Employment Opportunities template is so detailed.

As you can see from Figure 18.8, the template begins with a summary list of job openings by title. Each item in the list is linked to a detailed summary of the job.

**FIGURE 18.8.**

*Summary of job openings.*

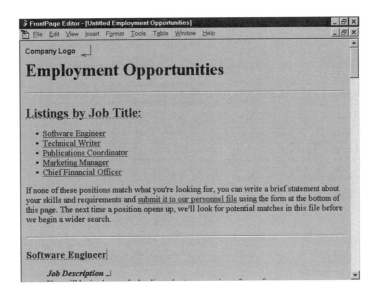

Replace the sample job titles with the current employment opportunities. The easiest way to update link text is to place the insertion point within the link text, type the new job title, and then delete any unnecessary text. If you do not insert your title in this way, you might accidentally delete the hypertext reference.

The main section of the page is the area used to describe the employment opportunities within your organization. As Figure 18.9 shows, each job opening is organized by title, with areas for job description, requirements, and more information.

**FIGURE 18.9.**

*Detailed descriptions of employment opportunities.*

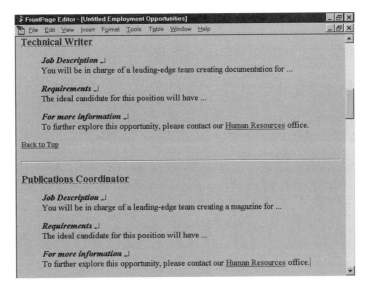

Throughout the main section of the page, you will find links labeled "Back to Top." Readers can use these links to jump to the top of the Listings by Job Title section of the page.

The final section of the page contains a form that allows readers to apply for the positions you have offered. Part of this form is shown in Figure 18.10. Although these questions are good for getting you to think about the type of questions you should ask, you will probably want to create a form that allows readers to enter the electronic version of their résumé.

**FIGURE 18.10.**

*Obtaining information from the prospective employee with a form.*

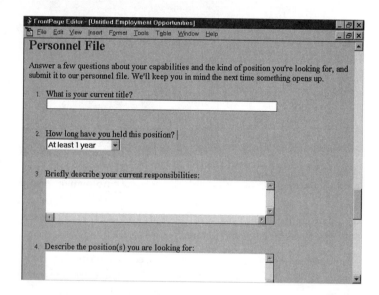

By default, the form uses the Save Results box and stores the data in HTML format to a file called `persfile.htm`. You can change the form handler and default file using the Form Properties box. To access this dialog box, select a form element, press Alt+Enter or select Properties from the File menu, and then click the Form button.

## Press Release

Press releases tell the world what the company is doing, and your Web site is definitely the place to showcase this information. Most sites have a section dedicated to press releases, and to public relations in general. The Press Release template provides a good starting point for your PR needs and is designed for a single press release. After you replace the text in square brackets with the necessary information, paste the body of your press release into the document as requested.

Figure 18.11 shows the Press Release template.

**FIGURE 18.11.**

*The Press Release template.*

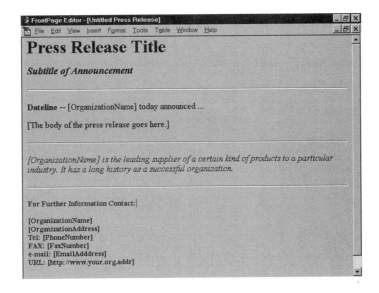

## Directory of Press Releases

To give your press releases clear organization, you might want to use the Directory of Press Releases template. As shown in Figure 18.12, the template begins with an index to the current month's, the previous month's, and older press releases. Within these sections, each entry should link to your press release pages.

**FIGURE 18.12.**

*The Directory of Press Releases template.*

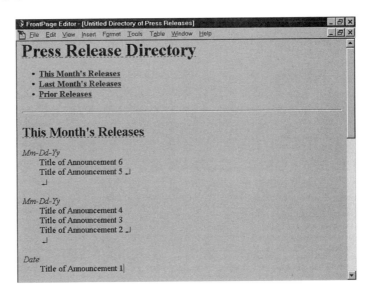

# Product Description

The product description page shown in Figure 18.13 and Figure 18.14 can help you showcase an individual product. Like many template pages, the product description page begins with a topic index that links to the key sections of the page.

**FIGURE 18.13.**

*Topic index for the product description page.*

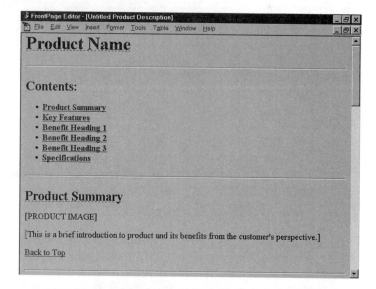

**FIGURE 18.14.**

*Defining key features of your product.*

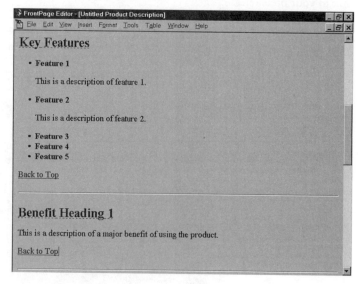

Although you usually will not want to use all the sections included in the template, you can use the section topics and subtopics as a guide to help you design a thorough product description page. As with other templates, you will want to replace the sample text with your product information.

# Product or Event Registration

The heart of this template is a registration form. Customers can use the form to register products or to sign up for events, such as conferences. Although comments in the template suggest that the text in square brackets is what you should fill in, you should probably replace the generalized questions and subject headings.

As shown in Figure 18.15, the first section of the form is used to obtain contact information from the user. The list is quite exhaustive and you generally will not want to gather all the contact information. Therefore, use the form as a guide to help you select the necessary input and then delete the unnecessary input.

**FIGURE 18.15.**

*Gathering contact information from the user for registration purposes.*

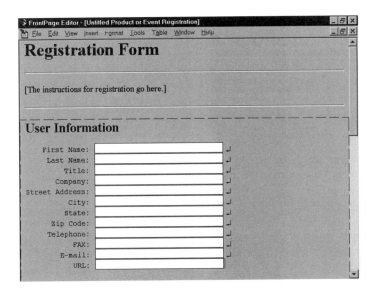

The second section of the template is used to obtain product- or event-specific information from the user, such as the product serial number. Figure 18.16 shows this section of the template.

By default, the form uses the Save Results box and stores the data in HTML format to a file called reginfo.htm. You can change the form handler and default file using the Form Properties box. To access this dialog box, select a form element, press Alt+Enter or select Properties from the File menu, and then click the Form button.

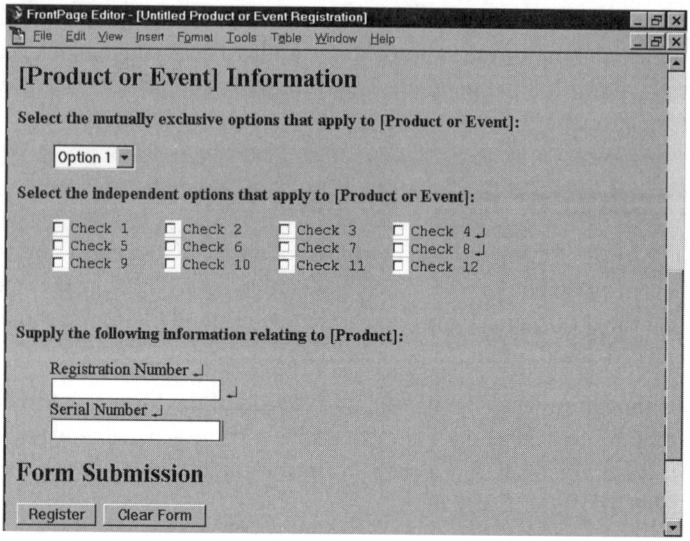

**FIGURE 18.16.**

*Obtaining product or event information.*

## Software Data Sheet

Software data sheets generally provide information related to product pricing, availability, and system requirements. This data is often tied in directly with product information such as benefits and key features, which can be included on the data sheet page, the product information page, and sometimes on both pages depending on your needs and the complexity of the software product.

Figure 18.17 shows the first section of the software data sheet. As with other templates, this template provides a terrific guide for the type of information you should include on a data sheet page. You should start by snapping a couple of screen shots of your product in action and including them on the page.

> **TIP**
>
> Whenever you use images, keep in mind my 14-second rule. Large screen shots slow down the loading of the page considerably. Use thumbnail images with descriptions of what the screen shots show instead. This allows users to click the thumbnail to see the larger image if they want to.

**FIGURE 18.17.**

*The Software Data Sheet template.*

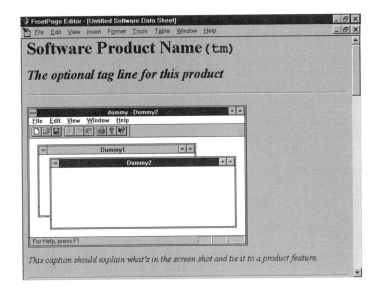

## Office Directory

Figure 18.18 shows the first section of the Office Directory template. Although the Office Directory template is designed for organizations with worldwide office locations, any business with multiple offices can use the concept of an office directory page. Simply put, the directory page tells your customers where your offices are.

**FIGURE 18.18.**

*The Office Directory template.*

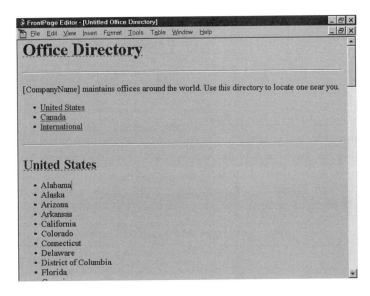

Organizations as large as those implied by the template will probably want to link to separate pages that contain office listings either by state or by country. Small organizations, even those with offices located within a single metropolitan area, probably will not want to use this template. However, you can still use the concepts introduced by the template. The main concept is to organize your office locations based on geographic areas. These geographic areas can be cities, states, or countries.

## User Registration

Often, sections of a Web site are restricted to those who have registered with your Web server using a form such as the one shown in Figure 18.19. User registration is used to track visitors and can provide valuable statistics.

**FIGURE 18.19.**

*The User Registration template.*

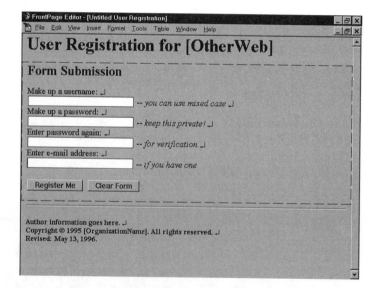

By default, the form handler for this page is the Registration box. Although you probably will not want to change the form handler, you can change the default file used as the database for user information. You can do this from the Form Properties box. To access this dialog box, select a form element, press Alt+Enter or select Properties from the Edit menu, and then click the Form button. Alternatively, you can right-click on the form and select Form Properties on the popup menu that appears.

> **TIP**
>
> If you are not using the Personal Web server, you might not be able to use self-registration. To see whether your server software with installed FrontPage extensions supports self-registration, try exporting the page to your Web server. The FrontPage Explorer will test for this capability and flag the page with a red triangle in the Outline view if there is a problem.

Because of how the self-registration process works, you must save this page to the Root Web. After users fill out and submit the registration form, they will become registered users of another Web on the server. This other Web must already exist before you save this page and must be specified in the Results tab of the Settings for Form Handler Properties box. If the Form Properties box is open, you can access the Settings for Form Handler Properties box by clicking the Settings button. In the Web Name field, you can enter the name of the target Web, which cannot be the Root Web. (See Chapter 20, "Automation with FrontPage's WebBots," for complete details on setting up the registration bot and the Results tab.)

The registration box tracks the username and password throughout the current session, which allows the user continued access to your restricted Web site. The next time the user visits the restricted Web site, he or she will be asked to enter the username and password.

# Templates for Meetings, Lectures, and Seminars

Meetings, lectures, and seminars are a part of professional organizations and career tracks. The templates in this section can help you announce these events to the world or strictly to employees who have access to the corporate intranet.

## Meeting Agenda

The Meeting Agenda template covers all the important details related to meetings. You can use the template shown in Figure 18.20 to ensure that your meeting announcement is thorough. As with other templates, replace the generic text with detailed information and delete the sections you do not need.

**FIGURE 18.20.**

*The Meeting Agenda template.*

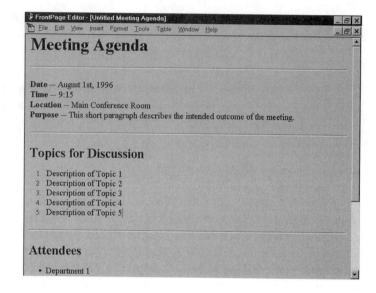

**FIGURE 18.21.**

*The Lecture Abstract template.*

## Lecture Abstract

Thousands of seminars and workshops are organized every year. A key part of these seminars and workshops is the lectures. Usually, attendees want to know what the lectures will be about beforehand. You can use the Lecture Abstract template shown in Figure 18.21 to help you develop a page that covers all the key information attendees will want.

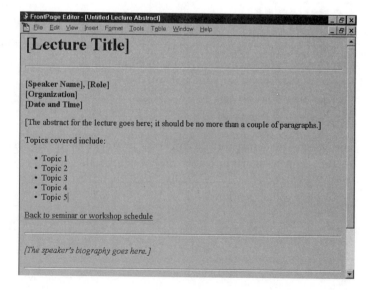

## Seminar Schedule

Seminars, workshops, and conferences are organized in much the same way. You can use the template partially depicted in Figure 18.22 to help you develop a list of sessions and speakers. Generally, each lecture title should be linked to a lecture abstract page.

**FIGURE 18.22.**

*The Seminar Schedule template.*

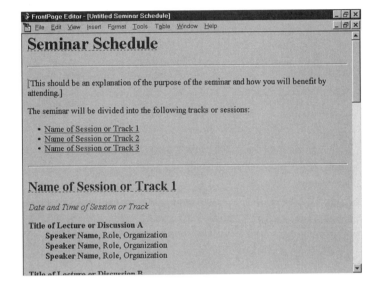

# Templates for Online Publications

This section discusses the main templates you can use for online publications. Most online publications have key elements, such as a table of contents, bibliography, and glossary.

## Table of Contents

The Table of Contents template is shown in Figure 18.23. You will use the Table of Contents template with the Table of Contents bot to automatically generate an index to your Web site. (See Chapter 20 for complete details on using the Table of Contents bot.)

## Bibliography

The Bibliography template is shown in Figure 18.24. You will use this template to create a bibliography for your online publication. Unlike print publications, your online publication can contain hypertext links to the bibliography page. You can also include links to additional references sites or to works on the Web.

**FIGURE 18.23.**

*The Table of Contents template.*

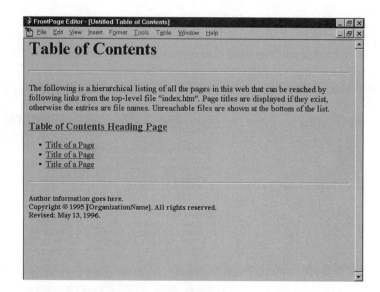

**FIGURE 18.24.**

*The Bibliography template.*

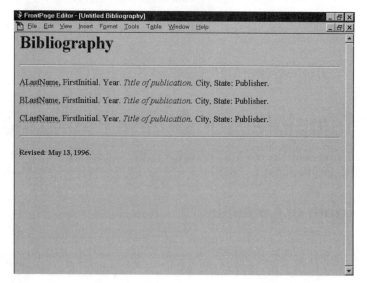

# Glossary of Terms

The Glossary of Terms template can be used to create a comprehensive glossary for your on-line publication. As shown in Figure 18.25, the glossary page is organized into two main sections. The first section contains an index to the actual terms. The second section contains the words and their definitions. This allows readers to click the first letter of the word or phrase they want to see defined. For example, if you click Z, the browser jumps to the section containing words starting with the letter Z.

**FIGURE 18.25.**

*The Glossary of Terms template.*

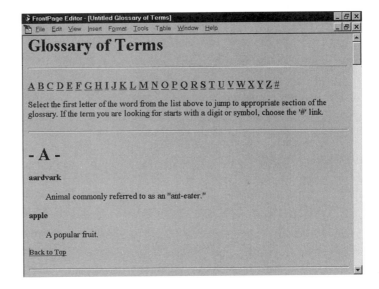

Throughout the page, you will find links labeled "Back to Top." Readers can use these links to jump back to the alphabetical index.

# Templates with Forms

Many types of pages are designed for a specific type of form. In earlier sections, you saw some of these pages. This section looks at a group of miscellaneous forms that should be useful in your Web publishing operation as well. All forms can be used to collect additional data automatically. This data includes the date and time the form was submitted, the name of the user submitting the form, the name of the host providing services to the user, and the type of browser used.

## Confirmation Form

Whenever a user submits a form, a confirmation page can be displayed to show that the form was submitted successfully. This page uses the Confirmation bot to automatically insert values for input fields, such as the UserName, UserEmail, UserTel, and UserFax fields shown in Figure 18.26.

Most Web publishers use confirmation pages, and you probably will want to as well. You can use the Confirmation Form template as the basis for your default confirmation page. Figure 18.26 shows this page. (See Chapter 20 for complete details on using the Confirmation bot.)

**FIGURE 18.26.**

*The Confirmation Form template.*

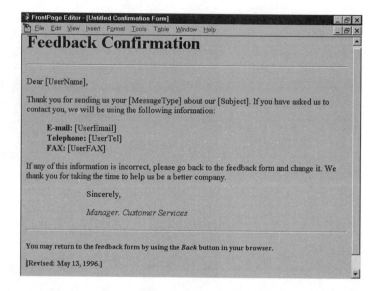

**NOTE**

Keep in mind that if you do not specify a confirmation page, the Save Results, Registration, and Discussion bots create one automatically. You define the URL to the confirmation page in the Results tab of the Settings for Form Handler Properties box. On the page with the form for which you would like to create a confirmation page, open the Form Properties box, and then access the Settings for Form Handler Properties box by clicking the Settings button. In the URL for Confirmation Page field, enter the name of the confirmation page.

## Feedback Form

Getting feedback from customers is essential. The template shown in Figure 18.27 provides a good starting point for some of the questions you might want to ask visitors to your Web site.

By default, the form uses the Save Results bot and stores the data in a text database with fields separated by tabs. The destination file is `feedback.txt` in a private directory. You can change the form handler and default file using the Form Properties box. To access this dialog box, select a form element, press Alt+Enter or select Properties from the File menu, and then click the Form button.

**FIGURE 18.27.**

*The Feedback Form template.*

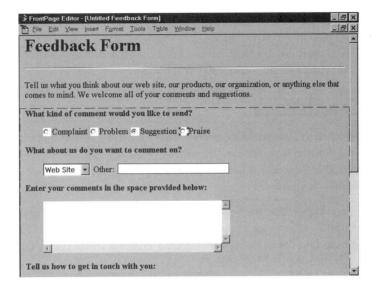

## Guest Book

As you surf the Web, you will find that many sites use guest books. Guest books have been around for centuries, and it should be no surprise that Web entrepreneurs adopted the idea to obtain both a listing of visitors and comments from those visitors. Figure 18.28 shows the Guest Book template, which includes a single text area for submitting comments.

**FIGURE 18.28.**

*The Guest Book template.*

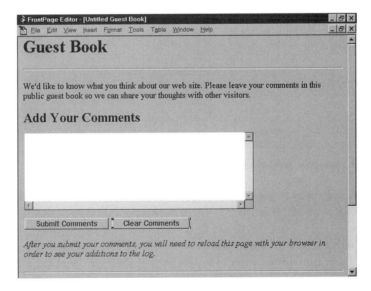

By default, the form uses the Save Results bot and stores the data in an HTML file called guestlog.htm. You can change the form handler and default file using the Form Properties box. To access this dialog box, select a form element, press Alt+Enter or select Properties from the File menu, and then click the Form button.

# Search Page

The Search Page template creates a page that lets you search through the full text of your Web site. Whenever you save a Web page or recalculate links, FrontPage creates a text index to your site. Using the Search bot and the search page, you can allow users to access and retrieve information from this index.

If you plan to use the Search bot, the template shown in Figure 18.29 is the perfect starting point. As you can see, the page includes the search form and detailed information on the search process and query syntax. (See Chapter 20 for complete details on using the Search bot.)

**FIGURE 18.29.**

*The Search Page template.*

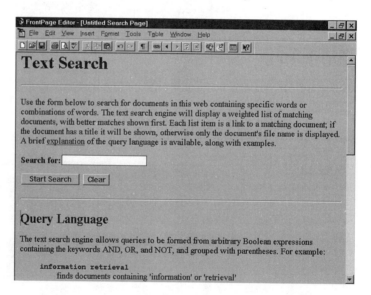

# Survey Form

Another way to gather information from visitors to your site is with a survey like the one shown in Figures 18.30 and 18.31. This survey is not meant to be usable; rather, it is designed to help you create your own survey. Therefore, your first step will be to replace the sample questions with ones more appropriate for your survey. Like many other templates, the first part of the survey contains an index to key sections of the page. Within the major sections, the template includes a number of sample questions.

**FIGURE 18.30.**

*Creating a survey.*

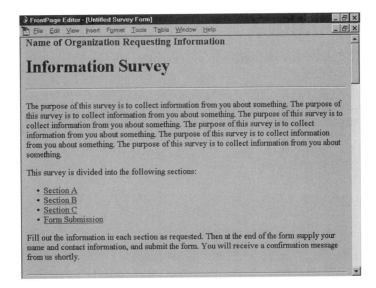

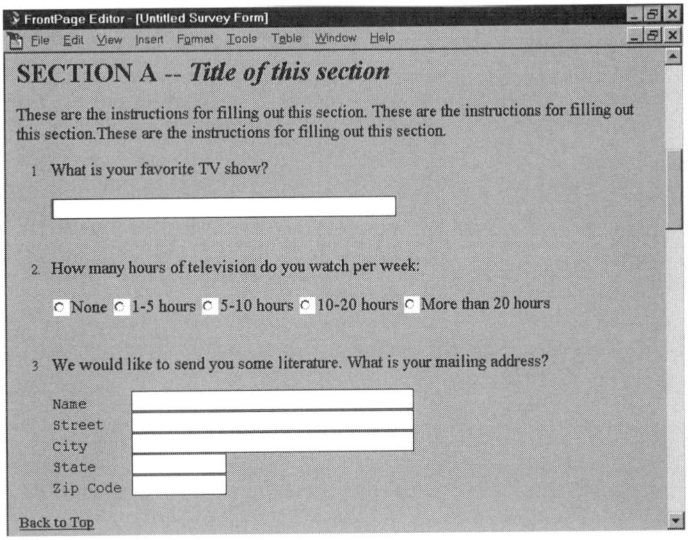

**FIGURE 18.31.**

*Sample survey questions.*

By default, the form uses the Save Results bot and stores the data in a text database with fields separated by tabs. The destination file is survresp.txt. You can change the form handler and default file using the Form Properties box. To access this dialog box, select a form element, press Alt+Enter or select Properties from the File menu, and then click the Form button.

# Summary

Old and new Web publishers alike might want to base their pages on an appropriate template. Not only will creating Web pages with templates save you time, but also the templates themselves are guides that can help you design better pages. If you target your pages correctly, you can use templates regardless of whether you plan to publish on the corporate intranet or on the World Wide Web.

# Instant Web Sites with FrontPage's Web Wizards

**19**

*by William Robert Stanek*

**IN THIS CHAPTER**

With the ready-to-use Web sites included in FrontPage, you can create an instant Web site that will dazzle the masses. These ready-to-use Web sites bring new definition to the meaning of templates and range from basic one-page sites to advanced sites with dozens of pages. This chapter discusses how to create an instant Web site that will meet your needs whether you plan to set up a complete corporate intranet or a site on the World Wide Web. Even if you do not plan to use an instant Web site, you should read this chapter to gain an understanding of the various sites you can create to establish your Web presence.

# Saving Time with Instant Web Sites

You can create a wide range of Instant Web sites with Web templates and Web wizards. As you might expect, you build basic Webs with templates and advanced Webs with wizards. A Web template contains outlines for a specific set of pages, such as all the pages that relate to a customer support Web. A wizard helps you automatically generate content for a complex Web, such as one that will help you build a presence on the World Wide Web.

Both Web templates and wizards contain helpful guidelines to make development of a particular type of site easier. Like page templates, the guidelines provided do not ask specific questions concerning design and layout of the page. However, they do cover just about every major issue you should consider when developing a specific type of site, which gives you valuable insight into the specific areas your site should cover.

As you know, you create Webs in the FrontPage Explorer. To base a new site on a template or wizard, select New from the File menu (or press Ctrl+N), and then choose the template or wizard you want to base your site on. Next, select a name and a server for your Web. After you enter this information, FrontPage either creates your Web based on a template or launches the appropriate Web wizard.

## EDITING TECHNIQUES FOR WIZARD PAGES

FrontPage wizards understand a whole range of editing commands, including cut, copy, paste, and undo. This allows you to select text on any wizard page and copy it to the clipboard, paste text on the clipboard into a field, and unerase text that you accidentally deleted.

Here is how you can use these editing commands:

- Cut: Select the text and then press Ctrl+X. This action places text on the clipboard.
- Copy: Select the text and then press Ctrl+C. This action places text on the clipboard.
- Paste: With text on the clipboard, move to the field into which you want to paste text, and press Ctrl+V.
- Undo: You can undo a paste, cut, or other deletion of text by pressing Ctrl+Z.

> Because the clipboard is a standard object, you can copy text to the clipboard in other applications and then paste it into a wizard field. For example, you can copy the company phone number from an MS Word document and paste it into a relevant wizard field.

Each instant Web contains default pages and images that you can use as a road map to help you design a terrific site. Most Webs have at least one top-level page. A top-level page, like a home page, is the page that most visitors start on and use to access other areas of your Web.

As a designer of dozens of commercial and intranet Web sites, I was surprised to see how comprehensive the instant Webs in FrontPage really are. By using an advanced Web wizard, such as the corporate presence Web, you can literally cut days off the development time of your Web site. In some cases, this represents thousands of dollars in time and resource savings.

To better understand how instant Webs can save you time and money, let's look at each of the Webs available in FrontPage. By examining each of the available Webs, you can gain a thorough understanding of what types of sites you can build and how the sites are designed.

**NOTE**

> When you create documents with templates, FrontPage automatically adds comments that guide you through the process of designing the page. To allow you to see the page as it will appear in the reader's browser, these preset comments do not appear in the figures in this chapter.

# The Normal and Empty Webs

The normal and empty Webs are the most basic Webs available. If you have been following the examples in this book, you have probably already used the normal Web. When you use the normal Web, the FrontPage Explorer creates a Web with a single page based on the normal page template. By default, the normal Web is selected when you open the New Web dialog box. To use this Web, you simply press the Enter key or the OK button without making a selection.

The empty Web, as the name implies, creates a new Web that has no contents. You can use the empty Web when you want to create a new site from scratch. However, with all the ready-to-use Webs available, I do not know why you would ever want to use this Web.

# The Discussion Web Wizard

The discussion Web wizard creates a discussion forum for your corporate intranet or Web site. Creating and managing this advanced Web is explored in Chapter 27, "Creating and Managing Discussion Groups."

# The Customer Support Web

Hundreds of companies have online customer support areas. An online customer support area can serve your customers 24 hours a day, 365 days a year. Customers can access the area when they have problems, regardless of whether it is 3 a.m. or 12 noon.

The customer support Web is a fairly advanced Web, with over 20 HTML pages designed to help you provide world-class customer support. Ideally, this Web would be a separate area of a larger site and not your only presence on the Web.

## The Welcome Page

The top-level page of the Customer Support Web is called the Welcome page and appears in Figure 19.1. The Welcome page, like most pages in this Web, has three main sections: a header, body, and footer.

**FIGURE 19.1.**

*The Welcome page.*

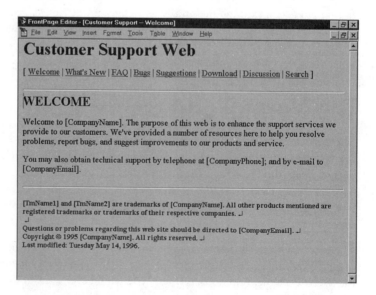

An Include bot adds the standard document header to the document. You cannot update this section directly; instead, you update the associated template page. To see what page you should update, select the header by clicking on it, and then open the Include Bot Properties box by double-clicking the left mouse button or pressing Alt+Enter. As you can see, the header includes links to all the key areas of the customer support Web. Generally, you will not want to update the header itself. (See Chapter 20, "Automation with FrontPage's WebBots," for complete details on the Include bot.)

Unlike the other sections of the page, you can—and should—edit the body of the document. Because the purpose of this page is to welcome visitors and tell them about your services, you should include two or three paragraphs describing the features of your online customer support Web.

An Include bot also adds the standard document footer to the document. You should edit the footer immediately. To do this, right-click on the Include Bot and choose Open `footer.htm`, which opens the footer document for editing. With the footer document open, you can edit the properties for the Include Bot and the text on the page. Start by replacing the text in brackets with text appropriate for your company. The footer page also includes a TimeStamp bot. If you do not like the style of the time stamp, you can change this by opening the TimeStamp bot's properties box. (See Chapter 20 for complete details on the TimeStamp bot.)

# The What's New Page

The What's New page of a customer support Web has a slightly different goal and scope from the What's New page on your main Web. The page should track product updates, the availability of patches, release schedules, and other product related information.

Figure 19.2 shows the What's New page. The page has a standard header and footer like other pages in this Web. You will want to update the body of this page immediately. The body section contains links to the download page and a technical notes page. The easiest way to update the link text is to place the insertion point within the link text, type in your new link text, and then delete the unnecessary text. If you do not update the link text in this way, you might accidentally delete the link.

# The FAQ Page

A FAQ is a list of frequently asked questions and their answers. Your customer support Web should contain a comprehensive FAQ page that answers common questions that your support staff handles. You might also want to include tips and tricks that make using your software, products, or services easier. The FAQ page included in the support Web and shown in Figure 19.3 is a starting point.

If you do not already have a list of commonly asked questions, ask your support team to help you make the list. They will probably be very glad to help you, especially when they consider how the page will make their jobs easier.

**FIGURE 19.2.**

*The What's New page.*

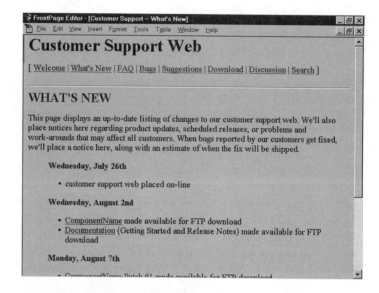

**FIGURE 19.3.**

*The FAQ page.*

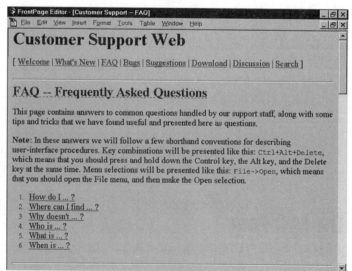

# The Bug Reporting and Information Page

Very few software products do not have bugs. Bugs are software glitches, the worst of which cause systems to crash. The purpose of the Bugs page shown in Figures 19.4 and 19.5 is two-fold. Customers should be able to report bugs they have found in the software so you can fix them. Customers should also be able to see a list of known bugs.

Most customer support areas include a bug reporting and information page for each major product that the company produces. Ideally, you would not only list the known bugs, but would also tell the customer how to get around each bug and perhaps where to download a patch that fixes the bug.

**FIGURE 19.4.**

*Customers should be able to report bugs quickly and easily.*

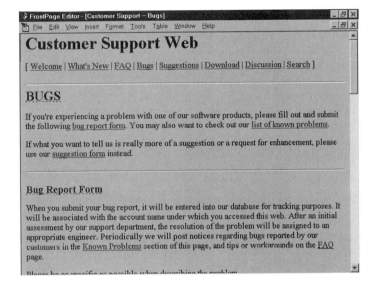

**FIGURE 19.5.**

*Customers should be able to find a list of known bugs as well.*

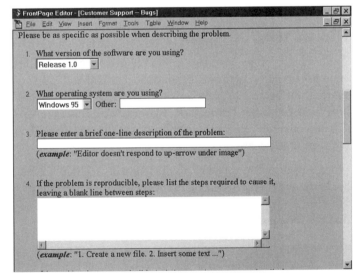

# The Suggestions Page

A suggestions page opens an extremely important communications channel with your customers. Although you will certainly get suggestions that won't be useful, you might be surprised at how many truly wonderful ideas your customers have for enhancing your products and improving your customer service. The Suggestions page shown in Figure 19.6 allows customers to make suggestions concerning your Web site, company, products, services, support, and even your marketing style.

**FIGURE 19.6.**

*Suggestions pages are a great way to learn from your customers.*

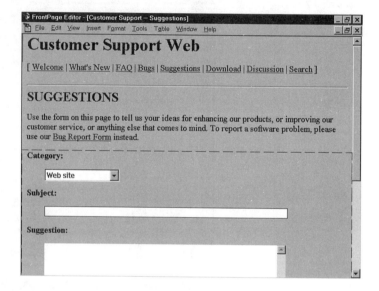

## The Download Page

The Download page provides a common area for downloading patches, updates, and other customer support related files. Beyond the standard header and footer, the page contains many sections. As Figure 19.7 shows, the first of these sections introduces the page and provides a link to the file formats bookmark. The next section is an index for the updates, patches, and other files that the reader can download from this page. You should replace the link titles with more appropriate text.

When a reader clicks on a link in the Contents section, his browser displays the appropriate bookmark within the document, such as those shown in Figure 19.8. When providing files on the Web, it's helpful to use some form of compression to reduce download time. This shows that you are considerate of the customer's time.

---

**TIP**

You should provide files in at least two compressed formats if possible, such as ZIP and compressed TAR. ZIP is an extremely popular compression technique. Zipped files can be decompressed on just about any system as long as the reader has an unzip utility. The compressed tape archive (TAR) format is another popular format. Although TAR utilities are available for most systems, the TAR format is primarily for readers who access the Web via a UNIX-based server.

**FIGURE 19.7.**

*A template for downloading updates and enhancements.*

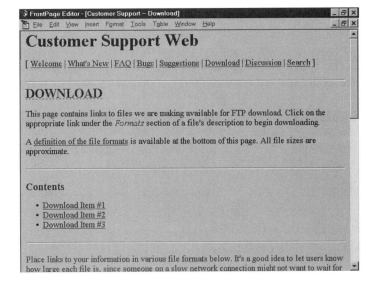

**FIGURE 19.8.**

*Key areas are linked from the top of the page.*

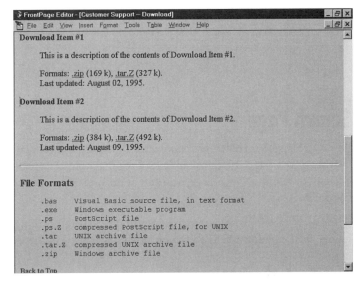

# The Discussion Area

No customer support Web would be complete without a discussion area in which company employees and customers can discuss your products. This area contains four pages: a home page, table of contents, search page, and posting page. The home page for this area is the same page the reader accesses when he clicks on the Discussion link from another area of the Web. The table of contents, search, and posting pages have common headers and footers designed for the discussion area.

The centerpiece of the discussion area is the page shown in Figure 19.9. On this page, readers can post material to the discussion area. All current postings to the discussion group are available from the table of contents page. The table of contents updates whenever new material is posted. Readers can also search through the postings using a search page. (See Chapter 27 for more information.)

**FIGURE 19.9.**

*Posting to the Customer Support group.*

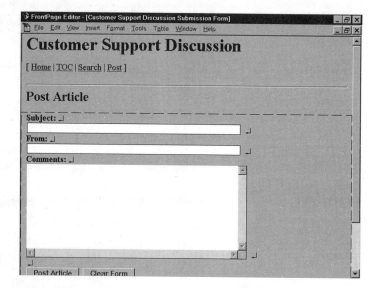

# Search Page

The search page lets readers search through the full text of your customer support Web. Whenever you save a page or recalculate links, FrontPage creates a text index to your site. Using the Search bot and the search page, you can allow users to access and retrieve information from this index.

The search page is partially shown in Figure 19.10. A great thing about this page is that it includes detailed information on the query language used in the search process.

# The Technical Notes Page

Hidden among the many pages provided with the customer support Web is the technical notes page, used to describe problems and solutions. Initially, this page is accessible only from the

What's New page. However, if you plan to provide technical notes to your readers, you should add links to the page throughout the support Web. For example, you might want to create links to this page from the bug page and the download page.

**FIGURE 19.10.**

*Search the Customer Support Web.*

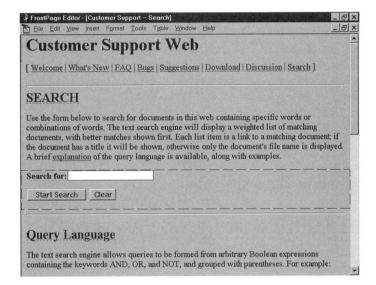

## The Personal Web

The personal Web is a simple yet well-designed Web that consists of a single page—your home page. The personal Web is primarily useful in intranet environments and as part of a large business-oriented Web site. Figure 19.11 shows the header section of the home page, which contains an index to the page's key sections.

To understand why the page is really best-suited for your corporate intranet, you only have to look at the employee information and current project sections. As you can see from Figure 19.12, these sections ask you to list information you probably would not want to release to the general public, such as your manager's name and the names of those you supervise.

The remaining sections on the page are good guides to the type of information you can use on any home page. Most home pages contain links to the publisher's favorite sites called a *hot list*. Most home pages also contain biography and contact information. Some home pages contain personal interests and areas for comments and suggestions.

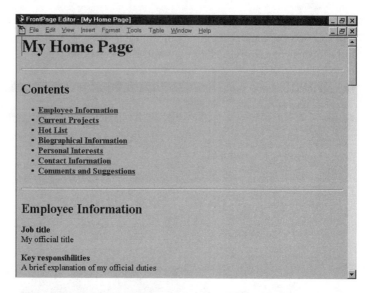

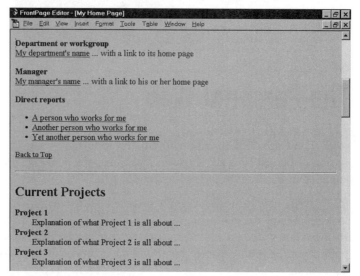

# The Personal Home Page Wizard

The Personal Home Page Wizard helps you create a personalized home page. This wizard is an oddball and is the only wizard discussed in this chapter that you can start in the FrontPage Editor. The page created by the wizard is based on the home page template included in the personal Web, which is why this wizard is examined in this chapter and not in the previous chapter. In fact, if you run the wizard and accept all the default values, the Personal Home Page Wizard creates a page nearly identical to the home page in the personal Web.

There are advantages to using the Personal Home Page Wizard. When you use the wizard, you can adjust just about every aspect of the home page. You can select the sections that you want to include and exclude, change the order of the sections, adjust the default text, and add personal information.

If you want to create an instant home page, I recommend trying both the Personal Home Page Wizard and the personal Web template. In this way, you can learn firsthand which one best fits your needs.

# The Project Web

No matter what company or department you work in, you are probably a part of one or more projects. Your project team's goal is to get the job done, whether the job entails designing a new car, developing an application, or putting together an advertising campaign. The project Web can help you ensure that your project stays on track and accomplishes its goals.

Just as you might not want to release information on your boss and those you supervise, you probably would not want the general public to know the status of the company projects. Thus, the project Web is another Web best-suited for the corporate intranet. The project Web includes the following:

- A home page where you can list What's New with the project and access key pages within the Web.
- A page where you can list the members of the project team and their contact information.
- A page for your schedule, complete with sections for events, milestones, and deliverables.
- Two discussion areas for tracking discussions related to the project.
- An archive page so that you can reference and link to all the documents generated by the project team and its members.

## The Project Home Page

The top-level page of this Web is called the project home page and appears in Figure 19.13. The page provides a starting point for the project Web and lists what's new with the project. Like most pages in this Web, the project home page has three main sections: a header, a body, and a footer.

An Include bot adds the standard header and footer to the document using an Include bot. You cannot update these sections directly; you update the associated template page instead. Unlike the header and footer, you can (and should) edit the body of the document directly. Start by replacing the default text with text that is specific to your project.

**FIGURE 19.13.**

*The project home page.*

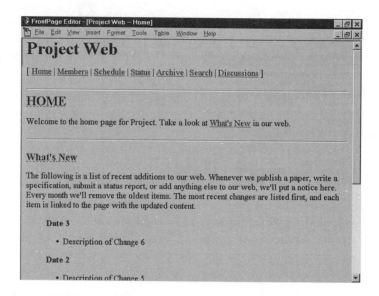

**FIGURE 19.13.**

*The project home page.*

## The Members Page

You can use the members page to create a complete listing of the members of the project team. The page consists of two main sections. The first section, shown in Figure 19.14, contains an index of member names linked to the detailed listing shown in Figure 19.15. As shown, the second section can contain photos and contact information for each member of the project team.

**FIGURE 19.14.**

*The index to the members page.*

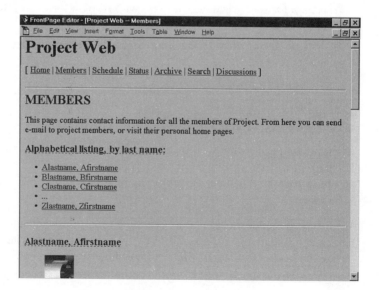

**FIGURE 19.15.**

*Member information.*

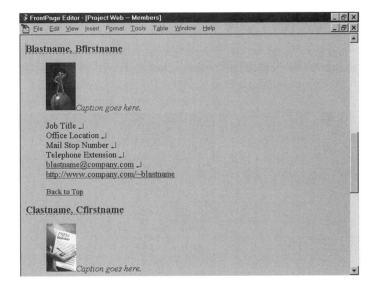

# The Schedule Page

The schedule page helps the project stay on track. Figure 19.16 shows part of the schedule page. The page begins with an area for a prioritized list of items that the team is working on week-by-week.

Use the concepts that the page introduces to help you develop a schedule page suitable for your project. Project team members can use the schedule page as a quick reference for all the events, milestones, and deliverables related to the project.

**FIGURE 19.16.**

*The schedule page.*

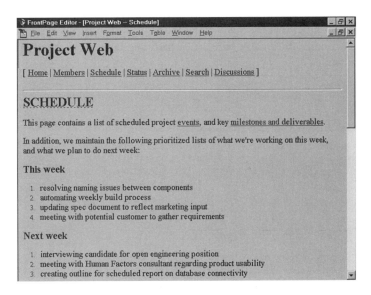

## The Status Page

Another key page in the project Web is the status page, shown in Figure 19.17. The status page helps all the members of the project team track the monthly, quarterly, and yearly reports for your project. Management might also find it useful to track the status page as a reference.

**FIGURE 19.17.**

*The status page.*

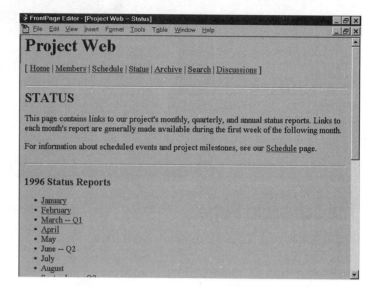

## The Archive Page

The archive page provides a common area for referencing and linking to all the documents that the project team and its members generate. You can also use it to create links to software and utilities that the members of the project team might need. Figure 19.18 shows the introduction to the archive page. The remaining sections of the page are organized much like the download page in the Customer Support Web described earlier in this chapter.

**FIGURE 19.18.**

*The archive page.*

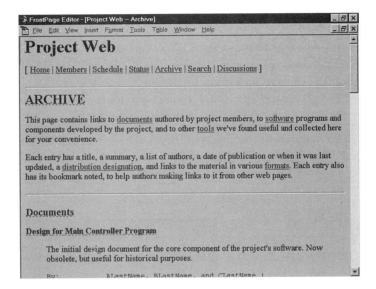

## The Search Page

The search page lets project members search through the full text of your project Web. Whenever you save a page or recalculate links, FrontPage creates a text index to your site. Using the Search bot and the search page, you can enable users to access and retrieve information from this index. The search page is partially shown in Figure 19.19.

**FIGURE 19.19.**

*Search the project Web.*

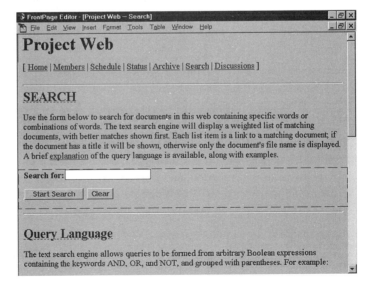

## The Discussion Area

As shown in Figure 19.20, the project Web includes two complete discussion areas. The first discussion relates to project requirements. The second discussion builds a knowledge base for the project by tracking common questions and answers. Although you could redefine the purposes of these discussions simply by changing the text where appropriate, the requirements and knowledge base discussions are great for most projects.

Each discussion area contains four pages: a home page, a table of contents page, a search page, and a posting page. The home page for the area is the same page the reader accesses when he clicks on the Discussion link from another area of the Web. The table of contents, search, and posting pages have common headers and footers designed for their respective discussion areas.

**FIGURE 19.20.**

*The project Web includes two discussion areas.*

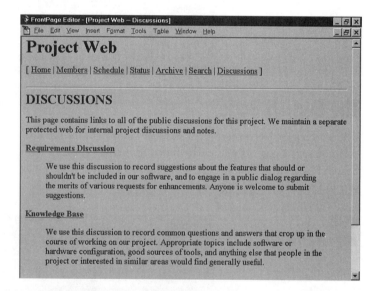

# The Corporate Presence Wizard

The corporate presence Web is by far the most advanced Web included with FrontPage, so advanced in fact that you need a Web Wizard to help you build it. As the name of the Web implies, this Web is designed to help your company (or the company you work for) establish a presence on the Web. This Web is designed to be your company's main site on the World Wide Web. It can help you build the site, step by step.

The key pages of the corporate presence Web include the following:

A corporate home page

A table of contents page

A What's New page

Press release pages

A directory of your company's products and services

Pages for individual products and services

Pages for obtaining feedback from your customers

A search page

As you can see from the page listing, the pages included in this Web are similar to the templates discussed in Chapter 18, "Creating Web Pages with FrontPage's Templates." What makes this Web unique and powerful is that just about every aspect of the Web is tuneable to your needs via the wizard.

To start, select New from the File menu (or press Ctrl+N), and then choose the Corporate Presence Wizard from the New Web dialog box. Next, select a name and a server for your Web. After you enter this information, FrontPage launches the Corporate Presence Wizard.

Figure 19.21 shows the first page of the Corporate Presence Wizard. The buttons at the bottom of the dialog box are standard throughout the Web creation process. At any time, you can move to the previous or next phase of the creation process using the Back or Next buttons. When you have fully defined the Web, click the Finish button and the FrontPage Editor creates the Web you have designed.

**FIGURE 19.21.**

*Getting started with the Corporate Presence Wizard.*

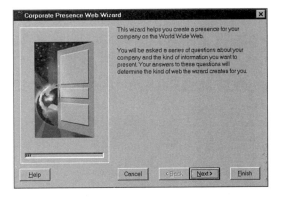

# Determining the Pages for Your Web

Now that you have started the Corporate Presence Wizard, click on the Next button. This displays the wizard page shown in Figure 19.22, from which you can select the type of pages you want to include in your Web.

To get a general idea of what these pages are used for, you can refer back to the templates in Chapter 18. Keep in mind, though, that the pages you create with the wizard are based on templates designed specifically for the corporate presence Web. In most cases, you will want your corporate presence Web to include all of the possible pages.

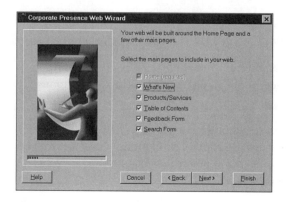

# Choosing Topics for Your Home Page

After you have selected the type of pages for your Web, you can continue by clicking Next. The next page in the Corporate Presence Wizard lets you select the topics you want to appear on the corporate home page.

As the page shown in Figure 19.23 implies, the home page is the first thing most visitors to your Web will see. For this reason, you should let visitors know immediately what your company does and what the company represents.

Small to mid-sized businesses should include the company mission and profile on the home page, because not all users who visit may be familiar with the company. However, most large businesses will want to include the company mission and profile on a separate company background page. Still, I recommend selecting all the available topics. You can always delete sections you do not want to use later.

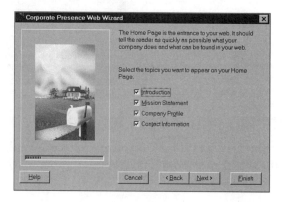

# Defining the What's New Page

If you chose to include a What's New page, the wizard next displays the screen shown in Figure 19.24. This page helps you choose topics for your What's New page.

What's New pages usually provide readers with an update history for a Web site, and they are often among the most visited pages. You can also use the What's New page to tell your potential customers about new developments within the company, which is a powerful tool for establishing your corporate presence in cyberspace. For this reason, the Corporate Presence Wizard includes changes to the Web site, a directory of press releases, and recent reviews of the company—all on the same page. This is a winning combination, and you will probably want to use all three topics on your What's New page.

**FIGURE 19.24.**

*Selecting topics for your What's New page.*

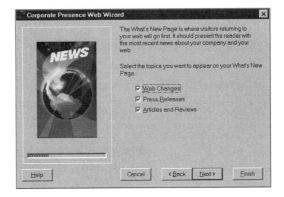

# Creating Product and Service Pages

If you selected the products and services option earlier, clicking the Next button takes you to the page shown in Figure 19.25. Most companies sell products or services—some companies offer both. On this page, you can choose how many products and services pages you want to create.

> **NOTE**
>
> Zero is an acceptable value for the Products and Services fields. If you enter a zero in one of the fields, you will not be able to select the related options in later pages. If you enter a zero in both fields, you will skip wizard pages that relate to products and services.

**FIGURE 19.25.**

*Creating product and service pages.*

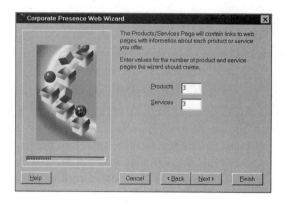

After entering the number of product and service pages you would like the wizard to create, click on the Next button. As you can see from Figure 19.26, the wizard then lets you select the topics for your product and services pages.

Keep in mind that you are specifying default topics for all product and service pages. If you are unsure about the type of product or service information you would like to provide on the Web, select all the available options and make a determination when you see the completed templates.

**FIGURE 19.26.**

*Selecting topics for the product and service pages.*

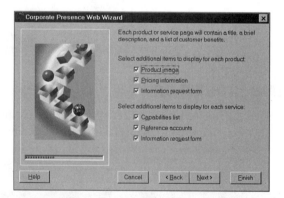

# Creating the Feedback Page

Getting feedback from customers is extremely important, which is why the Corporate Presence Wizard creates a Feedback page for you. As you can see from Figure 19.27, the feedback page enables you to collect a lot of information from the reader—perhaps too much. If you really want to know what visitors think, do not ask them for too much personal information. Their e-mail addresses and perhaps their full names should suffice in most instances.

**FIGURE 19.27.**

*Determining input for the feedback page.*

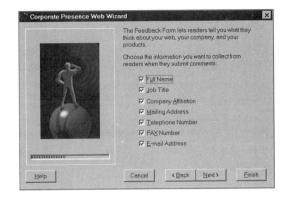

As shown in Figure 19.28, you can store the data gathered from the feedback form in two key formats: ASCII text or HTML. Data in a text format is easily manipulated, which is good if you want to do any follow-up processing. Data in HTML format is easy to read, but not easily manipulated. You can change this selection later by opening the page in the FrontPage editor and changing the properties associated with the feedback form.

**FIGURE 19.28.**

*Storing feedback data.*

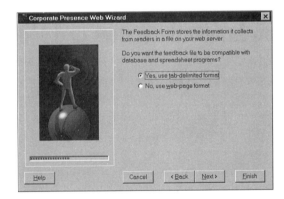

# Creating the Table of Contents Page

Like an index, a table of contents for a Web site is useful but usually difficult to build and maintain. FrontPage automates this process and enables you to build a table of contents page that gets automatically updated when you make changes to the Web structure. As shown in Figure 19.29, you can also create links to pages in the Web that are not linked to other pages and identify top-level pages with a bullet.

---

> **NOTE**
>
> Although I recommend using this page, it could grow unwieldy if your site has a lot of pages. If that happens, you might want to remove the WebBot that is making automatic updates to the page. You might also want to delete links to low-level pages.

**FIGURE 19.29.**

*Determining the style of the table of contents page.*

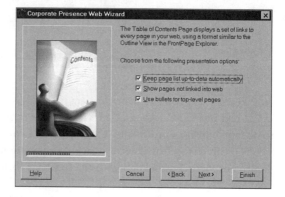

# Creating Standard Headers and Footers

One way to create a cohesive look and feel for your Web is to use standard headers and footers. Using Include bots, FrontPage makes the process of creating and maintaining standard headers and footers relatively effortless. You merely select the style of header and footer you want to use from the wizard page shown in Figure 19.30.

For the header, you have three options. If you select Company Logo, an image you specify appears as a banner on all your pages. If you select Page Title, the title of the page (as defined in the page properties dialog box) appears as a level one heading below the banner. If you select Links to your main Web pages, an image map with links to the top-level pages in the Web appears. You can define the style of this image map on a later page. For a clean and clear style, you might want to use the logo and the image map.

For the footer, you have four options. Without the links on either the top or bottom of the page, readers cannot navigate your Web. For this reason, the Corporate Presence Wizard lets you advance to the next page only when you choose a location for the links. Putting links to key pages in both the header and the footer is a good design technique.

You will find that most Web pages contain the e-mail address of the Webmaster and some copyright notices. The footer is the appropriate place for this information. Finally, notifying the reader of the date the page was last modified is useful, especially if you plan to make frequent updates to your Web. A WebBot that tracks the last time you updated the page handles this feature. However, do you want readers making judgments about the accuracy of your information based on a timestamp? If you do not plan to update all your pages on at least a quarterly basis, you might not want to include a timestamp.

> **TIP**
>
> A series of bots adds the header and footer information to your documents. Although you can edit the properties for these bots on a page-by-page basis, you generally cannot easily redefine the header and footer for all pages. However, the company logo is added to pages with an Include bot that references an HTML document called `logo.htm`. If you edit the `logo.htm` page, you can define a new banner for all pages within your Web. You can edit the links section of the header and footer as well. An Include bot that references an HTML document called `navbar.htm` adds the links.

**FIGURE 19.30.**

*Defining standard headers and footers.*

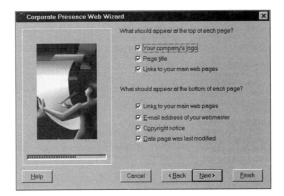

## Choosing a Presentation Style

The next page in the wizard lets you select a presentation style for all the pages in your Web. As you can see from Figure 19.31, these styles go from plain to cool. Keep in mind that the presentation style really only applies to the default graphics used in the Web. Generally, the wizard creates graphics for

> Header and footer page links
>
> Default page title graphics
>
> Fancy horizontal rules
>
> Buttons

If you choose the plain style, it replaces the default graphics with text links. If you choose any other style, your pages will use the default graphics as shown when you make the selection.

**FIGURE 19.31.**

*Selecting a presentation style.*

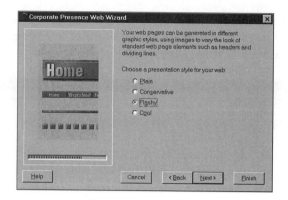

## Choosing Colors for the Web

Choosing a standard color scheme for your pages is a sound design technique. Figure 19.32 shows the wizard page that lets you define page colors. If you have been following along with your computer, clicking on the Next button should take you to this wizard page. The color options you choose apply to all the pages in your Web.

The two most basic options on this page are whether to use custom colors or default colors. If you choose custom colors, you can define the color of backgrounds, text, links, visited links, and active links. If you choose default colors, you cannot make color selections. Most Web publishers want to create custom colors for their pages.

The Background area of this page enables you to select either a background pattern or color. The wizard provides a good variety of background patterns that should fit most Web publishers' needs. Patterns add visual variety to your pages and can enhance your Web's design significantly. However, if you do not want to use a background pattern, select None from the Background pull-down menu. You can now select a background color. Click on the box next to the Color field to open the Color dialog box.

The Text area of this page enables you to set colors for normal text and links. You can set the color for text and links in the Color dialog box.

The sample document shown in the left half of the page changes to match your selections. This gives you a good idea of how the color and background options you choose will affect your pages.

> **TIP**
>
> FrontPage stores the color definitions for your Web in a style sheet page called Web Colors. This page resides in a private directory with the page URL `style.htm`. Through the Link View in the FrontPage Explorer, you can open this page for editing.

**FIGURE 19.32.**

*Choosing colors for the Web.*

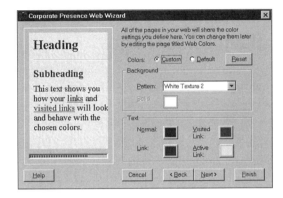

# Adding an "Under Construction" Icon

As you can see from Figure 19.33, the next page enables you to add an "under construction" icon to unfinished pages. This serves as a visual cue to visitors that the page is not yet finished. When you first create your Web, most of your pages will be unfinished, so if you decide to use this icon, you'll likely use it in a lot of places.

> **CAUTION**
>
> The "under construction" icon is extremely frustrating for users, especially if it is used in many places on your Web site. After all, who wants to browse a site where every link leads to a dead end? So, instead of publishing an unfinished site, polish your site until it shines and then publish it.

**FIGURE 19.33.**

*Adding an "under construction" icon.*

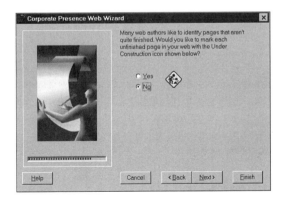

# Adding the Company Name and Contact Information to Your Pages

Your company name plays an important part in building your Web presence. All of your pages should include either the full name of your company or an abbreviated name. Some of your pages should include the company's address as well. To avoid the tedium of having to add this information to dozens of pages, the Corporate Presence Wizard lets you define this information using the page shown in Figure 19.34.

You must not leave any of these fields blank. Therefore, if you click on the Next button with the empty field shown in Figure 19.34, the Explorer displays a prompt that tells you to fill in the address field. After you specify this information, the wizard takes care of adding it to pages where needed.

**FIGURE 19.34.**

*Adding key information to your pages.*

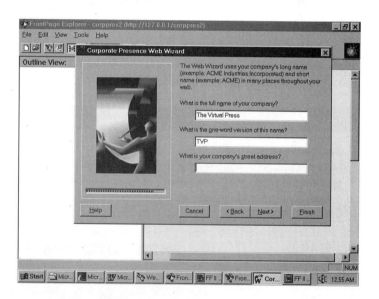

Contact information beyond the company's address is also important. On the next page, shown in Figure 19.35, you specify phone, fax, and e-mail addresses. Again, because this information must appear on key pages within your Web, you cannot leave any of these fields blank, which means that you would need to fill in the two fields on the page shown in Figure 19.35 before you advance to the next page.

# Creating a To-Do List

The final page in the Corporate Presence Wizard enables you to automatically generate a To-Do list for your new Web. The To-Do list contains a list of tasks that you should perform to complete the Web. You should generate the To-Do list because it gives you a clear idea of what you need to do next.

**FIGURE 19.35.**

*Completing the necessary contact information.*

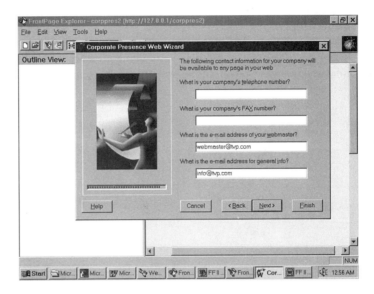

Now that you are done defining your Web, click on the Finish button. When you do this, the wizard starts creating the Web. After the wizard creates the Web, it generates the To-Do list. If you created all the available pages, you have a To-Do list with seven items similar to the one shown in Figure 19.36. Use this list as a guideline to help you complete the design of your Web. After you complete the tasks on your To-Do list, look at and edit each and every page in your Web.

**FIGURE 19.36.**

*Use the To-Do List to help you complete the design.*

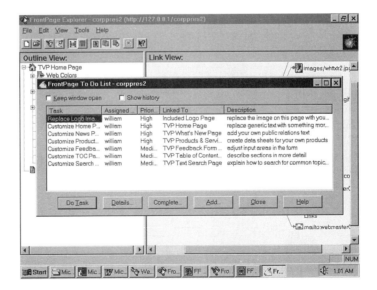

# Summary

Creating an instant Web site is easy with the Web templates and wizards included in FrontPage. A Web template contains outlines for a specific set of pages, such as all the pages that relate to a customer support Web. A wizard helps you automatically generate content for a complex Web, such as one that would help you build a presence on the World Wide Web. Both Web templates and wizards contain helpful guidelines to make development of intranet and Web sites easier.

# Automation with FrontPage's WebBots

**20**

*by William Robert Stanek*

**IN THIS CHAPTER**

WebBots greatly streamline the development process and eliminate the need to write your own scripts or add complicated HTML commands. With a WebBot you can collect the results from forms, automatically add navigation bars, create pages with full text searches, allow registered users to access key areas of your Web site, and much more. There is no programming involved at all.

# How To Use WebBots

Throughout this book, I have talked about bots. As you have seen, you can use bots to automate many Web publishing tasks.

The FrontPage Editor makes the process of adding WebBots to pages very easy. The first step is to move the insertion point where you want the bot. Next, open the Insert menu and select Bot. On the Insert Bot window, shown in Figure 20.1, select the bot you want to use by double-clicking on the appropriate key words. Alternatively, you can select the appropriate key words and then click on the OK button or press Enter on the keyboard.

**FIGURE 20.1.**

*Inserting bots onto the page.*

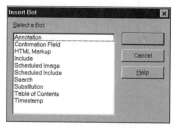

In FrontPage, the WebBot maintenance process is also very easy. When you move your pointer over an area of the page containing a WebBot, the pointer changes from an arrow to a robot. The robot icon indicates that a bot is embedded in this area of the page. You access a properties dialog box associated with the bot by double-clicking when the robot icon is visible. With this dialog box open, you can change the characteristics of the bot.

# How Do WebBots Work?

FrontPage includes more than a dozen WebBots. You can think of each WebBot as a program or script that runs when needed.

Some WebBots affect your Web site only when you add or update the bots in the FrontPage Editor. This means they have no effect when a user browses the Web. Most WebBots automatically update themselves at runtime. This means the bots either run immediately when viewed or start when the user performs an action in the page, such as submitting a fill-out form. Bots that run immediately make updates to the page in browsers and in the FrontPage Editor.

All WebBots that automatically update themselves at runtime depend on FrontPage server extensions. Therefore, you must either use the Personal Web Server to provide Web services or install the FrontPage server extensions for your server.

---

**CAUTION**

If you cannot use the FrontPage server extensions with your server, you are going to have problems with many of the WebBots. The following are the primary bots to watch out for:

> The Confirmation Field bot
>
> The Discussion bot
>
> The Registration bot
>
> The Save Results bot
>
> The Search bot

These bots execute when a user submits a fill-out form and will not work without the FrontPage server extensions. Other bots might present problems as well because they add material to the page when loaded into a browser.

In the commercial version of FrontPage, when you export pages from your Web, FrontPage should update your pages appropriately. Keep in mind that thereafter, you lose the functionality of the WebBot.

---

# Using the Annotation WebBot

The annotation bot enables you to automate the process of creating and maintaining annotations. Annotations appear in the FrontPage Editor and in the source markup for your page, but they do not appear when the reader views the page in a browser.

To use this bot, select Annotation from the Insert Bot dialog box. This opens the dialog box shown in Figure 20.2. Enter your annotation and close the bot's dialog box by clicking on the OK button. For complete details on using the annotation bot, see "Adding Comments to Your Documents" in Chapter 8, "Creating Web Documents with FrontPage."

**FIGURE 20.2.**

*Using the Annotation WebBot.*

**CAUTION**

Anyone can view the source markup for your page. Do not insert annotations that you do not want anyone else to read.

# Using the Confirmation Field WebBot

The Confirmation Field WebBot echoes a user's input to a form on a special page called a confirmation page. You can create confirmation fields for forms handled by Save Results bots, Discussion bots, and Registration bots. However, you must specify the URL of a confirmation page that you create to hold the input.

## Specifying the Confirmation Page

You can specify the confirmation page at any time by accessing a form element's properties box and clicking on the Form button. This opens the dialog box shown in Figure 20.3. After you choose the appropriate handler from the pull-down menu in the Form Handler area of the Form Properties box, click on the Settings button to define settings for the handler.

**FIGURE 20.3.**

*Selecting a form handler.*

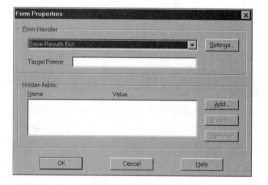

The Save Results handler has two configuration pages that you can access by clicking on the Results or Advanced tab. You can specify the confirmation page's URL in the URL of confirmation page field of the Results tab, as shown in Figure 20.4.

The Registration handler has three configuration pages that you can access by clicking on the Registration, Results, or Advanced tabs, respectively. As with the Save Results handler, you can specify the confirmation page's URL in the URL of confirmation page field of the Results tab, as shown in Figure 20.5.

**FIGURE 20.4.**

*Setting a confirmation page for the Save Results handler.*

**FIGURE 20.5.**

*Setting a confirmation page for the Registration handler.*

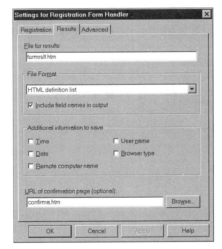

The Discussion handler has two configuration pages that you can access by clicking on the Discussion or Article tab. As with the other two previously discussed handlers, you can specify the confirmation page's URL in the URL of confirmation page field of the Discussion tab. See Figure 20.6.

# Associating Fields with Values

Chapter 11, "Using Forms and the Form Page Wizard," explored how to create forms. As you might recall, each input field has two attributes:

Name     The key word associated with the input field

Value    The value of the field

**FIGURE 20.6.**

*Setting a confirmation page
for the Discussion handler.*

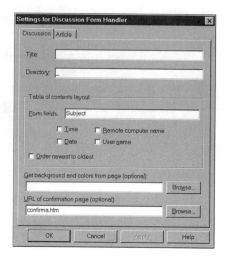

When you create a form, you should note the names of each field that you want to echo on a confirmation page. With this list of field names, you can open your confirmation page and insert the Confirmation Field bot as appropriate. You must insert one bot for each field that you want to confirm.

---

**TIP**

To view the properties for any field, open the properties dialog box associated with the field by moving the mouse pointer over the field and double-clicking.

---

To use this bot, select Confirmation Field from the Insert Bot dialog box. This opens the dialog box shown in Figure 20.7. In the Name of Form Field To Confirm field, enter the name of the form field you want to echo on this page. For all form fields except radio buttons, use the name in the Name field. For radio button fields, use the name in the Group Name field. When you are finished, click on the OK button.

**FIGURE 20.7.**

*Using the Confirmation
Field bot.*

---

**NOTE**

You should use this bot only on form confirmation pages. When the reader displays the page, the Confirmation Field bot updates the field and your page appears with appropriate values.

---

# The Confirmation Field WebBot in Action

Before you use the Confirmation Field bot, you should create a fill-out form such as the one shown in Figure 20.8. This form lets registered users submit questions to the company's customer support staff. The form asks for key information that confirms the identity of the user.

**FIGURE 20.8.**

*A customer support form for registered users.*

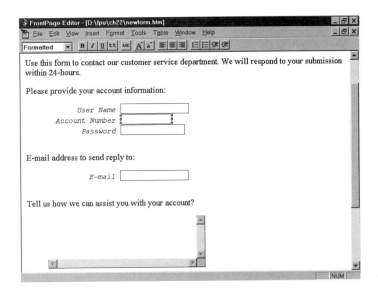

You should appropriately name each input field in the form. For this example, the fields you want to track are the user's account number and e-mail address. To verify the field names, you can open the properties box associated with the input field. Figure 20.9 shows the properties box for the input field for the user's account number. Note that the name of the field is `Account_number`. You should write all the field names down on a piece of scratch paper.

**FIGURE 20.9.**

*Verifying field names.*

Next, you should ensure that you have set a URL for the confirmation page. Afterward, you can create a confirmation page, such as the one shown in Figure 20.10. When you insert a Confirmation Field bot, the bot asks you to enter the name of the field, which is then inserted into the page within square brackets. This page has two confirmation fields, one for `Account_number` and one for `Account_email`. You can update the properties of these bots at any time by moving the mouse pointer over the confirmation field and double-clicking.

---

> **NOTE**
>
> At the bottom of Figure 20.10, you'll see a two-link navigation menu within square brackets. Do not confuse the confirmation fields in square brackets with a similar technique used to highlight navigation links.

**FIGURE 20.10.**

*A typical confirmation page.*

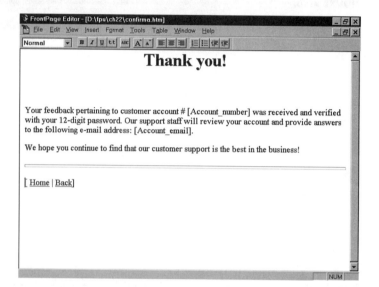

## Using the Discussion Bot

Discussion groups enable users to interact on the Web, and the Discussion bot automates this process. Creating discussion groups and using the Discussion bot handler is the subject of Chapter 27, "Creating and Managing Discussion Groups."

## Using the HTML Markup WebBot

You can use the HTML Markup bot to insert HTML elements not directly supported by FrontPage. To invoke the HTML Markup bot, open the Insert menu and select Bot. In the Insert Bot window, select the HTML Markup bot by double-clicking on HTML Markup. Alternatively, you can select HTML Markup and then click on the OK button or press Enter on the keyboard. Next, enter the HTML tag or element with the appropriate attributes in the HTML Markup Bot Properties box. Figure 20.11 shows this dialog box.

FrontPage does not verify the markup you insert with this bot in any way. All markup that FrontPage does not support directly appears highlighted, generally with a yellow background and blue text. The full tag does not appear. Instead, the FrontPage Editor uses the syntax <?> to designate non-standard HTML markup. Although you can see the <?> designator in the FrontPage Editor, it does not appear in a Web browser. Browsers that support the markup will display the appropriate element.

**FIGURE 20.11.**

*Using the HTML Markup bot.*

# Using the Include WebBot

The Include bot helps create standardized page sections throughout your Web by enabling you to merge a page into an existing page. This function was used in many of the pages created by the Web templates and wizards in the previous chapter to add standard headers, footers, and navigation bars to pages.

When you view a page in a browser or in the FrontPage Editor, all Include bots are replaced with the contents of the pages they reference. These pages must come from the same Web. If you change the contents of a page referenced by an Include bot, the change is made to every page in the Web that has the Include bot inserted in it.

> **TIP**
>
> Sometimes you might not want a page that you are including to be accessible to those who visit your Web site. If this is the case, create a subdirectory within your Web site called _private and store the page in this directory. Visitors to your Web cannot access files in the _private directory.

To insert the Include Bot into a page, open the Insert menu and select Bot. In the Insert Bot window, select the Include bot by double-clicking on the word Include. Alternatively, you can select Include and then click on the OK button or press Enter on the keyboard. This opens the dialog box shown in Figure 20.12.

**FIGURE 20.12.**

*Using the Include bot.*

In the Include Bot Properties box, enter the URL of the page to include. If you do not know the URL of the page, click on the Browse button to select a URL from a list of page URLs in the current Web. When you are finished, click OK to close the Include Bot Properties box.

When you close the box, you see a message telling you that FrontPage is retrieving the included page and inserting it into the current page. You cannot edit any elements contained on the included page. You must open and edit the original page to make any changes.

> **TIP**
>
> You can insert material before an Include bot that is the first element on the page. Simply move the insertion point before the included elements and press Enter. Alternatively, you can select the included elements by clicking on them and pressing Enter.

# Using the Registration WebBot

By default, all users have access to your Web. You can restrict access to a Web in two key ways:

- Require users to register before entering a restricted Web.
- Allow only users registered by the Web administrator to access a restricted Web.

In both instances, when a user tries to enter the restricted Web, the Registration bot asks him to enter his user name and password using the dialog box shown in Figure 20.13. If the user has not registered with the Web and tries to enter information in this dialog box, the Registration bot takes him to a page set up for registration failures. From this page, the user can get to the registration form.

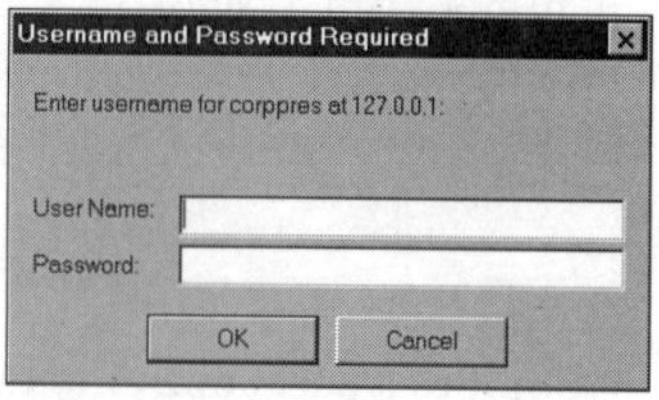

**FIGURE 20.13.**

*Users must specify user name and password to access restricted Webs.*

If the user has registered with the Web, the Registration bot grants him access to the Web and remembers his user name and password throughout the current session. However, the next time the user visits the Web, he will be prompted again for his user name and password, which again will be good for an entire session.

> **CAUTION**
>
> The Web administrator and any other users registered by the Web administrator can access the restricted Web. For this reason, you should always use very secure passwords, especially for the Web administrator. I recommend using a password that is at least six characters long and includes numbers and wild card characters, such as !, @, #, $, and ?.

The first method allows any user to access a Web as long as he registers beforehand. A user is typically able to register using a simple registration form that asks him to select a user name and password, which means access to the Web is virtually unlimited. The next section covers creating registration forms.

The second method allows only a specific set of users to access a Web. The Web administrator grants these users access, and each user must specify the user name and password that the administrator assigned him in order to enter the Web. At any time, the Web administrator can revoke the access privileges. Restricted access Webs created by Web administrators are covered in Chapter 26, "Managing Security for the Personal Web Server."

# Creating a User Registration Form

To allow users to register for a Web, you must create a registration form. Because of the way permissions are set, you should always register users using a form page located in the Root Web. This form should grant them access to another Web at your site.

> **NOTE**
>
> For instance, if your Web site is at www.tvp.com, then your Root Web is at
>
> http://www.tvp.com/
>
> To register users for the corppres Web at http://www.tvp.com/corppres/, you would create a registration form that was located in the base Web, such as
>
> http://www.tvp.com/registr.htm

In the FrontPage Explorer, open the Web you want to register users for, and then select Permissions from the Tools menu. This opens the Web Permissions dialog box shown in Figure 20.14. In the Settings tab, select Use Unique Permissions For This Web, and then click on the Apply button.

EDITING
TECHNIQUE

**FIGURE 20.14.**

*Setting Web permissions.*

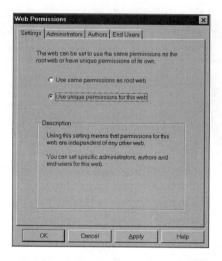

Next, in the End Users tab shown in Figure 20.15, select Registered Users Only, and click on the OK button, which closes the dialog box.

**FIGURE 20.15.**

*Setting user permissions.*

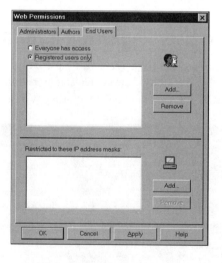

Now, open the Root Web, which is the first entry in the Open Web dialog box and labeled as `<Root Web>`. With the Root Web as your current Web, you can now open a new page in the FrontPage Editor and save it to the Root Web. Start by selecting New from the File menu. In the New Page dialog box, select the User Registration template, and click on the OK button.

You can use the page created by the editor as the basis for your registration page. Delete any text that you do not want to include and change the text associated with the registration form as appropriate for your Web. Next, check the names associated with each input field.

# Configuring the Registration WebBot

Now that you have created a registration page, you need to configure the Registration bot for use on your Web. With the registration page open, select any field and open its properties box, and then click on the Form button to open the Form Properties box. The Registration bot should be selected as the Form Handler by default. Next, click on the Settings button to define settings for the handler. This opens the dialog box shown in Figure 20.16.

**FIGURE 20.16.**

*Configuring the Registra-
tion handler.*

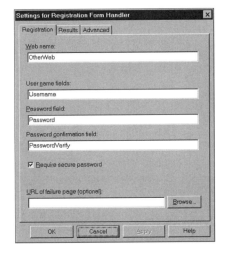

As you can see from Figure 20.16, the Registration handler has three configuration pages. You can access these by clicking on the Registration, Results, or Advanced tab. Although the Registration tab contains unique settings, the Results and Advanced tabs are exactly the same as those used for the Save Results handler, covered in "Saving the Results of the Form" in Chapter 11.

The first tab you should look at is the Registration tab. In the Web Name field, enter the name of the Web for which you are registering users. The name must match the Web name as shown in the Open Web dialog box.

All registration forms should have user name, password, and password confirmation fields. You should verify that the field names you used in your registration form match those shown in the Registration tab. If they do not match, enter the correct field names.

If you want to ensure that users have passwords that follow sound security practices, check the Require secure password field. In FrontPage, a secure password has six or more characters and does not partially match the user name.

The final field for which you might want to specify information is the URL of failure page field. All registration forms use default failure pages unless you specify another page. Figure 20.17 shows a failed registration using the default failure page. Although the default page is fairly basic, it gets the job done.

**FIGURE 20.17.**

*The default page for failed registrations.*

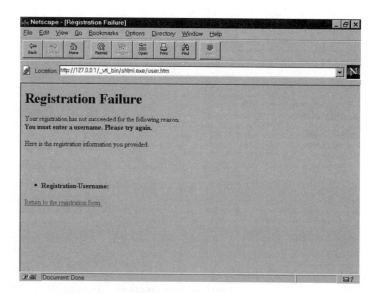

Next, you should review the settings in the Results and Advanced tabs. The key field you should check is the URL for the confirmation page in the Results tab. All registration forms use default confirmation pages unless you specify another page.

Figure 20.18 shows a confirmed registration using the default confirmation page. This page confirms the user's registration and lets the user access the restricted Web. To ensure that users can register for your Web, your home page in the Root Web should have a link to the registration page.

**FIGURE 20.18.**

*The default page for
confirmed registrations.*

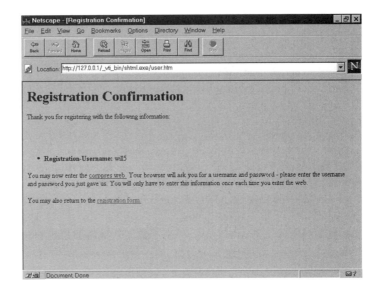

# Using the Save Results WebBot

The Save Results bot lets you save form data to a file or database. This is the most common type of form handler. For detailed information on the Save Results Bot, see "Saving the Results of the Form" in Chapter 11.

# Using the Scheduled Image WebBot

Sometimes you might want to display images at your site for a specific period of time. For example, an advertiser wants to run a two-week ad in your magazine. You sign the advertiser to a contract stating this and ask him to specify the start date of the advertisement. Armed with this information, you place a Scheduled Image bot on the pages where the ad will appear and schedule it so that the ad begins on the advertisers start date, displays for 14 days, and then is replaced with your standard logo.

The previous example gives one instance of when you might want to use the Scheduled Image bot. Obviously, there are many other times when you might want to use this bot. The primary reason to use this bot is to include an image in a page with the intent of replacing the image at a later date and time.

> **CAUTION**
>
> The Scheduled Image and Include bots execute only when changes occur to a Web. Thus, to ensure that the Scheduled Image or Include bot runs when you want it to, you should make some type of change to your Web daily, such as incrementing the value of a configuration variable.

To insert the Scheduled Image bot into a page, open the Insert menu and select Bot. In the Insert Bot window, select the Scheduled Image bot by double-clicking on Scheduled Image. Alternatively, you can select Scheduled Image and then click on the OK button or press Enter on the keyboard. This opens the dialog box shown in Figure 20.19.

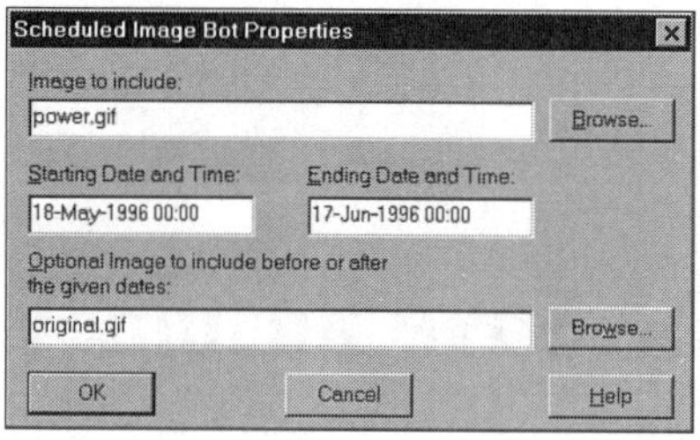

**FIGURE 20.19.**

*Using the Scheduled Image bot.*

In the Scheduled Image Bot Properties box, enter the URL of the image to include. If you do not know the image's URL, click on the Browse button to select a URL from a list of images in the current Web.

Next, you can specify the dates when the image should appear on the page. In the Starting Date and Time field, enter the starting date in the following form:

DD-MMM-YY HH:MM

Here's an example:

25-Aug-96 23:00

> **NOTE**
>
> The date stamp uses a 24-hour clock. This means that you enter 1 a.m. as 01:00 and 1 p.m. as 13:00. If the Starting Date and Time is earlier than the current date and time, the image appears on the page immediately.

In the Ending Date and Time field, enter the date to stop including the image. This is the final field you can define for an optional image to display when the included image is not being displayed. Click on the Browse button to select a URL from a list of images in the current Web. Click OK to close the properties box.

# Using the Scheduled Include WebBot

Sometimes you might want to display a standard header, footer, or section of a page for only a specific period of time. With the Scheduled Include bot, you can insert a page into the current page for a fixed time period.

To insert the Scheduled Include bot into a page, open the Insert menu and select Bot. In the Insert Bot window select the Scheduled Include bot by double-clicking on Scheduled Include. Alternatively, you can select Scheduled Include and then click on the OK button or press Enter on the keyboard. As you can see from Figure 20.20, you configure this bot almost identically to the Schedule Image bot.

**FIGURE 20.20.**

*Using the Scheduled Include bot.*

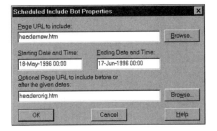

In the Scheduled Include Bot Properties box, enter the URL of the page to include. If you do not know the page URL, click on the Browse button to select a URL from a list of pages in the current Web. Next, specify the dates when the Include should appear in the page. In the Starting Date and Time field, enter the starting date. If the starting date and time is earlier than the current date and time, the page appears immediately.

In the Ending Date and Time field, enter the date to stop including the page. You can also define a page to display before and after the scheduled page appears. Click on the Browse button to select a URL from a list of pages in the current Web. When you are finished, click OK to close the properties box.

# Using the Search WebBot

The Search bot provides a full text-searching capability for your Web. When a user submits a form created by the Search bot, the Search bot returns a list of all pages in the current Web containing the user's search words. The user can then access any of the pages by clicking on the page title.

---

**NOTE**

You can place any pages that you do not want users to search, such as header and footer pages, in a subdirectory called _private. The Search bot does not search in this directory.

---

The Search bot is the only bot that creates its own search form that you can place on any page. To insert the Search bot and its associated search form into a page, open the Insert menu and select Bot. Next, select the Search bot in the Insert Bot dialog box. This opens the dialog box shown in Figure 20.21.

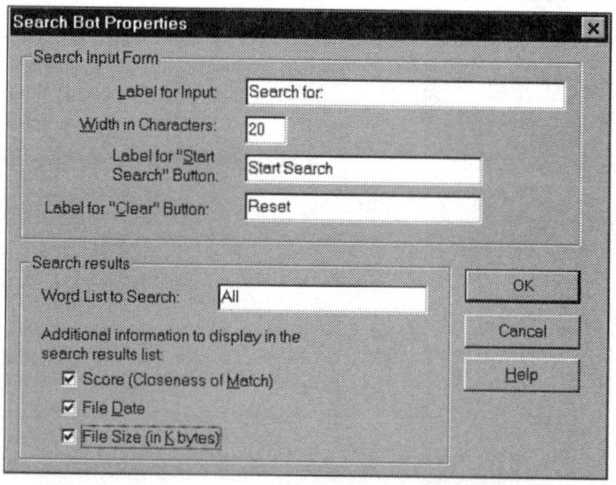

**FIGURE 20.21.**

*Using the Search bot.*

| Search Bot Properties | ☒ |
|---|---|
| **Search Input Form** | |
| Label for Input: | Search for: |
| Width in Characters: | 20 |
| Label for "Start Search" Button: | Start Search |
| Label for "Clear" Button: | Reset |
| **Search results** | |
| Word List to Search: | All |
| Additional information to display in the search results list: | |
| ☑ Score (Closeness of Match) | |
| ☑ File Date | |
| ☑ File Size (in K bytes) | |

Buttons: OK, Cancel, Help

---

**TIP**

You can also use the search page template to create a new page with a search form. A key reason to use this template is that it includes detailed information on the query language that the user might need.

---

## Conducting a Search with the Search Bot

A sample search form appears in Figure 20.22. In the search form, I entered the search words writer and writing. When I click on the Start Search button, the Search bot conducts a full-text search of the current Web and inserts the results into the current page.

As you can see in Figure 20.23, the Search bot found 82 documents matching the search criteria. Because the Search bot was set up to return a score, file size, and file date, documents containing the search words were ranked by these three criteria.

#### Chapter 20

**FIGURE 20.22.**

*A sample search form.*

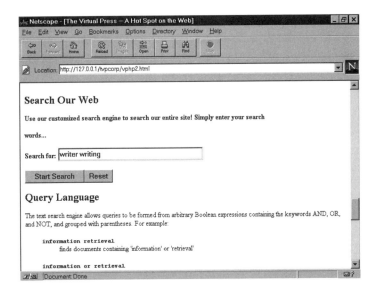

**FIGURE 20.23.**

*The Search bot returns the results.*

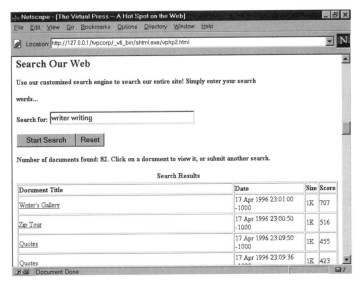

# Configuring the Search Bot and the Search Form

To customize the search form and the search results, change the Search bot's default property values. As you saw in Figure 20.21, the Search Bot Properties box has two key areas.

The Search Input Form area defines the way the search form looks in your Web page. The form is very simple, with a label for the input box, a one-line text box that accepts input, and two labeled buttons. To change the way the form looks, simply change the default labels. Here's a list of the fields and how they are used:

| | |
|---|---|
| Label for Input | The label for the one-line text box. The default is `Search For:`. |
| Width in Characters | The width of the one-line text box. By default the character width of the text box is 20. |
| Label for "Start Search" button | The label for the button that starts the search. The default is `Start Search`. |
| Label for "Clear" button | The label for the button that clears the form. The default is `Reset`. |

The Search Results area defines the ways you can manipulate the results of a search. Results appear based on matches for the search words and can be ranked by the following criteria:

| | |
|---|---|
| Score | The scoring mechanism tries to rank the relevancy of the page based on the number of times the search words appear on the page. |
| File Date | The date the file was created or the last time the file was updated. |
| File Size | The size of the file. |

---

**TIP**

Although scoring is the most common way to rank the relevancy of files, many Web publishers prefer to use all three ranking statistics. The file's modification date tells the user how current the document is. The file's size indicates how much data the file contains.

---

# Using the Substitution WebBot

Just as you might sometimes want to insert standard headers and footers into your pages, you might also want to include standard segments of text. For example, most pages include contact information. Wouldn't it be great to be able to instantly change the contact information if one of the addresses is no longer valid? Well, with the Substitution bot, you can make instant updates to your pages.

To insert the Substitution bot into a page, open the Insert menu and select Bot. In the Insert Bot dialog box select the Substitution bot. This opens the dialog box shown in Figure 20.24.

The Substitute with field has a pull-down menu that lets you select any of the default configuration variables, as well as any configuration variables that you have added to the Web.

**FIGURE 20.24.**
*Using the Substitution bot.*

# Using Default Configuration Variables

When a reader views a page containing a Substitution bot, the bot replaces a temporary variable with its value. This variable is called a *configuration variable* because the Web administrator can configure it and is valid throughout the Web.

FrontPage tracks key information for all pages created, such as who created the page and who last modified the page. To view the settings for the default variables associated with any page, select the page in the FrontPage Explorer, and then open the Properties dialog box by selecting Properties from the Edit menu or by pressing Alt+Enter.

As you can see from Figure 20.25, the Properties dialog box has two tabs: General and Summary. Four default configuration variables are defined by the fields in the Summary tab:

Author    The user name of the person who created the page, as defined in the Created by field of the FrontPage Explorer's Properties dialog box.

ModifiedBy    The user name of the person who most recently modified the page, as defined in the Modified by field of the FrontPage Explorer's Properties dialog box.

Description    A description of the current page, as defined in the Comments field of the FrontPage Explorer's Properties dialog box.

Page-URL    The page URL of the page, as defined in the Page URL field of the FrontPage Explorer's Properties dialog box.

**FIGURE 20.25.**
*The FrontPage Explorer's Properties box.*

# Defining New Configuration Variables

Defining new configuration variables is easy. Start by selecting Web Settings from the FrontPage Explorer's Tools menu to open the Web Settings dialog box shown in Figure 20.26. The Web settings dialog box has three tabs. The Parameters tab shows any user-defined configuration variables, and you can use it to add, modify, and remove user-defined configuration variables.

**FIGURE 20.26.**

*The Parameters tab.*

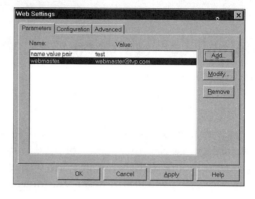

To add a configuration variable, click on the Add button, which opens the Add Name and Value dialog box shown in Figure 20.27. In the Name field, enter the name of the configuration variable you want to define. Although the name can be any length, it cannot contain the colon character (:). In the Value field, enter the value you want associated with the new configuration variable. The value can be a text string of any length. When you are done, click on the OK button. Repeat the procedure to define additional configuration variables.

**FIGURE 20.27.**

*Defining new configuration variables.*

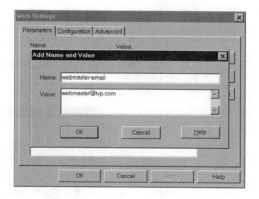

# Using the Table of Contents WebBot

Like an index, a table of contents is useful but usually difficult to build and maintain. FrontPage allows you to instantly add a table of contents to your Web.

FrontPage builds the table of contents by examining all the links contained in the top-level page you specify and then recursively examining the lower level pages for links to other pages. If the Web contains pages that are not linked to any other pages, these pages are either excluded (by default) or included (by selecting a property setting for the bot that builds the table of contents).

To build a table of contents for the current Web, insert the Table of Contents bot into a page or create a new page based on the Table of Contents template. To set properties for the Table of Contents, open the bot's properties box, which is shown in Figure 20.28.

**FIGURE 20.28.**

*Using the Table of Contents bot.*

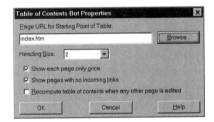

Each of the fields in the properties box enables you to customize the table of contents. You can use these fields as follows:

| | |
|---|---|
| Page URL for Starting Point of Table | Enables you to specify the URL of the top-level page you want the bot to examine and build the table of contents from. If you do not know the page URL, click on the Browse button to get a list of pages in the current Web. |
| Heading Size | Enables you to specify the size of the heading to use for the first entry in the table of contents. If you want no headings, select none. |
| Show each page only once | Ensures that each page appears only once in the table of contents. Otherwise, pages linked from more than one page will be listed once for each link. |
| Show pages with no incoming links | Ensures that pages not linked to other pages appear in your table of contents. |
| Recompute table of contents when any other page is edited | Ensures that the table of contents is automatically updated when any page in the Web is edited. |

# Using the TimeStamp WebBot

Telling visitors to your Web when a page was last modified is useful, especially if you plan to make frequent updates to your Web. Use the TimeStamp bot to do this.

To insert the TimeStamp bot into a page, open the Insert menu and select Bot. In the Insert Bot window, select the TimeStamp bot by double-clicking on TimeStamp. Alternatively, you can select TimeStamp and then click on the OK button or press Enter on the keyboard. As you can see from Figure 20.29, you configure this bot almost identically to the Schedule Image bot.

**FIGURE 20.29.**

*Using the TimeStamp bot.*

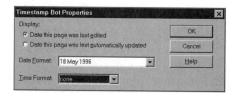

In the Display field in the TimeStamp Bot Properties dialog box, select the type of page modifications you want to track. A page is considered "edited" when you save it to the server. A page is considered "updated" whenever FrontPage touches the document. This happens when you save the page to the server, when you upload the page to a Web, and when the page's links are recalculated.

Your timestamp can include both a date and a time. Select the date format from over a dozen styles using the Date Format field's drop-down menu. Select the time format from one of three time formats in the Time Format field's drop-down menu. If you do not want to use a date or time, you can choose the drop-down menu option None. Although both the Time Format and Date Format fields allow you to select None, you should not set both fields to None, because that defeats the purpose of using the TimeStamp bot.

# Summary

FrontPage includes more than a dozen WebBots. WebBots are useful for automating even the most advanced tasks, and they can be easily added to any page. Some WebBots only affect your Web when you add or update the bots in the FrontPage Editor. Most WebBots automatically update themselves at runtime. Bots that run immediately make updates to the page in browsers and in the FrontPage Editor.

All WebBots that automatically update themselves at runtime depend on FrontPage server extensions. Therefore, if you plan to use WebBots that execute at runtime, you must either use the Personal Web Server to provide Web services or install the FrontPage server extensions for your server.

# PART

# VI

# Using the FrontPage Developer's Kit

# Introducing the FrontPage Developer's Kit

**21**

*by William Robert Stanek*

**IN THIS CHAPTER**

FrontPage is the most powerful Web publishing and administration tool available. Not only can you personalize FrontPage, but you can also create customized tools to meet your specific needs. These tools can include new templates for pages and Webs, wizards for creating pages and Webs, and programs that automate publishing tasks. To create customized tools for FrontPage publishing, you use the FrontPage Developer's Kit. The Developer's Kit has everything you need to help you customize FrontPage publishing.

This chapter introduces the Developer's Kit. In addition to learning how to obtain and install the kit, you will get a detailed look at what the kit contains and how to use the kit with FrontPage.

# Using the Developer's Kit

The FrontPage Developer's Kit was created to help developers extend the functionality of FrontPage. You use this kit to create templates, wizards, utilities, and CGI scripts for use with FrontPage. Although this kit is primarily for developers who have some experience in programming and automation with object linking and embedding (OLE), the kit is meant to be easy to use regardless of your experience.

As you have seen in this book, templates are used as the basis for pages and Webs. Using the Developer's Kit, you can also create templates for frame-enhanced documents. These templates are called *framesets*. You learn all about creating framesets in Chapter 22, "Creating Your Own Templates." The good news is that you do not need any programming or OLE automation experience to create templates for pages, frames, and Webs.

Wizards are also used to create pages and Webs. As you have seen in this book, wizards aid the content creation process by presenting options that help you customize pages and Webs. Unlike templates, wizards are programs that run on your system and interface with FrontPage. To create a wizard, you need to use a programming language, such as Visual Basic or Visual C++. To interface with FrontPage, your program uses OLE automation. Thus, if you plan to create wizards, you should be familiar with programming and OLE automation. You learn how to create wizards in Chapter 23, "Creating Your Own Wizards."

> **NOTE**
>
> Visual Basic and Visual C++ are the best programming languages for creating FrontPage wizards because of their visual development nature. Creating the graphical interface for wizards is easy and quick if you use either of these languages.

Another use for OLE automation is to create utilities that can be used with FrontPage. An example of a FrontPage publishing utility is the Publishing Wizard you learn about in Chapter 36, "Designing and Publishing a Web Site." This wizard allows you to use the File Transfer

Protocol to publish Webs. Using this wizard, you can transfer Webs to servers that do not support FrontPage extensions.

The Developer's Kit also helps you create CGI scripts that interface with the Personal Web Server. Again, the interface to FrontPage is handled with OLE automation. See Chapter 30, "Writing CGI Scripts," to learn more about CGI scripts.

# Obtaining and Installing the Developer's Kit

Microsoft has plans to integrate the Developer's Kit into the commercial release of FrontPage. If the version of FrontPage you purchased does not include the Developer's Kit, you can obtain the kit from Microsoft's Web site at no charge. To do so, visit Microsoft's home page for FrontPage at the following URL:

```
http://www.microsoft.com/frontpage/
```

From this page, you can follow links to the section containing the Developer's Kit. If you obtain the Developer's Kit from Microsoft's Web site, you will need to install it on your system. All the files in the FDK are compressed into a ZIP file that you have to uncompress using a ZIP utility such as PKZIP.

**CAUTION**

The Developer's Kit's ZIP file contains subdirectories. ZIP utilities that run from the DOS prompt do not automatically unpack your files into multiple directories. So, if your ZIP utility runs from the DOS prompt, be sure to use the -d flag to preserve the directory structure, as shown in the following example:

```
pkunzip -d fpdevkit.zip
```

At the time of this writing, the ZIP file for the Developer's Kit is 583KB. You need approximately 1.5MB of hard drive space to uncompress the ZIP file, which means that initially you need 2.1MB of free space on your hard drive. After you successfully uncompress the Developer's Kit, you can delete the original ZIP file.

# What's in the Developer's Kit

The FrontPage Developer's Kit is quite extensive and includes many examples. These examples show you how to create templates, wizards, utilities, and CGI scripts that interface with

FrontPage. Each specific type of example has its own directory under the base installation directory for the Developer's Kit. These directories have the following names:

```
template
wizards
utility
cgi
```

The sections that follow examine the contents of these directories and discuss how you can use the examples to help you customize FrontPage. You might want to review what the Developer's Kit contains, and then read this part of the book in its entirety before studying the examples.

# The Template Examples

The `template` directory is in the base installation directory of the FrontPage Developer's Kit. The `template` directory contains template examples for pages, Webs, and frames with each example organized into subdirectories.

The `template/pages` directory has a page template containing a simple table stored in the subdirectory `tablepag.tem`. The template was created with the FrontPage Editor Save as Template option. When you use this option of the Editor, you create an HTML document with the `.htm` extension and a document that stores template information with an `.inf` extension. Files with the `.inf` extension are formatted like Windows INI files and contain parameters for the template, such as the template name and directory.

The `template/webs` directory contains a Web template stored in the subdirectory `testcorp.tem`. This sample Web template was created with the Web Template Maker Utility and was based on the Corporate Presence Web. The Web Template Maker Utility is one of the utilities included in the Developer's Kit. With this useful tool, you can base a Web template on any existing Web.

The `template/frames` directory contains a frameset called `sample.frm`. The `.frm` extension is used to indicate that the document is a frameset. You can use the sample document to help you create your own framesets.

# The Wizard Examples

The `wizards` directory under the base installation of the FrontPage Developer's Kit contains sample wizards. Most of these wizards are programmed in Visual Basic 4, which is one of the easiest programming languages to learn and use. Because wizards are programs, you can run them just as you would any other program.

> **TIP**
>
> You can use the Windows Explorer to run any wizard. All you need to do is change to the directory containing the executable file and double-click the appropriate icon. Before you run a wizard, you should start the FrontPage Explorer and the Personal Web Server.

To better understand the sample wizards, change to the appropriate subdirectory, list the files, and examine all files except the binary executable file using a word processor or standard ASCII text editor. When you list and examine the files in wizard directories, you should see immediately that wizards are more complex than templates, and not only because there are more files involved. Because most of the wizard examples are written in Visual Basic, the wizard directories contain seven files that end with the extensions shown in Table 21.1.

### Table 21.1. Files in wizard directories.

| Extension | Description |
| --- | --- |
| .exe | The binary executable file for the wizard |
| .inf | A Windows INI-formatted file that specifies parameters for the wizard, such as the wizard name and directory |
| .log | A file that logs errors that occur when the wizard runs |
| .frm | A form written in Visual Basic and used to create the wizard |
| .frx | Another Visual Basic file containing program information |
| .vbp | File used to set up program information for wizards written in Visual Basic |
| .vbz | File used to set up flags, dependencies, and so on for wizards written in Visual Basic |

## Examining the Page Wizards

The `wizards/pages` directory has subdirectories for two simple wizards: `hello.wiz` and `calendar.wiz`. Both wizards are created with Visual Basic and use the seven types of files described in Table 21.1.

The Hello Page Wizard has three setup pages and is used to create a page that greets visitors to your Web site. Figure 21.1 shows the document this wizard creates. Because this example is so basic, it is the best example to examine piece by piece to learn more about creating wizards. When you look through the files used to create the Hello Page Wizard, start with the file named `Hello.frm`.

**FIGURE 21.1.**

*Document created by the Hello Page Wizard.*

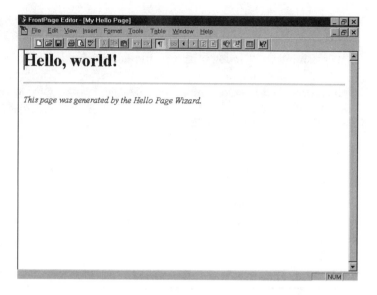

Like the Hello Page Wizard, the Calendar Page Wizard has three setup pages. As you can see from Figure 21.2, this wizard creates a document with a nicely formatted calendar for a specific month and year. The Calendar Page Wizard is a great example of how to create a useful wizard. Examine this wizard starting with the file named `Calendar.frm` to learn how to manage dates in your wizards and generate fairly complex documents that use tables.

**FIGURE 21.2.**

*Document created by the Calendar Page Wizard.*

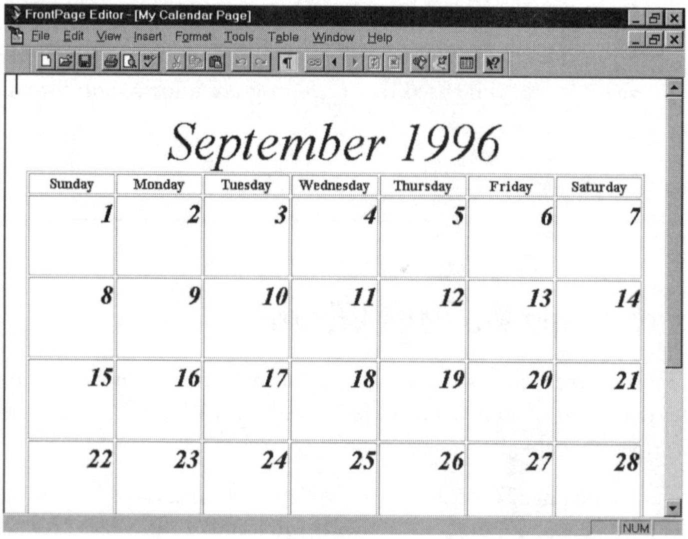

Pages you create with the Hello Page or Calendar Page Wizards are loaded into the FrontPage Editor. Thus, you can study these wizards to learn how OLE automation is used to access and launch the FrontPage Editor.

## Examining the Web Wizards

The `wizards/webs` directory contains two sample Web wizards: `helloweb.wiz` and `realest.wiz`. Both wizards are programmed in Visual Basic and use the seven types of files described previously in Table 21.1.

The Hello Web Wizard creates a Web based on the same HTML document used by the Hello Page Wizard. Examine this Web to learn how to create OLE hooks to the FrontPage Explorer. You also can learn a lot about the difference between creating Webs and creating files by doing a line-by-line comparison between the Hello Page Wizard files and the files used by the Hello Web Wizard. Start by comparing the file named `HelloWeb.frm` to the file named `Hello.frm`.

The Real Estate Wizard is one of the most complex examples in the FrontPage Developer's Kit. This wizard creates a Web customized for real estate information. Because of the complexity of this Web wizard, you should examine its files only after you've looked at the other Web wizards.

## Code Modules and Libraries

Sample wizards are not the only programs in the `wizards` directory. This directory also contains directories for Visual Basic modules and Visual C++ object libraries.

The `wizards/vb` directory has utility procedures to help you create wizards. The file `botgen.bas` contains a series of Visual Basic procedures that lets you insert different types of WebBots into output strings. In this way, your wizards can create pages that use WebBots. The file `htmlgen.bas` has Visual Basic procedures for handling HTML documents. The file `wizutil.bas` has miscellaneous utility procedures you can use in your wizards. You can use these procedures to add meta-information to documents, add files to a list of files you want to update or create, look up or set parameters for the wizard, and much more.

The `wizards/vc` directory contains object and type libraries for use with Visual C++. You can use these libraries in OLE automation. The files `webber.tlb` and `webber.odl` are used with the OLE identifier `FrontPage.Explorer.1.1`. The files `wpe.tlb` and `wpe.odl` are used with the OLE identifier `FrontPage.Editor.1.1`.

## The Developer's Kit Utilities

There are three very useful utilities in the Developer's Kit: the API Test Utility, the Web Template Maker, and a helper application called fplaunch. These utilities are written in Visual Basic and use OLE automation to interface with FrontPage. Not only are the utilities useful, but you also can learn a great deal by examining their source code.

## The API Test Utility

The API Test Utility is a test suite of all the OLE automation functions you can use with FrontPage. You can use the source code in the `utility/apitests` directory as a starting point for any wizard you create. In fact, you can usually cut procedures out of the source code and paste them directly into your wizard's source code. When you run the utility by executing the `apitests.exe` binary executable file, you see the dialog box shown in Figure 21.3.

**FIGURE 21.3.**

*Using the API Test Utility.*

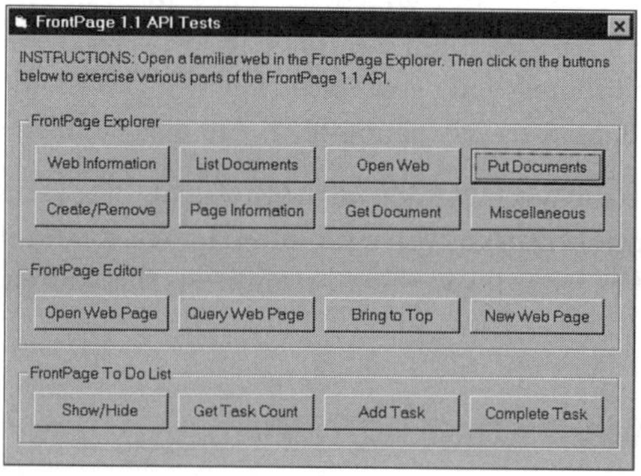

Each push button in the dialog box enables you to test a specific set of related OLE automation functions. Most functions display a form that prompts you to enter information. For example, if you press the button labeled Web Information, the dialog box shown in Figure 21.4 is displayed. This dialog box lets you test OLE procedures that get a Web's title, URL, and meta-information.

**FIGURE 21.4.**

*Testing OLE procedures.*

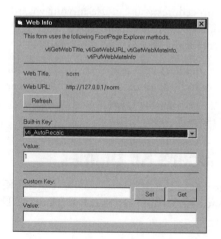

# The fplaunch Utility

The fplaunch utility is an extremely useful helper application that uses OLE automation to create an authoring interface between your Web browser and FrontPage. Using fplaunch, you can create HTML documents with links that access the FrontPage Explorer, open a specified Web, and then open a page for editing in the FrontPage Editor. To learn how to create your own helper applications, examine the source code in the utility/fplaunch directory.

Because you can set an optional user name parameter, fplaunch is a useful utility for Web administrators and anyone else authoring pages in your Webs. Before you can use fplaunch, you need to do the following:

1. Configure your Web server and browser so that they recognize fplaunch parameter files, which end in the .fpl extension.
2. Create an fplaunch parameter file and a document that references the parameter file.

## Configuring Your Server and Browser

As with most helper applications, you need to ensure that your server and browser correctly identify files used by the helper application. To do this, you must update server and browser configuration files.

Because fplaunch parameter files should end in the .fpl extension, you configure your server to send files with this extension as a new MIME type. On most servers, MIME types are stored in a specific configuration file. For the Personal Web Server, the configuration file is called mime.typ and is located in the FrontPage Webs/Server/conf directory. You need to edit this file and add the following entry to the end of the file:

```
application/x-fplaunch        fpl
```

### NOTE

The exact number of spaces between the MIME type and the extension designator does not matter. MIME types are broken down into basic categories, such as application. The application type identifies binary data that can be executed or used with another application. Each data type category has a subtype associated with it. MIME subtypes are defined as primary data types, additionally defined data types, and extended data types. The primary subtype is the primary type of data adopted for use as MIME content types. Additionally defined data types are additional subtypes that have been officially adopted as MIME content types. Extended data types are experimental subtypes that have not been officially adopted as MIME content types. You can easily identify extended subtypes because they begin with the letter x followed by a hyphen, such as x-fplaunch. The x-fplaunch subtype identifies an extended data type in fplaunch format.

After you save the MIME configuration file, restart the Personal Web Server. You are now ready to configure your browser for use with fplaunch. You do this by setting preferences from an options menu within the browser. Figure 21.5 shows the Preferences menu for helper applications in Netscape Navigator 3.

The helper application configurations shown in the figure are the default settings. If you visit a Web site using the Netscape browser with the sample helper application configuration and select a link to an image file in TIFF format, the browser would ask what helper application you want to use to display the file. If you select a page link to an image file in JPEG or GIF format, the browser would display the file because it has direct support for JPEG and GIF images.

**FIGURE 21.5.**

*Setting helper application preferences in Netscape.*

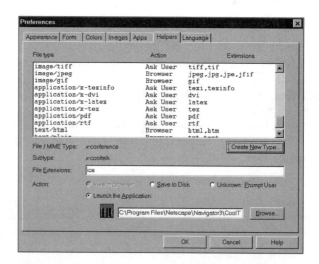

To set a helper application in Netscape Navigator 3, click the Create New Type button. This action opens the Configure New MIME Type dialog box that lets you enter the MIME type and subtype. In the MIME Type field, enter the keyword: `application`. In the MIME SubType field, enter the keyword: `x-fplaunch`. After you enter this information, click the OK button to close the Configure New MIME type dialog box.

In the File Extensions field of the dialog box shown in Figure 21.5, enter the extension: `fpl`. In the Action field, select the radio button labeled Launch the Application. Next, click on the Action field's Browse button. This will open the Select an appropriate viewer dialog box. Using this dialog box, you search through your file system until you identify the file path to the binary executable for the `fplaunch` application. When you are finished, click OK. After you double-check the accuracy of your helper application entry, click OK in the Preferences dialog box.

## Creating and Referencing a Parameter File

Creating a parameter file to use with fplaunch is easy. All you need to do is create an ASCII text file that sets the parameters that enable OLE automation to perform its magic on the FrontPage Explorer. There are three mandatory parameters and one optional parameter:

| Parameter | Description |
|---|---|
| Web server name | The host name or IP address of the server storing the Web you want to access |
| Web name | The name of the Web you want to access |
| user name | Optional user name to enter in the login dialog |
| page URL | In the named Web, the page URL of the file you want to edit |

> **NOTE**
>
> All users must authenticate themselves to FrontPage, even if you set the user name parameter. When a user activates a link to fplaunch, she is prompted to enter her user name and password before FrontPage opens the Web for editing.

Use each of these parameters in the order presented and enter them on separate lines. Here is a sample parameter file called `startcorp.fpl`:

```
http://www.tvpress.com
corpres
william
index.htm
```

When a user clicks on a link containing a reference to `startcorp.fpl`, his browser starts fplaunch, fplaunch reads the parameter file, and then the server asks the user to authenticate with the user name filled in as `william`. The user can enter a new user name and password or enter a valid password for the user `william`. After authentication, the FrontPage Explorer loads a Web called `corpres` from the server at `http://www.tvpress.com` and opens the file called `index.htm` for editing in the FrontPage Explorer.

> **NOTE**
>
> The parameter file *must* be placed in the subdirectory for your Web. If you installed FrontPage to the default location, the location of your Web is `FrontPage Webs\ Content\`*yourweb_name*. Keep in mind, all entries in the parameter file *must* be valid. If you are practicing with FrontPage, you are probably using a local server with the server name as `http://127.0.0.1`.

After you save the parameter file to the subdirectory for your Web, you must create a document that references the parameter file.

> **TIP**
>
> The hypertext reference to the parameter file is best entered as a page link. You can create page links in the Current Web tab of the Create Link dialog box.

## The Web Template Maker

The Web Template Maker creates Web templates that are based on existing Webs. The source code and binary executable file for the template maker are in the `utility/webtmpl` directory. Before you use the Web Template Maker, start the Personal Web Server and the FrontPage Explorer, and then open a Web on the server that has the Webs you want to use as the basis for templates.

Next, start the Web Template Maker. The list of existing Webs is displayed by title in the Available Webs area of the Template Maker dialog box. Select a Web to base a template on by moving the mouse pointer over the name of the Web and clicking the mouse pointer. In the New Web Template area of the dialog box shown in Figure 21.6, enter a title, name, and description for the template. The template name must be unique. You should also enter a unique title for the template.

When you finish defining the template, click the Make Web Template button to create the new template. From then on, when you select New from the File menu in the FrontPage Explorer, your new template will be available for use. To refresh the list of existing Webs after you create a new template, click the Refresh Web List button.

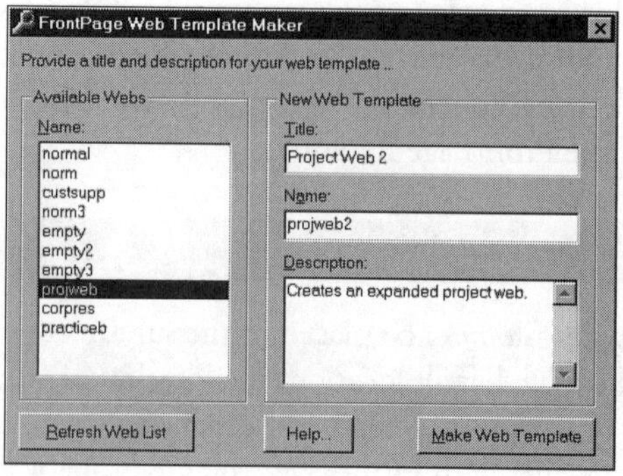

**FIGURE 21.6.**

*Creating templates with the Web Template Maker.*

# Examining the CGI Scripts

CGI scripts are external programs that run on Web servers. Originally, CGI scripts were used to perform advanced publishing tasks, such as processing input from fill-in forms and image maps. Because these tasks are automated in FrontPage, you primarily use CGI scripts to do advanced follow-up processing of form input. Also, if your server does not support FrontPage Server Extensions, you might need to use CGI scripts to perform general processing for forms and image maps as well.

The CGI scripts in the Developer's Kit are in the cgi directory under the base installation of the Developer's Kit. Because most CGI scripts are written in a UNIX shell or C, three of the four sample scripts are written in C. After you read Chapter 30, examine these scripts.

## Using the Hello Script

The cgi/hello directory has a simple CGI script written in C called Hello. The purpose of this script is to generate a simple HTML document that says, "Hello CGI world." Listing 21.1 shows a similar but more useful script called Thanks.c. This script is used to thank customers for submitting a form and provides a link back to your Web's home page.

### Listing 21.1. The Thanks.c script.

```
/* Thanks.c: a small script written in C that uses standard input and output */

#include <stdio.h>

int main (argc, argv)
int argc;
char *argv[];
{
printf("Content-type: text/html\n\n");
printf("<HTML>\n");
printf("<HEAD>\n");
printf("<TITLE>Thank, you!</TITLE>\n");
printf("</HEAD>\n");
printf("<BODY>\n");
printf("<H1>Thanks for submitting your comments to the customer
➥support staff!</H1>\n");
printf("<P>\n");
printf("<P><A HREF=\".\">Return to our home page.</A></P>\n");
printf("</BODY>\n");
printf("</HTML>\n");

return 0;
}
```

# Using the `cgiwin32` Script

The `cgiwin32` script is designed as an interface to the original CGI-WIN interface created for Windows 3.1 servers. Using this script written in C, you can use programs created for CGI-WIN with FrontPage-compatible servers. All you have to do is create a link to the CGI-WIN script. You can add the link as an extra path argument to the `cgiwin32.exe` program in the URL that calls the script. For example, to link a script called `crunch.exe`, you could use the following URL:

```
cgi-bin/cgiwin32.exe/crunch.exe
```

In Chapter 11, "Using Forms and the Form Page Wizard," you read about forms and form handlers. All forms need a handler, such as the Registration bot or a custom CGI script. To use a CGI script, you must select the Custom CGI Script handler in the Forms Properties dialog box shown in Figure 21.7.

**FIGURE 21.7.**

*Using CGI scripts in your pages.*

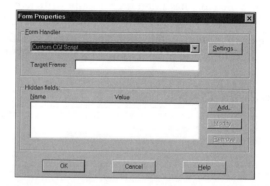

Next, click the Settings button. Then you must specify the script that will process the input in the Action field, as shown in Figure 21.8. You must use the full URL with the extra path information. When you have finished filling out information in the Settings For Custom Form Handler dialog box, click the OK button.

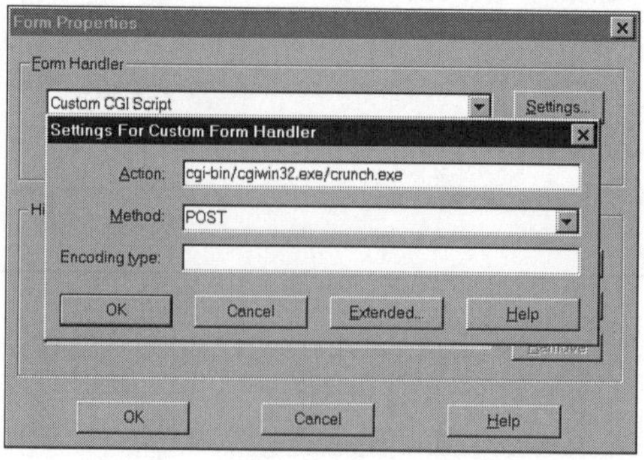

**FIGURE 21.8.**

*Enter the name of the script with the extra path information in the Action field.*

## Using Script Handlers

The `cgi/olecgi` and `cgi/olecgi/vb` directories contain utilities for creating CGI script handlers. Using these utilities, you can create a gateway between the standard I/O interface used in CGI and dynamic linked libraries that can be used with OLE servers. Although most of the examples in these directories are written in C, the OLE DLLs themselves are written in Visual Basic.

The examples in these directories are meant to be used together. Because the examples are fairly advanced, wait until you are very comfortable with CGI, OLE, and programming concepts before you examine them.

# Summary

The Developer's Kit was created to help you extend the functionality of FrontPage. With the Developer's Kit, you can create templates, wizards, utilities, and CGI scripts. Although you do not need to have experience in programming and OLE automation to create templates, you do need this experience to create wizards, utilities, and CGI scripts.

# Creating Your Own Templates

**22**

*by William Robert Stanek*

**IN THIS CHAPTER**

After learning what the FrontPage Developer's Kit contains and how you can use it, you should be ready to create your own templates. There are three types of templates in FrontPage: page templates, Web templates, and frameset templates. Although page templates and Web templates are discussed in many chapters of this book, frameset templates are only discussed in this chapter. As you will see, creating frameset templates is a rather advanced subject.

# The Basics of Creating Templates

Most template basics you already know. Page templates usually create a single page. Web templates usually create a set of related pages. Frameset templates create a frame-enhanced page. Any page created by a template can contain images, WebBots, references to multimedia objects, and links.

The way you access a template depends on the type of template you want to use. To create a new page based on a page template, you select New from the File menu in the FrontPage Editor. To create a new Web based on a Web template, you select New Web from the File menu in the FrontPage Explorer. To create a frame-enhanced page, you use the FrontPage Editor's Frames Wizard, which can be started by selecting New from the File menu and then clicking Frames Wizard in the New Page dialog box.

## Template Directories

All templates are stored in special directories on your hard drive. When you installed FrontPage, you had to select a base installation directory. The template directories are in this base installation directory. The default path to the FrontPage base installation directory is `Program Files\Microsoft FrontPage`.

If you change to the FrontPage base installation directory or examine this directory with Windows Explorer, you will find a directory called `pages`. This directory is used to store the page templates and wizards used by the FrontPage Editor. As you can see from Figure 22.1, all page templates are stored in separate subdirectories under the `pages` directory.

The FrontPage base installation directory also contains a directory called `webs`. This directory is used to store the Web templates and wizards used by the FrontPage Explorer. As you can see from Figure 22.2, all Web templates are stored in separate subdirectories under the `webs` directory.

In Figures 22.1 and 22.2, note the naming structure for page and Web templates. All page and Web template directories are named with a `.tem` extension, such as `normal.tem` and `glossary.tem`. If you examine the template directories, you will find that all templates are defined by HTML pages named with an `.htm` extension and a parameter file named with an `.inf` extension.

**FIGURE 22.1.**

*Page templates are stored in separate directories.*

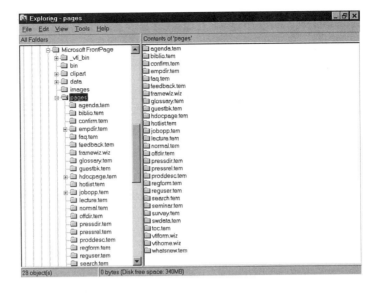

**FIGURE 22.2.**

*Web templates are stored in separate directories.*

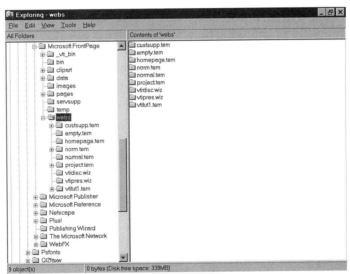

The directory and naming structure for frameset templates is different from the directory and naming structure for pages and Webs. Because frameset templates are used only by the Frames Wizard, they are in the `pages\framewiz.wiz` directory. All frameset templates are defined in a single frame definition file that ends with a `.frm` extension. Frame definition files are discussed in the section titled "Creating Templates for Frames."

# Creating the Parameter File for Pages and Webs

All templates for pages and Webs must have a parameter file. This file is a plain ASCII text file that ends with the .inf extension and is formatted similarly to a Windows INI file.

> **NOTE**
>
> When you create parameter files in a word processor, be sure to save the file in ASCII text format.

Because of the way FrontPage looks for parameter files, the parameter file must use the base name of the template directory. If your template is stored in a directory named mytemplate.tem, for example, the parameter file for this template must be in a file named mytemplate.inf.

As with Windows INI files, your parameter files are broken down into several sections. Each section is named with an identifier set off by square brackets. For example, a section containing information about the template is in a section with the identifier [info].

Template parameters are placed after section identifiers, with one parameter on each line, and are entered as name-value pairs. Each name-value pair identifies a parameter by name and the value associated with the parameter separated by an equal sign (=), such as title=Sample template. Parameter files can have four sections: info, FileList, MetaInfo, and TaskList. Only the info section is mandatory for all parameter files. Additionally, because the FrontPage Editor does not refer to the optional sections, you should only use them for Web templates used by the FrontPage Explorer.

## The Parameter File Information Section

The information section of the parameter file has the identifier [info]. This section is used to specify general information about the template including the title, description, and indexing information.

Whenever you open the New Page dialog box in the FrontPage Editor, FrontPage reads the information section of all page templates in order to provide you with a title and description of the page templates. Similarly, when you open the New Web dialog box in the FrontPage Explorer, FrontPage reads the information section for all Web templates in order to provide you with a title and description of the Web templates. If, for some reason, FrontPage cannot find the parameter file, FrontPage displays the base name of the directory in which the template is stored.

The information parameters are designated by the following names:

title              This parameter is the title of the template, such as Normal Web.

| description | This parameter is the description of the template, such as `Creates a new Web with a single page that is based on the Normalpage template.` |
|---|---|
| NoIndexRenaming | This parameter tells FrontPage not to rename index files published on external servers. If you do not set this value, files called `index.htm` are renamed automatically to the name used for index files on the external server, such as `welcome.htm`. To disable index renaming, set this parameter as `NoIndexRenaming=1`. |

> **NOTE**
>
> Generally, index files are used when users point their browsers to a directory instead of a page. Because FrontPage renames index files automatically, you should not reference index files directly. Instead of using the index filename of `index.htm` in your links, use the link `./`, which forces the server to serve the renamed index document to the user.

The following is a sample information section for a parameter file:

```
[info]
title=Internet Resource Web
description=Create a Web designed to showcase Internet resources
NoIndexRenaming=1
```

# The Parameter File `FileList` Section

By default, when a new Web is created in the FrontPage Explorer, all files in the Web template directory are used to create the Web. All you have to do is move the files you want to include on the Web into the Web template directory, and they will be used to create the Web. Generally, all filenames are converted to lowercase. Additionally, the URLs to these files matches their filenames.

Using the optional `FileList` section of the parameter file, you can selectively include files from the template directory and specify the URL for the files, which can be different from the filename. Another use for the `FileList` section is to enable you to include files that are in subdirectories of the Web template, such as files you've placed in the Web's _private or cgi-bin directory. If you do not make specific entries for files in template subdirectories, the files will not be included in any Webs based on your template.

> **NOTE**
>
> Only valid Web subdirectories can be used. Valid subdirectories for Webs include _private for hidden files, cgi-bin for CGI scripts, and images for images used in the Web.

You enter files in the `FileList` section one per line in the form *filename=URL*. When you specify only the filename, the file URL will be the same as the filename. The only exception to this rule is that images with the `.gif`, `.jpg`, and `.jpeg` extensions are generally stored in a subdirectory called `images`, which means the URL path to images on most newly created Webs is `images/`*filename*.

> **CAUTION**
>
> When you include the directory structure in the filename, you use the backslash as the directory separator. However, when you include the directory structure in the URL, you use the forward slash as the directory separator.

The following is a sample `FileList` section that uses the concepts discussed in this section:

```
[FileList]
pageone.htm=
pagetwo.htm=
pagethree.htm=
pagefour.htm=
header.htm=_private/header.htm
footer.htm=_private/footer.htm
images\newpage.gif=images/house.gif
images\newtext.gif=images/new.gif
```

## The Parameter File `MetaInfo` Section

The meta-information section of the parameter file has the identifier `[MetaInfo]`. Using this optional section, you can specify meta-information parameters for Webs created with your template. The primary use for meta-information parameters is for configuration variables, but these parameters can also be used to set variables used by the Substitution WebBot.

To make handling meta-information easier, the parameter names are not case-sensitive. The parameter name `WEB_HOST` is interpreted the same as the parameter name `web_host` or `Web_Host`. All parameter names beginning with the prefix `vti_` are reserved for Web administration.

The following is a sample meta-information section for a parameter file:

```
[MetaInfo]
WebMaster=william@tvp.com
ContactEMail=info@tvp.com
CompanyName=TVP, Inc.
```

## The Parameter File `TaskList` Section

Whenever you create complex Web templates, you will probably want to provide users with pointers as to how they can best use the Web based on the template. One way to do this is to provide a series of tasks that the user can perform after creating the new Web. Using the `TaskList` section of the parameter file, you can assign tasks to the To Do list.

Each task you assign can have six attributes:

| | |
|---|---|
| `TaskName` | The name of the task to be performed |
| `Priority` | The priority of the task entered as an integer value from 1 to 3, where 1 is for high-priority tasks, 2 is for medium-priority tasks, and 3 is for low-priority tasks |
| `CreatedBy` | The name of the person or template that created the task |
| `URL` | The page or file the task refers to, such as `homepage.htm` |
| `Cookie` | An additional identifier for a specific bookmark within the referenced page |
| `Comment` | A description of the task to be performed |

As with other parameters, you enter tasks one per line. Each task must be identified by a unique task number, such as `Task01` or `Task02`. Attributes for a task are separated by the vertical bar character (¦) and must be entered in the following form:

```
TaskNum=TaskName¦Priority¦CreatedBy¦URL¦Cookie¦Comment
```

Even if you do not use an attribute, you must account for it. For example, most tasks will not use the `Cookie` attribute. Here is the form for tasks that do not use the `Cookie` attribute:

```
TaskNum=TaskName¦Priority¦CreatedBy¦URL¦¦Comment
```

The following is a sample `TaskList` section for a parameter file:

```
[TaskList]
task1=Replace Banner Image¦1¦Internet Resource Web¦_private/logo.htm¦¦replace
➥the temporary image on this page with your banner
task2=Customize Home Page¦1¦Internet Resource Web¦index.htm¦¦customize the
➥headings and text to meet your needs
task3=Add Link¦1¦Internet Resource Web¦index.htm¦#resources¦update the bookmark
```

# Creating Page Templates

The easiest template to create is a page template. You create new templates in the FrontPage Editor by using an existing page as the basis for the template. Start by opening the page you want to use as the basis for your template, and then select Save As from the File menu. In the Save As dialog box, click the As Template button. This action opens the dialog box shown in Figure 22.3.

As you can see in Figure 22.3, the Save As Template dialog box has three fields: Title, Name, and Description. You use the Title field to enter a title for the template. The FrontPage Editor displays this title in the New Page dialog box. By default, the template is named after the template on which the current page is based. You must change the template name in the Name field to create a new template. In the Description field, enter a description of the template. The template description is visible in the New Page dialog box when a user clicks on the template title.

**FIGURE 22.3.**

*Creating a new page template with the Save As Template dialog box.*

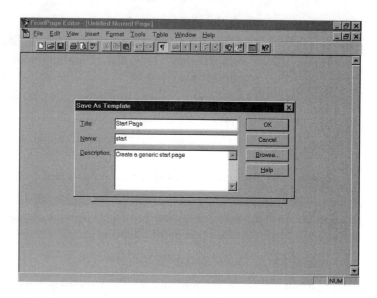

When you use the Save As Template option of the FrontPage Editor, the page template and its parameter file are created automatically. All images, HTML pages, and miscellaneous files associated with the page template are stored in the same directory. The name of the directory is based on the template name with the .tem extension. After creating a page with the template, users can save the page to the current Web or to a file. If the page is saved to the current Web, the FrontPage Editor will update the page so that the image links point to the images subdirectory and will place images in this subdirectory.

Although creating page templates with the FrontPage Editor is very easy, sometimes you might want to create your templates by hand. One reason that you might want to do this is to practice with a simple page template before you try to create a more advanced Web template.

To create a page template by hand, change to the FrontPage base installation directory, which is usually Program Files\Microsoft FrontPage, and then change to the pages directory. In the pages directory, create a subdirectory for your new template with the .tem extension. Keep in mind that template names are based on the name of their related directories, which don't have the .tem extension.

Next, move your template page and associated files to the directory you just created. Finally, create a parameter file with the .inf extension. Parameter files for pages only have an info section, so a sample parameter file for a page is as follows:

```
[info]
title=Internet Resource Page
description=Create a page that has links to useful Internet resources.
```

# Creating Web Templates

Although creating a Web template can be a lot of work, it is also very rewarding. After you create a Web template exactly as you like it, the template is available to anyone authoring Webs on your server. You could also distribute your custom Web to others. With the FrontPage Developer's Kit installed on your system, you can create Web templates by hand or by using the Web Template Maker.

## Using the Web Template Maker

The easiest way to create Web templates is to use the Web Template Maker utility. This utility was discussed in Chapter 21, "Introducing the FrontPage Developer's Kit." When you use the Web Template Maker, you are basing the Web template entirely on a Web you created in FrontPage. The utility does the following tasks:

- Creates a directory for your Web template
- Creates subdirectories for images, CGI scripts, private files, and WebBot source files as necessary
- Moves all files in the original Web to template directories
- Generates a parameter file based on the original Web that includes existing meta-information and To Do tasks

Generating a Web template automatically is a definite time-saver. Keep in mind that before you can generate a template, you must create a Web to base the template on. Additionally, before you use the Web Template Maker, you must perform these steps:

1. Start the Personal Web Server.
2. Start the FrontPage Explorer.
3. Open a Web in the FrontPage Explorer.

Sometimes after you create a template with the Web Template Maker, you might want to customize the parameter file. Therefore, even if you plan to use the Web Template Maker, you should read the next section on creating Web templates by hand.

## Creating a Web Template by Hand

When you create a Web template by hand, you have complete control over what is in the Web and how parameters for the Web are defined. To create a Web template, change to the FrontPage base installation directory, which is usually `Program Files\Microsoft FrontPage`, and then change to the `webs` directory.

In the `webs` directory, create a subdirectory for your new template with the `.tem` extension. Template names are based on the name of their related directory. The structure of files and subdirectories within the template directory should follow the structure of FrontPage Webs.

The next step is to change to the template directory and create subdirectories for images, CGI scripts, and private files as necessary. The subdirectory for images should be called images. The subdirectory for CGI scripts should be called cgi-bin. The subdirectory for private or hidden files should begin with the underscore character and is usually called _private. After the directory structure for template files is in place, you can move files into the appropriate directories.

To find pages you created in FrontPage, change to the base installation directory for Web content, which is, by default, FrontPage Webs\content. Then change to the Web directory containing the file you want to move. Figure 22.4 shows the contents of a Web called custsupp on my file system.

As you can see in the figure, the path to this Web is FrontPage Webs\content\custsupp. Note also that the Web has many subdirectories and that you would not move any files from most of the subdirectories. In particular, you should only move files in the _private, cgi-bin, images, and _vti_shm directories. Also, you do not want to move any access control files (#haccess.ctl) that might be in these directories.

**FIGURE 22.4.**

*Locating Web files on your file system.*

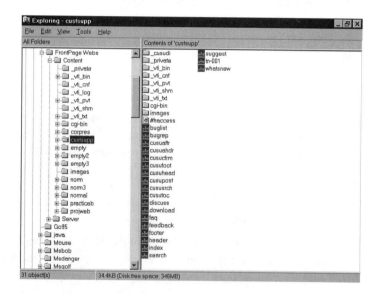

The main problem you face when moving files created in FrontPage is that pages with WebBots are saved in two forms: source and HTML. The source document for pages with WebBots is the one you want to move into the appropriate template directory. This document references the WebBots in a usable form. You will use the source document in place of the HTML document that lacks the WebBot information.

You will find the WebBot source documents in a private directory called _vti_shm. When you move the source document to the Web template directory, do not place it in a directory called _vti_shm. Instead, place the source file in the same directory in which you would have placed the HTML document that the source file is used with.

After you move all the necessary files to template directories, create the parameter file. The key to creating the parameter file is to ensure all references to files in subdirectories are entered in the parameter file appropriately. To demonstrate this process, suppose you created a template called `sample.tem`. If you move a file called `header.htm` to the `sample.tem\_private` directory, the entry in the parameter file for the header document should read as follows:

```
_private\header.htm=_private/header.htm
```

Parameter files for Web templates should have the following sections:

```
    info
    FileList
```

Parameter files for Web templates can include these sections as well:

```
    MetaInfo
    TaskList
```

# Creating Templates for Frames

The Frames Wizard is used to create frame-enhanced pages from frameset templates. Although frameset templates contain definitions for the layout of frames within a page, they do not contain detailed content as standard HTML pages do. Instead, frameset pages include default text based on the way you created the frameset. Figure 22.5 shows the default text for the banner page that is created by the Banner with Nest Table of Contents frameset template.

**FIGURE 22.5.**

*Banner page created by the Banner with Nest Table of Contents frameset template.*

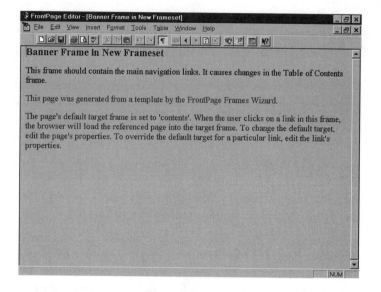

The first line of text on the banner page is the title of the page:

```
Banner Frame in New Frameset
```

The second line of text is the description as entered into the frameset template:

```
This frame should contain the main navigation links.
It causes changes in the Table of Contents frame.
```

The third line of text is generated automatically to show how the page was created:

```
This page was generated from a template by the FrontPage Frames Wizard.
```

The last line of text is entered when you set a target for the page:

```
The page's default target frame is set to 'contents'. When the user clicks on
a link in this frame, the browser will load the referenced page into the target
frame. To change the default target, edit the page's properties. To override
the default target for a particular link, edit the link's properties.
```

When you install FrontPage, there are only a few banner templates. These templates are located in the directory associated with the Frames Wizard. To find this directory, change to the FrontPage base installation directory, which is usually `Program Files\Microsoft FrontPage`, and then change to the `pages` directory. The `pages` directory contains a directory called `FrameWiz.wiz`. This directory contains the available frameset templates and is where you must store your frameset templates.

If you examine the contents of the `FrameWiz.wiz` directory, you will find that framesets are not placed in separate directories. Each frameset is defined in a single parameter file that ends with the `.frm` extension. As with other parameter files used in FrontPage, the frameset parameter file follows the format of Windows INI files.

Frameset parameter files have two types of sections. The first section is always an information section with the identifier [info]. Other sections in the parameter file relate to the frames used in the frameset. Each frame in the frameset must have a section that describes it. This section is identified by the frame name used in the layout specification for the frameset.

# Creating Frameset Files

The information section of the frameset file has the identifier [info]. This section specifies information about the frameset including the title, description, and layout. Whenever you start the Frames Wizard and decide to create a frame-enhanced page based on a template, the Frames Wizard reads the information section for all frameset templates to provide the title, description, and layout information for the page.

The information parameters are designated by the following names:

| | |
|---|---|
| title | This parameter is the title of the frameset, such as Banner with TOC. |
| description | This parameter is a full description of the frameset, such as Creates a frame-enhanced page with a banner and sidebar. |
| noframesURL | This parameter assigns an alternate page for browsers that do not support frames. Although your frameset file must contain this parameter, you cannot assign it a value. The Frames Wizard assigns this value if necessary. |
| layout | This parameter specifies the layout of the frameset using a special notation described in the section "Defining the Frameset Layout." |

The following code is a sample information section for a frameset template:

```
[info]
title=Banner with Sidebar
description=Creates a frame-enhanced document with a banner and sidebar
noframesURL=
layout=[R(15%,85%)F("banner",[C(20%,80%)F("sidebar","main")])]
```

The Frames Wizard uses the layout parameter to display a preview graphic with the frame names displayed. After you define the information section, you need to create a section for each frame used by the frameset. Section names must match the frame names. In the sample information section, three frames are identified: banner, sidebar, and main. The section identifiers for the sample frames would be [banner], [sidebar], and [main].

All sections that describe the individual frames use the following parameters:

| | |
|---|---|
| title | This parameter is the title of the frame, such as Banner. |
| description | This parameter is a full description of the frame, such as A page on which you can place your banner. |
| URL | This parameter is the page URL for the frame. Although you must include this parameter, you cannot assign it a value. The Frames Wizard assigns this value dynamically when the page is created. |

| marginWidth | This parameter specifies the width of the frame's margin. If you do not specify a value, FrontPage uses the default value of 1. When the frame-enhanced page is created, this value can be overridden. |
| --- | --- |
| marginHeight | This parameter specifies the height of the frame's margin. If you do not specify a value, FrontPage uses the default value of 1. When the frame-enhanced page is created, this value can be overridden. |
| scrolling | This parameter specifies whether scroll bars are displayed. If you do not specify a value, FrontPage uses the default value of auto, which means scroll bars are used if necessary. A value of Yes means scroll bars are always displayed. A value of No means scroll bars are never displayed. When the frame-enhanced page is created, this value can be overridden. |
| noresize | This parameter turns off the capability to resize the frame. If you do not specify a value, FrontPage uses the default value of False, which means the frame can be resized. |
| target | This parameter is the name of the frame to target when a user clicks on a link in this frame. |

The following section defines a frame:

```
[banner]
title=Page Banner
description=This frame should contain a banner for the page. It causes
➥changes in the sidebar frame.
URL=
marginWidth=1
marginHeight=1
scrolling=auto
noresize=False
target=sidebar
```

# Defining the Frameset Layout

The most difficult frameset task is building the layout notation. As you saw in the previous section, the layout notation can seem confusing. What does the following code tell you?

```
layout=[R(15%,85%)F("banner",[C(35%,65%)F("contents","main")])]
```

To understand this notation, consider that frames are organized much like tables, with each window divided into one or more rows and columns. You count the rows for a window as the number of horizontal frame partitions. You count the columns for a window as the number of vertical frame partitions. The square brackets in the layout notation are used to identify the major sections for rows and columns. The definitions for rows and columns are entered in the way the frames divide the main window.

# Layout Attributes

Using the rows attribute R, you can define the number and size of the rows to display in the browser window. The vertical size of a row is expressed as a percentage of the window size with multiple row assignments separated by commas. The number of rows is equal to the number of items in the comma-separated list, which is enclosed in parentheses. In the example, two rows are defined with the notation R(15%,85%).

Using the columns attribute C, you can define the number and size of the columns to display in the browser window. The size of a column is expressed as a percentage of the window size, with multiple column assignments separated by commas. The number of columns is equal to the number of items in the comma-separated list, which is enclosed in parentheses. In the example, two columns are defined with the notation C(35%,65%).

> **NOTE**
>
> The size of the browser window can vary substantially, depending on the display mode and sizing being used. By expressing the size of frames as a percentage of the total window size, you are ensuring that all of the window is filled. To ensure your frames work well on other systems, view the frame-enhanced document with different frame-capable browsers and at various display modes.

The values you assign for rows and columns should be between 1 and 100. Always follow the value with a percent sign. If the total of all percentages assigned is greater than 100, the values are scaled down to 100. If the total of all percentages assigned is less than 100, the relative sizes are scaled up to 100.

The frames attribute, F, always follows a row or column size assignment, and the frames it deals with are enclosed within parentheses. All frame assignments for a row or column are made within the opening and closing parentheses. Each frame assignment is separated by a comma. The example includes two frame assignment sets. The first assignment set pertains to the rows: [R(15%,85%)F("frame1","frame2")]. The second assignment set pertains to the columns: [C(35%,65%)F("frame1","frame2")].

Any of the row assignments can be substituted with a new column assignment. Similarly, any column assignment can be substituted with a new row assignment. This is why the column assignment in the example can replace the assignment for the second row's frame. The following code is a generalized format for the sample frameset layout:

```
[R(15%,85%)F("r1frame1",[C(35%,65%)F("c1frame1","c2frame2")])]
```

Now that you know the frameset notation, you can read the layout of the sample frameset:

```
R(15%,85%)
```

In this code, the window is divided into two rows. The first row is assigned 15 percent of the screen area. The second row is assigned 85 percent of the screen area.

```
F("banner",[C(35%,65%)F("contents","main")])
```

The frame definition states that the first row has only one frame named banner and that the second row has multiple columns. These columns are defined as follows:

C(35%,65%) The second frame has two columns. The column row is assigned 35 percent of the total area for the frame. The second column is assigned 65 percent of the total area for the frame.

F("contents","main") The frame definition states that the first column has a frame called contents and the second column has a frame called main.

# Working with Frameset Layouts

Understanding the frameset layout notation is not an easy thing. The examples in this section should help you better understand the notation and ensure that you can create your own custom framesets.

The way columns and rows of frames are displayed depends on how you make row and column assignments. Each column assignment you make after your row assignments will divide successive rows of frames into columns. Conversely, each row assignment you make after your column assignments will divide successive columns of frames into rows.

In the example that follows, three rows are defined. The second row is divided by two columns of equal size. The other two rows extend across the entire width of the screen. Figure 22.6 shows how the following sample layout is displayed:

```
layout=[R(25%,50%,25%)F("main",[C(50%,50%)F("logo1","logo2")],"footer")]
```

By changing the order of the column and row assignments, you create an entirely different window. The next example has two columns of equal size. The first column is divided by three rows. The second column extends down the full length of the window. Figure 22.7 shows how this sample layout is displayed:

```
layout=[C(50%,50%)F([R(25%,50%,25%)F("logo1","main","footer")],"logo2")]
```

**FIGURE 22.6.**

*Creating frames using the layout notation.*

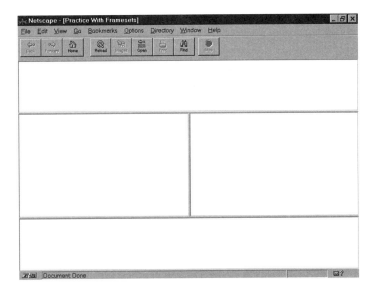

**FIGURE 22.7.**

*A new window created by reversing column and row frames.*

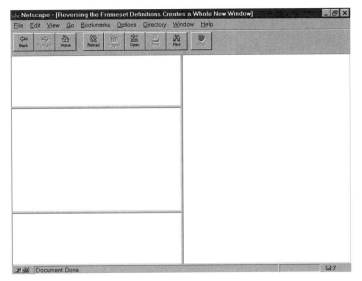

# Summary

Use the examples in this chapter to help you create customized templates. You can create templates for pages, Webs, and framesets. Although page templates are the easiest to create, you can, with practice, create templates for Webs and framesets. After you create a template, be sure to move it to the appropriate directory.

# Creating Your Own Wizards

# 23

*by William
Robert Stanek*

**IN THIS CHAPTER**

Wizards aid the content development process for pages and Webs. Unlike templates, which are based on HTML documents and parameter files, wizards are programs that run on your system and use OLE to interface with FrontPage.

Before you create wizards, you should learn the basics of programming and OLE automation. This chapter does not examine these basics. Instead, the chapter focuses on the specific concepts you use to create wizards.

# The Basics of Creating Wizards

Most wizards basics you already know. Using a series of setup pages, wizards help you design pages and Webs. Although a distinction exists between page wizards and Web wizards, the only real restriction on a wizard is what FrontPage tool it works with.

Generally, you use the FrontPage Editor to access page wizards and the FrontPage Explorer to access Web wizards. To design a new page with a page wizard, you select New from the File menu in the FrontPage Editor, and then select the wizard you want to use. To design a new Web with a Web wizard, you select New Web from the File menu in the FrontPage Explorer, and then select the wizard you want to use.

All wizards are written in a programming language such as Visual Basic or Visual C++. The way wizards communicate with FrontPage is through OLE automation. Just as you put templates in specific directories, you put wizards in specific directories as well.

## Wizard Directories

All wizards are stored in special directories under the FrontPage base installation directory. The default path to the FrontPage base installation is `Program Files\Microsoft FrontPage`.

If you change to the FrontPage base installation directory or examine this directory with the Windows Explorer, you will find a directory called `pages`. This directory stores the page templates and wizards used by the FrontPage Editor. The FrontPage base installation directory also contains a directory called `webs`. This directory is used to store the Web templates and wizards used by the FrontPage Explorer.

As with templates, all wizards must have unique names within the `pages` or `webs` directory. All wizard directories are named with a `.wiz` extension, such as `framewiz.wiz` and `vtipres.wiz`. If you examine the wizard directories, you will find that all wizards have a binary executable file with an `.exe` extension and a parameter file named with an `.inf` extension. By default, the base name of the executable file and the parameter file must match the base name of the directory that the wizard is in.

Most wizards have other files in their directories as well. For example, the directory for the Frames Wizard contains frameset files with the `.frm` extension, and the directory for the Corporate Presence Wizard contains all the fancy GIF and JPEG images used with the wizard.

# Creating the Parameter File for Wizards

All wizards must have a parameter file. This file is a plain ASCII text file that ends with the .inf extension and is formatted similarly to a Windows INI file. Because of the way FrontPage looks for parameter files, the parameter file must use the base name of the wizard directory. If your template is stored in a directory named mywizard.wiz, for example, the parameter file for this wizard must be in a file named mywizard.inf.

Unlike template parameter files that have several sections, wizard parameter files have only one section, an information section with the identifier [info]. This section is used to specify general information about the wizard including the title, a description, the name of the executable file, and whether the wizard has editing capabilities.

Whenever you open the New Page dialog box in the FrontPage Editor, FrontPage reads the information section for all page wizards in order to provide a title and description in the dialog box. Similarly, when you open the New Web dialog box in the FrontPage Explorer, FrontPage reads the information section for all Web wizards in order to provide a title and description in the dialog box. If, for some reason, FrontPage cannot find the parameter file, FrontPage displays the base name of the directory in which the wizard is stored.

Valid parameters for wizards are designated by the following names:

title
: This parameter is the title of the wizard, such as Corporate Presence Wizard.

description
: This parameter is the description of the wizard, such as Design a new Web to help you establish a corporate presence on the Web.

editor
: This parameter is used to specify that the wizard can function as an editor in addition to a content generator. An example of a wizard that is both an editor and a generator is the Frames Wizard. If you do not specify a value of 1 for this parameter, FrontPage assumes that the wizard cannot function as an editor.

exename
: This parameter is the name of the binary executable file for the wizard. You can use this parameter to override the default value that specifies that the name of the executable file must match the base name of the wizard's directory.

The following is a basic parameter file that does not use the editor or exename parameters:

```
[info]

title=My Wizard
description=Design a new page.
```

The following parameter file uses all available parameters:

```
[info]

title=Internet Resource Wizard
```

```
description=Design a new resource page.
editor=1
exename=resources.exe
```

# Creating Your Wizard's Interface

With wizards, Microsoft tried to create programs that let you design advanced content using a self-explanatory interface. As you've seen in this book, the interface is not always particularly self-explanatory, especially when you deal with very advanced wizards. However, the interface Microsoft developed goes a long way toward easing the content creation process, and you should consider the general design concepts that went into creating the existing wizards.

The interface used for wizards is fairly standardized; it includes a set of buttons that are displayed throughout the page or Web creation process. These buttons are generally labeled Back, Next, Cancel, Help, and Finish. The Back and Next buttons enable users to move to the previous or next phase of the creation process. The Cancel button enables users to quit the wizard without creating the page or Web. The Help button opens a Windows Help file. The Finish button enables users to create what they've designed. When a button is not a valid option, the button is usually grayed out to indicate that it cannot be pressed. Other buttons, like the Finish button, are only visible at certain stages of the creation process.

Beyond buttons, your wizard should allow users to design pages and Webs using a series of setup pages. Generally, each setup page lets users select from a set of related design options or enter related information. Each setup page in your wizard should have explanatory text. The most detailed explanatory text is usually found on the wizard's initial setup page.

Another wizard design concept you should study is the use of graphics. Most of the images you will find on the existing wizards are positioned on the left side of setup pages and are always above the buttons, which are positioned on the bottom of the setup pages.

# Tracking Wizard Parameters Using Temporary Files

An important aspect of any wizard you create is its ability to communicate with FrontPage. Part of this communication process means that your wizard should be able to track key parameters and their values.

When you start a wizard in the FrontPage Editor or Explorer, the wizard is passed a single parameter that specifies the path to a temporary parameter file. As with other parameter files, the file is in Windows INI format with section identifiers. Unlike the parameter file discussed in the previous section, this temporary file exists only when the wizard is running and is updated as necessary to track changes made by the user and other essential system information. The file has three sections related to input, environment, and output settings, which have the identifiers of `[input]`, `[environment]`, and `[output]` respectively.

# Input Parameters

The input section is used to track built-in parameters, such as the directory path to the wizard's executable file and the full path to its INF file. When a wizard is started, input parameters are passed to it automatically.

The input parameters for page and Web wizards are identified as follows:

| | |
|---|---|
| Dir | This parameter is the full path to the wizard directory. |
| Inf | This parameter is the full path to the wizard's parameter file, which has an .inf extension. |
| Blocking | This parameter determines whether the temporary file is deleted before the wizard exits. If the parameter is set with a value of 0, the file is deleted before the wizard exits. If the parameter is set with a value of 1, the file is not deleted before the wizard exits. Generally, you will use a value of 1 when you want to pass output back to the program that started the wizard, in which case the launching program will delete the temporary file after it reads the parameters it needs. |
| Editing | This parameter determines whether the wizard can be used as an editor. This parameter relates directly to the editor parameter in the wizard's INF file. If the Editing parameter is set with a value of 0, the wizard cannot be used as an editor. If the parameter is set with a value of 1, the wizard can be used as an editor. |

Some input parameters can only be used with the page wizard:

| | |
|---|---|
| PageURL | The URL that the page should be saved with, which is a relative URL in the current Web |
| PageTitle | The title for the new page |
| PageFile | The full path to the file being edited, which is set only if the value of the Editing parameter is 1 |

Another useful parameter that you can use only with page wizards is the destination parameter. In general, when a page wizard finishes, the page it creates is loaded into the FrontPage Editor. However, if the wizard generates content that cannot be edited by the FrontPage Editor, the wizard should load the page to the current Web or to a file on the user's file system instead. You use the destination parameter to specify where the file should be loaded or stored.

By default, the destination parameter is set to editor, which means the page generated by the wizard should be loaded into the FrontPage Editor using OLE automation. You can change the default destination by setting a value of either web or disk. If the destination parameter is set to web, the page is saved to the current Web. If the destination parameter is set to disk, the page is saved to a file on the user's file system.

The following input parameters can only be used by Web wizards:

| | |
|---|---|
| WebName | The name of the current Web |
| ServerName | The name of the host server or its IP address |
| Proxy | The proxy server currently being used |
| User | The name of the user who is accessing the FrontPage Explorer |

The following is a sample input section for the temporary parameter file:

```
[input]

PageURL=index.htm
PageTitle=My Home Page
Dir=D:\Program Files\Microsoft FrontPage\Pages\FramesWiz.wiz
Inf=D:\Program Files\Microsoft FrontPage\Pages\FramesWiz.wiz\frameswiz.inf
Blocking=0
Editing=0
```

## Environment Parameters

The environment section is used to track standard environment variables such as the name of the computer or path settings. Like input parameters, environment parameters are set automatically. Additionally, environment parameters are unique to the computer you are using. To check environment variable settings on your Windows 95/NT system, type the keyword set at the MS-DOS prompt.

When I enter the set command on my system, I see that these environment variables are set as follows:

```
TMP=C:\WINDOWS\TEMP
TEMP=C:\WINDOWS\TEMP
PROMPT=$p$g
winbootdir=C:\WINDOWS
COMSPEC=C:\WINDOWS\COMMAND.COM
NBACKUP=C:\NBACKUP
CLASSPATH=.;C:\JAVA\LIB\;C:\JAVA\LIB\CLASSES.ZIP;
PATH=C:\MSBOB;C:\WINDOWS;C:\WINDOWS\COMMAND;C:\NBACKUP;C:\JAVA\BIN;
windir=C:\WINDOWS
BLASTER=A220 I5 D1 H5 P330 T6
```

## Output Parameters

Unlike the input and environment sections of the temporary file, the output section is empty when the wizard is started and is written to only if the input blocking parameter is set to 1 or the destination parameter is set to disk.

The primary output parameter recognized by FrontPage is ExitStatus, which is used to set the status of the wizard. A value of error indicates that an error has occurred. A value of cancel indicates that the user canceled the creation of the page or Web—usually by pressing a button labeled Cancel. A value of ok indicates that the wizard completed successfully. If you do not set the `ExitStatus` parameter, FrontPage assumes that an error has occurred. For this reason, you should always set this parameter.

Other output parameters are used only if the `destination` parameter is set to the value of `disk`. These parameters include the number of files created by the wizard, which is set with the `FileCount` parameter, as well as a `File` and `Url` parameter for each file the wizard creates. The `File` and `Url` parameters are used as keys and end with a suffix that indicates the position of the key, such as `File1`, `Url1`, `File2`, and `Url2`. The `File` parameter indicates the full path to the file, and the `Url` parameter sets the page URL.

A wizard that generated three files might create the following output section:

```
[output]

ExitStatus=ok
FileCount=3
File1=c:\temp\wiz01.tmp
Url1=index.htm
File2=c:\temp\wiz02.tmp
Url2 = banner.htm
File3=c:\temp\wiz03.tmp
Url3=footer.htm
```

# Putting Temporary Parameter Files in Perspective

All files generated by your wizard should be written to the `temp` directory under the FrontPage base installation directory. The default path to this directory is `Program Files\Microsoft FrontPage\temp`. To ensure a consistent naming structure, all temporary files your wizard creates should end with the `.tmp` extension.

For the temporary parameter file, you might want to follow the naming scheme used by Microsoft, which consists of the following:

- Naming the file with the prefix `wiz`
- Adding a unique numeric identifier
- Using the `.tmp` extension

A sample filename using this structure is `wiz5190.tmp`.

If you have used wizards, you will find a number of temporary files in the `temp` directory. Examining these files can tell you a lot about how temporary parameter files are used. The following is a sample file from my file system:

```
[Input]

Dir=C:\Program Files\Microsoft FrontPage\pages\framewiz.wiz
Inf=C:\Program Files\Microsoft FrontPage\pages\framewiz.wiz\framewiz.inf
Blocking=0
Editing=0
```

```
[Environment]

TMP=C:\WINDOWS\TEMP
TEMP=C:\WINDOWS\TEMP
PROMPT=$p$g
winbootdir=C:\WINDOWS
COMSPEC=C:\WINDOWS\COMMAND.COM
NBACKUP=C:\NBACKUP
CLASSPATH=.;C:\JAVA\LIB\;C:\JAVA\LIB\CLASSES.ZIP;
PATH=C:\MSBOB;C:\WINDOWS;C:\WINDOWS\COMMAND;C:\NBACKUP;C:\JAVA\BIN;
CMDLINE=WIN
windir=C:\WINDOWS
BLASTER=A220 I5 D1 H5 P330 T6

[Output]

ExitStatus=cancel
```

A final note on parameter files is that you should not use a temporary parameter file when you want to retain option settings selected by the user. If you've used the wizards in FrontPage, you probably noticed that the first time you use a wizard you see default settings, but thereafter, you see the last settings you made in the wizard.

To preserve option settings, store the settings in a wizard initialization file. Name this file with the .ini extension so that you can identify it as an initialization file and put it in the data directory under the FrontPage base installation directory. The default path to this directory is `Program Files\Microsoft FrontPage\data`.

To get an idea of how you can save option settings, examine the following option settings based on the selections I made using the Corporate Presence Wizard:

```
[Settings]

DoFeedbackPage=True
DoWhatsNewsPage=True
DoProductsPage=True
DoSearchPage=True
DoTOCPage=True
DoHomePage=True
DoHomeContactInfo=True
DoHomeIntro=False
DoHomeMission=True
DoHomeProfile=False
DoNewsArticles=False
DoNewsPressReleases=False
DoNewsWhatsNew=True
ProductOption=0
NumProducts=3
NumServices=3
DoFeedbackAddress=False
DoFeedbackCompany=True
DoFeedbackEmail=True
DoFeedbackFAX=True
DoFeedbackName=True
DoFeedbackTelephone=True
DoFeedbackTitle=False
FeedbackFileFormat=0
```

```
TOCAutoRecalc=False
TOCBullets=True
TOCOrphans=False
DoBottomLinks=False
DoBottomCopyright=False
DoTopLogo=True
DoTopTitle=True
DoTopLinks=True
DoBottomWebmasterAddress=True
DoBottomDateModified=True
DoProductImage=False
DoProductInfoRequest=True
DoProductPricing=True
DoServiceCapabilities=False
DoServiceInfoRequest=True
DoServiceReferences=False
StyleOption=1
UnderConstructionOption=0
CompanyLongName=ACME Industries Inc.
CompanyShortName=ACME
CompanyAddress=123 Web Way, Cambridge MA 02138
CompanyPhone=617-555-1212
CompanyFAX=617-555-1212
CompanyWebMaster=webmaster@yourcompany.com
CompanyEmail=info@yourcompany.com
ShowToDoList=True
LinkColor=0xff0000
VisitedLinkColor=0x800080
TextColor=0x0
BackgroundColor=0xc0c0c0
ActiveLinkColor=0xff
BackgroundImage=0
ColorSettingsOption=0
```

# Determining Where Your Wizard Should Look for Key Files

Any wizard you create should be able to run on someone else's computer. However, if your wizard references hard file paths, the wizard will only work properly on systems where FrontPage is installed exactly as you've installed it. The key to ensuring the portability of your wizard is to not use hard file paths.

Instead, you should look up the file paths in the initialization file for FrontPage, which will always be stored in the Windows directory. The FrontPage initialization file is called frontpg.ini. Using this file, you can determine the location of the FrontPage base installation directory and the base installation directory for FrontPage Webs. The FrontPageRoot variable tells you the location of the FrontPage base installation directory. The PWSRoot variable tells you the location of FrontPage Webs. These variables are in the FrontPage 1.1 section of the INI file.

The following is an example of what the INI file looks like:

```
[FrontPage 1.1]

FrontPageRoot=C:\Program Files\Microsoft FrontPage
PWSRoot=C:\FrontPage Webs
FrontPageLangID=0x0410
FrontPageLexicon=C:\Program Files\Microsoft FrontPage\bin\mssp2_en.lex
FrontPageSpellEngine=C:\Program Files\Microsoft FrontPage\bin\mssp232.dll
CheckedHostName=tvp.com

[Ports]

Port 80=

[Port 80]

servertype=frontpage
serverconfig=C:\FrontPage Webs\Server\conf\httpd.cnf
authoring=enabled
frontpageroot=C:\Program Files\Microsoft FrontPage
```

# Using OLE Automation in Your Wizards

The key to communication between your wizard and FrontPage is OLE automation. If you are familiar with Windows programming, you probably already know how OLE automation works. Basically, with OLE automation your wizard can make procedure calls to the FrontPage Explorer, the FrontPage Editor, and the FrontPage To Do List. These procedure calls can cause the program they call to perform specific actions. For example, a procedure call can cause the FrontPage Editor to start and load a page for editing. Likewise, a procedure call can cause the FrontPage Explorer to launch.

Each of the FrontPage tools you can access with OLE has a specific set of procedures. The set of OLE procedures that a program can use is collectively referred to as its OLE interface.

Because the automation interface used in FrontPage is still evolving, your OLE automation code should use macros of function wrappers to localize calls to OLE procedures. In this way, you can easily update your code for compatibility with the next major release of FrontPage.

All applications capable of being accessed with OLE automation must be registered in the Windows Registry. The FrontPage interfaces for version 1.1 have the following identifiers in the Windows Registry:

- FrontPage.Explorer.1.1
- FrontPage.Editor.1.1
- FrontPage.ToDoList.1.1

You will use these identifiers to specify which tool you want to connect to. You also can use the FrontPage tools with a generic identifier that resolves to the current release of FrontPage installed on the user's system:

- FrontPage.Explorer
- FrontPage.Editor
- FrontPage.ToDoList

> **NOTE**
>
> You will probably have to update your wizard programs for compatibility with future releases of FrontPage. When you use the specific identifier, you will always have to update your wizard for the new versions of FrontPage. When you use the generic identifier, you might run into compatibility problems if the interface changes in future versions of FrontPage. If you use the generic identifier, however, you might not recognize that the problem is with version compatibility.

# Programming the Wizard

Now that you know wizard basics, what parameters the wizard can use, and what files the wizard should create, you are almost ready to program the wizard. Before you begin, consider carefully what programming language you will use. The language you select must support OLE automation. As stated earlier, both Visual Basic and Visual C++ are good choices for programming languages. Not only is it easy to create graphical interfaces with Visual Basic and Visual C++ languages, but the OLE programming examples in the next chapter also use these languages.

After you read about the OLE automation procedures supported by FrontPage and how they are used, you might want to spend a few hours examining the sample wizards included in the FrontPage Developer's Kit. You will be amazed at how much code you can reuse.

Most of the wizards you create will use three common types of routines:

- Routines that establish a connection to the OLE server and perform a procedure
- Routines that check the status of the FrontPage Explorer before performing an OLE procedure
- Routines that write HTML pages to files

**NOTE**

For detailed information on the OLE procedures used in the examples you will find in this section, see Appendix B, "ActiveX Control Automation Command Reference."

# Establishing a Connection to the OLE Server

One very important step you should perform before calling an OLE procedure is to establish a connection to the automation server's exported object interfaces. Typically, you do this by creating an object with an object type of the application you want to connect to. After the connection is established, you have access to the object's OLE interface and can make procedure calls. When you're finished making procedure calls, release the connection with the OLE automation server.

A key concept when using OLE automation is to minimize the amount of time when an open OLE connection exists. Otherwise, you might run into serious problems when users close the application they are using or change the application's state in a way that will cause your OLE procedures to fail. Most programmers open and close the OLE connection inside a single procedure.

To put these OLE concepts in perspective, Listing 23.1 shows a sample procedure written in Visual C++ that demonstrates these concepts and uses a generalized OLE identifier.

### Listing 23.1. An OLE procedure in Visual C++.

```
#include "target.h"

// Initiate the procedure
void IncludeEvent()
{

// Establish connection to the automation server and handle possible error
IWebber explorer;
COleException error;

if(!explorer.CreateDispatch("FrontPage.Explorer",&error))
{
AfxMessageBox("Error connecting to FrontPage Explorer. Check server status.");
return;
}

// Make procedure call to the FrontPageExplorer
explorer.vtiBringToTop();

// Release the connection with the OLE automation server
explorer.ReleaseDispatch();

}
```

Listing 23.2 shows the same procedure written in Visual Basic.

## Listing 23.2. An OLE procedure in Visual Basic.

```
' Initiate the procedure
Function IncludeEvent()
{
Dim explorer as Object

' Establish connection to the automation server and handle possible error
Set explorer = CreateObject("FrontPage.Explorer")

' Make procedure call to the FrontPageExplorer
explorer.vtiBringToTop

' Release the connection with the OLE automation server
Set explorer = Nothing

}
```

# Checking the Status of the Explorer When Necessary

The main OLE interface in FrontPage is for the FrontPage Explorer. Whenever your wizards use OLE hooks that access or alter the current Web, you will need to write a procedure that ensures a Web is open in the FrontPage Explorer. The routine shown in Listing 23.3 checks the URL of the current Web in the FrontPage Explorer before adding a task to the To Do List. This routine is written in Visual Basic.

## Listing 23.3. Checking the Explorer before calling a To Do List procedure.

```
Private Sub AddTask()

' Initialize variables
    Dim todolist As Object
    Dim webber As Object
    Dim webURL As String
    Dim ret As Boolean
    Dim url As String
    Dim priority As Integer

    MousePointer = 11

' Ensure a Web is open in the FrontPage Explorer
Set webber = CreateObject("FrontPage.Explorer.1.1")
    webURL = webber.vtiGetWebURL

' Close the connection to the Explorer
    Set webber = Nothing
```

*continues*

## Listing 23.3. continued

```
' If the length of the webURL variable is 0, no Web is currently open
' in the FrontPage Explorer. Handle the error by exiting.
    If Len(webURL) = 0 Then
        MsgBox "No Web is currently open in the Explorer."
Exit Sub
    End If

' Set the task priority based in user selection
    If optionHigh Then priority = 1
    If optionMedium Then priority = 2
    If optionLow Then priority = 3

' Add task to the current Web's To Do List
Set todolist = CreateObject("FrontPage.ToDoList.1.1")
    ret = todolist.vtiAddTask(txtTask, priority, txtCreator, txtURL,
    txtCookie, txtComment)

' Display error message if could not add the task
    If Not ret Then
        MsgBox "Failed to add task for To Do List."
    End If

' Close the connection to the To Do List
    Set todolist = Nothing

    frmGetURL.Tag = ""

    MousePointer = 0

End Sub
```

# Writing HTML Pages to Files

Your wizards must also generate HTML documents based on the user's selections. Generally, the wizard will write HTML documents to files, with each file containing the HTML markup for one page. Listing 23.4 shows a sample routine written in Visual Basic that writes an HTML page to a file.

## Listing 23.4. Writing an HTML page to a file.

```
Public Sub CreatePage(pagepage As String)

' Initialize variable for file
    Dim ff As Integer

' Initialize variable for new line
    Dim nl As String

' Initialize variable for standard string
    Dim str As String
```

```
' set new line variable to ASCII new line line value
    nl = Chr$(10)

' set file variable to FreeFile
    ff = FreeFile

' set up error handling
    On Error GoTo BadFile

' open file on file system for output
    Open pagefile For Output As #ff

' Build and write the HTML page
    Print #ff, "<HTML>"
    Print #ff, "<HEAD>"
    Print #ff, "<TITLE>" & TitleTag & "</TITLE>"
    Print #ff, "</HEAD>"
    Print #ff, "<BODY BGCOLOR=" & BGColorTag & " TEXT=" & TXColorTag & ">"

    str = "H" & (cmbStyle.ListIndex + 1)   ' H1, H2, or H3
    Print #ff, "<" & str & ">" & ResourceTitle & "</" & str & ">"

    Print #ff, "<P>" & ParaText1 & "</P>"
    Print #ff, "<UL>"
    Print #ff, "<LI>" & P1ListItem1
    Print #ff, "<LI>" & P1ListItem2
    Print #ff, "<LI>" & P1ListItem3
    Print #ff, "<LI>" & P1ListItem4
    Print #ff, "</UL>"

    Print #ff, "<P>" & ParaText2 & "</P>"
    Print #ff, "<OL>"
    Print #ff, "<LI>" & P2ListItem1
    Print #ff, "<LI>" & P2ListItem2
    Print #ff, "<LI>" & P2ListItem3
    Print #ff, "<LI>" & P2ListItem4
    Print #ff, "</OL>"

    If chkCredit Then
        Print #ff, "<HR SIZE=5>"
        Print #ff, "<P><EM>This page was generated by the Internet
        ➥Resource Wizard.</EM></P>"
    End If

    Print #ff, "</BODY>"
    Print #ff, "</HTML>"

' close the page file
    Close #ff

' on error exit the subroutine
BadFile:
    Exit Sub

End Sub
```

# More OLE Automation with FrontPage

The previous section introduced basic OLE concepts. Wizards use OLE automation to communicate with three FrontPage components: the FrontPage Explorer, the FrontPage Editor and the FrontPage To Do List. Each component has a specific set of OLE procedures that it recognizes.

## Using OLE Automation with the FrontPage Explorer

Most procedures your wizards use will need to interface with the FrontPage Explorer. Using the FrontPage Explorer OLE interface, you can do the following:

- Create a Web
- Delete a Web
- Add files to a Web
- Remove files from a Web
- Get the URL of the current Web
- Get the title of the current Web
- Retrieve a list of files in the current Web
- Get meta-information variables for Webs and pages
- Set meta-information variables for Webs
- Launch the To Do List application

The procedures you use to perform these tasks are restricted by the FrontPage Explorer's OLE interface. For FrontPage version 1.1, the only OLE procedures you can use are the following:

```
vtiBringToTop
vtiCancelRequests
vtiCreateWeb
vtiEditWebPage
vtiGetDocToFile
vtiGetPageList
vtiGetWebMetaInfo
vtiGetWebPageMetaInfo
vtiGetWebTitle
vtiGetWebURL
vtiIsPageInWeb
vtiOpenWeb
vtiPromptOpenWeb
vtiPutDocument
```

```
vtiPutDocuments
vtiPutWebMetaInfo
vtiPutWebPageMetaInfo
vtiRefreshWebFromServer
vtiRemoveWeb
vtiSetWebRecalcDependencies
```

The FrontPage Explorer has the most extensive OLE interface. One of the most common reasons your wizards will access this interface is to open a Web. Listing 23.5 shows a sample procedure for opening a Web that is written in Visual Basic. As you study the example, pay particular attention to the way OLE procedure calls are made.

### Listing 23.5. Opening a Web using OLE.

```
Private Sub OpenWeb()

MousePointer = 11

' Initialize variables
Dim webber As Object
Dim ret As Integer

' Open a Web on the specified server
Set webber = CreateObject("FrontPage.Explorer.1.1")
ret = webber.vtiOpenWeb(Server, Web, User)

' Close the connection to the Explorer
Set webber = Nothing

MousePointer = 0

End Sub
```

Another common task your wizards might need to do is to create a Web. Listing 23.6 provides a sample procedure for creating a Web.

### Listing 23.6. Creating a new Web.

```
Private Sub CreateWeb()

MousePointer = 11

' Initialize variables
Dim webber As Object
```

*continues*

## Listing 23.6. continued

```
Dim ret As Long

' Create the new Web on the server
Set webber = CreateObject("FrontPage.Explorer.1.1")
ret = webber.vtiCreateWeb(Server, Web)

' Close the connection to the Explorer
Set webber = Nothing

MousePointer = 0

End Sub
```

Listing 23.7 shows a sample procedure for removing a Web. Removing a Web is trickier than creating a new Web or opening an existing Web. Before you remove a Web, you must ensure that there is an open Web in the FrontPage Explorer. You must also ensure that you do not accidentally delete the Root Web. To handle these tasks, check the value returned by the vtiGetWebURL procedure before removing the Web.

## Listing 23.7. Removing Webs.

```
Private Sub RemoveWeb()

MousePointer = 11

' Initialize variables
Dim webber As Object
Dim ret As Long
Dim webURL As String

' vtiGetWebURL returns an empty string if there is no current web
' AND if the current Web is the RootWeb
Set webber = CreateObject("FrontPage.Explorer.1.1")
webURL = webber.vtiGetWebURL

' Remove the Web if there is a current Web AND it is not the RootWeb
If Len(webURL) > 0 Then
     ret = webber.vtiRemoveWeb("/" & Web)
     If ret <> 1 Then
     MsgBox "An error occurred while trying to remove the web '" & Web &
     ➥"'. The Web may not exist on the server."
End If
Else
     MsgBox "A Web must be open in the FrontPage Explorer."
End If

' Close the connection to the Explorer
Set webber = Nothing

MousePointer = 0

End Sub
```

# Using OLE Automation with the FrontPage Editor

The FrontPage Editor is primarily used for creating and editing pages. Because pages are not as complex as Webs, there is no need for an extended interface between wizards and the FrontPage Editor. You will use the FrontPage Editor OLE interface to perform basic editor tasks including the following:

- Creating a new empty page
- Opening an existing page from the current Web or local file system
- Determining whether a page is currently being edited

Although most of the OLE automation hooks to the FrontPage Editor are designed to be used by other FrontPage components, your wizards can use any of the available OLE procedures. These procedures are as follows:

```
vtiBringToTop
vtiNewWebPage
vtiOpenWebPage
vtiQueryWebPage
```

Although the FrontPage Editor OLE interface is not as extended as the FrontPage Explorer interface, you will find many uses for Editor procedures in your wizards. One of the tasks your wizards might need to do is to create a new page. Listing 23.8 shows a sample procedure written in Visual Basic for creating new pages.

### Listing 23.8. Creating new pages.

```
Private Sub CreateNewPage()

' Initialize variables
Dim editor As Object
Dim page As Object

'Create new HTML page
Set editor = CreateObject("FrontPage.Editor.1.1")
Set page = editor.vtiNewWebPage("homepage.htm", "", "")

' Close the connection to the Editor
Set editor = Nothing

End Sub
```

Another task you might want to perform is to bring the FrontPage Editor to the front of the display. Listing 23.9 shows a sample procedure to do this task.

## Listing 23.9. Bringing the FrontPage Editor to the front.

```
Private Sub BringFront()

' Initialize variable
Dim editor As Object

MousePointer = 11

' Bring editor to front
Set editor = CreateObject("FrontPage.Editor.1.1")
editor.vtiBringToTop

' Close the connection to the Editor
Set editor = Nothing

MousePointer = 0

End Sub
```

A more advanced task you might want your wizard to perform involves checking to see whether a page is currently loaded in the FrontPage Editor. Using the `vtiQueryWebPage` procedure, you query the editor to see whether a page is loaded. Because this procedure can check the URL of the Web the page came from, you should ensure that a Web is open in the FrontPage Explorer before making the procedure call to the FrontPage Editor.

Listing 23.10 shows a sample procedure for querying the FrontPage Editor.

## Listing 23.10. Querying the Editor.

```
Private Sub QueryEditor()

' Initialize variables
Dim editor As Object
Dim webber As Object
Dim webURL As String
Dim ret As Long
Dim url As String

' Ensure a Web is open in the FrontPage Explorer
Set webber = CreateObject("FrontPage.Explorer.1.1")
webURL = webber.vtiGetWebURL

' Close the connection to the Explorer
Set webber = Nothing

' Display error message and exit if no current web
If Len(webURL) = 0 Then
    MsgBox "Cannot continue. No Web is open in the FrontPage Explorer."
Exit Sub
End If

MousePointer = 11
```

```
' Routine for Querying the Editor and displaying a message.
Set editor = CreateObject("FrontPage.Editor.1.1")
ret = editor.vtiQueryWebPage(url, webURL)
If ret = 1 Then
     MsgBox "Document is open in the FrontPage Editor."
Else
     MsgBox "Document is not open in the FrontPage Editor."
End If

' Close the connection to the Editor
Set editor = Nothing

MousePointer = 0

End Sub
```

# Using OLE Automation with the FrontPage To Do List

The FrontPage To Do List helps you manage tasks related to creating and editing Webs. All tasks have a set of attributes that describe the purpose of the task. When tasks are completed, they are removed from the To Do List.

As with the FrontPage Editor, there is no need for an extended interface between wizards and the FrontPage To Do List. Usually, you will use the interface to perform the following tasks:

- Add new tasks to the To Do List
- Remove accomplished tasks from the To Do List
- Hide the To Do List
- Display the To Do List

Like the FrontPage Editor OLE interface, the FrontPage To Do List OLE interface is designed primarily to be used by other FrontPage components. Still, your wizards can use any of the available OLE procedures. These procedures include the following:

```
vtiAddTask
vtiAddTaskAskUser
vtiCompletedTaskByUrl
vtiGetActiveCount
vtiHide
vtiShow
vtiWorkedOnTaskByUrl
```

The most common reason you will use the OLE interface to the To Do List is to add tasks. Listing 23.11 shows a sample procedure written in Visual Basic for adding tasks. As with other code examples in this chapter, you should follow the logic of the code, paying particular attention to the way OLE procedure calls are made.

## Listing 23.11. Adding tasks.

```
Private Sub AddTask()

' Initialize variables
Dim todolist As Object
Dim webber As Object
Dim webURL As String
Dim ret As Boolean
Dim url As String

MousePointer = 11

' Ensure a Web is open in the FrontPage Explorer
Set webber = CreateObject("FrontPage.Explorer.1.1")
webURL = webber.vtiGetWebURL

' Close the connection to the Explorer
Set webber = Nothing

' If the length of the webURL variable is 0, no web is currently open
' in the FrontPage Explorer. Handle the error by exiting.
If Len(webURL) = 0 Then
    MsgBox "A Web must be open in the Explorer."
Exit Sub
End If

' Add task to the current Web's To Do List
Set todolist = CreateObject("FrontPage.ToDoList.1.1")
ret = todolist.vtiAddTask(Task, priority, Creator, URL, Cookie, Comment)

' Display error message if could not add the task
If Not ret Then
    MsgBox "Could not add task for To Do List."
End If

' Close the connection to the To Do List
Set todolist = Nothing

frmGetURL.Tag = ""

MousePointer = 0

End Sub
```

Other important procedures you might use with the To Do List interface are those that mark tasks as completed. Note the use of the URL and Cookie parameters to find a particular task. Listing 23.12 shows how you could use Visual Basic to write a procedure that marks tasks as completed.

## Listing 23.12. A procedure for marking tasks as completed.

```
Private Sub TaskCompleted()

' Initialize variables
Dim todolist As Object
Dim webber As Object
Dim webURL As String
Dim ret As Boolean
Dim url As String
Dim priority As Integer

MousePointer = 11

' Mark specific task as completed
Set todolist = CreateObject("FrontPage.ToDoList.1.1")
ret = todolist.vtiCompletedTaskByUrl(URL, Cookie)

' Display error message if could not mark the task
If Not ret Then
     MsgBox "Could not mark task as completed."
End If

' Close the connection to the To Do List
Set todolist = Nothing

MousePointer = 0

End Sub
```

# Summary

Use the concepts discussed in this chapter to help you create customized wizards. Your wizards can use OLE automation to communicate with the FrontPage Explorer, the FrontPage Editor, and the FrontPage To Do List.

The FrontPage Explorer, the FrontPage Editor, and the FrontPage To Do List each use a specific set of OLE procedures. You can use these procedures to create wizards that communicate with FrontPage. After you create a wizard, be sure to move it to the appropriate directory.

## IN THIS PART

# Managing Your Web

VII

**PART**

# Using Web Servers with FrontPage

# 24

*by John Jung*

**IN THIS CHAPTER**

FrontPage in itself is an impressive WYSIWYG HTML editor. However, Microsoft has also thrown in a Windows NT/95–based Web server, called the Personal Web Server, with the FrontPage package. You might be wondering what to do with this server. This chapter explains why you might need a Web server and how to use the one included with FrontPage.

# Why You Might Need a Web Server

Is it really important to have a Web server along with an HTML editor? Absolutely. The Personal Web Server brings with it many different uses for everybody, from an individual creating his own Web page to an organization looking to create a presence on the Net. The bundling of a full-fledged Web server makes FrontPage the front-runner in being the end-all Web package.

## Why Individuals Might Need One

Although an individual might not really need a Web server, there are times when having one would be useful. One such instance is when you're designing and maintaining large Web pages. This situation typically occurs in large organizations where each internal group has its own Web space. In this situation, groups typically have to design their Web pages without direct access to the Web server, so the Webmaster of each group has to maintain the content of the group's Web page. This all adds up to a lot of bookkeeping on the part of each group's Webmaster.

Another use an individual might have for a Web server is in creating CGI scripts. Most advanced HTML elements, such as forms and image maps, depend on CGI scripts to work. Directory location, server type, and other technical information are often needed in CGI script creation. Traditionally, creating these scripts required the Web author to get this information from the Webmaster. If there was some miscommunication between you and the Webmaster, your CGI script would probably fail. Consequently, such scripts were created through trial and error. Also, tracking down buggy parts of CGI scripts could be problematic because you might need to look at system files.

By including a Web server with FrontPage, both problems are easily resolved. Complicated Web sites are easier for the Webmaster to manage because she can easily check links when changes are made. If the Webmaster adds, moves, or removes Web pages, she can easily try out the latest links on the Personal Web Server. Also, CGI scripts can now be tested and debugged without needing to put them on the actual Web server. Rather than guessing how a particular script might behave, you can test it. All these capabilities make the Personal Web Server an invaluable tool for Web authors. Web pages and CGI scripts can now be correct the first time they're pushed out to the actual Web server.

# Why an Individual Might Not Need One

Although there are some good reasons why you would find a Web server useful, there are also reasons why it's not useful. For one thing, if you're designing very simple Web pages, you really don't need a Web server. You don't need a Web server to see how the <H1> tag will look or how your tables will come out. You can correctly view and test these and other simple aspects of Web pages with a Web browser.

Another reason you might not want a Web server is because you're low on disk space. The typical Web server uses 6 to 10 megabytes of disk space for the server software alone. The content of the Web server takes up additional disk space. Although having a Web server might be useful, you have to ask yourself if it's a luxury you can afford. Is it worth 10 megabytes of disk space just to verify your CGI scripts?

# Why Organizations Might Need One

Organizations might need a Web server because they're looking to establish a Web presence. A Web presence can be a benefit for any size of company or organization. For companies that already have an Internet domain, a Web presence can provide great customer support. Along with being able to provide sales material, a company can distribute information for customers. Such information might include frequently asked technical support questions, bug reports, or software updates.

# Why Organizations Might Not Need One

Although a Web server might be beneficial for many businesses, it's certainly not right for all businesses. If you're running a corner drug store, does it really make sense to have a Web presence? Probably not. Although it might be interesting to let people order things from your store through the Net, it's probably not very practical. Ask yourself whether you will really generate that much business just by being on the Web. Also, do you have the money to spare to pay someone to host your Web page? Some Web service providers can charge over $2,000 a year for a Web presence.

Another reason why a company might not need a Web page is because it isn't on the Internet. Although many technology-based and large organizations have a Web presence just to inform others, your organization might not fit the bill. Ed's CompuHut, for example, might benefit from having a Web presence, but it might not have the manpower to run its own Web server. It would be best, and cheapest, for Ed to use his own resources for the task. But would he benefit that much from the extra exposure, and can he afford to redirect his small staff into designing Web pages?

# Why Use the Personal Web Server?

You've decided that you could use a Web server. So why should you use the Personal Web Server that comes with FrontPage? (Just because it's included doesn't mean that you should necessarily use it.) One reason to use the Personal Web Server is that it's extremely flexible. It can talk to other Web servers if server extensions have been installed. This flexibility makes it possible for an organization to use the Personal Web Server as its main Web server. From there, the organization can access other Web servers for different needs. For example, if you're running a Web site that allows people to purchase things over the Net, you can have the catalog of items running on a Personal Web Server and have a commerce Web server accessed when needed.

Another reason that you should use the Personal Web Server is because FrontPage is an integrated package. Any changes made on any Web page are instantly available. This integration allows for a faster and easier method of updating information for different departments. Most traditional Web servers, especially corporate ones, have a staging area. Web pages are created and modified in the staging area before they are published to the outside world. With the Personal Web Server and FrontPage working together, this area is no longer needed.

# Installing the Personal Web Server

The Personal Web Server is easy to install. Most of the default options can be used, and at the end of the process, you'll have a fully functional Web server.

## Specifying a Directory

The Personal Web Server is automatically installed as part of the Typical installation of FrontPage. You can also use the Custom option to install only certain pieces of the product, such as just the client applications, the Personal Web Server, or the server extensions. By default, FrontPage is installed to the `C:\Program File\Microsoft FrontPage` folder. You can easily change this location as needed using the Browse button. The installation is very simple, and if the defaults are sufficient for your purposes, there is no reason to change them.

## Checking Your Connection

The Personal Web Server operates like most other HTTP servers. The server communicates over Port 80 and requires TCP/IP as a transport for the HTTP information. The server application is a WIN32 application, so a requirement for operation is a 32-bit TCP/IP stack. The Personal Web Server will not operate with 16-bit TCP/IP stacks. If you do not know whether you have the necessary 32-bit TCP/IP stack, FrontPage ships with a TCP/IP Test application that you can run to test whether the Personal Web Server will run on your system. This application, though very simple in scope, gives the most important information you need to set up your Web server, as you can see in Figure 24.1.

**FIGURE 24.1.**

*The FrontPage TCP/IP Test application details the TCP/IP information for your computer.*

The information that this application captures is the same information that will be used by the installation program when you install FrontPage. This information is stored in the configuration files for your server and can be changed manually if needed by editing those files as you'll see later in the chapter. If your TCP/IP stack is configured correctly, FrontPage should discover the information similar to what you see in this dialog. The information that is returned by the TCP/IP Test application is what you would use for a URL to your site. The Personal Web Server uses this same information as its identity.

---

**TIP**

If you publish your URL for others to see, always refer to the URL as TCP/IP Test application lists it, and always include the trailing slash (/) character. Without the slash, the URL is not complete; it is missing the path portion of the URL. When a server receives a URL without path information, it has to issue a server fix to correct the URL with an assumed path equal to the root of the server. This fix is a potential cause for performance problems because the server has to execute this fix on every URL received in this manner.

---

You can use either the hostname or the IP address for your server because the hostname is actually just a convenient way to reference the server for human readability. When you enter a hostname in a URL, the request is sent to a Domain Name Server (DNS) to translate the host name to an IP address. Then the request is routed to the appropriate network address. Without the DNS, you would all have to remember numbers like 199.177.202.10 or 198.105.232.30 instead of names like www.mcp.com or www.microsoft.com, which are the hostnames of those same IP addresses.

---

**NOTE**

The hostname localhost and TCP/IP address 127.0.0.1 are reserved names. This hostname and IP address refer to the local machine. You should be able to open Web pages on your local machine using a URL of http://localhost/ or http://127.0.0.1/ instead of your fully qualified domain name.

---

After you have this information, it is quite simple to install the Personal Web Server and begin to build the content using FrontPage. Though you won't be asked during installation to input the information, FrontPage will use the information to configure the Personal Web Server. When installing FrontPage, if you chose the Custom installation from the opening dialog, you are given the option to only install the portions of the program that you need to install. You could, for instance, install the client software on your main PC and the Personal Web Server and server extensions on another PC that would be dedicated for Web traffic.

## Defining the Administrator

During installation of the Personal Web Server, you will be asked to provide an administrative name and password. You will be asked to enter this information before the FrontPage Explorer can open a Web for editing. FrontPage enforces this built-in authentication so that only authorized administrators or authors can change the content of your Web. If you later add individual authors, they will be shown a similar dialog before authoring access is allowed.

The Personal Web Server fully supports HTTP basic authentication, and a version of this mechanism is used to allow access for authoring as well as to add access restrictions to sections of your Web.

## Starting Up the Personal Web Server

After the server is installed, you will need to start the Personal Web Server before using it the first time using the shortcut for the Personal Web Server from the Start/Programs/Microsoft FrontPage folder. After you have verified that the server is running as you want it to, you will probably want to have the server start automatically by adding a shortcut to the server in the Startup folder. Then, as long as you are logged in to the computer, your server will be running, and people can access your content.

If you are running Windows NT 4.0 or you have Windows 95 set to provide separate profiles for each user, your Web server will only run when the user that installed the server is logged in. If this is not the behavior you want, edit the registry in Windows 95 to add the Personal Web Server executable vhttpd32.exe to the Run key in the registry. In Windows NT, you can use the servany.exe file from the Resource Kit to run the server as an NT service. When run as a service, the Personal Web Server will run no matter who is currently logged in to the PC. You could also log in as the administrator account when you create the Startup folder shortcut so that the shortcut will be seen by all users.

> **CAUTION**
>
> If you choose to edit the registry in Windows 95, the key you need to edit is the following:
>
> HKEY_LOCAL_MACHINE\SOFTWARE\Microsoft\Windows\CurrentVersion\Run
>
> You need to add a string value to this key using the information in the other values as examples. Using the Registry Editor incorrectly can cause serious system-wide

problems that could require you to reinstall Windows 95 to correct them. Microsoft cannot guarantee that any problems resulting from the use of Registry Editor can be solved. Use this tool at your own risk.

After you make the appropriate changes, the Personal Web Server will automatically start up so anyone can connect to your server the next time you reboot your PC.

# Using the Personal Web Server

The Personal Web Server that comes with FrontPage is pretty straightforward (see Figure 24.2). You can manually start it up from the command line, or you can use Windows 95's Start button. It's also automatically started every time you try to access a Web that it controls.

**FIGURE 24.2.**

*The Personal Web Server that comes with FrontPage is smart enough to start when needed.*

## What Is the Personal Web Server?

The Personal Web Server is, as its name implies, a Web server for individuals. That's not to say that it's limited or doesn't have a lot of features. Quite the contrary. It has all the standard features you'd expect from a typical shareware Web server. The only difference is that it doesn't implement any sophisticated features. For example, it doesn't support SSL (Secure Sockets Layer). SSL allows Web browsers to securely send data, such as credit card numbers, across the Internet. The Personal Web Server is more than adequate for most needs, however.

## What Is Supported?

As mentioned before, the Personal Web Server supports a number of standard Web Server features. It supports such things as CGI scripts, which are useful for image maps and form fields. It also provides for built-in support for image maps that follow either NCSA or CERN formats. Client-side image maps in the form of Netscape or Microsoft extensions to HTML are also supported. The Personal Web Server also provides built-in support for O'Reilly's Website. This support means that if you're already running a Web server with that software, FrontPage will have no problems with it.

# The Server Administrator Program

Because you're running the Personal Web Server, you're probably your organization's Webmaster. To adequately manage the Personal Web Server, you'll need to run the Server Administrator program. From Windows 95, select the Start button, choose Programs|Microsoft FrontPage, and then select the Server Administrator menu item to display the program's main interface (see Figure 24.3) where you can control how the Personal Web Server behaves. Each of these features is discussed in Chapter 25, "Personal Web Server Administration."

**FIGURE 24.3.**

*The Web Server Administration Program is the Webmaster's main tool to maintain the Personal Web Server.*

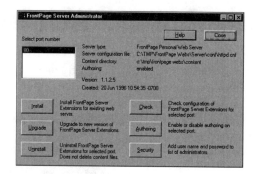

# The FrontPage Explorer

Although the Server Administrator program gives you a great deal of control, part of a Webmaster's function still lies within the FrontPage Explorer. In this program, you can easily create, copy, and delete Webs from any FrontPage Web server for which you are the Webmaster. You can also specify who is and isn't a Webmaster for each particular Web. Similarly, you can control who can and can't create Web pages for each Web. Finally, the FrontPage Explorer gives the Webmaster the ability to specify whether a certain Web is publicly accessible. By default, every Web is publicly viewable, but this situation might not always be desirable.

# Using Server Extensions

FrontPage extensions allow Windows 95, Windows NT, and UNIX Web servers to directly interface with a FrontPage server. To fully utilize the extensions, you must have a Personal Web Server running somewhere on your network. This machine will be accessed by the other Web servers when the extension is triggered.

## What Exactly Is an Extension?

Extensions are just separate programs that run on the remote Web server. These programs, which are available for a large number of UNIX platforms, enhance existing Web servers. After the extensions have been installed, you'll be able to access Webs stored on a Personal Web computer. This kind of access gives you the ability to have the best of both worlds. You can have a Personal Web Server running on a Windows NT machine to perform the regular Web server functions. In addition, you can have a commercial Web server that takes care of secure transmissions.

## How Do I Get Them?

You can get FrontPage extensions by pointing your Web browser to `http://www.microsoft.com/frontpage/freestuff/agreement.htm`. Fill out the form to be taken to the corresponding download page. Select the UNIX platform you want the extension for and choose from compressed tar and uncompressed tar format. Depending on the platform you have, the extension can take up to 9 megabytes of disk space.

## Installing Extensions

Extensions are very easy and straightforward to install, especially if you already have a Web server installed. Simply uncompress, if necessary, and untar the file you downloaded. Next, modify the configuration files of the existing Web server to point to the extensions. Finally, restart your Web server, and you'll be able to access FrontPage Webs.

The FrontPage extensions come with their own barebones Web server administration program (see Figure 24.4). This program allows you to easily shut down and restart the entire Web server that the extensions are installed on. After the extensions are installed, FrontPage will be able to talk to that Web server.

**FIGURE 24.4.**

*The FrontPage Server Extensions give you a simple interface for maintaining the server.*

# Multihoming

A very useful, though somewhat limited, feature of the Personal Web Server is the support of multihoming. Traditionally, multihoming isn't available on all Web server software. Consequently, to add it into some UNIX Web servers would require you to recompile the server itself. Making a computer multihoming-capable also requires some work.

Most individuals will have no need to use the multihoming capability. Even though multihoming is a useful feature, it's still not necessary for everyone. This feature is mainly useful for companies and Internet Service Providers (ISPs). Even though you might never need to use multihoming, it's a useful tool to have if you need it.

## What Is Multihoming?

Multihoming is the capability for one computer on one domain name to pretend to be another domain name. One computer can then appear to be many different computers. Suppose you're the Webmaster for the company mycom.com. The company spawns a subsidiary that makes a different product and has the domain name mycom2.com.

Now, traditionally, to provide an Web presence for both companies, you would need two computers: one computer to be the Web server for mycom.com and another computer to be the Web server for mycom2.com. Multihoming enables you to use one computer as the Web server for mycom.com and mycom2.com. At the same time, both Web sites look different from each other.

Probably the best example of multihoming in progress is with Web Service Providers (WSPs). WSPs typically offer the service of domain hosting, which means that the WSP makes its multihome-capable Web server act as your server. You don't need to dedicate any computing power to handle Web access. The WSP's computers will take care of everything for you.

## Multihoming Methods

There are two different methods of multihoming. Each has its advantages and disadvantages. Fortunately, FrontPage supports both methods of multihoming. The first method is to have multiple Web servers running on one machine. The computer running the many Web servers has already been configured to have different domain names. Each Web server is configured to listen for a different domain name so that when a particular domain name is accessed, only that Web server is working. This method of multihoming has the advantage that each Web server can run independently of the other. If you need to change the content of one Web, you don't have to take down everybody else. You also have the ability to run one type of server for one customer and another type for another customer. If one customer needs to have secure data transmissions, you can start up a commerce server for him only. The obvious downside to this setup is that you can use valuable system resources running multiple instances of the same program. Consequently, you're going to need a fairly powerful and well-loaded computer for this task. Buying the extra necessary hardware could cost you a significant amount of money.

Another method of multihoming is to have one Web server running one set of configuration. The configuration tells the Web server to listen to different domain names and retrieve the appropriate content. The more people who access all the mulithomed domains, the greater the impact on the Web server. The clear advantage with this method of multihoming is that you're only running one process. Although the process might be running a lot and taking up lots of resources, it's not taking up as much as having many servers running at once. Another advantage of this method is that when you upgrade the software, you're only upgrading one program. The problem with this approach to multihoming is that if you do upgrade the software, everybody's affected. Another problem is that you'll have a harder time running specific Web servers for specific customers.

## Listening for Other Hosts

Currently, multihoming is most widely supported on UNIX machines. This isn't because the UNIX Web server software is superior; it's because UNIX is capable of listening to multiple domain names. If a UNIX system receives data intended for two different domains, it will route the data correctly. To get a UNIX machine to listen to multiple domains, you have to initialize the network devices to listen to the domains. For example, using a Solaris machine as the root, you would have to type in something similar to the following:

```
ifconfig le0:1 www.mycom1.com up
ifconfig le0:2 www.mycom2.com up
```

This code enables your computer to respond to incoming traffic directed for www.mycom1.com and www.mycom2.com. Now that your computer is looking for multiple domains, you have to get the Web server to do the same. This is often a simple matter of modifying a configuration file; for NCSA-based servers, this configuration file is the httpd.conf file. Most Web servers pretend to be a particular host by using the specifications of ServerName and BindAddress in the httpd.conf file. To have a Web server be the server for www.mycom1.com, you would have to add the following code to this file:

```
ServerName www.mycom1.com
BindAddress www.mycom1.com
```

## Connecting FrontPage to a Multihomed System

Now that you have your Web server configured for multihoming, you'll want to hook it into FrontPage. This is easily accomplished by installing the FrontPage server extension. Download the appropriate extension for your Web server, and install it on that machine. After you've done that, a file called we####.cnf will be placed in the /usr/local/frontpage directory. The #### refers to the port number that the Web server for that domain is listening to. You must rename the we####.cnf file to hostname:port.cnf. The host name refers to the name of that domain's Web server, and port is the number that the server is installed on.

# Configuring FrontPage

After you have the Web server and the FrontPage extensions up and running, you have to deal with some other issues. First and foremost is that the FrontPage Server Extensions are basically CGI scripts that run under the server itself. Consequently, the Web server's CGI scripts must be run as the same user as the HTTP server itself. Probably the best way to implement this is to have the HTTP server and CGI scripts run as the FrontPage user account. This gives your UNIX system the most security and gives FrontPage the most flexibility.

You can also configure the FrontPage Server Extensions themselves by modifying the configuration files. Because each multihomed server has its own configuration file in /usr/local/ frontpage, you can configure each system independently. Table 24.1 gives you a complete list of the parameters, what they do, and acceptable values.

## Table 24.1. FrontPage Server Extensions parameters.

| *Parameter* | *Function* | *Values* |
|---|---|---|
| NoExecutableCgiUploads | Prevents files uploaded to the cgi-bin directory from being executable files | 0 = Files have the execute permission set<br>1 = Files don't have the execute permission set |
| NoSaveResultsTo AbsoluteFile | Prevents Discussion, Registration, and Save Results WebBots from writing to an absolute file | 0 = Can write to absolute file<br>1 = Can only write to relative file |
| NoSaveResultsPipeTo | Prevents Discussion, Registration, and Save Results WebBots from sending output to any other program | 0 = Can send output to another program<br>1 = Can't send output to another program |
| NoSaveResultsToLogDir | Stops the Discussion, Registration, and Save Results WebBots from writing to the _vti_log directory | 0 = Allows writing to _vti_log<br>1 = Doesn't allow writing to _vti_log |
| PreserveTagCase | Keeps the existing case (upper or lower) of HTML tags | 0 = Does not preserve the case<br>1 = Preserves the case |
| ReformatHtml | Allows FrontPage to reformat Web pages that contain WebBots | 0 = Disables reformatting<br>1 = Enables reformatting |

| Parameter | Function | Values |
|-----------|----------|--------|
| SaveResultsPipeToAllows | Restricts which programs the Discussion, Registration, and Save Results WebBots send output to | A list of space-separated programs |
| TextMemory | Indicates how many megabytes text indexing will allocate for internal indexing | Any numeric value |
| UpperCaseTags | Converts all HTML tags to uppercase characters | 0 = Does not convert characters<br>1 = Converts all characters |

# Summary

This chapter explained the advantages and disadvantages of having a Web server. Although a Web server gives individuals the ability to write cleaner, and better, advanced Web pages, that might not be enough of a reason to install a server. And although companies could benefit from having an integrated HTML editor and Web server, they might not need one.

If you think a Web server would be useful to you, you should seriously consider using the Personal Web Server. This Web server, which comes with FrontPage, is straightforward and versatile. It can talk to other Web servers that have FrontPage extensions installed on them. Also, the Personal Web Server comes with the capability to multihome different domains. Although individuals won't have a need for this capability, conventional companies and some Internet-based companies will find it invaluable.

# Personal Web Server Administration

# 25

*by John Jung*

**IN THIS CHAPTER**

The inclusion of the Personal Web Server with FrontPage raises a number of issues. These aren't new issues, just issues that many people haven't had to deal with before. Because FrontPage has both a Web server and an HTML editor, it becomes very easy to set up a Web page. Consequently, many people who've never had a chance to be a Webmaster can now be one.

In this chapter, you learn the following:

- The basics of Web server administration
- How to administer the Personal Web Server on Windows 95/NT
- How to administer the Personal Web Server from the command line
- How to manage and check your Web pages
- How to recalculate links
- How to manage and verify your links

# Being a Webmaster

The word *Webmaster* means different things to different people. The role of a Webmaster is rather nebulous and unclear. Before you can understand what FrontPage lets you do as a Webmaster, you need to understand the various aspects of being a Webmaster.

## Webmaster as Web Author

Probably the most traditional definition of a Webmaster is the person who's in charge of Web page design. This person knows HTML codes inside and out and can whip out CGI scripts in no time. Most people will think of the Webmaster as the person who develops the organization's main Web page. Oftentimes this person is put in charge of the machine that's running the Web server software. This kind of Webmaster might also be able to use paint programs to create fancy images for Web pages.

The Webmaster will also probably know some technical aspects of the Web server. This knowledge enables her to answer commonly asked questions, such as how image map definition files should be formatted. The Webmaster might also be in charge of the Web server hardware and software itself. But it's unlikely that she'll be asked to deal with any computers beyond the Web server.

## Webmaster as Network Administrator

A lesser-known definition of the Webmaster is a network administrator. Because the Web server must be able to talk to other computers on the network, certain networking issues relate to managing the Web server. For Web servers that sit on the Internet, the Webmaster has a number of things to worry about. The most obvious is the security of the Web server software and computer itself. The Webmaster must ensure that CGI scripts aren't malicious or can't be manipulated by others to become dangerous.

Another concern for this sort of Webmaster is making sure the computer can talk to other computers. Because the Web server sits on the Internet, it has to be able to correctly resolve host names and perform similar tasks. In large companies, this isn't usually a concern because this sort of task should already be done by the network administrator. However, many small companies use one computer to perform multiple tasks. It's not uncommon for a small company to have one system as the e-mail server, domain name server, FTP server, and Web server. Consequently, if the system is moved or its functions are broken up, the network connection must be maintained.

Web servers that sit on intranets involve different concerns. Because they're outside the realm of outside systems, Webmasters don't have to worry about security as much. In large companies, intranet Web server security takes the form of restricting information to only designated people. For example, the research and development group might want to keep the latest specifications under wraps. This secrecy prevents the sales and marketing group from prematurely releasing untested, or unimplemented, features or functionality.

## Combining Both Jobs

For small- and medium-sized companies, a Webmaster is both a Web author and a network administrator. Because the company's network isn't particularly large, it's still probably managed by one person. Consequently, the company probably doesn't have a budget for two people. Instead, such companies opt to have the systems and network administrator learn HTML. This person is then put in charge of creating Web pages and maintaining the Web server hardware and software.

Larger companies usually divide Webmaster tasks between two or more people. The network administrator often has a number of ongoing issues that he deals with regularly, such as Internet connectivity, intranet connectivity, and network security. He's got a full load of things to do as it is and doesn't have time for Web page design. Consequently, the company would much rather get an HTML expert and make him a Webmaster.

## FrontPage Support for Webmasters

FrontPage's Personal Web Server is primarily aimed at Webmasters who are Web authors. All the configuration and variables that the Personal Web Server allows are related to the server itself. There are some settings that relate to the network, but few things of great technical detail. There are no provisions for setting up routing tables and the like.

FrontPage's Web server also lets you control user access. You can define other Webs underneath the top-level Web for your site. This Root Web is what all other sub-Webs are connected to. As Webmaster, you can decide which users get access to which Webs. You assign usernames and passwords. You can even create lower-level Webmasters by assigning to people in charge of their group's Web page Webmaster-like privileges. These privileges extend only to the Webs you specifically designate. This capability enables you to distribute your Webmastering authority to others, who'll know better what they need. All these user-access features are covered in detail in the Chapter 26, "Managing Security for the Personal Web Server."

# Configuration

In most installations, there is no need to change the configuration of your server. If you have installed the server properly and you are able to browse its contents using Internet Explorer, the server is running. But sometimes you might need to change the server from its default operation. You might need to run the server on a different port, for example. Or you might need to add a new MIME type to serve a new data type or add access restrictions to a portion of your Web.

You can do each of these tasks in FrontPage by directly editing the server configuration files. If you accept the installation defaults, the server's configuration and access information is located in the C:\FrontPage Webs\Server\conf folder. The four main configuration files are called httpd.cnf, srm.cnf, mime.typ, and access.cnf. If you are familiar with the UNIX NCSA servers, you recognize three of those names as similar to the configuration files for those servers, which are named with a four letter extension of .conf. The contents of these files are very similar as well, and Microsoft even points you to http://hoohoo.ncsa.uiuc.edu/ for more details on the configuration! The mime.typ file details the MIME types that the server recognizes.

The following sections look at each of these files in turn to see what settings might commonly need changing. The first three are discussed as configuration files, and the access.cnf file is discussed in the section on access control.

## Settings in the httpd.cnf File

The httpd.cnf file is the main configuration file for your Personal Web Server. This file contains the location of the server root, which is the location of the vhttpd32.exe server executable file. The httpd.cnf file is also where you will find the port number on which the server listens for HTTP requests. Listing 25.1 shows a portion of this file.

### Listing 25.1. Partial listing of the httpd.cnf file.

```
# ServerRoot: The directory the server's config, error, and log files
# are kept in. This should be specified on the startup command line.
#
# Format: ServerRoot <path>
#
ServerRoot e:/frontpage\ webs/server/
# Port: The port the standalone listens to. 80 is the network standard.
#
Port 80
```

You likely will never need to change any of these settings. But if, for example, you manually move the server files from the e: drive to another drive, you could change the `ServerRoot` directive to the new location to allow the server to run and find its other files. The other configuration files use the `ServerRoot` as the default starting location for their files, so when you change this one directive, you do not need to change the other files. Another common reason to change this file is if you want to run the server on a different port than the default Port 80. You might already have another Web server installed on Port 80, and you just want to install the Personal Web Server for testing purposes. You could change the `Port` directive line to read something like the following, which would cause the server to listen to Port 8080 instead of Port 80:

```
Port 8080
```

> **NOTE**
>
> You might have encountered a location on the Web with a URL like `http://www.someplace.com:8080/`. This URL shows that the server is running on Port 8080, a common alternative to Port 80. Also note that without the `:8080` portion of the URL, a client browser will fail to connect to the server.

After you make any changes to this or the other configuration files, you must stop and restart the Personal Web Server for the changes to take effect. And it is always a good idea to make a copy of these files before you make any changes! FrontPage already ships an original unedited version of these files named with an `.org` extension, as in `httpd.org`, but you still should make sure that you have a backup copy of these files for safety's sake.

## Settings in the `srm.cnf` File

The Server Resource file (`srm.cnf`) contains settings that control the document layout for your server and the file and folder names that a client is allowed to see. This file defines the location of your `DocumentRoot`, which is the location for the content of your Web. As you see in Listing 25.2, this file also determines the default directory index file, which is the file that the server will attempt to load when a URL ends without a filename, as in `http://www.where.com/`.

### Listing 25.2. Partial listing of the `srm.cnf` file.

```
# DocumentRoot: The directory out of which you will serve your
# documents. By default, all requests are taken from this directory, but
# aliases may be used to point to other locations.
#
DocumentRoot e:/frontpage\ webs/content
# DirectoryIndex: Name of the file to use as a pre-written HTML
# directory index. This document, if present, will be opened when the
```

*continues*

## Listing 25.2. continued

```
# server receives a request containing a URL for the directory, instead
# of generating a directory index.
#
 DirectoryIndex index.htm
# AccessFileName: The name of the file to look for in each directory
# for access control information. This file should have a name which is
# blocked from appearing in server-generated indexes!
#
AccessFileName #haccess.ctl
```

As you can see from this listing, the DocumentRoot for this server is at e:\frontpage webs\content, but notice also that instead of normal \ (backslash) path delimiters you would expect in Windows NT or Windows 95, the srm.cnf file uses the UNIX / (forward slash) character. This character reveals the UNIX roots of the Personal Web Server and is the way paths are delimited throughout all of the configuration files. As with the httpd.cnf file, there is not normally a reason to change the settings in the srm.cnf file. But, for instance, if you already were using the popular EMWAC HTTPS Web server for NT whose default directory index filename is default.htm, you could change the DirectoryIndex line so that you could easily use your existing files without having to rename them.

### NOTE

The European Microsoft Windows Academic Consortium (EMWAC) created the first popular HTTP server for Windows NT; this server is still easy to use and configure. Dr. Chris Adie was the author of this server and is also responsible for many of the other tools that are available from the EMWAC server at the following URL:

http://emwac.ed.ac.uk/

This server was eventually shipped by Microsoft as part of the Windows NT Resource Kit and was also the base for the commercial Purveyor Web server from Process Software.

Listing 25.3 shows another section of the srm.cnf file that might interest you.

## Listing 25.3. Another section of the srm.cnf file.

```
# AUTOMATIC DIRECTORY INDEXING
# ============================
# The server generates a directory index if there is no file in the
# directory whose name matches DirectoryIndex.
# FancyIndexing: Whether you want fancy directory indexing or standard
#
FancyIndexing off
# IconsAreLinks: Whether the icons in a fancy index are links as
# well as the file names.
IconsAreLinks off
```

```
# AddIcon tells the server which icon to show for different files or filename
# extensions. In preparation for the upcoming Chicago version, you should
# include explicit 3 character truncations for 4-character endings. Don't
# rely on the DOS underpinnings to silently truncate for you.
AddIcon /icons/text.gif     .html   .htm    .txt    .ini
AddIcon /icons/image.gif    .gif    .jpg    .jpe    .jpeg   .xbm    .tiff
➡.tif    .pic    .pict     .bmp
AddIcon /icons/sound.gif    .au     .wav    .snd
AddIcon /icons/movie.gif    .mpg    .mpe    .mpeg
AddIcon /icons/binary.gif   .bin    .exe    .bat    .dll
AddIcon /icons/back.gif     ..
AddIcon /icons/menu.gif     ^^DIRECTORY^^
AddIcon /icons/dblank.gif      ^^BLANKICON^^
# DefaultIcon is which icon to show for files which do not have an icon
# explicitly set.
DefaultIcon /icons/unknown.gif
```

If you are familiar with directory indexing, you might be able to figure out what the settings in this section are used for. Most Web servers have the capability to show you a file directory when a default document is not found. This capability has become a common alternative to an FTP server. If FancyIndexing is turned off, and you access a folder that doesn't have a default document, the server generates a display like the one shown in Figure 25.1. If you turn on FancyIndexing, you see a display similar to the one in Figure 25.2. Another change you can make is to enable IconsAreLinks so that the icons that are shown in these server-generated listings (see Figure 25.3) are links to the files as well as the filenames.

**FIGURE 25.1.**

*When the* FancyIndexing *directive in the* srm.cnf *file is set to* off, *a simple directory listing is automatically generated.*

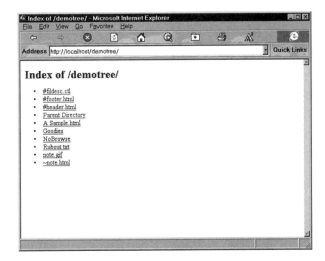

**FIGURE 25.2.**

*When the* FancyIndexing *directive in the* srm.cnf *file is set to* on, *a fancy directory listing is generated.*

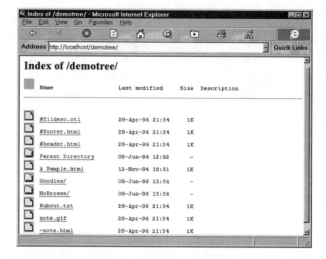

**FIGURE 25.3.**

*When you also set the* IconsAreLinks *directive in the* srm.cnf *file to* on, *the fancy directory listing adds the icons as file links in addition to the filename.*

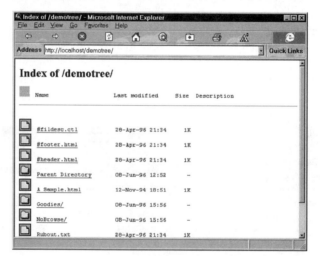

You could also create custom icons to use in place of the default icons to represent the types of files you have in these directories. These icons are specified using an AddIcon directive as in the following line:

```
AddIcon /icons/text.gif    .html   .htm    .txt    .ini
```

Note that you specify an icon to represent a specific file extension and that you can have a single icon represent multiple file types. If you are going to use this feature often and plan on creating multiple icons for different file types, use the default icons as samples so that your icons are the same size. Having icons of the same size makes for a uniform display.

# The `mime.typ` File

A Web server is essentially a file pump. It sends a file to the client when requested. This file can be any type of file; the server doesn't care. Without the existence of MIME types, a Web server and client would have a hard time deciding the content of files. MIME types define the content of files so that the Web server and client can communicate consistently. Listing 25.4 is a partial listing of the `mime.typ` file that ships with FrontPage. If you need to add a content type to your Web, you add a line to this file.

**Listing 25.4. Partial listing of the `mime.typ` file.**

```
text/html                    html htm
text/plain                   txt
application/octet-stream     bin exe
application/oda              oda
application/pdf              pdf
application/postscript       ai eps ps
audio/basic                  au snd
audio/x-aiff                 aif aiff aifc
audio/wav                    wav
image/gif                    gif
image/ief                    ief
image/jpeg                   jpeg jpg jpe
image/tiff                   tiff tif
application/zip              zip
# Microsoft types
application/msword           doc dot
application/ms-access        mdb
application/ms-excel         xls
application/ms-powerpoint    ppt
application/ms-project       mpp
application/ms-publisher     pub
application/ms-schedule      scd
```

This example shows several common file types that you will likely be familiar with. MIME types are listed as type/subtype, with the most common types encountered being text, application, and audio. When the server gets a request for a specific URL, it parses the URL, and if the request resolves to one of the MIME types, the server sends a Content header to the client defining the data that will follow. The content is then sent to the client, who now knows what kind of data to expect.

Remember that undefined MIME types should not be arbitrarily assigned. The MIME RFC1521 specifically requires that undefined types be preceded with an `x-` to signify the type. So if you have an application called myapp that creates `.myf` files that are currently undefined, you would need to use a MIME type similar to `application/x-myfile myf` to specify that the content type is not currently accepted as a standard MIME type.

> **TIP**
>
> For more information on MIME types, check out the hypertext version of RFC1521 at the following URL:
>
> `http://www.oac.uci.edu/indiv/ehood/MIME/MIME.html`

# The `access.cnf` File

The `access.cnf` file controls who can access all the files on the server. You can use the contents of this file to restrict access to individual directories on your server. You can restrict access based on host name or IP addresses so that only clients from certain locations can access your content.

Usually, the settings in this file should only be changed if you want to institute server-wide access restrictions. If you want to restrict access to individual directories, you can use `#htaccess.ctl` files, which you might have noticed earlier in Listing 25.2. The content of these files is similar to the format used in the `access.cnf` file and allows a very fine granularity to the authentication that the Personal Web Server supports. Let's look at the `access.cnf` file in Listing 25.5 to understand the format of this file.

### Listing 25.5. Partial listing of the `access.cnf` file.

```
# The following access configuration establishes unrestricted access
# to the server's document tree. There is no default access config, so
# _something_ must be present and correct for the server to operate.
# This should be changed to whatever you set ServerRoot to.
<Directory e:/frontpage\ webs/server>
Options Indexes
</Directory>
## This should be changed to whatever you set DocumentRoot to.
#<Directory e:/frontpage\ webs/content/>
## This may also be "None", "All", or "Indexes"
#Options Indexes
## This controls which options the #HACCESS.CTL files in directories can
## override. Can also be "None", or any combination of "Options", "FileInfo",
## "AuthConfig", and "Limit"
#AllowOverride All
## Controls who can get stuff from this server.
#<Limit GET>
#order allow,deny
#allow from all
#</Limit>
#</Directory>
# You may place any other directories you wish to have access
# information for after this one.
```

To understand the format of this file, you need to understand the original NCSA HTTPD server that it is based on. The structure is based on concepts originally developed for a UNIX environment. The file is a simple sequential list of access directives. Because the file is sequentially read when the server starts, the order of the directives in this file is important. If you want to deny unrestricted access for only a single folder on your server, it is best to add that directive at the end of the `access.cnf` file rather than at the beginning. If you changed the `<Directory...>` section in Listing 25.5 to read the following, you would lock out all accesses to your server!

```
<Directory e:/frontpage\ webs/server>
<Limit GET>
deny from all
</Limit>
</Directory>
```

If you are going to require access authentication on your server, you need to think it through before you implement it! There are generally three ways of thinking when it comes to access restrictions for a site. One is the wide open "allow all" approach. Any and all accesses are allowed. The opposite is what you just read with a significant change. The change would be to limit access to everyone *except* certain people. Instead of totally closing the site, you can open the site to certain host names using a format such as this:

```
<Directory e:/frontpage\ webs/server>
<Limit GET>
order deny, allow
deny from all
allow from *.ingr.com
</Limit>
</Directory>
```

Remember that the file is read sequentially. Here, you've told the server to deny everybody first, and then allow those from any host name that has the string ".ingr.com" in the host name. This will result in everyone except those from `ingr.com` domain being denied access to this server. If you reverse the directives in the `order deny, allow` line to read `order allow, deny` instead, the file would be processed in such a manner that the `deny from all` would be the last directive, and again, no access would be allowed!

The third way that access restrictions are usually used is kind of a hybrid approach. You start with a wide-open server and add access restrictions on a single directory basis using `#htaccess.ctl` files. If you are not careful, this scheme can become very difficult to keep track of. You might intend to restrict access to a specific subfolder, and place the `#htaccess.ctl` file in the wrong location and therefore lock out a section of the server that you weren't intending. The default `#htaccess.ctl` file is shown in Listing 25.6.

548

### Listing 25.6. The default `#htaccess.ctl` file.

```
# -FrontPage-
IndexIgnore #haccess.ctl */.??* *~ *# */HEADER* */README* */_vti*
<Limit GET>
order deny,allow
deny from all
allow from all
</Limit>
<Limit POST PUT>
order deny,allow
deny from all
</Limit>
AuthName default_realm
AuthUserFile e:/frontpage\ webs/content/_vti_pvt/service.pwd
AuthGroupFile e:/frontpage\ webs/content/_vti_pvt/service.grp
```

The `#htaccess.ctl` file is a very powerful tool. As you can see from this listing, you can put any directives in this file to modify the standard settings of the server. Because configuration files are read sequentially, settings in this file will be loaded when an attempt is made to get a file from the folder that this file resides in.

You can place a copy of this file in any folder to restrict access on a folder and subfolder level. I mentioned that you could also use this file to add or change MIME types on-the-fly in a given folder. If you want to serve self-extracting archive files from a certain folder, you might need to change the MIME type from the usual `application/octet-stream` to something such as `application/x-sfx-archive` so that the Internet Explorer would offer the File | Save As dialog for a file of this unknown type. To change a MIME type on-the-fly like this, you would need to place an `#htaccess.ctl` file in the folder in which you want to change the defaults with the single line:

```
AddType application/x-sfx-archive exe
```

Then, any time a client clicks on a link in this folder with an `.exe` file extension, the server would send the file with a content type of `application/x-sfx-archive`.

# The Basics of Web Server Administration

As a Webmaster, you have a number of issues to contend with. In addition to creating new Webs under your root Web, you have to work with users. You have to create user accounts and enable whatever privileges you want to grant them. You're also responsible for helping other people when they're having problems with their Web pages. Many UNIX Web servers have built-in facilities, through UNIX itself, to help you handle these tasks. Because FrontPage can run on Windows 95, you must program these capabilities into the Personal Web Server.

You can do most of the day-to-day Webmaster activities from the FrontPage Explorer. This is because most of the time you'll want to change individual Webs, not the entire server. The only times you should access the Server Administrator program are when you're affecting the entire Web site by doing such things as moving the port of the Web server or changing the server type.

## Creating Sub-Webs

When you first start up FrontPage's Personal Web Server, a default Web, the <Root Web>, has already been defined for you. This <Root Web> is the main Web that people see when they enter your organization's host name. You can easily create sub-Webs that hang off of this main Web by starting FrontPage Explorer and selecting File | New Web. The screen shown in Figure 25.4 appears. In the Web Server pull-down list field, specify the Web server you want to use. Next, type in the name of the new sub-Web to create in the Web Name field.

**FIGURE 25.4.**

*Type in the name of the Web that you want to create.*

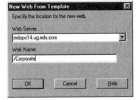

## Changing Web Server Types

FrontPage lets you install FrontPage extensions, which basically make other Web servers talk to FrontPage. If you've updated the Web server on the other machine, you can easily update FrontPage itself. Follow these steps:

1. Shut down the Personal Web Server and run the Server Administrator program (see Figure 25.5).
2. Select the port for the FrontPage extension you want to uninstall, and click the Uninstall button.
3. Verify that the server running on the other, non-FrontPage machine is working fine. When it is, you can install the FrontPage extensions for that server.
4. Click the Install button, and a new dialog box appears (see Figure 25.6).
5. Click the Server Type drop-down list and select the new server type. Depending on which server you choose, you are asked something that applies to that server.
6. Restart the Personal Web Server, and everything will work just fine.

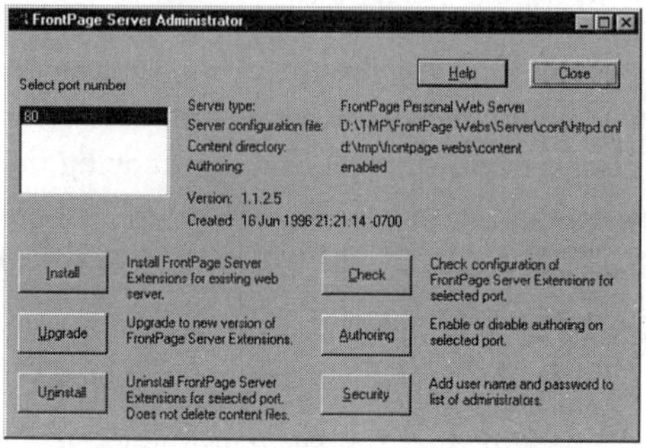

**FIGURE 25.5.**

*When doing some administration task that affects the entire Web, you have to use the Server Administrator program.*

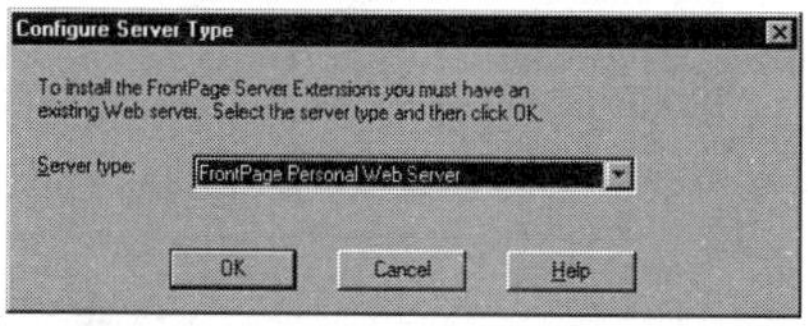

**FIGURE 25.6.**

*Select the new server type that you want to install.*

# Managing Webs

FrontPage gives you a great deal of flexibility in managing Webs. You can define administrators that manage individual Webs or define another Web site–wide Webmaster, such as yourself. Administrators have other abilities in addition to being able to create Web pages for their particular Web. For example, administrators can manage and verify links of every page in their Web calls (see "Managing and Verifying Links," later in this chapter). Administrators can also determine whether they want to make their particular Web password-protected.

Along with such routine abilities, each administrator can create accounts. These can be accounts for other administrators or Web authors. A Web author is someone who has access to FrontPage, and his sole responsibility is to create Web pages. These accounts enable people with access to FrontPage to focus on their tasks. The Webmaster can deal with issues that relate to the entire Web, such as creating new sub-Webs. The administrators for each Web can watch over the content and integrity of their Webs. Finally, authors focus on creating content for the Webs they have access to. Chapter 26 talks about creating administrator and author accounts.

# Administering the Personal Web Server from the Command Line

Sometimes you might want to run the Personal Web Server from the command line. You might need to do this when you're logged in from a remote machine onto a Windows NT computer. Or perhaps you want to set up a batch file that maintains a Web server. Whatever the case may be, you need to be able to manage the Personal Web Server from the command line. You have to start the FrontPage Personal Web Server Administrator program (found at

\Microsoft FrontPage\bin\fpsrvadm.exe) with a set of command-line options. Table 25.1 gives you a complete list of the available options, their arguments, and their functions.

## Table 25.1. Personal Web Server command-line options.

| Switch | Parameter | Function |
|---|---|---|
| -o, -operation | operation_type (install, upgrade, uninstall, check, recalc, enable, disable, security, putfile, or recalcfile) | The specified option is performed. |
| -p, -port | port_number | The port_number indicates what port number is to be used for the specified operation. |
| -w, -web | webname | This option specifies the name of the Web. To specify the <Root Web>, use " ". |
| -r, -root | front_page_root_dir | This option specifies the directory where the FrontPage extensions are installed. |
| -t, -type | server_type (ncsa, ncsa-manual-restart, apache, apache-manual-restart, cern, cern-manual-restart, netscape, netscape-manual-restart, or omi) | This option specifies the server type. |
| -s, -servconf | server_config_file | This option is the filename of the server configuration file. By default, the server configuration file is located under the directory where the server is installed. |
| -m, -multihost | hostname | This option is the host name for the multihosting server configuration. |
| -u, -username | username | This option is the administrator's username. This option is required in install and security operations. |
| -pw, -password | password | This option is the administrator's password. This option is required in install and security operations. |

*continues*

**Table 25.1. continued**

| Switch | Parameter | Function |
|---|---|---|
| -i, -ipaddress | internet_address | This option defines the allowable Internet addresses for a Web administrator. This option follows the standard four-part IP numbering scheme. |
| -d, -destination | destination_URL | This option specifies the destination URL for a document specified by the -w machine. |
| -f, -filename | filename | This option is the full pathname for a file on the Web server. |

Some examples might help you understand how to use these command-line options. If you want to create the new sub-Web Corporate for an existing <Root Web> that's running on Port 80, you type in the following:

```
fpsrvadm -o install -p 80 -w Corporate
```

To create an administrator for this new Web, type in the following line:

```
fpsrvadm -o security -p 80 -u Corpadm -pw Corpadm -w Corporate
```

# Managing and Verifying Links

Eventually, after each of your Webs has been updated and changed numerous times, you'll have broken links. Fixing these links can be a rather daunting task for anybody, especially on large sites. Before FrontPage, there was no easy way to make sure that links in an entire Web site were valid. The best way that a Webmaster could check the links were to follow them by hand. A less tedious method of checking the validity of your links was to wait until someone complained and then fix the broken link. Fortunately, FrontPage makes link management much easier.

## Verifying Links

FrontPage can automatically check and verify each link in an entire Web. To use this feature, you must load a particular Web as the Web's administrator or the site's Webmaster. Next, select Tools | Verify Links to display the Verify Links dialog box (see Figure 25.7). This dialog box has a complete list of all links that point outside of the current Web. Even links to Webs in another part of the same Web site are considered outside links. You can use the scroll bar at the bottom of the dialog box to see more information about a particular link.

To have FrontPage check and verify the links, click the Verify button. As it's checking links, FrontPage will update each entry it has checked. You can stop the verification process at any time by clicking the Stop button. To resume a stopped verification procedure, click the Resume button.

**FIGURE 25.7.**

*FrontPage gives you a list of all the links that it's going to try to verify.*

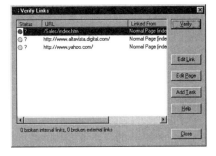

By default, any link that FrontPage hasn't checked will have a yellow dot and a question mark next to it. This mark indicates that the status of the link is uncertain and should be checked. After a link has been verified, a green dot and the word *OK* show up next to its entry. Any links that can't be verified because they don't exist or the network connection times out have a red dot and the word *Broken* next to their entries. Figure 25.8 gives you an example of three links and their status. You can modify a particular link by selecting it and clicking the Edit Link button. Similarly, you can modify the page with the link by highlighting the link and clicking Edit Page. You can add a broken link to your To Do list by selecting it and clicking Add Task.

**FIGURE 25.8.**

*As the links are being verified, FrontPage updates the status of each link.*

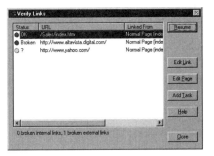

# Recalculating Links

Because FrontPage allows multiple authors to work on multiple links, you might need to check out the links from time to time. FrontPage's recalculate link feature updates all the views for the currently selected Web. What this feature enables you to do is see the changes that another author has recently put in. The recalculate link feature will also re-create all WebBots being used in the current Web. If that weren't enough, the recalculate link feature also updates the text index that the Search WebBot uses. Because the recalculate link feature does so many things, it can take quite a long time to finish, especially for large Webs. That's why when you're in the FrontPage Explorer and select Tools | Recalculate Links, you're asked to confirm the procedure (see Figure 25.9).

**FIGURE 25.9.**

*Because recalculating all the links in a Web can take a while, FrontPage wants to make sure you want to proceed.*

# Summary

Just because you have a Web server doesn't mean you'll necessarily know what to do with it. Most of the fine-tuning aspects of the Personal Web Server are buried under configuration files. If you've worked on other Web servers, these files are probably very similar.

But there's a lot more to being a Webmaster than simply configuring a Web server. As much fun as that might be, you, the Webmaster, have to make sure that the server is running fine. To this end, FrontPage gives you a number of useful tools to help you keep your Web server working. You can verify hypertext links, take a look at any given Web at any time, and run the server from the command line. The command-line options let you run the server remotely or through a series of batch files.

# Managing Security for the Personal Web Server

## 26

*by John Jung*

Webmasters typically deal with HTML or CGI scripting questions. But they're also expected to maintain the integrity of the Web server itself. Traditionally, Web servers were run from UNIX machines, which made security a very important issue. Sometimes the Web servers had to interface with proxies and talk through firewalls. In some cases, the Webmasters were in charge of the proxies and firewalls themselves.

The security issues that face a Webmaster running the Personal Web Server are much different. Along with the traditional security issues of talking with proxies and firewalls, there are new concerns. The focus in this chapter is primarily on security as it relates to Web page creation. Although there are still some concerns about restricting access to the Web server, this process is not as technical as it once was. This chapter explains the security issues that relate to the use of the Personal Web Server.

# Internet Security Issues

Web servers that are directly accessible through the Internet have mainly server access issues. That is, you have to be careful of people accessing the Web server from the Internet. Webmasters also have to keep a watchful eye on the activities of the Web server itself. They have to watch out for tasks that the Web server performs that might jeopardize its security.

## Remote Access

For traditional Web servers that are run from UNIX machines, having remote users accessing the Web server is always a security issue. The Webmaster must make sure that user accounts on the Web server have secure passwords. He must also be sure that the latest security patches for various UNIX functions have been applied. UNIX Webmasters have to worry about people being able to hack into their servers.

For people running a Web server on a Windows 95 machine, however, these issues aren't as prevalent. This is because Windows 95 machines don't offer many of UNIX's features; in particular, Windows 95 doesn't offer the ability to remotely log into a computer over the Internet. Consequently, running Web servers from Windows 95 machines is less of a security risk. Because there is no way into a Windows 95 computer, there are fewer risks of the system being hacked into.

For those who want to have some of the power of UNIX but the friendliness of Windows 95, Windows NT is a good option. Windows NT makes much better use of the system's resources and offers better system protection than Windows 95. However, it keeps many of the aspects of UNIX that are missing from Windows 95. These aspects include true user and group permissions and better networking. Although running a Windows NT Web server might be more work than a Windows 95 server, it's well worth the effort.

## Content Control

Being a Webmaster also means being in charge of the content of the entire site. For both large and small companies, this responsibility involves ensuring that whatever is publicly available follows company standards. For example, the Webmaster must make sure that Web pages on an Internet Web server don't hold confidential information. Company Web pages also can't contain copyrighted images, such as those from comic strips, movies, or magazines. Finally, the Webmaster of a corporate Web page must ensure that the content isn't offensive. Pictures of nude people, offensive language, and similar content must be removed.

Another aspect of content control is that not all pages are accessible to everyone. A large business has many different groups, and each group has a particular focus. A particular group might want to limit its Web page to certain people. This practice is not uncommon in large service-oriented companies where groups focus on particular customers. Each group can have a private Web page that only certain, specially designated people can visit. This kind of page enables customers and their corresponding group to be able to view private information.

## CGI Scripts

Another security concern with Internet-accessible Web servers is CGI scripts because the Web server typically runs CGI scripts itself. This means that whatever permissions the Web server has when it is running, the CGI scripts will have as well. Because most UNIX Web servers run as either root (the superuser) or a regular user with extra functions, the CGI scripts can have extraordinary permissions. Consequently, the Webmaster must ensure that all CGI scripts are not potentially malicious. A possible approach to get around malicious CGI scripts is to not allow anyone to create them. This is an acceptable method for many small- and medium-sized companies.

# Intranet Security Issues

An intranet Web server is one that is accessible from within a particular domain. For large companies, internal Web servers are intranet Web servers. Intranet Web servers allow large companies to distribute private company information easily. Because the information is often sensitive, intranet Web servers aren't accessible to outsiders. Just because the Web server isn't available to the world at large doesn't mean that security can be relaxed, however.

## Content Control

For many companies, content control means that the Webmaster must keep track of who has access to what. For example, the Webmaster wouldn't want an author from one group modifying the Web page for another group. Typically, tracking access isn't a problem with UNIX Web servers because UNIX has well-defined user control. If the author of a page didn't want anybody to change her home page, she would set her permissions accordingly.

Unfortunately, Windows 95 doesn't have such controls. Although there are definite user accounts and different user configurations, little file control exists. Anybody can sit down on any Windows 95 machine and delete and modify any and all files. This makes running a Web server for a large intranet site unworkable under Windows 95. There is an acceptable alternative that comes in the form of Windows NT. It does have many of the user control security measures that Windows 95 lacks. Also, because it's built on top of the Windows interface, you don't need to learn UNIX commands.

## CGI Scripts

Intranet Web servers, like Internet ones, should also be careful of CGI scripts. It might seem a little weird to be afraid of coworkers, but that's what security is all about. If an employee has created a potentially malicious CGI script, this script could cause problems if he leaves the company. If he's laid off or fired, he could easily use his script's malevolent aspects and cripple the Web server. Although this action could just result in some downtime for the intranet Web server, it could also have more dire consequences.

# Setting Access Permissions

FrontPage comes with a number of facilities to help you, the Webmaster, control access to Webs. This control comes in the form of restricting who creates Web pages as well as who reads them. Most of this control takes place in the FrontPage Explorer, where permissions are set on a per-Web basis.

## Access Permissions for the Entire Web

All the Webmaster tasks might be too much for one person to handle, especially in a large company. Fortunately, you can define additional Webmasters for the entire Web site by first bringing up the FrontPage Server Administrator program. Next, click on the Security button to display the Administrator name and password dialog box (see Figure 26.1). Now type in the username for the new Webmaster, type in his password, and confirm his password.

**FIGURE 26.1.**

*If you have more than one Webmaster for your entire site, you can add him from this dialog box.*

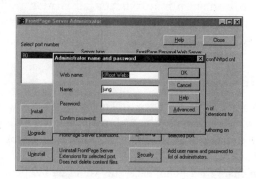

> **TIP**
>
> You can create an account for Webmasters in sub-Webs from this dialog box as well. All you have to do is type in the entire name of the sub-Web to define the new Webmaster. Just remember that you can't display a list of sub-Webs, so you have to know the exact name of the sub-Web.

## Access Permissions for Administrators

FrontPage makes it very easy for the site's Webmaster to delegate authority. For particularly large sites, lots of different groups are probably looking to publish lots of different information. Because it's unrealistic for one Webmaster to watch over all the content, FrontPage allows for lower-level Webmasters so that each group can set up its own Webmaster to watch over the content of its particular Web. The main Webmaster still has complete jurisdiction over everything.

You can define Webmasters for certain Webs from the FrontPage Explorer. As a higher-level Webmaster, load a particular Web into the FrontPage Explorer. Next, click on Tools|Permissions to display a dialog box. Select the Administrators tab to display the Web Permissions dialog box (see Figure 26.2). This dialog box shows an alphabetical list of all Webmasters who have control over the current Web. Removing a Webmaster is a simple matter of selecting the Webmaster to remove and clicking the Remove button.

**FIGURE 26.2.**

*As the site's Webmaster, you can control who else has Webmaster abilities in a particular Web.*

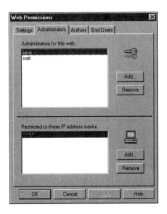

You can easily add a Webmaster for the current sub-Web by clicking the Add button. When adding a new Webmaster, you are presented with a new dialog box (see Figure 26.3). Type in the Webmaster's username and password and confirm the password for the new Webmaster. When you click the OK button, the new Webmaster will be created. You can also restrict the abilities of the new Webmaster by clicking the Advanced button to open a dialog box where you can enter a numeric TCP/IP address. Whatever address you put in restricts the new Webmaster to that particular machine. You can widen the domain of that Webmaster by entering an asterisk (*) in one of the TCP/IP address fields.

**FIGURE 26.3.**

*To create a new Webmaster, just type in his name and his password twice.*

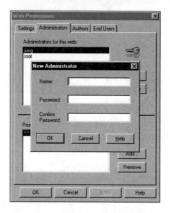

## Access Permissions for Authors

After you've defined the Webmasters for a particular Web, you have to define some authors for that Web. Although Webmasters of a certain Web can be authors, other users inside your domain can also be authors. To define authors, open the Web Permissions dialog box and click the Authors tab (see Figure 26.4). Any Webmaster for this Web can add or remove authors by using the buttons on the right side of the dialog box. Adding and removing authors works the same as adding or removing a Webmaster.

**FIGURE 26.4.**

*Defining authors works the same way as defining Webmasters.*

## Access Permissions for Users

You might need a sub-Web that's not available to everyone. With most traditional Web servers, the Webmaster of the entire site has to use CGI scripts to restrict access to certain Webs. These scripts are told which sub-Webs are password-protected. The Webmaster must also be in charge of the usernames and passwords for each protected sub-Web. Although some of these functions can be delegated to others, maintaining Web access permissions is still a lot of work for the Webmaster.

In FrontPage, such password protection is very easily implemented. The Webmaster of any particular sub-Web can easily turn on or off the password protection. All she has to do is display the Web Permissions dialog box and click the End Users tab (see Figure 26.5). If the Registered Users Only option is selected, the Webmaster can add or remove users. The mechanism for adding and deleting end user accounts is the same as for authors. When someone tries to access a password-protected sub-Web, that person is asked for a username and password. If the Everyone Has Access option is selected, no password protection is implemented.

> **NOTE**
>
> The password protection extends to the entire sub-Web, not an individual page. You can't password-protect just one page with FrontPage. If you want to password-protect an individual page, you should create a sub-Web for it. Then you can password-protect just that sub-Web.

**FIGURE 26.5.**

*Webmasters can control who does and doesn't have access to an entire sub-Web.*

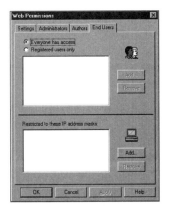

## The Authentication Process

Whenever someone tries to access the Web as an author, administrator, or user, a process takes place. This process, known as the authentication process, is used for both Web modifications and Web viewing. This isn't to say that there is one process for intranet accesses and another for Internet accesses. The processes are in place for certain procedures; they are not dependent on the location of the person accessing the Web.

## Internal Authentication

The internal authentication process begins when someone tries to access the Web in order to modify it. Whether this is a modification of the Web page itself or just of its permissions, the internal authentication process is used. FrontPage controls the internal authentication process. This process begins when someone tries to access a Web with the FrontPage Explorer. The user is presented with a dialog box from his Web browser (see Figure 26.6), where he enters his name and password. When he enters the correct information, he is given access to the Web.

**FIGURE 26.6.**

*When you try to access a protected Web page, Netscape presents this dialog box.*

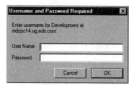

## External Authentication

The external authentication process occurs when someone tries to access a Web. This process occurs regardless of where the machine requesting the Web is located, so machines on both the Internet and intranet are subject to this authentication method. Typically, no authentication is needed on these Webs because most Web pages you create are visible by everybody. However, if you password-protect a Web, the user has to enter a valid username and password before she can access that Web.

## Firewalls

You have just purchased a car. It's blue with four doors. Is an alarm enough to secure it? In case the car disappears, its color and the fact it has four doors won't make much difference. I'm sure you wouldn't be so casual about it. You probably would have insurance for it and would list its vehicle identification number, any accessories it has, plate numbers, and so on. But believe it or not, many companies treat the security of their network assets—especially data communication and internetworking assets—very lightly. Often there are no security policies or any sort of recordkeeping; the security of their systems depends on less information than you have about your car.

That's where firewalls come in; but a firewall alone will not secure your network. It is only part of a broader area of Web site and networking security in general. The complexities of firewalls, their components, and how to create them are far beyond the scope of this book. However, this section covers some fairly general ground on them and discusses how FrontPage works with them.

A firewall separates an internal network from the Internet. It screens and filters all connections coming from the Internet to the internal network, and vice versa, through a single, concentrated security checkpoint. You cannot reach the Internet from the internal network, nor vice versa, unless you pass through this checkpoint. Some systems even require you to log onto the firewall. A firewall protects you against the electronic version of vandalism and helps you manage a variety of aspects of your gate to the Web by keeping the jerks out and enabling you to concentrate on your job.

> **TIP**
>
> Using FTP, you can get information on firewalls from mailing-list archives at the following URL:
>
> `ftp://ftp.greatcircle.com/ub/firewalls`
>
> A firewall toolkit and papers are available at the following URL:
>
> `ftp://ftp.tis.com/ub/firewalls`

## Protection

A firewall greatly improves network security and reduces risks to servers on your network by filtering inherently insecure services. As a result, your network environment is exposed to fewer risks because only selected protocols are able to pass through the firewall.

For example, a firewall could prohibit certain vulnerable services such as NFS from entering or leaving a protected network. This prohibition provides the benefit of preventing the services from being exploited by outside attackers while permitting people to use these services with a greatly reduced risk of exploitation. Services such as NIS or NFS that are particularly useful on a local area network can be enjoyed and used to reduce the server management burden without exposing the network to outside threats.

The problem with firewalls, though, is that they limit access to and from the Internet. In some configurations, you might decide to use a proxy server (which the "Proxy Service" section of this chapter explores in more detail) to filter the inbound and outbound access your policy has determined to be safe. Although not necessary, proxies can be very useful.

## Access Control

A firewall can provide access control to site systems. For instance, some servers can be made reachable from outside networks, whereas others can be effectively sealed off from unwanted access. Depending on the level of risk you are willing to take in your Web site, you should watch out for outside access to the internal network servers, except for special cases such as mail servers or RAS services. When setting up access control systems, keep the following rule in mind: Never provide access to servers or services unless it is required. A good rule of thumb in access control is to keep the available servers and services to a minimum. This will limit the number of possible break-in points on your system.

# Security

A firewall can be less expensive for an organization than security measures on individual machines because all (or most) modified software and additional security software can be located on the firewall system instead of distributed on each server or machine. In particular, one-time password systems and other add-on authentication software can be located at the firewall rather than on each system that needs to be accessed from the Internet.

Other solutions to your Web site security could involve modifications at each server system. Although many techniques are worthy of consideration for their advantages and are probably more appropriate than firewalls in certain situations, firewalls tend to be simpler to implement because only the firewall needs to run specialized software. However, if you have a package-filtering firewall or require your users to log onto the firewall, you need either a router that filters the packages or a dedicated machine.

> **CAUTION**
>
> Don't neglect internal security just because you have a firewall. If a hacker cracks in, your network will be exposed unless you have some internal security policies in place.

# Privacy

Privacy should be of great concern for every Web site because what normally would be considered innocuous information might contain clues that would be useful to a hacker. By using a firewall, Web sites can block access from services such as Finger and Domain Name Service (DNS). Finger displays information about users such as their last login time, whether they've read mail, and other items. But Finger can also reveal information to hackers about how often a system is used, whether the system has active users connected, and whether the system could be attacked without attracting the attention of administrators and other monitoring systems.

Some sites have independent internal and external DNS setups. The internal DNS setups would have everything, all the names and IP addresses of your Web site. The external setup, which is the one accessible from the Internet, would not have all the names and IP addresses available, only those important to other Internet servers. Some Web administrators feel that by blocking this information they are hiding material that otherwise would be useful to hackers.

## Logging and Statistics

By having all access to and from the Internet passing through a firewall, you can log accesses and provide valuable statistics about network usage.

> **TIP**
>
> A firewall with appropriate alarms that sound when suspicious activity occurs can also provide details on whether the firewall and network are being probed or attacked.

You should have a log of your Web site usage statistics and evidence of probing for a number of reasons. The first reason is to know whether the firewall is withstanding probes and attacks so that you can determine whether the controls on the firewall are adequate. Another reason is to track your Web server usage statistics as input for network requirements studies and risk-analysis activities.

# Proxies

Proxies are another form of security for networks. They are often applications running on a particular machine that control access. Proxies are often used to send data from inside the firewall to the Internet at large. You can think of a proxy as a second line of defense for your network security.

Proxy services allow through only those services for which there is a proxy. If an application gateway only contains proxies for FTP and Telnet, only FTP and Telnet are allowed into the protected subnet. All other services are completely blocked. This degree of security is important. A proxy makes sure that only trustworthy services are allowed through the firewall and prevents untrustworthy services from being implemented on the firewall without your knowledge.

> **NOTE**
>
> If you have used TIA (The Internet Adapter), slirp, or TERM, you probably are familiar with the concept of redirecting a connection. Using these programs, you can redirect a port. Proxy servers work in a similar way by opening a socket on the server and allowing the connection to pass through.

# Proxy Service

A *proxy* is a special HTTP server that typically is run on a firewall. A proxy basically does the following:

- Receives a request from a client inside the firewall
- Sends this request to the remote Web server outside of the firewall
- Reads the response
- Sends the response back to the client

Usually, all of the clients in a subnet use the same proxy. This enables the proxy to efficiently cache documents that are requested by several clients.

> **NOTE**
>
> The fact that a proxy service is not transparent to the user means that either the user or the client will have to be "proxified." Either the user is instructed on how to manage the client in order to access certain services (Telnet, FTP), or the client, such as Web clients, should be made proxy-aware.

# How Proxies Work with Web Servers

Proxying permits high-level logging of client transactions, which includes the client IP address, date and time, URL, byte count, and success code. Another characteristic of proxying is its capability to filter client transactions at the application protocol level. It can control access to services for individual methods, servers, domains, and so on.

Technically speaking, when a client requests a normal HTTP document, the HTTP server gets only the path and keyword portion of the requested URL. It knows its host name and that its protocol specifier is `http:`. When a proxy server receives a request from a client, HTTP is always used for transactions with the proxy server, even when accessing a resource served by a remote server using another protocol, such as Gopher or FTP.

A proxy server always has the information necessary to make a request to remote hosts specified in the request URL. Instead of specifying only the pathname and possibly search keywords to the proxy server, the full URL is specified. In this way, a proxy server behaves like a client to retrieve a document, by calling the same protocol that the client would call to perform the retrieval. However, the proxy creates an HTTP document containing the requested resource to return to the client. A Gopher or FTP directory listing, for example, is returned to the client as an HTML document.

Therefore, a proxy server has a hybrid function. It must act as both client and server—a server when accepting HTTP requests from clients connecting to it, and a client (to the remote server) when retrieving the documents for its own client.

**NOTE**

A complete proxy server must be compatible with all of the Web protocols, especially HTTP, FTP, Gopher, WAIS, and NNTP.

# Using Proxies and Firewalls with FrontPage

With all the complexities involved in a firewall and proxy server, talking to one might be complicated. It's not. All you really need is to set up a proxy server somewhere on your network. That job is left up to the Webmaster who's also the network administrator. There are entirely too many aspects of proxy servers and firewalls for FrontPage to cover. The only aspect that FrontPage lets you do is to define an HTTP proxy.

## Defining Proxies

To define an HTTP proxy with FrontPage, a Webmaster must load in a particular Web. Presuming that he is an authorized Webmaster for that Web, he can click Tools|Proxies to display the dialog box shown in Figure 26.7. With this dialog box, you can define an HTTP proxy server by typing in the host name in the HTTP Proxy field. In addition to the host name, you should specify a colon (:) followed by the port number that the proxy is using. FrontPage will automatically take care of the communication between it and the proxy server.

**FIGURE 26.7.**

*All you have to do to use a proxy server is define its host name and port number.*

You can also define other hosts on the same network that are inside the firewall. Simply enter the host names and optional port numbers of the servers in the List of Hosts without Proxy field. These hosts will then be able to use FrontPage as a pseudo proxy. These hosts will be able to talk to the FrontPage host, which in turn will talk to the proxy server itself. Use a comma to separate multiple entries in the list.

# When FrontPage Uses Proxies

After you've defined a proxy server, that server name will only be used when you try to access the Internet. For example, when you try to use the Open Location command to point to a Web page outside the firewall, the proxy server will be used. Similarly, when you try to open a link to an external Web page with the Editor, the proxy server will be used. Finally, FrontPage will access the proxy server if you try to use the Follow Link command in the Editor to follow an external Web page.

# Encryption

Some people need to send secure data with a Web server. To secure data, the Web server can encrypt the data to be sent. This form of data protection is typically used when you want to conduct transactions across the Net. Most methods of data encryption for Internet transmission are fairly secure. This feature is often the domain of advanced Web servers, so it is not available with all Web servers. Such is the case with the FrontPage Personal Web Server, which has no provision for data encryption.

If FrontPage accesses an encryption-capable Web server, the encrypted data merely passes through FrontPage without ever being looked at. What this means is that you can safely send encrypted data *through* the Personal Web Server. You can't send encrypted data *with* the Personal Web Server.

# Accessing Your Server

After all the Web pages are created for your Web, you'll want to be able to access your Web server. You can access the Web server from both inside and outside the firewall, and each kind of access raises different issues to consider. Fortunately, with proxy servers in place, accessing your Web server is not a problem.

## Accessing Your External Server from Inside the Firewall

If you're sitting behind a firewall, accessing an external Web server isn't a problem. Follow these steps:

1. Start up the FrontPage Explorer and select File|Open Web to display a dialog box similar to Figure 26.8.
2. Type the complete host name for the external Web server that you're trying to access into the Web Server field.
3. Click the List Webs button to display a list of existing FrontPage Webs.
4. Select the Web that you want to work on, and then click the OK button.

**FIGURE 26.8.**

*You can access an external
Web server from behind a
firewall without a problem.*

Depending on the type of firewall you're sitting behind, you might run into some problems. These problems all point back to your firewall blocking the data being sent through the firewall. It's not necessarily blocking your data going out, but rather data going in. The best way around this situation is to use an HTTP proxy server that allows both sides of a firewall to talk to each other. Without the proxy server, and depending on your firewall, you might not be able to access an external Web server.

## Accessing Your Server from Outside the Firewall

Suppose you're trying to access a Web server from outside a firewall. If the Web server you're trying to access is Internet-accessible, you will have no problems. You can access the internal Web server from outside the organization's domain. However, if the internal Web server you're trying to access is behind a firewall, you'll have a problem. The only way to access an internal Web server from outside the firewall is with a proxy server. If your organization doesn't have a proxy server in place, you won't be able to work on the internal server at all.

# Summary

Web server security is a very important part of being a Webmaster. It includes security for the Web server itself as well as its content. For maintaining content security, FrontPage gives you a good set of tools. These tools take the form of defining accounts for other Web administrators and Web authors. In keeping with the theme of maintaining content security, you can restrict access to certain Webs by defining user accounts for end users for each Web. User accounts enable you to have part of your Web site be public while another part is private.

Another purpose of Web server security is to prevent unauthorized people from accessing your system. Two methods of doing this include firewalls and proxy servers. FrontPage gives you a very basic mechanism for communicating with them. Actually setting up firewalls and proxy servers are matters best left to the organization's network administrator. The complex issues involved in firewalls and proxy servers are beyond the scope of FrontPage.

# Creating and Managing Discussion Groups

**27**

*by John Jung*

No matter how big an organization becomes, it always needs to hear from its customers, whether it's through customer response forms or the total sales every month. If you're already on the Web, one useful form for getting customer feedback is a discussion board. Discussion boards often allow users and your own employees to communicate with each other. Whether it contains a gripe session or troubleshooting help, a discussion board is useful for any organization.

# What Are Discussion Groups?

Despite its rather straightforward definition, a discussion group can take many different forms. Some groups are open-ended where anybody and everybody can post to them. With another kind of group, the authorship is much more regulated, and user accounts are explicitly given. I'll briefly cover the good and bad points for using each kind of group. Perhaps the best way to compare open-ended and restricted discussion groups is with talk radio. Some talk-radio shows air nationally, and consequently, you hear all the other caller's opinions. With a local talk show, the topic can be more focused to a particular audience. This isn't to imply that one is necessarily better than the other—just that they are different.

## Open-Ended Discussion Groups: the Usenet Model

One aspect of the Internet that many people find enjoyable is Usenet. On Usenet, anybody and everybody can read and write to each other in public on almost any topic they want. This makes Usenet a great public forum where you can get, or give, help to anybody on the Net. The only real problem with Usenet is the sheer bulk of its entirety; Usenet has well over 12,000 newsgroups. Each of these newsgroups generally has a different topic from the other groups on Usenet.

## Pros and Cons of Open-Ended Discussion Groups

Probably one of the best aspects of Usenet is its complete openness. Because anybody can post anything they want, all opinions are heard equally. Consequently, if a point is argued or defended well, then the author will probably command respect. This makes it possible for minority opinions to be exposed to everybody at large. In this respect, Usenet is great for allowing everyone a complete perspective on any given topic. Another benefit of an open-ended discussion group is the many different viewpoints from the rest of the Internet. If you have a problem with something and you live far from civilization, Usenet can bring you a great deal of help. You don't necessarily need to drive many miles just to get an opinion; you can simply post your query to Usenet. Its many inhabitants will typically respond with some useful answers.

The obvious downside of an open-ended discussion forum such as Usenet is the easy abuse of it. It's far too easy for people to post topics that are unrelated to a particular newsgroup. Anybody who's read Usenet long enough knows how annoying chain letters and advertisements can be. These messages are often posted to entirely too many newsgroups, most of which have nothing to do with the article in question. Another downside of a discussion group such as Usenet is that everybody can post. Without someone to regulate what's posted, there is little accountability. What this means is that literally anybody can write to almost any Usenet newsgroup and disrupt the ongoing discussions.

Usenet does have some moderated newsgroups where the content is filtered out. With moderated newsgroups, a small number of people are in charge of all posts that appear in a particular newsgroup. That's not to say that only a handful of people actually write the content; rather, they are the editors. A post bound for a moderated newsgroup is routed to the moderator, who then decides whether it should be posted to the entire newsgroup. This allows a moderator to filter out all the venom and pointless arguments. Some people dislike the concept of a moderator, claiming that the moderator is imposing his own viewpoints on a newsgroup. Although this is certainly true, a moderated newsgroup has few realistic alternatives. It is almost impossible to present completely objective information in a newsgroup with only one moderator.

# Restricted Discussion Groups: the BBS Model

Another popular model for a discussion group is a restricted discussion forum. This model is frequently seen in BBSs (bulletin board systems) around the country. The big difference between the two models of discussion groups is how many people can access them. Although almost anybody on the Internet can access Usenet, very few people can access BBS discussion groups. This isn't to say that BBSs are actively restrictive; it's just that each one is located in its own particular area. Consequently, the users closest to a BBS will be able to participate in that system's discussion. The rest of the country, and indeed the world, is left out because of prohibitive long distance phone bills.

# Pros and Cons of Restricted Discussion Groups

On the whole, restricted discussion groups tend to be more focused. They're usually more focused not only on content, but also on information. That is, because the discussion group participants have been filtered already, there will be fewer voices to be heard. This means that most mainstream opinions will be heard, and no extremes. If you post a query to a restricted discussion group, you may or may not get an answer. If you send that same message to a Usenet newsgroup, you'll almost always get a reply. You'll get an answer, whether it's right or wrong. Also, depending on the criteria for restricting access to a discussion group, the content could be very helpful. The moderator of a moderated discussion group has a certain flavor, and he'll impose it over his group. If a BBS catered to only writers, any queries about writing hints or the like will garner more useful replies. On Usenet, whether people know something or not, they'll volunteer their opinions.

The downside of a restricted discussion group is a lack of information. Suppose you wanted to ask for car help on a BBS devoted to writing; chances are, you wouldn't get too much help. You might have to go to a car BBS or post the question to an open-ended forum, such as Usenet. Another downside to a restricted discussion board is the problem of stagnation. After awhile, all the "old hats" at a BBS will tend to dominate the discussion boards. Because the discussion has fewer participants, there tend to be fewer new topics. Most of the old timers have already expressed their opinions to each other, and few want to explain themselves again. Open discussion boards tend to have a constantly changing mix of new participants.

## Which One Is Right for You?

With all this talk about discussion boards, you're probably trying to figure out which one is right for you. As with anything else, it all depends on what you want to do with it. If you're the Webmaster in charge of setting up a corporate Web site, you might want an open-ended discussion board. This will allow users of your product to freely and openly talk to your employees, as well as other users. They can exchange useful information for technical support, upcoming releases, and the like. Although anybody can post anything they want, you can easily moderate over the newsgroup.

You can opt for a private discussion board if you're only the Webmaster for a particular group within your company. This will allow only the customers that your group serves to participate. Although there is more work involved with creating user accounts for everybody, the discussion will remain more focused. Your customer can ask questions of your group, and replies will be focused to that particular person. Any technical support will be very personalized and appropriate to the customer. Another benefit with having a closed-off discussion board is the ability to disseminate proprietary information.

# Creating a Discussion Group

One of the more difficult tasks for a traditional Webmaster is creating a discussion board because of the amount of time required for setting it up and writing the CGI scripts. After you finish these tasks, you can easily export and modify the board for anybody else who needs it. It is the initial creation that is difficult. Fortunately, FrontPage takes a great deal of the difficulty out of creating discussion boards.

# The Discussion Board as a New Web

Probably the easiest way to create a discussion board is to create a new Web for it. From the FrontPage Explorer, simply click File | New Web and select the Discussion Web Wizard option. Next, specify the name of the new Web you're creating. After you log in as the Webmaster for this Web, you're presented with an introductory screen (see Figure 27.1). The discussion board creation wizard asks you a series of questions. Based on your answers, the wizard creates a new discussion board that is tailored to your choices.

**FIGURE 27.1.**

*FrontPage makes creating a discussion board a simple matter of going through a wizard.*

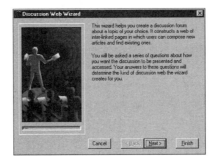

# Features of the Discussion Board

The FrontPage Discussion Web Wizard offers a great deal of power for what it does. It features a number of options that you can easily disable or enable at creation time. For example, the first choice you see when you start the wizard is what primary options to enable (see Figure 27.2). You can let every user see a list of the current discussion by enabling the Table of Contents option. Similarly, you can allow people to search the text of messages by turning on the Search Form option.

**FIGURE 27.2.**

*You can enable or disable a wealth of features from this dialog box.*

One of the most useful features of any newsreader is the capability to display threads. A thread is a series of messages that are related to each other. When you follow a thread from the beginning, you can see where the topic started and where it began to diverge. Particularly large discussions have many subthreads running through them. When people first load your discussion board, you can allow them to see the existing threads by checking the Threaded Replies option. The Confirmation Page is a simple Web page that tells the author that his message has been posted.

After you've specified what main features you want enabled, you can type in the name of the board itself. FrontPage will automatically convert your input into the name of a folder. The folder that is created will hold all the data files related to this discussion board. The name of the folder is displayed under the title you specify for the discussion forum (see Figure 27.3).

**FIGURE 27.3.**

*Be sure to make a note of the name of the folder that FrontPage will create.*

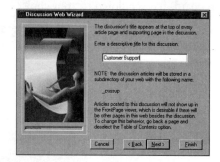

## Different Types of Discussion Boards

You next have to determine what fields for the message each writer has to specify. After this, you see the dialog box shown in Figure 27.4. This dialog box is asking the very simple question of whether you want a public or private discussion board. The default is to create an open discussion forum so that anybody can post to it. You can change this by clicking the Yes option. If you restrict access to your discussion board, FrontPage will prompt you. It will remind you that the Web in which the discussion board resides must be restricted. If you've made the discussion board a separate Web, this won't be a problem.

**FIGURE 27.4.**

*You can specify whether the discussion board should be private.*

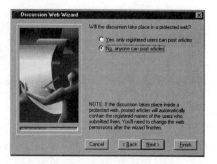

The next two questions the wizard will present to you relate to the Table of Contents. You can specify how the messages are listed, as well as whether the discussion board will be the home page for the Web. The second option allows you to easily create a discussion board in an existing Web. You might not want to use this option if you want your message board to be private.

# Look and Feel

FrontPage also enables you to easily control the look and feel of the discussion board. This is done with the next three questions the wizard will ask you. If you've enabled message searching on this discussion board, the wizard will ask you how search results should be displayed (see Figure 27.5).

**FIGURE 27.5.**

*When people search your discussion board, you can control how the results will be shown.*

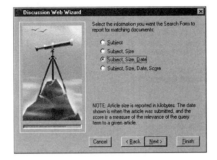

The next question is probably the most important look-and-feel issue you have to deal with (see Figure 27.6). You're given the ability to specify the general display of all the Web pages in the discussion board. You can control the background color or image for the pages and various link colors. Although this might not sound impressive, it makes all your messages appear consistently. For sites that are run by an organization, it's imperative for the Web pages to have a consistent look; this option from FrontPage achieves it.

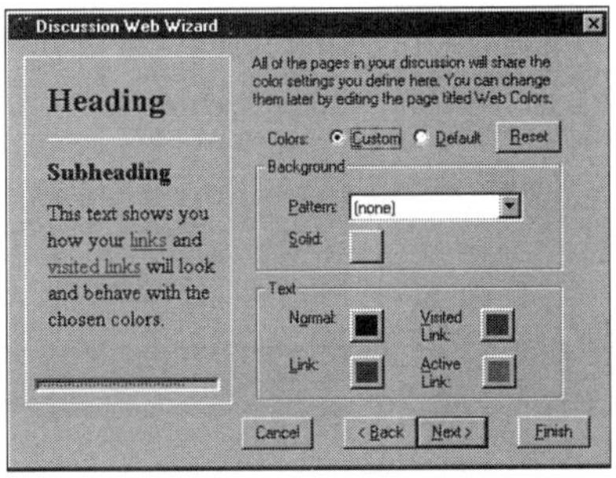

**FIGURE 27.6.**

*You can control how all the Web pages in the discussion board will look.*

After you indicate your color preference for the discussion board, you see Figure 27.7. This dialog box enables you to control how each message in the discussion board is displayed—not the general color and look and feel, but the general layout. You can have FrontPage use general Web pages so that all browsers can view your board. If you want to target Netscape users, you can specify frames-specific layouts. If you choose to use frames, you can indicate the size and shape of each frame (see Chapter 13, "Using Frames and the Frames Wizard").

**FIGURE 27.7.**

*You can choose to use frames or generic Web pages for the layout of each message.*

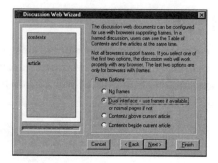

# How Discussion Groups Are Logged and Updated

After you've answered all the Discussion Web Wizard's questions, your discussion board is created. People will now be able to access your discussion forum and post whatever they want. Typically, you'll want to post some sort of welcome message before everybody else posts. This will act as a springboard to spur other people to write in your discussion board.

## Posting and Replying to Messages

Your new discussion board is updated every time anybody posts to it. When someone accesses your Web page, she sees a display similar to Figure 27.8. Any messages are displayed under the first horizontal rule. You can post a new message to the discussion board by clicking the Post button. You see a new window where you simply enter the information in the form fields (see Figure 27.9). After you're done, you click the Post Message button at the bottom of the Web page. If you're currently viewing a message, you can also reply to it. This will bring up a window similar to Figure 27.9. The main difference is that the Subject field has already been filled in for you. You can simply type in your message as if you were posting a new message.

> **NOTE**
>
> If the discussion board you're creating is password-protected, users won't have to fill in their usernames. These fields will be filled in automatically by FrontPage for each poster.

**FIGURE 27.8.**

*This newly created discussion board is waiting for someone to contribute something.*

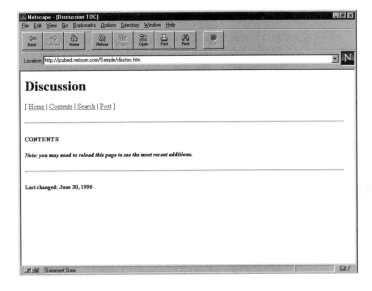

**FIGURE 27.9.**

*When you post a new message, you have to enter the subject, your name, and the message.*

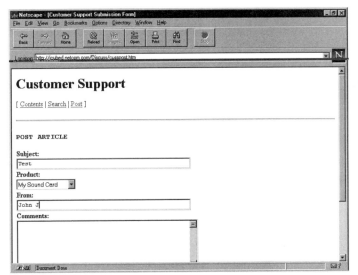

# How Threading Works

When you first create the discussion board, you can enable FrontPage's threading capability. If used, threads allow users to more easily follow flows of discussions as they evolve. Each reply message is placed at the end of the thread in relation to the original message. As more and more people reply to the different articles in the thread, subthreads develop. FrontPage displays all threads by indenting each article in a particular subthread (see Figure 27.10). Those articles in the same thread are points in which the thread separated into another tangent. It's very likely that subthreads will develop subthreads of their own. When you reply to any message, it adds to the thread or subthread.

**FIGURE 27.10.**

*Threads can easily show how a discussion on a certain topic has evolved.*

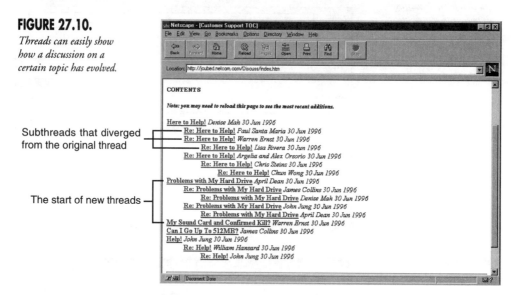

Subthreads that diverged from the original thread

The start of new threads

## Where the Files Are

FrontPage keeps track of all the files for a discussion group in one central location. During the creation process for a discussion board, you're asked to name the board. When you enter a name, the name is modified and used as the folder name (refer to Figure 27.3). All the data files associated with a discussion board are stored in that folder. Generally speaking, the files are stored in `\FrontPage Webs\Content\`*webname*`\`*discussion board name*. If you create a Web called Sales with a discussion group called Customer Support, the directory is `\FrontPage Webs\Content\Sales\_cussup\`. Table 27.1 has a list of all the critical files that each discussion board depends on and where they're located.

**Table 27.1. Disk Location for discussion board data files.**

| File Location (Relative to \FrontPage Webs\Content\ Web Name) | Purpose |
| --- | --- |
| `\Group Name` | The name you gave the discussion board under the `Web name` Web. |
| `\cusscfrm.htm` | After a user posts an article, this Web page is displayed indicating that the post was received. This file will not be created if you disable the |

| File Location (Relative to<br>`\FrontPage Webs\Content\`<br>`Web Name`) | Purpose |
|---|---|
| | option during the creation of the discussion board. |
| `\cusspost.htm` | This is the Web page that users use when they want to post an article to your discussion group. |
| `\cusssrch.htm` | This is the Web page that users use when they want to search the discussion board. This file is only created if you want to let people search your discussion board. |
| `\index.htm` | The table of contents for the discussion board. |
| `\_private\cussahdr.htm` | This file holds the header that appears at the top of posted articles. This file has links to Next, Previous, Reply, and Up. |
| `\_private\cussaftr.htm` | This file holds the footer that appears at the bottom of posted articles. By default, this page is blank. |
| `\_private\cusshead.htm` | The generic header for all messages. By default, it contains everything up to, and including, the first horizontal rule. |
| `\_private\cussfoot.htm` | The generic footer for all messages. By default, it contains everything after, and including, the last horizontal rule. |
| `\_private\cussstyl.htm` | The sample Web page that has the color configuration for all messages. |
| `\Group Name\########.htm` | The actual body for the message of the corresponding article number. |
| `\Group Name\_vti_cnf\########.htm` | This file holds various information about the corresponding article, including relational links, creation date, and related information. |
| `\Group Name\_vti_shm\########.htm` | The file contains the page that's presented when somebody wants to reply to an article. |

# Managing Discussion Groups

Another daunting task in managing a discussion group is maintaining it. You have to be able to check the content of the messages and change them if necessary. You might also want to purge old articles because of disk space considerations or simply because they're old. Whatever the case might be, you'll sometimes need to perform some form of maintenance on the board. Although FrontPage doesn't give you direct capabilities to manage your discussion board, it does simplify the task.

## Traditional Group Handling

Traditionally, most Web-based message board systems had a small set of functions accessible to the moderator. He could easily delete messages or entire threads from a discussion board. Occasionally, he had the power to directly modify the content of each message. This typically wasn't necessary because the moderator often had direct access to the Web pages that made up the articles. In fact, in many cases, the role of a moderator was held by the Web administrator.

## Getting a View from Above

Although FrontPage doesn't directly provide support for message boards, it makes managing them fairly intuitive. Essentially, the discussion board is a series of Web pages with certain attributes that link them to each other. FrontPage takes advantage of this by making the FrontPage Explorer a bit more intelligent. You can easily look at all the messages in a discussion group by first opening up the Web. Next, select Tools | Web Settings and choose the Advanced Tab (see Figure 27.11). Enable the Show Documents in Hidden Directories option, and click the OK button. FrontPage should automatically ask if you want the view of the Web to be refreshed, and you should answer Yes. After it's done updating, switch to the summary view and you'll see all the Web pages for the discussion group (see Figure 27.12). All messages posted by users are named ########.htm with the # characters representing digits.

**FIGURE 27.11.**

*If you want to see all the data files in the discussion board, have FrontPage show the files in hidden directories.*

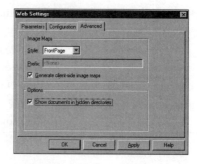

**FIGURE 27.12.**

*In the summary view, FrontPage presents you with a complete list of all the data files for the discussion board.*

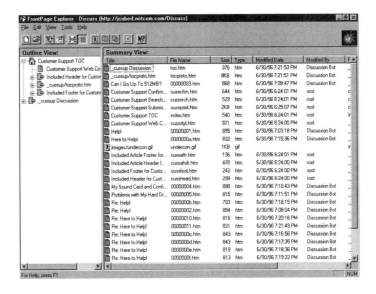

## Deleting Individual Messages

One of your jobs as moderator of the discussion board is removing messages. Sometimes, somebody will post something offensive or inappropriate that must be removed. Other times, you might want to remove a message because it's too old to be relevant. Regardless of the need, FrontPage provides an easy mechanism for removing any unwanted message.

Simply get a summary view of the entire discussion board and locate the article you don't want. Highlight it, click the right mouse button, and select the Delete option. The message is removed and all links are updated accordingly. That means that if the article was in the middle of a thread, the Next and Previous links are fixed.

> **CAUTION**
>
> After a message is deleted, there is no method for retrieving it. If you need to keep a backup of the message, such as for archiving purposes, save the message first.

## Modifying Individual Messages with FrontPage

Another job of a moderator is modifying an existing message. For whatever reason—the author used too many profanities, wrote a rambling message, or whatever—you'll have to change it. This task is also very intuitive using FrontPage's Explorer. Because each article in the discussion board is a Web page, simply get a summary view of the discussion forum. Next, select the article number that you want to change and highlight it. Click the right mouse button and select the Open option, which will load the article into the FrontPage Editor. You can then simply edit the article as you would any other Web page.

> **TIP**
>
> If you modify an article, be sure to let people know that you've changed it. It's generally considered good form to do this so that the author doesn't get blindsided. He might have written one thing, but someone could argue with him over an edit that you made. Be sure to include some text in the edited text that indicates that you modified the original and why.

# Summary

Discussion boards can be very useful tools for any organization, large or small. It allows both employees and users to talk about whatever interests them. Because you'll be creating the discussion board, you can control the direction of the discussion. FrontPage provides a very easy-to-use wizard mechanism for creating many types of discussion forums. You can control everything from the general look and feel to what features to enable.

In addition to providing various aesthetic controls, FrontPage also gives you tools to work with your discussion group. You can decide whether the discussion board is open to everybody or restricted in its access. FrontPage also gives you full editorial control over the content of the discussion board. You can delete existing articles or simply edit them. You accomplish all of this without any special interface from FrontPage. FrontPage is flexible enough to handle all your modifications and adjust all affected files.

# Troubleshooting FrontPage

# 28

*by John Jung*

No matter how well documented FrontPage is, or how proficient you are, you're bound to run into problems. Some of the problems can be solved by digging through the help files. You might even be able to get some help from Microsoft's Internet-based knowledge base. Although you can *find* the information you're looking for, it could take a while.

As with most other Microsoft products, FrontPage comes with a rather extensive context-sensitive help file. To help you get used to the software, FrontPage even includes its own help file to help you learn about the product. Unfortunately, the help files are broken into different components, some tied to each other. This ensures that when you look things up, you'll come back to something you've already read. Unfortunately, this isn't always what you want. Sometimes you'll desire a different angle on your problem.

# Solving Problems with the Editor

The Microsoft FrontPage Editor is a very versatile WYSIWYG HTML editor. It can occasionally get a little confusing, especially to people new to FrontPage. The fact that FrontPage makes extensive use of the network frequently causes problems. Fortunately, these problems aren't devastating and can easily be remedied.

## Problems Saving a Web Page

If you started up the FrontPage Editor by itself, and not from the FrontPage Explorer, you could have a number of problems. One of the more significant ones is that it becomes extremely difficult for you to access any Web page on a local Web. If you know the full URL for the local Web page you want to work on, you can access it. Unfortunately, you won't be able to save any changes you make (see Figure 28.1).

**FIGURE 28.1.**

*The FrontPage Editor prevents you from saving the page into a non-existent Web.*

This occurs because FrontPage doesn't know who you are. Consequently, it doesn't know what permissions you have. The best way to get around this problem is to start the FrontPage Explorer. When it's up and running, choose the Web where you want to save the Web page. You'll have to enter your username and password to the system before you can access any pages. Finally, assuming you have the proper permissions for that Web, you'll be able to save your work.

## Imagemap Display Problem

FrontPage enables you to create client-side imagemaps right on a Web page. Traditionally, imagemaps were implemented with a number of files that, when used together, made up the imagemap. The problem with this approach is that some Web browsers, such as text-based browsers, couldn't handle imagemaps. People with slow Net connections who turned off the automatic loading of images had the same problem. Client-side imagemaps implement imagemap capability from within a Web document itself. Consequently, it is suddenly possible for everybody to access an imagemap. Chapter 10, "Enhancing Your Web Publication with Images—the Easy Way," gives you more information about what imagemaps are used for and how to create them.

If you're creating a client-side imagemap, it's possible that you won't see the clickable regions. Don't panic. All your hotspots are still in place, you just can't see them. When you put an image on your Web page, the FrontPage Editor suddenly has two display modes: the Web page and the imagemap. The Web page display mode is shown when you click anywhere on your Web page outside an image. You can navigate through the Web page, and everything you do will take place on it. However, if you move your mouse cursor over an imagemap hotspot, nothing shows up. The imagemap display mode shows you the entire Web page as well, but all the links for the imagemap become visible. If you don't see any imagemap regions, simply click inside an image and everything should be fine.

## Forms and Text

If you're designing complex Web pages, you'll probably want to add form fields. Unfortunately, because form fields are rather complicated, it's possible that you might not get the results you want. Probably the most common problem you'll encounter when working with forms is trying to put forms and text in the same line. By default, when you create a form field, FrontPage puts it on its own line, as its own object. You can't move the form field object into another line with text or graphics. As a result, it might not seem possible to put forms and text on the same line.

If you're faced with such a situation, don't despair. You *can* put in a form field on the same line as text. When you insert a form field, it isn't inserted into the document at the cursor location. It's inserted into the next blank line after your cursor. If you want to add text before or after the form field, you must create the form field first. After that, you can position your text cursor in the form field region, and type in the text you want. This method enables you to put form fields before and after the text in the form field region.

# Solving Problems with the Explorer

The best way to minimize the number of problems you might encounter with the FrontPage Editor is to use the FrontPage Explorer. This Explorer takes care of a number of access problems you might encounter with the Editor. However, while you're getting around some problems for the FrontPage Editor, you're getting new problems for the Explorer.

# Problems Accessing a Local Web

Suppose that you want to add something to a Web page on your Web but you can't. There are a number of problems that could be impeding you. First check to make sure that you have an account on the Web. If you don't have an account on it, you'll have to talk to your Web administrator, or Webmaster. That person will be able to create a Web authoring account for you for the Web in question.

If you already have such an account, make sure that you've typed in your username and password correctly. Also, make sure that you have an account for the Web that you're trying to access. Just because you have an account on one Web doesn't mean you have access to all Webs. This is true even if the two Webs are being run from the same Web site. FrontPage enables Web administrators and Webmasters to restrict where Web authors can go. It's possible that you're trying to access a Web that's off-limits to you.

You might be unable to access a local Web because Web authoring has been disabled. The Webmaster, or Web administrator, has the ability to disable authoring for a particular Web. That's not to say that just the page you want to work on has been disabled, but your entire Web has been disabled. If you're working in a group in a large company, it's possible that your group's Web has authoring disabled. This isn't something to panic about, because it's possible that the Webmaster is doing some maintenance on your Web. He might be upgrading the software or backing up the content.

# Problems Accessing Remote Web Pages

One of the most common problems with the FrontPage Explorer is accessing Web pages outside your Web. You'll encounter this problem when you try to have FrontPage Explorer verify all the links in your Web page. Unfortunately, if you run into this sort of problem there's very little you can do about it. In all likelihood the reason you can't get a remote Web page is because of network issues. The best thing to do is tell your Webmaster about the problem.

Another possible cause of this problem is that you're running FrontPage from a stand-alone computer. Because the system isn't on any network, it won't be able to resolve or connect to any host name. As a result, if you connect to the Internet through a modem, you can't access any other computer on the Net. Unfortunately, unlike most other Winsock applications, FrontPage does not attempt to connect to the Net when necessary.

# Web Pages Don't Exist

Because FrontPage is a multiuser environment, you might get a message from one of your colleagues. Suppose that she tells you that she just finished a Web page, and that the one you're working on should link into it. If you try to access her new Web page and can't find it, the problem could lie with the FrontPage Explorer. The FrontPage Explorer loads in the attributes for a particular Web when you first access it. This means that if changes are made after you first accessed the Web, they won't be seen. Fortunately, you can force the FrontPage Explorer to update the attributes for the current Web. This can be done by clicking on Tools|Recalculate Links, from the FrontPage Explorer, causing FrontPage to re-evaluate all the links and data information for the currently loaded Web.

# Solving Problems with the Personal Web Server

The Personal Web Server that comes with FrontPage is derived from an NCSA Web server. It is straightforward and its interface is easy to use. That's not to say it's a perfect Web server, but the Personal Web Server is at least familiar to veteran Webmasters. Because it's based on a UNIX Web server, when something goes wrong, it might not be easy to fix. The FrontPage Web Server Administrator program doesn't give you an option to work on the files directly. Consequently, you'll have to break out a text editor and directly modify the configuration files.

## Changing Port Numbers

Although changing port numbers isn't a problem, it is certainly a commonly requested feature. In a completely fresh and Windows-specific Web server, this could be accomplished in a number of ways. However, because FrontPage is an NCSA-derivative, you have to modify its configuration files. To change the port number of a Web server, you first have to start up the FrontPage Server Administrator program. Next, shut down the Web server that you want to change the port number for. Finally, start up a text editor and modify that Web server's httpd.conf file. Go to the entry that states "Port =" and change the value from 80 to some other number.

By default, Web servers "listen" to port 80 of all machines. However, you might want to change it to suit your particular setup. Situations in which you'll want a different port number include running a multihoming environment, running a Web server through a firewall, and similar circumstances. Whatever the case may be, changing a port number is easy, but not intuitive.

## Problems Installing Internet Information Server

The Internet Information Server (IIS) is a very good intranet package for Windows NT. It offers FTP, Gopher, and Web access in a package that's easy to work with. Your organization could very well be running IIS, and as a result, you might want to have FrontPage be able to hook into it. Fortunately, Microsoft has made a FrontPage Extension for the Internet Information Server. If you're having problems installing the Internet Information Server Extension, you simply might not be using Windows NT. IIS was written with the Windows NT operating system in mind, and consequently depends a great deal on Windows NT features that aren't in Windows 95.

An incorrect version of the software also might be preventing you from installing the extensions. Which software? The operating system or FrontPage could be at fault. The Internet Information Server extensions can only be installed on Windows NT 3.51 Server. Furthermore, that system must have the NT Server Pack #3, or later, installed on the system. You also have to be careful of which FrontPage version you're running. You might run into problems installing the IIS Extensions if you're not using the released version of FrontPage 1.1.

## Problems Accessing Web Pages

As a Webmaster, you might receive complaints about inaccessible Web pages, either on your server or at a remote site. These problems are different; after all, one is a problem with your site, and the other is a possible problem with another site. However, they are similar problems and have some similar solutions.

Internal Web pages might be inaccessible because the Web in question is password protected. While you, the Webmaster, can enable or disable password-protection on a Web, so can Web administrators. It's possible that the Web administrator for the page in question has made his Web protected. You can easily get around a page access problem by disabling password protection for a Web. This can be done by loading the Web in question into the FrontPage Explorer. Next, select Tools|Permissions, and choose the End Users tab. Simply disable the Web password protection and quit out of the Explorer.

If your users could also have problems trying to access external Web pages, you must make sure that the host name of the Web in question is actually up. You can verify this by using the standard UNIX utility, ping, and trying to access the remote host. If there is no response, the host could be down, or routing to that host is unavailable. To make sure that your site isn't at fault, try to ping a computer outside your domain. If it succeeds, then it's probably a network problem with the destination host name. If it fails, your network connection could be down. You should contact your organization's Internet Service Provider (ISP) and report your problem.

A possible cause for Web page access problems both into and out of your site, is the proxy server. If your organization uses a proxy server in conjunction with a firewall, the proxy server could be at fault. It could be offline or misconfigured to disallow any communication on port 80, the default port for HTTP. You should talk with your network administrator to verify that the proxy server is running properly. If it is, also have him check that proxy servicing is enabled for the ports on which the Personal Web Server is running.

# Solving Problems Accessing Your Web: No Network Access

Even though FrontPage was designed to work on a network, it works fine if you're not on one. However, if you're not on a network, you can still have some problems. The most common problems are that Webs on the FrontPage server aren't available.

# Can't Access a Local Web

If you're trying to access an existing Web and you just started a machine, you might have problems. Typically, the Personal Web Server starts up automatically when needed. This isn't a problem for people running Windows 95 or Windows NT with more than 12MB of physical memory. For those of you who fall into that category, you could have problems with the Personal Web server starting up. Regardless of how much virtual memory you've allocated for Windows 95, the server will, in all likelihood, start up after a message has been displayed (see Figure 28.2). This is because the disk drive is slower than the processor in your system.

**FIGURE 28.2.**

*FrontPage is complaining that there isn't a server, but in fact the server started up too late.*

It's not that the server won't start up, but just that it starts up too late. Consequently, it's possible that you'll get an error message about a Web server not running on a particular port. Because the Personal Web Server is automatically started when needed, it should be running after you get the error message. If not, simply start the Web server manually. After you've confirmed that the Personal Web Server is up and running, try to access the Web again. However, the underlying problem is still there, which is that you don't have enough memory. You should seriously consider getting more memory, especially if you want to make extensive use of FrontPage.

# Can't Open Up a Web

When you're not on a network you might sometimes have difficulty starting the FrontPage Editor. This often happens because you have the Personal Web Server and FrontPage Explorer already running. If you try to open a particular Web page, you get an error message about certain modules not being able to run. Although FrontPage recommends that you quit out of other running applications, that might not be enough.

This problem occurs because, once again, the system you're running has insufficient memory. That's not to say that it doesn't have enough physical RAM, just not enough total memory. It's possible that the drive that Windows 95 is using for the swap file is filled up. You should delete unnecessary files from that particular drive, and then try to access the Web. FrontPage's minimum system requirement is 12MB of memory. Make sure that you have at least that much in combined physical and virtual memory.

# Solving Problems Accessing Your Web on the Network

After you have FrontPage up and running on a network, intranet or Internet, you might still run into problems. This is especially true if your computer is the one running the Personal Web Server. If you're not familiar with your system's configuration, this could be the source of some of your problems.

## Unable To Access Your Webs

From time to time you'll probably get reports about users having problems accessing one of your Webs. The Internet is basically a series of interconnected computers, all talking to each other. If one of those computers, between you and the person reporting the problem, goes down, the network will seemingly go down. Consequently, it's likely that your Web will not always be accessible to everyone at all times. As a result, if you get one or two e-mails complaining about inaccessibility of your Web, you can probably ignore it.

On the other hand, if you receive e-mail about your Web from a number of different people, there's probably a problem. You should first check your network connection. Using the UNIX utility ping, try to reach a random set of computers outside your network. If you can't reach any of them, it could be that you, or your ISP, are having problems. You also can attempt to track down the specific host that's giving you problems by using the traceroute UNIX utility. Whereas ping just tells you whether it can talk to another computer, traceroute tells you how it's getting there. You should inform your network administrator about what you've found as soon you have results.

Another possible problem arises if you're in a multihoming environment. After you've checked your network connection, you should check each of the computers that you're multihoming for. Make sure that the Web servers are running on each of those systems. Also, you should check to make sure that the FrontPage Extensions are properly installed on each of those systems.

If your system can talk to the Internet and you're still having problems, you might want to look at your proxy server (if you have one). Proxy servers are used, often in conjunction with firewalls, to help watch over network traffic. This is often simply monitoring the traffic between the organization and the Internet. If you are using a proxy server, it's possible that the server has malfunctioned, shut down, or crashed. Whatever the case may be, you should report your problem to the network administrator as soon as possible.

## Can't Locate a Particular Web Page

When your Personal Web Server is on the Net another problem you might face is an unavailable page. In this case, you should use the FrontPage Explorer, load the Web in question, and try to find the page itself. If the link that was followed was outside your organization, inform the Web author of that link concerning the page in question. This will enable the Web author to either remove his link, or remove the page altogether.

If the link that was followed was from one of your Webs, you should load the Web into the FrontPage Explorer. Next, load the Web page in question and inform that Web's administrator. It's possible that the Web administrator in question has a reason for having a dead link. It could be that he, or his organization, is planning to put in a page there but hasn't gotten around to it. Whatever the case may be, you can probably safely defer the problem to the Web administrator.

# Solving Problems Publishing Your Web

You might be enabling people to publish Web pages through the Personal Web Server. What "publishing of Web pages" means is that the Web pages are worked on in a staging area. When they're ready to be released, they are "published" and pushed out to the external Web server. It's possible that this is the method your organization has chosen to handle each group's Web page. Or, it's possible that you're working for an ISP, and this is how you want your users to make their pages publicly available.

## Authors Can't Talk to Your Server

Before authors can publish their Web pages, they have to be able to communicate to your Web server. If they are complaining that their system isn't established to the Personal Web Server, there could be a few problems. One of the most basic occurs when the author isn't logged onto your network. This is especially true if you work for an Internet Service Provider, where people dial into your system. Unlike most other Internet-based applications, FrontPage does not start up the dialup routine. As a result, it's possible that the user is trying to upload his Web page to you without actually connecting to the Web. Make sure that the user is logged on to your system to begin with.

Another possible difficulty is that there's a problem between your system and the author's. You can check the network connection through the usual suite of tools. If you're working at an ISP, you probably won't be able to check the connectivity to the author's computer. However, you can have the telephone company check the telephone connection between the remote modem and your company's computer. If there are any problems with the connectivity, the telephone company should fix it automatically. If they determine that the connection between your company's building and the remote modem is fine, you should check your building's telephone wiring. (Obviously, checking telephone wiring requires a trained professional from the telephone company.)

## Authors Can't Copy Their Webs

One of the most typical methods of publishing your Web pages with FrontPage is to copy the Web. That is, the Web author loads his Web into the FrontPage Explorer and tries to copy it to the external Web server. This method is a good one because it enables each author to develop his pages independently. This also enables authors to test everything on their system, minimally impacting the Web server itself. However, because it's probable that you'll have authors from all over the world, the Internet is involved, which means that there could be network problems while an author is trying to publish his Web page.

If a few authors can't publish their Web pages, you should check the network connection. Check the network connection between the Web server and the author's computer. You can use the usual `ping` and `traceroute` utilities to help you. It's also possible that the drive with the Web content is filled up, and the copy operation is failing. The obvious solution to this problem is to delete or move unneeded files.

# Problems Moving Your Web

A possibility exists that you won't always be with the same Internet Service Provider. It's also possible that you won't be working for the same company forever. Consequently, there might come a time when you need to move your Web. This obviously only extends to your personal Webs, because you won't have access to your group's Web when you leave. Those duties will be given to someone else to maintain and update.

## Missing Files

While you're creating Web pages, you'll almost definitely create links. There are a number of acceptable protocols that a URL can take, such as `gopher://`, `ftp://`, and so on. Another such protocol is `file://`, which refers to a file on the local computer's drive. The file that's going to be accessed isn't stored on the server's hard drive, but on the client's. Although this might not be used very often on the Internet itself, it's more likely to be used on intranets. It might be practical to have a URL point to a common network drive and access a particular document.

As a result of the way the `file://` protocol behaves, when you move the Web you might suddenly have some broken links. FrontPage usually does a good job of keeping track of which files go where. But the `file://` protocol could easily be overlooked while you're moving your Web. Be sure to check your Web for any URLs that use the `file://` protocol and manually copy the files over.

# Unable To Connect to Web Server

Problems with connecting to a Web server typically arise when you move or copy the Web server somewhere else. Some Web authors may have hardcoded the host name of the Web server. That is, they've put the actual IP host name in a URL they used in a link. Consequently, when you move the Web to a new computer and a new host name, those links could very well break. This is especially true if the old Web server has been given to another person. So, when people try to access once valid links, they'll try to talk to the old computer. That system might not even be running the Personal Web Server, and it isn't likely to have the same content.

To fix this problem, first take the old Web server completely off the network. Next, start up the Personal Web Server on the new computer and have FrontPage verify all links. If there are any broken links, they are probably due to the hardcoding of the old host name. Correct the problem by eliminating the `http://` protocol, and simply refer to the Web from the top level. This will make it easier if, and when, you move the Web in the future.

# Summary

FrontPage is an incredibly detailed and involved HTML editor and Web server. Although this is mostly something to be praised, there are some aspects of it that can lead to problems. Most often, these problems are the result of a bad or questionable network connection. Be it an intranet-based Web server or an Internet Service Provider providing Web services, the problems and solutions are pretty similar. Most of the time, they can be tracked down and fixed by a veteran network administrator.

Another source of common problems is due to lack of knowledge on the part of Web authors of how the Web works. There are certain "good" and "bad" aspects in creating a Web page. As a result, there's a good chance that some "bad" aspects of Web design will creep in. To help minimize this problem, be sure to have FrontPage check and verify all links. This should be done periodically and when something major happens to the Web server.

PART

VIII

# Advanced Issues: Multimedia, CGI, and Indexed Databases

# Adding Sound and Video to Web Pages

**29**

*by William Robert Stanek*

**IN THIS CHAPTER**

Multimedia is the driving force behind the phenomenal popularity of the World Wide Web. By adding sound and video, you can create visually stunning, highly interactive, dynamic pages that will entice readers to visit your page time after time. This chapter is filled with insider tips and techniques for incorporating multimedia into your publications.

# Live Documents in Real-Time

Direct support of multimedia, plug-ins, Java, and VRML is making live multimedia publications on the Web a reality. Behind this first wave of inline multimedia capabilities is a second wave carrying even more advanced capabilities. This new wave of technology is bringing with it the capability to create live documents that either execute or update in real-time.

Using inline multimedia, you can create documents with full-motion video and soundtracks. Innovations such as RealAudio enable you to create soundtracks that begin playing almost as soon as they are accessed. Plug-ins, such as the Macromedia Director plug-in available for the Netscape Navigator, enable browsers to incorporate features from advanced multimedia tools.

The Java programming language is poised to storm the applications development marketplace like no other programming language before it. In the coming months, you will find that if a browser developer wants to be taken seriously in the race to develop the ultimate browser, his or her browser will *have* to support Java. Web users will demand this, because their favorite destination sites will increasingly employ Java applets. (See Chapter 34, "Writing Java Applets," for more information on the Java programming language.)

The hottest innovation for VRML is the live application engine. Using a live application engine, you can transform static 3-D worlds into worlds filled with live animation. Although point-and-click in a 3-D environment is fun, nothing compares to entering a 3-D world with spinning, moving, and flying objects that race by and, based on your actions, intelligently interact. If you want to create live VRML documents, learn all you can about Microsoft's ActiveVRML and the Moving Worlds VRML 2.0 specification.

ActiveVRML is based on the VRML 1.0 specification. Both ActiveVRML and Moving Worlds are specifically designed to meet the needs of Web publishers who want to create multimedia interactive animation.

With VRML 2.0, you can leave behind the static and lifeless VRML 1.0 worlds and enter worlds rich in interaction and animation. VRML 2.0 includes many realism enhancements for objects and backgrounds. For example, publishers can automatically generate irregular terrain. There are additions for generating spatial 3-D sound, which allows publishers to create sounds that grow louder as you approach and fade as you move away.

Some of the best enhancements for VRML 2.0 are the ones that help publishers create animation. The best VRML animation is triggered by user events, but best of all, every movement in a Moving World can trigger new events. When you walk up to a virtual house and ring the bell, an eerie voice can tell you to come in, and the front door can slowly open. To allow for timed-events, you can include counters that track the time. For example, a grandfather clock can echo out the time precisely on the hour and half hour.

VRML 2.0 also lets you detect object collisions, which gives substance to every virtual object. Now that you can detect when objects collide, you can ensure that the virtual tourists to your world can't walk through walls—unless you want them to.

If all this sounds complicated, consider the following example. A visitor to your VRML world is racing toward a black hole you've created in the center of your cyber-galaxy. Your VRML world file feeds data to the appropriate program modules according to the speed and direction they are traveling. Using this input, you can vary the sounds the visitor hears as he or she speeds up or slows down. You can decrease the intensity of celestial bodies as the visitor begins to enter the black hole's gravitational field, and so on.

Using these same live functions, you could create a live cybermall populated by the visitors to the mall. Here, your real-time world would change as visitors move around the mall. Doors could open and close. Visitors could chat with each other. They could interact with information desk personnel to find the products they are looking for.

If the VRML cybermall just described seems far off, consider browsers such as the Sesame Navigator from Ubique that let you invite friends to cybersurf with you. Although Sesame Navigator uses HTML to create what it calls Virtual Places, it is only a matter of time before someone integrates this capability into VRML.

**NOTE**

You can learn more about these innovations at the following Web sites:

**RealAudio**

`http://www.realaudio.com/`

**ActiveVRML**

`http://www.microsoft.com/`

**The Moving Worlds VRML 2.0**

`http://webspace.sgi.com/moving-worlds/`

**VRML resource**

`http://www.sdsc.edu/vrml/`

**Sesame Navigator**

`http://www.vplaces.com/index.htm`

# Enhancing Your Web Publication with Sound

Many Web publishers are experimenting with sound in their publications. These publishers have found that Web users everywhere find sound fascinating and often visit sites solely to obtain sound clips. You can include many types of sound in your publications. Here are some ideas:

- You can use digitized voice messages to provide greetings, installation instructions, and author introductions.

- You can include music to let readers listen to the latest songs, to add soundtracks to your publications, or simply to entertain.

- You can add digitized sound effects to your publications to heighten the mood or drama of your publication.

- You can add simple tones as warnings and audible cues.

Technologies revolving around sound are growing at an explosive pace on the Web. You might be surprised to find that you can include internal and external sound clips in your publications. A few months ago, it would have been impossible to add a soundtrack to a publication. Now, not only can you include a soundtrack for your publications, but you can include multiple soundtracks for publications that play on cue when the part of the page containing the sound clip appears in the browser's viewing area. The potential uses of internal sound files are phenomenal and will take Web publishing to a new high. (See the "Creating Documents with Soundtracks" section in this chapter for more information.)

Although support for internal sound files is just beginning, support for external sound files is already widespread. Readers can access external sound files by activating a hypertext link to the sound file. You can easily create a link to a sound file in the FrontPage Editor.

In the editor, select the text or image that identifies the link, and then either choose Edit|Link or click the Link button. This opens the Create Link dialog box. In the Create Link dialog box, click on either the Current Web tab or the World Wide Web tab.

To create a link from the Current Web tab, enter the relative or page URL for the sound file in the Page field, such as rainstorm.wav. If you do not know the URL, click on the Browse button. From the Current Web dialog box, select the page or file you want to link to, and then click the OK button.

To create a link from the World Wide Web tab, select the HTTP protocol from the list of supported protocols. The editor creates the protocol portion of the URL in the URL field. In the URL field, enter the absolute URL of the sound file to which you want to link, such as http://tvp.com/idn/intro.wav. Click OK.

When a reader clicks on the link, the browser downloads the sound file to his or her computer. If a sound player is available and configured for use in the reader's browser, the sound file plays. If a sound player is not available, the browser stores the sound file on the reader's hard disk for later playing.

Many browser packages come with a sound player, especially commercial browser packages. The Netscape Navigator package includes a sound player called NAPLAYER. NAPLAYER can play most popular sound formats including AU, SND, AIFF, and AIFF-C.

Browsers know which sound player to launch based on the file type extension (`.au`, `.aiff`, `.wav`, and so forth) of the external sound file referenced in your document. When a reader accesses a link to a WAV file, the browser checks a configuration table to see which application should play the sound file. For this reason, you should always name your Web files with the appropriate extension. If the file is in WAV format, name it with a `.wav` extension. If the file is in AIFF format, name it with an `.aiff` extension.

# When and How To Use Sound

Deciding when and how to use sound is one of the most important choices you as the Web publisher have to make. You can use sound in your publications in many ways, but it's especially useful for enhancing and supplementing the text and images on the page. Although adding sound to your documents is easy (using links to external sound files), there are many concepts to consider before adding sound.

Most computer systems come equipped with all the necessary equipment to create sound files:

- A sound card with an analog-to-digital converter
- An audio tool
- A microphone

If your computer does not have this equipment, you can purchase a sound kit, such as the Sound Blaster Pro 16 kit from Creative Labs.

The first step in making a recording is generally to plug a microphone into the sound input jack on your sound card. Using a microphone to make recordings is an analog-to-digital process that most computers can handle. If you want to record a digital audio source, such as music from a compact disc or digital audio tape, you can record directly into the audio jack of the sound card. When you do this, the digital source is usually automatically converted to analog and then back to digital.

> **NOTE**
>
> It might seem strange to convert a digital signal to an analog signal so that you can record it in digital format. However, the conversion is necessary because most computers and sound cards do not support digital inputs. If you want to make a *true* digital-to-digital

recording, you will need to obtain specialized equipment. Fortunately, however, most of the time you will not need specialized equipment. Most CD and DAT players have an internal analog-to-digital converter that outputs analog sound on a standard output jack. Using an extension cord that connects the output jack of the CD or DAT player to the input jack of the computer, you can make recordings. Keep in mind, however, that the conversion process from digital to analog and back to digital could degrade the audio signal.

You can use digitized voice to personalize your Web publications. You can provide a prerecorded greeting from your CEO or marketing specialist, or from the author of the latest work you are featuring. Not only can digitized voice add a personal touch to your publication, but it also has many practical uses. You can use a sound file to provide commentary on the document's subject matter, which can give readers wonderful insight into the author's thoughts. Before you can add the digitized voice file to your page, you must create the sound file. You can create digitized voice files using a microphone and the audio tool that came with your computer.

You can also use your microphone and audio tool to create or record sound effects. Useful sound effects include doors slamming, horns honking, and jet engines roaring. If you want to add the splashing sounds of a spring rainstorm to your publication, you can record the sounds using a standard tape recorder, and then later digitize the sounds. To do this you could connect the output of your tape recorder to the input of your computer's sound card. Alternatively, you could simply press Play on the recorder and use your computer's microphone and audio tool to record the sounds from the recorder's speaker. You could also hold your computer's microphone near an open window to record your street noises or rainstorm sounds directly.

The key to linking sound files to your documents is to do it in an unobtrusive way. Although you do not want to say "Click here to access a sound file," you want to let the reader know the format and size of the sound file. One way to do this would be to simply insert the information within the link, like so:

sound of thunder (760KB WAV)

Or you could add it after the link:

Greetings from our CEO! (150KB AU)

Consider very carefully the sampling rate for your recordings. You might be surprised to learn that sound files gobble up 150KB to 10MB of hard disk space per minute. A voice-quality recording sampled at 8kHz uses approximately 150KB per minute. Voice-quality recordings, also referred to as 8-bit mono recordings, are useful for all general-purpose recordings, including recordings of digitized voice, sound effects, and simple tones. A high-fidelity recording sampled at 44.1kHz uses approximately 10MB per minute. High-fidelity recordings, also referred to as 16-bit stereo recordings, are useful whenever you want to make stereo recordings to include recordings of music from compact disc or digital audio tape.

The primary difference between a mono recording and a stereo recording is the number of audio channels used. Mono recordings use only one audio channel. Stereo recordings use two audio channels. When mono recordings play on a system equipped for stereo playback, the same channel plays in both the left and right speakers. When stereo recordings play on a system equipped for stereo playback, one channel goes to the left speaker and the other channel goes to the right speaker. Although a growing number of computers can play stereo sound files, the average computer does not have stereo speakers. The average computer can play only 8-bit mono sound.

Although 8kHz and 44.1kHz are the most commonly used sampling rates, some Web publishers use other rates as well. One rate you might see is 22.05kHz, which is one half the 44.1kHz sampling rate. Many Web publishers use this rate to record one channel or the mono equivalent of a stereo recording. This is useful because it cuts in half the size of the resulting file. Instead of using 10MB per minute, the 22.05kHz sound file uses 5MB per minute.

Another sampling rate you might see is 22kHz for stereo sound files and 11kHz for mono sound files. Because the sound is sampled at a lower rate, the resulting files use less disk space. You might see this sample rate used on Macintosh computers with System 7 and on Windows systems.

Don't forget, you can create sound clips using an audio tool. Most computer systems come with an audio tool capable of recording sound from the computer's standard input. Using an audio converter, you can convert to and from the popular sound formats discussed in the next section.

# Sound Formats

When adding sound files to your publication, you should try to keep the length of the recording to a minimum. The smaller the file, the more quickly the reader can download and play back the file. You have already seen one way to reduce the size of the file (by reducing the sampling rate). Another way to reduce the file size is to use an audio format that compresses the sound file. One such format is MPEG, developed by the Moving Pictures Expert Group.

## Using MPEG Sound

MPEG is the world standard in audio and video compression. Just as JPEG images and other graphic images can be compressed, so can digital audio and video. MPEG is a technical standard for compression, not a compression algorithm. Manufacturers who follow the MPEG standard develop or obtain a proprietary compression algorithm to achieve what the standard defines. A compression algorithm is a program that uses an advanced mathematical formula to squeeze audio and video into smaller disk spaces. Using MPEG, you can compress a 10MB sound file into 1MB or even 1/2MB of disk space.

When you compress files, there is a tradeoff between compression and the quality of the playback. The higher the compression ratio, the more information is squeezed out of the recording, and the lower is the quality of the playback. For MPEG audio you might want to use a compression ratio of 7:1 to 12:1. MPEG audio players are available for most computer systems, including Amiga, DOS/Windows, Mac, and UNIX. You can use MPEG audio to produce high-quality stereo sound sampled at 44.1kHz; because the files are compressed, the resulting files are small compared to other stereo formats.

The sound format you should use depends on your publishing needs and the projected needs of your readers. Each computer platform has its own sound format. In fact, most computer platforms have several formats, which makes it difficult to adapt sound for use on different systems. This is why industry standards, such as MPEG, are so important.

## Using AU Sound

Although MPEG audio is used widely, other formats are even more prevalent on the Web. Some of these formats are so popular they seem to be industry standards. Sun Microsystem's audio format AU is one of these formats.

Sun's audio format is also called the μ-law format. AU formatted sound files use the `.au` extension. The AU format originated on Sun workstations and in the UNIX environment. Although the AU format is not a high-quality format, it enjoys wide usage because many platforms support it. Audio players are available for just about every computer platform, including Amiga, Atari, DOS/Windows, Mac, and UNIX. AU sound files with a sample rate of 8kHz are the most common and offer fair sound quality that is a close equivalent to that of a telephone receiver.

## Using AIFF and AIFF-C Sound

There are two audio formats associated with Apple's Audio Interchange File Format. AIFF is a basic format that supports high-quality stereo sound. AIFF-C is an advanced format that enables you to compress audio files up to a ratio of 6:1. Using these formats, you can create sound files sampled at a variety of rates. The most popular sampling rates are 16-bit stereo at 44.1kHz and 8-bit mono at 8kHz.

On most systems, AIFF files use the `.aiff` extension and AIFF-C files use the `.aifc` extension. Because DOS/Windows systems limit extensions to three letters, both AIFF and AIFF-C files use the `.aif` extension on DOS/Windows computers. Because Apple originally developed these formats, the formats are primarily used on Macintosh systems. Most audio players that support AIFF also support AIFF-C and audio players are available for just about every computer platform, including Amiga, DOS/Windows, Mac, and UNIX.

## Using WAV Sound

Microsoft's Waveform audio format is another popular format. WAV-formatted sound files use the .wav extension. The proprietary WAV format originated on Windows systems and is capable of producing high-quality sound. Using WAV, you can create sound files sampled at a variety of rates. The most popular sampling rates are 16-bit stereo at 44.1kHz and 8-bit mono at 8kHz. Audio players are available for just about every computer platform, including Amiga, DOS/Windows, Mac, and UNIX.

## Using SND Sound

The SND format is a basic format used in various ways on different systems. On some UNIX systems, audio files saved with the .snd extension are actually AU sound files. DOS/Windows systems use a basic sound format saved with the .snd extension as well. Macintosh systems also use a basic sound format that is saved with the .snd extension. On System 7 for Macintosh, popular sampling rates for SND formatted sound files are 22kHz for stereo sound and 11kHz for mono sound.

## Using MIDI and MOD Sound

Other popular formats include the Musical Instrument Digital Interface (MIDI) format and digital music files in module (MOD) format. MIDI sound files are not sampled like other sound files, and they contain instructions for how and when to play electronic synthesizers. Using MIDI, you can create very advanced soundtracks that use a very small amount of disk space. To playback MIDI sound files, you need a MIDI player.

Modules (MODs) refer to a group of sound formats. MOD files are not sampled, and they contain sets of digital music samples and sequencing information for those samples. There are more than 100 MOD formats. The three most popular of these formats are MOD, S3M, and MTM. Although MODs originated on the Amiga, any computer system using a compatible audio player can play popular MOD formats.

## Summing It All Up

Table 29.1 shows the popular audio formats and summary information for each format. As you have seen, audio players are available for a variety of sound formats on most computer platforms. However, if you want to ensure that a particular group of users can play your sound file, you should use a sound format that originated on their system.

**Table 29.1. Popular audio formats.**

| Format | Extension | MIME Type | Common Sample Rates | Compression |
|--------|-----------|-----------|---------------------|-------------|
| AIFF | .aif/.aiff | audio/x-aiff | 44.1kHz, 16-bit stereo | None |
| | | | 8kHz, 8-bit mono | None |
| AIFF-C | .aif/.aifc | audio/x-aiff | 44.1kHz, 16-bit stereo | 6:1 |
| | | | 8kHz, 8-bit mono | 6:1 |
| AU/µ-law | .au | audio/basic | 8kHz, 8-bit mono | None |
| MPEG | .mp2 | audio/mpeg | 44.1kHz, 16-bit stereo | 20:1 |
| SND | .snd | audio/basic | 22kHz, stereo | None |
| | | | 11kHz, mono | None |
| WAV | .wav | audio/x-wav | 44.1kHz, 16-bit stereo | None |
| | | | 8kHz, 8-bit mono | None |

# Finding Sound Resources on the Internet

One of the best places on the Web to find sound resources is Yahoo. At Yahoo, you can find links to hundreds of resources related to sound. The following links take you to some of Yahoo's most popular sound pages:

Yahoo's multimedia sound page
`http://www.yahoo.com/Computers_and_Internet/Multimedia/Sound/`

Yahoo's MIDI sound page
`http://www.yahoo.com/Entertainment/Music/Genres/Computer_Generated/MIDI/Sounds/`

Yahoo's MOD music page
`http://www.yahoo.com/Computers_and_Internet/Multimedia/Sound/MOD_Music_Format/`

Another great place to find resources related to sound is the World Wide Web Virtual Library. The WWW Virtual Library maintains an audio index and a music department. You can find these areas at the following addresses:

Audio index at the WWW Virtual Library
`http://www.comlab.ox.ac.uk/archive/audio.html`

Music Department of the World Wide Web Virtual Library
`http://syy.oulu.fi/music.html`

If you are looking for sound archives, this popular archive contains lots of Sun AU sounds and a large collection of Ren & Stimpy sounds:

`ftp://ftp.ee.lbl.gov/sounds/`

Another good sound archive can be found at Sunsite. Although Sunsite maintains a multimedia archive, the best stuff is in these sound directories:

AU sounds

`http://sunsite.unc.edu/pub/multimedia/sun-sounds`

WAV sounds

`http://sunsite.unc.edu/pub/multimedia/pc-sounds`

Music

`http://sunsite.unc.edu/pub/multimedia/music`

To stay current with audio concepts and resources, you might want to participate or lurk in the newsgroups related to sound. Here are some newsgroups you might be interested in:

```
alt.binaries.sounds.misc
alt.binaries.sounds.midi
alt.binaries.sounds.mods
alt.binaries.sounds.movies
alt.binaries.sounds.music
alt.binaries.sounds.tv
alt.binaries.sounds.utilities
```

# Creating Documents with Soundtracks

Sound is a powerful enhancement to any document. Internet Explorer 2.0 introduced another innovation for Web publications by enabling you to create documents with soundtracks. Internet Explorer 2.0 directly supports audio files in Microsoft's WAV format, Sun Microsystem's AU format, or in the MIDI format. You add a soundtrack to a document using the HTML Markup bot. This basic Web bot enables you to add non-standard HTML markup that FrontPage will not check.

To create a soundtrack for a document, use the `<BGSOUND>` tag. The `<BGSOUND>` tag has the following attributes:

```
SRC
LOOP
LOOPDELAY
```

The source audio file you specify with the `SRC` attribute starts playing when it finishes downloading. By default, the sound file plays only once. You can change this default using the `LOOP` attribute. The `LOOP` attribute specifies the number of times the audio file plays. You can set the loop to a specific value, such as `LOOP=5`. If you want the soundtrack to continue to loop as long as the reader is on the page, you can set the value to `LOOP=INFINITE` or `LOOP=-1`. To set a delay time between loops you can use the `LOOPDELAY` attribute.

To invoke the HTML Markup bot, open the Insert menu and select Bot. On the Insert Bot window, select the HTML Markup bot by double-clicking on the word HTML Markup. Alternatively, you can select HTML Markup and then click on the OK button or press Enter on

EDITING
TECHNIQUE

the keyboard. Next, enter the <BGSOUND> tag with the appropriate attributes in the HTML Markup Bot Properties window. The HTML Markup bot then inserts the reference to your background sound on the page.

---

**TIP**

When you move your pointer over the non-standard markup designator, you see a robot icon. This icon indicates that a WebBot is embedded in the page. You access an edit window associated with the bot by double-clicking when the robot icon is visible.

---

Figure 29.1 shows the markup used to add a soundtrack that will play three times. Other examples of the <BGSOUND> tag follow:

```
<BGSOUND SRC="RAINSTORM.WAV" LOOP=INFINITE>
```

```
<BGSOUND SRC="waves.au" LOOP=5 LOOPDELAY=30>
```

**FIGURE 29.1.**

*Adding a reference to a soundtrack.*

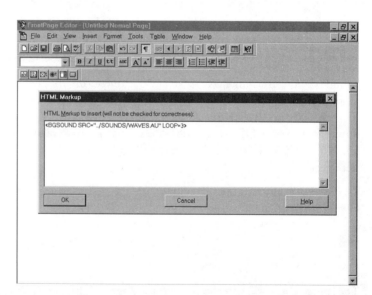

---

**NOTE**

If you are testing a sound that you do not want to loop, you can choose Refresh from your browser's View menu to play the sound again. Keep in mind that currently only Internet Explorer version 2.0 and 3.0 support this extension.

# Enhancing Your Web Publication with Video

Video is another explosive medium that Web publishers are experimenting with. Web users are just as fascinated with video as they are with sound, and they often seek out sites solely to find video clips. There are two basic types of video: digitized motion video and animation. The ways to create animation and video are closely related. This is because animation is a series of still images, while video is a series of still representations of movement.

The idea of computer-generated animation is very simple. You draw a series of still images and play them back in near real-time as if they were motion video. You can create many special effects using animation, such as bouncing a ball across the screen, creating a spinning globe, or even making a tiny sun rise and set. The ways you can use animation in your Web publications are limited only by your imagination.

Generally, digitized motion video refers to video recorded on a video camera that is subsequently digitized for playback on a computer. Although early video productions were nothing more than digitized home videos, these productions attracted tremendous interest from multimedia enthusiasts and Internet users around the world. The applications for using digitized video in your Web publications are limitless.

Another major advance in Web publishing is that you can now include video clips in your Web publications. Thanks to the development team at Microsoft, not only can you create publications with a digitized video sequence, but you can also control how the video will be played back and when. (See the section titled "Using Dynamic Sources to Create Inline Motion Video" to learn more about using internal video clips in your publications.)

Although browser support for video and animation sequences used within Web pages has only recently become possible, there is strong support for external video and animation sequences. Readers can access external video and animation sequences by activating a hypertext link to the video file. You can easily create a link to a video file in the FrontPage Editor.

In the editor, select the text or image that identifies the link, and then either choose Link from the Edit menu or click the Link button. This opens the Create Link dialog box. In the Create Link dialog box, click on either the Current Web tab or the World Wide Web tab.

To create a link from the Current Web tab, enter the relative or page URL for the video file in the Page field, such as `niagara_falls.mov`. If you do not know the URL, click the Browse button. From the Current Web dialog box, select the page or file you want to link to, and then click on the OK button.

To create a link from the World Wide Web tab, select the HTTP protocol from the list of supported protocols. The editor creates the protocol portion of the URL in the URL field. In the URL field, enter the absolute URL of the video file you want to link, such as `http://www.tvpress.com/hello.avi`. When you are done, click OK.

When a reader clicks on the link, the video file downloads to his or her computer. If a video player is available and configured for use in the reader's browser, the video file plays. If a video player is not available, the video file is stored on the reader's hard disk for later playing. Browsers know which video player to launch based on the file type extension (`.avi`, `.mov`, `.mpeg`, and so forth) of the external sound file referenced in your document. Consequently, you should always name your video files with an appropriate extension.

You should also let readers know the format and size of the video file. One way to do this would be to simply insert the information into the text of your publication as follows:

```
Preview our newest Microsoft AVI movie, Cool Waves (4.5MB).
```

Before you add video or animation to your publications, there are many concepts you should consider. The most important matters you should think about are when and how to use video and animation in your publications.

# When and How To Use Video

Adding video to your publications is more complicated than adding other media. Primarily this is because video production merges concepts for still images, motion, and audio. When creating video, you need to understand multimedia concepts related to still images, moving images—which are basically a series of still images that change in time—and audio. However, as you have seen in previous sections, adding multimedia to your publications is easy if you know the standards and related concepts.

Video signals are broadcast using a broadcast standard. NTSC is the broadcast standard in North America and Japan. PAL is the broadcast standard for most of Europe. Although there are other broadcast standards, such as SECAM used in France and variations of PAL used in some European countries, NTSC and PAL are the broadcast standards in widest use.

When you create or incorporate a video sequence into your publication, you will probably use your local broadcast standard. However, consider where the audience for your publication resides. If you are in North America and your primary audience is in Europe, you should create a PAL version of your video sequence. Having to switch between broadcast standards in a finished video can cause problems and affect the quality of the playback. To avoid problems, you should use video equipment that supports both NTSC and PAL. However, specialized video equipment to convert your video sequence to other broadcast standards is available. There are also programs that enable you to display digitized PAL on an NTSC monitor and vice versa.

The key differences between PAL and NTSC are in the number of horizontal and vertical scan lines used and in how the images are interlaced for playback. NTSC-PAL and PAL-NTSC software converters take advantage of how the variance in horizontal and vertical scan lines affects the physical screen size. Most of these converters simply convert the horizontal and vertical scan lines to a pixel size for the screen on which to display your images. The result is a screen of slightly different proportions than what you are used to.

The NTSC standard specifies that broadcast quality video should be displayed at 60 fields per second. The images are interlaced, with the odd and even horizontal lines alternating during each pass. This means that actually only 30 distinct frames appear each second. When you create real-time video or animation sequences for your publications, you will also use the rate of 30 frames per second. If you are digitizing video sequences, you'll capture 30 video frames to create one second of motion video. If you are creating an animation sequence, you'll use a series of 30 still images to create one second of animation.

Many Web publishers create video sequences by capturing them one frame at a time. The primary reason for this is that video digitizing equipment until recently was priced out of the reach of most small publishers. Thanks to recent advances in technology, however, the prices for video digitizing equipment are falling fast. If you plan to create your own video sequences, check the current pricing. You might be surprised at how affordable the equipment is.

Creating thirty frames for a single second of motion video is a lot of work, which is why most digital video sequences are less than a minute in duration. A one-minute video sequence uses 1800 frames. Here's where you want to go back and review the concepts covered earlier. Each video frame can eat up lots of disk space, depending on the pixel bit depth and size of the image. A full-screen (640×480) 24-bit video frame uses as much as 1MB of disk space. Multiply that by 1800 and you will find that each minute of motion video can gobble up as much as 1.8GB of disk space. To top it off, that's 1.8GB of disk space without audio. Add another 10MB per minute for stereo sound sampled at 44.1kHz.

Because video sequences can get so large, there are many techniques for reducing the resulting file size. The primary technique used is compression. When compressing video sequences, you select a compression ratio and a quality setting. A compression ratio is the ratio at which video and accompanying audio, if any, is compressed. Some video formats let you compress files as much as 200:1. A 200:1 compression ratio means that your video sequence is squeezed into a space approximately 1/200th of its original size. Although such a large compression ratio seems attractive, you cannot squeeze that much information out of a file without losing valuable data that directly affects the quality of the playback.

A quality setting, which is often used with compression, is a reality check describing the tradeoff you want to make between the resulting file size and its quality during playback. A general range for quality setting is from 1 to 100. The higher the quality setting, the larger the resulting file will be and the better its playback quality. Quality settings can be confusing, because a quality setting of 75 does not mean the resulting file will have 75 percent of the information. The compression ratio describes how much information to squeeze out of the file. The quality setting keeps the ratio of compression realistic when compared to your need for a quality playback.

Generally, your goal should be to select the highest compression ratio and lowest quality setting that provide playback quality you feel is acceptable. Try several combinations of compression ratios and quality settings. You should never use a quality factor of 100, and you will probably not notice any loss of playback quality using a quality factor of 90.

Although compression is the major technique used to reduce the size of your video files and thus decrease the download time as well, compression alone is often not enough. Many video producers limit the width and height of the video to save disk space and increase playback speed as well. A common size providing good playback speed with an acceptably sized playback window is 160×120. A video recorded at 160×120 is 16 times smaller than a video recorded at 640×480.

You can save disk space and reduce the download time in other ways as well. For the audio portion of the recording, you could use 8-bit mono instead of 16-bit stereo; 8-bit mono sound saves disk space and generally provides a fair quality playback. For the video format, you could use an 8-bit pixel depth instead of a 24-bit pixel depth. Although you can use the 16.7 million colors offered by true 24-bit color to create sharp, high-quality videos, most computers can display only 256 colors anyway. A video recorded in 256 colors is at least three times smaller than a video recorded in 16.7 million colors.

# Video Formats

Although video technology is fairly new, it is advancing at an explosive pace. Video formats are also advancing. Autodesk's original flick format, FLI, has been widely used to create animation sequences, but it is being replaced by the updated flick format, FLC. Because animation and digitized video sequences both display a series of still images that change over time, many Web publishers use popular video formats to create animation sequences.

The most popular video formats are MPEG and QuickTime. MPEG offers advanced compression technology and quality playback. Apple's QuickTime format is a close second to MPEG, offering quality playback and basic compression techniques. Another format working its way into the mainstream is Microsoft's AVI format. The AVI format offers features similar to those of QuickTime. The MPEG, QuickTime, and AVI formats offer quality solutions for video production and editing. As a result, the video format you use will most likely depend on the computer platform you prefer to work with and the video format that originated on that platform. The popular video formats and summary information for each format appear in Table 29.2.

**Table 29.2. Popular video formats.**

| Format | Extension | MIME Type | Compression |
|---|---|---|---|
| AVI | .avi | video/x-msvideo | Yes |
| MPEG-1 | .mpeg, .mpg, .mpe | video/mpeg | Yes |
| MPEG-2 | .mpeg, .mpg, .mpe | video/mpeg | Yes |
| QuickTime | .mov, .qt | video/quicktime | Yes |

The MPEG format is the world standard in video, yet it enjoys the most usage on UNIX systems. If you plan to use a UNIX platform, you will probably want to use MPEG. Apple originally developed the QuickTime format. If you plan to use a Macintosh, you will probably want to use QuickTime. Microsoft originally developed the AVI format. If you plan to a Windows-based system, you will probably want to use AVI. Although these guidelines are true most often, let's explore these formats to help you make a more educated choice of video format for your publications.

## Using the AVI Format

With the large installed base of Windows systems, it should come as no surprise that Microsoft's AVI format is gaining widespread popularity. AVI-formatted video files use the .avi extension. The AVI format is also referred to as the Video for Windows format. Video for Windows is a video production software package sold by Microsoft. The software package includes a suite of tools for creating and editing video sequences, including VidCap, VidEdit, Media Player, BitEdit, PalEdit, and WaveEdit.

Using VidCap, you can capture video in real-time or step through the frames individually. The key to using VidCap in real-time is to make sure your computer is fast enough to process a video frame and save it to disk before the next frame enters the capture hardware. If the processing time exceeds the time it takes for the next frame to enter the capture hardware, you must use the step-frame capture mode.

VidCap processes the audio input with the frames as well. In real-time mode, the software captures the audio as it plays. In step-frame mode, the software captures the video frame and audio associated with the frame separately. VidCap accepts NTSC and PAL video sources as inputs.

Using VidEdit, you can create and edit audio and video sequences. VidEdit displays video and audio segments as separate entities that you can edit in a variety of ways. You can cut out video frames and edit them individually with or without their associated audio segment. You can also cut audio segments for editing and paste them into the video sequence in any order. In this way, you can create an entire new soundtrack for a video segment. With VidEdit, you can save video files in AVI format using a variety of compression algorithms.

VidEdit plays FLC, FLI, DIB, and AVI video formats. You can use the Video for Windows Converter to convert Apple QuickTime to the AVI format. You can also edit your WAV files associated with a video sequence separately using WaveEdit.

Media Player enables you to play your video and audio sequences separately or together. Media Player plays videos in AVI format and audio in WAV format. Usually, the Media Player is included with Windows as an accessory. If it is not, you can obtain run-time versions of the Media Player free.

BitEdit is a handy drawing tool that enables you to easily touch up your video files. Yet because BitEdit supports over a dozen popular image formats including GIF, you can use BitEdit to convert still images into AVI animation.

PalEdit is a handy editor for color palettes that enables you to perform many necessary tasks for color mapping. You can modify any color in a particular palette, modify the entire palette, reduce the number of colors in a palette, and even copy colors from one palette to another.

> **TIP**
>
> If you are looking for information on the AVI format, visit Microsoft at
>
> `http://www.microsoft.com/`

## MPEG Format

The MPEG format is the industry standard for video. The MPEG standard has several progressive levels, but only two of these levels have been implemented. Although MPEG Level 1 became the world standard in video several years ago, MPEG Level 2 was implemented in 1995. MPEG video files use the `.mpeg`, `.mpg`, or `.mpe` extension.

> **TIP**
>
> The best place on the Web to find information on MPEG is the Moving Pictures Expert Group (MPEG) Frequently Asked Questions (FAQ) page. At the MPEG FAQ page, you can find tools, detailed information on the MPEG standard, and information on making MPEG videos. The URL for the MPEG FAQ is
>
> `http://www.crs4.it/HTML/LUIGI/MPEG/mpegfaq.html`
>
> An alternate source for the MPEG FAQ is here:
>
> `http://www.lib.ox.ac.uk/internet/news/faq/by_category.mpeg-faq.html`

Another great site for technical information on MPEG is the MPEG resource list from the University of Minnesota's graphics and visualization lab. The list contains detailed examples of how to create MPEG video and then convert it to and from popular formats. You can find the MPEG resource list on the Web at

`http://www.arc.umn.edu/GVL/Software/mpeg.html`

## Using MPEG Level 1

MPEG Level 1 is the first and most versatile standard that the Moving Pictures Expert Group implemented. MPEG Level 1 video plays at roughly 30 frames per second. Although there are tricks to make the image window larger, MPEG-1 usually displays at a resolution of 352×240 pixels or less. You can compress MPEG Level 1 files using either software or hardware encoders. Most Web publishers use MPEG-1 software encoders, which are very inexpensive. In fact, you can find free MPEG-1 software encoders on the Internet.

Although MPEG-l software encoders are inexpensive and friendly, MPEG-1 *hardware* encoders are fast and efficient. The time savings that MPEG-1 hardware encoders offer is often a selling point in itself, especially if you plan to create multiple video sequences or are on a tight time schedule. Generally, as you create a video sequence, you must experiment with many different compression and quality settings until you find the optimal setting. Each time you use a different setting, you must compress the file and test the playback quality. An MPEG-1 hardware encoder's efficiency is another selling point. A more efficient compression routine can generally create a more compact and higher-quality video file.

Although the MPEG-1 standard is not associated with a single compression algorithm, MPEG-1 compression algorithms are generally more advanced than the algorithms used by AVI or QuickTime. Using MPEG-1 compression, you can compress video sequences up to 100:1. Many Web publishers use MPEG-1 compression because it produces no noticeable quality loss at compression ratios of 7:1 to 12:1. Even with compression ratios of up to 20:1, there is often little noticeable quality loss.

MPEG-1 players are available for all computer systems, including Amiga, Atari, Macintosh, DOS/Windows, and UNIX. Although early MPEG video players did not support audio tracks, most current MPEG players now support 16-bit stereo at sample rates up to 44.1kHz.

## Using MPEG Level 2

MPEG Level 2 is a high-quality video standard that the Moving Pictures Expert Group implemented in 1995. MPEG Level 2 video offers Web publishers true full-screen playback capability. Using MPEG-2, you can play 30 video frames per second at a resolution of 720×480 pixels.

Although the MPEG-2 standard is not associated with a single compression algorithm, MPEG-2 compression algorithms are the most advanced video compression algorithms in use today. Using MPEG-2 compression, you can compress video sequences up to 200:1 with no noticeable quality loss at compression rates at high as 30:1.

The drawback to using MPEG-2 compression is that you need an MPEG-2 video encoder chip to compress the video sequence and an MPEG-2 decoder chip to decompress the video sequence. This means that in order to play your recording, users need a video board with an MPEG-2 decoder chip. Although you can purchase video processing equipment with MPEG-2 encoder and decoder chips for around $2500, it will be some time before standard computer video boards include MPEG-2 decoder chips.

## QuickTime Format

Apple's QuickTime format is one of the most popular formats on the Internet, so popular in fact that the Netscape Navigator 3.0 includes direct support for it. QuickTime video files usually have the `.mov` or `.qt` extension. Macintosh systems have special software and hardware facilities for handling multimedia, and the QuickTime format takes full advantage of these facilities by separating video data into a resource fork and a data fork. The resource fork contains information necessary for system resources such as the Macintosh's multimedia hardware. The data fork contains the actual bits and bytes.

To play QuickTime videos on other systems, the two data forks must be merged into a single data fork. The process of merging the data forks is called "flattening;" if someone ever tells you to flatten your QuickTime video, this is what they are talking about. Although the process may sound complicated, there are tools you can use to flatten QuickTime videos at the press of a button.

Apple includes QuickTime players with current versions of System 7. If you own a Macintosh and do not have a QuickTime player, you can obtain one for free at the Apple QuickTime site highlighted in the resource section that follows. You can also find free QuickTime players for Windows and UNIX X Window systems.

---

**TIP**

Apple's QuickTime site is the place to find information on QuickTime. The site contains the latest players for the various systems QuickTime supports, lists of useful utilities, and even QuickTime videos. You will find Apple's QuickTime site on the Web here:

```
http://quicktime.apple.com/
```

## Finding Video Resources on the Internet

Dozens of sites on the Web have video archives. The problem is that most of these sites are on servers maintained by universities, and sometimes when a site gets too popular, the site closes. To stay current with the changes, you might want to visit the multimedia section at Yahoo:

```
http://www.yahoo.com/Computers_and_Internet/Multimedia/Video/
```

If you own a Macintosh, visit this page at Yahoo:

```
http://www.yahoo.com/Computers_and_Internet/Software/Macintosh/Multimedia/
```

One of the most popular movie archives on the Internet is the MPEG Movie Archive. At the MPEG Movie Archive, you can find nearly a hundred MPEG movies. The archive contains several categories of movies, including Super Models, Animation, Movies & TV, Music, Racing, Space, and a miscellaneous category. Recently the site closed down because it became too popular, but the developers of the site say the site is back permanently. You can find the archive at the main site or at one of the mirror sites:

Main site
```
http://www.eeb.ele.tue.nl/mpeg/index.html
```

Mirror site
```
http://ftp.luth.se/pub/misc/anim/
```

Mirror site
```
http://www.wit.com
```

Rob's Multimedia Lab, sponsored by the Association for Computing Machinery at University of Illinois Urbana/Champaign campus, is a comprehensive resource for all things related to multimedia. The front door to the site contains dozens of links, but you can also go straight to the good stuff, which includes an image archive, a sound archive, and an MPEG movie archive:

Image archive
```
http://www.acm.uiuc.edu:80/rml/Gifs/
```

Sound archive
```
http://www.acm.uiuc.edu:80/rml/Sounds/
```

MPEG movie archive
```
http://www.acm.uiuc.edu:80/rml/Mpeg/
```

# Using Dynamic Sources to Create Inline Motion Video

Internet Explorer 2.0 takes the prize for developing one of the most innovative enhancements to the HTML specification. Using Internet Explorer's dynamic sources, you can incorporate motion video directly into your publication. Although the Internet Explorer currently supports motion video only in Microsoft's AVI format, direct browser support for inline video is a major step toward true multimedia Web publications.

The development team at Microsoft considered very carefully how to incorporate video into publications, and devised a way to incorporate video into existing pages without altering the way users without the Internet Explorer browser see the page. This key concept for dynamic sources avoids leaving a gaping hole in the document where the video should be. To do this, the developers decided to extend the image tag and add an attribute called DYNSRC, which allows you to specify a SRC image and a DYNSRC video. Users with an Internet Explorer-capable browser see the video, and users without an Internet Explorer-capable browser see the image.

Adding a dynamic source to an existing image is easy. To start, select the image using one of the following techniques:

1. Click on the image.

2. Move the pointer to the left or right side of the image, and then click the left mouse button and drag the pointer over the image.

3. Move the insertion point to the left or right side of the image, and then press Shift+left arrow key or Shift+right arrow key.

After you have selected the image, open the Image Properties dialog box with any of the following methods: pressing Alt+Enter, selecting Properties from the Edit menu, or double clicking on the image.

Next, click on the Extended button. This opens the Extended Attributes dialog box shown in Figure 29.2. This dialog box shows all currently defined extensions. As you can see from Figure 29.2, the current image has a dynamic source extension.

**FIGURE 29.2.**

*Extending the Image tag.*

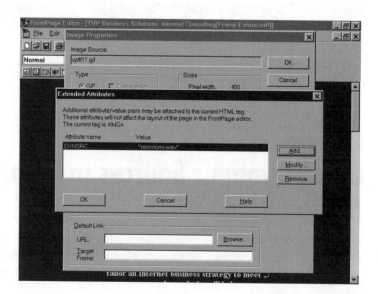

To define a dynamic source for your image, click the Add button. This opens the Set Attribute Value dialog box shown in Figure 29.3. In the Name field, enter DYNSRC. In the Value field, enter the relative or absolute URL to your video file, such as

```
SUNSET.AVI
```

or

```
http://tvp.com/idn/hello.mpeg
```

**FIGURE 29.3.**

*Adding a dynamic video source.*

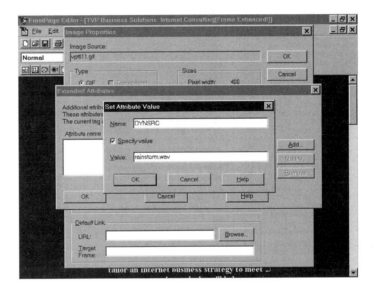

To allow more control over the video, the following attributes for the <IMG> tag were also introduced by Microsoft:

```
CONTROLS
LOOP
LOOPDELAY
START
```

## Controls for the Video

By default, user controls for the video do not appear. To add a basic set of user controls below the video frame, you use the CONTROLS attribute. The basic controls include play, stop, fast forward, and reverse. Although there is only one set of controls at this time, Microsoft has plans to offer more control over the style and functionality of the controls.

With the Set Attribute Value dialog box displayed in the FrontPage Editor, you can add this attribute. In the Name field, enter CONTROLS. No value is associated with this attribute, so don't enter a value in the Value field. Instead, deselect the Specify Value field as shown in Figure 29.4.

**FIGURE 29.4.**

*Adding controls.*

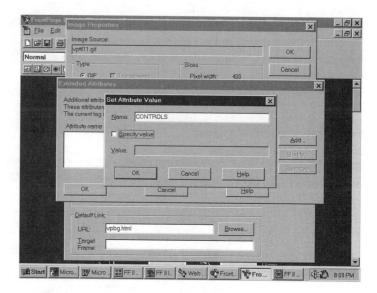

# Looping the Video

Inline videos normally play only once. You can change this default using the LOOP attribute. The LOOP attribute specifies the number of times the video plays. You can set the loop to a specific value, such as 3. If you want the video to continue to loop as long as the reader is on the page, you can set the value to INFINITE or -1.

Using the LOOPDELAY attribute, you can specify how long the video waits before looping, in milliseconds. The video clip defined with the attributes shown in Figure 29.5 will play once, and then wait two seconds before playing the video the second and final time.

**FIGURE 29.5.**

*Looping the video.*

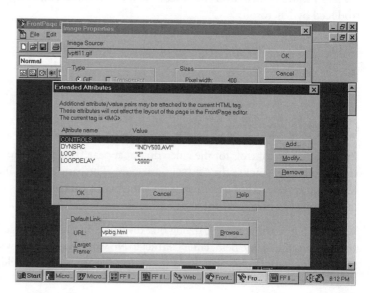

## Starting the Video

The START attribute enables you to set the video so that it plays automatically. You can set this in one of two ways: the video plays automatically when the file opens, or the video plays automatically when the user moves the mouse over the video. The values you use to do this are as follows:

```
FILEOPEN
MOUSEOVER
```

Internet Explorer creates an interesting way to use these values by enabling you to combine them. The video clip defined with the attributes shown in Figure 29.6 will start when the file finishes downloading and repeat whenever the user moves the mouse cursor over the video.

**FIGURE 29.6.**

*Determining how the video will start.*

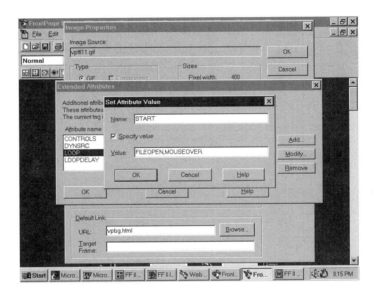

# Examples of Video in Web Pages

The traditional way to reference video in Web pages is as an external resource. In the Movies and TV page at the MPEG Movie Archive, readers can download a video to their computers by clicking on any of the underlined links. To play the video, you need a helper application such as an MPEG video player. This way to reference video in your documents is not very exciting, but that hasn't deterred the 3.5 million users who visited the MPEG Movie Archive.

Compare the static MPEG Movie Archive page to the dynamic source video on the Microsoft page at the following address. The coffee cup on the page comes to life when you move the mouse pointer over the graphic. It twirls around as steam rises from the cup, swirling round and round. Now isn't that more exciting than a lifeless page? You can visit this demo, created by Microsoft, at the following address:

```
http://www.microsoft.com/workshop/author/roberth/set2/dynsrc.htm
```

**TIP**

Recently, Microsoft released a format called the ActiveMovie streaming format (ASF). This new video format is revolutionizing the way multimedia files are used on the Internet. With ASF, Web publishers can create Web documents with realtime video. To learn more about ASF, visit Microsoft's Interactive Media Home Page at

`http://www.microsoft.com/imedia/`

# Summary

Everywhere you look on the Web, you will find Web publications that use multimedia. Web publishers use sound and video to enhance their pages and to attract readers. You can use multimedia to convey your message in a way more powerful than text alone. Multimedia can help sell your products and services. It can even show the rest of the world what your part of the world looks like.

Although images are a basic medium for your publications, you can also use sound and video. Both sound and video offer Web publishers a powerful way to express their ideas and reach readers. In fact, many Web users seek out sites that feature sound and video.

# Writing CGI Scripts

**30**

*by William Robert Stanek*

**IN THIS CHAPTER**

Using CGI scripts, you can create powerful, personalized, and professional Web publications that readers can really interact with. CGI scripts are external programs that act as gateways between the Web server and other applications. You can use CGI scripts to process input from readers and thus open a two-way communication channel with your readers. Reader input can be data from fill-out forms, keywords for a database query, or values that describe the reader's browser and connection.

Your CGI scripts can use this input to add entries to an index, to search databases, to create customized documents on the fly, and much more. Yet the most wonderful thing about CGI scripts is that they hide their complexities from users. If you've used a fill-out form or an image map on the Web, you've probably used a gateway script and probably didn't even know it. This is because everything seems to happen automatically. You enter data, click a mouse button, and a moment later a result is displayed. Learning what actually happens between the click of the mouse button and the display of the result is what this chapter is all about. This chapter explains what you need to know about CGI scripts—what they are, how to use them, and why to use them.

Although FrontPage enables you to easily add WebBots to pages that use forms, WebBots generally do not perform any post-submission processing. With CGI scripts, you can process input from forms automatically and generate output directly to the reader based on the results of the processing.

# What Are CGI Scripts?

CGI scripts are external programs that run on the Web server. You can use CGI scripts to create highly interactive Web publications. The standard that defines how external programs are used on Web servers and how they interact with other applications is the common gateway interface. The three words that comprise the name of the standard—common, gateway, and interface—describe how the standard works:

> **Common:** By specifying a common way for scripts to be accessed, CGI enables anyone, regardless of their platform, to pass information to a CGI script.
>
> **Gateway:** By defining the link or gateway between the script, the server, and other applications, CGI makes it possible for external programs to accept generalized input and pass information to other applications.
>
> **Interface:** By describing the interface or the way external programs can be accessed by users, CGI reduces the complex process of interfacing with external programs to a few basic procedures.

The developers of CGI worked these key concepts into the CGI standard to create a powerful and extendible advanced feature for Web publishers that shields readers of your publications from its complexities. The reader need only click on an area of an image map or submit the fill-out form after completing it. Everything after the click of the mouse button seems to happen automatically, and the reader doesn't have to worry about the how or why. As a Web publisher, understanding how CGI scripts work is essential, especially if you want to take advantage of the ways CGI can be used to create powerful Web publications.

Although the reader sees only the result of his submission or query, behind the scenes many things are happening. Here is a summary of what is taking place:

1. The reader's browser passes the input to the Web server.
2. The server, in turn, passes the input to a CGI script.
3. The CGI script processes the input, passes it off to another application if necessary, and sends the output to the Web server.
4. The Web server passes the output back to the reader's browser. The output from a CGI script can be anything from the results of a database search to a completely new document generated based on the reader's input.

On UNIX systems, CGI scripts are located in a directory called `cgi-bin` in the `usr` file system and CGI utilities are located in a directory called `cgi-src` in the `usr` file system. On other systems, your Web server documentation will explain in what directories CGI scripts and utilities should be placed.

# Choosing a Programming Language for Your CGI Scripts

CGI scripts are also called *gateway scripts*. The term *script* comes from the UNIX environment, in which shell scripts abound, but gateway scripts don't have to be in the format of a UNIX script. You can write gateway scripts in almost any computer language that produces an executable file. The most common languages for scripts are

Bourne Shell
C Shell
C/C++
Perl
Python
Tcl
Visual Basic

Two up-and-coming scripting languages are

JavaScript
VBScript

The best programming language to write your script in is one that works with your Web server and meets your needs. Preferably, the language should already be available on the Web server and you should be proficient in it (or at least have some knowledge of the language). Keep in mind, most user input is in the form of text that must be manipulated in some way, which makes support for text strings and their manipulation critically important.

The easiest way to determine if a language is available is to ask the Webmaster or system administrator responsible for the server. Because most Web servers operate on UNIX systems, you might be able to use the following UNIX commands to check on the availability of a particular language:

```
which
whereis
```

You can use either which or whereis on UNIX systems. You would type which or whereis at the shell prompt and follow the command by a keyword on which you want to search, such as the name of the programming language you want to use. To see if your UNIX server supports Perl, you could type either

```
which perl
```

or

```
whereis perl
```

Perl, C/C++, and UNIX shell are the most popular languages for scripts, so the sections that follow will look briefly at these languages, with emphasis on why and when to use them. Each section contains a checklist for features and systems supported, which can be interpreted as follows:

- Operating system support: The operating systems on which the language can be used.
- Programming level: The difficulty of the language to use and learn.
- Complexity of processing: The complexity of the tasks you can process with the language.
- Text-handling capabilities: The ability of the language to manipulate text and strings.

The sections on common scripting languages are followed by close-ups on the newest scripting languages: JavaScript and VBScript. Both JavaScript and VBScript are hot topics on the Net right now. If you want to be on the cutting edge of Internet technologies, these are languages you want to keep both eyes on.

# Using UNIX Shell

**Operating system support:** UNIX
**Programming level:** Basic
**Complexity of processing:** Basic
**Text-handling capabilities:** Moderately Advanced

The UNIX operating system is in wide use in business, education, and research sectors. There are almost as many variations of the UNIX operating system as there are platforms that use it. You will even find that platforms produced by the same manufacturer use different variants of the UNIX operating system. For example, DEC has variants for the Dec-Alpha, Decstation, and Dec OSF.

What these operating systems have in common is the core environment on which they are based. Most UNIX operating systems are based on Berkeley UNIX (BSD), AT&T System V, or a combination of BSD and System V. Both BSD and System V support three shell scripting languages:

> Bourne shell
> C shell
> Korn shell

---

**TIP**

You can quickly identify the shell scripting language used by examining the first line of a script. Bourne shell scripts generally have this first line:

```
#!/bin/sh
```

C shell scripts generally have a blank first line or the following:

```
#!/bin/csh
```

Korn shell scripts generally have this first line:

```
#!/bin/ksh
```

---

All UNIX shells are interpreted languages, which means the scripts you create do not have to be compiled. Bourne shell is the most basic shell. C shell is an advanced shell with many features of the C programming language. Because Bourne shell uses a completely different syntax than C shell, scripts written in Bourne are not compatible with scripts written in C. If you create a script in Bourne shell and later want to use C shell to interpret the script, you must rewrite the script for C shell.

Many programmers often want to merge the simplicity of Bourne shell with the advanced features of C shell, and this is where Korn shell comes in handy. Korn shell has the same functionality as the Bourne shell and also incorporates many features of the C shell. Any shells you've written in Bourne shell can be interpreted directly by the Korn interpreter. This saves time rewriting a script when you later find you want to use a feature supported by Korn. Although the Korn shell is gaining popularity, Bourne and C shell are the two most widely used UNIX shells.

Some differences in Bourne, C, and Korn shell are visible only if you are at the shell prompt and using a particular shell. You can change your current shell any time from the shell prompt by typing:

/bin/sh to change to Bourne shell

/bin/csh to change to C shell

/bin/ksh to change to Korn shell

Usually, you will see visible differences between the various shells immediately. For example, the default command prompt for Bourne shell is the dollar sign, while the default command prompt for C shell is usually your host name and user ID followed by a colon. Beyond this, C shell supports a history function, aliasing of commands, and many other controls that the Bourne shell does not. However, to the CGI programmer, these differences are generally not important. Your primary concern should be the features that the shell directly supports and how scripts behave when executed in it.

Bourne shell is the smallest of the shells and the most efficient. Consequently, a Bourne shell script will generally execute faster and use less system resources. When you want more advanced features, such as arrays, you will want to use Korn shell. Korn shell has more overhead than Bourne shell and requires slightly more system resources. When you want to make advanced function calls or assignments, you will want to use C shell. Because C shell is larger than Bourne and Korn shell, scripts written in C shell generally have higher overhead and use more system resources.

Although UNIX shells have good built-in facilities for handling text, such as sed, awk, and grep, they are not as powerful or extensible as traditional programming languages. You should consider using shell scripts when you want to perform simple tasks and moderately advanced text or file manipulation.

# Using C/C++

**Operating system support:** UNIX, DOS, Windows, Mac, and others
**Programming level:** Advanced
**Complexity of processing:** Advanced
**Text-handling capabilities:** Difficult to use

When you want your scripts to perform complex tasks, you call in the big guns. Two of the most advanced languages used in CGI scripts are C and C++. C is the most popular programming language in use today. C++ is the object-oriented successor to C. Both C and C++ are advanced programming languages that require you to compile your scripts before you can use them. A major advantage of C and C++ is that they enjoy widespread use, and versions are available for virtually every operating system you can think of.

The primary time to use C (rather than C++) is when your scripts must execute swiftly and use minimal system resources. C was developed more than 20 years ago, and it has been gaining popularity ever since. CGI programmers use C because compiled C programs are very small—tiny compared to programs with similar functionality programmed in other languages. Small programs use minimal system resources and execute quickly. However, C is a very complex language with difficult-to-use facilities for manipulating text. Therefore, if you are not proficient in C, you should be wary of using C to perform advanced text string processing.

The primary time to use C++ is when certain functions of your scripts will be reused and when long-term development costs are a major concern. C++ is an object-oriented language that enables you to use libraries of functions. These functions form the core of your CGI scripts and can be reused in other CGI scripts. For example, you can use one function to sort the user's input, another function to search a database using the input, and another function to display the output as an HTML document. However, C++ is an object-oriented language that is very different from other languages. If you have not used an object-oriented language before, are not familiar with C, and plan to use C++ for your CGI scripts, you should be prepared for a steep learning curve.

# Using Perl

**Operating system support:** UNIX, DOS, Windows, Mac, and others
**Programming level:** Advanced
**Complexity of processing:** Advanced
**Text handling capabilities:** Easy to use

If you want to be on the inside track of CGI programming, you should learn and use the Practical Extraction and Report Language (Perl). Perl combines elements of C with UNIX shell features such as awk, sed, and grep to create a powerful language for processing text strings and generating reports. Because most of the processing done by CGI scripts involves text manipulation, Perl is rapidly becoming the most widely used language for CGI scripts. As with C and C++, a major advantage of Perl is its widespread use. Versions of Perl are available for virtually every operating system you can think of. You can use Perl to perform the following tasks:

- Easily manipulate files, text, and processes.
- Extract text strings and manipulate them in complex ways.
- Quickly and easily search files, databases, and indexes.
- Print advanced reports based on the data extracted.

Perl, like Bourne and C shell, is an interpreted language. However, Perl does not have the limitations of most interpreted languages. You can use Perl to manipulate extremely large amounts of data, and you can quickly scan files using sophisticated pattern-matching techniques. Perl strings are not limited in size. The entire contents of a file can be used as a single string. Perl's syntax is similar to C's. Many basic Perl constructs, such as if, for, and while statements, are used just as you use them in C.

> **TIP**
>
> Like a UNIX shell script, a Perl script will usually specify the path to the source routines in the first line. Therefore, the first line of a Perl script should specify the path to where Perl is installed on the system. This path is usually
>
> ```
> #!/usr/local/perl
> ```
>
> or
>
> ```
> #!/usr/local/bin/perl
> ```

Perl is surprisingly easy to learn and use, especially if you know the basics of C or UNIX shell. Perl scripts are usually faster than UNIX shell scripts and slightly slower than compiled C/C++ scripts. You should use Perl whenever you have large amounts of text to manipulate.

# Using JavaScript

JavaScript is a scripting language based on the Java programming language developed by Sun Microsystems. This powerful up-and-coming scripting language is being developed by Netscape Communications Corporation, and as you might have guessed, the Netscape Navigator 2.0/ 3.0 fully supports JavaScript.

Netscape Navigator 2.0/3.0 interprets JavaScript programs embedded directly in an HTML page, and just like Java applets, these programs are fully interactive. JavaScript can recognize and respond to mouse clicks, form input, and page navigation. This means your pages can "intelligently" react to user input. The JavaScript language resembles the Java programming language—with a few important exceptions, as you can see from the comparisons in the following lists:

JavaScript is

- An interpreted language
- Object-based, but lacks classes and inheritance
- Embedded in HTML
- Loosely typed with variable data types, not declared
- Checked at runtime
- Secure: cannot write to hard disk

Java is

- Compiled to bytecode before execution on client
- Object-oriented and uses classes with inheritance
- Referenced from HTML, but source code is separate

- Strongly typed with variable data declared
- Checked at compile time and at runtime
- Secure: cannot write to hard disk

JavaScript is designed to complement the Java language and has some terrific features for Web publishers. You could create a JavaScript program that passes parameters to a Java applet. This would enable you to use the JavaScript program as an easy-to-use front-end for your Java applets. Furthermore, because a Web publisher is not required to know about classes to use JavaScript and to pass parameters to a Java applet, JavaScript provides a simple solution for publishers who want to use the features of the Java language but don't want to learn how to program in Java.

This powerful up-and-coming scripting language is featured in Chapter 32, "Using JavaScript in Your Web Pages."

## Using VBScript

With VBScript, Microsoft proves once again that it understands the tools developers need. Visual Basic Script is a subset of Visual Basic and is used to create highly interactive documents on the Web. Similar to JavaScript, programs written in VBScript are embedded in the body of your HTML documents.

Visual Basic Script also enables dynamic use of OLE scripting management with ActiveX Controls. The object linking and embedding of scripts enables Web publishers to dynamically embed VBScript runtime environments. Basically, this enables you to use VBScripts as plug-in modules. You can, for example, embed a VBScript program in your Web document that calls other VBScript programs to use as plug-ins. The exact plug-in calls could be dynamically selected based on user input.

This powerful scripting language is featured in Chapter 33, "Using VBScript in Your Web Pages."

# Why Use CGI Scripts?

At this point, you might be worried about having to program. You might also be wondering why you would want to use gateway scripts at all. These are valid concerns. Learning a programming language isn't easy, but as you will see later, you might never have to program at all. Dozens of ready-to-use CGI scripts are freely available on the Web. Often you can use these existing programs to meet your needs.

The primary reason to use CGI scripts is to automate what would otherwise be a manual and probably time-consuming process. Using CGI scripts benefits both you and your reader. The reader gets simplicity, automated responses to input, easy ways to make submissions, and fast ways to conduct searches. Gateway scripts enable you to automatically process orders, queries, and much more. CGI programs are commonly used for the following purposes:

- Process input, typically search strings, and output a document containing the results of the search.

- Validate user identification and password information and grant readers access to restricted areas of the Web site.

- Process input from image maps and direct the reader to associated documents.

- Add the reader's feedback or survey responses to a database or index.

- Track visitors to Web pages and post continually updated numbers to the Web page as it is accessed.

- Generate documents based on the type of browser the reader is using.

- Perform post-submission processing and possibly output results for the reader.

FrontPage WebBots perform many of the things that CGI scripts are used for. In fact, the only common CGI tasks FrontPage has not automated are the last three items in the previous list.

# How CGI Scripts Work

Gateway scripts are used to process input submitted by readers of your Web publications. The input usually consists of environment variables that the Web server passes to the gateway script. Environment variables describe the information being passed, such as the version of CGI used on the server, the type of data, the size of the data, and other important information. Gateway scripts can also receive command-line arguments and standard input. To execute a CGI script, the script must exist on the server you are referencing. You must also have a server that is both capable of executing gateway scripts and configured to handle the type of script you plan to use.

Readers pass information to a CGI script by activating a link containing a reference to the script. The gateway script processes the input and formats the results as output that the Web server can use. The Web server takes the results and passes them back to the reader's browser. The browser displays the output for the reader.

The output from a gateway script begins with a header containing a directive to the server. Currently there are three valid server directives: Content-type, Location, and Status. The header can consist of a directive in the format of an HTTP header followed by a blank line. The blank line separates the header from the data you are passing back to the browser. Output containing Location and Status directives usually are a single line. This is because the directive contained on the Location or Status line is all that the server needs, and when there is no subsequent data, you do not need to insert a blank line. The server interprets the output, sets environment variables, and passes the output to the client.

Any transaction between a client and server has many parts. These parts can be broken down into the following eight steps:

1. Client passes input to a server.
2. Server sets environment variables pertaining to input.
3. Server passes input as variables to the named CGI script.
4. Server passes command line input or standard input stream to CGI script if present.
5. Script processes input.
6. Script returns output to the server. This output always contains a qualified header, and a body if additional data is present.
7. Server sets environment variables pertaining to output.
8. Server passes output to client.

FrontPage enables you to set properties for forms using the Form Properties box. You can access this box whenever you add a form element by clicking on the Form button in the element's Properties box or by opening the element's Properties box and clicking on the Form button. This dialog box has two main areas. The Form Handler area defines the type of handler that will process the input from the form. The Hidden Fields area defines form fields not visible to the user.

To use a CGI script, select the Custom CGI Script form handler. Next, click the Settings button. This opens the Settings For Custom Form Handler dialog box shown in Figure 30.1. As you can see, this dialog box has three fields: Action, Method and Encoding Type. The next three sections discuss the values you can use for these fields.

**FIGURE 30.1.**

*Using CGI scripts.*

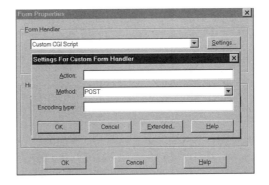

# The Action Field

The Action field specifies the action to be performed when a form is submitted. Because a form without a defined action will not be processed in any way, you should always specify a value for the Action field. You can define an action for your forms as the URL to a gateway script to be executed or as an actual action.

By specifying the URL to a gateway script, you can direct input to the script for processing. The URL provides a relative or an absolute path to the script. Scripts defined with relative URLs are located on your local server. Scripts defined with absolute URLs can be located on a remote or local server. Most CGI scripts are located in the cgi-bin directory. You could access a script in a cgi-bin directory by setting the Action field to

```
http://tvp.com/cgi-bin/your_script
```

You can also use the Action field to specify an actual action to be performed. The only action currently supported is mailto, which enables you to mail the contents of a form to anyone using their e-mail address. Most current browser and server software support the mailto value. To use the mailto value, set the Action field as follows:

```
mailto:name@host
```

Here, name is the user name and host is the host machine the user is located on, as in the following example:

```
mailto:publisher@tvp.com
```

A form created using the previous example would be sent to publisher@tvp.com. The mailto value provides you with a simple solution for using forms that does not need to be directed to a CGI script to be processed. This is great news for Web publishers who don't have access to CGI and can't use FrontPage server extensions. Because the contents of the form are mailed directly to an intended recipient, the data can be processed offline as necessary. You should consider using the mailto value for forms that don't need immediate processing and when you don't have access to CGI or FrontPage server extensions but would like to use forms in your Web publications.

## The Method Field

The Method field specifies the way the form is submitted. There are currently two acceptable values:

```
GET
POST
```

The preferred submission method is POST, the default value used by FrontPage. POST sends the data as a separate input stream via the server to your gateway script. This enables the server to pass the information directly to the gateway script without assigning variables or arguments. The value of an environment variable called CONTENT_LENGTH tells the CGI script how much data to read from the standard input stream. Using this method, there is no limit on the amount of data that can be passed to the server.

GET appends the retrieved data to the script URL. The script URL and the data are passed to the server as a single URL-encoded input. The server receiving the input passes it to two variables: the script URL to SCRIPT_NAME and the data to QUERY_STRING.

Assigning the data to variables on a UNIX system means passing the data through the UNIX shell. The number of characters you can send to UNIX shell in a single input is severely limited. Some servers restrict the length of this type of input to 255 characters. This means you can append only a limited amount of data to a URL before truncation occurs. You lose data when truncation occurs, and losing data is a bad thing. Consequently, if you use GET, you should always ensure that the length of data input is small.

## The Encoding Type Field

The Encoding Type field specifies the MIME content type for encoding the form data. The client encodes the data before passing it to the server. The reason for encoding the data from the fill-out form is not to prevent the data from being read, but rather to ensure that input fields can be easily matched to key values. By default, the data is x-www-form-encoded. This encoding is also called URL encoding. If you do not specify an encoding type, the default value is used automatically.

Although in theory you can use any valid MIME type, such as text/plain, most forms on the Web use the default encoding, x-www-form-encoded. MIME stands for Multipurpose Internet Mail Extensions. HTTP uses MIME to identify the type of object being transferred across the Internet. The purpose of encoding is to prevent problems you would experience when trying to manipulate data that has not been encoded in some way.

You do not have to set a value for this field. However, if you wanted to strictly specify the default encoding, you would set the Encoding Type field to the following value:

```
x-www-form-encoded
```

# Input to CGI Scripts

When a user activates a link to a gateway script, input is sent to the server. The server formats this data into environment variables and checks to see whether additional data was submitted via the standard input stream.

## Environment Variables

Input to CGI scripts is usually in the form of environment variables. The environment variables passed to gateway scripts are associated with the browser requesting information from the server, the server processing the request, and the data passed in the request. Environment variables are case-sensitive and are normally used as described in this section. Although some environment variables are system-specific, many environment variables are standard. The standard variables are shown in Table 30.1.

As later examples show, environment variables are set automatically whenever reader input is passed to a server. The primary reason to learn about these variables is to better understand how input is passed to CGI scripts, but you should also learn about these variables so that you know how to take advantage of them when necessary.

## Table 30.1. Standard environment variables.

| Variable | Function |
|---|---|
| AUTH_TYPE | Specifies the authentication method and is used to validate a user's access. |
| CONTENT_LENGTH | Used to provide a way of tracking the length of the data string as a numeric value. |
| CONTENT_TYPE | Indicates the MIME type of data. |
| GATEWAY_INTERFACE | Indicates the version of the CGI standard the server is using. |
| HTTP_ACCEPT | Indicates the MIME content types the browser will accept, as passed to the gateway script via the server. |
| HTTP_USER_AGENT | Indicates the type of browser used to send the request, as passed to the gateway script via the server. |
| PATH_INFO | Identifies the extra information included in the URL after the identification of the CGI script. |
| PATH_TRANSLATED | Set by the server based on the PATH_INFO variable. The server translates the PATH_INFO variable into this variable. |
| QUERY_STRING | Set to the query string (if the URL contains a query string). |
| REMOTE_ADDR | Identifies the Internet Protocol address of the remote computer making the request. |
| REMOTE_HOST | Identifies the name of the machine making the request. |
| REMOTE_IDENT | Identifies the machine making the request. |
| REMOTE_USER | Identifies the user name as authenticated by the user. |
| REQUEST_METHOD | Indicates the method by which the request was made. |
| SCRIPT_NAME | Identifies the virtual path to the script being executed. |
| SERVER_NAME | Identifies the server by its host name, alias, or IP address. |
| SERVER_PORT | Identifies the port number the server received the request on. |
| SERVER_PROTOCOL | Indicates the protocol of the request sent to the server. |
| SERVER_SOFTWARE | Identifies the Web server software. |

# AUTH_TYPE

The AUTH_TYPE variable provides access control to protected areas of the Web server and can be used only on servers that support user authentication. If an area of the Web site has no access control, the AUTH_TYPE variable has no value associated with it. If an area of the Web site has access control, the AUTH_TYPE variable is set to a specific value that identifies the authentication scheme being used. Otherwise, the variable has no value associated with it. A simple challenge-response authorization mechanism is implemented under current versions of HTTP.

Using this mechanism, the server can challenge a client's request and the client can respond. To do this, the server sets a value for the AUTH_TYPE variable and the client supplies a matching value. The next step is to authenticate the user. Using the basic authentication scheme, the user's browser must supply authentication information that uniquely identifies the user. This information includes a user ID and password.

Under the current implementation of HTTP, HTTP 1.0, the basic authentication scheme is the most commonly used authentication method. To specify this method, set the AUTH_TYPE variable as follows:

```
AUTH_TYPE = Basic
```

# CONTENT_LENGTH

The CONTENT_LENGTH variable provides a way of tracking the length of the data string. This tells the client and server how much data to read on the standard input stream. The value of the variable corresponds to the number of characters in the data passed with the request. If no data is being passed, the variable has no value.

As long as the characters are represented as octets, the value of the CONTENT_LENGTH variable will be the precise number of characters passed as standard input or standard output. Thus, if 25 characters are passed and they are represented as octets, the CONTENT_LENGTH variable will have the following value:

```
CONTENT_LENGTH = 25
```

# CONTENT_TYPE

The CONTENT_TYPE variable indicates the data's MIME type. MIME typing is a feature of HTTP 1.0 and is not available on servers using HTTP 0.9. The variable is set only when attached data is passed using the standard input or output stream. The value assigned to the variable identifies the MIME type and subtype as follows:

```
CONTENT_TYPE = type/subtype
```

MIME types are broken down into basic type categories. Each data type category has a primary subtype associated with it. The basic MIME types and their descriptions are shown in Table 30.2.

**Table 30.2. Basic MIME types.**

| Type | Description |
| --- | --- |
| application | Binary data that can be executed or used with another application |
| audio | A sound file that requires an output device to preview |
| image | A picture that requires an output device to preview |
| message | An encapsulated mail message |
| multipart | Data consisting of multiple parts and possibly many data types |
| text | Textual data that can be represented in any character set or formatting language |
| video | A video file that requires an output device to preview |
| x-world | Experimental data type for world files |

MIME subtypes are defined in three categories: primary, additionally defined, and extended. The primary subtype is the primary type of data adopted for use as MIME Content-Types. Additionally defined data types are additional subtypes that have been officially adopted as MIME Content-Types. Extended data types are experimental subtypes that have not been officially adopted as MIME Content-Types. You can easily identify extended subtypes because they begin with the letter x followed by a hyphen. Table 30.3 lists common MIME types and their descriptions.

**Table 30.3. Common MIME types.**

| Type/Subtype | Description |
| --- | --- |
| application/mac-binhex40 | Macintosh binary-formatted data |
| application/msword | Microsoft word document |
| application/octet-stream | Binary data that can be executed or used with another application |
| application/pdf | ACROBAT PDF document |
| application/postscript | PostScript-formatted data |
| application/rtf | Rich Text Format (RTF) document |

| *Type/Subtype* | *Description* |
| --- | --- |
| application/x-compress | Data that has been compressed using UNIX compress |
| application/x-dvi | Device-independent file |
| application/x-gzip | Data that has been compressed using UNIX gzip |
| application/x-latex | LATEX document |
| application/x-tar | Data that has been archived using UNIX tar |
| application/x-zip-compressed | Data that has been compressed using PKZip or WinZip |
| audio/basic | Audio in a nondescript format |
| audio/x-aiff | Audio in Apple AIFF format |
| audio/x-wav | Audio in Microsoft WAV format |
| image/gif | Image in GIF format |
| image/jpeg | Image in JPEG format |
| image/tiff | Image in TIFF format |
| image/x-portable-bitmap | Portable bitmap |
| image/x-portable-graymap | Portable graymap |
| image/x-portable-pixmap | Portable pixmap |
| image/x-xbitmap | X-bitmap |
| image/x-xpixmap | X-pixmap |
| message/external-body | Message with external data source |
| message/partial | Fragmented or partial message |
| message/rfc822 | RFC-822–compliant message |
| multipart/alternative | Data with alternative formats |
| multipart/digest | Multipart message digest |
| multipart/mixed | Multipart message with data in multiple formats |
| multipart/parallel | Multipart data with parts that should be viewed simultaneously |
| text/html | HTML-formatted text |
| text/plain | Plain text with no HTML formatting included |
| video/mpeg | Video in the MPEG format |
| video/quicktime | Video in the Apple QuickTime format |
| video/x-msvideo | Video in the Microsoft AVI format |
| x-world/x-vrml | VRML world file |

Some MIME Content-Types can be used with additional parameters. These Content-Types include text/plain, text/html, and all multipart message data. The charset parameter is used with the text/plain type to identify the character set used for the data. The version parameter is used with the text/html type to identify the version of HTML used. The boundary parameter is used with multipart data to identify the boundary string that separates message parts.

The charset parameter for the text/plain type is optional. If a charset is not specified, the default value charset=us-ascii is assumed. Other values for charset include any character set approved by the International Standards Organization. These character sets are defined by ISO-8859-1 to ISO-8859-9 and are specified as follows:

```
CONTENT_TYPE = text/plain; charset=iso-8859-1
```

The version parameter for the text/html type is optional. If this parameter is set, the browser reading the data interprets the data if the browser supports the version of HTML specified. The following document conforms to the HTML 3.2 specification:

```
CONTENT_TYPE = text/html; version=3.2
```

The boundary parameter for multipart message types is required. The boundary value is set to a string of 1 to 70 characters. Although the string cannot end in a space, the string can contain any valid letter or number and can include spaces and a limited set of special characters. Boundary parameters are unique strings that are defined as follows:

```
CONTENT_TYPE = multipart/mixed; boundary=boundary_string
```

## GATEWAY_INTERFACE

The GATEWAY_INTERFACE variable indicates the version of the CGI specification the server is using. The value assigned to the variable identifies the name and version of the specification used as follows:

```
GATEWAY_INTERFACE = name/version
```

The current version of the CGI specification is 1.1. A server conforming to this version would set the GATEWAY_INTERFACE variable as follows:

```
GATEWAY_INTERFACE = CGI/1.1
```

## HTTP_ACCEPT

The HTTP_ACCEPT variable defines the types of data the client will accept. The acceptable values are expressed as a type/subtype pair. Each type/subtype pair is separated by commas, as in

```
type/subtype, type/subtype
```

Most clients accept dozens of MIME types. The following identifies all the MIME Content-Types accepted by this client:

```
HTTP_ACCEPT = application/msword, application/octet-stream,
application/postscript, application/rtf, application/x-zip-compressed,
audio/basic, audio/x-aiff, audio/x-wav, image/gif, image/jpeg, image/tiff,
image/x-portable-bitmap, message/external-body, message/partial,
message/rfc822, multipart/alternative,
multipart/digest, multipart/mixed, multipart/parallel, text/html,
text/plain, video/mpeg, video/quicktime, video/x-msvideo
```

## HTTP_USER_AGENT

The HTTP_USER_AGENT variable identifies the type of browser used to send the request. The acceptable values are expressed as *software type/version* or *library/version*. The following HTTP_USER_AGENT variable identifies the Netscape Navigator Version 2.0:

```
HTTP_USER_AGENT = Mozilla/2.0
```

As you can see, Netscape uses the alias Mozilla to identify itself. The primary types of clients that set this variable are browsers, Web spiders, and robots. Although this is a useful parameter for identifying the type of client used to access a script, keep in mind that not all clients set this variable.

Here's a list of software type values used by popular browsers:

> Arena
> Enhanced NCSA Mosaic
> Lynx
> MacWeb
> Mozilla
> NCSA Mosaic
> NetCruiser
> WebExplorer
> WinMosaic

These values are used by Web spiders:

```
Lycos
MOMSpider
WebCrawler
```

## PATH_INFO

The PATH_INFO variable specifies extra path information and can be used to send additional information to a gateway script. The extra path information follows the URL to the gateway script referenced. Generally, this information is a virtual or relative path to a resource that the server must interpret. If the URL to the CGI script is specified in your document as

```
/usr/cgi-bin/formparse.pl/home.html
```

then the PATH_INFO variable would be set as follows:

```
PATH_INFO = /home.html
```

## PATH_TRANSLATED

Servers translate the PATH_INFO variable into the PATH_TRANSLATED variable. They do this by inserting the default Web document's directory path in front of the extra path information. For example, if the PATH_INFO variable was set to home.html and the default directory was /usr/documents/pubs, the PATH_TRANSLATED variable would be set as follows:

```
PATH_TRANSLATED = /usr/documents/pubs/home.html
```

## QUERY_STRING

The QUERY_STRING specifies a URL-encoded search string. You'll set this variable when you use the GET method to submit a fill-out form, or when you use an ISINDEX query to search a document. The query string is separated from the URL by a question mark. The user submits all the information following the question mark separating the URL from the query string. Here is an example:

```
/usr/cgi-bin/formparse.pl?string
```

When the query string is URL-encoded, the browser encodes key parts of the string. The plus sign is a placeholder between words, as a substitute for spaces:

```
/usr/cgi-bin/formparse.pl?word1+word2+word3
```

Equal signs separate keys assigned by the publisher from values entered by the user. In the following example, response is the key assigned by the publisher, and never is the value entered by the user:

```
/usr/cgi-bin/formparse.pl?response=never
```

Ampersand symbols separate sets of keys and values. In the following example, response is the first key assigned by the publisher, and sometimes is the value entered by the user. The second key assigned by the publisher is reason, and the value entered by the user is "I am not really sure". Here is an example:

```
/usr/cgi-bin/formparse.pl?response=sometimes&reason=I+am+not+really+sure
```

Finally, the percent sign is used to identify escape characters. Following the percent sign is an escape code for a special character expressed as a hexadecimal value. Here is how the previous query string could be rewritten using the escape code for an apostrophe:

```
/usr/cgi-bin/formparse.pl?response=sometimes&reason=I%27m+not+really+sure
```

## REMOTE_ADDR

The REMOTE_ADDR variable is set to the Internet Protocol (IP) address of the remote computer making the request. The IP address is a numeric identifier for a networked computer. The REMOTE_ADDR variable is associated with the host computer making the request for the client and could be used as follows:

```
REMOTE_ADDR = 205.1.20.11
```

## REMOTE_HOST

The REMOTE_HOST variable specifies the name of the host computer making a request. This variable is set only if the server can figure out this information using a reverse lookup procedure. If this variable is set, the full domain and host name are used as follows:

```
REMOTE_HOST = www.tvp.com
```

## REMOTE_IDENT

The REMOTE_IDENT variable identifies the remote user making a request. The variable is set only if the server and the remote machine making the request support the identification protocol. Further, information on the remote user is not always available, so you should not rely on it even when it *is* available. If the variable is set, the associated value is a fully expressed name that contains the domain information as well, such as

```
REMOTE_IDENT = william.www.tvp.com
```

## REMOTE_USER

The REMOTE_USER variable is the user name as authenticated by the user, and as such is the only variable you should rely upon to identify a user. As with other types of user authentication, this variable is set only if the server supports user authentication and if the gateway script is protected. If the variable is set, the associated value is the user's identification as sent by the client to the server, such as

```
REMOTE_USER = william
```

## REQUEST_METHOD

The REQUEST_METHOD specifies the method by which the request was made. For HTTP 1.0, the methods could be any of the following:

```
GET
HEAD
POST
```

```
PUT
DELETE
LINK
UNLINK
```

The GET, HEAD, and POST methods are the most commonly used request methods. Both GET and POST are used to submit forms. The HEAD method could be specified as follows:

```
REQUEST_METHOD = HEAD
```

## SCRIPT_NAME

The SCRIPT_NAME variable specifies the virtual path to the script being executed. This is useful if the script generates an HTML document that references the script. If the URL specified in your HTML document is

```
http://tvp.com/cgi-bin/formparse.pl
```

the SCRIPT_NAME variable is set as follows:

```
SCRIPT_NAME = /cgi-bin/formparse.pl
```

## SERVER_NAME

The SERVER_NAME variable identifies the server by its host name, alias, or IP address. This variable is always set and could be specified as follows:

```
SERVER_NAME = tvp.com
```

## SERVER_PORT

The SERVER_PORT variable specifies the port number on which the server received the request. This information can be interpreted from the URL to the script if necessary. However, most servers use the default port of 80 for HTTP requests. If the URL specified in your HTML document is

```
http://www.ncsa.edu:8080/cgi-bin/formparse.pl
```

the SERVER_PORT variable is set as follows:

```
SERVER_PORT = 8080
```

## SERVER_PROTOCOL

The SERVER_PROTOCOL variable identifies the protocol used to send the request. The value assigned to the variable identifies the name and version of the protocol used. The format is *name/version*, such as HTTP/1.0. The variable is set as follows:

```
SERVER_PROTOCOL = HTTP/1.0
```

### SERVER_SOFTWARE

The SERVER_SOFTWARE variable identifies the name and version of the server software. The format for values assigned to the variable is *name/version*, such as CERN/2.17. The variable is set as follows:

```
SERVER_SOFTWARE = CERN/2.17
```

# CGI Standard Input

Most input sent to a Web server is used to set environment variables, yet not all input fits neatly into an environment variable. When a user submits actual data to be processed by a gateway script, this data is received as a URL-encoded search string or via the standard input stream. The server knows how to process actual data by the method used to submit the data.

Sending data as standard input is the most direct way to send data. The server simply tells the gateway script how many 8-bit sets of data to read from standard input. The script opens the standard input stream and reads the specified amount of data. Although long URL-encoded search strings might get truncated, data sent on the standard input stream will not. Consequently, the standard input stream is the preferred way to pass data.

# Clarifying CGI Input

You can identify a submission method when you create your fill-out forms. Under HTTP 1.0, there are two submission methods for forms:

- The HTTP GET method uses URL-encoded search strings. When a server receives a URL-encoded search string, the server assigns the value of the search string to the QUERY_STRING variable.

- The HTTP POST method uses the standard input streams. When a server receives data by the standard input stream, the server assigns the value associated with the length of the input stream to the CONTENT_LENGTH variable.

Let's create a sample Web document containing a form with three key fields: NAME, ADDRESS, and PHONE_NUMBER. Assume the URL to the script is http://www.tvp.com/cgi-bin/survey.pl and the user responds as follows:

```
Sandy Brown
12 Sunny Lane WhoVille, USA
987-654-3210
```

Identical information submitted using the GET and POST methods is treated differently by the server. When the GET method is used, the server sets the following environment variables and then passes the input to the survey.pl script:

```
PATH=/bin:/usr/bin:/usr/etc:/usr/ucb
SERVER_SOFTWARE = CERN/3.0
SERVER_NAME = www.tvp.com
GATEWAY_INTERFACE = CGI/1.1
SERVER_PROTOCOL = HTTP/1.0
SERVER_PORT=80
REQUEST_METHOD = GET
HTTP_ACCEPT = text/plain, text/html, application/rtf, application/postscript,
audio/basic, audio/x-aiff, image/gif, image/jpeg, image/tiff, video/mpeg
PATH_INFO =
PATH_TRANSLATED =
SCRIPT_NAME = /cgi-bin/survey.pl
QUERY_STRING = NAME=Sandy+Brown&ADDRESS=12+Sunny+Lane+WhoVille,+USA
&PHONE_NUMBER=987-654-3210
REMOTE_HOST =
REMOTE_ADDR =
REMOTE_USER =
AUTH_TYPE =
CONTENT_TYPE =
CONTENT_LENGTH =
```

When the POST method is used, the server sets the following environment variables and then passes the input to the survey.pl script:

```
PATH=/bin:/usr/bin:/usr/etc:/usr/ucb
SERVER_SOFTWARE = CERN/3.0
SERVER_NAME = www.tvp.com
GATEWAY_INTERFACE = CGI/1.1
SERVER_PROTOCOL = HTTP/1.0
SERVER_PORT=80
REQUEST_METHOD = POST
HTTP_ACCEPT = text/plain, text/html, application/rtf, application/postscript,
audio/basic, audio/x-aiff, image/gif, image/jpeg, image/tiff, video/mpeg
PATH_INFO =
PATH_TRANSLATED =
SCRIPT_NAME = /cgi-bin/survey.pl
QUERY_STRING =
REMOTE_HOST =
REMOTE_ADDR =
REMOTE_USER =
AUTH_TYPE =
CONTENT_TYPE = application/x-www-form-urlencoded
CONTENT_LENGTH = 81
```

The following POST-submitted data is passed to the gateway script via the standard input stream:

```
NAME=Sandy+Brown&ADDRESS=12+Sunny+Lane+WhoVille,+USA&PHONE_NUMBER=987-654-3210
```

# Output from CGI Scripts

After the script has completed processing the input, the script should return output to the server. The server will then return the output to the client. Generally, this output is in the form of an HTTP response that includes a header followed by a blank line and a body. Although the CGI header output is strictly formatted, the body of the output is formatted in the manner you specify in the header. For example, the body can contain an HTML document for the client to display.

# CGI Headers

CGI headers contain directives to the server. Currently there are three valid server directives:

- Content-type
- Location
- Status

A single header can contain one or all of the server directives. Your CGI script would output these directives to the server. Although the header is followed by a blank line that separates the header from the body, the output does not have to contain a body.

## Content-Types Used in CGI Headers

The Content-Type field in a CGI header identifies the MIME type of the data you are sending back to the client. Usually the data output from a script is a fully formatted document, such as an HTML document. You could specify this in the header as follows:

```
Content-Type: text/html
```

## Locations Used in CGI Headers

The output of your script doesn't have to be a document created within the script. You can reference any document on the Web using the Location field. The Location field references a file by its URL. Servers process location references either directly or indirectly depending on the location of the file. If the server can find the file locally, it passes the file to the client. Otherwise, the server redirects the URL to the client and the client has to retrieve the file. You can specify a location in a script as follows:

```
Location: http://www.tvpress.com/
```

> **NOTE**
>
> Some older browsers don't support automatic redirection. Consequently, you might want to consider adding an HTML-formatted message body to the output. This message body will be displayed only if a browser cannot use the location URL.

## Status Used in CGI Headers

The Status field passes a status line to the server for forwarding to the client. Status codes are expressed as a three-digit code followed by a string that generally explains what has occurred. The first digit of a status code shows the general status as follows:

1XX    Not yet allocated

2XX    Success

3XX    Redirection

4XX    Client error

5XX    Server error

Although many status codes are used by servers, the status codes you pass to a client via your CGI script are usually client error codes. For example, let's say the script could not find a file, and you have specified that in such cases, instead of returning nothing, it should output an error code. Here is a list of the client error codes you might want to use:

`Status: 401 Unauthorized Authentication has failed`. User is not allowed to access the file and should try again.

`Status: 403 Forbidden`. The request is not acceptable. User is not permitted to access file.

`Status: 404 Not found`. The specified resource could not be found.

`Status: 405 Method not allowed`. The submission method used is not allowed.

# Clarifying CGI Output

Creating the output from a CGI script is easier than it might seem. All you have to do is format the output into a header and body using your favorite programming language. This section contains two examples. The first example is in the Perl programming language. The second example is in the UNIX Bourne shell.

If you wanted the script to output a simple HTML document using Perl, here is how you could do it:

```
#!/usr/bin/perl
#Create header with extra line space
print "Content-Type: text/html\n\n";
#Add body in HTML format
print <<"MAIN";
<HTML><HEAD><TITLE>Output from Script</TITLE></HEAD>
<BODY>
<H1>Top 10 Reasons for Using CGI</H1>
<P>10. Customer feedback.</P>
<P>9. Obtaining questionnaire and survey responses.</P>
<P>8. Tracking visitor count.</P>
<P>7. Automating searches.</P>
<P>6. Creating easy database interfaces.</P>
<P>5. Building gateways to other protocols.</P>
<P>4. HTML 2.0 Image maps.</P>
<P>3. User Authentication.</P>
<P>2. On-line order processing.</P>
<P>1. Generating documents on the fly.</P>
</BODY>
MAIN
```

If you wanted the script to output a simple HTML document in Bourne shell, here's how you could do it:

```
#!/bin/sh
#Create header with extra line space
echo "Content-Type: text/html"
#Add body in HTML format
cat << MAIN
<HTML><HEAD><TITLE>Output from Script</TITLE></HEAD>
<BODY>
<H1>Top 10 Reasons for Using CGI</H1>
<P>10. Customer feedback.</P>
<P>9. Obtaining questionnaire and survey responses.</P>
<P>8. Tracking visitor count.</P>
<P>7. Automating searches.</P>
<P>6. Creating easy database interfaces.</P>
<P>5. Building gateways to other protocols.</P>
<P>4. HTML 2.0 Image maps.</P>
<P>3. User Authentication.</P>
<P>2. On-line order processing.</P>
<P>1. Generating documents on the fly.</P>
</BODY>
MAIN
```

The server processing the output sets environment variables, creates an HTTP header, and then sends the data on to the client. Here is how the HTTP header might look coming from a CERN Web server:

```
HTTP/1.0 302 Found
MIME-Version: 1.0
Server: CERN/3.0
Date: Monday, 4-Mar-96 23:59:59 HST
Content-Type: text/html
Content-Length: 485

<HTML><HEAD><TITLE>Output from Script</TITLE></HEAD>
<BODY>
<H1>Top 10 Reasons for Using CGI</H1>
<P>10. Customer feedback.</P>
<P>9. Obtaining questionnaire and survey responses.</P>
<P>8. Tracking visitor count.</P>
<P>7. Automating searches.</P>
<P>6. Creating easy database interfaces.</P>
<P>5. Building gateways to other protocols.</P>
<P>4. HTML 2.0 Image maps.</P>
<P>3. User Authentication.</P>
<P>2. On-line order processing.</P>
<P>1. Generating documents on the fly.</P>
</BODY>
```

# Summary

The common gateway interface opens the door for adding advanced features to your Web publications. This workhorse running quietly in the background enables fill-out forms, database queries, index searches, and creation of documents on the fly. FrontPage allows you to easily add WebBots to pages that use forms. However, WebBots generally do not perform any post-submission processing. With CGI scripts, you can process input from forms automatically and generate output directly to the reader based on the results of the processing.

Although CGI enhancement is a click of the mouse button away for most readers, CGI enhancement means extra work for Web publishers. Still, the exponential payoff associated with CGI enhancing your Web publications makes the extra effort truly worthwhile.

# Search Engines and Indexed Databases

# 31

*by Willam Robert Stanek*

**IN THIS CHAPTER**

The hypertext facilities of the World Wide Web put the world's most powerful search engines at your fingertips. Search engines are the gateways to the vast storehouses and databases available on the Web. Thousands of Web search engines are used every day, and if you've browsed the Web, you know that online searches are easy to perform. You simply enter keywords and press Enter, and the search engine takes over.

A *search engine* is an application specifically designed and optimized for searching databases. Search engines can race through megabytes of information in nanoseconds. They achieve this terrific speed and efficiency thanks to an application called an *indexer*. An indexer is an application specifically designed and optimized for indexing files. Using the index built by the indexer, the search engine can jump almost immediately to sections of the database containing the information you are looking for. Thus, creating an indexed database of documents at your Web site requires two applications: a search engine and an indexer. The search engine and indexer are normally a part of a larger application, such as a Wide Area Information Server (WAIS).

The trick to creating Web documents that provide access to a search engine lies in knowing how to integrate the capabilities of the search engine using the existing structure of hypertext and CGI. This chapter unlocks the mysteries of search engines and indexed databases.

# When To Use a Search Engine or Indexed Database

As you learned in Chapter 20, "Automation with FrontPage's WebBots," FrontPage includes a powerful search engine in the form of a WebBot. This WebBot, called the Search bot, provides a full text-searching capability for your Web site. When the user submits a form containing search words, the Search bot returns a list of all pages in the current Web that contain matches for the search words.

Although the Search bot is a great search engine, there are two specific reasons that you might have to (or want to) use a different type of search engine:

■ You cannot use FrontPage Server Extensions with your current Web server software or do not plan to install the server extensions for your server.

■ You have advanced or unique needs for which the Search bot is not well-suited.

In the first case, you will probably know immediately that you cannot use the Search bot. However, before you decide against the Search bot, obtain the most current list of servers supported by FrontPage extensions. You might be pleasantly surprised when you discover that extensions are available for your server and you only have to download and install them. You can find this list of available server extensions in the FrontPage area of Microsoft's Web site:

```
http://www.microsoft.com/frontpage/
```

In the second case, you might have a more difficult time determining when the Search bot will not meet your needs. Full-text searches are powerful, and the results are displayed quickly using the Search bot. In most cases, the Search bot is exactly what you need at your Web site. However, if your needs are advanced or unique, the Search bot will not meet your needs. For example, if you want to display the search results in a customized format that includes a list of keywords used in the matching pages, you would not want to use the Search bot.

To better understand when not to use the Search bot, let's reexamine the properties you can associate with this search engine. Figure 31.1 shows the Search Bot Properties dialog box.

**FIGURE 31.1.**

*Search bot properties.*

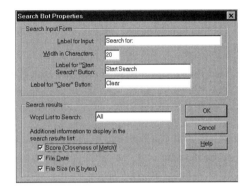

The Search Input Form area defines the way the search form looks in your Web page. The form is very simple with a label for the input box, a one-line text box that accepts input, and two labeled buttons.

The Search Results area defines the ways you can manipulate the results of a search. Results are displayed based on matches for the search words and ranked by score, file date, and file size.

These property settings put limits on the way you can use the Search bot and the way the Search bot displays results. Any time your search needs are outside what the Search bot provides, you will want to consider using another search engine and indexing method.

At this point, you've probably decided whether or not you will use the Search bot. If you've decided to use the Search bot, great! Still, I recommend reading the rest of this chapter to give you a firm understanding of search engines and indexers. This chapter examines many of the search engine and indexing options currently available. The chapter also explains in great detail how search engines and indexers work.

# What Are Indexers and How Are They Used?

The index for *Microsoft FrontPage Unleashed* is an invaluable resource for quickly finding information in this book. Using the index, you can quickly find the topic or subtopic you want to learn more about. You do this by following an alphabetical listing of keywords selected by the human indexer who combed the manuscript in search of the gems you would be interested in.

The indexer used the text of the entire book to create an alphabetical list of keywords and related concepts. The alphabetical listing is broken down into categories and subcategories. The first categories are broad and divided based on the letters *A* to *Z*. Next, the broad categories are subdivided based on keywords. The keyword categories are sometimes further divided based on related concepts. For quick reference, a page number is associated with keywords and their related concepts. You've probably noticed that articles such as *a, an*, and *the*, and prepositions such as *in, with*, and *to*, are never listed in the index. This is because the indexer has a list of hundreds of common words that should be excluded from the index because they occur too often to be helpful.

A computer-coded indexer builds an index in much the same way. The indexer application uses a list of common words to figure out which words to exclude from the index, searches through the list of documents you specified, and finally, builds an index containing the relevant associations between the remaining words within all the specified documents. Because most indexers build a full-text index based on your documents, the index is often larger than the original files. For example, if your Web site has 15MB of data in 125 documents, the indexer would create an index slightly larger than 15MB.

Most indexers enable you to add to or subtract from the list of common words. Often you can do this simply by editing an appropriate file or by creating a *stop word* file. A stop word file contains an alphabetized list of words that the indexer should ignore. Most indexers have a predefined stop word file, but you can override it to use a list of stop words that you create yourself instead.

Another type of word list used by indexers is the *synonym list*. Synonym lists make it easier for readers to find what they need on your Web site without knowing the exact word to use in the search. Each line of a synonym file contains words that can be used interchangeably. A search for any word in the list will be matched to other words in the same line. Instead of getting no results from the search, the reader will get a list of results that match related words.

Let's say a reader wants to learn how forms are processed on the server but doesn't know the right keyword to use to get a relative response. This line from a synonym file could be used to help the reader find what she is looking for:

```
cgi cgi-bin script gateway interface programming
```

Before you use a synonym list, you should think carefully about the words you will use in the list. Synonym lists are used by the indexer program to create an index. Any modifications of the lists will not be used until the database is reindexed. This means any time you change the synonym list you will have to reindex your Web site.

# What Are Search Engines and How Are They Used?

Hundreds of search engines are used in commercial and proprietary applications. Usually search engines are part of a larger application, such as a database management system.

When Web publishers looked for indexing and searching solutions, they looked at the search engines available and found that most of them were not well-suited for use on the World Wide Web. Primarily this was because these search engines weren't designed to be used on distributed networks.

One solution Web publishers did find is the *Wide Area Information Server*, or *WAIS*. WAIS is a database retrieval system that searches indexed databases. The databases can contain any type of file, including text, sound, graphics, and even video. The WAIS interface is easy to use and you can perform a search on any topic simply by entering a keyword and pressing Enter. When you press the Enter key, the WAIS search engine takes over. You can find both commercial and freeware versions of WAIS.

WAIS was developed as a joint project whose founders include Apple Computer, Dow Jones, Thinking Machines, and the Peat Marwick group. In the early days of WAIS, Thinking Machines maintained a free version of WAIS suitably titled freeWAIS. This version of WAIS enjoys the widest usage. freeWAIS is now maintained by the Clearinghouse for Networked Information Discovery and Retrieval. CNIDR started handling freeWAIS when the founders of WAIS turned to commercial ventures such as WAIS, Inc.

Today, CNIDR is the primary developer of WAIS technology. CNIDR's goal is to develop new software for use in networked information discovery and retrieval. Recent developments at CNIDR include an integrated software package called Isite that includes an indexer, search engine, and communication tools to access databases.

You can find more information on CNIDR and download the latest version of freeWAIS at

```
http://cnidr.org/
```

# Using a Search Engine

The largest database on the Web, the Lycos Catalog of the Internet, enables you to perform searches precisely as described earlier in the chapter. Lycos indexes over 90 percent of Internet sites using a powerful indexer called a Web crawler. The Web crawler uses URLs at Web sites to find new information, and thus can index every page at a Web site and even find new Web sites. Lycos combines the Web crawler with a powerful search engine. Using the search engine, Web users can find the information they are looking for in a matter of seconds.

---

**NOTE**

A Web *crawler* is a generalized term for an indexer that searches and catalogs sites using the links in hypertext documents. By using the links, the indexer crawls through a document and all its related documents one link at a time.

---

The Lycos search engine is characteristic of the dozens of search engines you will find on the Web that use WAIS or are modeled after WAIS. You can enter a query at Lycos using the simple one-box form shown in Figure 31.2. By default the Lycos search engine finds all documents matching any keyword you type in the query box. Because the exclusion list for Lycos contains articles, prepositions, and other nonuseful words for searching, you can enter a query just as a complete sentence, such as

```
What is WAIS?
Where is WAIS?
How do I use WAIS?
```

**FIGURE 31.2.**

*The Lycos search engine.*

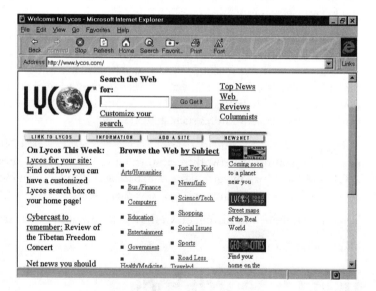

You can enter as many keywords as you want on the query line. Because the search is not case-sensitive, the keywords do not have to be capitalized as shown. If you type in two keywords that are not on the exclusion list, the search engine assumes that you want to search on both words. Therefore, if you entered

```
WAIS Web
```

the search engine would search its index for all documents containing either WAIS or Web. Although you could specify the "or" explicitly in a search, such as WAIS OR Web, you generally do not have to. Again, this is because the OR is assumed whenever you do not specify otherwise. To search the index only for documents containing both WAIS and Web, you could use the following:

```
WAIS AND Web
```

Here, the AND tells the search engine you are only interested in documents containing the words WAIS and Web. You can combine the basic functions of logical OR and logical AND in many ways. Because you will often be searching for material on a specific subject, you can use multiple keywords related to the subject to help you get better results on your searches. For example, if you are looking for publishers on the Web, you might try the following keywords:

```
book
fiction
magazine
nonfiction
publisher
publishing
```

Often your main topic will reveal dozens or hundreds of relevant sites. As Figure 31.3 shows, a single search on the keyword "WAIS" at Lycos returned over 26,000 matches. The Lycos search engine returns a summary of each document matching the search. The summary is in the form of an abstract for small documents and a combined outline and abstract for long documents. However, most search engines return a two-line summary of the related document that includes the size, type, and title of the document.

**FIGURE 31.3.**

*The results of a Lycos search.*

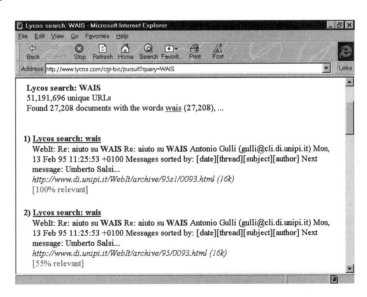

Documents matching your search are weighted with what should be the most relevant documents displayed first and what should be the least relevant documents displayed last. These scores are usually on a 0.0 to 1.0 scale or a 0 to 1,000 scale. The most relevant documents have a high score, with the highest score being 1.0 or 1,000. The criteria used to figure out relevancy aren't the greatest, but they do work most of the time. These criteria are

- Number of words that match the search string
- The proximity of the words to each other in the document

The overall scores based on these two criteria are used to present the matching documents in order from most relevant to least relevant. Although this method of ranking by relevance is used widely, you can see how it could mislead Web users. This is the primary reason that other descriptive features, such as a title and summary, are provided with the search results.

# Accessing a WAIS Database

Originally, you could only access a WAIS database using a WAIS client. WAIS clients have built-in functions and are used much like other clients. Yet few people want to download a new type of client onto their system and learn how to use it, especially when the client can be used only for the specific purpose of searching a database. If you've ever used a WAIS client, you know they aren't the friendliest clients on the block. This is why Web users prefer to use their browsers, which provide a simple interface to just about every resource on the Internet.

Currently, most Web users access WAIS databases using a simple fill-out form, such as the one shown in Figure 31.2. When a user enters data into the form, the data is passed to the server and directed to a gateway script designed for search and retrieval. The script does five things:

1. Processes the input
2. Passes the input to the search engine
3. Receives the results from the search engine
4. Processes the results
5. Passes the output to the client

As you can see, the gateway script creates the interface between the client browser and WAIS. Creating a gateway script to interface with WAIS is not an extremely complex process. Although you could create such a script using fewer than 100 lines of Perl code, there are dozens of ready-made WAIS gateways already available. Some of these WAIS gateways are simple and involve efficient Perl scripts packed into a few kilobytes of file space. Other WAIS gateways are part of all-in-one software packages that contain an indexer and search engines as part of a WAIS server and a gateway script to create the Web to WAIS interface. The sections that follow discuss five freeware options for WAIS gateways.

# Basic WAIS Gateways

Three ready-made solutions for processing the information from WAIS searches are

```
wais.pl
son-of-wais.pl
kidofwais.pl
```

## wais.pl

The very first WAIS gateway, a Perl script called `wais.pl`, is a quick-and-dirty solution for accessing WAIS. The `wais.pl` script was created by Tony Sanders and is included with the NCSA Web server software. You can obtain `wais.pl` from NCSA's FTP server at

```
ftp://ftp.ncsa.uiuc.edu/Web/httpd/Unix/ncsa_httpd/cgi/wais.tar.Z
```

## son-of-wais.pl

Although you'll find that `wais.pl` is used widely on the Web, it is slowly being replaced by its offspring: `son-of-wais.pl` and `kidofwais.pl`. The `son-of-wais.pl` script is the second evolution of `wais.pl`. This Perl script created by Eric Morgan beats its generic parent hands down because it is more advanced than the original and more robust. You can obtain `son-of-wais.pl` from NCSU at

```
http://dewey.lib.ncsu.edu/staff/morgan/son-of-wais.html.
```

## kidofwais.pl

The third evolution of `wais.pl` is a script called `kidofwais.pl`. This script, created by Michael Grady, is a somewhat advanced WAIS gateway programmed entirely in Perl. The features of `kidofwais.pl` include debugging, multiple formatting options, table titles, and more. You can obtain `kidofwais.pl` from UIUC at

```
http://www.cso.uiuc.edu/grady.html.
```

The results of a search on the word "computer" using the `kidofwais.pl` script are shown in Figure 31.4. Many Web publishers prefer the clean output of `kidofwais.pl`. As you can see, matches are generally displayed on a single line of a bulleted list. Each item on the list is displayed in ranked relevance order with the scores omitted. The title, size, and type of matching documents form the basis of each list item.

**FIGURE 31.4.**

*Search results using the* kidofwais.pl *script.*

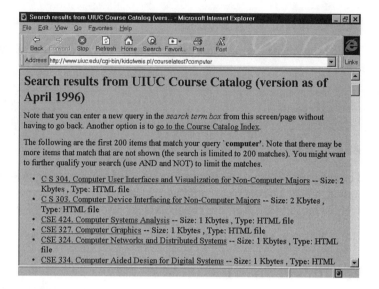

## Advanced WAIS Gateways

Two advanced and powerful solutions for your WAIS needs are

SFgate

wwwwais.c

## SFgate

Created by Miao-Jane Lin and Ulrich Pfeifer, SFgate is one of the most advanced freeware WAIS gateways. Unlike other gateways discussed so far, SFgate uses a group of shell scripts to create a smooth and feature-rich interface to your WAIS server. This WAIS gateway is several orders of magnitude larger than other WAIS gateways and uses more than 500KB of disk space. In the days of 2GB hard drives, 500KB of disk space is negligible, but when you compare this to the kidofwais.pl script that is only 24KB in size, you can easily see that SFgate is certainly a more involved gateway. Fortunately, the SFgate distribution includes an installation routine and good documentation.

SFgate provides you with advanced control over the search options. Not only can you search on a keyword, but you can also tell SFgate the specific areas of the indexed database to search. You can search by document type, title, author, date, and contents. You can also tell SFgate precisely how to format the search results. Increased flexibility in the search parameters and output style produces more meaningful results. You can learn more about SFgate and download the latest version at

http://ls6-www.informatik.uni-dortmund.de/SFgate/SFgate.html

## `wwwwais.c`

The `wwwwais.c` gateway is proof positive that you can pack a lot of power into a small C script. Created by Kevin Hughes of EIT and packed into 54KB of C code, `wwwwais.c` is arguably the most powerful freeware WAIS gateway. EIT uses the `wwwwais.c` gateway to search the databases at its Web site. Figure 31.5 shows the results from a `wwwwais.c` search using EIT's `wwwwais.c` gateway.

As you can see, the output from `wwwwais.c` is similar to other WAIS gateways discussed previously. Matches are generally displayed in a numbered list. Each item on the list is displayed in ranked relevance order. The title, size, type, and ranked score of the matching documents form the basis of each list item. You can download the latest version of this WAIS gateway at

```
http://www.eit.com/software/wwwwais/
```

**FIGURE 31.5.**

*Using* `wwwwais.c`.

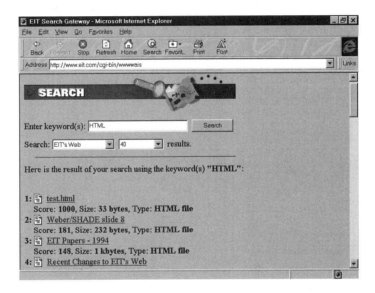

# How WAIS Gateways Work

The best way to see how a WAIS gateway really works is to examine the actual code for a script. Ideally, the script should be slightly advanced, but not too advanced so that its interworkings cannot be easily studied. Because the `son-of-wais` script is slightly advanced and does not have much clutter and housekeeping, you should study the code for `son-of-wais.pl` shown in Listing 31.1.

If you go through the code line by line, you will see that the first part of the script begins with an overview of changes Eric Morgan made to `wais.pl`. This section also contains contact information. Because documentation makes it easier to use and maintain a script, good programmers always add documentation to a script.

After the overview, the code assigns configuration variables. Because these variables will be unique to your Web server, you will need to update them accordingly. Follow the inline documentation to update the paths to where your data is stored on the server, and be sure to update the contact and title information. One variable that you should pay particular attention to is the one that sets the location of the search engine to be used to perform the search. In the script, the variable is $waisq. Using waisq and waissearch to access WAIS databases is discussed later in this chapter.

The next section creates the output to waisq. The brevity of this section of the code surprises most beginning Web programmers. Yet, keep in mind that waisq is the actual script performing the search against your WAIS database.

The final section of the script creates the output. Although the actual code for the search fills only a handful of lines, massaging the output and creating the textual portion of the output fills dozens of lines. You can modify the output message to suit your needs. However, the output page should contain the general information provided in the script, which ensures that the readers know how to use the index if they've had problems. If you follow the script, you can see that brief summaries for documents matching the search are displayed according to their relevance. Ranked relevance is described by scores associated with the documents.

Listing 31.1 shows the code for the son-of-wais.pl script.

## Listing 31.1. The `son-of-wais.pl` script.

```perl
#!/usr/bin/perl
#
# wais.pl — WAIS search interface
#
# $Id$
#
# Tony Sanders <sanders@bsdi.com>, Nov 1993
#
# Example configuration (in local.conf):
#     map topdir wais.pl &do_wais($top, $path, $query, "database", "title")
#
# Modified to present the user "human-readable" titles, better instructions as
# well as the ability to do repeated searches after receiving results.
#
# by Eric Lease Morgan, NCSU Libraries, April 1994
# eric_morgan@ncsu.edu
# http://www.lib.ncsu.edu/staff/morgan/morgan.html
# To read more about this script try:
# http://www.lib.ncsu.edu/staff/morgan/son-of-wais.html
#
# where is your waiq binary?
$waisq = "/usr/users/temp/wais/freeWAIS-0.202/bin/waisq";

# where are your source files?
$waisd = "/usr/users/temp/gopher/data/.wais";

# what database do you want to search?
```

```
$src = "ncsu-libraries-www";

# what is the opening title you want to present to users?
$openingTitle = "Search the NCSU Libraries Webbed Information System";

# after searching, what to you want the title to be?
$closingTitle = "Search results of the NCSU Libraries Information System";

# specify the path to add
# this is the same path your subtracted when you waisindexed
$toAdd = "/usr/users/temp/www/httpd/data/";

# specify the leader to subtract
# again, this is the same string you added when you waisindexed
$toSubtract = "http://www.lib.ncsu.edu/";

# who maintains this service?
$maintainer = "<A HREF=http://www.lib.ncsu.edu/staff/morgan/morgan.html>
Eric Lease Morgan</A> (eric_morgan@ncsu.edu)";

# and when was it last modified?
$modified = "April 15, 1994";

# you shouldn't have to edit anything below this line,
except if you want to change the help text

sub extractTitle {
  # get the string
  $theFile = $headline;

  # parse out the file name
  $theFile =~ s/^.*$toSubtract//i;

  # Concatenate the "toAdd" variable with the file name
  $theFile = $toAdd.$theFile;

  # open the file
  open( DATA, $theFile) ¦¦ die "Can't open $theFile\n";

  # read the file and extract the title
  $linenum = 1;
  $foundtitle = 0;
  $humanTitle = "(No title found in document!) Call $maintainer.";
  while ( $line = <DATA>) {
    last if ($linenum > 5);
    $linenum++;
    if ($line =~ s/^.*<title>//i ) {
      chop( $line);
      $line =~ s!</title>.*$!!i;
      $humanTitle = $line;
      $humanTitle =~ s/^\s*//;
      $humanTitle =~ s/\s*$//;
      $foundtitle = 1;
      last;
    }
  }

  # close the file
```

*continues*

## Listing 31.1. continued

```perl
    close (DATA);

    # return the final results
    return $humanTitle;
    }

sub send_index {
    print "Content-type: text/html\n\n";

    print "<HEAD>\n<TITLE>$openingTitle</TITLE>\n<ISINDEX></HEAD>\n";
    print "<BODY>\n<H2>", $openingTitle, "</H2>\n";

    print "<p>";
    print "This is an index of the information on this server. ";
    print "To use this function, simply enter a query.<P>";
print "Since this is a WAIS index, you can enter complex queries.
    For example:<P>";
    print "<DT><b>Right-hand truncation</b> (stemming) queries";
    print "<DD>The query 'astro*' will find documents containing the words";
    print " 'astronomy' as well as 'astrophysics'.<P>";
    print "<DT>Boolean '<b>And</b>' queries";
print "<DD>The query 'red and blue' will find the <B>intersection</b> of
    all";
    print " the documents containing the words 'red', and 'blue'.";
    print "The use of 'and' limits your retrieval.<p>";
    print "<DT>Boolean '<b>Or</b>' queries";
    print "<DD>The query 'red or blue' will find the <B>union</b> of all the";
    print " documents containing the words 'red' and 'blue'.";
    print "The use of 'or' increases your retrieval.<p>";
    print "<DT>Boolean '<b>Not</b>' queries";
print "<DD>The query 'red not green' will find the all the documents
    containing";
print " the word 'red', and <b>excluding</b> the documents containing the
    word 'green'.";
    print "The use of 'not' limits your retrieval.<p>";
    print "<DT><b>Nested</b> Boolean queries";
print "<DD>The query '(red and green) or blue not pink' will find the
    union of all";
print " the documents containing the words 'red', and 'green'. It will
    then add (union)";
print " all documents containing the word 'blue'. Finally, it will exclude all
    documents";
    print " containing the word 'pink'";
    print "<HR>";
    print "This page is maintained by $maintainer, and it was last modified on
    $modified.<p>";
}

sub do_wais {
#    local($top, $path, $query, $src, $title) = @_;

    do { &'send_index; return; } unless defined @ARGV;
    local(@query) = @ARGV;
    local($pquery) = join(" ", @query);

    print "Content-type: text/html\n\n";
```

```
    open(WAISQ, "-¦") ¦¦ exec ($waisq, "-c", $waisd,
                                    "-f", "-", "-S", "$src.src", "-g", @query);

    print "<HEAD>\n<TITLE>$closingTitle</TITLE>\n<ISINDEX></HEAD>\n";
    print "<BODY>\n<H2>", $closingTitle, "</H2>\n";

    print "Index \`$src\' contains the following\n";
    print "items relevant to \`$pquery\':<P>\n";
    print "<DL>\n";

    local($hits, $score, $headline, $lines, $bytes, $type, $date);
    while (<WAISQ>) {
        /:score\s+(\d+)/ && ($score = $1);
        /:number-of-lines\s+(\d+)/ && ($lines = $1);
        /:number-of-bytes\s+(\d+)/ && ($bytes = $1);
        /:type "(.*)"/ && ($type = $1);
        /:headline "(.*)"/ && ($headline = $1);            # XXX
        /:date "(\d+)"/ && ($date = $1, $hits++, &docdone);
    }
    close(WAISQ);
    print "</DL>\n";
    print "<HR>";
    print "This page is maintained by $maintainer.<P>";

    if ($hits == 0) {
        print "Nothing found.\n";
    }
    print "</BODY>\n";
}

sub docdone {
    if ($headline =~ /Search produced no result/) {
        print "<HR>";
        print $headline, "<P>\n<PRE>";
# the following was &'safeopen
        open(WAISCAT, "$waisd/$src.cat") ¦¦ die "$src.cat: $!";
        while (<WAISCAT>) {
            s#(Catalog for database:)\s+.*#$1 <A HREF="/$top/$src.src">
            [ccc]$src.src</A>#;
            s#Headline:\s+(.*)#Headline: <A HREF="$1">$1</A>#;
            print;
        }
        close(WAISCAT);
        print "\n</PRE>\n";
    } else {
        $title = &extractTitle ($headline);
        print "<DT><A HREF=\"$headline\">$humanTitle</A>\n";
        print "<DD>Score: $score, Lines: $lines, Bytes: $bytes\n";
    }
    $score = $headline = $lines = $bytes = $type = $date = '';
}

eval '&do_wais';
```

# How To Create an HTML Document for a WAIS Gateway

Creating an HTML document for your WAIS gateway is easy. All you have to do is create a document with a fill-out form that sends the proper values to your WAIS gateway of choice. Depending on the WAIS gateway you choose, this can be a simple one-line form for entering keywords or a complex multiple-line form for entering keywords as well as search and retrieval options. This form would look much like the form used for the Search bot, but it doesn't need the submit and reset buttons. The `wwwwais.c` script passes the value of the user's input to the WAIS search engine you have installed on your system.

> **TIP**
>
> If a form has only one input field, the submit and reset buttons are not necessary. When the user presses return, the form will be automatically submitted.

Forms designed for use with the `SFgate` script can be as simple or complex as you make them. This is because `SFgate` gives you advanced control over how searches are performed and the way results are formatted. Figure 31.6 shows the search section of an advanced form designed to be used with `SFgate`. Figure 31.7 shows how users could be allowed to alter your default search and debug parameters.

**FIGURE 31.6.**

*An advanced form for use with* SFgate.

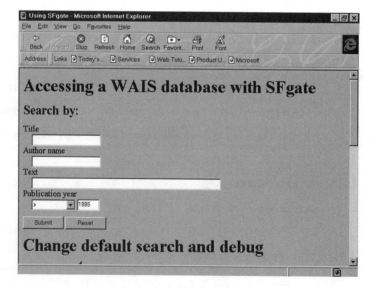

**FIGURE 31.7.**

*Setting additional search and debug parameters.*

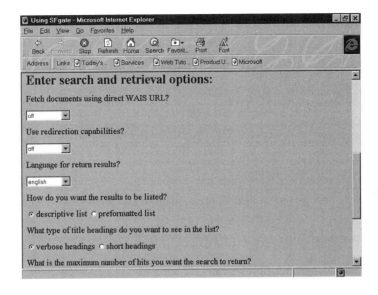

The form used with the `SFgate` script has many fields. You can assign the `NAME` field to key values that have special meaning to `SFgate`. The primary search and retrieval parameters are `ti`, `au`, `text`, and `py`. The title parameter `ti` enables keyword searches of titles. The author parameter `au` enables keyword searches of the authors of documents indexed in the database. The text parameter `text` enables keyword searches of the full text of documents indexed in the database. The publication year parameter `py` is used to search based on the date the indexed documents were published.

The `database` variable defines the name of the WAIS database you want to search. Here, this variable is assigned to a hidden input field; in this way, you could use `SFgate` to search different databases at your Web site. You could even let the user search different databases at your Web site using the same form, by changing the input field for the database from a hidden field to one the user can manipulate.

Most of the additional search variables are set to default values automatically and do not have to be specified. Specifying parameters for these variables enables you to provide additional controls to users. The debug parameters are used for testing and troubleshooting problems and are not normally included in your final search form.

# Installing a WAIS Gateway

Installing a WAIS gateway might not be as easy as you think. This section looks at installing basic and advanced WAIS gateways.

## Configuring Basic WAIS Gateways

Installing one of the basic WAIS gateways—`wais.pl`, `son-of-wais.pl`, and `kidofwais.pl`—is easy. You simply obtain the script, move it to an appropriate directory, such as `cgi-bin`, and modify the configuration parameters in the beginning of the script. The easiest gateway to configure is `wais.pl`. Configuring `wais.pl` involves modifying four lines of code at the beginning of the script:

1. Set the path to the search engine, which is normally `waisq` if you've installed the freeWAIS server:

   ```
   $waisq = "/usr/local/bin/wais/waisq";
   ```

2. Specify the location of the directory containing your WAIS databases:

   ```
   $waisd = "/usr/local/wais.db/";
   ```

3. Specify the actual indexed database for the search:

   ```
   $src = "sitedb.src"
   ```

4. Specify the title for the HTML document used to display the results:

   ```
   $title = "Search Results"
   ```

If all WAIS gateways were as easy to configure as `wais.pl`, Web publishers would have no problems creating an interface to WAIS. Although configuring `son-of-wais.pl` and `kidofwais.pl` is slightly more difficult, the scripts have good step-by-step documentation.

## Configuring Advanced WAIS Gateways

Advanced WAIS gateways present more problems to Web publishers because there are more options and variables involved. This section looks at configuring an advanced WAIS gateway called `wwwais.c`.

To install EIT's `wwwais.c`, you have to make a minor modification to the source code, compile the source code, move the compiled script to an appropriate directory, and update the configuration file.

### Preparing the `wwwais.c` Script

Because the `wwwais.c` gateway uses a separate configuration file, you can install the configuration file wherever you would like. For this reason, you must specify the path to the configuration file in the source code. This minor modification is easy to make. You simply edit the source code using your favorite editor. To ensure the configuration file is easy to find if you need to update it later, you might want to place the file in the same directory as the configuration file for your Web server, such as

```
/usr/local/httpd/conf/wwwais.conf
```

> **NOTE**
>
> Because you specify the full path to the configuration file in the source code, you can name the file anything you want. In the previous example, the configuration file is called wwwwais.conf.

After you've modified the source code, you can compile it using your favorite C compiler, such as gcc. The wwwwais.c script should compile without errors. After the program is compiled, you can move it to an appropriate directory on your Web server. Usually this directory is your server's cgi-bin directory. After moving the script, make sure the script is executable.

## Updating the wwwwais.c Configuration File

The wwwwais.c configuration file enables you to set many useful parameters for searching indexed databases and displaying the results. The configuration file contains parameters that can be passed to wwwwais.c. Variables are specified by variable name and associated value. The space between the variable name and value is necessary.

Listing 31.2 is an example of a wwwwais configuration file.

### Listing 31.2. Sample wwwwais configuration file.

```
# WWWWAIS configuration file

# If PageTitle is a string, it will be a title only.
# If PageTitle specifies an HTML file, this file will be prepended to
# wwwwais results.
PageTitle "waistitle.html"

# The self-referencing URL for wwwwais.
SelfURL "http://www.tvpress.com/cgi-bin/wwwwais"

# The maximum number of results to return.
MaxHits 40

# How results are sorted. This can be "score", "lines", "bytes",
# "title", or "type".
SortType score

# AddrMask is used to specify the IP addresses of sites authorized access
# to your database
# Only addresses specified here will be allowed to use the gateway.
# These rules apply:
# 1) You can use asterisks in specifying the string, at either
#    ends of the string:
#    "192.100.*", "*100*", "*2.100.2"
# 2) You can make lists of masks:
#    "*192.58.2,*.2", "*.100,*171.128*", ".58.2,*100"
# 3) A mask without asterisks will match EXACTLY:
```

*continues*

## Listing 31.2. continued

```
#      "192.100.58.2"
# 4) Define as "all" to allow all sites.
AddrMask all

# The full path to your waisq program.
WaisqBin /usr/local/bin/waisq
# The full path to your waissearch program.
WaissearchBin /usr/local/bin/waissearch
# The full path to your SWISH program.
SwishBin /usr/local/bin/swish

# WAIS source file descriptions.
# These represent the path to the indexed databases
# For SWISH sources:
#      SwishSource full_path_to_source/source.swish "description"
SwishSource /usr/local/httpd/wais/index/index.swish "Search our Web"
SourceRules replace "/usr/local/www/" "http://www.tvpress.com/"
# For waisq sources:
#      WaisSource full_path_to_source/source.src "description"
WaisSource /usr/local/httpd/wais/index/index.src "Search our Web"
SourceRules replace "/usr/local/www/" "http://www.tvpress.com/"
WaisSource /usr/local/httpd/wais/index/index.src "Search our Web"
SourceRules replace "/usr/local/www/" "/"
SourceRules prepend "http://www.tvpress.com/cgi-bin/print_hit_bold.pl"
SourceRules append "?$KEYWORDS#first_hit"
# For waissearch sources:
#      WaisSource host.name port source "description"
WaisSource quake.think.com 210 directory-of-servers "WAIS directory of servers"

# Do you want to use icons?
UseIcons yes

# Where are your icons kept?
IconUrl http://www.tvpress.com/software/wwwwais/icons

# Determining file type based on suffix.
# Suffix matching is not case sensitive is entered in the form:
#      TypeDef .suffix "description" file://url.to.icon.for.this.type/ MIME-type
# You can use $ICONURL in the icon URL to substitute the root icon directory.
# You can define new documents types and their associated icons here
TypeDef .html "HTML file" $ICONURL/text.xbm text/html
TypeDef .txt "text file" $ICONURL/text.xbm text/plain
TypeDef .ps "PostScript file" $ICONURL/image.xbm application/postscript
TypeDef .gif "GIF image" $ICONURL/image.xbm image/gif
TypeDef .src "WAIS index" $ICONURL/index.xbm text/plain
TypeDef .?? "unknown" $ICONURL/unknown.xbm text/plain
```

When you update the configuration file for use on your system, you will want to look closely at every line of the file containing a parameter assignment. Because you will need to change almost every parameter assignment, you should be wary of any assignments that you do *not* change. The most important updates to the configuration file involve specifying the proper paths to essential files on the system. Here's how you should assign these essential values:

| SelfURL | The URL path to wwwwais.c. |
|---|---|
| WaisqBin | The full path to your waisq program. |
| WaissearchBin | The full path to your waissearch program. |
| SwishBin | The full path to your SWISH program. SWISH is similar to wwwwais.c and will be discussed later in the chapter. |
| SwishSource | The location of local databases indexed with SWISH and a brief description. If there are multiple SwishSource lines, the user will be prompted to specify the database to search. |
| WaisSource | Local WAIS databases will be accessed with waisq, and remote WAIS databases will be accessed with waissearch. For local WAIS databases, you must specify the location of the database and a brief description. All local database names should include the .src extension. For remote WAIS databases, you must specify a host name, port, database name, and description. All remote database names should *not* include the .src extension. |
| SourceRules | The action to take on the results. Valid actions are |

| | append | Add information after the results. |
|---|---|---|
| | prepend | Add information before the results. |
| | replace | Replace the local path with a URL path so Web users can access the documents. |

| TypeDef | The MIME type definition. Allows the script to match filename extensions to MIME types. Any MIME types not configured are assigned to the type unknown. |
|---|---|

## Passing Additional Parameters to wwwwais.c

You can pass additional parameters to wwwwais.c as input from a fill-out form or with environment variables set in a script that calls wwwwais.c. Any additional parameters you reference will override parameters set in your configuration file. The simple form used earlier to pass keywords to wwwwais.c can be easily updated to accommodate these additional parameters. The variables you can set include the following:

| host | The name of the remote host machine to search with waissearch. The host information should include the domain, like this: |
|---|---|
| | `host=tvp.com` |
| iconurl | The URL path to icons. The iconurl should include the transfer protocol, like this: |
| | `iconurl=http://tvp.com/icons/` |
| isindex | The keywords to search on. |

| | |
|---|---|
| `keywords` | The keywords to search on. |
| `maxhits` | The maximum number of matches to return after a search. |
| `port` | The port number to contact the remote host machine on. |
| `searchprog` | The search engine to use. This variable can be set to |

| | |
|---|---|
| `searchprog=swish` | A local search using SWISH |
| `searchprog=waisq` | A local search using `waisq` |
| `searchprog=waissearch` | A remote search using waissearch |

| | |
|---|---|
| `selection` | The indexed database to use as specified by the description set in the configuration file. |
| `sorttype` | The sorting method for the results. This variable can be set to |

| | |
|---|---|
| `sorttype=bytes` | Sort by the byte size of the documents |
| `sorttype=lines` | Sort by the number of lines |
| `sorttype=score` | Sort by score |
| `sorttype=title` | Sort by document title |
| `sorttype=type` | Sort by document type |

| | |
|---|---|
| `source` | Specifies the indexed database to search. |
| `sourcedir` | Specifies the directory of the indexed database. |
| `useicons` | Specifies whether icons based on file type are used. This can be set to |

| | |
|---|---|
| `useicons=no` | Do not use icons |
| `useicons=yes` | Use icons |

| | |
|---|---|
| `version` | Provides the version number of your WAIS applications. The default value false can be set to `true` as follows: |
| | `version=true` |

You can use either the GET or POST method to submit data from an HTML form to `wwwwais.c`. You can set variables yourself using hidden fields or allow the users to set these variables using input fields. The `wwwwais.c` script supports the PATH_INFO variable as well. This means you can add additional parameters to the end of the URL path to `wwwwais.c` in URL-encoded format. You could create a form with additional parameters already added to the URL path by setting them in the Action field of the Settings For Custom Form Handler dialog box, like so:

```
/cgi-bin/wwwwais/useicons=yes&maxhits=50&sorttype=score
```

To set parameters in a script that calls `wwwwais.c`, you will use environment variables. Any of the variables discussed earlier can be changed into an environment variable that `wwwwais.c` will recognize by putting `www` before the variable name. All variable names should be in uppercase. Listing 31.3 is a simple `csh` script to show how you could set variables and call `wwwwais`.

**Listing 31.3. A `csh` script to set variables for `wwwwais`.**

```
!/bin/csh
#Shell script for setting environment variables for wwwwais
setenv WWWW_USEICONS = yes
setenv WWWW_MAXHITS = 50
setenv WWWW_SORTTYPE = type
#Call wwwwais
/usr/local/cgi-bin/wwwwais
exit
```

# Building an Indexed Database

So far this chapter has discussed the basics of indexers, search engines, WAIS, and WAIS gateways. Now that you have read the section on accessing a WAIS database, you should understand how WAIS gateways work and how to create an HTML document for a WAIS gateway. The next step is to install a search and retrieval application that includes an indexer and a search engine.

As I mentioned earlier in this chapter, one of the most widely used Wide Area Information Servers is freeWAIS. The freeWAIS server is actually a series of scripts for building and searching an indexed database. An alternative to freeWAIS is SWISH. Developed by the team at EIT Corporation, the Simple Web Indexing System for Humans offers ease of installation and use.

## Installing and Configuring freeWAIS

There are many versions of freeWAIS in use on the Internet. The two main variants you might be interested in are the standard freeWAIS package and the freeWAIS-sf package. Standard freeWAIS is the most widely used WAIS system. The freeWAIS-sf package is optimized for use with `SFgate`.

You can find information on the current version of freeWAIS and obtain the source code at these locations:

```
http://www.eit.com/software/
http://cnidr.org/
ftp://ftp.cnidr.org/pub/NIDR.tools/freewais/
```

You can find information on the current version of freeWAIS-sf and obtain the source code at these locations:

```
http://ls6-www.informatik.uni-dortmund.de/SFgate/SFgate.html
ftp://mirror-site/mirror-dir/SFgate/
ftp://mirror-site/mirror-dir/freeWAIS-sf-1.2/freeWAIS-sf/
```

After you download the source to your computer from one of the preceding locations and uncompress the source as necessary, you can begin installing and configuring freeWAIS. Both variants of freeWAIS include essentially the same applications. These applications include

```
waisserver

waisq

waissearch

waisindex
```

## Using `waisserver`

The `waisserver` program is the primary server program. You need to run `waisserver` only if you want to be able to search locally available databases. Before you start the `waisserver`, you will need to know three things:

1. The port on which you want the `waisserver` to allow connections. This port is normally 210. You invoke `waisserver` with the -p option to set the port number.

2. The directory where your source databases are located. The `waisserver` program will allow any database in the specified directory to be searched. You invoke `waisserver` with the -d option to set the directory path to your indexed WAIS databases.

3. How you want errors to be treated. Although tracking errors is not mandatory, it is a sound administrative practice. You invoke `waisserver` with the -e option to specify a log file for tracking errors.

To start `waisserver`, you should change directories to where `waisserver` is installed. In the following example, `waisserver` answers requests on port 210, source databases are in /usr/local/ httpd/wais/sources and errors are logged in /usr/local/httpd/logs/wais.log. To start waisserver using these options, you would type the following all on one line:

```
./waisserver -p 210 -d /usr/local/httpd/wais/sources -e
➥/usr/local/httpd/logs/wais.log &
```

> **NOTE**
>
> The ampersand symbol puts `waisserver` in the background. If you do not put the server process in the background, the server will stop running when you exit. Additionally, to ensure `waisserver` is started if the host computer is rebooted, you should update the appropriate configuration files. Here's what you could add to the `rc.local` file on most UNIX systems so that `waisserver` is started automatically:
>
> ```
> #Added to start the waisserver process
> #waisserver is used to enable searching of the local WAIS databases
> /usr/local/httpd/wais/waisserver -p 210 -d /usr/local/httpd/wais/sources -e
> ➥/usr/local/httpd/logs/wais.log &
> ```

# Using `waisq` and `waissearch`

The `waisq` and `waissearch` programs search WAIS databases for the information you're looking for. The `waisq` search engine looks in databases on the local host, and `waissearch` looks in databases on remote machines. The `waissearch` program does things remotely by contacting WAIS servers on different machines, each of which has its own database. In order for `waissearch` to work properly, you must tell it a host name and a port to which to connect. Additionally, the remote host must have a WAIS server of its own running on the port you specified. Because your WAIS gateway will call `waisq` or `waissearch` for you, you generally do not access these search engines directly.

# Using `waisindex`

The `waisindex` program creates indexed WAIS databases. When you create an index, you can index all or any portion of the files on the host computer. Generally, files are indexed into a database according to their directory. If you want files to be indexed, you can specify the following:

■ The directory in which the files to be indexed reside. You invoke `waisindex` with the `-d` option to set the directory path to the files you want to index.

■ Whether you want `waisindex` to recursively index subdirectories. You invoke `waisindex` with the `-r` option to specify that you want subdirectories to be indexed.

■ The name of the source database, including the file path. Indexed WAIS databases end with the `.src` extension, but are named *without* the `.src` extension.

■ Whether you want `waisindex` to index the full contents of the document or just the filename. The default is to index the full contents of the documents. For files indexed with the `nocontents` flag, only the filenames are indexed.

You can specify these additional parameters if you choose:

■ How you want errors to be treated. Although tracking errors is not mandatory, it is a sound administrative practice. You invoke `waisindex` with the `-e` option to specify a log file for tracking errors.

■ The level of detail for logging what `waisindex` is doing on your system. You invoke `waisindex` with the `-1` option to specify logging verbosity. The higher the number, the more verbose and detailed the logging will be.

■ The amount of system memory and resources to use during the indexing. You invoke `waisindex` with the `-m` option to specify the amount of memory and resources to use for indexing. The higher the number, the more system resources will be used.

To run `waisindex`, you should either change to the directory where `waisindex` is installed or specify the full path to the program. In the following example, `waisindex` is located in the `/usr/local/httpd/wais` directory, the verbosity of the output is `small`, errors are logged in

/usr/local/httpd/logs/waisindex.log, the directory to index is /users/webdocs, the path to the database is /usr/local/httpd/wais/sources, and the name of the database is webdocuments. To run waisindex using these options, you would type the following all on one line:

```
/usr/local/httpd/wais/waisindex -l 1 -d /users/webdocs -e/usr/local
➥/httpd/logs/wais.log -r /usr/local/httpd/wais/sources/webdocuments
```

Although you could run waisindex by hand whenever you needed to reindex your site, the best way to handle indexing is to set up a cron job to handle the task. In UNIX environments, cron jobs are run automatically at times you specify. Most systems have multiple cron tables. Jobs in a cron table are run by the owner of the cron tab, which is normally located in the /usr/spool/cron/crontabs directory.

You will usually want to update your indexes daily, especially on a host that changes frequently. The best time to run waisindex is when system usage is low. Often, this is in the early morning hours. To add a statement to the root cron table to update your index daily at 1 a.m., you could insert the following lines:

```
# Root Cron
# Entry added to build waisindex
00 01 * * * /usr/local/httpd/wais/waisindex -l 1 -d /users/webdocs -e/usr/
➥local/httpd/logs/wais.log -r /usr/local/httpd/wais/sources/webdocuments
```

Although the previous example assumes you want to index only a single directory and its subdirectories, you can add additional statements to the cron tab to build additional indexed databases. This solution for indexing your site works best on simple document structures. If your host has a complex document structure, there are two solutions:

- Build the index using links.
- Build the index using a script.

## Building a WAIS Index Using Links

You can add links from your document directories to a base directory that you will index using the -r option to recursively index subdirectories. To do this, you could create a base directory, such as /users/webdocs, add subdirectories to this directory, and link your document directories to the subdirectories. Here's how you would do this on most UNIX systems that enable symbolic links:

```
$ mkdir /users/webdocs
$ cd /users/webdocs
$ mkdir HTML
$ mkdir TEXT
$ mkdir PDF
$ mkdir GIF
$ ln -s /users/webdocs/HTML /usr/local/httpd/docs/html
$ ln -s /users/webdocs/TEXT /home/users/local/text
$ ln -s /users/webdocs/PDF /usr/bin/adobe/acrobat/docs
$ ln -s /users/webdocs/GIF /usr/local/images/samples/gif
```

Now if you ran the command defined earlier, you would index all the appropriate directories you have linked to the /users/webdocs directory. Keep in mind that the actual database would be located in the /usr/local/httpd/wais/sources directory and would have the name webdocuments.src. The waisindex program adds the .src extension to the database name to indicate that the file is a source file.

## Building a WAIS Index Using a Script

For the most complex document structures, you will want to use a shell script. A script also enables you to easily specify the types of files you want to be indexed and the types of files you want to ignore.

The following csh script by Kevin Hughes of EIT can be used to index documents at your site using waisindex. Documents you don't want to index the contents of, such as GIF images, are specified with the nocontents flag. This flag tells waisindex to index only the filename and not the contents. You can see this in the code from Listing 31.4.

### Listing 31.4. A csh script for indexing documents using waisindex.

```
#! /bin/csh

set rootdir = /usr/local/www
#       This is the root directory of the Web tree you want to index.

set index = /usr/local/httpd/wais/sources/index
#       This is the name your WAIS indexes will be built under.
#       Index files will be called index.* in the /usr/local/httpd/wais/sources
#       directory, in this example.

set indexprog = /usr/local/httpd/wais/waisindex
#       The full pathname to your waisindex program.

set nonomatch
cd $rootdir
set num = 0
foreach pathname ('du $rootdir | cut -f2 | tail -r')

        echo "The current pathname is: $pathname"
        if ($num == 0) then
                set exportflag = "-export"
        else
                set exportflag = "-a"
        endif
        $indexprog -l 0 -nopairs -nocat -d $index $exportflag $pathname/*.html
        $indexprog -l 0 -nopairs -nocat -d $index -a $pathname/*.txt
        $indexprog -l 0 -nopairs -nocat -d $index -a $pathname/*.c
        $indexprog -nocontents -l 0 -nopairs -nocat -d $index -a $pathname/*.ps
        $indexprog -nocontents -l 0 -nopairs -nocat -d $index -a $pathname/*.gif
        $indexprog -nocontents -l 0 -nopairs -nocat -d $index -a $pathname/*.au
        $indexprog -nocontents -l 0 -nopairs -nocat -d $index -a $pathname/*.hqx
        $indexprog -nocontents -l 0 -nopairs -nocat -d $index -a $pathname/*.xbm
```

*continues*

## Listing 31.4. continued

```
        $indexprog -nocontents -l 0 -nopairs -nocat -d $index -a $pathname/*.mpg
        $indexprog -nocontents -l 0 -nopairs -nocat -d $index -a $pathname/*.pict
        $indexprog -nocontents -l 0 -nopairs -nocat -d $index -a $pathname/*.tiff
        @ num++
end
echo "$num directories were indexed."
```

The following script for indexing directories based on file type was created by Michael Grady from the University of Illinois Computing & Communications Services Office. This Perl script is based on the csh script in Listing 31.4. Although both scripts are terrific and get the job done right, the Perl script offers more control over the indexing. Listing 31.5 shows the actual code for the script.

## Listing 31.5. A Perl script for indexing documents using `waisindex`.

```
#!/usr/local/bin/perl
# Michael Grady,  Univ. of Illinois Computing & Communications Services Office
# Perl script to index the contents of a www tree. This is derived from a csh
# script that Kevin Hughes of EIT constructed for indexing files.

$rootdir = "/var/info/www/docs";
#        This is the root directory of the Web tree you want to index
$index = "/var/info/www/wais-sources/ccso-main-www";
#        This is the name and location of the index to be created
$indexprog = "/var/info/gopher/src/fw02sf/bin/waisindex";
#        The full pathname of the waisindex program
$url = "http://www.uiuc.edu";
#        The main URL for your Web. No slash at the end!

$numdir = $num = 0;

# Generate a list of directory names, then for each directory, generate an
# array of all the filenames in that directory except for . and .. . Sort this
# list so that if there is an .htaccess file in that directory, it comes near
# the front of the list. We assume that if you've bothered to put special
# access controls into a directory, then maybe you don't want these files
# indexed in a general index. You of course can remove this restriction if you
# want. Then we separate all the files in the directory into two lists: one
# list is those file types for which it is appropriate to index the contents of
# the files, and the second list are those whose file types are such we don't
# want to index the contents, just the filename (gif, for instance). Then
# if there are any files in either of these lists, we call waisindex to index
# them. The first time we index, we do not include the -a flag, so that the
# index replaces the current one. Every subsequent call to waisindex includes
# the -a flag so that we then add to the new index we are building. We include
# the -nopairs option on all waisindex calls, because this saves a lot of
# unused info from being put into the index.

# If this is run by cron, redirect print statements to file (or /dev/null).
# Probably want to add a "-l 0" option to the waisindex call also.
#open (LOGIT, ">>/tmp/waisindex.run");
#select LOGIT;
```

```
# Put in the appropriate path on your system to each of the commands
# "du", "cut" and "tail", in case you want to run this from a cronjob and
# these commands are not in the default path. Note that "du" will not follow
# symbolic links out of this "tree".
open (PATHNAMES,"/usr/bin/du $rootdir ¦ /usr/bin/cut -f2 ¦/usr/bin/tail -r ¦");
DO_PATH: while ( $pathname = <PATHNAMES>) {
        chop $pathname;

        # The following are "path patterns" that we don't want to
        # follow (subdirectories whose files we do not want to index).
        # Add or subtract from this list as appropriate. These may
        # be directories you don't want to index at all, or directories
        # for which you want to build their own separate index.
        next DO_PATH if $pathname =~ /uiucnet/i;
        #next DO_PATH if $pathname =~ /demopict/i;
        next DO_PATH if $pathname =~ /images/i;
        next DO_PATH if $pathname =~ /testdir/i;

        print "Current pathname is: $pathname\n";
        $numdir++;
        @contents = @nocontents = ();
        opendir(CURRENT_DIR, "$pathname")
                        ¦¦ die "Can't open directory $pathname: $!\n";
        @allfiles = sort (grep(!/^\.\.?$/, readdir(CURRENT_DIR)));
        closedir(CURRENT_DIR);

        DO_FILE: foreach $file (@allfiles) {
                        # skip directories that contain a .htaccess file
                        # note this is NOT smart enough to be recursive (if a
                        # directory below this does not itself contain an
                        # .htaccess file, it WILL be indexed).
                next DO_PATH if $file eq '.htaccess';
                        # filetypes for which we want to index contents
                $file =~ /\.html$/i &&
                    do { push(@contents, "$pathname/$file"); next DO_FILE;};
                $file =~ /\.te?xt$/i &&
                    do { push(@contents, "$pathname/$file"); next DO_FILE;};
                $file =~ /\.pdf$/i &&
                    do { push(@contents, "$pathname/$file"); next DO_FILE;};
                #$file =~ /\.ps$/i &&
                    #do { push(@contents, "$pathname/$file"); next DO_FILE;};

                        # filetypes for which we DON'T want to index contents
                $file =~ /\.gif$/i &&
                    do { push(@nocontents, "$pathname/$file"); next DO_FILE;};
                #$file =~ /\.au$/i &&
                    #do { push(@nocontents, "$pathname/$file"); next DO_FILE;};
                #$file =~ /\.mpg$/i &&
                    #do { push(@nocontents, "$pathname/$file"); next DO_FILE;};
                #$file =~ /\.hqx$/i &&
                    #do { push(@nocontents, "$pathname/$file"); next DO_FILE;};
        # Comment out the above lines to your liking, depending on what
        # filetypes you are actually interested in indexing.
#       For instance, if the ".mpg" line is commented out, then
#       MPEG files will *not* be indexed into the database (and thus
#       won't be searchable by others).
        } # end DO_FILE loop
```

*continues*

## Listing 31.5. continued

```
        if ($#contents >= 0) {          # Index if any files in list.
            @waisflags = ("-a", "-nopairs");
            @waisflags = ("-nopairs") if $num == 0;
            $num ++;
            system($indexprog, "-d", $index, @waisflags, "-t", "URL",
                        $rootdir, $url, @contents);
        }
        if ($#nocontents >= 0) {        # Index if any files in list.
            @waisflags = ("-a", "-nopairs");
            @waisflags = ("-nopairs") if $num == 0;
            $num ++;
            system($indexprog, "-d", $index, @waisflags, "-t", "URL",
                        $rootdir, $url, "-nocontents", @nocontents);
            # note that "-nocontents" flag must follow any -T or -t option
        }
} # end DO_PATH loop

close(PATHNAMES);
print "Waisindex called $num times.\n";
print "Tried indexing $numdir directories.\n";
# end of script
```

# Testing the WAIS Database

After you have installed freeWAIS, started `waisserver`, and built an index, you will want to test your new WAIS system. You can do this using `waisq`. If the database was indexed with the command

```
00 01 * * * /usr/local/httpd/wais/waisindex -l 1 -d /users/webdocs -e/usr/
➥local/httpd/logs/wais.log -r /usr/local/httpd/wais/sources/webdocuments
```

you could invoke `waisq` as follows to test the database:

```
/usr/local/httpd/wais/waisq -m 40 -c /usr/local/httpd/wais/sources -f -
➥-S webdocuments -g Stanek
```

This command tells `waisq` to return a maximum of 40 matches and to search the `webdocuments` source file located in the `/usr/local/httpd/wais/sources` directory for the keyword `Stanek`. If all goes well and some documents actually contain the keyword, the server should respond with output similar to the following:

```
Searching webdocuments.src . . . Initializing connection . . . Found 28 items.
```

After this, the server should produce output containing the search word used and the results of the query. Keep in mind that this output will normally be interpreted by your WAIS gateway. The WAIS gateway will process this output, create a document containing the results, and send the document to the client originating the search.

# Installing and Configuring SWISH

SWISH, the Simple Web Indexing System for Humans, is an easy-to-use alternative to freeWAIS. SWISH is good choice if you want to experiment with indexing and search engines. Besides being easy to install, SWISH creates very small indexes compared to a WAIS index. Using the environment variables PLIMIT and FLIMIT, you can squeeze what otherwise would be a large index into about one-tenth of the file space. Because a smaller file is quicker to search, SWISH can display results faster than many other search engines. However, there is a trade-off between file size and search results. A smaller file contains less data, and the smaller the file size, the less accurate the results of the search.

SWISH has a couple of limitations. Because it can search only local SWISH databases, you will need to use another indexing system if you need to access remote hosts. Additionally, SWISH works best with small to medium size databases, so if you have a large site with hundreds of megabytes of files to index, you might want to use freeWAIS instead of SWISH.

You can find information on the current version of SWISH and obtain the source code from EIT corporation at

```
http://www.eit.com/software/
```

After you download the source to your computer from the EIT Web site and uncompress the source as necessary, you can begin installing and configuring SWISH. The first step is to change directories to the SWISH source directory and update the config.h file. If you've just uncompressed SWISH, you should be able to change directories to swish/src or simply src. In the config.h file, you will need to set parameters for your specific system. This file is also where you update the PLIMIT and FLIMIT variables that control the size of your index files. After you set those parameters following the inline documentation, you can compile SWISH. SWISH compiles fine with any C compiler, even plain old gcc.

# Setting Up the SWISH Configuration File

The next step is to edit the SWISH configuration file. This file is usually located in the src directory and is used to configure environment variables for search and retrieval results. After you've updated the configuration file, you can name it anything you want, such as swish.conf. Listing 31.6 is a sample configuration file for SWISH.

### Listing 31.6. A sample SWISH configuration file.

```
# SWISH configuration file

IndexDir /usr/webdocs
# This is a space-separated list of files and directories you want to index.

IndexFile /usr/local/httpd/swish/sources/index.swish
```

*continues*

## Listing 31.6. continued

```
# This is the name your SWISH indexed database.

IndexAdmin "William Stanek publisher@tvp.com"
IndexDescription "Index of key documents at the Web site"
IndexName "Index of TVP Web site"
IndexPointer "http://tvp.com/cgi-bin/wwwwais/"
# Additional information that can be used to describe the index,
# the WAIS gateway used, and the administrator

FollowSymLinks yes
# If you want to follow symbolic links, put yes. Otherwise, put no.

IndexOnly .html .txt .c .ps .gif .au .hqx .xbm .mpg .pict .tiff
# Only files with these suffixes will be indexed.

IndexVerbose yes
# Put this to show indexing information as SWISH is working.

NoContents .ps .gif .au .hqx .xbm .mpg .pict .tiff
# Files with these suffixes won't have their contents indexed,
# only their file names.

IgnoreLimit 75 200
# To ignore words that occur too frequently, you will want to
# set this parameter. The numbers say ignore words that occur
# in this percentage of the documents and occur in at least this
# many files. Here, ignore words that occur in 75% of the files
# and occur in over 200 files. If this variable is not set SWISH
# uses a default setting

IgnoreWords SwishDefault
# This variable allows you to set your own stop words.
# To do this, you replace the word SwishDefault with a space
# separate list of stop words. You can use multiple assignments
# if necessary
```

The most important variables in the configuration file are `IndexDir` and `IndexFile`. The `IndexDir` variable enables you to specify the files and directories to index. If you enter multiple directories and filenames, you should be sure to separate them with spaces. You can make more than one `IndexDir` assignment if necessary. The `IndexFile` variable tells SWISH where to store the index. Because SWISH does not add the `.src` extension to the filename, you can name the file anything you want. However, you might want to use an extension of `.swish` so you know the file is a SWISH-indexed database.

# Compiling and Running SWISH

After you've updated the configuration file, you can move the compiled SWISH program, `swish`, and the configuration file to an appropriate directory, such as

```
/usr/local/httpd/swish/
```

To run SWISH and index the files and directories specified in the configuration file, change directories to where SWISH is located and type the following:

```
./swish -c /usr/local/httpd/swish/swish.conf
```

Based on the settings in the previously defined configuration file, when SWISH finishes indexing your site, the indexed database will be located here:

```
/usr/local/httpd/swish/sources/index.swish
```

Because SWISH lets you specify the full path to the configuration file, you can have different configuration files for different databases. To use SWISH with a gateway, you must ensure that the script has been modified to work with SWISH or is SWISH-friendly. To modify a gateway so that it is SWISH-friendly, you might only have to change the path for its search engine from its current setting to the full path to the SWISH executable. An example of a SWISH-friendly gateway is wwwwais.c. The wwwwais.c program enables you to set the path to SWISH executables and sources. Here are the settings that make the program SWISH-friendly:

```
# The full path to your SWISH program.
SwishBin /usr/local/bin/swish

# WAIS source file descriptions
# These represent the path to the indexed databases
# For SWISH sources:
#    SwishSource full_path_to_source/source.swish "description"
SwishSource /usr/local/httpd/wais/index/index.swish "Search our Web"
SourceRules replace "/usr/local/www/" "http://www.tvpress.com/"
```

# Summary

Building an indexed database and creating Web documents that access the database via a gateway requires a lot of effort on the part of the Web publisher. Yet if you take the process one step at a time, you can join the thousands of Web publishers who have indexed their Web sites and thus provide to Web users the ability to search the site quickly and efficiently. Enabling the interface from a fill-out form in your Web document to an indexed database involves these steps:

1. Obtaining the appropriate software. If you use freeWAIS, the package includes waisserver, waisq, waissearch, and waisindex. These programs will handle searching and indexing. You will also need to select a gateway, such as wwwwais.c.

2. Installing and configuring the software.

3. Building your indexed databases.

4. Creating a fill-out form to submit data to the gateway.

5. Testing the search capabilities of the index.

# Using JavaScript in Your Web Pages

# 32

*by Rick Darnell*

**IN THIS CHAPTER**

JavaScript, a scripting extension to HTML, extends your capability to respond to user events without the need for client-server communication or CGI scripting.

In the past, a form typically was submitted to the server for all processing, whether it meant checking a ZIP code or putting information in a database. Each time information was passed back and forth between client and server it slowed down the process, due to inherently slow communication lines. JavaScript eliminates much of the client-server communication by shifting responses to user events to the client side. Because network transmission is not required, the process goes much faster.

# Getting to Know JavaScript

JavaScript is more closely related to a programming language than to HTML tags. JavaScript cannot exist, however, outside of HTML. To function, it must be included as part of a page.

## What Is JavaScript?

JavaScript was developed by Netscape in conjunction with Sun's Java. You may also know it as LiveScript—the first name it had before the collaboration with Sun.

### JAVASCRIPT ISN'T JAVA

Java is an object-oriented programming language used to create stand-alone applications and applets, special "mini" applications for Web pages. Java is compiled into machine-independent bytecodes, which are in turn interpreted by the Java virtual machine on the host computer. Writing Java programs is easiest when you have some background in programming, such as with C or C++.

JavaScript shares some of the same syntax and structure as Java but provides a much smaller and simpler language for people with HTML or CGI experience. It is interpreted along with the rest of the page at load time. JavaScript only resides within an HTML document and provides for greater levels of interactivity than basic HTML commands.

For example, JavaScript enables the HTML author to respond to user-initiated events, such as mouse clicks and form activity, without the need for client-server interaction. The result provides quicker operation for the end user, and less load on the server.

Although similarities exist between Java and JavaScript, the languages are different and are intended for different uses. A simple form-handling routine that would require a significant amount of coding in Java represents a basic task for JavaScript, but creating a browser such as HotJava in JavaScript is impossible.

> Java applets occupy a defined space on the screen, much as an image or other embed-
> ded item. Although it can communicate with another applet on the same page,
> communicating with a page's HTML elements requires a substantial amount of code.

JavaScript does not represent a watered-down version of Java for programming beginners. Although it is related to Java, JavaScript provides a solution for client-side scripting in an era
when users with high-powered machines get bogged down by client-server communication.

Although many ways exist to control the browser from within a Java applet, simple tasks such
as computing a form or controlling frame content become complicated affairs. JavaScript bridges
the gap by enabling HTML authors to implement basic HTML functionality and interactivity
without hours and hours of codewriting.

The other side of the coin for JavaScript means you have a much smaller set of objects, methods, and properties to work with, and they all focus toward dealing with HTML content. For
example, JavaScript does not have the capability to control network connections or download
files.

# Why Is JavaScript So Hot?

Although it is based on programming, JavaScript is simple enough to be within easy reach of
anyone who feels comfortable with HTML coding. It greatly expands the capabilities of typical HTML pages, without a great deal of hassle.

Consider the following example:

```
<SCRIPT LANGUAGE="javascript">
document.writeln("This page last changed on "+document.lastModified());
</SCRIPT>
```

When the page loads, some basic information about itself also is included, such as the time and
date the page was saved. Without any further communication with the server, JavaScript accesses the date and displays it for the user. You don't need to remember to update a line of
HTML or include a link to a CGI script—once the JavaScript line appears, the process is automatic.

JavaScript also includes the capability to effectively manage multiple frames. Although a page
cannot be redrawn, you can control the content in other frames by loading them with new
URLs or managing form input.

**NOTE**

Frames allow multiple document windows simultaneously within one browser. Each
frame can scroll, hyperlink, reload, and do all of the other things possible with a single

browser window. Frames enable creation of useful document groups, such as combining menu and navigation bars with content.

They are created with the FRAMESET tag, with each individual frame defined using FRAME SRC=*URL* NAME="*name*", as follows:

```
<HTML>
<FRAMESET ROWS="20%,80%">
    <FRAME SRC="MenuBar.htm" NAME="menu" noresize>
    <FRAMESET COLS="20%,80%">
        <FRAME SRC="NavBar.htm" NAME="nav" noresize>
        <FRAME SRC="Home.htm" NAME="body">
    </FRAMESET>
</FRAMESET>
</HTML>
```

Note the nested framesets for creating frames within frames. Be careful when using frames. Although you can break down the browser screen into individual units, it can slow down displays and turn the screen into an unintelligible jigsaw puzzle, especially for a user screen with less than 800×600 resolution.

Assigning names can make referencing frames easier, although it can happen in JavaScript using the frames array.

When you create a frame, JavaScript adds an entry to its frames array. In the preceding example, JavaScript creates three entries:

```
document.frames[0].name //"menu"
document.frames[1].name //"nav"
document.frames[2].name //"body"
```

As a general rule, JavaScript always begins numbering with 0, even in arrays. For more information on creating and working with frames, see Chapter 13, "Using Frames and the Frames Wizard."

One major power JavaScript has is its capability to handle forms and their elements. Using JavaScript, the information on a form can be validated and checked before it is sent to the server, saving valuable processing and communication time on the server. Client-side form processing also localizes the process, making it much harder for end users to send incompatible data that could cause damage to the server.

Additional characteristics now represent a part of form elements in the shape of events and event handlers. For INPUT TYPE= tags such as BUTTON and TEXT, the page author can check for mouse clicks, changed text, focus, and even change the content of form elements. In addition, submission of forms and other information is controlled by substituting custom actions for the standard submit button formats.

## How to Use JavaScript Now

Most HTML editors that handle nonstandard HTML tags will allow creation and editing of JavaScript sections of your pages. Several resources available for learning the syntax and idiosyncrasies of JavaScript appear at the end of this chapter.

> **TIP**
>
> One of the most useful sites is the JavaScript online documentation at `http://home.netscape.com/eng/mozilla/Gold/handbook/javascript/index.html`, which is also available as a downloadable file.

For users to take advantage of your JavaScript-empowered pages, they need to use a compatible browser. The list of these browsers keeps expanding and should include most of the popular applications by the beginning of 1997.

> **WARNING**
>
> The JavaScript API is not entirely stabilized yet. As Netscape continues its own development and collaboration with Sun, the implementation and workability of some features may change. You should always try your script on more than one browser and platform combination to ensure that your solutions function as planned.

The current browser choices include Netscape Navigator (2.0 and later) and Microsoft Internet Explorer (3.0 and later). Sun HotJava is also scheduled for JavaScript compatibility, although it hasn't been included in any of the beta implementations. NCSA Mosaic also includes support for Java and JavaScript on its wish list, although no date has been set for implementation.

> **TIP**
>
> Like many sites that provide a host of compatibilities, some of which are mutually exclusive, it shows good manners to offer your page in a generic version if crucial content is not usable with a non-JavaScript browser. You can also offer a link to sites where a compatible browser is available for downloading.

# Creating Scripts

Creating scripts is really quite simple, although you must use proper syntax to ensure success. Although a knowledge of object-oriented programming will prove useful to anyone creating functions with JavaScript, it is not a necessity.

# New Language, New Terminology

Objects, methods, properties, classes—an object-oriented world has taken off, and a whole new batch of terminology has cropped up to go with it. This section provides a quick primer on the basic terms that are used in conjunction with an object-oriented language such as JavaScript.

---

**TIP**

JavaScript is case-sensitive. For example, if your variable is called Bob, you can also have a BOB, bob, and boB, and each one will be unique.

---

## Objects

Objects are at the heart of any object-oriented programming language, and JavaScript is no different. An object is a software model, typically used to represent a real-world object along with a set of behaviors or circumstances. In JavaScript, built-in objects can also represent the structure, action, and state of an HTML page.

In object-oriented terminology, the actions are called methods and the states are called properties. Both of these terms are covered later in this section.

To build an object, you need to know something about it. Consider a squirrel as an example. A squirrel has several physical properties, including sex, age, size, and color. It also has properties relating to its activity, such as running, jumping, eating peanuts, or tormenting dogs. Its methods relate to changes in behavior or state, such as run away, stop and look, or twitch tail and chatter.

This example may seem all well and good, but how do you represent this idea as an object in JavaScript? The basic object creation is a two-step process, beginning with defining a function that outlines the object and then creating an instance of the object. (See Listing 32.1.) Using some of the properties listed in the preceding example, you make a JavaScript squirrel.

### Listing 32.1. A JavaScript object definition for a squirrel.

```
function squirrel(color) {
    this.color = color;
    this.running = false;
    this.tormentingDog = false;
}

var groundSquirrel = new squirrel("brown")
```

The first part of the script with the `function` tag outlines the initial state for any given squirrel. It accepts one parameter, called `color`, which becomes a property, and adds two more properties called `running` and `tormentingDog`, both set to false by default.

By itself, the function does nothing—it has to be invoked and assigned to a variable. This is what happens in the next step, where a variable called `groundSquirrel` is created and given the color brown. The following code shows how the object and its properties are represented:

```
groundSquirrel.color // "brown"
groundSquirrel.running // false
groundSquirrel.tormentingDog // false
```

Now, to implement the object as part of an HTML page (see Figure 32.1), include the object definition between the HEAD tags. To see the object in motion, use Listing 32.2.

### Listing 32.2. Use the JavaScript definition of a squirrel in an HTML document similar to this one.

```html
<HTML>
<HEAD>
<TITLE>The Squirrel Page</TITLE>
<SCRIPT language="javascript">
<!--
function squirrel(color) {
    this.color = color;
    this.running = false;
    this.tormentingDog = false;
}

// -->
</SCRIPT>
</HEAD>
<BODY>
Making a squirrel...
<BR>
<SCRIPT LANGUAGE="javascript">
var brownSquirrel = new squirrel("brown");
document.writeln("brownSquirrel.color = "+brownSquirrel.color);
document.writeln("<BR>brownSquirrel.running = "+brownSquirrel.running);
document.writeln("<BR>brownSquirrel.tormentingDog =
➥"+brownSquirrel.tormentingDog);
</SCRIPT>
</BODY>
</HTML>
```

# Class

A class represents the definition for a type of object. Although classes are in Java and not in JavaScript, it is helpful to understand classes because many discussions about either language may refer to them.

**FIGURE 32.1.**

*The squirrel page creates a simple object and displays its properties.*

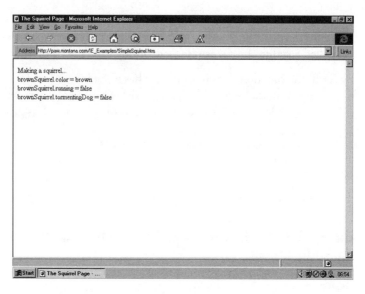

```
Making a squirrel...
brownSquirrel.color = brown
brownSquirrel.running = false
brownSquirrel.tormentingDog = false
```

Simply stated, a class relates to an object as a blueprint relates to a bicycle. A blueprint contains all the information about the bicycle, but you can't ride it. To ride a bicycle, you need to create an instance of it. In object-oriented terminology, this process is called instantiation.

Classes can also have inheritance, which means they take on the behavior of other classes. A 10-speed bicycle and a tandem bicycle have bicycle characteristics, but different specific features and functions. They are considered subclasses of the bicycle class.

Although a JavaScript function has a definition similar to a class, it can operate without instantiation.

## Property

Properties are the individual states of an object, typically represented as variables. In the squirrel example, `color`, `running`, and `tormentingDog` all represent properties of `squirrel`. An object's properties can include any of the valid JavaScript variable types.

---

**WHICH TYPE IS WHICH?**

A variable's type is the kind of value it holds. Several basic variable types are offered by JavaScript, including string, boolean, integer, and floating-point decimal.

JavaScript utilizes loose casting, which means that a variable can assume different types at will, as in the following example:

```
squirrel.color = "pink"
...statements...
squirrel.color = 30
```

Both color values are valid. In Java, this would cause an error because it incorporates tight casting. After a variable is assigned a type in Java, it can't be changed.

Loose casting can make life easier when working with JavaScript. When building strings, for example, you can add a string to an integer, and the result will be a string, as in the following example:

```
value = 3;
theResult = value + "is the number." //Results in "3 is the number."
```

The downside is that sometimes you can easily forget what a variable thinks it is. It's a good idea to keep variables to their original type unless absolutely necessary.

Object properties are accessed using the object's name, followed by a period and the name of the property.

```
squirrel.color
```

Assigning a new value to the property will change it.

```
squirrel.color = "pink"
```

## Function

A JavaScript function is a collection of statements that are invoked by using the name of the function and a list of arguments, if used. As a general rule, if you use a set of statements more than once as part of a page, it will probably be easier to include them as a function. Also, any activity used as part of an event handler should be defined as a function for ease of use.

Functions normally appear in the HEAD portion of the HTML document to ensure that they are loaded and interpreted before the user has a chance to interact with them.

The syntax to define a function is as follows:

```
function functionName ([arg1] [,arg2] [,...]) {
...statements...
}
```

An example of a function that automatically generates a link to an anchor called top at the top of the current page could look like this:

```
function makeTopLink (topLinkText) {
    var topURL = "#top";
    document.writeln(topLinkText.link(topURL));
}
```

This function accepts a text string as its one argument and generates a hypertext link similar to using the HTML A HREF tags.

```
makeTopLink("Return to the top.");
makeTopLink("top");
```

## Method

If properties represent the current conditions of the object, methods serve as the knobs and levers that make it perform. Consider the squirrel example again. Defining a squirrel seemed easy enough, but what about making it do something? First, the methods need to be defined as JavaScript functions.

The first method for the squirrel makes him run and quit tormenting the dog.

```
function runAway() {
    this.running = true;
    this.tormentingDog = false;
    document.writeln("The squirrel is running away.");
}
```

The second method makes the squirrel stop moving and tease the dog.

```
function twitchTailChatter () {
    this.tormentingDog = true;
    this.running = false;
    document.writeln("The squirrel is being annoying.");
}
```

One more method would help you see what happens to the squirrel as his state changes.

```
function showState() {
    document.writeln("<HR><BR>The state of the squirrel is:<UL>")
    document.writeln("<LI>Color: "+this.color+"</LI>");
    document.writeln("<LI>Running: "+this.running+"</LI>");
    document.writeln("<LI>Tormenting dog: "+this.tormentingDog+"</LI>");
    document.writeln("</UL><HR>");
}
```

### TIP

You can include HTML tags in text written to the browser screen using JavaScript's write and writeln methods. These methods are interpreted like any other HTML text, so formatting can occur for generated content.

Now that you have three methods defined, you need to make them a part of the object. This step amounts to including the method names as part of the object definition.

```
function squirrel(color) {
    this.color = color;
    this.running = false;
    this.tormentingDog = false;
    this.runAway = runAway;
    this.twitchTailChatter = twitchTailChatter;
    this.showState = showState;
}
```

Finally, the last step is including the whole package as part of an HTML document, such as Listing 32.3, and seeing whether it works (see Figure 32.2).

### Listing 32.3. Using the JavaScript definition of a squirrel and its behavior requires an HTML document similar to this one.

```
<HTML>
<HEAD>
<TITLE>The Squirrel Page</TITLE>
<SCRIPT language="javascript">
<!--
function runAway() {
    this.running = true;
    this.tormentingDog = false;
    document.writeln("The squirrel is running away.");
}

function twitchTailChatter () {
    this.tormentingDog = true;
    this.running = false;
    document.writeln("The squirrel is being annoying.");
}

function showState() {
    document.writeln("The state of "+this.name+" is:<UL>")
    document.writeln("<LI>"+this.name+".color: "+this.color+"</LI>");
    document.writeln("<LI>"+this.name+".running: "+this.running+"</LI>");
    document.writeln("<LI>"+this.name+".tormenting dog:
    ➥"+this.tormentingDog+"</LI>");
    document.writeln("</UL><HR>");
}

function squirrel(color,squirrelName) {
    this.name = squirrelName;
    this.color = color;
    this.running = false;
    this.tormentingDog = false;
    this.runAway = runAway;
    this.twitchTailChatter = twitchTailChatter;
    this.showState = showState;
    document.writeln("A squirrel is born...");
}
```

*continues*

## Listing 32.3. continued

```
// -->
</SCRIPT>
</HEAD>
<BODY>
<SCRIPT LANGUAGE="javascript">
var brownSquirrel = new squirrel("brown","brownSquirrel");
brownSquirrel.showState();
brownSquirrel.twitchTailChatter();
brownSquirrel.showState();
brownSquirrel.runAway();
brownSquirrel.showState();
</SCRIPT>
</BODY>
</HTML>
```

**FIGURE 32.2.**

*The browser screen displays the activity of the JavaScript object as each method is executed.*

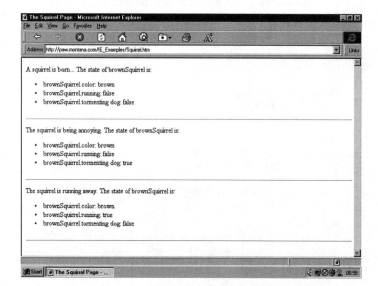

# The Script Tag

As seen in the previous examples in this chapter, JavaScript requires its own special tag to mark its beginning and end. The basic form of the tag appears in the following code:

```
<SCRIPT [LANGUAGE="JavaScript"]>
...statments...
</SCRIPT>
```

A problem can develop when a user views a page embedded with JavaScript statements with an incompatible browser.

Note the following two figures (Figure 32.3 and Figure 32.4). Both use the same HTML document, which includes JavaScript statements; however, Figure 32.3 is viewed with Internet Explorer 3.0, and Figure 32.4 is viewed with NCSA Mosaic.

**FIGURE 32.3.**

*A JavaScript-compatible Internet Explorer 3.0 displays this HTML document and processes the JavaScript commands contained in it.*

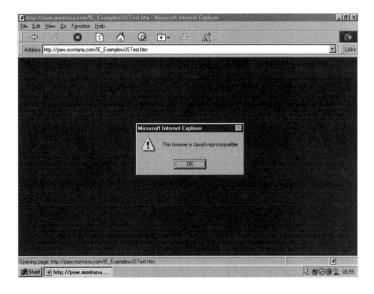

**FIGURE 32.4.**

*The NCSA Mosaic browser is not yet JavaScript compatible. The SCRIPT tags are ignored and the commands are processed like any other text.*

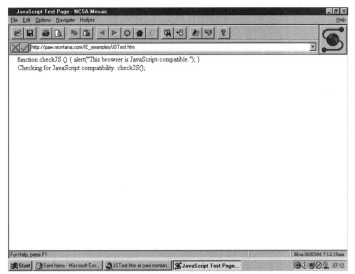

## Listing 32.4. The contents of the HTML document used in Figures 32.3 and 32.4.

```
<HTML>
<HEAD>
<TITLE>JavaScript Test Page</TITLE>
<SCRIPT>
function checkJS () {
    alert("This browser is JavaScript-compatible.");
}
</SCRIPT>
</HEAD>
<BODY>
Checking for JavaScript compatibility.
<SCRIPT>
checkJS();
</SCRIPT>
</BODY>
</HTML>
```

An incompatible browser ignores the SCRIPT tags and displays the JavaScript commands as any other text. For a document including any length of JavaScript, the result produces a screen full of commands and characters otherwise unintelligible to the user.

# Hiding Scripts from Incompatible Browsers

To prevent an older or incompatible browser from incorrectly processing your JavaScript code, you must correctly use HTML comment tags.

To hide your JavaScript, you must nest a set of HTML comment tags inside the SCRIPT tags. A JavaScript comment tag (two forward slashes) must appear just before the closing comment tag to prevent it from being processed as another line of JavaScript and causing a syntax error (see Figure 32.5).

```
<SCRIPT LANGUAGE="JavaScript">
<!--  Note: An opening HTML comment tag.
...statements...
// --> Note: A JavaScript comment tag (two forward-slashes),
➥followed by a closing HTML comment tag.
</SCRIPT>
```

With proper placement and usage, JavaScript can add vital functionality to your HTML pages without interfering with the capability of incompatible browsers to interpret the document. Remember, however, that if your page depends on JavaScript for including crucial information or operability, it shows common courtesy to warn users and, if possible, supply a generic version of the document.

**FIGURE 32.5.**

*NCSA Mosaic with the additional HTML comment tags displays the non-JavaScript content and passes over the part it can't interpret.*

# Placing Scripts on the Page

The SCRIPT tag can appear in either the HEAD or BODY section, although its placement will determine when and how the script gets used.

If placed in the HEAD portion of the document, the script is interpreted before the page is completely downloaded (see Figure 32.6). This order works especially well for documents that depend on functions. The script is loaded and ready before the user has a chance to interact with any event that actually invokes the function (see Figure 32.7).

**Listing 32.5. Placing functions in the HEAD portion of the document ensures that they are interpreted before the rest of the document.**

```
<HTML>
<HEAD>
<SCRIPT LANGUAGE="javascript">
function printMessage(msgStr) {
    document.writeln("<HR>");
    document.writeln(msgStr);
    document.writeln("<HR>");
}
alert("Function is loaded and ready.");
</SCRIPT>
</HEAD>
<BODY>
Welcome to the body of an HTML page.
<SCRIPT LANGUAGE="javascript">
printMessage("I just called a function from the body.")
</SCRIPT>
</BODY>
</HTML>
```

**FIGURE 32.6.**

*The initial screen displayed by Listing 32.5. Note that the first line of JavaScript text and the alert box have appeared, but the text contained in the* BODY *portion of the document has not.*

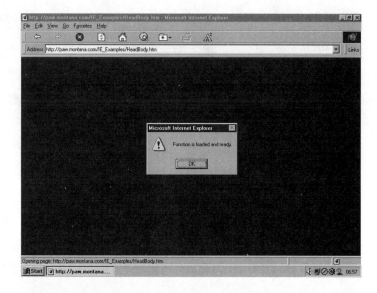

**FIGURE 32.7.**

*The rest of the display generated by Listing 32.5 shows the HTML text in the body of the page and executes the function that was defined in the head.*

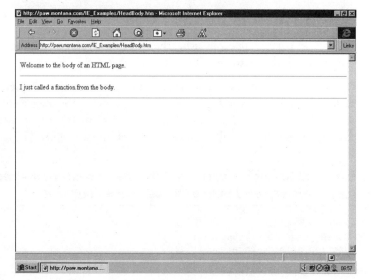

# Using JavaScript in Your Web Page

Many uses exist for JavaScript, and more continue to appear all the time as developers experiment with the possibilities opened with interactive HTML.

This section shows a few areas and examples to get you started.

**SCROLLING TICKER DISPLAYS**

A JavaScript ticker, which scrolls a message across the status bar, is absent from this list of applications. With Internet Explorer's MARQUEE tag and the availability of multi-featured Java ticker applets, the JavaScript ticker no longer provides an efficient use of browser capability.

# Validating Forms

Using CGI scripts to validate forms wastes precious user time and server time to conduct a process which is now easier and faster on the client's computer. The time required for client-server communication is reduced, along with the lengthy development necessary for CGI scripts.

With its capability to interact with form elements, JavaScript seems ideally suited to validate information directly on the HTML page. This setup localizes the process and takes advantage of the under-utilized client machine. Checking information on the client side also makes it much harder for users to send incompatible or damaging data to the server.

Several methods exist to implement form validation, and most include adding a JavaScript function as the action of a submit button. The HTML definition of the submit button could look like this:

```
<INPUT TYPE="BUTTON" NAME="SUBMIT" VALUE="SUBMIT"
➥onClick="checkInformation(this.form)">
```

checkInformation is a function that provides verification for the form to ensure that the information meets CGI script expectations. If not, it should return to the document without submitting the form contents to the server. It can also return focus to the offending items. If everything passes inspection, then the function can also use the submit method.

```
function checkInformation(thisForm) {
    ...validation statements ...;
    if (validationPassed) {
        thisForm.submit(); }
    return;
}
```

Each form element becomes part of a form object with JavaScript. By using the name of the form as the name of the object, you can access each of the elements. If a name is not used, you can also use the forms array. The first form on the page is forms[0], the next is forms[1], and so on.

For an example, look at the following form definition.

```
<FORM NAME="validation">Enter your user name and identification in the boxes.<BR>
Your name: <INPUT TYPE="text" NAME="userName" VALUE=""><BR>
User ID: <INPUT TYPE="text" NAME="userID" WIDTH="9" VALUE=""><BR>
```

```
<INPUT TYPE="button" NAME="button" VALUE="Submit" onClick="checkID(this.form)">
</FORM>
```

Each element in this form is represented in JavaScript as follows:

```
document.validation.userName
document.validation.userID
document.validation.button
```

The last element, a button, includes an event handler that calls the function `checkID` with the current form as the argument. Note that you don't need the name of the form in the call because the contents are passed as an argument in `this.form`. In the function (see Listing 32.6), the form is referred to as the name of the argument, `formID`.

### Listing 32.6. A function to ensure that the length of two form elements are correct before submitting the form.

```
function checkID(formID) {
    val validUser = true;
    val validID = true;
    if (formID.userName.length != 10) {
        validUser = false;
        formID.userName.value = "Invalid Entry"; }
    if (formID.userID.length != 9) {
        validID = false;
        formID.userName.value = "Error"; }
    if (validUser && validID) {
        formID.submit(); }
    else {
        alert("Please try again."); }
}
```

To understand the function, you work through it section by section. First, two boolean variables are initialized. These flags indicate whether or not the validation has been passed when it comes time to check at the end of the function.

Next, the length of a form element named `userName` is checked. If the value doesn't equal 10 (represented in JavaScript by `!=10`), then the valid flag is set to false, and the form element receives a new value, which is reflected immediately on the page.

The same process is repeated for the next form element, `userID`. At the end, if both flags are true (logical and is represented by `&&`), the form is submitted using the `submit` method. If either or both of the flags are false, an alert screen appears.

## Random Numbers

JavaScript includes a method of the `Math` object that generates random numbers, but in its current form, it only works on UNIX machines. Another way of generating somewhat-random numbers exists using a user-defined function instead of the built-in method. It is referred to as a calculated random number and can reveal its biases and true non-random nature if used repeatedly over a short period of time.

To ensure compatibility for a script across platforms, any script depending on random numbers shouldn't depend exclusively on the `random` method, and instead should rely on a generated number created by a function similar to the i.

```
function UnixMachine() {
    if (navigator.appVersion.lastIndexOf('Unix') != -1)
        return true
    else
        return false
}

function randomNumber() {
    if UnixMachine()
        num = Math.random()
    else
        num = Math.abs(Math.sin(Date.getTime()));
    return num;
}
```

If the client machine has a UNIX base, `randomNumber` will use the built-in function. Otherwise it generates a number between 0 and 1 by generating a sine based on the time value.

## JAVASCRIPT TIME

Time in JavaScript is measured as the number of milliseconds elapsed since midnight on January 1, 1970, and is accessed by using the `Date` object or an instance of it. The `Date` object is dynamic, ever changing with the time. An instance of the object returns a static value, depending on the current value of `Date` or the date parameter passed to it.

The time is based on the client machine, not the server. One idiosyncrasy occurs in JavaScript's representation of time elements. The `getMonth` and `setMonth` methods both return a value from 0 (January) to 11 (December). When using these two methods, make sure to convert to the 1-12 system the rest of the world recognizes.

```
var birthday1 = new Date(96,1,11);
document.writeln(birthday1.getMonth()); //Returns a 1 (February)
var birthday2 = new Date("January 11, 1996 06:00:00");
document.writeln(birthday2.getMonth()); //Returns a 0 (January)
```

If you need a constant stream of random numbers, a sine wave pattern will become evident. In this case, it becomes necessary to show some variation in the process by adding more variation into the calculation. You can do this by substituting a different computation (`cos`, `log`) at various intervals of time.

# Status Bar Messages

With event handlers and the `window.status` property, JavaScript enables your browser to display custom messages in the status bar that respond to user actions. One of the most popular implementations is a descriptive line for hyperlinks (see Figure 32.8).

```
More information is available from
<A HREF="http://www.microsoft.com" onMouseOver="window.status=
➥'The Microsoft Home Page';return true">
Microsoft Internet Explorer</A>.
```

**FIGURE 32.8.**

*A simple addition to the
A HREF tag enables page
authors to include useful
status bar messages to
respond to actions such as
placing the mouse over a
hyperlink.*

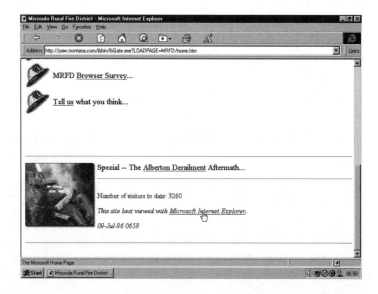

One problem with the `status` property is that it becomes the default message until a browser-generated message overrides it, or `status` is set to a different value. In the preceding example, `The Microsoft Home Page` remains in the status bar until another message preempts it.

To work around this problem requires the use of a timer. After passing the mouse over the hyperlink, the message displays, but only for a short time, after which the status bar is reset to a blank display. This setup requires two functions—one to write the message and set the timer, and one to erase the message.

```
timerLength = 1.5;
function writeStatus(str) {
    timeoutVal = timerLength * 1000;
    setTimeout("clearStatus()",timeoutVal);
    window.status = str;

}
function clearStatus() {
    window.status = "";
}
```

This method of generating status bar messages requires more lines of code but results in a cleaner operation for custom hyperlink messages. The message appears for the number of seconds assigned to `timerLength`, after which the `clearStatus` function is called to write a null string to the display. To invoke the new method, use the following example:

```
<a href="http://www.microsoft.com/"
➥onMouseOver="writeStatus('Microsoft Home Page'); return true;">
Microsoft</A>
```

Another possibility for this method of generating status bar displays includes making a copy of the old value of `window.status` and restoring it when the timer expires.

# Controlling Browser Behavior

One of the important and powerful capabilities of JavaScript is controlling various aspects of browser behavior and appearance. This feature comes in handy for implementing demonstrations and tours by adding the capability to spawn new browser windows with controllable levels of functionality.

The command syntax to create a new browser window is as follows:

```
windowVar = window.open("URL", "windowName" [, "windowFeatures"])
```

*windowVar* represents the name of a variable that holds the information about the new window.

*URL* refers to an address for the contents of the new window and can be blank.

*windowName* represents how the window will be referred to in frame and window references.

*windowFeatures* provides a list of the individual features of the browser that should be included or excluded. If blank, all features are enabled. If only some features appear, any unmentioned features are disabled.

To include a feature, use the syntax *windowFeature*=yes or *windowFeature*=1. Conversely, to disable a feature use *windowFeature*=no or *windowFeature*=0.

The features include `toolbar` for the row of buttons at the top of the screen, `status` for the status bar at the bottom, `scrollbars` for the buttons and slides to control the part of the document viewed, `resizable` for user control over the size of the browser, and `width` and `height` in pixels for the initial size.

To open a plain window with hotlink-only navigation, use this code:

```
//Note: Setting one feature automatically sets all
//non-mentioned features to false.
window.open("URL", "windowName", "toolbar=no")
```

# JavaScript Resources on the Internet

JavaScript is used and talked about on the Internet frequently, making the Internet one of the first stops for information. You can find up-to-the-minute information on current implementations, bugs, work-arounds, and new and creative uses.

## Netscape

One of the first stops you make should be the home of the people who developed and implemented JavaScript. The Netscape site provides a place to look for new developments and documentation about JavaScript features.

The complete JavaScript online documentation (see Figure 32.9) also appears here and includes discussion of the advanced topic of JavaScript cookies, which store client-specific states between sessions or visits. The online manual is also available in a ZIP file that you can download, or check out a book such as *Teach Yourself JavaScript in a Week* by Arman Danesh from Sams.net Publishing, ISBN 1-57521-073-8.

You can access Netscape at

```
http://home.netscape.com/
```

The manual is located at

```
http://home.netscape.com/eng/mozilla/Gold/handbook/javascript/index.html
```

**FIGURE 32.9.**

*The Netscape site has an online manual on JavaScript, including objects, methods, and event handlers. It is also available for download in ZIP format.*

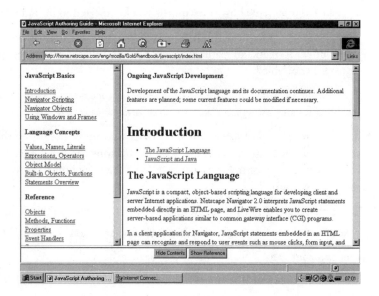

# Gamelan

This site provides one of the best places for examples of what other people are doing with JavaScript on the Web. Although Gamelan is more geared toward Java, it also includes one of the largest listings of JavaScript sites found anywhere on the Web. By perusing the examples here (see Figure 32.10), you can gain insight from others who have gone before you.

You can access Gamelan at

```
http://www.gamelan.com/pages/Gamelan.javascript.html
```

**FIGURE 32.10.**

*The Gamelan site offers one of the premier sites for JavaScript resources on the World Wide Web.*

# JavaScript Index

The JavaScript Index (see Figure 32.11) has a collection of real-life JavaScript examples and experiments, including a growing list of Web pages that illustrate some of JavaScript's features and capabilities. One of the pages included on the Index is a JavaScript Library, an expanding collection of source code from around the Web community.

You can access the JavaScript Index at

```
http://www.c2.org/~andreww/javascript/
```

**FIGURE 32.11.**

*The JavaScript Index has a solid source of examples and successful experiments from developers who are making JavaScript one of the fastest growing languages on the Internet.*

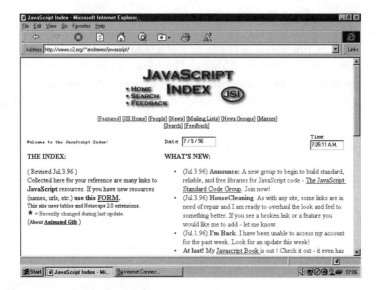

# The Unofficial JavaScript Resource Center

A well-designed site with a great deal of potential, the Unofficial JavaScript Resource Center (see Figure 32.12) remains shy on content in comparison with similar sites. Although it includes links to a variety of sites, this site also includes links to several tutorials.

You can reach the site at

```
http://www.intercom.net/user/mecha/java/index.html
```

**FIGURE 32.12.**

*The Unofficial JavaScript Resource Center, a growing resource, offers examples and tutorials for getting the most out of scripting on your Web pages.*

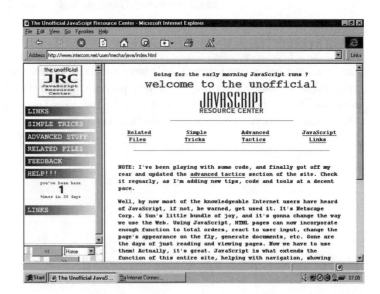

# Voodoo JavaScript Tutorial

The Voodoo JavaScript Tutorial (see Figure 32.13) contains a set of lessons covering the various aspects of including JavaScript on your Web pages. This project continues to evolve with new lessons added periodically, so you might want to check back periodically to see what's new.

You won't find much in the way of advanced material here, but what you find gives you more than enough to get beyond the beginner level.

You can access the site at

```
http://rummelplatz.uni-mannheim.de/~skoch/js/index.htm
```

**FIGURE 32.13.**

*The Voodoo JavaScript tutorial provides a good place to pick up the basics of working with JavaScript, in addition to other HTML features such as frames.*

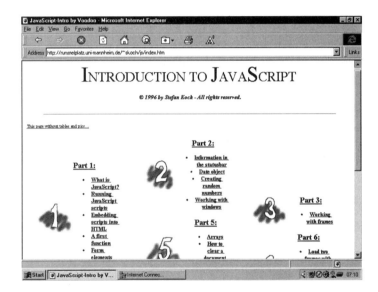

# JavaScript Newsgroup

This group is frequented by many of the JavaScript gurus and provides an excellent source of information, tips, and work-arounds. A high level of activity occurs and the threads move quickly, so make sure to check everyday if possible.

You can reach the JavaScript Newsgroup at

```
news://comp.lang.javascript
```

# netscape.navigator

It never hurts to have a direct line monitored by the folks who developed JavaScript at Netscape, and netscape.navigator remains the closest thing to that line. JavaScript topics are definitely in the minority in this group, but you can find them if you look.

Note the different news server. The title implies it's secure, but it seems to be readily available for browsing and posting.

Use this address to get there:

`news://secnews.netscape.com`

## JavaScript Digest

Much like a chain letter, this site serves as a running interactive discussion similar to the newsgroup. Once available in a digest format, it also comes in a standard form.

To subscribe, send a message to `listproc@inquiry.com` with the message, `set javascript mail ack`.

If you have problems receiving the digest, send a message to `listproc@inquiry.com` with the message body `help`. To unsubscribe to the list, send a message to `listproc@inquiry.com` with the message body `unsubscribe JAVASCRIPT`.

# Summary

JavaScript adds new functionality and interactivity to HTML pages that in the past you could only attain through learning CGI scripting languages such as Perl. By switching the bulk of interactive behavior to the client side, it has also improved the perceived speed of World Wide Web sites as seen by the user.

Although it does have its nuances and idiosyncrasies, taking the time to learn JavaScript will pay off in supporting Web pages with dramatically improved features and functions that users will want to visit again and again.

# Using VBScript in Your Web Pages

**33**

*by Sanjaya Hettihewa*

VBScript is Microsoft's scripting language for the Internet. Similar in functionality to JavaScript, VBScript has been designed to leverage the skills of millions of Visual Basic programmers to the Internet. Although JavaScript is a powerful scripting language, it is not as easy to learn and use as VBScript. VBScript can be used to easily create active Web pages. Because VBScript is supported by Microsoft, you will also see a great deal of VBScript/Windows NT/95/Office/ BackOffice integration. VBScript code is lightweight, fast, and has been optimized to be transmitted via the Internet. You should spend some time to learn how you can use VBScript to enhance a Web site by making it easier and more exciting to navigate. By the time you read this, you can expect to see VBScript supported by several other Web browsers in addition to Internet Explorer.

**CAUTION**

The current version of FrontPage is not VBScript aware. Because FrontPage is a WYSIWYG Web page development tool, you need to use the ActiveX Note Pad to insert VBScript code into Web pages. This will change when Microsoft releases the next version of FrontPage (version 2.0).

# Introduction to VBScript

VBScript is a subset of Microsoft Visual Basic and is upwardly compatible with Visual Basic for Applications (VBA). VBA is shipped with Microsoft Office applications to make it easier for developers to build custom solutions using Office applications. The capability to provide scripting, automation, and customization capabilities for Web browsers is a major feature of VBScript. If you are already familiar with Visual Basic, very shortly, you will be able to leverage your skills to the Internet using VBScript. Even if you are not familiar with another programming language, after reading this chapter you will be able to create active Web pages using VBScript. However, familiarity with a programming language makes it easier for you to grasp various concepts such as recursion, type casting, and Boolean arithmetic. Several VBScript applications are included on the CD-ROM; experiment with them to become more familiar with VBScript. Visit the Microsoft VBScript home page for the most up-to-date information about VBScript.

**URL**

Visit the Microsoft VBScript information Web site for the latest information about VBScript.

```
http://www.microsoft.com/VBScript
```

# How VBScript Works

VBScript programs are defined between two HTML tags. Browsers that support VBScript read the VBScript program contained between the two HTML tags and execute it after checking for any syntax errors. VBScript works as shown in Figure 33.1.

**FIGURE 33.1.**

*How VBScript works.*

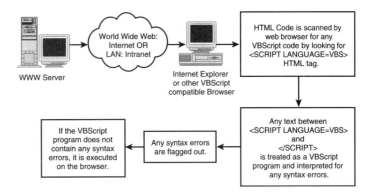

As you can see in Figure 33.1, a VBScript program is part of a regular HTML file and is enclosed between the two HTML tags <SCRIPT LANGUAGE=VBS> and </SCRIPT>. When a Web browser that supports VBScript encounters the <SCRIPT LANGUAGE=VBS> HTML tag, all text between that tag and </SCRIPT> is treated as a VBScript program and is interpreted for syntax errors. If any syntax errors are detected, they are flagged by the VBScript interpreter as shown in Figure 33.2.

**FIGURE 33.2.**

*Syntax errors in VBScript programs are flagged by the VBScript interpreter.*

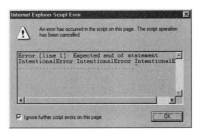

If the code does not contain any syntax errors, it is executed on the Web browser. In order to hide VBScript code from "technologically challenged" Web browsers, VBScript code can be enclosed in two HTML comment tags as shown in the following lines:

```
<SCRIPT LANGUAGE=VBS>
<!-- To hide VBScript code from technologically challenged browsers
… VBScript code …
!-->
</SCRIPT>
```

# Hello World!

Writing the classic Hello World program with VBScript is very easy. For the purpose of this example, you will be shown how to create a Web page similar to the one in Figure 33.3. This Web page has three buttons. The first button displays a message box with a greeting; the second button displays the current time; and the third button displays today's date.

> **NOTE**
>
> The author used several of this chapter's examples in the book *Web Site Developer's Guide for Windows NT*. Therefore, some of this chapter's figures retain that title. If you follow the code listings in this chapter, you will get slightly different results for titles.

**FIGURE 33.3.**

*The classic Hello World program written with VBScript.*

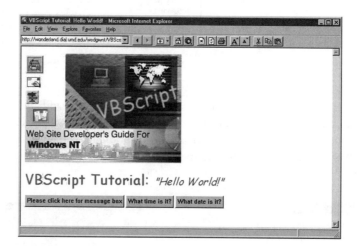

If you would like to experiment with the VBScript application shown in Figure 33.3, it is located on the CD-ROM that accompanies this book. Various key elements of the Hello World VBScript program are outlined next.

## The Hello World Dialog Box

As shown in Figure 33.4, the Hello World dialog box is shown each time a user clicks on the `Please click here for message box` button in Figure 33.3. If you look at the HTML page containing the VBScript program, you see that the command button associated with the Hello World dialog box is named `BtnHello` (`NAME="BtnHello"`). As you can see from Listing 33.1, the `OnClick` event is associated with the `BtnHello` subroutine. Each time a user clicks on the `Please click here for message box` button in Figure 33.3, the Web browser invokes the `BtnHello_OnClick` subroutine, and any VBScript code defined in that subroutine is executed.

The `BtnHello_OnClick` subroutine is a very simple VBScript subroutine. The first three lines create strings displayed by the dialog box in Figure 33.4. Note how the string concatenation operator (&) is used in line 4 to merge two strings into one and assign the result to a variable. Details on the concatenation operator can be found in Appendix C, "VBScript Reference." The result is then displayed in a message box, as shown in Figure 33.4.

**NOTE**

Lines numbers in various code segments are not part of the VBScript code. The line numbers are only there for reference purposes.

### Listing 33.1. The `BtnHello_OnClick` subroutine.

```
1: Sub BtnHello_OnClick
2:   titleString = "FrontPage Unleashed"
3:   helloString = "Hello world! Welcome to the fun filled "
4:   helloString = helloString & "world of VBScript programming!"
5:   MsgBox helloString, 0, titleString
6: End Sub
```

**FIGURE 33.4.**

*The Hello World dialog box.*

## Time Dialog Box

The `BtnTime_OnClick` subroutine is very similar to the `BtnHello_OnClick` subroutine. The only difference is the fact that rather than concatenating two strings, it concatenates a string with the result of a function. The `time` function returns the current time. As shown in Figure 33.5, line 3 of Listing 33.2 displays the current time in a dialog box.

### Listing 33.2. The `BtnTime_OnClick` subroutine.

```
1: Sub BtnTime_OnClick
2:   timeString = "So, you want to know the time? The time is " & time
3:   MsgBox  timeString , 0, "Time Dialog Box"
4: End Sub
```

**FIGURE 33.5.**

*Time dialog box.*

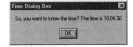

# Date Dialog Box

The Date dialog box displays the current date in a dialog box, as shown in Figure 33.6. As you can see in line 2 of Listing 33.3, the result of one function (`date`) can be used as an argument of another function (`DateValue`).

### Listing 33.3. The `BtnDate_OnClick` subroutine.

```
1: Sub BtnDate_OnClick
2:   dateString = "Today's date is " & DateValue(date)
3:   MsgBox  dateString , 0, "Date Dialog Box"
4: End Sub
```

**FIGURE 33.6.**

*The Date dialog box.*

For your reference, the full source code of the Hello World program appears in Listing 33.4.

### Listing 33.4. The Hello World Web page.

```
<!--
 1996 Sanjaya Hettihewa (http://wonderland.dial.umd.edu)
All Rights Reserved.
!-->

<HTML>
<HEAD>
<TITLE>VBScript Tutorial: Hello World!</TITLE>
</HEAD>

<BODY BGCOLOR="#FFFFFF" TEXT="#0000FF"
      LINK="#B864FF" VLINK="#670000" ALINK="#FF0000">

<IMG SRC="vbscript.jpg"><P>

<B><FONT FACE="Comic Sans MS" SIZE=6 COLOR=RED>
VBScript Tutorial: <FONT></B>
<I><FONT FACE="Comic Sans MS" SIZE=5 COLOR=BLUE>
  "Hello World!" </I><P><FONT>

<form>
<INPUT TYPE=BUTTON VALUE="Please click here for message box"
       NAME="BtnHello">
<INPUT TYPE=BUTTON VALUE="What time is it?"
       NAME="BtnTime">
<INPUT TYPE=BUTTON VALUE="What date is it?"
       NAME="BtnDate">
</form>
<SCRIPT LANGUAGE=VBS>
<!-- To hide VBScript code from technologically challenged browsers
```

```
Sub BtnHello_OnClick
 titleString = "FrontPage Unleashed"
 helloString = "Hello world! Welcome to the fun filled "
 helloString = helloString & "world of VBScript programming!"
 MsgBox helloString, 0, titleString
End Sub

Sub BtnTime_OnClick
 timeString = "So, you want to know the time? The time is " & time
 MsgBox  timeString , 0, "Time Dialog Box"
End Sub

Sub BtnDate_OnClick
 dateString = "Today's date is " & DateValue(date)
 MsgBox  dateString , 0, "Date Dialog Box"
End Sub
!-->
</SCRIPT>

</BODY>

</HTML>
```

# Applications of VBScript

The various control structures and commands that can be used to create VBScript programs are outlined in Appendix C. The next few sections are devoted to applications of these commands and control structures to demonstrate how you can use VBScript to create active Web pages.

## Simple Calculator

Using the various functions and control structures covered in Appendix C, you can create a simple calculator using VBScript, as the following example shows. If you want to experiment with the source code of the calculator program, it is included on the CD-ROM. The type of calculator that you will develop is shown in Figure 33.7.

You or your Web page visitor can enter operators and numbers into the calculator either by using the numeric buttons shown in Figure 33.7 or simply by typing them into one of the three textboxes. Before proceeding any further, you should experiment with the calculator program and find out how it works. When the Simple Calculator Web page is first invoked and numbers are typed in using various command buttons, they appear in the left textbox. After a valid operator is entered into the operator textbox, numbers entered next appear on the right textbox. At this point, if the Evaluate button is clicked, the VBScript program evaluates the expression entered and returns its value in a dialog box, as shown in Figure 33.8.

After the user clicks the OK button in the dialog box shown in Figure 33.8, the result of the calculation is copied to the first textbox, as shown in Figure 33.9. The user can then continue performing calculations using results of previous calculations.

**FIGURE 33.7.**

*The Simple Calculator application.*

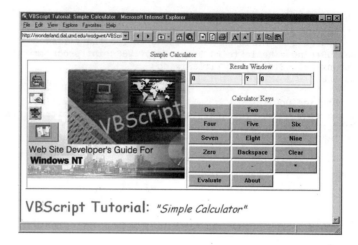

**FIGURE 33.8.**

*When the Evaluate button is pressed, the VBScript program calculates the expression entered and returns its value in a dialog box.*

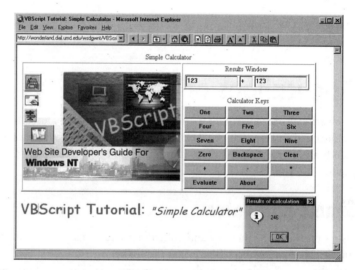

Let's now examine the calculator program in detail so you can learn how it works. The VBScript subroutine in Listing 33.5 displays a dialog box similar to the one shown in Figure 33.10, when a user clicks on the About button. Note how the string concatenation operator is used in line 4 to merge two strings.

**Listing 33.5. The `BtnAbout_OnClick` subroutine.**

```
1: Sub BtnAbout_OnClick
2:   titleString = "FrontPage Unleashed"
3:   helloString = "Simple VBScript calculator by "
4:   helloString = helloString & "Sanjaya Hettihewa."
5:   MsgBox helloString, 64, titleString
6: End Sub
```

**FIGURE 33.9.**

*The result of a calculation is copied to the first textbox so that it can be used as part of another calculation.*

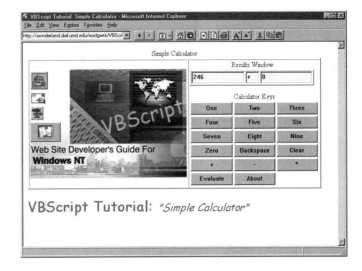

**FIGURE 33.10.**

*The About dialog box.*

Error checking is an important part of any application. One of VBScript's strengths is its ability to perform various error checks when users enter data into a form. By using the OnChange event, you can check the value of a textbox that has recently been changed by the user. The subroutine shown in Listing 33.6 makes sure the user enters a valid number into a textbox that is used to obtain an operand from the user. The error-checking subroutine for the second operand is similar. Note how Chr(10) is used to create a multiline string. As you can see in Figure 33.16, when a user enters an invalid number, the subroutine in Listing 33.6 informs the user and resets the textbox.

### Listing 33.6. The Operand1Box_OnChange subroutine.

```
 1: Sub Operand1Box_OnChange
 2:   IF (NOT IsNumeric(Operand1Box.Value)) THEN
 3:     MsgBoxString = "Do not type invalid characters "
 4:     MsgBoxString = MsgBoxString & "into the Results Window! "
 5:     MsgBoxString = MsgBoxString & chr(10)
 6:     MsgBoxString = MsgBoxString & "Results Window will now be reset."
 7:     MsgBox MsgBoxString , 48 , "Invalid input detected!"
 8:     Operand1Box.Value = 0
 9:   END IF
10: End Sub
```

**FIGURE 33.11.**

*Invalid numbers entered by users are detected by the* Operand1Box_OnChange *subroutine.*

A similar subroutine is used to check whether operators entered into the operator textbox are valid. The code in Listing 33.7 verifies that operators entered into the operator textbox are valid. Note how the underline character (_) is used to join a long expression that spans several lines. If an invalid operator is entered, it is detected by the OperatorBox_OnChange subroutine, the textbox is reset, and the user is informed of the invalid input, as shown in Figure 33.12.

**Listing 33.7. The OperatorBox_OnChange subroutine.**

```
 1: Sub OperatorBox_OnChange
 2:  IF (NOT((OperatorBox.Value = "+" ) OR _
 3:     (OperatorBox.Value = "-" ) OR _
 4:     (OperatorBox.Value = "*" ) OR _
 5:     (OperatorBox.Value = "?" ))) THEN
 6:     MsgString = "Do not type invalid characters "
 7:     MsgString = MsgString & "into the operator text box! "
 8:     MsgString = MsgString & chr(10)
 9:     MsgString = MsgString & "The operator text box will now be reset."
10:     MsgString = MsgString & chr(10) & chr(10)
11:     MsgString = MsgString & "Valid input: +, -, *"
12:     MsgBox MsgString , 48 , "Invalid input detected!"
13:     OperatorBox.Value = "?"
14:  END IF
15: End Sub
```

**FIGURE 33.12.**

*Invalid operators entered into the operator textbox are detected by the* OperatorBox_OnChange *subroutine.*

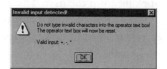

The Delete button deletes characters entered into one of the operand textboxes. The subroutine associated with the Delete button, BtnDelete_OnClick, is a smart function subroutine. As shown in line 2 of Listing 33.9, the subroutine first examines the operator textbox and determines whether a calculation has already been performed. If so, it knows that any numbers added should appear on the textbox to the right and deletes a digit from that textbox. If not, a digit from the left textbox is deleted.

**Listing 33.9. The BtnDelete_OnClick subroutine.**

```
 1: Sub BtnDelete_OnClick
 2:  IF (OperatorBox.Value = "?") THEN
 3:     IF ((Len (Operand1Box.Value) > 0) AND (Operand1Box.Value <> 0)) THEN
```

```
 4:          Operand1Box.Value = Left (Operand1Box.Value,
                                 Len (Operand1Box.Value) - 1)
 5:      IF (Len (Operand1Box.Value) = 0) THEN
 6:          Operand1Box.Value = 0
 7:      END IF
 8:      END IF
 9:   ELSE
10:      IF ((Len (Operand2Box.Value) > 0) AND (Operand2Box.Value <> 0)) THEN
11:          Operand2Box.Value = Left (Operand2Box.Value,
                                 Len (Operand2Box.Value) - 1)
12:      IF (Len (Operand2Box.Value) = 0) THEN
13:          Operand2Box.Value = 0
14:      END IF
15:      END IF
16:   END IF
17: End Sub
```

The Evaluate button calculates two operands using an operator and returns a value as shown in Figure 33.8. As you can see in line 2 of Listing 33.10, the `BtnEvaluate_OnClick` subroutine first checks the operator textbox. If a valid operator is found, it performs a calculation and displays it using a dialog box. If not, a dialog box similar to the one shown in Figure 33.13 is displayed. Afterwards, as shown in lines 17 and 18, the operand textboxes are reset so that additional calculations can be performed. Note that the result of the calculation is copied in line 17 to the left operand box so that the result of the calculation can be used as part of another calculation.

## Listing 33.10. The `BtnEvaluate_OnClick` subroutine.

```
 1: Sub BtnEvaluate_OnClick
 2:   IF (OperatorBox.Value = "?") THEN
 3:      MsgBoxString = "A valid operator is required to carry out "
 4:      MsgBoxString = MsgBoxString & "an evaluation."
 5:      MsgBoxString = MsgBoxString & chr(10)
 6:      MsgBoxString = MsgBoxString & "Valid operators are: +, -, *"
 7:      MsgBox MsgBoxString , 48 , "Invalid operator!"
 8:   ELSE
 9:      IF (OperatorBox.Value = "+")   THEN
10:         answer = CDbl(Operand1Box.Value) + CDbl(Operand2Box.Value)
11:      ELSEIF (OperatorBox.Value = "-")   THEN
12:         answer = CDbl(Operand1Box.Value) - CDbl(Operand2Box.Value)
13:      ELSEIF (OperatorBox.Value = "*")   THEN
14:         answer = CDbl(Operand1Box.Value) * CDbl(Operand2Box.Value)
15:      End IF
16:      MsgBox answer , 64 , "Results of calculation"
17:      Operand1Box.Value = answer
18:      Operand2Box.Value = 0
19:   END IF
20: End Sub
```

The `AddDigit` subroutine adds a digit selected via one of the calculator buttons into one of the operand textboxes. As shown in line 4 of Listing 33.11, if a valid operator is not present, digits are added to the left textbox. However, if a valid operator is present, this means that the user has either entered a valid number to the left textbox or that it contains a result of a previous calculation (in which case, the digit selected by the user is added to the right textbox). When adding digits, it is possible that the user might try to add too many digits. This is taken care of in lines 9 and 16, where a separate subroutine informs the reader by displaying a dialog box similar to the one shown in Figure 33.14.

## FIGURE 33.13.

*The operands are evaluated only if a valid operator is found.*

## Listing 33.11. The `AddDigit` Subroutine.

```
1: Sub AddDigit ( digit )
2:   REM Just in case there are any preceeding zeros or spaces
3:   Operand1Box.Value = CDbl (Operand1Box.Value)
4:   IF ( OperatorBox.Value = "?") THEN
5:       IF ( Len ( Operand1Box.Value ) < 14 ) THEN
6:           Operand1Box.Value = Operand1Box.Value & digit
7:           Operand1Box.Value = CDbl (Operand1Box.Value)
8:       ELSE
9:           TooManyDigits
10:      END IF
11:  ELSE
12:      IF ( Len ( Operand2Box.Value ) < 14 ) THEN
13:          Operand2Box.Value = Operand2Box.Value & digit
14:          Operand2Box.Value = CDbl (Operand2Box.Value)
15:      ELSE
16:          TooManyDigits
17:      END IF
18:  END IF
19: End Sub
```

## FIGURE 33.14.

*The* `AddDigit` *subroutine prevents users from entering too many digits into a textbox.*

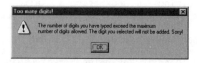

For your reference, the full source code of the Calculator application is given in Listing 33.12.

## Listing 33.12. The complete Calculator Web page code.

```
<!--
(C) 1996 Sanjaya Hettihewa (http://www.NetInnovation.com/)
All Rights Reserved.
Permission is hereby given to modify and distribute this code
as you wish provided that this block of text remains unchanged.
```

```
! -->

<HTML>
<HEAD>
<TITLE>VBScript Tutorial: Simple Calculator</TITLE>
</HEAD>


<TABLE COLSPEC="L20 L20 L20" BORDER=2 WIDTH=10 HEIGHT=10>
<CAPTION ALIGN=top>Simple Calculator</CAPTION>
<TR><TD>
<BODY BGCOLOR="#FFFFFF" TEXT="#0000FF"
      LINK="#B864FF" VLINK="#670000" ALINK="#FF0000">
<IMG ALIGN=TOP SRC="vbscript.jpg">
<TD>

<TABLE BORDER=2 >
<CAPTION ALIGN=top>Results Window</CAPTION>
 <TD>
 <input type=text size=14 maxlength=14 name="Operand1Box" value="0">
 <input type=text size=1 maxlength=1 name="OperatorBox" value="?">
 <input type=text size=14 maxlength=14 name="Operand2Box" value="0">
 </TD>
</TABLE>

<TABLE COLSPEC="L20 L20 L20" >

<CAPTION ALIGN=top>Calculator Keys</CAPTION>
<TR>
 <TD><INPUT TYPE=BUTTON VALUE="One" NAME="BtnOne"></TD>
 <TD><INPUT TYPE=BUTTON VALUE="Two" NAME="BtnTwo"></TD>
 <TD><INPUT TYPE=BUTTON VALUE="Three" NAME="BtnThree"></TD>
</TR>
<TR>
 <TD><INPUT TYPE=BUTTON VALUE="Four" NAME="BtnFour"></TD>
 <TD><INPUT TYPE=BUTTON VALUE="Five" NAME="BtnFive"></TD>
 <TD><INPUT TYPE=BUTTON VALUE="Six" NAME="BtnSix"></TD>
</TR>
<TR>
 <TD><INPUT TYPE=BUTTON VALUE="Seven" NAME="BtnSeven"></TD>
 <TD><INPUT TYPE=BUTTON VALUE="Eight" NAME="BtnEight"></TD>
 <TD><INPUT TYPE=BUTTON VALUE="Nine" NAME="BtnNine"></TD>
</TR>
<TR>
 <TD><INPUT TYPE=BUTTON VALUE="Zero" NAME="BtnZero"></TD>
 <TD><INPUT TYPE=BUTTON VALUE="Backspace" NAME="BtnDelete"></TD>
 <TD><INPUT TYPE=BUTTON VALUE="Clear" NAME="BtnClear"></TD>
</TR>
<TR>
 <TD><INPUT TYPE=BUTTON VALUE="+" NAME="BtnPlus"></TD>
 <TD><INPUT TYPE=BUTTON VALUE="-" NAME="BtnMinus"></TD>
 <TD><INPUT TYPE=BUTTON VALUE="*" NAME="BtnMultiply"></TD>
</TR>

<TR>
 <TD><INPUT TYPE=BUTTON VALUE="Evaluate" NAME="BtnEvaluate"></TD>
 <TD><INPUT TYPE=BUTTON VALUE="About" NAME="BtnAbout"></TD>
```

*continues*

## Listing 33.12. continued

```
</TR>

</TABLE>

</TR>
</TABLE>

<P>

<B><FONT FACE="Comic Sans MS" SIZE=6 COLOR=RED>
VBScript Tutorial: <FONT></B>
<I><FONT FACE="Comic Sans MS" SIZE=5 COLOR=BLUE>
 "Simple Calculator" </I><P><FONT>


<SCRIPT LANGUAGE=VBS>
<!-- To hide VBScript code from technologically challenged browsers

Sub BtnAbout_OnClick
 titleString = "FrontPage Unleashed"
 helloString = "Simple VBScript calculator by "
 helloString = helloString & "Sanjaya Hettihewa."
 MsgBox helloString, 64, titleString
End Sub

Sub Operand1Box_OnChange
 IF (NOT IsNumeric(Operand1Box.Value)) THEN
    MsgBoxString = "Do not type invalid characters "
    MsgBoxString = MsgBoxString & "into the Results Window! "
    MsgBoxString = MsgBoxString & chr(10)
    MsgBoxString = MsgBoxString & "Results Window will now be reset."
    MsgBox MsgBoxString , 48 , "Invalid input detected!"
    Operand1Box.Value = 0
 END IF
End Sub

Sub Operand2Box_OnChange
 IF (NOT IsNumeric(Operand2Box.Value)) THEN
    MsgBoxString = "Do not type invalid characters "
    MsgBoxString = MsgBoxString & "into the Results Window! "
    MsgBoxString = MsgBoxString & chr(10)
    MsgBoxString = MsgBoxString & "Results Window will now be reset."
    MsgBox MsgBoxString , 48 , "Invalid input detected!"
    Operand2Box.Value = 0
 END IF
End Sub

Sub OperatorBox_OnChange
 IF (NOT((OperatorBox.Value = "+" ) OR _
    (OperatorBox.Value = "-" ) OR _
    (OperatorBox.Value = "*" ) OR _
    (OperatorBox.Value = "?" ))) THEN
    MsgString = "Do not type invalid characters "
    MsgString = MsgString & "into the operator text box! "
    MsgString = MsgString & chr(10)
    MsgString = MsgString & "The operator textbox will now be reset."
```

```
      MsgString = MsgString & chr(10) & chr(10)
      MsgString = MsgString & "Valid input: +, -, *"
      MsgBox MsgString , 48 , "Invalid input detected!"
      OperatorBox.Value = "?"
  END IF
End Sub


Sub BtnOne_OnClick
  IF (IsNumeric(Operand1Box.Value)) THEN
      AddDigit ( 1 )
  ELSE
      ResetResultsWindow
  END IF
End Sub
Sub BtnTwo_OnClick
  IF (IsNumeric(Operand1Box.Value)) THEN
      AddDigit ( 2 )
  ELSE
      ResetResultsWindow
  END IF
End Sub
Sub BtnThree_OnClick
  IF (IsNumeric(Operand1Box.Value)) THEN
      AddDigit ( 3 )
  ELSE
      ResetResultsWindow
  END IF
End Sub
Sub BtnFour_OnClick
  IF (IsNumeric(Operand1Box.Value)) THEN
      AddDigit ( 4 )
  ELSE
      ResetResultsWindow
  END IF
End Sub
Sub BtnFive_OnClick
  IF (IsNumeric(Operand1Box.Value)) THEN
      AddDigit ( 5 )
  ELSE
      ResetResultsWindow
  END IF
End Sub
Sub BtnSix_OnClick
  IF (IsNumeric(Operand1Box.Value)) THEN
      AddDigit ( 6 )
  ELSE
      ResetResultsWindow
  END IF
End Sub
Sub BtnSeven_OnClick
  IF (IsNumeric(Operand1Box.Value)) THEN
      AddDigit ( 7 )
  ELSE
      ResetResultsWindow
  END IF
End Sub
```

*continues*

## Listing 33.12. continued

```
Sub BtnEight_OnClick
 IF (IsNumeric(Operand1Box.Value)) THEN
    AddDigit ( 8 )
 ELSE
    ResetResultsWindow
 END IF
End Sub
Sub BtnNine_OnClick
 IF (IsNumeric(Operand1Box.Value)) THEN
    AddDigit ( 9 )
 ELSE
    ResetResultsWindow
 END IF
End Sub
Sub BtnZero_OnClick
 IF (IsNumeric(Operand1Box.Value)) THEN
    AddDigit ( 0 )
 ELSE
    ResetResultsWindow
 END IF
End Sub

Sub BtnDelete_OnClick
 IF (OperatorBox.Value = "?") THEN
    IF ((Len (Operand1Box.Value) > 0) AND (Operand1Box.Value <> 0)) THEN
       Operand1Box.Value = Left (Operand1Box.Value,
                                 Len (Operand1Box.Value) - 1)
    IF (Len (Operand1Box.Value) = 0) THEN
       Operand1Box.Value = 0
    END IF
    END IF
 ELSE
    IF ((Len (Operand2Box.Value) > 0) AND (Operand2Box.Value <> 0)) THEN
       Operand2Box.Value = Left (Operand2Box.Value,
                                 Len (Operand2Box.Value) - 1)
    IF (Len (Operand2Box.Value) = 0) THEN
       Operand2Box.Value = 0
    END IF
    END IF
 END IF
End Sub

Sub BtnClear_OnClick
 Operand1Box.Value = 0
 Operand2Box.Value = 0
 OperatorBox.Value = "?"
End Sub

Sub BtnPlus_OnClick
 OperatorBox.Value = "+"
End Sub

Sub BtnMinus_OnClick
 OperatorBox.Value = "-"
End Sub

Sub BtnMultiply_OnClick
```

```
   OperatorBox.Value = "*"
End Sub

Sub BtnEvaluate_OnClick
 IF (OperatorBox.Value = "?") THEN
    MsgBoxString = "A valid operator is required to carry out "
    MsgBoxString = MsgBoxString & "an evaluation."
    MsgBoxString = MsgBoxString & chr(10)
    MsgBoxString = MsgBoxString & "Valid operators are: +, -, *"
    MsgBox MsgBoxString , 48 , "Invalid operator!"
 ELSE
    IF (OperatorBox.Value = "+")   THEN
       answer = CDbl(Operand1Box.Value) + CDbl(Operand2Box.Value)
    ELSEIF (OperatorBox.Value = "-")   THEN
       answer = CDbl(Operand1Box.Value) - CDbl(Operand2Box.Value)
    ELSEIF (OperatorBox.Value = "*")   THEN
       answer = CDbl(Operand1Box.Value) * CDbl(Operand2Box.Value)
    End IF
    MsgBox answer , 64 , "Results of calculation"
    Operand1Box.Value = answer
    Operand2Box.Value = 0
 END IF
End Sub

Sub AddDigit ( digit )
 REM Just in case there are any preceeding zeros or spaces
 Operand1Box.Value = CDbl (Operand1Box.Value)
 IF ( OperatorBox.Value = "?") THEN
    IF ( Len ( Operand1Box.Value ) < 14 ) THEN
       Operand1Box.Value = Operand1Box.Value & digit
       Operand1Box.Value = CDbl (Operand1Box.Value)
    ELSE
       TooManyDigits
    END IF
 ELSE
    IF ( Len ( Operand2Box.Value ) < 14 ) THEN
       Operand2Box.Value = Operand2Box.Value & digit
       Operand2Box.Value = CDbl (Operand2Box.Value)
    ELSE
       TooManyDigits
    END IF
 END IF
End Sub

Sub ResetResultsWindow
 MsgBoxString = "Do not type invalid characters "
 MsgBoxString = MsgBoxString & "into the Results Window! "
 MsgBoxString = MsgBoxString & chr(10)
 MsgBoxString = MsgBoxString & "Use Calculator keys instead. "
 MsgBoxString = MsgBoxString & "Results Window will now be reset."
 MsgBox MsgBoxString , 48 , "Invalid input detected!"
 Operand1Box.Value = 0
 Operand2Box.Value = 0
 OperatorBox.Value = "?"
End Sub

Sub TooManyDigits
```

*continues*

## Listing 33.12. continued

```
MsgBoxString = "The number of digits you have typed "
MsgBoxString = MsgBoxString & "exceed the maximum"
MsgBoxString = MsgBoxString & chr(10)
MsgBoxString = MsgBoxString & "number of digits allowed. "
MsgBoxString = MsgBoxString & "The digit you selected will "
MsgBoxString = MsgBoxString & "not be added. Sorry!"
MsgBox MsgBoxString , 48 , "Too many digits!"
End Sub

!-->
</SCRIPT>

</BODY>
</HTML>
```

# Labeling an Image

You can also use VBScript to label a graphic when the mouse is moved over it. The VBScript program in Listing 33.13 labels an image. When the Web page containing the VBScript program is first invoked, it looks similar to Figure 33.15. Note that the description textbox contains the string Hello! Select a link, please.

**FIGURE 33.15.**

*Textbox contains the string* Hello! Select a link, please. *when the VBScript Web page is first invoked.*

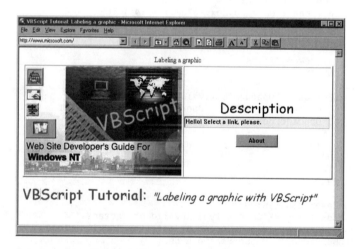

At this point, if the mouse is moved over the graphic in Figure 33.15, the value of the textbox changes.

As you can see in Figure 33.16, there are four icons in the graphic to the left of the browser window. When the mouse is moved over any of these icons, the textbox lists the description of the textbox. For example, when the mouse is over the bulletin board icon, the value of the textbox in Figure 33.17 changes to Post messages on an online discussion forum. Now, let's discuss various key subroutines of the label image program.

**FIGURE 33.16.**

*When the mouse is moved over the graphic, the value of the textbox changes to* No link selected. Please select a link!.

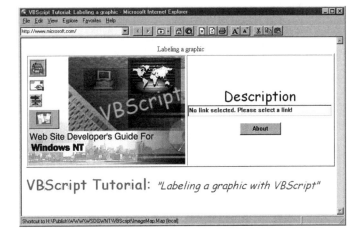

**FIGURE 33.17.**

*When the mouse cursor is over one of the icons of the image, the value of the textbox changes the icon's description.*

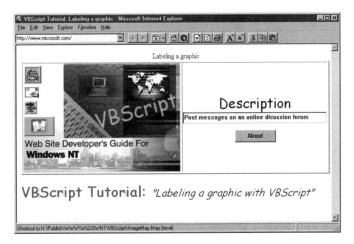

In order to detect mouse movement over the graphic in Figure 33.17, a special identification code needs to be assigned to the graphic. This is done in line 1 of the following code excerpt.

```
1: <A ID="ImageMapGraphic" HREF="ImageMap.Map">
2: <IMG  ALIGN=TOP SRC="vbscript.jpg" ALT="Sample Graphic" ISMAP BORDER=0>
3: </A>
```

The ImageMapGraphic_MouseMove is the heart of the VBScript shown in Figure 33.17. When the mouse is moved over the graphic, the subroutine in Listing 33.13 is activated. When the mouse pointer falls in a predetermined region of the graphic, the textbox is updated with the description of the region the mouse pointer is over, as shown in line 4 of Listing 33.13. The HotSpot subroutine simply returns true if the mouse coordinates passed into the HotSpot subroutine fall within a certain region of the graphic.

## Listing 33.13. The `ImageMapGraphic_MouseMove` subroutine.

```
 1: Sub ImageMapGraphic_MouseMove(keyboard,mouse,xPosition,yPosition)
 2:
 3: IF (HotSpot(xPosition, yPosition,  2, 5, 70, 41)) THEN
 4:    Description.Value = "Main Homepage"
 5: ELSE IF (HotSpot(xPosition, yPosition,  2, 49, 70, 82)) THEN
 6:    Description.Value = "Send Feedback"
 7: ELSE IF (HotSpot(xPosition, yPosition,  2, 84, 70, 117)) THEN
 8:    Description.Value = "Site Map"
 9: ELSE IF (HotSpot(xPosition, yPosition,  2, 119, 70, 164)) THEN
10:    Description.Value = "Post messages on an online dicussion forum"
11: ELSE
12:    Description.Value = "No link selected. Please select a link!"
13: END IF
14: END IF
15: END IF
16: END IF
```

If you want to experiment with the VBScript program in Listing 33.14, it is on the CD-ROM that accompanies this book. For your reference, the full source code of the Label Image application appears in Listing 33.14.

## Listing 33.14. Labeling a graphic.

```
<!--
(C) 1996 Sanjaya Hettihewa All Rights Reserved.
    http://www.NetInnovation.com/
    Permission is hereby given to modify and distribute this code
    as you wish provided that this block of text remains unchanged.
!-->

<HTML>
<HEAD>
<TITLE>VBScript Tutorial: Labeling a graphic</TITLE>
</HEAD>

<BODY BGCOLOR="#FFFFFF" TEXT="#0000FF"
          LINK="#B864FF" VLINK="#670000" ALINK="#FF0000">

<TABLE COLSPEC="L20 L20 L20" BORDER=2 WIDTH=10 HEIGHT=10>
<CAPTION ALIGN=top>Labeling a graphic</CAPTION>
<TR><TD>

<A ID="ImageMapGraphic" HREF="ImageMap.Map">
<IMG  ALIGN=TOP SRC="vbscript.jpg" ALT="Sample Graphic" ISMAP BORDER=0>
</A>

</TD><TD>

<CENTER><FONT FACE="Comic Sans MS" SIZE=6 COLOR=Black>
Description<FONT></CENTER>
<input type="text" name="Description"
      Value="Hello! Select a link, please." size=45><P>
```

```
<CENTER><INPUT TYPE=BUTTON VALUE="About" NAME="BtnAbout"></CENTER>

</TD><TD>

</TR>
</TABLE>

<P>

<B><FONT FACE="Comic Sans MS" SIZE=6 COLOR=RED>
VBScript Tutorial: <FONT></B>
<I><FONT FACE="Comic Sans MS" SIZE=5 COLOR=BLUE>
 "Labeling a graphic with VBScript" </I><P><FONT>
</TD></TR>
</TABLE>

<SCRIPT LANGUAGE="VBS">
<!-- To hide VBScript code from  technologically challenged browsers

Sub BtnAbout_OnClick
  titleString = "FrontPage Unleashed"
  helloString = "Labeling a graphic with VBScript by "
  helloString = helloString & "Sanjaya Hettihewa."
  MsgBox helloString, 64, titleString
End Sub

Sub ImageMapGraphic_MouseMove(keyboard,mouse,xPosition,yPosition)

IF (HotSpot(xPosition, yPosition,  2, 5, 70, 41)) THEN
  Description.Value = "Main Homepage"
ELSE IF (HotSpot(xPosition, yPosition,  2, 49, 70, 82)) THEN
  Description.Value = "Send Feedback"
ELSE IF (HotSpot(xPosition, yPosition,  2, 84, 70, 117)) THEN
  Description.Value = "Site Map"
ELSE IF (HotSpot(xPosition, yPosition,  2, 119, 70, 164)) THEN
  Description.Value = "Post messages on an online dicussion forum"
ELSE
  Description.Value = "No link selected. Please select a link!"
END IF
END IF
END IF
END IF

End Sub

Function HotSpot ( mouseX, mouseY, TopX , TopY, BottomX, BottomY)
 HotSpot = (mouseX >= TopX) AND _
           (mouseX <= BottomX) AND _
           (mouseY >= topY) AND _
           (mouseY<=bottomY)
End Function

!-->
</SCRIPT>

</BODY>
</HTML>
```

# VBScript Programming with the ActiveX Control Pad

The ActiveX Control Pad is a useful application for inserting ActiveX controls into Web pages. With it, you can create richly interactive multimedia Web pages using an easy to use graphical user interface. This section focuses on how you can use the ActiveX Control Pad to insert ActiveX controls to Web pages. Although the following example performs a very simple task, it demonstrates how the ActiveX Control Pad can be used to automate ActiveX controls using VBScript. For additional information about VBScript programming with the ActiveX Control Pad, visit `http://WWW.NetInnovation.com/`.

## Creating a Clock with VBScript

This exercise demonstrates how you can use the ActiveX Control Pad to create a clock. Before proceeding any further, download and install the ActiveX Control Pad on your system. The ActiveX Control Pad is available from `http://www.microsoft.com/intdev/author/cpad/`.

After installing the ActiveX Control Pad, invoke it by executing the Microsoft ActiveX Control Pad icon located in the Microsoft ActiveX Control Pad Start Menu folder. When it is first invoked, the Active Control Pad looks similar to the window in Figure 33.18.

**FIGURE 33.18.**

*The ActiveX Control Pad.*

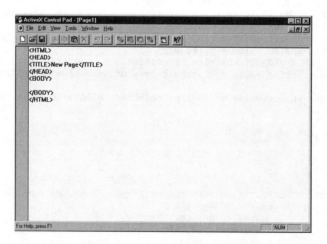

In order to create the clock, two ActiveX controls (Microsoft Forms 2.0 Label and Timer Object) have to be inserted into the Web page in Figure 33.19. The Microsoft Forms 2.0 Label displays the time, and the Timer Object updates the Microsoft Forms 2.0 Label each second. These two controls can be inserted by selecting Edit | Insert ActiveX Control from the menu bar and using the Insert ActiveX Control dialog box (see Figure 33.19).

**FIGURE 33.19.**

*The Insert ActiveX Control dialog box is used to insert ActiveX controls to Web pages.*

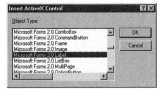

> **NOTE**
>
> When Inserting ActiveX controls, make sure the cursor is between the two HTML tags `<BODY>` and `</BODY>` before invoking the dialog box.

When inserting the two ActiveX controls, Microsoft Forms 2.0 Label and Timer Object, you will see a Properties dialog box for each ActiveX control. Change values of the Properties dialog box of the Microsoft Forms 2.0 Label ActiveX Control to match the values of the dialog box in Figure 33.20. Similarly, modify values of the Properties dialog box of the Timer Object to match the values of the dialog box in Figure 33.21. After modifying the values, click on the Cancel button of each dialog box.

**FIGURE 33.20.**

*Values of the Properties dialog box of the Microsoft Forms 2.0 Label ActiveX control.*

After inserting the two ActiveX controls, you need to automate them with VBScript. You can do this by using the Script Wizard. Select Tools | Script Wizard to invoke the Script Wizard dialog box shown in Figure 33.22. If this dialog box looks somewhat complicated, do not worry; it is very easy to use. After you understand how it works, you'll love the Script Wizard. As you can see in Figure 33.22, the top half of the Script Wizard is comprised of two frames. The left frame contains various events and the right frame contains various actions of ActiveX controls that have been inserted into the Web page being edited.

**FIGURE 33.21.**

*Values of the Properties
dialog box of the Timer
Object ActiveX control.*

Because the clock has to be updated each second, select the `Timer` event of the `IeTimer1` object in the left frame as shown in Figure 33.22. Afterwards, select the `caption` attribute of the `Label1` object as illustrated in Figure 33.22.

**FIGURE 33.22.**

*The Script Wizard assigns
actions to various events of
ActiveX controls.*

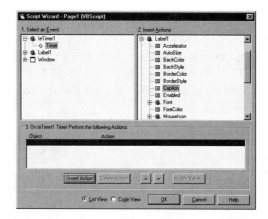

Press the Insert Action Button. The dialog box in Figure 33.23 appears. This dialog box assigns a value to the caption of `Label1` object each time the `Timer` action is triggered.

**FIGURE 33.23.**

*The Change `Label1`
Caption dialog box (used to
type in string expressions).*

Because the caption of `Label1` has to be updated with the value of a VBScript function that returns the current system time, press the Custom button of the dialog box shown in Figure 33.23. The Change `Label1` Caption dialog box shown in Figure 33.24 appears. Type `Time` (the name of the VBScript function that returns the current time) in the Change `Label1` Caption dialog box and press the OK button. Next, press the OK button of the Script Wizard dialog box shown in Figure 33.22. See Listing 33.15 for the Web page that you just created with the ActiveX Control Pad.

**FIGURE 33.24.**

*The Change* Label1
*Caption dialog box (used
to type in VBScript
expressions).*

## Listing 33.15. HTML code of the ActiveX/VBScript Clock application.

```
<HTML>
<HEAD>
<TITLE>New Page</TITLE>
</HEAD>
<BODY>
    <OBJECT ID="Label1" WIDTH=137 HEIGHT=31
     CLASSID="CLSID:978C9E23-D4B0-11CE-BF2D-00AA003F40D0">
        <PARAM NAME="ForeColor" VALUE="0">
        <PARAM NAME="BackColor" VALUE="14286843">
        <PARAM NAME="Size" VALUE="3620;811">
        <PARAM NAME="SpecialEffect" VALUE="1">
        <PARAM NAME="FontHeight" VALUE="360">
        <PARAM NAME="FontCharSet" VALUE="0">
        <PARAM NAME="FontPitchAndFamily" VALUE="2">
    </OBJECT>
    <SCRIPT LANGUAGE="VBScript">
<!--
Sub IeTimer1_Timer()
Label1.Caption = Time
end sub
-->
    </SCRIPT>
    <OBJECT ID="IeTimer1" WIDTH=39 HEIGHT=39
     CLASSID="CLSID:59CCB4A0-727D-11CF-AC36-00AA00A47DD2">
        <PARAM NAME="_ExtentX" VALUE="1005">
        <PARAM NAME="_ExtentY" VALUE="1005">
        <PARAM NAME="Interval" VALUE="1000">
    </OBJECT>
</BODY>
</HTML>
```

Note how the HTML code of Listing 33.15 appears in the ActiveX Control Pad. As you can see in Figure 33.25, a button is present in the left side margin next to the VBScript code and each of the two ActiveX controls. To modify attributes of the ActiveX controls or assign additional events and actions, click one of the buttons in the left side margin.

Select File | Save to save the ActiveX/VBScript Clock application. After you have saved it, it can be viewed with any Web browser that supports ActiveX, such as Internet Explorer, as shown in Figure 33.26.

**FIGURE 33.25.**

*Buttons in the left side margin can be used to modify attributes of ActiveX controls as well as VBScript code.*

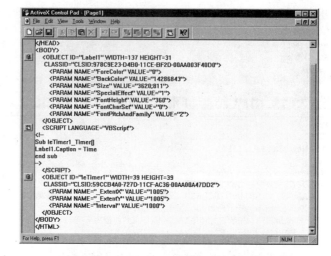

**FIGURE 33.26.**

*ActiveX/VBScript Clock application.*

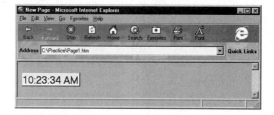

# Summary

VBScript, a subset of Visual Basic, is an easy-to-use scripting language that you can use to create active Web pages. It enables Web-site developers to create various client-side solutions and make a Web site easier and more interesting to navigate.

A Web site's success depends on how well it is publicized on the Internet. The next chapter focuses on writing Java applets for your Web site. Java is more complicated than scripting languages such as VBScript and JavaScript, but it can do much more.

# Writing Java Applets

# 34

*by Rick Darnell*

**IN THIS CHAPTER**

Java is one of the hottest topics on the World Wide Web, and for good reason. It offers expanded portability for Web content, including sound and animation, without the use of plug-ins or other helper applications, and independent of host hardware. In this sense, Java has helped promote a change in the way page developers think about content on the World Wide Web, similar to the way the World Wide Web changed the way people think about the Internet.

# Getting To Know Java

Java is an object-oriented programming language developed by Sun Microsystems, Inc. Although not initially conceived as a way to expand the interactivity and capability of Web pages, it didn't take long for people to see how the platform-independent nature of Java made an ideal fit with the nature of the Internet.

In the past, when an author developed a page with special content beyond the constraints of HTML, an important decision had to be made: either use helper-applications or shift the necessary processing to the server. The first solution meant that some content would be inaccessible to some users if they didn't have the helper application or if a helper was unavailable for their system. The second solution meant excluding some content because inherently slow modem lines made animation and sounds unworkable over normal network connections.

Enter Sun's Java. By utilizing a key feature of Java—platform independence—Java applets can implement sound, animation, and other user interactivity regardless of platform.

## What Is Java?

Sun Microsystems makes it clear whenever introducing Java that "Java is a simple, robust, secure, object-oriented, platform-independent, dynamic programming environment."

At first, all of this Java talk can sound like a lot of voodoo. After you strip away the hype, however, it's easy to see how Java works effectively for implementing simple solutions to potentially complicated challenges in a distributed environment.

## Simple

Java was designed with C and C++ programmers in mind. C and C++, however, had many hard-to-understand, rarely used features that the Java developers felt caused more pain than benefit. Important functions that come standard to every program, such as memory allocation and pointer arithmetic, are automatically handled by the Java system without needing any acknowledgment from the programmer.

In addition, Java is relatively small. Because of the need to run on a wide variety of platforms, Java applications tend to be smaller than the multi-megabyte applications that predominate the marketplace. The overhead to run a Java program includes 40KB for the basic interpreter and classes, plus an additional 175KB for the standard libraries and threading.

# Robust

Java programs must be inherently reliable because any piece of Java byte must be capable of running on any platform. For this reason, a great deal of emphasis is placed on checking for bugs and problems early in the development process, beginning with basic language implementation.

A pointer serves as a popular example. C++, a close cousin of Java, used extensive pointer arithmetic to keep track of arrays and other memory variables. This setup enabled programmers to take full advantage of a specific platform, but it also created problems when pointers went awry, overwriting memory and corrupting data.

The Java compiler checks for a wide variety of errors beyond basic syntax, including type casting and method invocations. If you've made a mistake or mistyped, chances are good that your mistake gets flagged by the compiler, which is a far better place than by the interpreter at runtime.

# Secure

Running in a distributed environment, such as an intranet or the World Wide Web, requires safeguards for client computers; a potentially hostile piece of code can do a great deal of damage by erasing files, formatting disks, and creating other types of damage. Given the way applets are implemented—automatic load and run—you need to ensure the integrity of any piece of code distributed to a broad and uncontrolled audience. Java uses three security procedures to make the end user safe from malicious attacks:

- Bytecode verification
- Memory layout control
- File access restrictions

## Bytecode Verification

After a piece of Java code is loaded into memory, it enters the interpreter, where it gets checked for language compliance before the first statement is executed. This process ensures against corruption or changes to the compiled code between compile time and runtime.

## Memory Layout

Next, the memory layout is determined for each of the classes, preventing would-be hackers from forging access by deducing anything about the structure of a class or the machine it's running on. Memory allocation is different for each class, depending on its structure and the host machine.

## File Access Restrictions

After that, the interpreter security continues to monitor the activity of the applet to make sure it doesn't access the host file system, except as specifically allowed by the client or user. You can extend some implementations of this specific feature to include no file access, period.

Though no system can guarantee 100 percent security, Java goes a long way to ensure the protection of client systems from its applets.

## Object-Oriented

Object-oriented, probably one of the most overused and confusing terms in computer lingo, really has a simple and easy-to-understand meaning. It facilitates creating clean and portable code by breaking software down into coherent units.

In other words, object-oriented programming focuses on the ways of interacting with data, rather than the programming language. For example, if you're going to mow the lawn, are you going to be concerned about starting the lawnmower or about the type of socket used to install the spark plug? In object-oriented programming, the focus is on the lawnmower.

Objects become the basic building blocks of the application. Because of their modularity, an object can change without requiring major revision of the other program elements.

## Platform-Independent

This feature is probably the most important one. One compiled piece of Java code can run on any platform with a Java compiler. Currently, the list of platforms includes Windows 95, Solaris, and Macintosh, but that list should grow significantly in the near future. By its very nature, Java does not contain any "implementation-specific" syntax. This format means a byte is an 8-bit integer and a float is a 32-bit IEEE 754 floating point number, no matter where the applet runs.

## Dynamic

One benefit of the object-oriented code is the dynamic nature of the resulting programs. By using inherited interfaces—a set of methods without instance variables or implementation—updating a class library does not affect the capability of the rest of the program to interact with it.

## Why Is Java So Hot?

Java holds a great deal of promise for the World Wide Web and computers in general because it provides a solution to the problem of incompatible platforms. Internets and intranets are no longer expected to include similar or directly compatible machines (all UNIX, all Macintosh, or all PC). Because it has a neutral architecture, the same application written in Java can be used by anyone on the network, without concern for what kind of machine the developer used.

For stand-alone applications, Java's object-oriented structure gives an easy method to upgrade. The class for the upgrade or extension of the application is downloaded into the appropriate class library; then you can run the updated features.

With its modeling capabilities, Java represents a good choice for implementing advanced Web capabilities and content, such as virtual reality sites or Web crawlers powered by intelligent agents.

## How To Use Java Now

Probably the simplest way to implement Java is through embedding applets in your HTML pages. A wide variety of applets are already available for inclusion, such as the animation applet included with the Java Developer's Kit, and a plethora of "ticker" display applets.

> **NOTE**
>
> Although Java applets are spreading quickly, they do not come with all browsers. Netscape's Navigator and Sun's HotJava support Java applets, and Microsoft's Internet Explorer is scheduled to include applet functionality with its 3.0 release. NCSA Mosaic has included Java compatibility in its wish list for future upgrades to its product, but no word has been given on when that might happen.
>
> If your browser is not Java-compatible, the applet section of the HTML page is ignored.

# How Applets and Applications Are Different

Java applications work similarly to stand-alone programs, such as your browser or word processor. They don't require a third-party intermediary, such as HotJava or the applet viewer. Applets require a Java-compatible browser or the applet viewer for viewing. They operate similarly to other objects embedded in HTML documents, such as Shockwave or RealAudio files, which require assistance to run.

> **NOTE**
>
> The HotJava browser developed by Sun is a Java application that was written and implemented entirely in the Java language.

The fact that applets run on a host system makes them especially suspect and leads to several key security restrictions. Applets have limited capability to interact with their host platform. An applet cannot write files or send files to a printer on the local system. In addition, it cannot read local files or run local applications. Although no system is 100 percent secure, Java goes to great lengths to ensure the integrity of applets generated under its banner.

Java is not bulletproof, however. As soon as it was proclaimed "secure," a dedicated group of programmers went to work to find security holes. And they found them. Through cooperative efforts between Sun, Netscape, Microsoft, and others, these are being corrected, but it's still a dangerous world. There are reports of "black Java" applets that are hostile enough to format system drives and pass secure information across the Internet.

There are a few things you can do to protect yourself and your system.

- Use only the most up-to-date versions of software.
- If your system allows screening applets at the firewall, take advantage of it. If there are applets you'd like to use, make them available internally.
- Don't browse a Java site unless you know it's clean.

As discussed in the introduction, the compiled byte code is checked extensively for illegal operations and is verified again on the host system before the applet is run. Although these security features limit the scope and capabilities of an applet, they also help ensure against "Trojan horse" viruses and other shenanigans by less-than-scrupulous programmers.

With all of the security features built in, you don't want to implement word processors, spreadsheets, or other interactive applications in Java applets. If you require these programs, consider building a full Java application, which does not contain the security restrictions of an applet.

## JAVA APPLETS AND JAVASCRIPT

It has been said a million times, but if you have just started using Java, it bears repeating. Java isn't JavaScript. JavaScript isn't Java.

Java, in applet or application form, is a compiled language with classes and inheritance. HTML pages can include a reference to Java applets, which then are downloaded and run when a compatible browser finds the tag.

JavaScript is an object-based, client-side scripting language developed by Netscape, but it does not include classes or inheritance. JavaScript exists on the HTML page and is interpreted by a compatible browser along with the rest of the page.

Although they share some common syntax and terminology, the two items work differently and have different uses. Confusing Java and JavaScript only leads to a steeper learning curve.

# HotJava

HotJava (see Figure 34.1) represents one of the first applications written entirely in Java. In its initial release, HotJava primarily showed how applets could be included as part of an HTML document. Now, it functions more like a full-featured browser, supporting all of HTML 1 and 2 specifications. Support for HTML 3.2 is also in the process of integration.

> **TIP**
>
> To download a copy of HotJava, point your browser to `http://java.sun.com/java.sun.com/hotjava.html`. The file size is approximately 3MB.

**FIGURE 34.1.**

*The HotJava browser is one of the first stand-alone applications written entirely in the Java language.*

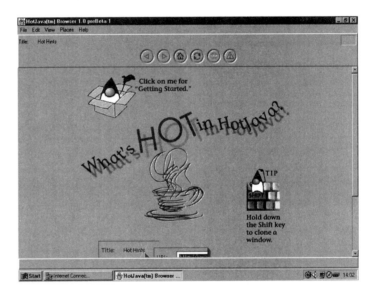

HotJava operates differently from most browsers in its basic functioning. Settings, preferences, and other basic maintenance screens are stored in the form of HTML documents and classes.

Stripped down to its most basic level, HotJava knows nothing about anything. Classes are added to the browser so that it can understand HTML, e-mail, sound files, and other specialty items. As new content and new formats are developed for Web pages, Java will only require the addition of another class. You won't need a complete upgrade to a new version to take advantage of the latest developments.

# Applet Viewer

During applet development and testing, sometimes it's easier to bypass the unnecessary overhead of a browser. If your browser doesn't support applets, you still need a way to view the applets. At this point, the Java Applet Viewer (see Figure 34.2) comes in handy.

**FIGURE 34.2.**

*The Java Applet Viewer enables the programmer to view embedded Java applets without the use of a browser. Only the applet is displayed, and the rest of the HTML is ignored.*

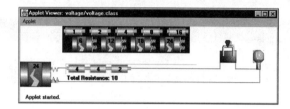

## Using the Applet Viewer

The Applet Viewer searches the HTML document for the `<APPLET>` tag, as shown in Listing 34.1.

**Listing 34.1. A simple HTML document containing an applet tag.**

```
<HTML>
<HEAD>
<TITLE>The animation applet</TITLE>
</HEAD>
<BODY>
<APPLET CODE="Animator.class" WIDTH=460 HEIGHT=160>
<PARAM NAME=imagesource VALUE="images/beans">
<PARAM NAME=endimage VALUE=10>
<PARAM NAME=pause VALUE=200>
</APPLET>
</BODY>
</HTML>
```

Using the information contained within the tag, it opens a window and runs the applet. Other HTML information on the page is ignored—only the applets appear.

The Java Applet Viewer is distributed with the Java Developer's Kit and is found in the same directory as the Java compiler and interpreter. To run the Applet Viewer, use the following steps:

1. Create a document that references your applet with the appropriate tags and parameters. See Listing 34.1 for an example.

2. From a command line prompt, type `appletviewer [path/]filename.html`.

   If the Applet Viewer launches from the same directory as the HTML document, you don't need the path name. Otherwise, the path is relative to your current location in the directory structure. The extension `.htm` is also valid for the viewer.

3. Any applets found in the HTML document are loaded and run, with each applet in its own instance of the Applet Viewer.

4. Although you cannot change the initial parameters contained within the HTML page from the Applet Viewer, you can start the applet from the beginning by choosing Applet|Restart. To load it again from memory, select Applet|Reload.

5. Leave the applet by choosing Applet|Quit.

---

**TIP**

The Applet Viewer Reload function will not work if the application was launched from the same directory as the HTML document and classes. For applets, create a subdirectory from your class directory called HTML, and place all of your classes and HTML files in it. Call the Applet Viewer from the parent directory by using `appletviewer html\`*`filename`*`.html`. This way, you can make changes to the applet, compile it, and use the Reload function to see your changes.

---

# Creating Java Applets

Creating Java applets is easier if you already have a background in programming. With Java's tight structure, the basic format of an applet is fairly straightforward. You walk through an example here.

---

**TIP**

You can access online tutorials and documentation for Java and object-oriented programming from the Sun site:

`http://java.sun.com/`

---

## Applet ABCs

At its simplest, an applet consists of two parts—the class declaration and a `paint` method. The following snippet contains a breakdown of the common elements for any applet:

```
import java.awt.Graphics;

public class MyApplet extends java.applet.Applet {
    public void paint (Graphics g) {
        your statements here;
    }
}
```

The first line includes a copy of the Graphics class from Java's Abstract Windowing Toolkit (AWT), which contains the methods needed for putting graphics, including text, lines, and dots, on the browser screen. This line can also be represented as import java.awt.Graphics if more than the Graphics class will be used.

Second, the actual applet is declared. It is public, meaning it is available to any other class, and it is a subclass of Java's Applet class, which provides the behavior necessary for interaction with the host browser.

The third section defines a method called paint, which the Java interpreter looks for to put the information on the screen. It is public to the class, and void indicates it does not return a value when it is completed. Its one parameter is an instance of the Graphics class imported on the first line of the program, which is referred to as g. This reference could just as easily be called bob or hammer, but g is the commonly used convention.

## Displaying with Paint

Now that the applet is defined, you need to make it do something. For the paint method, include the following line.

```
g.drawString("Hava a nice day.",50,25);
```

After compiling the code and inserting it into an HTML document (see "Using an Applet on a Web Page" later in this chapter), you get something that looks like Figure 34.3.

### COMPILING AN APPLET

To convert your source code into a usable class, type javac MyApplet.java at the command prompt. If any errors are reported, check your spelling and syntax and try again.

**FIGURE 34.3.**

MyApplet *displays a simple message on the screen.*

Of course, applets can do much more. If you include some other AWT classes, the text can look better. First, you need the classes that control the font and display color.

```
import java.awt.Font;
import java.awt.Color;
```

Now, after the class declaration, create a variable to hold a new setting for the text.

```
Font f = new Font("TimesRoman",Font.ITALIC,24);
```

After the `paint` method declaration, use the `Graphics.set` methods to set the display before writing to the screen.

```
g.setFont(f);
g.setColor(Color.red);
```

With this extra bit of effort, the applet now looks like the one in Figure 34.4.

**FIGURE 34.4.**

`MyApplet` *now displays in a larger font in red after some minor revisions to the code.*

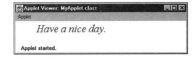

Again, this example is limited. The addition of a parameter to control the string would make it more useful to the HTML author. After the class declaration, declare the message as a variable.

```
String message;
```

A new method is also required to initialize the value of `message`.

## APPLET ACTIVITIES

In addition to `paint`, four major activities exist in the life of an applet. If any are omitted, default versions are provided in the `Applet` class. This setup is called *inheritance*. Providing new methods in the applet is called *overriding*.

The first activity is initialization, accomplished with the `init` method: `public void init() {...}`. This activity occurs once, immediately after the applet is loaded. Initialization includes creating objects, setting graphics, or defining parameters. It can only happen once in the applet's life.

The second activity is starting, accomplished with the `start` method: `public void start() {...}`. After initialization, activity begins. This activity can also happen if a user activity stopped the applet. Starting can happen many times in the life of an applet. The `paint` method is invoked somewhere in this method.

The next activity is stopping, accomplished with the `stop` method: `public void stop() {...}`. This activity can be an important method to include because by default the applet continues running and using system resources, even after the user has left the page with the applet. Like `start`, stopping can occur many times in the course of execution.

The last activity is destroying, accomplished with the `destroy` method: `public void destroy() {...}`. Destroying occurs when an applet throws out its own garbage after completing execution—when the applet is no longer needed or the user exits the browser. Java provides adequate coverage in this department, so you don't need to override this method unless you want to return specific resources to the system.

Initializing the message parameter requires overriding the `init` method for the applet.

```
public void init() {
    this.message = getParameter("message");
    if (this.message == null) {
        this.message = "Your message here."; }
    this.message = "A note from Java: " + this.message;
}
```

This method retrieves the value of the parameter in the HTML document. If a parameter named `message` is not found, then the value is null and `message` is set to the default string.

---

**TIP**

Java is case-sensitive for all of its variables, even when passed back and forth as parameters. Remember that a `Rose` by another name is not a `rose`.

---

Now you need to update the `paint` method so that it uses the string defined in `init`, rather than the literal string in the `drawString` method.

```
g.drawString(this.message);
```

Using the Applet Viewer again now generates the results in Figure 34.5.

**FIGURE 34.5.**

*The default message generated by* MyApplet, *after checking for a* message *parameter and finding none.*

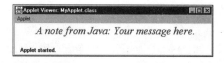

To place your own message in the applet, add a `<PARAM>` tag to the HTML source containing the applet. For more information, see "Passing Parameters to Applets" later in this chapter. The complete listing for `MyApplet` appears in Listing 34.2.

---

**TIP**

Listing 34.3 is a sample HTML file that can be used as the basis for inserting or testing applets. Saved in a generic form, it is a very reusable piece of code.

---

**Listing 34.2. A simple applet for displaying text on-screen. Note the use of the parameter in the `init` method.**

```
import java.awt.Graphics;
import java.awt.Font;
import java.awt.Color;
```

```
public class MyApplet extends java.applet.Applet {
    Font f = new Font("TimesRoman",Font.ITALIC,24);
    String message;

    public void init() {
        this.message = getParameter("message");
        if (this.message == null) {
            this.message = "Your message here."; }
        this.message = "A note from Java: " + this.message;
    }

    public void paint(Graphics g) {
        g.setFont(f);
        g.setColor(Color.red);
        g.drawString(this.message,50,25);
    }
}
```

## Listing 34.3. A sample of an HTML document that can display `MyApplet`.

```
<HTML>
<HEAD>
<TITLE>The MyApplet</TITLE>
</HEAD>
<BODY>
<HR>
<APPLET CODE="MyApplet.class" WIDTH=400 HEIGHT=50>
<PARAM NAME=message VALUE="Here I am.">
</APPLET>
<HR>
</BODY>
</HTML>
```

# Using an Applet on a Web Page

Using applets on a Web page is a two-part process. First, you must make sure your classes and related files, such as images and audio clips, appear in a directory accessible to the HTML page. One common location is in a `classes` subdirectory of the HTML documents.

Second, the applet tag that refers to the class is inserted in the Web page, along with any parameters the applet needs to function.

# All About the Applet Tag

The `<APPLET>` tag is used to insert the applet on a page, and it takes the following syntax:

```
<APPLET CODE="appletName.class" [CODEBASE="pathToClass"] WIDTH=xxx
➡HEIGHT=xxx [ALIGN= ]>
```

```
[<PARAMETER name=parameterName value=parameterValue>]
</APPLET>
```

The required line of code identifies the name of the applet, `CODE`, and the size it will appear on the page.

The optional parameter `CODEBASE` indicates a relative path to the class if it is not stored in the same directory as the HTML file. `ALIGN` works similarly to the parameter in the `<IMG SRC>` tag by controlling the positioning of HTML text adjacent to the applet's space.

> **TIP**
>
> `FrontPage` does not yet include support for inserting applets. Use the HTML Markup Bot to insert the tags.

# Passing Parameters to Applets

Parameters are used to pass information to applets about their environment and how they should behave in the current HTML document. Some applets have one method of running and don't accept any parameters. Most, however, contain some user-definable parameters that can be changed.

The `<PARAM>` tag enables you to pass information to the applet. The syntax is this:

```
<PARAM NAME=paramName VALUE=paramValue>
```

The parameter of the name is case sensitive and must exactly match the parameter name in the applet. If the applet does not provide exceptions for mismatched data types, an incompatible value could cause it not to function. For example, if a parameter looks for a string and you enter an integer, the applet could fail to operate.

# Applets for Fun and Utility

This section provides a selection of applets available on the CD-ROM that you can use on your own Web pages.

## Animator

Probably one of the most frequently used applets is the Java animator applet (see Figure 34.6), which comes with the Java Developer's Kit and provides a quick-and-easy way to add animation to your Java-powered page.

**FIGURE 34.6.**

*The Animator applet is used to display a series of images with an option for frame-specific sounds and soundtracks.*

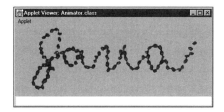

Animator also supports synchronized sound with the animation, but the sound must use the Sun .AU format. No other sound formats are supported yet.

Implementing the applet requires a set of GIF or JPG files containing the images that form the animation.

A wide variety of parameters exist and control the operation of Animator. Here's the breakdown and syntax.

`<APPLET CODE="Animator.class" WIDTH=`*number* `HEIGHT=`*number*`>`: Width should be at least the width in pixels of the widest frame, whereas height should reflect the size of the tallest frame. Smaller values will result in the image being clipped.

`<PARAM NAME=IMAGESOURCE VALUE="`*pathInfo*`">`: Points to the directory that contains the animation frames. The default directory is the same as the HTML document. By default, the files are named T1.gif, T2.gif, and so on.

`<PARAM NAME=STARTUP VALUE="`*filename*`">`: An image that is displayed while the applet loads and prepares to run.

`<PARAM NAME=BACKGROUND VALUE="`*filename*`">`: An image file for use as a background for the animation.

`<PARAM NAME=BACKGROUNDCOLOR VALUE="`*color,color,color*`">`: The color for the animation background, represented as an RGB value with a number from 0 to 255 for each of the settings.

`<PARAM NAME=STARTIMAGE VALUE=`*number*`>`: The first frame in the animation, by default 1.

`<PARAM NAME=ENDIMAGE VALUE=`*number*`>`: The last frame in the animation.

`<PARAM NAME="NAMEPATTERN" VALUE="`*dir/prefix%N.suffix*`">`: A pattern to use for generating names based on `STARTIMAGE`, `ENDIMAGE`, or `IMAGES`. (See above.)

`<PARAM NAME="PAUSE" VALUE=`*`number`*`>`: Number of milliseconds to pause between images default—can be overridden by `PAUSES`.

`<PARAM NAME="PAUSES" VALUE="`*`number`*`|`*`number`*`|...">`: Millisecond delay per frame, with each value separated by a vertical bar. Blank uses a default `PAUSE` value.

`<PARAM NAME="REPEAT" VALUE=true>`: If true, the animation will continue as a loop.

`<PARAM NAME="POSITIONS" VALUE="x@y|x@y...">`: Screen positions (`X@Y`) for each frame, represented in pixels and separated by vertical bars. A blank value will use the previous frame's position.

`<PARAM NAME="IMAGES" VALUE="`*`number`*`|`*`number`*`|...">`: Used to define an explicit order for frames, which becomes useful if your frames are out of order or if you want to reverse the sequence (such as `"1|2|3|2|1"`).

`<PARAM NAME="SOUNDSOURCE" VALUE="aDirectory">`: Indicates the directory with the audio files. The default is the same directory as the class.

`<PARAM NAME="SOUNDTRACK" VALUE="aFile">`: An audio file to play throughout the animation as background music.

`<PARAM NAME="SOUNDS" VALUE="aFile.au||||||bFile.au">`: Plays audio files keyed to individual frames.

`<PARAM NAME="HREF" VALUE="aURL">`: The URL of the page to visit when the user clicks the animation (if not set, a mouse click pauses/resumes the animation).

# Clock

This applet displays an analog clock on-screen (see Figure 34.7), complete with a sweeping second hand. Right now, no way exists to control the appearance of the clock. It would, however, be a relatively simple matter to add a parameter to control the size of the clock, whether the second hand appears, and display of the date and time underneath.

The time is determined by the host machine. It occupies little computer space for a computer implementation of an analog clock—just more than 3KB.

```
<applet code="Clock2.class" width=170 height=150>
</applet>
```

**FIGURE 34.7.**

*The Clock applet, a small and simple local-time clock to include on a Web page.*

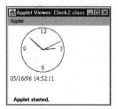

# Nervous Text

Nervous Text (see Figure 34.8) works like combining the basic HTML heading with a strong dose of really strong coffee and a slab of double chocolate cake. The letters jitter and jump around like Mexican jumping beans on a hot pan.

**FIGURE 34.8.**

*The Nervous Text applet moves each letter around in a frantic haphazard fashion.*

Nervous Text takes a string of text as its lone parameter. If not included, the default text is "HotJava." You can also modify the applet's source code to achieve more flexibility, including controlling the size and color of the font.

```
<PARAM NAME=text VALUE="string">
```

# Ticker (`http://www.uni-kassel.de/fb16/ipm/mt/java/ticker.htm`)

This applet (see Figure 34.9) provides one example of the many "ticker tape" applets available. It is one of the improved versions, which has made the extra effort to reduce flicker and provide additional control over the text.

The Ticker applet takes a variety of parameters, described here.

`<PARAM NAME=msg VALUE="string">`: The message to display.

`<PARAM NAME=speed VALUE=number>`: The animation speed, expressed as the number of pixels per 100 milliseconds. The default is 10.

`<PARAM NAME=txtco VALUE="r,g,b">`: The color of the message, expressed as an RGB value with numbers from 0 to 255. If omitted, the default is black.

`<PARAM NAME=bgco VALUE="r,g,b">`: The color of the background. If omitted, the default appears as light gray.

`<PARAM NAME=shco VALUE="r,g,b">`: The color of the message shadow. If omitted, no shadow appears.

`<PARAM NAME=href VALUE="URL">`: The ticker can also serve as a hyperlink if the user clicks on the ticker. A relative or complete URL is legal.

`<PARAM NAME=hrefco VALUE="r,g,b">`: The color of the URL frame. If omitted, the default is blue.

`<PARAM NAME=start VALUE="yy, mm, dd">` and `<PARAM NAME=exp VALUE="yy, mm, dd">`: Dates to start and stop displaying the applet. If the page is viewed outside of these dates, as determined by the host machine, the ticker will not display its message. It will still occupy space on the screen, however. You can use either date parameter by itself.

`<PARAM NAME=exfill VALUE="r,g,b">`: If the local date falls outside of the start and stop parameters, the box becomes filled with this color.

**FIGURE 34.9.**

*The Ticker applet provides a flexible way to display scrolling messages on the browser screen.*

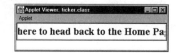

## Nuclear Power Plant

This little simulation (see Figure 34.10) really doesn't seem useful, unless you plan to run power plants in Russia. It does, however, show a good example of a user interface, object interaction, and animation. After the applet is initialized, you can select one of three powerplant crises— from pump failures to blown turbines. To prevent a meltdown, open and close valves and start pumps as necessary. If you don't work quickly enough, the core turns to mush and releases enough radioactivity to ruin everyone's day.

**FIGURE 34.10.**

*The Nuclear Plant applet, a creative use of Java as a learning tool and game implementation.*

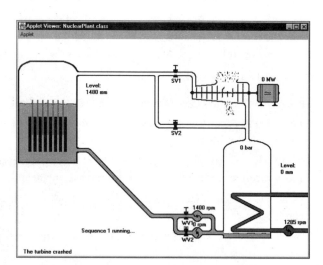

# Applet Sources on the Web

Many sources exist for applets on the Web that you can use. Make sure to check the licensing on the applet. Just because an applet appears on a page doesn't mean you can freely use it.

# JavaSoft (`http://java.sun.com/`)

JavaSoft, a subsidiary of Sun Microsystems, handles the Java products. Go to their Web site (see Figure 34.11) first when looking for information, documentation, updates, downloads, and other feedback.

**FIGURE 34.11.**

*The JavaSoft home page includes links to the Java Developer's Kit, HotJava, and other information of use to Java users and developers.*

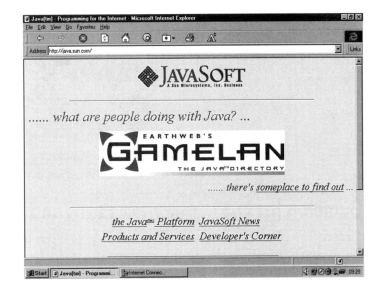

Originally part of the Sun Web site, JavaSoft received its own space to handle the dramatic increase in attention Java has received since its release.

# JavaWorld (`http://www.javaworld.com/`)

The first online publication devoted entirely to Java, JavaWorld (see Figure 34.12) comes out monthly and includes news and views about Java developments, along with hands-on tips and tricks. Programming contests are a regular feature, and many articles include links to Java-powered sites, source code, and other helpful items.

# Part VIII

**FIGURE 34.12.**

*JavaWorld includes interviews with the movers and shakers in the Java realm, along with hands-on examples, tutorials, and contests.*

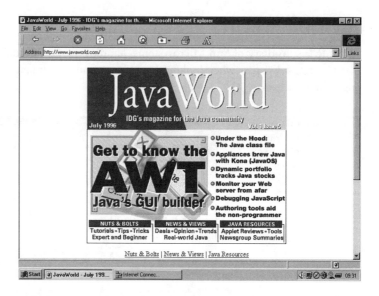

# Gamelan (`http://www.gamelan.com/`)

This site shows you what the rest of the world is doing with Java. Links appear here to some of the best applets to date for the viewing, and you can download some for use on your pages. It also includes a page devoted to JavaScript for links devoted to pages utilizing Java's cousin.

Some of the innovative productions found here include animators, tickers, network utilities, and a Learn to Dance applet.

**FIGURE 34.13.**

*Gamelan was developed specifically for the development and advancement of Java. As such, it maintains a comprehensive list of links to applications and applets available on the Web.*

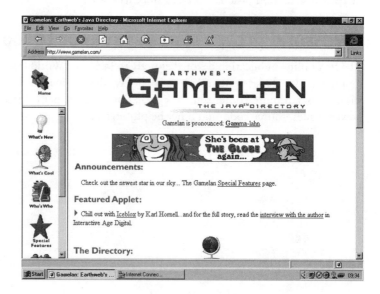

## `alt.lang.java`

Although not technically a source for applets, this newsgroup provides a great source of information about Java and its uses. Following the threads can also lead to Java applets and applications, where you can learn from people already making the most of this new language.

# Summary

Java use keeps spreading quickly as more and more hardware and software manufacturers pledge support to the language and concepts. Even if you never have the chance to delve deep into the intricacies of building an applet or application from scratch, an understanding of the basics will help you take full advantage of the powerful capabilities available.

**IN THIS PART**

# Putting It All Together

# Designing and Publishing a Home Page

**35**

*by William Robert Stanek*

**IN THIS CHAPTER**

Publishing on the World Wide Web might provide your ticket to success. Success can be measured in many ways. Your success might include increased sales, attracting new clients, or simply gaining widespread visibility for your ideas. Every success story has a beginning and in Web publishing, the first step involves creating a Web document to tell the world who you are and what you represent.

As the Web publisher, you are responsible for more than the content and quality of the information you provide. You must also make the information friendly and usable. The HyperText Markup Language provides the easiest markup language for creating friendly, usable, and informative documents. This chapter takes you through the seven steps necessary to create and publish a Web document. These steps include the following:

1. Develop a strategy.
2. Define the document structure.
3. Create the document.
4. Add features to the document.
5. Proof the document.
6. Test the document.
7. Publish the finished document.

# Developing a Strategy

The Web represents the ultimate forum for your ideas. By adding sound, graphics, and video, you can create visually stunning, highly interactive, dynamic documents that will entice readers to visit your site time after time. You have only a few minutes, however, to convince readers to read your Web publication. If you do not, they will go somewhere else for their information needs as quickly and as effortlessly as you can change the channel on your television with a remote control. Thus, you should carefully organize your ideas and develop a specific strategy before creating a Web document.

Creating your Web document can either be a continuous struggle or a logically flowing process. Take the time to organize your ideas. Not only will the payoff result in a better product, but it also means time and resource savings. Your strategy should focus on four areas:

- The purpose of the document.
- The scope of the document.
- The audience for the document.
- The structure of the document.

# Defining the Purpose of the Document

The purpose of the document focuses on the reason you are creating the document. Are you creating a Web document to tell the world about your latest book? Are you creating a Web document to tell the world about a service you offer? Are you creating a Web document simply because you want to share your ideas or expertise?

If your purpose is to sell a service or a product to Web users, do not hide that fact; come right out and say it. This approach ensures that readers become informed about what they are reading. Value the readers' time, and they will probably return if they need the product or service later.

If your purpose is to provide an Internet community service, make sure the readers know that, too. You can build tremendous goodwill by simply providing free information. So why not share a bit of your expertise with the world?

# Defining the Scope of the Document

Another key concept to keep in mind is scope. Scope sometimes is defined in terms of the focus and size of the project. As you organize your thoughts, determine the subject matter you will discuss and how broadly or narrowly you will cover the subject. Will your document have a broad focus and cover many topics related to computer games? Or will it have a narrow focus and cover very specific topics related to Multi-User Dimensions (MUDs)?

After you determine the focus, you should determine the level of detail for the document's subject matter. You could briefly discuss many topics, or you could discuss a few topics at length. If you decide you want to cover a few specific topics at length, you might want to cover the topics on a single Web document. If you want to cover many topics at length, however, you might want to present your ideas on a series of documents with increasing levels of detail. For example, the initial document serves as an overview document discussing the popularity of Multi-User Dimensions. From this document readers can access other documents that discuss the features of specific MUDs in detail. From the detailed document, readers can access other documents that cover newsgroups, mailing lists, and Web sites related to a specific MUD and so on. Documents set up in progressive levels of detail shows the basic format for a Web site. For more information on setting up a Web site, see Chapter 36, "Designing and Publishing a Web Site."

# Defining the Audience for the Document

Developing a strategy with your audience in mind represents an essential element of your success, yet determining the group you want the work to reach does not always occur easily. On the Web, you can reach an extremely diverse global audience, and words written in your native language might be read by people from dozens of countries. A document that specifically focuses on resources for U.S. writers might exclude or alienate writers from dozens of other countries. A document written in Spanish might be read by native speakers from the many Spanish-speaking countries in the world or by the millions of people who speak Spanish as a second language.

> **TIP**
>
> Although English is the dominant language used on the Web, it is not the only language in use on the Web. Many European Web publishers create documents in several languages; consequently, millions of people who otherwise couldn't read the document can access the information. If you have proficiency in a second language, you might want to consider publishing your ideas in both your native and secondary language. You have nothing to lose and everything to gain by ensuring your publication can reach the largest audience possible.

As you consider the potential audience for your ideas, products, or services, focus on specific ideas of who, what, why, and how:

- Who do you want to reach?
- What will this group of people consider interesting?
- Why would they want to buy your product or service?
- How will you reach them?

Tell yourself you are writing a document for anyone interested in extreme sports who is between the age of 16 and 35. Readers want your service because you are the only such service featuring excursions in the Australian outback and the mountains of New Zealand. You plan to reach readers by featuring a virtual tour and offering a 2-for-1 discount that only Web surfers can use. Got the idea?

# Defining the Document Structure

Before you start creating the actual document, you should carefully consider how you want to organize the document. Getting organized becomes extremely important. Not only does it save you time, but it also helps you create a better document. The quality of your document convinces readers your document is worth reading.

You can write out the initial structure for your document as an outline or simply as notes you scratch down during a brainstorming session. As you write down your ideas, focus on the purpose, scope, and audience you defined earlier. The following are the key areas of the document that you want to concentrate on:

- The introductory section: Introduce the document and provide readers with a brief overview of what lies ahead.
- The main features: Showcase the content of your site.

■ The hook: Give readers a reason to come back to your site.

■ The final section: Close the document in style.

After you develop the basic concept for the document, you might want to try to improve your ideas through freethinking, brainstorming, or storyboarding. These and other techniques for unleashing your creativity and better organizing your publications are explored in-depth in Chapter 7, "Organizing and Information," of *Electronic Publishing Unleashed*, published by Sams.

# Creating the Document

Creating the document serves as the next step. You can use the knowledge you gain as you create your first document as a stepping stone to more advanced projects.

With this in mind, you can create your first document for fun or business, but you should try to keep the document simple. If you don't know what type of document you want to create, try creating a document that involves something you find interesting or that revolves around a subject about which you have expertise. For example, I love books. I could spend hours in the local library just wandering the aisles looking for books on any of a hundred topics. One of the first Web documents I created relates directly to my interest in reading and writing. I called this document the Writer's Gallery and, as Figure 35.1 shows, I designated it as "A place for anyone who loves the written word."

> **NOTE**
>
> The examples in this chapter show how the Writer's Gallery looked in the early stages of development. You can visit the current incarnation of the Writer's Gallery on the Web at http://tvp.com/vpwg.html.

> **TIP**
>
> Creating Web documents in FrontPage is easy. If you haven't already created a Web for your use, create one now by selecting New Web from the File menu in the FrontPage Explorer. So that you can create your own home page following the techniques you learn in this chapter, you should base the new Web on the normal Web template.

**FIGURE 35.1.**

*The Writer's Gallery: a document on the Web.*

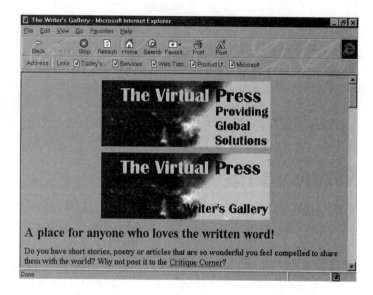

As you create your Web document, you will want to use the strategy and structure you developed. My strategy for the Writer's Gallery was to create a document for anyone who was as interested in the written word as I was. Although I was not trying to sell a service to the people who read the document, I wanted to make the document an interesting place to visit, and I planned to freely share my knowledge of Web resources related to writing. Readers would have an interest in the Writer's Gallery because it provided a resource for many different areas related to the written word. The primary audience I focused on was writers, but I made sure the document would also interest readers and anyone who might want writing resources.

# Adding Features to the Document

After you create the basic outline of the document, you can add features to the document. You want to include features in the document that add to its visual impact and that make the document interactive.

## Introducing the Document

The primary way to increase the visual impact of your document is to use images. You can use images to enhance all aspects of your document. As Figure 35.1 shows, the first section of the Writer's Gallery document uses a graphical logo to introduce the document. This section also provides an overview of what readers can expect to find at the site.

The overview gives Web surfers who have an interest in writing a reason to continue reading the document. The organization of this part of the document becomes critically important. In this area, you want to establish the purpose of the document and grab the reader's attention.

# Creating the Main Features of the Document

Although images represent the most obvious features that can add to the visual impact of the document, other features that can add to the visual impact of the document include using line breaks to create a column of text and adding horizontal rules to visually divide the document into sections. You can also add any of several types of lists to your document, which can add to the visual impact of the document by clearly organizing material.

The more useful your document is, the more powerful it becomes. The key to increasing the usefulness of your document and its impact on readers lies in interactivity. To increase the interactive nature of your document, you can create links to other documents on the Web. Interactivity was added to the Writer's Gallery page using three interactive lists.

The first list included in the page is a glossary list, as shown in Figure 35.2. A glossary list helps relate the key terms with related phrases. Adding interactivity to your glossary list is easy, and you can include links wherever they make sense.

**FIGURE 35.2.**

*More interactive lists.*

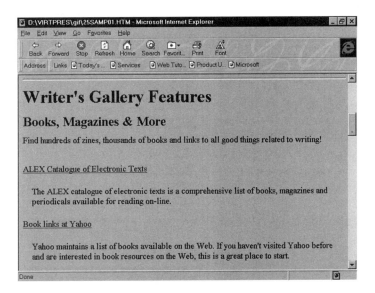

The second list included in the page is the bulleted list shown in Figure 35.3. A bulleted list was used because the items have no specific order.

As you can see from Figure 35.4, the final list has a numbered list. Instead of providing a simple list of resources, you can include links that enable readers to jump to the resources in your list.

**FIGURE 35.3.**

*Using a linked bulleted list.*

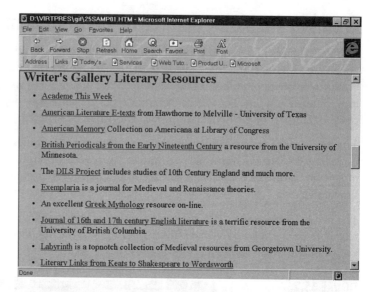

**FIGURE 35.4.**

*A numbered list of important resources.*

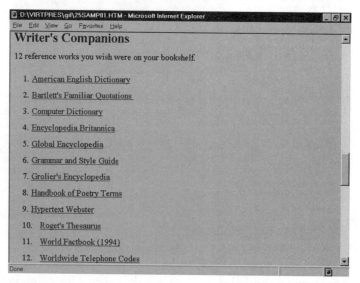

# Creating Additional Pages

All your information doesn't have to appear on a single page. As Figure 35.5 shows, you can provide a link to other pages containing additional resources. The header `Newsgroups for Writers` contains links that will take readers to a document called `wnewsgroups.html`.

In your first document, these additional areas don't have to contain dozens of resources or even be finished. If the area is under construction, however, tell readers the area is under construction. To do this, you can use an image such as a warning sign. Because most pages on the Web are "under construction," meaning that they constantly change and grow, you should remove the warning signs when these areas have useful content.

> **CAUTION**
>
> The construction areas shown in Figure 35.5 serve as examples only. Normally, you would not include links to multiple pages that are under construction. Pages like that become frustrating for readers. If a linked section of your document has bare bones content, warn the reader before they access the section as you see in this example. You may prefer to wait until you have useful content for the page and then add a link to the page.

**FIGURE 35.5.**

*All your information doesn't have to appear on a single page.*

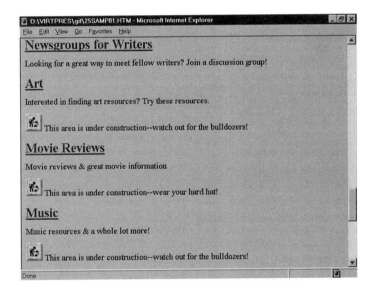

## Bringing Visitors Back

Growth potential provides a key attraction for Web surfers. Web surfers like to visit sites that continue to change and grow. Add a section to your document that gives readers a reason to return to the site. The Writer's Gallery also has a section that continues to change over time called Critique Corner, which Figure 35.6 shows.

**FIGURE 35.6.**
*Include a section of the
document that will grow
to give readers a reason
to revisit the site.*

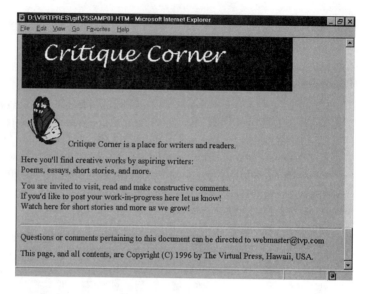

## Finishing the Document

In addition to providing readers with another area to explore in the future, the final section of
the document, shown in Figure 35.6, provides contact and copyright information. Well-
designed documents provide a point of contact for questions, technical or otherwise, about the
document. Typically, the point of contact for technical questions is called the Webmaster, an
electronic mail alias. A mail alias is a generic mail address that you can assign to an individual
or group who will receive mail directed to the Webmaster. The mail address for the Webmaster
is typically `webmaster@yourcompany.com`.

If you cannot use a mail alias, your site can still have a Webmaster. In this case, you could use
the following:

```
This page was webmastered by william@tvp.com.
```

You could also use a special type of link that starts a create mail session in the reader's browser.
To do this, you create a link that uses the `mailto` protocol. The `mailto` reference shown in Figure
35.7 tells the reader's browser to open a create mail session that will be sent to `william@tvp.com`.
This type of link enhances the interactivity of the page and provides a mechanism for getting
feedback from readers. Don't forget to anchor the link to the page with text or graphics that
readers can click.

The final section of your document should also contain copyright information. Adding a copyright notice to the document tells the world that the document is an intellectual property, and
as such, receives protection under U.S. and international copyright laws.

**FIGURE 35.7.**

*Creating a link with a*
mailto *reference.*

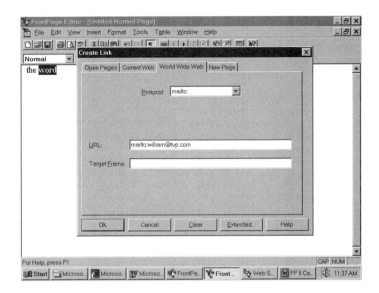

## The Complete Document

As you have seen, your Web document can have many features and still stay fairly basic. You should create a document that has enough features to attract visitors but doesn't become so complex that you never get it ready for publishing. You can always include places that will grow and bring visitors back.

Take a few minutes to examine the HTML code for the Writer's Gallery document shown in Listing 35.1. Because FrontPage allows you to create HTML documents in a WYSIWYG environment, you can easily forget that the documents contain markup code. This markup code can be viewed at any time by selecting HTML from the View menu in the FrontPage Editor.

### Listing 35.1. The Writer's Gallery Web page.

```
<HTML>
<HEAD>
<TITLE>The Writer's Gallery</TITLE>
</HEAD>
<BODY>
<P ALIGN=CENTER><IMG SRC="vpttl11.gif" ALT="The Virtual Press Present's">
</P>
<P ALIGN=CENTER><IMG SRC="wgttl.gif" ALT="The Writer's Gallery"></P>
<H2>A place for anyone who loves the written word!</H2>
<P>Do you have short stories, poetry or articles that are so wonderful
you feel compelled to share them with the world?  Why not post it to the
<A HREF="#CCorner">Critique Corner</A>?</P>
<P><IMG SRC="boom.gif" ALIGN="BOTTOM" ALT="* ATTN *">
Put a bookmark here.  Come back and visit!</P>
<HR>
```

*continues*

## Listing 35.1. continued

```
<H1>Writer's Gallery Features</H1>
<H2>Books, Magazines &amp; More</H2>
<P>Find hundreds of zines, thousands of books and links to all
good things related to writing!</P>
<DL>
<P><DT> <A HREF="gopher://rsl.ox.ac.uk/11/lib-corn/hunter">
ALEX Catalogue of Electronic Texts</A></P>
<DD>The ALEX catalogue of electronic texts is a comprehensive list of
books, magazines and periodicals available for reading on-line.
<P><DT> <A HREF="http://www.yahoo.com/Entertainment/Books/">
Book links at Yahoo</A></P>
<DD>Yahoo maintains a list of books available on the Web. If you haven't
 visited Yahoo before and are interested in book resources on the Web,
this is a great place to start.
<P><DT> <A HREF="http://white.nosc.mil/books.html">
Books and Libraries</A></P>
<DD>On the Web, there are many virtual libraries. These libraries
feature collections of creative works available for on-line viewing.
<P>
<DD>One of these virtual libraries is the
<A HREF="http://eryx.syr.edu/Main.html">ERIC Virtual Library</A>,
which is an educational resource.
</DL>
<H2>Writer's Gallery Literary Resources</H2>
<P>If you need a literary reference on the Web, this is a great
place to start.</P>
<UL>
<LI> <A HREF="http://chronicle.merit.edu">Academe This Week</A>
<P>
<LI> <a href="http://auden.fac.utexas.edu/~daniel/amlit/amlit.html">
American Literature E-texts</A> from Hawthorne to Melville -
University of Texas
<P>
<LI> <A HREF="http://rs6.loc.gov/amhome.html">American Memory</A>
Collection on Americana at Library of Congress
<P>
<LI> <A HREF="http://www.umn.edu/nlhome/m059/mh/britper.html">
British Periodicals from the Early Nineteenth Century</A>
a resource from the University of Minnesota.
<P>
<LI>The <a href="gopher://gopher.epas.utoronto.ca/11/cch/disciplines
➥/medieval_studies/keefer">DILS Project</A> includes studies of
10th Century England and much more.
<P>
<LI> <A HREF="http://www.clas.ufl.edu:80/english/exemplaria/">
Exemplaria</A> is a journal for Medieval and Renaissance theories.
<P>
<LI>An excellent <A HREF="http://info.desy.de/gna/interpedia/greek_myth
➥/greek_myth.html">Greek Mythology</A> resource on-line.
<P>
<LI> <A HREF="http://edziza.arts.ubc.ca/0c:/english/emlshome.htm">
Journal of 16th and 17th century English literature</A> is a terrific
resource from the University of British Columbia.
<P>
<LI> <A HREF="http://www.georgetown.edu/labyrinth/labyrinth-home.html">
Labyrinth</A> is a topnotch collection of Medieval resources
from Georgetown University.
```

```
<P>
<LI> <A HREF="http://coombs.anu.edu.au/~andrea/LiteraryLinks.html">
Literary Links from Keats to Shakespeare to Wordsworth</A>
<P>
<LI> <A HREF="http://gopher.well.sf.ca.us:70/1/Publications">
Literary Sites on the Internet</A>
<P>
<LI> <A HREF="http://www.artsci.wustl.edu/~jntolva/">Renaissance Studies
and E-texts</A> - University of Washington
</UL>
<H2>Writer's Companions</H2>
<P>12 reference works you wish were on your bookshelf.</P>
<OL>
<LI> <A HREF="gopher://uts.mcc.ac.uk/77/gopherservices/enquire.english">
American English Dictionary</A>
<P>
<LI> <A HREF="http://www.columbia.edu/~svl2/bartlett/">
Bartlett's Familiar Quotations </A>
<P>
<LI> <A HREF="http://wombat.doc.ic.ac.uk/">Computer Dictionary</A>
<P>
<LI> <A HREF="http://www.eb.com/">Encyclopedia Britannica</A>
<P>
<LI> <A HREF="http://www.halcyon.com/jensen/encyclopedia/">
Global Encyclopedia</A>
<P>
<LI> <A HREF="http://www.library.upenn.edu/grammar.html">
Grammar and Style Guide</A>
<P>
<LI> <A HREF="http://gagme.wwa.com/~boba/grolier.html">
Grolier's Encyclopedia</A>
<P>
<LI> <A HREF="http://www.cc.emory.edu/ENGLISH/Handbook/Handbook.html">
Handbook of Poetry Terms</A>
<P>
<LI> <A HREF="http://c.gp.cs.cmu.edu:5103/prog/webster">
Hypertext Webster</A>
<P>
<LI> <A HREF="gopher://odie.niaid.nih.gov:70/77/.thesarus/index">
Roget's Thesaurus</A>
<P>
<LI> <A HREF="http://www.ic.gov/94fact/fb94toc/fb94toc.html">
World Factbook (1994)</A>
<P>
<LI> <A HREF="http://www.digital.com/gnn/wic/refbook.10.html">
Worldwide Telephone Codes</A>
</OL>
<H2><A HREF="wnewgroups.html">Newsgroups for Writers</A></H2>
<P>Looking for a great way to meet fellow writers?
Join a discussion group!</P>
<H2><A HREF="vpwart.html">Art</A></H2>
<P>Interested in finding art resources? Try these resources.</P>
<P><IMG SRC="constr.gif">This area is under construction--watch out
for the bulldozers!</P>
<H2><A HREF="vpwart.html">Movie Reviews</A></H2>
<P>Movie reviews & great movie information</P>
<P><IMG SRC="constr.gif">This area is under construction--wear
your hard hat!</P>
```

*continues*

## Listing 35.1. continued

```
<H2><A HREF="vpwart.html">Music</A></H2>
<P>Music resources & a whole lot more!</P>
<P><IMG SRC="constr.gif">This area is under construction--watch out
for the bulldozers!</P>
<HR>
<H2><IMG SRC="ccorner.gif" ALT=""></H2>
<P><A NAME="CCorner"><P><IMG SRC="bfly.gif" ALT="">
Critique Corner is a place for writers and readers.</P>
<P>Here you'll find creative works by aspiring writers:<BR>
Poems, essays, short stories, and more.</P>
<P>You are invited to visit, read and make constructive comments.<BR>
If you'd like to post your work-in-progress here let us know!<BR>
Watch here for short stories and more as we grow!</P>
<HR>
<P>Questions or comments pertaining to this document can be directed
to webmaster@tvp.com</P>
<P>This page, and all contents, are Copyright (C) 1996 by
The Virtual Press, Hawaii, USA.</A></P>
</BODY>
</HTML>
```

# Proofing Your Web Document

Proofing represents the most neglected aspect of Web publishing. Time and time again Web documents appear with multiple typos and formatting inconsistencies—even at major sites. Documents with glaring typos and inconsistencies reflect poorly on you and your Web publishing practices.

Proofing is neglected in Web publishing primarily because of the ease with which ideas and words can be published electronically. You can create a document in FrontPage and publish it on the Web within minutes of finishing—seconds if you work fast enough. You do not have to spend hours checking spelling and grammar and generally poring over every punctuation mark on the document, worrying about whether you have missed something glaringly obvious that would cost a fortune in reprint of 10,000 copies. If you make a mistake, you just open the file, correct the mistake, and republish your masterpiece on the Web for the world to see. Right?

Wrong. The quality of your work directly reflects you. Thousands, and possibly millions, of people around the world will see your published document. Doesn't it seem worth a few hours of your time to ensure that days, weeks, or months of hard work gets the credibility it deserves?

The following list has a few tips to help you better proof your Web documents:

- Use spelling and grammar checkers to find the tedious errors, such as the typos or grammar mistakes you made because you hurried to meet a deadline, got worn out from long hours at the keyboard, or otherwise.

- Never rely solely on spelling and grammar checkers to find the critical errors; read the document several times, noting typos or inconsistencies you need to correct.

- For long documents or lengthy projects, reading the document three times, looking for specific problems each time, can often prove helpful. The first time you proofread, focus on the look of the document and if you find formatting inconsistencies and missing or misplaced items, correct them. The second time you proofread, check the logic and flow of ideas and words. The third time you proofread, scrutinize all the text on the document, checking syntax, spelling, capitalization, and punctuation.

- Always check images, figures, and charts on your document. Not only do you want to ensure that they appear consistent with your textual references, but you also want to check any text included in the graphics. You should even check images you believe do not contain text. You might find text and feel greatly relieved when you find and fix a typo you otherwise would have missed.

Some typos and inconsistencies slip by—the dragon wins every once in a while. If you find an error after you have already published your document, correct it.

# Testing Your Web Document

Testing all aspects of your Web document before you publish is crucial. At this stage in your Web publishing operation, you want to focus on the accuracy of your links and HTML markup. As you add features such as images and multimedia, however, you should test these features as well.

## Testing Your Links

One way to test links is to load the document in your browser and click the links one at a time. You want to ensure that all internal document links access the appropriate section that corresponds to the keyword you have designated. Watch out for multiple sections of the document labeled with the same keyword that can produce strange results. If you know that a section of your publication has a certain keyword as a label and the browser jumps to a different section of the document, check the keyword label in the section the browser displays. You probably mislabeled the keyword.

> **NOTE**
>
> You can use the FrontPage back link function to check internal and external links. FrontPage, however, won't tell you that a link leads to SciFi Channel's Dominion site at `http://www.scifi.com/` when the anchor text said the link was to the Internet Shopping Network at `http://www.internet.net/`.

You also want to ensure that all document links to other documents are valid and access the appropriate document. If you cannot access a document that you know should be available, check the syntax of your links. Did you specify the protocol correctly? Did you use the correct filename extension? Did you forget the tilde (~) symbol?

> **NOTE**
>
> In UNIX, the tilde symbol specifies the home directory of a user whose system name follows the tilde. Using the tilde symbol in a URL, you can refer to the Web documents in the user's home directory as follows:
>
> `http://www.aloha.com/~william/vphp.html`
>
> The Web server servicing this request would know to look in my home directory for the file called `vphp.html`. Although Web documents typically appear in a directory called `public_html` under the user's directory, Web servers know that when you use a tilde in a URL, you are referring to the directory containing the user's Web documents. The process of inferring a directory using the tilde is called mapping.

## Troubleshooting Problems in Your Document

What if everything looks okay, and you have fixed all the typos, but your browser still won't display the third sentence in bold face. This problem can usually be traced to your browser or to the code. You might want to check your browser's compatibility with character styles.

Your browser has to have the capability to display the physical style you have selected. Additionally, when displaying logical styles, the browser ultimately makes the decision about what style to display your text in. A quick way to check for a compatibility problem or a code problem is to display your document using a different browser. This browser should preferably support the specific style you want to use.

# Publishing Your Web Document on an External Server

Publishing your documents using the Personal Web Server occurs automatically. You simply create a Web and documents for that Web. As long as you have a connection to the Internet, the world can access your documents. Most Web publishers, however, don't have their own server and must use an Internet Service Provider's Web server.

When you use someone else's server, you might need to export your documents from FrontPage. If you cannot use FrontPage server extensions, you might also need to modify your documents, especially if they use WebBots. Through five authoritative chapters, Part VII of this book took an in-depth look at managing your Web. This section provides additional tips beyond what the other chapters already covered. You should refer back to Part VII to answer any specific questions you might have related to publishing and managing Webs.

# Checking the Name of the File

When moving files between different types of platforms, you should check the filename to ensure its appropriateness for the system you plan to move the file to. Some systems restrict the length of filenames. Other systems have case-sensitivity, meaning a file with a name in uppercase letters becomes a different file if saved in lowercase letters.

When you create documents using FrontPage templates, the documents generally have an .htm extension. Some systems do not recognize files with an .htm extension as an HTML document. Thus, after moving your file to a UNIX or Mac system, change the .htm extension to .html. For example, change home.htm to home.html. This change ensures that the UNIX or Mac Web server will recognize your file as an HTML document.

---

**TIP**

Before moving your file to a DOS/Windows 3.1 machine, the file must conform to DOS naming conventions. DOS filenames can have only eight characters and a three-character extension. If, for example, you had a file called my_home_document.html, you could change the name to homedocument.htm.

Watch out for wildcard characters in filenames. Although you can use wildcard characters on a Macintosh or UNIX system, you cannot use wildcard characters in filenames on a DOS machine.

When you change filenames, you must also change all links that reference the document. You can use FrontPage to help you automatically update these references.

In the FrontPage Explorer, select the page you want to rename in any of the views, and then press Alt+Enter or choose Properties from the Edit menu. Next, in the Page URL field, enter the new filename and then click the OK or Apply button. If any pages reference the page you changed, FrontPage will display the Confirm Updating Links dialog box to allow you to update these references automatically.

Generally, you should not use the Save As feature of the FrontPage Editor to create a file with a different filename or extension. When you use the Save As feature, you are actually creating a copy of the original file and both files will be a part of the current Web.

---

# Moving Your Files Yourself

To publish your documents, you need to move your files to a directory designated for Web documents on the external Web server. Typically this directory is mapped to a subdirectory in your home directory called `public_html`. Contact the server administrator to find out where to put your documents.

---

**TIP**

A mapped directory contains pointers to directories where the actual files reside. Web servers usually map directories to a subdirectory in a user's home directory that you can point to using the tilde followed by the user's system name. Setting up a Web server to map requests is easy. On most servers, your service provider or system administrator can enable this feature by setting a variable called `UserDir` to the subdirectory that will go to users' home directories, such as the following:

```
UserDir       public_html
```

If this variable has the setting as shown in the preceding example, requests to `http://www.your_provider.com/~you` would be mapped to the subdirectory called `public_html` in your account and a Web document called `home.html` could be accessed with the following URL:

```
http://www.your_provider.com/~you/home.html
```

---

You should follow the steps outlined in Chapter 25, "Personal Web Server Administration," for moving your documents. If you cannot use FrontPage functions to copy your Web to the new server, you need to export your files from FrontPage and move the files yourself. File Transfer Protocol (FTP) and modem transfer represent the two most common methods to transfer the files.

# Using FTP

FTP is a quick and easy way to transfer files, especially if you need to transfer files between UNIX systems. The best way to transfer files using FTP is to initiate a binary file transfer. Then you don't have to worry about which files are binary and which files aren't.

To start a binary transfer, you could type the following at the shell command prompt:

```
ftp hostname
bin
```

You can transfer multiple files between systems using the `mget` and `mput` commands. You use `mget` to retrieve multiple files from the host you connected to using FTP, and you use `mput` to send multiple files to the host you connected to using FTP. When you transfer multiple files between systems, another useful FTP command to know is `prompt`. Without toggling the prompt to the off position, your system will prompt you before sending or retrieving each file. Here's how you could toggle the prompt to the off position and retrieve all files that start with music and then quit:

```
ftp aloha.com
bin
prompt
cd /users/music/fun_stuff
mget music*
quit
```

## Modem Transfer

Many modem transfer protocols could work to transfer files. Some popular transfer protocols include

> ASCII
> Kermit
> Super-Kermit
> Xmodem
> Xmodem CRC
> Xmodem 1K
> Ymodem
> Ymodem batch or Ymodem-G
> Zmodem

Although these transfer protocols all seem popular, the most popular transfer protocol is the Zmodem transfer protocol. The reason for Zmodem's popularity comes from its ease-of-use and reliability. You can initiate a Zmodem transfer within your communication's program while connected to the Internet, and you only have to learn two commands:

```
rz     Receive via Zmodem transfer protocol.
sz     Send via Zmodem transfer protocol.
```

From your Internet account, you can type sz or rz at the shell prompt. If you type sz or rz and then press Enter, you get a brief summary of how to use the commands. The most basic format follows, where filename represents the name of the file to transfer:

```
rz filename
```

> **NOTE**
>
> If you own a Macintosh and you transfer files to a different computer platform, you should transfer your files as regular binary files. Other computer platforms cannot read Macintosh binary files and your files will be unreadable in this format.

# Moving Your Files with the Publishing Wizard

The FrontPage Publishing Wizard provides an automated tool for publishing individual files and even entire Webs on servers that do not support FrontPage Server Extensions. This wizard functions as a separate tool that runs as a stand-alone application, like the FrontPage Editor and the FrontPage Explorer. Although the commercial version of FrontPage might include the Publishing Wizard, you can obtain the source for this tool from the FrontPage area of Microsoft's Web site:

```
http://www.microsoft.com/frontpage/
```

If you installed the Publishing Wizard yourself, you start the Publishing Wizard by double-clicking the fppostit tool icon in the Publishing Wizard folder. Otherwise, you start the Publishing Wizard by double-clicking the appropriate tool icon in the Microsoft FrontPage folder.

When you start the Publishing Wizard, you see the dialog box shown in Figure 35.8. The buttons at the bottom of the dialog box are standard throughout the publishing process. At any time, you can move to the previous or next phase of the creation process using the Back or Next buttons. When you have completed all the necessary steps, you can press the Post button and the FrontPage Editor publishes your files.

> **NOTE**
>
> If this is the first time you are running the downloaded version, the first dialog box you see will ask you to accept Microsoft's licensing agreement for the Publishing Wizard. After you accept the agreement, you will see the dialog box shown in Figure 35.8.

**FIGURE 35.8.**

*Getting started with the Publishing Wizard.*

## Entering Server Information

To continue, press the Next button. On this wizard page, you must enter information about the server to which you want to post your files. As you can see from Figure 35.9, the

Publishing Wizard uses the file transfer protocol to transfer your files. You might need to contact your System Administrator or Webmaster to get this server information.

**FIGURE 35.9.**

*Entering server information.*

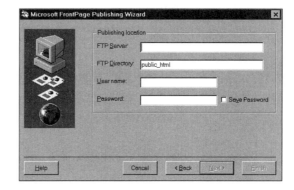

In the FTP Server field, you must enter the numeric IP address or the fully qualified host name of the server to which you want to transfer files, such as tvp.com. The name of the server you want to transfer files to is usually the same as that of your Web server because most Web servers also perform duties as an FTP server.

To publish your documents, you need to move your files to a directory designated for Web documents on the server. Usually, this directory is mapped to a subdirectory in your home directory called public_html. In the FTP Directory field, you must enter the name of the directory on the server where the Web will be stored. This directory path can be either absolute or relative. An absolute path to your Web directory can be /usr/httpd/docs/. A relative path to your Web directory could be public_html, the default value for the Publishing Wizard.

> **NOTE**
>
> Generally, when you log into a server, the directory you log into will be your home directory. Thus, if the directory designated for Web documents is public_html, you can use the relative path public_html.

Finally, in the User name and Password fields, enter your user name and password for the server. If you want the Publishing Wizard to remember your password, check the Save Password field. The Save Password feature proves useful if you make frequent updates to your Web. When you change your password on the server, however, you have to enter a new password. After you have defined all the fields on the server information page, click the Next button.

# Selecting the Web You Want to Publish

As shown in Figure 35.10, the next wizard page allows you to select the Web you want to publish from a list of currently defined Webs. Simply click the name of the Web you want to publish, and then click the Next button. Later, you will be given the option of publishing all or part of the Web.

**FIGURE 35.10.**

*Select the Web you want to publish from the list of current Webs.*

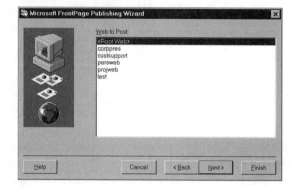

If any of the pages in the Web you want to publish contain elements that don't work without FrontPage Server Extensions, the next page you see contains a warning similar to the one shown in Figure 35.11. You will want to examine all the pages listed and remove unsupported elements. After writing down the page list, press the Next button.

**FIGURE 35.11.**

*The Warning page lists pages that have unsupported elements.*

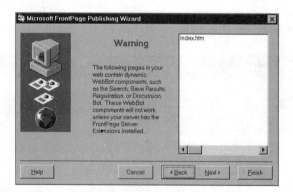

# Determining the Type of Files to Publish

After selecting a Web, you can select the type of files to publish using the page shown in Figure 35.12. As you can see from the figure, fields exist that enable you to post all the pages in the Web, post only the pages changed since the last post, not post pages listed on the warning page, and select the files to post. If you do not want to select the files to post from the Web, click the Post button to begin publishing your files.

**FIGURE 35.12.**

*Determining the type of files to publish.*

If you choose to select the files to post from the Web, you see the page shown in Figure 35.13 when you click the Next button. On this page, you can add or remove pages from the list of the pages you want to publish. You can add a page to the publishing list by double-clicking the page name in the Files in Web field. You can remove a page from the publishing list by double-clicking the page name in the Files to Copy field. Alternatively, you can click a page name and select the Add or Remove button as appropriate. The Clear button enables you to remove all the files listed in the Files to Copy field. When you finish, click the Post button.

**FIGURE 35.13.**

*Selecting individual pages to publish.*

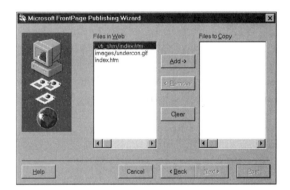

# Posting the Files

When you click the Post button, the Publishing Wizard begins publishing your files. As you can see from Figure 35.14, the wizard's first step logs in to the server you identified. Depending on your system's setup, you might be prompted by the dialer for your user name and password information. If this happens, enter your user name and password information as appropriate.

Provided that you entered all the server information correctly, the Publishing Wizard begins transferring pages. When the wizard finishes and all pages are transferred successfully, you see the page shown in Figure 35.15. You can click the Exit button to close the Publishing Wizard.

**FIGURE 35.14.**

*The Wizard's first step is to log in to the server.*

**FIGURE 35.15.**

*When all pages are published successfully, you see this page.*

If the Publishing Wizard experienced problems while trying to access the server, the wizard returns you to the server information page shown in Figure 35.9. After you update the server information, click the new button labeled Finish to take you to the last page of the Publishing Wizard. At this point, you can press the Post button to restart the transfer.

# Checking the Mode of the File

On some systems, files have strictly defined permissions that can be granted or denied to users. These permissions include the ability to read, write, and execute the file. Permissions generally are set by changing the mode attributed to the file. Make sure that files have the appropriately restricted mode for Web access. For example, 705 on a UNIX system means that you can read, write to, and execute the file, but others can only read and execute it.

**NOTE**

The command to change the mode of a file on a UNIX system is chmod. The chmod command enables you to set permissions for yourself, your associated group, and others. You can grant or deny permission to read, write, and execute the file. Permissions are generally set using a three-digit number that equates to the permissions you are setting.

The first digit sets the permissions for you, the owner of the file. The second digit sets the permissions for the group of users you are associated with on the UNIX system. The third digit sets the permissions for anyone else who can use the file. Read permissions are set by adding one to the digit count. Write permissions are set by adding four to the digit count. Execute permissions are set by adding two to the digit count.

A file with the mode of 000 has no permissions. If you changed the mode to 754, the file would be readable, writeable, and executable by you; readable and executable by anyone in your group; and readable by anyone else.

# Summary

Creating and publishing your first Web document seems easy if you follow the steps outlined in this chapter. Although your first document will be basic, developing a strategy can save you time and help you better organize your material. A good strategy focuses on the purpose, audience, scope, and structure of the document.

You can add to the visual impact of your document by adding features. Although images serve as powerful features to express your ideas and enhance your document, other features you can add include horizontal rules, line breaks, links, and lists. After you finish the document, proof your work and test the features you have added to the document so that you can proudly publish your document on the Web for the world to see.

# Designing and Publishing a Web Site

## 36

*by William Robert Stanek*

**IN THIS CHAPTER**

Creating and publishing your first Web page served as a starting point. The key to establishing a Web presence and building a name for yourself in cyberspace is to create a killer Web site that will stop Web surfers in their tracks. To do this, you must learn the basics of organizing, creating, and publishing a Web site where you can feature a collection of dozens or hundreds of pages. By following the steps outlined in this chapter, you can become one of the thousands of individuals successfully publishing in cyberspace.

The difference between a successful site and an unsuccessful site comes from attention to detail, good content, and good organization. Many books on the Internet and Web publishing discuss theories, cover key subjects, and show basic examples, but rarely follow a practical hands-on approach to Web publishing. Books without practical hands-on examples can leave you wondering where to start, how to start, and what to do when you finally manage to start. This chapter follows a hands-on approach for creating a Web site. Through practical, step-by-step examples, you learn how to create, organize, and publish your own Web site. The chapter goes on to tell you how you can publicize your site, a critical yet all too often neglected part of Web publishing. If you don't tell people your site exists, no one will know and no one will visit.

The following list provides eight steps for creating, publishing, and publicizing your Web site:

1. Define the Web site.
2. Learn Web site design concepts.
3. Create the Web site's content.
4. Learn about advanced linking of pages and publications.
5. Add rooms to your Web home.
6. Proof and test your Web site.
7. Publish your Web site.
8. Publicize your Web site.

# Defining Your Web Site

You build a Web site one step at a time, and the first step is simply defining what you want to publish on the Web. The basic components of a Web site are the pages you link together. These pages can contain text, graphics, and multimedia. The type of information you can publish on the Web has only the limits set by your imagination.

You can create a site that has many features, such as community services, product samples, and product information. For example, the Web site I created for The Virtual Press has the following features:

- Community service areas for writers, publishers, and job seekers
- Corporate background and history
- Information on products and services

- Online ordering center
- Personal information and resumé
- Product samples
- Web publications

Your Web site can be a commercial venture or simply an adventure. No strict rules say that you must publish either for fun or for profit. Your site can be for profit and still provide the Internet community with a useful resource containing information about you, your company, your products, and your services. Your site can serve as strictly informational with no sales information whatsoever, providing the Internet community with a fabulous free resource. You might desire to show the world that you have definitive expertise in a particular subject area, which might ultimately sell yourself, your ideas, or your company to consumers.

You should carefully consider what you want to publish on the Web. You can start by creating a list of your creative projects, the plans for your business, your favorite hobbies, and your areas of interest or expertise. You can use this list to help you decide on areas you might want to Web publish in. To help you manage the list, you might want to use the FrontPage To Do List. Each task in your list should focus on a specific aspect that you want to include in the site, such as a product information page or a resource page in your area of expertise.

# Web Site Design Concepts

Competing in a global marketplace requires planning from day one. Before you start building your Web site, you must establish objectives and define what you hope to gain from your Web presence. Establishing an identity for yourself and your company in cyberspace does not come easily. You must use your skills and ideas to sell yourself and your company to the world.

To establish a presence on tomorrow's Web, you must adopt a vision for success focused on global outreach. At the heart of this vision, you should have a strategy similar to the one you developed in the preceding chapter. This strategy should focus on the following:

- The goals of the site
- The audience for the site or key areas within the site
- The scope of the site's content

You must create a friendly Web site that continues to grow and change. The size of your site, however, won't sell your ideas and products. Your vision and ability to find your place in the world community will draw interest. You want to consider two major design concepts immediately:

- The general organization of your site
- The organization of your site's pages and files

# Getting Organized with FrontPage Webs

Whether you are thinking on a grand scale or a small scale, the organization of your information is the most important design issue in setting up a Web site. Carefully consider how you want to organize your site. The power of Web publishing is that you can seamlessly integrate complex presentations. Behind those complex presentations are dozens, possibly hundreds, of individual pages that can contain text, images, and multimedia. The result can either be an unfriendly place to visit and a nightmare to maintain or, if organized properly, a friendly place to visit and a joy to maintain.

FrontPage has built-in features to help you create a manageable infrastructure at your Web site. Whenever you create a new Web, you are actually creating a new subdirectory in your site's Root Web. Breaking down your site into several Webs makes the site as a whole more manageable. Instead of having to deal with 1,000 files in a single enormous Web, you would break the site down into several Webs of 200 to 300 files each. Each Web would contain the pages for a particular area of your Web, such as your customer service area.

Another reason for organizing what otherwise would be a single enormous Web into several smaller Webs is that FrontPage works best with Webs that are less than 500 pages. When your Web contains more than 500 pages, there will be a noticeable delay whenever you try to open, close, or update the Web. For example, one of the Webs I used with FrontPage during stress testing of the software contained over 650 files. My 133Mhz Pentium with 24MB RAM chugged and churned for an average of 45 seconds when I tried to open the Web.

Your site's Root Web should contain pages and files that pertain to the overall site or to the organization sponsoring the site. The best way to set up the base directory is to use an index or default page that pertains to the site as a whole. This default page serves as your home page and will most likely be the first page visitors to your site see. The address URL for your base directory usually looks something like this:

```
http://www.your_company.com/
```

or

```
http://www.your_service_provider.com/~you
```

In both cases, a browser accessing the URL would display the default page for your site. You will find a default page called index.htm in the Root Web used on FrontPage. You should replace this document with your own. If you use ISP's Web server with a virtual domain or an account with Web publishing privileges, the Root Web is normally published to a directory called public_html, which appears under your user directory. Keep in mind that the name of the default page might vary according to the server software of the ISP. If the filenames index.htm or index.html do not work for you, ask your ISP to tell you the name of the default page for the server.

> **NOTE**
>
> If the `public_html` directory was not created by your service provider, you can easily create it. On a UNIX or DOS-based system, type the following command:
>
> ```
> mkdir public_html
> ```
>
> The preceding command will make a directory called `public_html` for you. Before you type the command, you should ensure that you are in your user directory. One way to do this on a UNIX system is to type the command `cd` on a line by itself as follows:
>
> ```
> cd
> ```

# Organizing Your Site's Pages and Files

Your site's page and file structure can play a key role in helping you organize your ideas. Carefully consider how the outside world will regard the structure of your site. You can organize different types of information into Webs. You can organize your site into Webs that pertain to the projects or publications featured at the site. You can also organize the files within your directories into a logically named structure.

Each file that pertains to a particular presentation could use an element of the project's name to relate it to the project. Even if you plan to put individual projects in their own Webs, naming remains important, especially when you plan to publish multiple projects that are closely related. A book publisher who planned to publish extracts of her books on the Web would not want to name the parts of the first book:

```
page1.html
page2.html
page3.html
```

or

```
chapter1.html
chapter2.html
chapter3.html
```

A better naming scheme relates the parts of the project to the project itself, which helps avoid confusion when publishing additional projects and makes the site easier to maintain. Imagine a site with a dozen books that has identical names for the pages of the publications. What happens when the new employee you've hired moves pages 12 to 27 for your third book into the Web reserved for your first book?

To relate the parts of the project to the whole, you could prepend an abbreviation for the project or part of the project's title to the filenames. For example, *Microsoft FrontPage Unleashed*'s title could have the abbreviation FPU. You could then prepend the abbreviation to the component parts of the project as follows:

```
fpuch1index.html
fpuch1pg1.html
fpuch1pg2.html
fpuch1pg3.html
fpuch1title.gif
```

# Creating the Web Site's Content

A Web site functions as much more than pages linked together. It serves as your home on the Web, and as such, it should contain doorways that reduce communications barriers and help spread your ideas to a global audience. The first doorway you want to establish on the Web is the front door to your Web site, your home page. As the first thing most visitors to your site will see, your home page should seem friendly and inviting.

Creating a friendly and inviting home page involves much more than hanging up a virtual welcome mat. It involves creating a well-organized page that reflects who you are and what you plan to do on the Web. The page should follow a sound design that provides an overview of what the site has available. You can present an overview of content in many ways, but making it a sneak preview of what visitors to the site can expect to find can provide the best way to organize the overview.

Your sneak preview can tell the world that you are dull and unimaginative if you have a home page organized like the table of contents you would find in a print publication. A home page organized in such a pure linear fashion might seem like a logical way to go, but generally this design has only first-time visitors in mind. Although you want to attract new visitors, you also want to attract repeat visitors. If McDonald's attracted only one-time customers, they would have never sold billions of hamburgers. The key in business, even with a not-for-profit business, is building a customer base, and you cannot build a customer base if your customers only visit your site once. Thus, your sneak preview should convince users that they want to add this place to their hot list.

Designing a site with content for first-time and repeat visitors remains extremely important in creating an inviting place to visit. Yet, you also want your house on the Web to feel like a friendly place to visit. The friendliest sites on the Web consider the user's time and present information in the right level of detail based on your location within the site. Many houses exist on the Web that I visit. Some sites I visit often because they seem friendly, useful, or entertaining. Other sites I visit once and only once because they feel unfriendly and do not respect my time, or anyone else's. These sites often have the 50,000-byte graphics doing the greeting instead of the Web publisher. Anyone can create monstrous graphics and pitch them at the world, but it takes practice and skill to obtain a working balance between efficacy and grandeur.

The design of your site does not stop at your home page. The best sites on the Web have many special areas or mini-sites within the site. These mini-sites can be the star attractions, utilizing features that constantly change and grow. My house on the Web at tvp.com is no exception.

The design of the site has changed many times, but the features always had a design that kept first-time and repeat visitors in mind.

In addition to the community service area developed in Chapter 35, "Designing and Publishing a Home Page," some areas you might want to add to your first Web site include

- A home page
- A business background page highlighting your products and services
- A personal background page highlighting your achievements and telling the world who you are

Through step-by-step examples, the remainder of this chapter builds these pages. You can use similar pages to form the basis of your Web site and save hours of work.

# Advanced Linking of Pages and Publications

This section explores advanced techniques for linking the pages of your site. Page linking is extremely important. The more navigation mechanisms you provide within the site, the more easily visitors can find their way around.

Your site should follow a flowing design with multiple routes through the information infrastructure you have created. Readers should have the capability to advance from overview pages to more detailed pages within your site. They should also have a way back to your home page and should be able to start a new search from any level within the site.

Realize from the start that the Web structure enables users to enter your site at any level, and you will have a head start on many Web publishers. You can easily come across a Web page that gives users no indication of where the page is within the information infrastructure at the site. The worst of these pages become dead-end streets, with no way to return to the site's home page and no way to access any other information at the site. Finding a dead-end street on the Web becomes frustrating to say the least; however, dead-end streets occur because the creators lacked foresight. They either thought that all visitors would access the site starting from the front door, or they just never stopped to think about the consequences of creating such a page.

## Building a Friendly Home Page with Good Linking

The key to building a friendly and inviting home page rests in good linking. When I created The Virtual Press site, I considered very carefully the navigation mechanisms I would provide to readers. Although the site has changed many times over the years and has grown from a few dozen pages to a few thousand pages, the attention to user friendliness and ease of navigation has remained a constant. The current version of The Virtual Press home page is shown in Figure 36.1.

**FIGURE 36.1.**

*The Virtual Press Web site begins with a home page.*

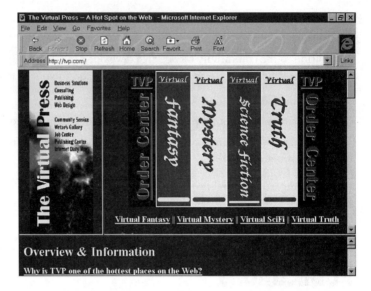

As you can see from Figure 36.1, the home page is broken down into three frames. You set up frames using the Frames Wizard. As discussed in Chapter 13, "Using Frames and the Frames Wizard," the contents of each frame are in a separately defined HTML document. When you create a frame-enhanced page, you should always create a separate version of the page for browsers that do not support frames. The Frames Wizard lets you specify this page as an alternate page URL.

## Linking the Side Frame

The left side frame is used to display TVP's logo, which is animated using client-pull technology. To create the animation, I rotated the axis of the logo image and saved each rotation as a different image. When these images are linked together in a sequence, they form an animation.

Client pull enables you to update documents at specified time intervals. With client pull, the server sends data to the client. When it is time to update the data, the client browser opens a new connection to the server and either retrieves new data or refreshes the current data. Afterward, the client closes the connection and waits until it is time to update the data again. FrontPage allows you to create documents that use client pull. You do this by setting a Meta variable with a refresh interval and the URL to the page to load after the time interval has passed. The refresh interval is specified as the number of seconds to wait before refreshing the current page or retrieving a specified page.

To set a Meta variable for any document open in the FrontPage Editor, select Page Properties from the File menu. In the Page Properties dialog box, click on the Meta button. Next, click on the Add button in the System Variables section of the Meta Information dialog box. In the Name field of the dialog box shown in Figure 36.2, enter the keyword Refresh; then in the

`Value` field, enter the time interval followed immediately by a semicolon, a space, and then the keyword URL. The value you set for the URL keyword must be the fully specified URL to the document or file you want to retrieve.

**FIGURE 36.2.**

*Using client pull by setting Meta variables.*

If you want to continue the animation, the document specified with the URL keyword should also have a `Refresh` Meta variable set. When you reach the last document in the animation sequence, you can make the animation loop infinitely by simply setting the URL keyword to the first document in the animation sequence. Here are sample values for the `Refresh` Meta variable in an animation sequence with eight documents that repeats infinitely:

`10; URL=http://www.tvpress.com/doc2.html`

`10; URL=http://www.tvpress.com/doc3.html`

`10; URL=http://www.tvpress.com/doc4.html`

`10; URL=http://www.tvpress.com/doc5.html`

`10; URL=http://www.tvpress.com/doc6.html`

`10; URL=http://www.tvpress.com/doc7.html`

`10; URL=http://www.tvpress.com/doc1.html`

Because I knew some users would get tired of the animation, I designed a mechanism for stopping the animation. Clicking on the logo image causes the animation to stop. When the animation is stopped, you can click on the logo again to restart it. Figure 36.3 depicts how the documents are linked together. To use a similar technique in your home page, link the logo to a document that contains the logo but does not have any Meta variables. This second document can then be linked back to the first document or file in your animation sequence. In this way, users can start and stop the animation by clicking on the logo.

**FIGURE 36.3.**

*Linking an animation that can be stopped and started.*

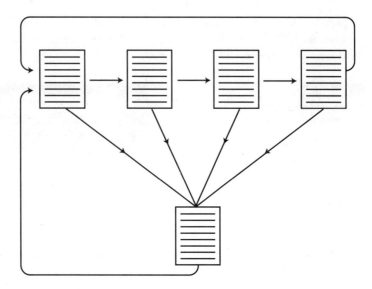

# Linking the Main Frame

The main frame contains the eyecatching front door to TVP's order center. Each book between the bookends is a clickable image that will take the reader to a key section of TVP's order center. Although these graphics appear large on-screen, they do not hog bytes. Under the images, a mini text menu provides readers with an alternate route to the order center. A text menu ensures that readers with a text-only browser can easily navigate the site. It also provides easy access to the order center for readers who might have turned off the graphics-loading capability of their browser.

Using the main frame's scroll bar, you can view additional sections of the page. One section on this page tells visitors about upcoming events at the site.

Informing visitors of upcoming events is extremely important. For large or complex Web sites, you might want to have a "What's New" page. A "What's New" page provides a great way to inform visitors of recent changes. Repeat visitors to your site will appreciate the effort because a "What's New" page makes it easier for them to use your Web site efficiently. You help them find new information faster, and ultimately, they return the favor by revisiting your friendly Web site.

As shown in Figure 36.4, the final section of the main frame provides contact and copyright information. You should always provide a point of contact for questions, technical or otherwise, about the site. Ideally, the contact name is linked to a mailto reference that lets visitors easily send e-mail to the point of contact. When you create links in the FrontPage Editor, mailto is one of the protocol options in the World Wide Web tab of the Create Link dialog box.

You should also provide a copyright notice to the pages of your site to tell the world that the site is an intellectual property and, as such, has protection under U.S. and international copyright laws. Instead of displaying complete copyright information on every page, you might want to create a link to a copyright page.

**FIGURE 36.4.**

*Always provide contact and copyright information.*

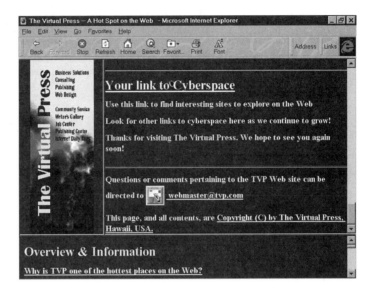

## Linking the Bottom Frame

The bottom frame contains a text-based menu that functions as the primary navigation mechanism to the key areas of the site. Figure 36.5 shows this menu in detail. Although I could have designed a cool image map to replace the text-based menu, I decided not to do this. Minimizing loading time whenever possible serves as an important concept in Web page design, especially when you consider that most Web users have a 14,400-bps modem. If your site has many attractions, you should consider using a text-based menu as the primary navigation mechanism.

**FIGURE 36.5.**

*Creating a text-based menu section for your frame-enhanced home page.*

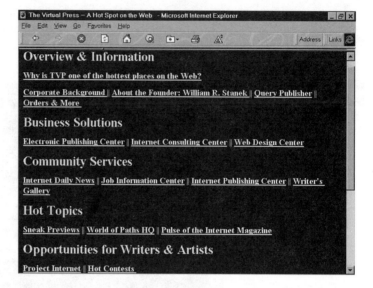

# Adding Rooms to Your Web Home

Your home on the Web should have many rooms. Filling those rooms with wonderful content doesn't always happen easily, especially when you have to choose which room to fill first. A new site should build its rooms a little at a time. You should start by building a solid framework for the site that tells the world who you are and what you plan to do. Show visitors you possess dedication to the development of a wonderful resource, and they will return to see the progress of your site even if it is in the early stages of development.

This section shows you how to build two more rooms for your site:

- A business-oriented background page
- A personal background page

Because these pages are part of the corporate background and history, they are placed in the Root Web. As you develop the areas of your Web site, keep in mind that you should create separate Webs for each key area. This will make your Web site more manageable.

## Your Business Background Page

All Web publishers—from well-known national or international companies to individual business people—should take the time to tell the world about their businesses. Too many sites on the Web offer products or services to the world and forget to tell the world who they are and what they represent. Your business background page provides essential background on what your site represents to the Internet community. This page can provide the background and history of your business. It can also provide an overview of products and services you currently offer or plan to offer.

Your business background page could contain four parts:

- Overview
- The selling points
- Product and service summary
- Additional and closing information

## Building the Overview Section

Your background page could begin with an overview that summarizes the background of your company or your business efforts in a few paragraphs. The summary should highlight the key points of your business and could focus on the following elements of your business:

- Mission
- Goals
- Objectives

Figure 36.6 shows the overview section on TVP's background page. The summary stays short and points out the corporate mission, goals, and objectives. Your summary should also be short and to the point.

**FIGURE 36.6.**

*A background page could begin with an overview.*

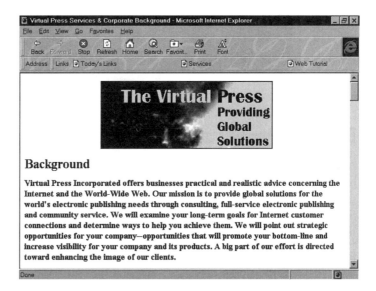

# Building in the Selling Points

Showing the world you are serious about business can become the purpose of the next section of your page. The design and content of the page tells the reader a great deal about who you are. You want to show the world that you are a professional. You also want to show the world you feel serious about business. If you are presenting a service to readers, you want to demonstrate why they should use your company and not one of the other companies they could jump to at the click of their mouse button. Showing that you know your subject area and have studied the market helps make your case.

The Virtual Press provides services to Internet-smart consumers and businesses. Figure 36.7 and Figure 36.8 demonstrate that we have studied the market.

**FIGURE 36.7.**

*Show the world you mean business and are a professional.*

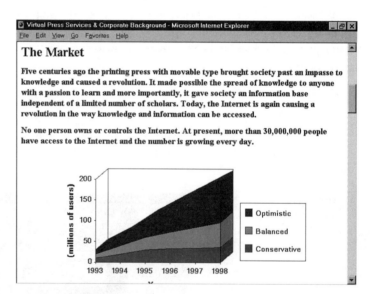

# Building a Product and Service Summary

After demonstrating your expertise and business savvy, you should provide readers with a list of your products or services. Ideally, your list will contain links to pages with detailed information that readers could access if they wanted more information. If you are just starting out, however, this spot can serve as an excellent place to tell readers what they can expect to see in the coming months. No Web site gets built overnight and readers know this.

Figure 36.9 shows the product and service summary for TVP. The summary appears as three lists. The first list pertains to books TVP publishes. The second list pertains to services TVP offers. The third list pertains to community service areas TVP maintains.

**FIGURE 36.8.**

*Demonstrate your expertise and business savvy.*

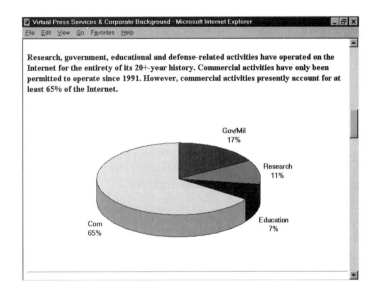

**FIGURE 36.9.**

*A product and service summary.*

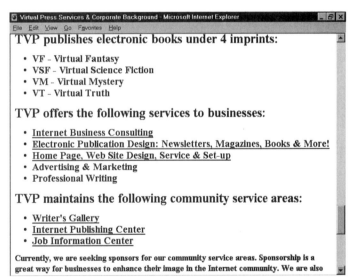

# Adding Information and Finishing the Page

The way you complete the page becomes as important as how you start the page. Don't create a dead-end for readers. At the very least, provide them with a way to easily return to your home page. Finish your background page with address and contact information, as shown in Figure 36.10.

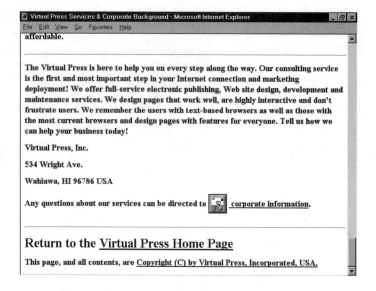

# Your Personal Background Page

Just as Web publishers sometimes neglect to tell the world about the background of their business, they also sometimes neglect to tell the world about themselves. Telling the world about yourself is extremely important, especially if you offer a service or product to Internet users. Again, the number of sites on the Web that offer services or products to Internet users and then fail to provide adequate credentials still seems amazing.

Why should anyone listen to your advice on rebuilding classic cars? Perhaps they should because you have worked as an auto mechanic for 20 years, rebuilt hundreds of cars, and won dozens of awards. No one will know these facts unless you tell them. The mechanic's background page could show a picture or contain a link to a picture of every award-winning car featured at the site.

**NOTE**

As you develop the page, keep in mind that a reader who visits your business background page might not visit your personal background page and vice versa. Consequently, you probably want to build some overlap into the material you cover on both pages.

Your background page could contain four main sections:

- Personal background summary
- Plans, goals, and objectives

- Credentials
- Additional and closing information

# Building in Your Personal Background Summary

Your background page should begin with a summary of your personal and professional life. You might want to keep the section short, usually three to five paragraphs will do. Project a positive image by touching on the high points of your life and career, not the low points.

This place can help bring down the barriers between you and the reader. You can do this by adding a few tidbits of personal information that show the reader the world isn't so large after all. You, the publisher, have a family, interests, and hobbies to match your ambitions and dreams.

Figure 36.11 shows the first section of my personal background page. To make the page as interactive as possible, the key links to other pages at the site appear in the summary. I also provided a link with a mailto reference so that readers can easily send me an e-mail message. Try to work links into your list as well; the more interactive you make your page, the better.

**FIGURE 36.11.**

*Show the world your personal side.*

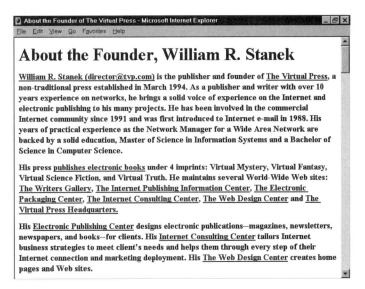

# Building in Your Plans, Goals, and Objectives

After you tell the world about yourself, tell the world about your plans, goals, and objectives for the Web site. These plans should serve as an overview and only provide as much or as little information as you feel comfortable providing. Figure 36.12 shows this section of the background page.

**FIGURE 36.12.**

*Tell the world a bit about your plans.*

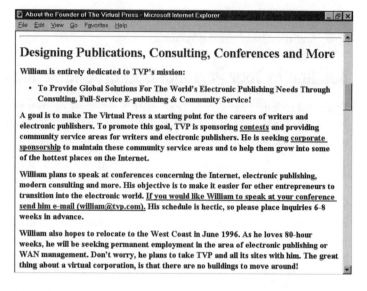

## Building in Your Credentials

After telling the world about your plans, back those plans up with your credentials. Here you should publish an electronic version of your resumé or simply outline the milestones in your professional career. A great way to present your resumé is as a series of bulleted lists, as shown in Figure 36.13.

**FIGURE 36.13.**

*Add your credentials with a Web version of your resumé.*

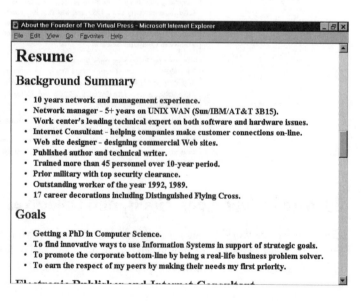

Whenever possible, work links into your resumé section as well. If you worked for IBM, then add a link to IBM's home page in the section of your resumé that outlines your job at IBM. The education section of your resumé also provides another good place to add links.

## Adding Information and Finishing the Page

The final section of the personal background page features contact and address information. Although this information might appear on your business background page, you should include the information here as well. As you can see from Figure 36.14, the page ends with a link back to the home page and provides copyright information as well.

**FIGURE 36.14.**

*Finish the page with links and contact information.*

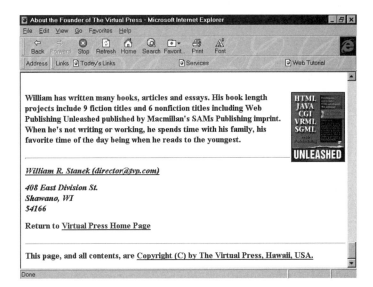

# Proofing and Testing the Web Site

Now that you have several finished pages and the makings of a wonderful site, you will want to test the site before you publish it. Make testing your Web site easier by checking the accuracy of your information one page at a time. Follow the advice on proofing and testing your pages discussed in Chapter 35, "Designing and Publishing a Home Page."

You can test the links used in your pages using the FrontPage Explorer's recalculate links feature. Don't forget that you have to individually test the Root Web and all the Webs in your site.

> **TIP**
>
> Browsers can change your window to the Web and different browsers might display your page in different ways. Always test features at your site with multiple browsers. I typically use three different browsers to test pages: Lynx, NCSA Mosaic, and Internet Explorer. Lynx, a text-only browser, can test features for readers with a text-only browser. NCSA Mosaic, a graphics-capable browser, tests images and features for the average reader. Internet Explorer, an advanced browser, supports its own unique extensions, Netscape extensions, and HTML 3.2 extensions. Internet Explorer can test the advanced features at the site.

# Publishing Your Web Site

Most Web publishers don't have their own server and must use an Internet Service Provider's Web server. When you use someone else's server, you have two publishing options. You can use the Publishing Wizard as discussed in Chapter 35, or you can export your documents from FrontPage and transfer them yourself.

While publishing your new site on an external server, you might encounter problems that you did not encounter when publishing your first page. Sometimes you just can't access your pages. The first thing you should do is to make sure all files are where they should be. Most of the time, HTML pages and associated files must be in very specific directories, such as the public_html directory, for the files to be accessed. If your files appear in the proper directory and you still can't access them, check the following:

- File and directory permissions
- File extensions
- Index files

## File and Directory Permissions

All operating systems flag files and directories with permissions. The permissions on files and directories are very important, especially on UNIX systems where the default file permissions are set according to an involved permission set. If you have problems accessing the file, check permissions on both the file and the directory where the file resides.

---

**NOTE**

On a UNIX system, a directory must be executable by the user to be readable. Typically, you want permissions on your public UNIX directories and files set so that users can access your files, but cannot write to the directory. The command you would use to put your files and directories in this mode is

```
chmod 705 filename
chmod 705 directory_name
```

Or

```
chmod 755 filename
chmod 755 directory_name
```

---

**NOTE**

On a DOS or Windows system, valid modes for files and directories include

```
System
Hidden
Read-only
Executable
```

If you have problems accessing files and directories, make sure the files are at least readable by the user. Your files and directories should not be hidden.

---

## File Extensions

The file extension you use should match the file type and format. Web servers can use the extension to determine what type of file you are trying to access. Web browsers can use the extension to determine what type of file you are retrieving and the action to take on the file. If you use a UNIX, Macintosh, or Amiga server, your HTML pages should have the extension `.html`. While your UNIX, Macintosh, or Amiga server might be configured to recognize the extension of `.htm` as a valid HTML document, it is often easiest to avoid a potential hassle and use the extension `.html`. If you use a Windows-based server, your HTML pages should have the extension `.htm`.

## Index Files

Most Web server software wants directories with HTML documents to have an index file. Servers will generally display the index when a user specifies a directory name instead of a filename, and if the index file doesn't exist, you might experience problems. The index file is sometimes called `index.html`, but not always. On a Macintosh server running MacHTTP or WebStar, each folder should have an index file called `default.html`.

> **NOTE**
>
> The lack of an index file can sometimes represent a security problem because most servers will display a list of the contents of a directory if no index document exists. If you are unable to use the filename `index.html` or `index.htm`, contact your Web administrator.

# Publicizing Your Web Site

You've published your Web site. You have a wonderful Web site or at least a start on what will become a wonderful Web site. Now you have to tell the world about it. In fact, you *must* tell the world about it. On the Internet, no road maps exist and unless you tell people you have created a new site, no one will find out. Thankfully, dozens of Web sites specialize in spreading the word about Web resources. These sites maintain databases that Web users can search or meander through using links to specific categories.

The good news is you can register your site with most of these sites for free. All you have to do is to tell the site where they can find you and what to expect.

In the past year, over a dozen new databases have appeared on the Web and soon dozens more will be available. Tracking down all these databases individually to ensure maximum exposure to the millions of Web users becomes difficult and time-consuming to say the least. Instead of spending an entire day registering your site, one solution would be to register your site only at the major databases, but then the question becomes which major databases. Here is a list of the major databases and the URL to their submission page:

Apollo: `http://apollo.co.uk/`

EINet Galaxy: `http://galaxy.einet.net/cgi-bin/annotate`

GNN: `http://www.gnn.com/gnn/wn/whats-new-form.html`

Harvest: `http://harvest.cs.colorado.edu/Harvest/brokers/register-with-CU-gatherers.html"`

HomeCom Global Village: `http://www.homecom.com/global/gc_entry.html`

InfoSeek: `http://www.infoseek.com/doc/FAQ/_How_do_I_get_my_web_page_inde.html`

Jump Station: `http://js.stir.ac.uk/jsbin/submit`

Lycos: `http://lycos.cs.cmu.edu/lycos-register.html`

New Rider's WWW Yellow Pages: `http://www.mcp.com/newriders/wwwyp/submit.html`

Nikos: `http://www.rns.com/www_index/new_site.html`

Open Text: `http://opentext.uunet.ca:8080/omw-submit.html`

Starting Point: `http://www.stpt.com/util/submit.html`

Web Crawler: `http://webcrawler.com/WebCrawler/SubmitURLS.html`

What's New Too: `http://newtoo.manifest.com/WhatsNewToo/submit.html`

Whole Internet Catalog: `http://gnn.com/gnn/forms/comments.html`"

World Wide Web Worm: `http://www.cs.colorado.edu/home/mcbryan/WWWadd.html`

World Wide Web Yellow Pages: `http://www.yellow.com/`

Yahoo: `http://www.yahoo.com/bin/add`

Another solution for registering your site with a database is to use a site that acts as a pointer to the databases. Pointer sites provide a way of automating the registration process, and using the fill-out form provided at the site, you can submit your information to multiple databases at the touch of a button. Currently, there are two primary pointer sites: Scott Banister's Submit It page and HomeCom's Pointers to Pointers page.

The Submit It page is shown in Figure 36.15. A great thing about the Submit It page is that all the database sites you see listed at the top of Figure 36.16 are automatically selected to receive your submission. You can tell the site is selected by the checkmark in the box associated with the database. If you don't want to register with a certain site, you would click the box to deselect the site and the checkmark would disappear.

After you complete the online form partially depicted in Figure 36.16, you can automatically register your site with more than a dozen Web databases. The key information you enter into this form includes your name, business address, e-mail address, site URL, site title, and a brief description of your site.

**FIGURE 36.15.**

*Use Submit It to register your site with more than a dozen databases.*

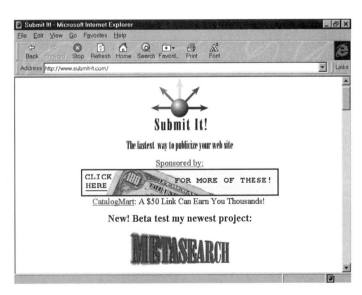

**FIGURE 36.16.**

*A fill-out form at Submit It makes submission easy.*

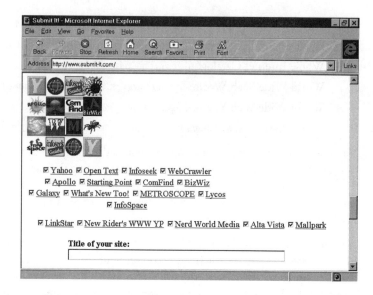

The Pointers to Pointers page is shown in Figure 36.17. This page has an organization very different from the organization of the Submit It page. Dozens of large, small, and specialized databases appear in a comprehensive list. Some databases are presented with a checkbox that you must select individually to place an automated submission. Other databases, particularly the specialized databases, are provided only as links that you must visit individually to submit your information.

HomeCom's page features a fill-out form for automatic submission to databases you have selected. This form appears partially depicted in Figure 36.18. The key information you enter into this form includes your name, business address, e-mail address, phone number, fax number, site URL, site title, and a brief description of your site.

**FIGURE 36.17.**

*Use Pointers To Pointers to register your site with large, small, and specialized databases.*

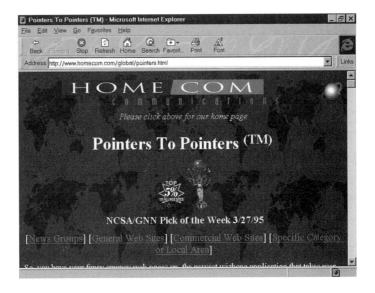

**FIGURE 36.18.**

*The Pointers To Pointers submission form.*

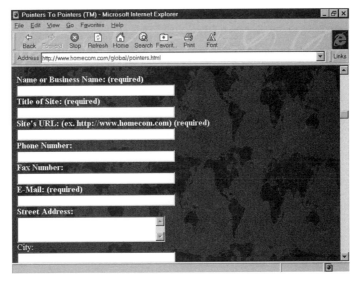

# Summary

Creating, publishing, and publicizing your first Web site remains easy if you follow the eight steps outlined in this chapter. If you follow the advice the examples present, your first Web site could have as many as four pages. These include your home page, business background page, personal background page, and the community service page developed in the previous chapter. Creating a Web site involves much more than creating pages; it involves developing a strategy and focusing on sound design concepts.

To attract visitors, your pages should seem friendly and inviting. One way to ensure your pages feel friendly is to design them with both first-time and repeat visitors in mind. You should also ensure that your site has no dead-ends. Dead-ends become frustrating and can easily be avoided by following a sound page design that includes adequate linking. You can use links to create image and text menus, to keep visitors informed, and to provide a feedback mechanism for readers. You can also use links to ensure that all your pages lead somewhere, even if it is only back to your home page.

# Planning and Developing an Intranet

by Mark L.
Chambers

**37**

**IN THIS CHAPTER**

In previous chapters, you've learned how to use Internet Explorer 3.0 to navigate the Internet, as well as how you can build your own Internet Web site with tools such as Internet Assistant, FrontPage, CGI scripts, and Java. At this point, you're ready to put your Web server online and begin to distribute your information to anyone around the world with an Internet connection.

However, another form of Web connection is growing in popularity nearly as fast as its big brother—and it might prove just as important as an Internet-based Web site to any office or business with a local area network! This new form of Web network, called an *intranet*, provides a method of distributing many types of information between different PCs on the same LAN using HTML technology.

In simple terms, intranets are like the Internet's Web on a much smaller scale, internal to a single company. How popular are they? Worldwide sales of intranet servers are forecast to grow from approximately 43,000 in 1995 to almost 2 million by 1999!

In this chapter, you'll find further definition of the important differences between an Internet Web site and an intranet Web site, including some of the pitfalls you might encounter while configuring your company's LAN for an intranet. You'll compare an intranet with traditional office-wide "groupware" technology, as well as look at design issues specific to an intranet Web site. You'll learn more about the many applications that you can develop for use by other departments within your company. Finally, you'll consider the future of the intranet and what applications might lie ahead.

# Intranet Essentials

Of course, Internet and intranet technologies are very similar in many ways, using the same base network protocol (TCP/IP) and the same language (HTML). For all practical purposes, a solid idea of what an intranet actually is has only coalesced within the last year or so.

Many companies still believe that they can use their existing Internet platform as the foundation for some of the applications that you'll see later in this chapter. The idea is to save money, of course, and reduce the hardware, software, and manpower required to run a Web site. The common question these days is, "Why do we need another Web computer just for company information?"

In this section, you'll learn why intranets are so popular, and why they warrant an investment of time, manpower, and money—even if your company already has an Internet site and a presence on the Web. You'll also learn the details of what you need in order to add an intranet to a company network that doesn't currently have an Internet connection.

## Internet versus Intranet

Unlike a Web site that allows connections through the Internet, an intranet site is designed with the internal needs of your company in mind, and this affects not only the appearance of your site but also the applications you'll add to it. The tools that you use remain the same. You still use HTML to build pages, for example. But the information you want to present to your fellow employees is usually quite different from the data you provide to the public on your Internet site. As a general rule, an intranet is best suited to a small or medium-sized company with a need to search, display, and update company data (although larger companies such as Ford and IBM have also implemented intranets). Figure 37.1 shows a typical intranet main menu with a set of common applications.

**FIGURE 37.1.**

*The top-level (or index level) of an intranet, showing some of the applications covered in this chapter.*

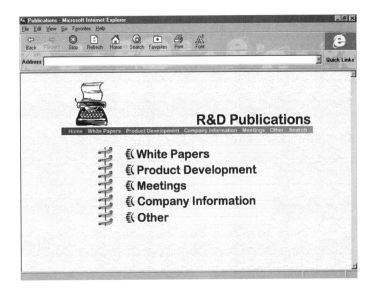

Let's examine some of the fundamental differences between an intranet and an Internet site:

■ **Teamwork.** On an Internet site, individuals usually access information independently of one another. In fact, on most Internet sites it's impossible to tell how many people are accessing the same page you are, or what they're doing. The only indication that others have visited the site is usually a "hit counter" that records how many visits are made to the page.

On the other hand, an intranet site allows your coworkers to work together as a team or communicate with each other, much like a more traditional company bulletin board system (or BBS). The same data can be shared and updated throughout your organization, using the familiar tools that employees are already using to browse the Internet! For example, group features for a typical intranet include discussion forums and project or meeting schedulers. Additionally, simple intranet applications such as these can take the place of some of the functions of traditional, expensive, company-wide *groupware* such as Lotus Notes.

■ **Security.** If your company has built a security firewall to prevent outsiders from accessing your LAN, your intranet server resides inside the firewall, where outsiders cannot access it. A firewall can be based on hardware or software technology; it prevents access from outside the LAN. Of course, your public Internet server exists outside any security firewall, or the public won't be able to reach it. If you have taken no security measures, it's strongly recommended that you do so before placing any company data meant for only internal use on an intranet site. Your company LAN administrator can tell you whether your LAN has security measures in place.

■ **Access**. As you've learned, the traditional Internet Web server is connected to the Internet via a direct wired connection—the faster, the better. However, an intranet server needs no connection to the Internet; it operates completely within the company's LAN.

In addition, an intranet can offer an alternate connection; it can be configured to handle individual calls directly from a modem (often called "dialup" access), allowing employees to search for information or update files from their home PC or from a laptop computer on the road. In fact, some commercial bulletin board systems with advanced TCP/IP features advertise themselves as the ideal framework for an intranet site (such as Mustang Software's WildCat or Galacticomm's WorldGroup).

■ **Content**. Let's face it. Browsing the Web on most Internet sites has been favorably compared to the display of billboards on a busy interstate. The vast majority of Internet sites available today simply involve an attractive HTML page with links to associated pages, perhaps with an FTP link or two. The closest thing to company information you're likely to find on an Internet site is probably a press release or company history.

An intranet is a different animal altogether; instead of entertaining visitors or presenting them with a selected menu of downloads, your site is designed from the beginning as a useful company tool. The intranet provides powerful applications and features that allow company-wide manipulation of data, group discussions, and even custom programs to search and display company records. An intranet, then, is strictly business; in fact, many intranets are text-only because the transmission of fancy graphics can double the amount of time needed to display a page!

Now that you're more familiar with the differences between an Internet site and an intranet site, let's examine what you'll need in order to operate an intranet (whether you currently have an Internet Web site or not).

# Hardware and Software Requirements

The traffic that you expect to visit your site will dictate the speed and capacity of your Internet server machine, and the same is true of your intranet platform: Make sure that you select a computer that is fast enough and has enough hard drive space!

Remember that after your intranet is operational and online, bringing it down to upgrade the hardware could be more than just a minor inconvenience. Make sure your intranet server is sufficient for the current size of your company, but also ensure that it can accommodate future growth.

Also, it's strongly recommended that you do not try to run both an Internet and an intranet site on the same PC. Performance will suffer, of course, but that's not as important as the issue of security. Sharing resources on the same machine between two servers greatly increases the chance that a document or company data meant for internal use only could be inadvertently displayed for the public to view. Additionally, if a machine running multiple servers happens to go down due to hardware failure or a lockup, you lose both of your Web sites. For these reasons, virtually every company with multiple Web servers dedicates a separate PC to each server.

With this in mind, here are the minimum requirements for an intranet server:

- A network-ready server PC running Windows 95 or Windows NT.
- A TCP/IP connection throughout the company. If the workstations on your network are currently connected to the Internet, it's likely that TCP/IP has already been implemented and you don't need to do anything else. However, if you're developing an intranet within a company with a network that doesn't support TCP/IP, your network administrator must add it.

---

**TIP**

If your company workstations are using Windows 3.11 or Windows 95, it's easy to configure the built-in TCP/IP stack for your intranet.

---

- One or more modems (if you're providing dialup access to your server). Modem connections usually require additional hardware and software on your server PC (or another PC on your network).
- Appropriate Web server software, such as FrontPage Web Server, installed on your server PC.
- A Web browser for each workstation, such as Internet Explorer 3.0.

That covers the basic requirements for your intranet site. Later in this chapter, you'll see additional commercial intranet Web applications, which are just now appearing on the market, that can greatly enhance your site. However, you'll be surprised by the applications you can create with these basic requirements.

Now it's time to start the actual planning of your intranet by introducing two important steps: identifying your audience and determining the content that the audience requires.

# Planning Your Intranet Site

At first glance, identifying the audience for a company intranet seems like a very easy task. After all, everyone in your organization will benefit from your intranet, so everyone will want to connect to it, right?

Similarly, selecting the data and applications that need to be provided by your intranet shouldn't be a problem; simply place all the company information you can get on the server, stick in a simple search engine, and you're ready to go.

Of course, both of these suppositions couldn't be farther from the truth, and few Webmasters would ever take such a course. However, it does underline the importance of planning. You'll save yourself a tremendous amount of work later (adding, deleting, and modifying content; restricting and granting access) by spending a small period of time planning realistically based upon your company's needs.

## Identifying Your Audience

First, let's consider who will use your intranet site within your company. Your goal is a simple one: Concentrate on providing access to the largest number of individuals who will consistently use the resources you feature on your site.

For some companies, this could indeed be everyone: for example, a small consulting firm of 10 to 20 people, or a real estate firm with less than 40 employees. Such companies are small enough not to overload your intranet server, and most individuals within the firm have similar needs for the same information. The smaller the organization, the less likely it is to need separate levels of security when it comes to company data. There are probably fewer departments and less specialization among employees.

Compare the possibilities for different audiences at a company with a large firm of 200 people or more. Employees are now grouped into distinct departments with different requirements for what they want to see online (and usually with different ideas of how to present and retrieve that data). Some company data undoubtedly needs a higher level of security. You must also consider the performance of your server PC: How well will it handle the traffic from a larger user base? Rather than provide everyone with access, it makes more sense to target those who will actually use your intranet.

Your company might be on either end of this spectrum, or it might fall somewhere between, but the process for determining your audience still involves the same three steps:

1.  **Determine constraints.** Will your intranet be limited to those in your own department or division within your company? If so, you might have already narrowed the scope of your intranet as much as necessary, unless there are separate groups in your company under the department level. If your intranet is company-wide, move to the next step.

2. **Identify relevance.** Although you haven't determined the exact content that you plan to deliver through your intranet, you still have a rough idea in mind of the data that you'll include. If your data is specific in nature or if viewing it requires a certain level of authority within your company, it's safe to say that you will be able to eliminate a portion of your fellow employees who either never need the information or are not allowed to see it. On the other hand, if your intranet site will offer data of general interest to everyone, this might not be a limiting factor.

3. **Examine priorities.** Finally, it's important to acknowledge that some employees within your company might have priority over others when it comes to your intranet. For example, if you plan to display ordering information within a mail-order firm, it's imperative that your salespeople and shipping crew have access to those records. However, marketing and personnel really don't need them, or they would have little use for them. Even if the information that your intranet provides needs to be distributed throughout the company, it pays to remember those employees that will use it the most!

After you've used these criteria to narrow your audience to those who will benefit the most from your intranet, you can determine whether all of those workers have access to a workstation and which of them will require training to use a Web browser. Identifying your intranet audience is also a requirement for planning the security measures that you're likely to need. You'll learn about these later, after you've decided on the content you'll offer on your site.

# Determining Content

The next phase of planning your intranet site centers on the data you'll provide to your users. You also make a first guess at the applications you'll offer to allow search and manipulation of that data.

As you saw earlier, it's likely that you already have a basic idea of what you'll offer on your site, and it might appear that this is a step you can skip. Perhaps content has already been determined by management, or you've met with key individuals in your company and discussed what their departments would like to see on a company intranet. This makes a good starting point, but unfortunately it's very easy to promise too much during the planning stages.

Before you set up your server and begin to gather information, code applications, or buy additional software, take a break and examine what you can actually deliver online (both now and in the future).

To plan the content of your site, keep these guidelines in mind:

- First, consider the scope of your audience. Is your site intended as a company-wide general resource? If so, the majority of the material you offer should apply to everyone, with little or no restrictions, and your applications must be easy to use for any employee. If your site is restricted to one or two departments, applications can be more complex, but you have to provide security as well.

■ Will your data be of value as an online resource? It's important to determine whether a specific set of data will benefit your users if you place it online. For example, would international sales records or meeting minutes from last year be of any use to your department? Typically, your users should be able to search or update information on your intranet server while online; your intranet site will suffer if you simply dump records and information into HTML format without some sort of logical order. As a general rule, if a topic isn't retrieved at least once every week by someone within your intranet, it's recommended that you simply maintain a printed list and not clutter your site with unneeded reference material.

■ Will your site offer archival information? If so, you might need additional hard drive space on your intranet server machine. If your server is dedicated to online discussion, ordering, or scheduling, you might decide to drop archival and general information entirely in favor of faster performance.

■ Who will maintain the site? Whether you or someone else will be responsible for your company's site, information must be updated and changes to the site must be made on a timely basis; this can include everything from updating a company phone list to handling hardware problems or backing up the server on a regular basis. Before you commit to adding information to your intranet site, consider the amount of work that will be required to maintain that information.

After you've determined the information that you'll furnish on your new intranet site, it's a good idea to request final approval of the content from those in charge. This extra step can save many headaches in the future, because you can be certain that what you're offering is indeed what was desired!

## Providing Security

As you learned earlier, intranet security is important if your company already has an Internet connection, or if your intranet will carry secure data that should not be distributed to some of its users. Today's Web server software might offer one or both of the following methods of security:

■ An IP address list or a range of IP addresses. This is the most common method of restricting access to an intranet, and it's typically used whenever the IP address of the workstation is permanently assigned by the network administrator. No logon or user action is required; the server automatically obtains this address at connection.

■ A name and password combination, similar to the logon procedure used by bulletin board systems. Because IP addresses generated for SLIP and PPP sessions are usually created dynamically, there's no way to add them to a permanent list. Therefore, if you're using a dialup connection to access your intranet, it's likely that you need to set up a name and password before making your first connection. For the same reason, most dialup Internet news and Internet e-mail servers require a name and password before granting access.

Of course, if your intranet will serve a single office with a network that's already using a standard login procedure—for example, a small business with 10 employees or less that is currently using the networking support built into Windows 95—you already have a basic security system in place. If there are any entry points into your LAN from the outside world, however, it's highly recommended that you implement at least one of the two security methods previously mentioned on your intranet server.

In this section, you learned the basics behind building an intranet site: the hardware and software requirements, how to plan for your audience, what information you should provide, and how you can safeguard your intranet from outside intrusion. In the next section, you'll see a comparison of intranets with commercial multiuser software packages (commonly called *groupware*). You'll also learn about many of the more popular applications currently being offered on intranets worldwide and how you can implement them on your site.

# Intranet Applications

One of the advantages that makes an intranet attractive is the low cost of the "raw material." HTML is relatively easy to learn and it's now supported as an integral part of Windows 95. Additionally, many of the best tools used to create Web pages are either free or relatively inexpensive. In fact, some of the simplest applications for your intranet in this section can be created in less than an hour!

In this section, you first see a comparison of intranet technology to traditional company-wide software packages that provide many of the same functions. You'll learn the advantages and disadvantages of each approach, and why the intranet is quickly becoming an attractive alternative.

The rest of this section is devoted to some of the most popular applications you can add to your intranet. Some applications are simple enough that you can easily write them yourself, and the more powerful features are available with commercial programs.

## Intranet versus Groupware

Although the intranet as an office tool is a relatively recent development, other software packages designed to allow employees to access company information have been popular for years. Program suites like these are called *groupware*; they're usually built around a proprietary database format and a multiuser interface, allowing coworkers to access and modify the same data at the same time. Lotus Notes is a good example of a popular groupware package, offering many of the same applications that are covered later in this chapter. Figure 37.2 shows a representative Lotus Notes menu. As a rule, however, a groupware package will be more powerful and offer more features than even the most sophisticated intranet.

**FIGURE 37.2.**

*Lotus Notes, a traditional groupware software suite that can handle multiple users at the same time across an entire network.*

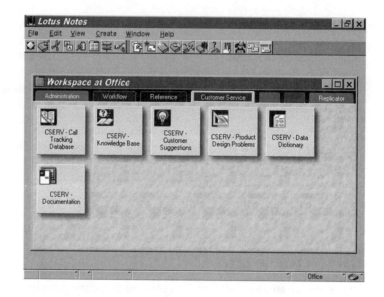

You might wonder, "Why should I bother building an intranet, then? Why not buy groupware instead?" Let's compare the two approaches to company-wide communications, and you'll learn why many firms are turning away from groupware in favor of an intranet.

## The Advantages of Groupware

In its simplest form, even a software package containing a network-aware word processor and spreadsheet can call itself groupware, but the name is more properly applied to comprehensive programs providing messaging, file transfer and retrieval, scheduling, database access, and document management to everyone within a company.

Typically, groupware is superior to an intranet system on these points:

- By its very nature, an integrated suite of applications written especially for groupware use offers features that an intranet server based on HTML simply cannot match. For example, a groupware system can provide network fax capability or support for videoconferencing.

- Groupware packages offer everything built in, with no menu system to create and no other applications to write or buy. Currently, an intranet is designed and built from the ground up, which takes more time and resources than some companies want to invest.

- Groupware offers professional technical support, ongoing development, and other benefits of commercial software. Often, an intranet is built and maintained by a single employee!

■ Unlike an intranet, a groupware program doesn't require TCP/IP. This is less important if you're adding an intranet server to a network that already carries TCP/IP support for an Internet site; but if your network doesn't currently include support, adding it can be a headache because it requires additional software and might require an investment in hardware as well.

# The Advantages of Intranets

So why are intranets so popular today? Let's examine some of the clear advantages of an intranet over a groupware suite:

■ For companies needing a basic company-wide information network, an intranet is much less expensive than purchasing a groupware package. Web servers and browsers are relatively inexpensive (or, in many cases, they're even built into the operating system), and the tools you use to create pages cost very little.

■ Employees can use their favorite Web browser to access your intranet, which means that you'll have fewer installation hassles and less training than with a groupware package. After all, many users will already be familiar with the Web and how to navigate it. Companies using more than one operating system need not worry about whether a Mac or UNIX browser is available, either.

■ HTML is relatively easy to learn, and tools exist for directly porting text and graphics from word processing and desktop publishing programs. Unlike a groupware solution, it's possible for someone other than an expensive in-house programmer to create new pages and even simple applications.

■ Finally, an intranet site is easily customized to exactly fit your company's needs, without extra features you don't want and would rather not buy. Unlike a "canned" groupware package, an intranet is an "open" architecture that can grow whenever the need arises, and you can choose from an ever-growing number of intranet commercial applications to add just the functions you need.

As you can see, an intranet is not the perfect solution for every company; much depends upon the amount you're willing to spend, the number of employees in your company, and the functions that you want the system to perform. If you need a turnkey system that will be up and running in a short time, an intranet is probably not as attractive as a groupware suite. However, if you're looking for an inexpensive company-wide system and you want to design it yourself, an intranet site is a natural solution.

In the next section, you'll explore some of what's possible today with an intranet, including applications you can create yourself.

# Possible Applications for Your Intranet

Often, an intranet is designed solely for the display of information throughout a company. Certainly, nothing is wrong with such a site; after all, HTML was designed expressly for the display and linking of text information. Your company might already have an online employee listing or a resource scheduling system in place, so why duplicate it on your intranet?

However, if you're looking to expand the functionality of your intranet beyond the basics, this section covers the details of each of the most popular applications available for you to add to your site.

## Document Display

As you learned earlier, a good starting point for any intranet site is a menu allowing the display of company documents. In fact, this is probably the most common function available on either an Internet or an intranet site; only the contents of the documents differ. Figure 37.3 shows an example of a document display application. Within FrontPage, a document display page is best created from the blank template.

**FIGURE 37.3.**

*It doesn't get any simpler than this: an intranet document display page.*

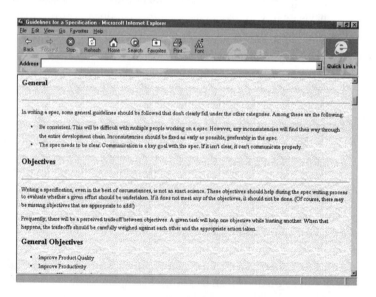

Note that document display and document retrieval are two different things in the intranet world:

- Unlike retrieval, the simple display of a document does not transfer it to the user's computer; the text is simply viewed online.

- If you're simply displaying a document, it must be converted to HTML format first.

- Because the contents of a display document are in HTML, it can also contain hypertext links to another page.

- Display does not require your browser to launch an FTP session.

Of course, converting large amounts of data to HTML format can be a time-consuming task—and reading a massive online document would probably prove just as bad! Therefore, document display on an intranet site is best reserved for documents of 10 pages or less that do not require constant updating, such as product feature lists, press releases, minutes, and white papers. If your company has a computer help desk, you can also create an excellent online troubleshooting guide for your support staff that might save countless calls.

If you're willing to take the time to create hypertext links within a document, you can make it easy for the reader to jump from inside the display of one document to another. However, sometimes this is actually unnecessary because static reference documents are usually self-contained and rarely require moving to another document. Also, in designing display pages and converting text for a company intranet, keep in mind that documents intended to be read on paper might not work as well online. Most computer users are less comfortable reading documents of several pages on a computer screen than reading that material printed on paper, so take the time to edit and shorten unnecessary sections of the text wherever possible.

## Document Retrieval

The second most common function for intranet sites is a menu allowing employees to receive binary files such as programs and word processing documents in their original format, usually with an option to search entries for a particular filename or keyword. Before the advent of intranet technology, many companies used electronic bulletin boards for the same purpose.

For example, a retrieval menu might subdivide company product information by operating system: By selecting the correct link for DOS, Windows 95, or Mac, you jump to a menu listing product information in the correct format. Each entry in the list is an FTP link to the document on the server, so by clicking on the filename, your browser would automatically retrieve the document (and possibly load it into the associated program).

Figure 37.4 shows an Adobe Acrobat document retrieved from this type of menu. Because the file carried the extension .PDF, Acrobat was launched and the retrieved file was loaded automatically! This is a great convenience if your company has standardized a specific word processor, graphics program, or spreadsheet.

Intranet retrieval menus are excellent for the following purposes:

- Distributing program upgrades and software drivers to workstation users across the network.

- Creating a company "publication guide," from which workers writing company documents such as memos and press releases can retrieve logos, fonts, and word processing templates for use in their work—whatever standard material is needed often throughout your company.

■ Archiving complete examples of standard company literature and manuals in .PDF format.

**FIGURE 37.4.**

*Helper applications can be used to display documents that do not exist natively in HTML or contain formatting that HTML does not support. Here, a desktop-published document (the company newsletter) can be retrieved from an intranet and viewed as it was originally designed.*

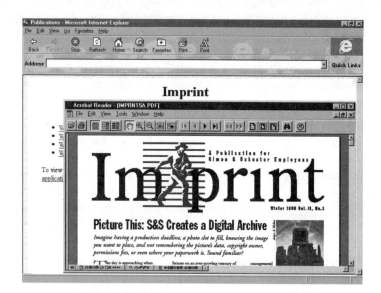

Because no conversion to HTML is necessary, an intranet Web administrator can assign the task of updating the retrieval menu to another employee with basic knowledge of HTML. After the administrator has granted the appropriate network rights on the server, updating such a menu is as simple as writing an entry with a new link and adding the corresponding files to the server. The employee need not even have physical access to the server because menu files can be updated offline and uploaded to overwrite the older versions.

Figure 37.5 shows another interesting example of document retrieval: This time, the files are images in two different sizes. The keyword search engine is an extra convenience, but it means a little additional work when adding images, because the person responsible for updating the server database must supply the file with more than just a filename. If the Browse display style is selected, each thumbnail is displayed along with the filename, and the List style simply displays the filenames as entries in a list.

#### Chapter 37

**FIGURE 37.5.**

*By clicking on the appropriate image, the production staff has immediate access to Simon & Schuster's online library of stock photographs.*

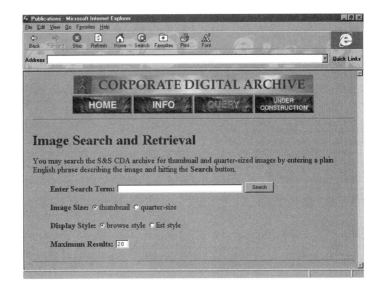

## Data Search and Display

A data search and display menu is quite similar to a document display menu. However, instead of displaying several pages of text in HTML format, the data display menu displays all the entries in a database that match your search criteria. Popular Internet search engines such as Yahoo! or Lycos work on this principle, returning entries with links to other Web pages that match the keywords or concepts you provide. Note, however, that no information on the server is updated by this type of application; although the list can be searched, the display is static.

In fact, data search and display menus are the real workhorses of any intranet, providing the basis for many applications. Figure 37.6 shows a typical search and display page application: a company-wide telephone directory, complete with a sophisticated search engine. As you can see, each entry returned might also be a link to a display page listing other phone numbers at that site.

Other typical uses for this basic intranet application include the following:

- Company client databases allow workers to search for those purchasing a particular product or based in a particular area. Each record could easily have a link to the client's Internet Web page or the client's e-mail address, adding convenience to the simple display of data.

- Employee databases highlight each worker's skills or knowledge base, creating a "knowledge cross-reference." If your company is constantly wondering which employee could perform a new task (or who has already done it), a knowledge cross-reference can be very valuable.

- Technical support databases contain known problems and workarounds for hardware or software, using symptoms and error codes as keys.

**FIGURE 37.6.**

*An example of an intranet-based database is Simon & Schuster's Corporate Telephone Directory. In this case, employees are able to look up phone numbers online, and the numbers are kept much more current than in printed directories.*

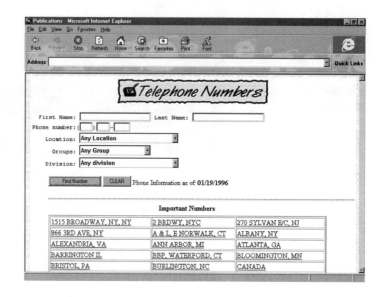

Within FrontPage, the Search Page template is a good example of an application using search and display.

When building search engines for your intranet pages, keep in mind that the user might not know the information for one or more fields. In the telephone directory example, for instance, you're not stuck simply because you don't know a person's name; you can search on location, group, or division within the company as well. Whenever possible, include enough search fields so that it's easy to display a range of data without depending upon the primary search key.

## Surveys, Questionnaires, and Feedback

Has a department within your company ever had to gather a specific piece of information from every employee? For example, perhaps the company picnic is approaching, and all 75 employees must select a main dish. Or, your marketing department has just finalized a new magazine advertisement and wants a general opinion from everyone within the company on how good it is. You could ask questions like these through company e-mail, or you might pass around a signup sheet, but compiling the results will be time-consuming (not to mention the headache of deleting countless e-mail replies). FrontPage includes a sample survey template.

An intranet site makes it easy for company management to stay in touch. Employees can submit ideas, requests, and complaints through an intranet page, or answer a company-wide survey using a simple form that can be filled out online. Paperwork is kept to a minimum, and replies are likely to be far more timely.

Figure 37.7 shows one possible application currently in use within a medium-sized company: a product requisition page, where workers can request additional hardware or software online.

Records submitted from this page are routed directly to purchasing, instead of the old paper method in which the requests were routed through several individuals before finally arriving at their destination.

**FIGURE 37.7.**

*This product requisition form is the perfect example of how an intranet can save any company time, effort, and paperwork.*

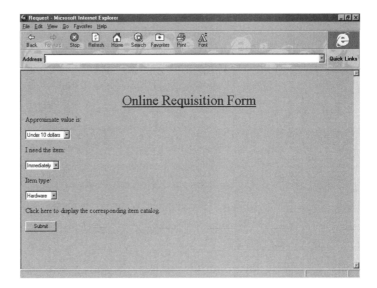

Commercial products are already available for feedback-style intranet applications that follow a regular process (such as submitting problem requests for software or the requisition page covered earlier). Workflow Metro from Action Technologies and Webflow from Ultimus both include prebuilt applications and enable you to design new ones quickly and easily.

In most cases, a feedback or survey page displays the form you've designed, accepts the input from the user, and saves the information on the server—perhaps displaying a simple page indicating that the submit step was successful. It is possible, however, for the server to run a CGI script to generate a tracking number or perhaps compile the results of a survey; these values can be displayed as part of the success page, so that the user receives a form of output as well.

**TIP**

When designing a form for one of these applications, use radio button groups and drop-down list controls whenever possible. Multiple choice fields are faster to complete and easier on the user than filling out a text field, and they ensure that the field returns a valid choice to the server. With a multiple choice field, you won't encounter a numeric value for a Yes/No question! Figure 37.8 shows an opinion poll form with multiple choice fields and radio button groups—a much better method of gauging employee reaction than requesting feedback through e-mail!

**FIGURE 37.8.**

*This intranet opinion poll is fast and easy for employees to complete, and the results are tabulated instantly.*

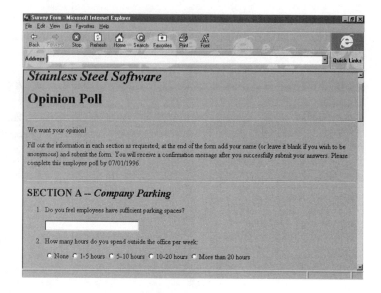

# Database Access

Most companies maintain some sort of database, either on a single machine (where only a single person can add, delete, or update records) or throughout the network. The more expensive network database servers can handle multiple instructions (or "queries") for the same record. SQL servers like these include high-level packages from Oracle, Sybase, and Microsoft.

On the surface, connecting your intranet to an SQL query database seems impossible. Typically, applications for these database servers are written in languages such as Visual BASIC or C. How can your intranet server offer access to these powerful database servers using only HTML?

With the recent growth in popularity of company intranets, there's a good possibility that you might be able to purchase a Web *front end* solution from the manufacturer of your database server. Many vendors have added proprietary products written especially for their database systems that process queries from a CGI script running on your server machine. This allows you to display a simple HTML form to accept a query request over your intranet and then display the results when the database returns the results to your server. Proprietary products using this technology include Oracle's WebServer and Sybase's Web.sql.

Records from smaller network database servers using Xbase technology can also be retrieved over an intranet in the same fashion; depending on the programming APIs supported by the database, it might be possible to view records and update them using only a combination of a CGI script and a Java applet.

Even if your database vendor doesn't currently offer an HTML processor, you might still be able to use a third-party program. For example, products such as NETAway's SQL-Surfer provide generic SQL access with full HTML and CGI compliance, including an SQL extension of HTML called SQL@Way. Allaire's Cold Fusion package enables you to write your own processor for generic SQL queries, and Object Manager from Tempest Products can orchestrate multiple applications written in different languages to handle database access.

Most of these programs require some knowledge of CGI, Java, or Perl, which most Web administrators are familiar with. However, if you're looking for a Web database solution that requires no programming at all, check out R:Web from Micorim. With R:Web, you simply design the Web database form onscreen, and the program delivers the scripts necessary to link any ODBC-compliant database to your form! Look for more easy-to-use WYSIWYG programs like these as intranets grow in popularity, increasing competition among software developers as a result.

## Resource Scheduling

Surprisingly enough, scheduling applications are not a common feature of intranet sites. After all, the paper method of tracking things is probably working fine for your company right now. Many Web administrators are not aware that HTML is powerful enough, while others simply don't feel that the function fits into the realm of an intranet site.

Nothing could be farther from the truth! As long as your intranet site is available to everyone in the company, you can throw away those paper logbooks and signup sheets! An intranet application can easily schedule company resources such as the following:

- Meeting rooms
- Exercise equipment or ball courts
- Audio/visual equipment
- Computer systems or laptops
- Company vehicles

These online schedules are available immediately to everyone within the company. Plus, your form can even record mileage driven or problems encountered with company equipment if necessary.

Figure 37.9 shows a meeting room resource scheduler currently in use on the intranet of a medium-sized company. The scheduler provides a graphical display that makes it easy to tell which hours a particular conference room will be occupied. To reserve a room for the current month or next month, you click on that day within either of the two small calendars on either side of the page title. This HTML display front-end works in concert with two separate CGI scripts that do the actual processing (one to return the occupied slots and one to process new reservations).

**FIGURE 37.9.**

*An intranet-based resource scheduler application for reserving company meeting rooms.*

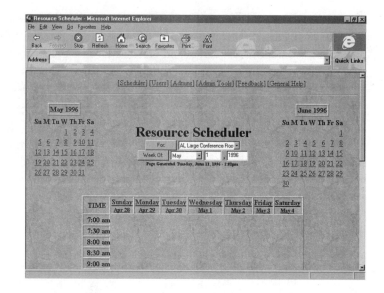

If you're planning an intranet or if you've just finished building your site, a resource scheduler makes a great first application to add. There's nothing like cutting paperwork and improving efficiency to justify your new intranet site!

## Discussion Forums

One of the primary uses for the company intranet today is the discussion forum. If you've ever read an Internet newsgroup or used a public message base on a bulletin board system, you'll find many similarities. A discussion forum is essentially an open, public message base where everyone can reply to any message.

Companies use intranet discussion forums in a myriad of ways. Of course, they're fine for informal general conversations by employees throughout the company. However, they can play an important role in the development of a project or product as well, acting as an ongoing open meeting where everyone can voice an opinion. Often, forums are used as open "suggestion boxes" by company management, or as continuing "think tank" conversations on future directions the company might take.

As in a BBS message base, forum messages are arranged into threads. A thread is composed of the original message that started a topic and all of the replies following in order. Threading makes it much easier to read an entire discussion on one topic from beginning to end, keeping the flow of the conversation intact.

Unlike its Internet cousin, however, an intranet discussion forum might offer the following additional features:

■ Embedded graphics, sounds, and Web forms within the message itself. For example, a software product development discussion message from a coworker might include a screenshot illustrating a new menu design, a binary voicemail attachment, and an HTML form requesting feedback from everyone within the group.

■ Embedded hypertext links within a message. Messages can include hypertext jumps to reference pages that should accompany the text, URLs for associated intranet pages, or FTP links for downloading the file mentioned within the text.

■ Depending on the forum software you select, the intranet administrator can assign different security levels for starting new topics, reading and posting messages, and reading replies.

If your company already has some form of electronic mail, you're probably familiar with *attachments*; most discussion forum products also allow the author to attach text files or binary files to the message, so that readers can download associated files while reading the message.

Microsoft's FrontPage provides support for a good entry-level discussion group. Users can create their own topics whenever they choose, or they can reply to individual messages. Replies appear threaded under the original topic, sorted further by date. The table of contents for a typical discussion built within FrontPage appears in Figure 37.10, and the message window itself appears in Figure 37.11.

**FIGURE 37.10.**

*A group discussion forum like this one may prove to be one of the most valuable and popular applications you can add to your intranet. Readers can click on any subject from this Table of Contents display to jump directly to that message. Note the indented message threads.*

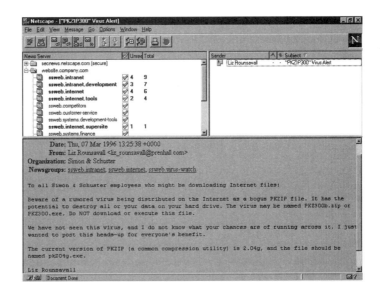

**FIGURE 37.11.**

*Posting a new message within an intranet discussion forum is as easy as replying to an e-mail message.*

Other third-party software adds even more functionality to the basic discussion forum feature set. For example, Digital's Workgroup Web Forum can sort messages by author and by date as well as by thread, making it easier to track down a particular message. Did you make a mistake in typing your message? Workgroup Web Forum also allows the author to change the text of a forum message after it has been posted, so that you can correct errors later. The forum software net.Thread, from net.Genesis, supports "moderated" forums in which messages must first be approved by the individual designated as the moderator. The moderator can also edit the text of the message before adding it to the forum.

# The Future of the Intranet

Throughout this chapter, you've seen applications that are commonly used today on corporate intranet sites around the world, and you've learned why the intranet is quickly becoming a viable alternative to traditional groupware.

However, like its Internet cousin, intranet technology is advancing on a daily basis. As the HTML language standard is enhanced and new helper applications appear, your intranet site can reap the benefits with powerful new features; in fact, upgrading the functionality of your intranet will often be as simple as distributing a new helper application throughout your company!

This final section introduces tomorrow's intranet technology—features that are only being used experimentally, or those that still need considerable work before they're widely used.

## Video Display and Video Conferencing

Full motion video is much more familiar to today's computer user than it was only two or three years ago; the video support within Windows (especially Windows 95) and the video featured in most of today's multimedia CD-ROM games and educational software has irrevocably changed the way that most of us look at computer technology.

During those same years, we also saw a parallel revolution occurring on the Internet, as more and more institutions and organizations began experimenting with sound and video across the global network. At first, these multimedia applications were simple diversions such as mounting a camera on a street corner and offering a video snapshot updated every few seconds, or adding sound clips to a Web page. More recently, these applications have matured into peer-to-peer live video and full-duplex voice communications over the Internet.

The intranet applications for live video are obvious: conferencing throughout your company, company-wide broadcasting, video training and technical support, individual discussions, and video "whiteboarding" (where everyone in a video conference can edit a graphic or document). With the proper equipment, you can actually add some of this state-of-the-art video technology to your intranet site for your company's use. A good example of current video display technology suitable for use as a helper application is the program Enhanced CU-SeeMe, from White Pine. This popular program requires a minimum of a 486-class PC with 256 color support and a TCP/IP bandwidth of at least a 28.8k SLIP/PPP modem connection (or a hardwired connection to the office TCP/IP network). Each workstation also needs a sound card, speakers, and a video camera such as the popular Connectix QuickCam. Figure 37.12 shows CU-SeeMe in action. The additional Reflector software allows video conferencing or group discussions.

**FIGURE 37.12.**

*With CU-SeeMe, coworkers can speak face-to-face anywhere within your company.*

Need more than person-to-person communications? White Pine also sells Reflector, which can concurrently distribute the video and audio from a CU-SeeMe broadcast to many workstations. Imagine the impact of a network-wide broadcast, in color, with your intranet as the foundation!

However, live video over TCP/IP still has its problems. For example, the quality of a live video feed is directly linked to the lowest bandwidth available throughout the network. ISDN and dialup connections to your intranet simply cannot handle the transmission of video data as well as a dedicated T1, and most office LANs are far slower. Additionally, the standard workstation provided by most companies would not be fast enough for live video to perform well.

# Voice Over an Intranet

Another popular multimedia feature that you can add to your intranet is two-way voice communications. Unlike the traditional Internet IRC chat or the chat areas on larger bulletin boards, where several people can type lines of text to one another in real time, voice products allow a conversation over a TCP/IP connection, just as if you had picked up a telephone and called another person.

You might be asking, "Why would my intranet site need to support voice communications? After all, anyone within the company can simply call another over the office phone system." Of course, that's true for local calls, but what about your foreign offices? Perhaps your company sends salespeople across the country, and they're constantly calling in to the office using a phone card. Any voice call that would normally be made over an expensive long distance phone connection can usually be made over a wired network or SLIP/PPP connection, saving your company a tremendous amount on its phone bill. And, depending upon the speed of the connection and the sound cards used by the PCs on either end, you might find that the sound quality of an intranet-based "telephone" call is almost as good as an actual long-distance call.

The requirements for a voice connection are similar to the requirements for a video link: a 486-class PC, a 14.4k SLIP/PPP connection (or a hardwired connection to the office TCP/IP network), a 16-bit full-duplex sound card (half-duplex requires one person to wait while the other talks, like a CB radio), a microphone, and speakers.

> **TIP**
>
> If your company intranet network isn't fast enough to support live video, it probably is still fast enough to provide quality voice communications.

Figure 37.13 shows Quarterdeck's WebTalk, one of the better Internet/intranet voice products available. Although the main screen doesn't look much like a telephone, it does give you some idea of the possibilities for global communications with its world map. To make a call, you must know the IP address of the person you're calling; WebTalk can either notify you of an incoming call (giving you the chance to refuse a call beforehand) or automatically pick up the "receiver" immediately.

**FIGURE 37.13.**

*Setting up WebTalk to make a voice connection over an office intranet.*

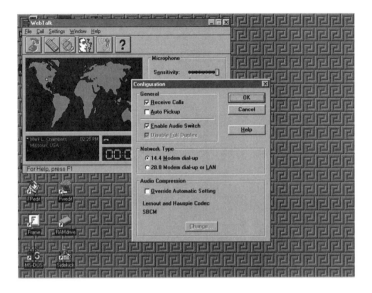

Other Internet voice products include NetSpeak's WebPhone, Internet Phone from VocalTec, and DigiPhone from Third Planet. Some of these competitors also include Web "answering machines," while higher-end software allows Web-based voice conference calls. Like video technology, the use of voice communication over the Web is just beginning to flourish, and you're likely to see many new and innovative uses for it in the next few years.

# Virtual Reality

Another brand-new technology that hasn't quite arrived yet for intranets is the virtual world, or VRML. VRML worlds currently range from a simple set of rooms depicted in cyberspace (in which you can walk between rooms) to a full-fledged three-dimensional outdoor discussion group with nearly real-time speech, where individuals are represented by images called *avatars* that they design themselves. Some VRML worlds even allow you to design your own building where others might enter and talk with you. Figure 37.14 shows a VRML world with avatars. Each character you see in this VRML world represents a real person somewhere on the Internet.

Unlike video technology, VRML worlds might not translate as well to the needs of a company intranet; they're probably better suited to the company Internet site, which can entertain the public as well as inform them. It's safe to assume that most companies would rather display live video for a conference than a meeting of 3-D animals in a setting like Stonehenge!

However, virtual reality does help illustrate just how exotic future intranet applications might become, as long as network bandwidth allows it. Would workers at your international division find it easier to navigate through the corridors of a virtual home office than to dig through a six month old copy of your corporate directory? Only time will tell as the technology driving the Web world advances.

**FIGURE 37.14.**

*Is this the foundation for a future virtual office?*

# Automation, Gophers, and Bots

When a "young" technology such as the Internet matures, one of the first demands from users is always convenience, and the same is true of the intranet. For example, consider a company employee searching through your intranet site for a specific day of meeting notes, a particular press release on a product that's a few years old, or perhaps even performing a general search on a common topic. Although you've made your search engine as easy as possible to use, wouldn't most people rather automate the search task and have it performed while they refill their coffee?

The idea of convenience is the driving force behind a growing number of automated "gopher" or "bot" technologies available for use on the Web. In its most basic form, you program an Internet/intranet bot with a search pattern (which can be simple or complex) and send it out to surf the Web for any and all information that might match that search pattern. Most bots also arrange the data within a synopsis, allowing you to quickly summarize the search; you can always send another bot that is more specific to garner additional information on anything interesting. Another interesting side of most automated bots is that they can also continue to work offline, even after you've turned off your computer.

Quarterdeck's WebCompass is an excellent example of an Internet-based bot that accesses large search engines such as Yahoo!, Lycos, and WebCrawler. Figure 37.15 shows the criteria for a WebCompass search for the topic "Batman," and Figure 37.16 shows the results returned by the program.

**FIGURE 37.15.**

*WebCompass from Quarterdeck enables you to automatically search for information using all of the larger Internet engines.*

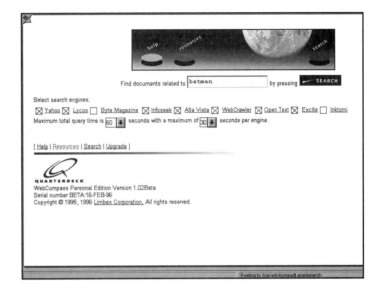

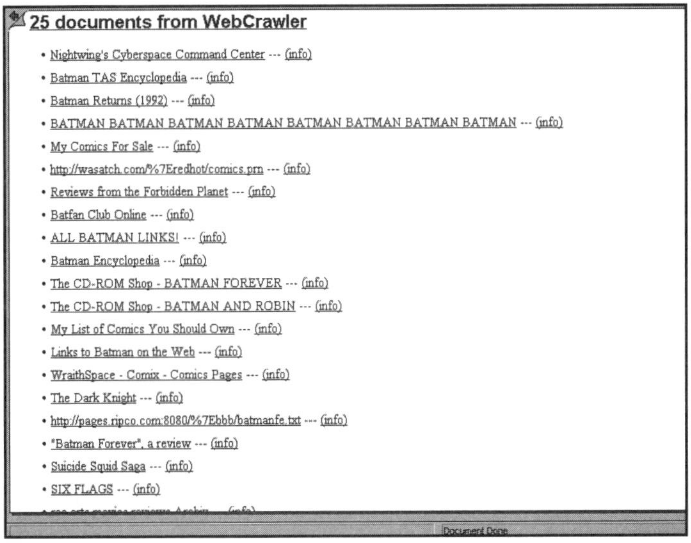

**FIGURE 37.16.**

*The results of a WebCompass search on "Batman."*

How does this technology affect your intranet site? Of course, the larger the site, the more convenient it will be for your users if they can create an automated bot. However, even smaller intranet sites can profit from the thorough searching that these automated programs can perform; for instance, the head of your financial department might program a bot that returns the following information from your intranet every business day when he turns on his computer:

■ All new information on your intranet site with an occurrence of the keywords "money," "finance," or "dollar."

- Any new press releases or public information.
- The latest progress reports on company products in development within R&D.
- Just for fun, a text file that your intranet server creates every day to describe what happened "today in history."

One company whose automation product is perfectly suited to the intranet world is General Magic, makers of the Telescript communications language. Employees can use automated Telescript programs called "agents" to perform complex searches throughout the Net, sort and arrange the data, and summarize it for quick use. Agents also continue searching and compiling data offline, so that the user's PC can be turned off and the agent will continue the search. The company also offers Active Web Server, which adds Telescript capability to any intranet or Internet Web server.

# Summary

In this chapter, you've been introduced to the idea of a self-contained, company-wide network based upon Internet technology, called an intranet. You've seen a comparison of a company intranet to the global Internet network and to traditional groupware software packages such as Lotus Notes. You've learned how to plan your intranet, and what applications are most popular on existing intranets. You also learned about the future of company intranets, including technologies such as video, voice, and automation that are currently "cutting-edge" in the Internet world.

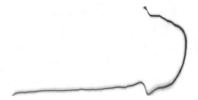

PART

X

**IN THIS PART**

# Appendixes

# HTML Reference

**A**

*by Dick Oliver*

This appendix is a reference to the HTML tags you can use in your documents. Unless otherwise noted, all the tags listed here are supported by both Netscape Navigator 3 and Microsoft Explorer 3.0. Note that some other browsers do not support all the tags listed, and some of the tags listed as (MS) might also be supported in the final shipping version of Netscape 3.

A few tags, most notably `<OBJECT>` and several new table tags, were not completely finalized when this book went to print. The proposed HTML style sheet specification is also not covered here. Refer to the Netscape (`http://home.netscape.com/`) or Microsoft (`http://www.microsoft.com/`) Web sites for details on these and other late-breaking changes to the new HTML 3.2 standard.

# HTML Tags

You use the following tags to create a basic HTML page with text, headings, and lists. An (MS) beside the attribute indicates Microsoft.

## Comments

| | |
|---|---|
| `<!-- ... -->` | Creates a comment. Can also be used to hide JavaScript from browsers that do not support it. |

## Structure Tags

| | |
|---|---|
| `<HTML>...</HTML>` | Encloses the entire HTML document. |
| `<HEAD>...</HEAD>` | Encloses the head of the HTML document. |
| `<BODY>...</BODY>` | Encloses the body (text and tags) of the HTML document. |

*Attributes:*

| | |
|---|---|
| `BACKGROUND="..."` | The name or URL of the image to tile on the page background. |
| `BGCOLOR="..."` | The color of the page background. |
| `TEXT="..."` | The color of the page's text. |
| `LINK="..."` | The color of unfollowed links. |
| `ALINK="..."` | The color of activated links. |
| `VLINK="..."` | The color of followed links. |
| `BGPROPERTIES="..."`(MS) | Properties of background image. Currently allows only the value FIXED, which prevents the background image from scrolling. |
| `TOPMARGIN="..."`(MS) | Top margin of the page, in pixels. |
| `BOTTOMMARGIN="..."`(MS) | Bottom margin of the page, in pixels. |

| | |
|---|---|
| **<BASE>** | Indicates the full URL of the current document. This optional tag is used within <HEAD>. |

*Attributes:*

| | |
|---|---|
| HREF="..." | The full URL of this document. |
| **<ISINDEX>** | Indicates that this document is a gateway script that allows searches. |

*Attributes:*

| | |
|---|---|
| PROMPT="..." | The prompt for the search field. |
| ACTION="..." | Gateway program to which the search string should be passed. |
| **<LINK>** | Indicates a link between this document and some other document. Generally used only by HTML-generating tools. <LINK> represents a link from this entire document to another, as opposed to <A>, which can create multiple links in the document. Not commonly used. |

*Attributes:*

| | |
|---|---|
| HREF="..." | The URL of the document to call when the link is activated. |
| NAME="..." | If the document is to be considered an anchor, the name of that anchor. |
| REL="..." | The relationship between the linked-to document and the current document; for example, "TOC" or "Glossary". |
| REV="..." | A reverse relationship between the current document and the linked-to document. |
| URN="..." | A Uniform Resource Number (URN), a unique identifier different from the URL in HREF. |
| TITLE="..." | The title of the linked-to document. |
| METHODS="..." | The method with which the document is to be retrieved—for example, FTP, Gopher, and so on. |
| **<META>** | Indicates meta-information about this document (information about the document itself)—for example, keywords for search engines, special HTTP headers to be used for retrieving this document, expiration date, and so on. Meta-information is usually in a key/value pair form. Used in the document <HEAD>. |

***Attributes:***

| | |
|---|---|
| `HTTP-EQUIV="..."` | Creates a new HTTP header field with the same name as the attribute's value; for example, `HTTP-EQUIV="Expires"`. The value of that header is specified by the `CONTENT` attribute. |
| `NAME="..."` | If meta-data is usually in the form of key/value pairs, `NAME` indicates the key; for example, `Author` or `ID`. |
| `CONTENT="..."` | The content of the key/value pair (or of the HTTP header indicated by `HTTP-EQUIV`). |
| `<NEXTID>` | Indicates the "next" document to this one (as might be defined by a tool to manage HTML documents in series). `<NEXTID>` is considered obsolete. |

# Headings and Title

| | |
|---|---|
| `<H1>...</H1>` | A first-level heading. |
| `<H2>...</H2>` | A second-level heading. |
| `<H3>...</H3>` | A third-level heading. |
| `<H4>...</H4>` | A fourth-level heading. |
| `<H5>...</H5>` | A fifth-level heading. |
| `<H6>...</H6>` | A sixth-level heading. |
| `<TITLE>...</TITLE>` | Indicates the title of the document. Used within `<HEAD>`. |

All heading tags accept the following attribute:

***Attributes:***

| | |
|---|---|
| `ALIGN="..."` | Possible values are `CENTER`, `LEFT`, and `RIGHT`. |

# Paragraphs and Regions

| | |
|---|---|
| `<P>...</P>` | A plain paragraph. The closing tag (`</P>`) is optional. |

***Attributes:***

| | |
|---|---|
| `ALIGN="..."` | Align text to `CENTER`, `LEFT`, or `RIGHT`. |
| `<DIV>...</DIV>` | A region of text to be formatted. |

***Attributes:***

| | |
|---|---|
| `ALIGN="..."` | Align text to `CENTER`, `LEFT`, or `RIGHT`. |

# Links

| | |
|---|---|
| `<A>...</A>` | With the HREF attribute, creates a link to another document or anchor; with the NAME attribute, creates an anchor that can be linked to. |

*Attributes:*

| | |
|---|---|
| `HREF="..."` | The URL of the document to be called when the link is activated. |
| `NAME="..."` | The name of the anchor. |
| `REL="..."` | The relationship between the linked-to document and the current document; for example, `"TOC"` or `"Glossary"` (not commonly used). |
| `REV="..."` | A reverse relationship between the current document and the linked-to document (not commonly used). |
| `URN="..."` | A Uniform Resource Number (URN), a unique identifier different from the URL in HREF (not commonly used). |
| `TITLE="..."` | The title of the linked-to document (not commonly used). |
| `METHODS="..."` | The method with which the document is to be retrieved—for example, FTP, Gopher, and so on (not commonly used). |
| `TARGET="..."` | The name of a frame that the linked document should appear in. |

# Lists

| | |
|---|---|
| `<OL>...</OL>` | An ordered (numbered) list. |

*Attributes:*

| | |
|---|---|
| `TYPE="..."` | The type of numerals to label the list. Possible values are A, a, I, i, 1. |
| `START="..."` | The value with which to start this list. |
| `<UL>...</UL>` | An unordered (bulleted) list. |

*Attributes:*

| | |
|---|---|
| `TYPE="..."` | The bullet dingbat to use to mark list items. Possible values are DISC, CIRCLE (or ROUND), and SQUARE. |
| `<MENU>...</MENU>` | A menu list of items. |
| `<DIR>...</DIR>` | A directory listing; items are generally smaller than 20 characters. |
| `<LI>` | A list item for use with <OL>, <UL>, <MENU>, or <DIR>. |

*Attributes*:

| | |
|---|---|
| TYPE="..." | The type of bullet or number to label this item with. Possible values are DISC, CIRCLE (or ROUND), SQUARE, A, a, I, i, 1. |
| VALUE="..." | The numeric value this list item should have (affects this item and all below it in <OL> lists). |
| <DL>...</DL> | A definition or glossary list. |

*Attributes*:

| | |
|---|---|
| COMPACT | Specifies a formatting that takes less white space to present. |
| <DT> | A definition term, as part of a definition list. |
| <DD> | The corresponding definition to a definition term, as part of a definition list. |

# Character Formatting

| | |
|---|---|
| <EM>...</EM> | Emphasis (usually italic). |
| <STRONG>...</STRONG> | Stronger emphasis (usually bold). |
| <CODE>...</CODE> | Code sample (usually Courier). |
| <KBD>...</KBD> | Text to be typed (usually Courier). |
| <VAR>...</VAR> | A variable or placeholder for some other value. |
| <SAMP>...</SAMP> | Sample text (seldom used). |
| <DFN>...</DFN> | A definition of a term. |
| <CITE>...</CITE> | A citation. |
| <B>...</B> | Boldface text. |
| <I>...</I> | Italic text. |
| <TT>...</TT> | Typewriter (monospaced) font. |
| <PRE>...</PRE> | Preformatted text (exact line endings and spacing will be preserved—usually rendered in a monospaced font). |
| <BIG>...</BIG> | Text is slightly larger than normal. |
| <SMALL>...</SMALL> | Text is slightly smaller than normal. |
| <SUB>...</SUB> | Subscript. |
| <SUP>...</SUP> | Superscript. |
| <STRIKE>...</STRIKE> | Puts a strikethrough line in text. |

# Other Elements

| | |
|---|---|
| **`<HR>`** | A horizontal rule line. |

*Attributes:*

| | |
|---|---|
| `SIZE="..."` | The thickness of the rule in pixels. |
| `WIDTH="..."` | The width of the rule in pixels or as a percentage of the document width. |
| `ALIGN="..."` | How the rule line will be aligned on the page. Possible values are `LEFT`, `RIGHT`, and `CENTER`. |
| `NOSHADE` | Causes the rule line to be drawn as a solid line instead of a transparent bevel. |
| `COLOR="..."` (MS) | Color of the horizontal rule. |
| **`<BR>`** | A line break. |

*Attributes:*

| | |
|---|---|
| `CLEAR="..."` | Causes the text to stop flowing around any images. Possible values are `RIGHT`, `LEFT`, `ALL`. |
| **`<NOBR>...</NOBR>`** | Causes the enclosed text not to wrap at the edge of the page. |
| **`<WBR>`** | Wraps the text at this point only if necessary. |
| **`<BLOCKQUOTE>... </BLOCKQUOTE>`** | Used for long quotes or citations. |
| **`<ADDRESS>...</ADDRESS>`** | Used for signatures or general information about a document's author. |
| **`<CENTER>...</CENTER>`** | Centers text or images. |
| **`<BLINK>...</BLINK>`** | Causes the enclosed text to blink irritatingly. |
| **`<FONT>...</FONT>`** | Changes the size of the font for the enclosed text. |

*Attributes:*

| | |
|---|---|
| `SIZE="..."` | The size of the font, from 1 to 7. Default is 3. Can also be specified as a value relative to the current size—for example, +2. |
| `COLOR="..."` | Changes the color of the text. |
| `FACE="..."` (MS) | Name of font to use if it can be found on the user's system. Multiple font names can be separated by commas, and the first font on the list that can be found will be used. |
| **`<BASEFONT>`** | Sets the default size of the font for the current page. |

*Attributes:*

| | |
|---|---|
| SIZE="..." | The default size of the font, from 1 to 7. Default is 3. |

# Images, Sounds, and Embedded Media

| | |
|---|---|
| `<IMG>` | Inserts an inline image into the document. |

*Attributes:*

| | |
|---|---|
| ISMAP | This image is a clickable image map. |
| SRC="..." | The URL of the image. |
| ALT="..." | A text string that will be displayed in browsers that cannot support images. |
| ALIGN="..." | Determines the alignment of the given image. If LEFT or RIGHT, the image is aligned to the left or right column, and all following text flows beside that image. All other values such as TOP, MIDDLE, and BOTTOM or the Netscape-only TEXTTOP, ABSMIDDLE, BASELINE, and ABSBOTTOM determine the vertical alignment of this image with other items in the same line. |
| VSPACE="..." | The space between the image and the text above or below it. |
| HSPACE="..." | The space between the image and the text to its left or right. |
| WIDTH="..." | The width, in pixels, of the image. If WIDTH is not the actual width, the image is scaled to fit. |
| HEIGHT="..." | The height, in pixels, of the image. If HEIGHT is not the actual height, the image is scaled to fit. |
| BORDER="..." | Draws a border of the specified value in pixels around the image. In the case of images that are also links, BORDER changes the size of the default link border. |
| LOWSRC="..." | The path or URL of an image that will be loaded first before the image specified in SRC. The value of LOWSRC is usually a smaller or lower resolution version of the actual image. |
| USEMAP="..." | The name of an image map specification for client-side image mapping. Used with `<MAP>` and `<AREA>`. |
| DYNSRC="..." (MS) | The address of a video clip or VRML world (dynamic source). |
| CONTROLS (MS) | Used with DYNSRC to display a set of playback controls for inline video. |
| LOOP="..." (MS) | The number of times a video clip will loop. (-1 or INFINITE means to loop indefinitely.) |

| | |
|---|---|
| START="..." (MS) | When a DYNSRC video clip should start playing. Valid options are FILEOPEN (play when page is displayed) or MOUSEOVER (play when mouse cursor passes over the video clip). |
| <BGSOUND> (MS) | Plays a sound file as soon as the page is displayed. |

*Attributes:*

| | |
|---|---|
| SRC="..." | The URL of the WAV, AU, or MIDI sound file to embed. |
| LOOP="..." (MS) | The number of times a video clip will loop. (-1 or INFINITE means to loop indefinitely.) |
| <EMBED> | Embeds a file to be read or displayed by a Plug-In application. |

**NOTE**

In addition to specifying the following standard attributes, you can specify applet-specific attributes to be interpreted by the Plug-In that displays the embedded object.

*Attributes:*

| | |
|---|---|
| SRC="..." | The URL of the file to embed. |
| WIDTH="..." | The width of the embedded object in pixels. |
| HEIGHT="..." | The height of the embedded object in pixels. |
| ALIGN="..." | Determines the alignment of the media window. Values are the same as the values for the <IMG> tag. |
| VSPACE="..." | The space between the media and the text above or below it. |
| HSPACE="..." | The space between the media and the text to its left or right. |
| BORDER="..." | Draws a border of the specified size in pixels around the media. |
| <NOEMBED>...</NOEMBED> | Alternate text or images to be shown to users who do not have a Plug-In installed. |
| <OBJECT> (MS) | Inserts an embedded program, control, or other object. (This tag was under revision when this book was printed; see the note at the beginning of this appendix.) |
| <MAP>...</MAP> | A client-side image map, referenced by <IMG USEMAP="...">. Includes one or more <AREA> tags. |
| <AREA> | Defines a clickable link within a client-side image map. |

*Attributes:*

| | |
|---|---|
| SHAPE="..." | The shape of the clickable area. Currently, only RECT is supported. |
| COORDS="..." | The left, top, right, and bottom coordinates of the clickable region within an image. |
| HREF="..." | The URL that should be loaded when the area is clicked. |
| NOHREF | Indicates that no action should be taken when this area of the image is clicked. |

# Forms

| | |
|---|---|
| **<FORM>...</FORM>** | Indicates an input form. |

*Attributes:*

| | |
|---|---|
| ACTION="..." | The URL of the script to process this form input. |
| METHOD="..." | How the form input will be sent to the gateway on the server side. Possible values are GET and POST. |
| ENCTYPE="..." | Usually has the value application/x-www-form-urlencoded. For file uploads, use multipart/form-data. |
| NAME="..." | A name by which JavaScript scripts can refer to the form. |

| | |
|---|---|
| **<INPUT>** | An input element for a form. |

*Attributes:*

| | |
|---|---|
| TYPE="..." | The type for this input widget. Possible values are CHECKBOX, HIDDEN, RADIO, RESET, SUBMIT, TEXT, SEND FILE, or IMAGE. |
| NAME="..." | The name of this item as passed to the gateway script as part of a name/value pair. |
| VALUE="..." | For a text or hidden widget, the default value; for a checkbox or radio button, the value to be submitted with the form; for Reset or Submit buttons, the label for the button itself. |
| SRC="..." | The source file for an image. |
| CHECKED | For checkboxes and radio buttons, indicates that the widget is checked. |
| SIZE="..." | The size, in characters, of a text widget. |
| MAXLENGTH="..." | The maximum number of characters that can be entered into a text widget. |
| ALIGN="..." | For images in forms, determines how the text and image will align (same values as the <IMG> tag). |

| | |
|---|---|
| **<TEXTAREA>...</TEXTAREA>** | Indicates a multiline text entry form element. Default text can be included. |

### *Attributes:*

| | |
|---|---|
| NAME="..." | The name to be passed to the gateway script as part of the name/value pair. |
| ROWS="..." | The number of rows this text area displays. |
| COLS="..." | The number of columns (characters) this text area displays. |
| WRAP="..." | Control text wrapping. Possible values are OFF, VIRTUAL, and PHYSICAL. |

| | |
|---|---|
| **\<SELECT\>...\</SELECT\>** | Creates a menu or scrolling list of possible items. |

### *Attributes:*

| | |
|---|---|
| NAME="..." | The name that is passed to the gateway script as part of the name/value pair. |
| SIZE="..." | The number of elements to display. If SIZE is indicated, the selection becomes a scrolling list. If no SIZE is given, the selection is a pop-up menu. |
| MULTIPLE | Allows multiple selections from the list. |

| | |
|---|---|
| **\<OPTION\>** | Indicates a possible item within a \<SELECT\> element. |

### *Attributes:*

| | |
|---|---|
| SELECTED | With this attribute included, the \<OPTION\> will be selected by default in the list. |
| VALUE="..." | The value to submit if this \<OPTION\> is selected when the form is submitted. |

# Tables

**NOTE**

Several additional table tags from the HTML 3.0 specification will be supported by all major browsers when that specification is complete. These new tags are not included in the follwing list. Refer to the Netscape or Microsoft Web sites for more details on these powerful new tags.

| | |
|---|---|
| **\<TABLE\>...\</TABLE\>** | Creates a table that can contain a caption (\<CAPTION\>) and any number of rows (\<TR\>). |

### *Attributes:*

| | |
|---|---|
| `BORDER="..."` | Indicates whether the table should be drawn with or without a border. In Netscape, `BORDER` can also have a value indicating the width of the border. |
| `CELLSPACING="..."` | The amount of space between the cells in the table. |
| `CELLPADDING="..."` | The amount of space between the edges of the cell and its contents. |
| `WIDTH="..."` | The width of the table on the page in either exact pixel values or as a percentage of page width. |
| `ALIGN="..."` (MS) | Alignment (works like `IMG ALIGN`). Values are `LEFT` or `RIGHT`. |
| `BACKGROUND="..."` (MS) | Background image to tile within all cells in the table that do not contain their own `BACKGROUND` or `BGCOLOR` attribute. |
| `BGCOLOR="..."` (MS) | Background color of all cells in the table that do not contain their own `BACKGROUND` or `BGCOLOR` attribute. |
| `BORDERCOLOR="..."` (MS) | Border color (used with `BORDER="..."`). |
| `BORDERCOLORLIGHT="..."` (MS) | Color for light part of 3D-look borders (used with `BORDER="..."`). |
| `BORDERCOLORDARK="..."` (MS) | Color for dark part of 3D-look borders (used with `BORDER="..."`). |
| `VALIGN="..."` (MS) | Alignment of text within the table. Values are `TOP` and `BOTTOM`. |

| | |
|---|---|
| `<CAPTION>...</CAPTION>` | The caption for the table. |

### *Attributes:*

| | |
|---|---|
| `ALIGN="..."` | The position of the caption. Possible values are `TOP` and `BOTTOM`. |

| | |
|---|---|
| `<TR>...</TR>` | Defines a table row containing headings and data (`<TR>` and `<TH>` tags). |

### *Attributes:*

| | |
|---|---|
| `ALIGN="..."` | The horizontal alignment of the contents of the cells within this row. Possible values are `LEFT`, `RIGHT`, and `CENTER`. |
| `VALIGN="..."` | The vertical alignment of the contents of the cells within this row. Possible values are `TOP`, `MIDDLE`, `BOTTOM`, and `BASELINE`. |
| `BACKGROUND="..."`(MS) | Background image to tile within all cells in the row that do not contain their own `BACKGROUND` or `BGCOLOR` attributes. |

| | |
|---|---|
| `BGCOLOR="..."` | Background color of all cells in the row that do not contain their own `BACKGROUND` or `BGCOLOR` attributes. |
| `BORDERCOLOR="..."`(MS) | Border color (used with `BORDER="..."`). |
| `BORDERCOLORLIGHT="..."`(MS) | Color for light part of 3D-look borders (used with `BORDER="..."`). |
| `BORDERCOLORDARK="..."`(MS) | Color for dark part of 3D-look borders (used with `BORDER="..."`). |

| | |
|---|---|
| `<TH>...</TH>` | Defines a table heading cell. |

### *Attributes:*

| | |
|---|---|
| `ALIGN="..."` | The horizontal alignment of the contents of the cell. Possible values are `LEFT`, `RIGHT`, and `CENTER`. |
| `VALIGN="..."` | The vertical alignment of the contents of the cell. Possible values are `TOP`, `MIDDLE`, `BOTTOM`, and `BASELINE`. |
| `ROWSPAN="..."` | The number of rows this cell will span. |
| `COLSPAN="..."` | The number of columns this cell will span. |
| `NOWRAP` | Does not automatically wrap the contents of this cell. |
| `WIDTH="..."` | The width of this column of cells, in exact pixel values or as a percentage of the table width. |
| `BACKGROUND="..."` (MS) | Background image to tile within the cell. |
| `BGCOLOR="..."` (MS) | Background color of the cell. |
| `BORDERCOLOR="..."` (MS) | Border color (used with `BORDER="..."`). |
| `BORDERCOLORLIGHT="..."` (MS) | Color for light part of 3D-look borders (used with `BORDER="..."`). |
| `BORDERCOLORDARK="..."` (MS) | Color for dark part of 3D-look borders (used with `BORDER="..."`). |

| | |
|---|---|
| `<TD>...</TD>` | Defines a table data cell. |

### *Attributes:*

| | |
|---|---|
| `ALIGN="..."` | The horizontal alignment of the contents of the cell. Possible values are `LEFT`, `RIGHT`, and `CENTER`. |
| `VALIGN="..."` | The vertical alignment of the contents of the cell. Possible values are `TOP`, `MIDDLE`, `BOTTOM`, and `BASELINE`. |
| `ROWSPAN="..."` | The number of rows this cell will span. |
| `COLSPAN="..."` | The number of columns this cell will span. |
| `NOWRAP` | Does not automatically wrap the contents of this cell. |
| `WIDTH="..."` | The width of this column of cells in exact pixel values or as a percentage of the table width. |
| `BACKGROUND="..."` (MS) | Background image to tile within the cell. |
| `BGCOLOR="..."` (MS) | Background color of the cell. |
| `BORDERCOLOR="..."` (MS) | Border color (used with `BORDER="..."`). |

*continues*

### *Attributes:*

| | |
|---|---|
| `BORDERCOLORLIGHT="..."` (MS) | Color for light part of 3D-look borders (used with `BORDER="..."`). |
| `BORDERCOLORDARK="..."` (MS) | Color for dark part of 3D-look borders (used with `BORDER="..."`). |

# Frames

| | |
|---|---|
| `<FRAMESET>...</FRAMESET>` | Divides the main window into a set of frames that can each display a separate document. |

### *Attributes:*

| | |
|---|---|
| `ROWS="..."` | Splits the window or frameset vertically into a number of rows specified by a number (such as 7), a percentage of the total window width (such as 25%), or an asterisk (*) indicating that a frame should take up all the remaining space or divide the space evenly between frames (if multiple * frames are specified). |
| `COLS="..."` | Works similar to `ROWS`, except that the window or frameset is split horizontally into columns. |
| `<FRAME>` | Defines a single frame within a `<FRAMESET>`. |

### *Attributes:*

| | |
|---|---|
| `SRC="..."` | The URL of the document to be displayed in this frame. |
| `NAME="..."` | A name to be used for targeting this frame with the `TARGET` attribute in `<A HREF>` links. |
| `<MARGINWIDTH>` | The amount of space to leave to the left and right side of a document within a frame in pixels. |
| `<MARGINHEIGHT>` | The amount of space to leave above and below a document within a frame in pixels. |
| `SCROLLING="..."` | Determines whether a frame has scroll bars. Possible values are `YES`, `NO`, and `AUTO`. |
| `NORESIZE` | Prevents the user from resizing this frame (and possibly adjacent frames) with the mouse. |
| `FRAMEBORDER="..."` (MS) | Specifies whether to display a border for a frame. Options are `YES` and `NO`. |
| `FRAMESPACING="..."` (MS) | Space between frames in pixels. |
| `<NOFRAMES>...</NOFRAMES>` | Provides an alternative document body in `<FRAMESET>` documents for browsers that do not support frames (usually encloses `<BODY>...</BODY>`). |

# Scripting and Applets

**\<APPLET\>**                Inserts a self-running Java applet.

---

**NOTE**

In addition to specifying the following standard attributes, you can specify applet-specific attributes to be interpreted by the Java applet itself.

---

*Attributes:*

| | |
|---|---|
| CLASS="..." | The name of the applet. |
| SRC="..." | The URL of the directory where the compiled applet can be found (should end in a slash / as in "http://mysite/myapplets/"). Do not include the actual applet name, which is specified with the CLASS attribute. |
| ALIGN="..." | Indicates how the applet should be aligned with any text that follows it. Current values are TOP, MIDDLE, and BOTTOM. |
| WIDTH="..." | The width of the applet output area in pixels. |
| HEIGHT="..." | The height of the applet output area in pixels. |

**\<SCRIPT\>**               An interpreted script program.

*Attributes:*

| | |
|---|---|
| LANGUAGE="..." | Currently only JAVASCRIPT is supported by Netscape. Both JAVASCRIPT and VBSCRIPT are supported by Microsoft. |
| SRC="..." | Specifies the URL of a file that includes the script program. |

# Marquees

**\<MARQUEE\>...\</MARQUEE\>** (MS)     Displays text in a scrolling marquee.

*Attributes:*

| | |
|---|---|
| WIDTH="..." | The width of the embedded object in pixels or percentage of window width. |
| HEIGHT="..." | The height of the embedded object in pixels or percentage of window height. |
| ALIGN="..." | Determines the alignment of the text outside the marquee. Values are TOP, MIDDLE, and BOTTOM. |
| BORDER="..." | Draws a border of the specified size in pixels around the media. |

*continues*

*Attributes:*

| | |
|---|---|
| BEHAVIOR="..." | How the text inside the marquee should behave. Options are SCROLL (continuous scrolling), SLIDE (slide text in and stop), and ALTERNATE (bounce back and forth). |
| BGCOLOR="..." | Background color for the marquee. |
| DIRECTION="..." | Direction for text to scroll (LEFT or RIGHT). |
| VSPACE="..." | Space above and below the marquee in pixels. |
| HSPACE="..." | Space on each side of the marquee in pixels. |
| SCROLLAMOUNT="..." | Number of pixels to move each time text in the marquee is redrawn. |
| SCROLLDELAY="..." | Number of milliseconds between each redraw of marquee text. |
| LOOP="..." (MS) | The number of times marquee will loop. (-1 or INFINITE means to loop indefinitely.) |

# Character Entities

Table A.1 contains the numeric and character entities for the ISO-Latin-1(ISO8859-1) character set. Where possible, the character is shown.

> **NOTE**
>
> Not all browsers can display all characters, and some browsers might even display characters different from those that appear in the table. Newer browsers seem to have a better track record for handling character entities, but be sure to test your HTML files extensively with multiple browsers if you intend to use these entities.

**Table A.1. ISO-Latin-1 character set.**

| Character | Numeric Entity | Character Entity (if any) | Description |
|---|---|---|---|
| | &#00;-&#08; | | Unused |
| | &#09; | | Horizontal tab |
| | &#10; | | Line feed |
| | &#11;-&#31; | | Unused |
| | &#32; | | Space |
| ! | &#33; | | Exclamation mark |
| " | &#34; | &quot; | Quotation mark |
| # | &#35; | | Number sign |

| Character | Numeric Entity | Character Entity (if any) | Description |
|---|---|---|---|
| $ | &#36; | | Dollar sign |
| % | &#37; | | Percent sign |
| & | &#38; | &amp; | Ampersand |
| ' | &#39; | | Apostrophe |
| ( | &#40; | | Left parenthesis |
| ) | &#41; | | Right parenthesis |
| * | &#42; | | Asterisk |
| + | &#43; | | Plus sign |
| , | &#44; | | Comma |
| - | &#45; | | Hyphen |
| . | &#46; | | Period (fullstop) |
| / | &#47; | | Solidus (slash) |
| 0–9 | &#48; - &#57; | | Digits 0–9 |
| : | &#58; | | Colon |
| ; | &#59; | | Semicolon |
| < | &#60; | &lt; | Less than |
| = | &#61; | | Equal sign |
| > | &#62; | &gt; | Greater than |
| ? | &#63; | | Question mark |
| @ | &#64; | | Commercial "at" |
| A–Z | &#65;-&#90; | | Letters A–Z |
| [ | &#91; | | Left square bracket |
| \ | &#92; | | Reverse solidus (backslash) |
| ] | &#93; | | Right square bracket |
| ^ | &#94; | | Caret |
| — | &#95; | | Horizontal bar |
| ` | &#96; | | Grave accent |
| a–z | &#97;-&#122; | | Letters a–z |
| { | &#123; | | Left curly brace |
| \| | &#124 | | Vertical bar |
| } | &#125; | | Right curly brace |
| ~ | &#126; | | Tilde |

*continues*

## Table A.1. continued

| *Character* | *Numeric Entity* | *Character Entity (if any)* | *Description* |
|---|---|---|---|
| | &#127;-   | | Unused |
| ¡ | &#161; | &iexcl; | Inverted exclamation |
| ¢ | &#162; | &cent; | Cent sign |
| £ | &#163; | &pound; | Pound sterling |
| ¤ | &#164; | &curren; | General currency sign |
| ¥ | &#165; | &yen; | Yen sign |
| ¦ | &#166; | &brvbar; or brkbar; | Broken vertical bar |
| § | &#167; | &sect; | Section sign |
| ¨ | &#168; | &uml; | Umlaut (dieresis) |
| © | &#169; | &copy; (Netscape only) | Copyright |
| ª | &#170; | &ordf; | Feminine ordinal |
| ‹ | &#171; | &laquo; | Left angle quote, guillemot left |
| ¬ | &#172; | &not; | Not sign |
| - | &#173; | &shy; | Soft hyphen |
| ® | &#174; | &reg; (Netscape only) | Registered trademark |
| ¯ | &#175; | &hibar; | Macron accent |
| ° | &#176; | &deg; | Degree sign |
| ± | &#177; | &plusmn; | Plus or minus |
| 2 | &#178; | &sup2; | Superscript two |
| 3 | &#179; | &sup3; | Superscript three |
| ´ | &#180; | &acute; | Acute accent |
| µ | &#181; | &micro; | Micro sign |
| ¶ | &#182; | &para; | Paragraph sign |
| · | &#183; | &middot; | Middle dot |
| ¸ | &#184; | &cedil; | Cedilla |
| 1 | &#185; | &sup1; | Superscript one |
| º | &#186; | &ordm; | Masculine ordinal |
| › | &#187; | &raquo; | Right angle quote, guillemot right |

| *Character* | *Numeric Entity* | *Character Entity (if any)* | *Description* |
|---|---|---|---|
| $^1/_4$ | &#188; | &frac14; | Fraction one-fourth |
| $^1/_2$ | &#189; | &frac12; | Fraction one-half |
| $^3/_4$ | &#190; | &frac34; | Fraction three-fourths |
| ¿ | &#191; | &iquest | Inverted question mark |
| À | &#192; | &Agrave; | Capital A, grave accent |
| Á | &#193; | &Aacute; | Capital A, acute accent |
| Â | &#194; | &Acirc; | Capital A, circumflex accent |
| Ã | &#195; | &Atilde; | Capital A, tilde |
| Ä | &#196; | &Auml; | Capital A, dieresis or umlaut mark |
| Å | &#197; | &Aring; | Capital A, ring |
| Æ | &#198; | &AElig; | Capital AE diphthong (ligature) |
| Ç | &#199; | &Ccedil; | Capital C, cedilla |
| È | &#200; | &Egrave; | Capital E, grave accent |
| É | &#201; | &Eacute; | Capital E, acute accent |
| Ê | &#202; | &Ecirc; | Capital E, circumflex accent |
| Ë | &#203; | &Euml; | Capital E, dieresis or umlaut mark |
| Ì | &#204; | &Igrave; | Capital I, grave accent |
| Í | &#205; | &Iacute; | Capital I, acute accent |
| Î | &#206; | &Icirc; | Capital I, circumflex accent |

*continues*

## Table A.1. continued

| Character | Numeric Entity | Character Entity (if any) | Description |
|---|---|---|---|
| Ï | &#207; | &Iuml; | Capital I, dieresis or umlaut mark |
| Đ | &#208; | &ETH; | Capital Eth, Icelandic |
| Ñ | &#209; | &Ntilde; | Capital N, tilde |
| Ò | &#210; | &Ograve; | Capital O, grave accent |
| Ó | &#211; | &Oacute; | Capital O, acute accent |
| Ô | &#212; | &Ocirc; | Capital O, circumflex accent |
| Õ | &#213; | &Otilde; | Capital O, tilde |
| Ö | &#214; | &Ouml; | Capital O, dieresis or umlaut mark |
| × | &#215; | | Multiply sign |
| Ø | &#216; | &Oslash; | Capital O, slash |
| Ù | &#217; | &Ugrave; | Capital U, grave accent |
| Ú | &#218; | &Uacute; | Capital U, acute accent |
| Û | &#219; | &Ucirc; | Capital U, circumflex accent |
| Ü | &#220; | &Uuml; | Capital U, dieresis or umlaut mark |
| Ý | &#221; | &Yacute; | Capital Y, acute accent |
| Þ | &#222; | &THORN; | Capital THORN, Icelandic |
| ß | &#223; | &szlig; | Small sharp s, German (sz ligature) |
| à | &#224; | &agrave; | Small a, grave accent |

| Character | Numeric Entity | Character Entity (if any) | Description |
|-----------|----------------|---------------------------|-------------|
| á | &#225; | &aacute; | Small a, acute accent |
| â | &#226; | &acirc; | Small a, circumflex accent |
| ã | &#227; | &atilde; | Small a, tilde |
| ä | &#228; | &aauml; | Small a, dieresis or umlaut mark |
| å | &#229; | &aring; | Small a, ring |
| æ | &#230; | &aelig; | Small ae diphthong (ligature) |
| ç | &#231; | &ccedil; | Small c, cedilla |
| è | &#232; | &egrave; | Small e, grave accent |
| é | &#233; | &eacute; | Small e, acute accent |
| ê | &#234; | &ecirc; | Small e, circumflex accent |
| ë | &#235; | &euml; | Small e, dieresis or umlaut mark |
| ì | &#236; | &igrave; | Small i, grave accent |
| í | &#237; | &iacute; | Small i, acute accent |
| î | &#238; | &icirc; | Small i, circumflex accent |
| ï | &#239; | &iuml; | Small i, dieresis or umlaut mark |
| ð | &#240; | &eth; | Small eth, Icelandic |
| ñ | &#241; | &ntilde; | Small n, tilde |
| ò | &#242; | &ograve; | Small o, grave accent |

*continues*

## Table A.1. continued

| *Character* | *Numeric Entity* | *Character Entity (if any)* | *Description* |
|---|---|---|---|
| ó | &#243; | &oacute; | Small o, acute accent |
| ô | &#244; | &ocirc; | Small o, circumflex accent |
| õ | &#245; | &otilde; | Small o, tilde |
| ö | &#246; | &ouml; | Small o, dieresis or umlaut mark |
| ÷ | &#247; | | Division sign |
| ø | &#248; | &oslash; | Small o, slash |
| ù | &#249; | &ugrave; | Small u, grave accent |
| ú | &#250; | &uacute; | Small u, acute accent |
| û | &#251; | &ucirc; | Small u, circumflex accent |
| ü | &#252; | &uuml; | Small u, dieresis or umlaut mark |
| ý | &#253; | &yacute; | Small y, acute accent |
| þ | &#254; | &thorn; | Small thorn, Icelandic |
| ÿ | &#255; | &yuml; | Small y, dieresis or umlaut mark |

# ActiveX Control Automation Command Reference

**B**

*by William Robert Stanek*

This appendix is organized using a reference guide and tutorial style that is easy to follow and reference quickly. You will find major sections for the FrontPage Explorer, the FrontPage Editor, and the FrontPage To Do List. Within the major sections, you will find listings of all the procedures you can use with a particular FrontPage Component.

Sections devoted to procedures are organized into four parts:

- A description of the procedure
- Parameters that the procedure uses, described in the order the parameters are used
- Values that the procedure returns
- A usage section with code examples written in Visual C++ and Visual Basic

# Using ActiveX Automation with the FrontPage Explorer

> **NOTE**
>
> ActiveX technology is simply Object Linking and Embedding (OLE) for use on the Internet.

The FrontPage Explorer's OLE interface provides a specific set of OLE commands that you can use in your wizards. This section highlights these commands.

## vtiBringToTop

The vtiBringToTop procedure brings the FrontPage Explorer to the front of the display and makes it active.

## Parameters

None

## Return Value

None

## Usage

Visual C++:

```
void vtiBringToTop();
```

Visual Basic:

```
vtiBringToTop
```

# vtiCancelRequests

The `vtiCancelRequests` procedure cancels any pending requests from the FrontPage Explorer to the Web server. This procedure has the same effect as pushing the Stop button on the FrontPage Explorer or FrontPage Editor toolbar.

## Parameters

None

## Return Value

None

## Usage

Visual C++:

```
void vtiCancelRequests();
```

Visual Basic:

```
CancelRequests
```

# vtiCreateWeb

The `vtiCreateWeb` procedure creates a new Web. All the rules for Web names apply when you create a Web. Keep in mind that the RootWeb is generally created when FrontPage is installed. All Webs you add afterward are children of the RootWeb and as such are stored in subdirectories under the RootWeb. Because this is a blocking procedure, it is expected to pass output back to the caller, which is usually the exit status of the wizard.

> **NOTE**
>
> Normally, FrontPage creates new Webs (when necessary) before launching a wizard. This means that most of the time you don't need to call this procedure directly.

## Parameters

*ServerName*: the host name or IP address of the Web server, which can include an optional port number. Examples: `www.your_company.com` and `www.your_company.com:8080`.

*WebName*: the name of the Web you want to create. Example: `your_web`.

## Return Value

The procedure returns the value of 1 to indicate success and the value of 0 to indicate failure.

## Usage

Visual C++:

```
long vtiCreateWeb(LPCTSTR szServerName, LPCTSTR szWebName);
```

Visual Basic:

```
vtiCreateWeb(ServerName as String, WebName as String) as Long
```

## vtiEditWebPage

The `vtiEditWebPage` procedure loads a page into the appropriate editor. Because you can use relative and absolute URL paths, the page can come from the current Web or from the Internet. The FrontPage Explorer determines the editor to use based on the extension of the file you are loading. Usually, the editor for HTML documents is the FrontPage Editor.

Because the procedure is non-blocking, it returns control immediately and does not wait until the page is loaded into an editor.

## Parameters

*PageURL*: the relative or absolute path to the file. For absolute paths, you should use the full hypertext reference. Examples: `http://www.your_server2.com/`, `banner.gif`, and `index.html`.

## Return Value

The procedure returns the value of 1 to indicate success and the value of 0 to indicate failure.

## Usage

Visual C++:

```
long vtiEditWebPage(LPCTSTR pszPageURL);
```

Visual Basic:

```
vtiEditWebPage(PageURL as String) as Long
```

# vtiGetDocToFile

The vtiGetDocToFile procedure retrieves a document and saves it to a local file on the user's file system. Because you can use relative and absolute URL paths, you can retrieve the page from the current Web or from the Internet. This call blocks until the file is finished downloading.

## Parameters

*URL*: the relative or absolute path to the file. For absolute paths, you should use the full hypertext reference. Examples: http://www.your_server2.com/, banner.gif, and index.html.

*FileName*: the full path to where the file should be saved on the user's file system. Example: C:\temp\newpage.htm.

## Return Value

The procedure returns the value of 1 to indicate success and the value of 0 to indicate failure.

## Usage

Visual C++:

```
long vtiGetDocToFile(LPCTSTR pszURL, LPCTSTR pszFilename);
```

Visual Basic:

```
vtiGetDocToFile(URL as String, FileName as String) as Long
```

# vtiGetPageList

The vtiGetPageList procedure returns a list of all the files of a specific type in the current Web. The list organizes files by URL and title.

There are three file types that you can request: HTML, Image, and All. HTML files have extensions that match the extensions expected by the vti_HtmlExtensions Web meta-information variable. Image files are those that have the .gif, .jpg, or .jpeg extensions. When you request all files, you see all files in the Web regardless of the file extension.

## Parameters

*DocType*: an integer value from 0–2 that identifies the type of document you want to see a listing of. If the value of *DocType* is 0, all files in the current Web are returned. If the value of

*DocType* is 1, only HTML files are returned. If the value of *DocType* is 2, image files are returned.

## Return Value

The procedure returns a string with two entries. The first entry is for the document title. The second entry is for the page URL of the document. If a document doesn't have a title, the page URL is inserted in the position normally reserved for the title. A newline character is used to separate each entry and all successive entries. If there is no current Web or there are no documents in the current Web, the result is an empty string. Examples:

```
"My Home Page\nindex.htm\nMy Link Page\nlinks.htm"
```

and

```
"My Home Page" & CHR$(10) & "index.htm" & CHR$(10) &
➡"My Link Page" & CHR$(10) & "links.htm".
```

> **NOTE**
>
> In Visual C++, the newline character is backslash n (\n). In Visual Basic, the newline character is CHR$(10).

## Usage

Visual C++:

```
CString vtiGetPageList(long lType);
```

Visual Basic:

```
vtiGetPageList(DocType as Long) as String
```

## vtiGetWebMetaInfo

The vtiGetWebMetaInfo procedure is used to get a meta-information variable associated with a Web. All Webs have meta-information lists, which contain name-value pairs for meta-information parameters. Parameters that begin with the prefix vti_ are reserved by FrontPage. As with other meta-information variables, the parameter names for Webs are not case-sensitive.

## Parameters

*Key*: a key word that identifies the meta-information variable you want to get.

Most parameter names associated with Webs are fixed and include

> `vti_AutoRecalc`: A variable used to track document dependency. A setting of 0 means dependency updating is turned off and a setting of 1 means dependency updating is turned on. Use the `vtiSetWebRecalcDependencies` procedure to set this variable. Example: `1`.

> `vti_CaseSensitiveURLs`: A variable used to track whether the server can use upper- and lowercase URLs. A setting of 0 means the server cannot use upper- and lowercase URLs: usually a Windows 3.1 server. A setting of 1 means the server can use upper- and lowercase URLs. Example: `1`.

> `vti_ExtenderVersion`: the current extender version. Example: `1.1.1.90`.

> `vti_FeatureList`: a space-separated list of features that are *not* supported by the current Web server. For many servers this string is empty. Most of the possible values relate to access control and have a prefix of AC. Values you might see when you check this variable include `vti_ACAll`, `vti_ACCreateNewUsers`, `vti_ACIPAddresses`, `vti_ACRegisteredEndUsers`, `vti_ServiceRemove`, and `vti_ServiceRename`. Examples: `vti_ServiceRename vti_ServiceRemove` and `vti_ACAll vti_ACCreateNewUsers vti_ACRegisteredEndUsers`.

> `vti_HtmlExtensions`: the extension the server expects for HTML documents. The list always ends with a period. Example: `.html.htm`.

> `vti_HttpdVersion`: the version of the server. Example: CERN/4.1.3.

> `vti_LongFilenames`: a variable used to track whether the server supports long filenames. A setting of 0 means the server does not support long filenames: usually a Windows 3.1 server. A setting of 1 means the server supports long filenames. Example: `1`.

> `vti_RestartManual`: a variable used to track whether the server needs to be manually restarted when a new Web is created. Some servers need to be restarted because they only read their configuration files when started. A setting of 0 means the server must be restarted each time a new Web is created. A setting of 1 means the server does not need to be restarted each time a new Web is created. Example: `0`.

> `vti_TextExtensions`: the extension the server expects for HTML documents. The list always ends with a period. Example: `.txt`.

> `vti_TimeCreated`: the date stamp for when the Web was created. Example: `26 Jun 1996 10:10:10 PST`.

> `vti_WelcomeNames`: a space-separated list of names the server uses for index documents. Examples: `index.html index.htm` and `welcome.html welcome.htm`.

# Return Value

The procedure returns a string containing the value of the requested key, or an empty string if the key doesn't exist.

# Usage

Visual C++:

```
CString vtiGetWebMetaInfo(LPCTSTR szKey);
```

Visual Basic:

```
vtiGetWebMetaInfo(Key as String) as String
```

# `vtiGetWebPageMetaInfo`

The `vtiGetWebPageMetaInfo` procedure is used to get a meta-information variable associated with a specific document in the current Web. All files in your Webs have meta-information lists, which are separate from the meta-information list for the Web the document is in.

# Parameters

*URL*: the name of the file in the current Web. Values for this parameter can reference subdirectories. Valid subdirectories for most Webs include `cgi-bin`, `images`, and `_private`. Examples: `newpage.htm`, `images\banner.gif`.

*KeyName*: a key word that identifies the meta-information variable you want to get. Entries beginning with the prefix `vti_` are reserved by FrontPage. As with other meta-information variables, the key names are not case-sensitive.

Most key names associated with documents are fixed and include the following:

> `vti_Author`: the author of the document. Example: `william`.
>
> `vti_Editor`: the editor for the document based on the document's file extension and settings in the FrontPage Explorer. Example: `FrontPage Editor`.
>
> `vti_ExtenderVersion`: the current extender version. Example: `1.1.2.0`.
>
> `vti_FileSize`: the byte size of the file. Example: `19525`.
>
> `vti_LinkInfo`: identifiers for links in the document using FrontPage link notation. Most wizards that use this variable delete the initial link identifier and use only the link references. Example: `FHUS¦newpage.htm FSUS¦images\banner.gif`.
>
> `vti_ModifiedBy`: the name of the person who last modified the document. Example: `william`.

vti_TimeCreated: the date stamp for when the document was created. Example: 26 Jun 1996 10:10:10 PST.

vti_TimeLastModified: the date stamp for when the document was last modified. Example: 31 Dec 1996 00:00:01 PST.

vti_Title: the title of the document. Example: My Home Page.

## Return Value

The procedure returns a string containing the value of the requested key, or an empty string if the key doesn't exist.

## Usage

Visual C++:

```
CString vtiGetWebPageMetaInfo(LPCTSTR szURL, LPCTSTR szKeyName);
```

Visual Basic:

```
vtiGetWebPageMetaInfo(URL as String, KeyName as String) as String
```

# vtiGetWebTitle

The vtiGetWebTitle procedure returns the title of the current Web, which is set by the Web's author in the FrontPage Explorer.

## Parameters

None

## Return Value

The procedure returns the title of the current Web as a string. If there is no current Web or if the current Web is the RootWeb, the procedure returns an empty string. If no title has been set, the return value is the same as the Web's URL. As a result, one way to see if the Web title has not been uniquely set is to compare the value returned by the vtiGetWebURL procedure to the value returned by the vtiGetWebTitle procedure.

## Usage

Visual C++:

```
CString vtiGetWebTitle();
```

Visual Basic:

```
vtiGetWebTitle as String
```

# vtiGetWebURL

The vtiGetWebURL procedure returns the URL of the current Web as a full hypertext reference. This means the URL includes everything from the http:// to the subdirectory for the current Web. Because the URL is in complete form, you can insert it into pages to reference the base document in a Web.

## Parameters

None

## Return Value

The procedure returns the URL of the current Web. Examples: http://www.your_company.com, http://www.your_company.com:8080, and http://www.your_company.com/sampleweb.

## Usage

Visual C++:

```
CString vtiGetWebURL();
```

Visual Basic:

```
vtiGetWebURL as String
```

# vtiIsPageInWeb

You use the vtiIsPageInWeb procedure to see whether a document exists in the current Web. You should always use this procedure before adding documents to the current Web.

## Parameters

URL: the name of the file you want to check, which is usually called the page URL. Values for this parameter can reference subdirectories. Valid subdirectories for most Webs include cgi-bin, images, and _private. Examples: newpage.htm, images\banner.gif.

## Return Value

The procedure returns a value other than zero if the document is in the Web, and 0 if the document is not in the Web.

# Usage

Visual C++:

```
BOOL vtiIsPageInWeb(LPCTSTR szURL);
```

Visual Basic:

```
vtiIsPageInWeb(URL as String) as Integer
```

# vtiOpenWeb

The vtiOpenWeb procedure is used to open a Web on a specified server that does not have to be the current server. Before the FrontPage Explorer opens the Web, the user must enter an appropriate username and password in the authorization dialog box.

Until the Web is open or an error occurs, the call blocks. Errors can occur if the user cannot validate his access to the server.

# Parameters

*ServerName*: the host name or IP address of the Web server, which can include an optional port number. Examples: www.your_company.com, www.your_company.com:8080.

*WebName*: the name of the Web you want to access with no initial slash. Use an empty string if you want the user to access the RootWeb. Example: your_web.

*User*: the username to place in the authorization dialog box. If this string is empty, the user has to enter both a username and password. If you set a value for this parameter, the user can change the username in the authorization dialog box.

# Return Value

The procedure returns a value other than zero if the Web is open, and 0 if the Web is not open.

# Usage

Visual C++:

```
BOOL vtiOpenWeb(LPCTSTR pszServer, LPCTSTR pszWebName, LPCTSTR pszUser);
```

Visual Basic:

```
vtiOpenWeb(Server as String, WebName as String, User as String) as Integer
```

# vtiPromptOpenWeb

The `vtiPromptOpenWeb` procedure tells the FrontPage Explorer to display the Open Web dialog box.

## Parameters

None

## Return Value

None

## Usage

Visual C++:

```
void vtiPromptOpenWeb();
```

Visual Basic:

```
vtiPromptOpenWeb
```

# vtiPutDocument

The `vtiPutDocument` procedure gets a single file from the user's file system and adds it to the current Web. Before updating the current Web, the FrontPage Explorer checks the authoring permissions of the user who opened the current Web. If the user has no authoring permissions, an error occurs. An error also occurs if there is no open Web.

> **TIP**
>
> To add several documents to the current Web, use the procedure `vtiPutDocuments`.

When a document is successfully added to the current Web, the server uses the FrontPage Server Extensions to expand any WebBots the page might contain. The server also regenerates documents linked to the uploaded document as necessary. The last thing the server does is refresh the Explorer views to ensure they show a current representation of the Web.

Because `vtiPutDocument` overwrites any existing document if there is a naming conflict, you should always check for an existing Web document with the same name before you use this procedure. Use the procedure `vtiIsPageInWeb` to perform this check.

# Parameters

*FileName*: the full path to the document on the user's file system, which can be an ASCII text or binary file. Example: `C:\FrontPage\newpage.htm`.

*URL*: the name of the file after you add it to the Web, which is usually called the page URL. Values for this parameter can reference subdirectories. However, this procedure cannot create new directories. Valid subdirectories for most Webs include `cgi-bin`, `images`, and `_private`. Examples: `newpage.htm`, `images\banner.gif`.

*BlockingRequest*: determines whether the procedure is blocking or non-blocking. Keep in mind that if this procedure is used as a non-blocking call, there is no way to determine when the request has completed. For this reason, you should normally set this parameter to True.

# Return Value

The procedure returns the value of 1 to indicate success and the value of 0 to indicate failure.

# Usage

Visual C++:

```
long vtiPutDocument(LPCTSTR szFileName, LPCTSTR szURL, BOOL bBlockingRequest);
```

Visual Basic:

```
vtiPutDocument(FileName as String, URL as String, BlockingRequest as Integer)
➥ as Long
```

# vtiPutDocuments

The `vtiPutDocuments` procedure gets multiple files from the user's file system and adds them to the current Web. Before updating the current Web, the FrontPage Explorer checks the authoring permissions of the user who opened the current Web. If the user has no authoring permissions, an error occurs. An error also occurs if there is no open Web.

Unlike the `vtiPutDocument` procedure, this procedure does not enable you to accidentally overwrite files. If a naming conflict occurs, a dialog box is displayed that enables users to overwrite the existing document or preserve it.

The method turns off document dependency updating while documents are being added to the current Web, which saves time. When all documents are successfully added to the current Web, the method turns on document dependency updating so that the server can use the FrontPage Server Extensions to expand any WebBots the page might contain. The server also regenerates documents linked to the uploaded document as necessary. However, the method does not instruct the server to update the FrontPage Explorer views. For this reason, your wizard should call the `vtiRefreshWebFromServer` procedure soon after executing the `vtiPutDocuments` procedure.

## Parameters

*FileName*: the full path to the document on the user's file system, which can be an ASCII text or binary file. Example: `C:\FrontPage\newpage.htm`.

*FileList*: a list of full paths to files on the user's file system, which can be ASCII text or binary. All file names in the list must be separated by the newline character. Example: `C:\FrontPage\newpage.htm\nC:\FrontPage\banner.gif`.

> **NOTE**
>
> If you are using Visual Basic, you might want to place `App.Path` and the file separator into a string before adding the name of a file in the current directory.

*UrlList* is a list of URLs for the files you are adding to the Web. This list must be in the exact order you used in the `FileList` parameter. Values for this parameter can reference subdirectories. However, this procedure cannot create new directories. Valid subdirectories for most Webs include `cgi-bin`, `images`, and `_private`. Example: `newpage.htm\nimages\banner.gif`.

## Return Value

The procedure returns a value other than zero if the call succeeds, and 0 if the call does not succeed.

## Usage

Visual C++:

```
BOOL vtiPutDocuments(LPCTSTR szFileList, LPCTSTR szUrlList);
```

Visual Basic:

```
vtiPutDocuments(FileList as String, UrlList as String) as Integer
```

## vtiPutWebMetaInfo

The `vtiPutWebMetaInfo` procedure is used to set the list of meta-information variables associated with a Web. When you use this procedure, you force FrontPage to update all documents that use meta-information variables.

Use the `vtiGetWebMetaInfo` procedure to retrieve a current list of meta-information variables.

Because this is a blocking procedure, it is expected to pass output back to the caller, which is usually the exit status of the wizard.

Before you use this procedure you should ensure that a Web is open in the FrontPage Explorer. You can do this by checking the string returned by the `vtiGetWebURL` procedure. If the string is empty, no Web is open in the FrontPage Explorer and you get an error if you try to use the `vtiPutWebMetaInfo` procedure.

## Parameters

*NameValuePairs*: a string containing a list of the names of the meta-information variables you are setting and their associated values. The colon character is used to separate variable names and values, and the newline character is used to separate name-value pairs. The server does not track the case of your variable names and stores the variables in all lowercase regardless of the original case. Examples: `webmaster:william@tvp.com\nphone:555-1212` or `"webmaster:william@tvp.com" & CHR$(10) & "phone:555-1212"`.

In Visual C++, the newline character is backslash n (`\n`). In Visual Basic, the newline character is: `CHR$(10)`.

## Return Value

The procedure returns the value of 1 to indicate success and the value of 0 to indicate failure.

## Usage

Visual C++:

```
long vtiPutWebMetaInfo(LPCTSTR szNameValuePairs);
```

Visual Basic:

```
vtiPutWebMetaInfo(NameValuePairs as String) as Long
```

# vtiPutWebPageMetaInfo

The `vtiPutWebPageMetaInfo` procedure sets meta-information variables associated with a specific page. Because this is a blocking procedure, it is expected to pass output back to the caller, which is usually the exit status of the wizard.

## Parameters

*PageURL*: the page in the current Web for which you want to set meta-information variables. Example: `index.htm`.

*NameValuePairs*: a string containing a list of the names of the meta-information variables you are setting and their associated values. The colon character is used to separate variable names and values, and the newline character is used to separate name-value pairs. The server does not track the case of your variable names and stores the variables in all lowercase regardless of the original case. Examples: `webmaster:william@tvp.com\nphone:555-1212` or `"webmaster:william@tvp.com" & CHR$(10) & "phone:555-1212"`.

> **NOTE**
>
> In Visual C++, the newline character is backslash n (`\n`). In Visual Basic, the newline character is `CHR$(10)`.

## Return Value

The procedure returns the value of 1 to indicate success and the value of 0 to indicate failure.

## Usage

Visual C++:

```
long vtiPutWebPageMetaInfo(LPCTSTR pszURL, LPCTSTR pszNameValuePairs);
```

Visual Basic:

```
vtiPutWebPageMetaInfo(PageURL as String, NameValuePairs as String) as Long
```

# vtiRefreshWebFromServer

The `vtiRefreshWebFromServer` procedure tells the FrontPage Explorer to refresh all its views of the current Web. The Explorer does this by placing a call to the server that checks for updates. If updates have been made, the Explorer's views are refreshed to reflect the current information.

Because this is a blocking procedure, it is expected to pass output back to the caller, which is usually the exit status of the wizard. You will usually want to call `vtiRefreshWebFromServer` after you upload documents using the `vtiPutDocuments` procedure.

> **TIP**
>
> Before you use this procedure, you should ensure that a Web is open in the FrontPage Explorer. You can do this by checking the string returned by the `vtiGetWebURL` procedure. If the string is empty, no Web is open in the FrontPage Explorer, and you get an error if you try to use the `vtiRefreshWebFromServer` procedure.

## Parameters

None

## Return Value

None

## Usage

Visual C++:

```
void vtiRefreshWebFromServer();
```

Visual Basic:

```
vtiRefreshWebFromServer
```

# vtiRemoveWeb

The `vtiRemoveWeb` procedure is used to remove a named Web from the current Web server. Before removing a Web, the FrontPage Explorer checks the permissions of the user who opened the current Web. If the user has no administrative permissions, an error occurs. An error also occurs if there is no open Web.

> **TIP**
>
> Before you use this procedure, you should ensure that a Web is open in the FrontPage Explorer. You can do this by checking the string returned by the `vtiGetWebURL` procedure. If the string is empty, no Web is open in the FrontPage Explorer and you get an error if you try to use the `vtiRemoveWeb` procedure.

## Parameters

*WebName*: the name of the Web to remove. The Web name must match that of a valid Web on the current server and should not reference the RootWeb. Additionally, the Web name must begin with a forward slash. Examples: `/myweb` and `/sampleweb`.

## Return Value

The procedure returns the value of 1 to indicate success and the value of 0 to indicate failure.

## Usage

Visual C++:

```
long vtiRemoveWeb(LPCTSTR szWebName);
```

Visual Basic:

```
vtiRemoveWeb(WebName as String) as Long
```

# vtiSetWebRecalcDependencies

The `vtiSetWebRecalcDependencies` procedure can be used to turn document dependency updating on or off in the current Web. The procedure does this by setting the value of the meta-information variable `vti_AutoRecalc`, which is a boolean value—a setting of 0 turns off dependency updating and a setting of 1 turns on dependency updating.

Although turning off document dependency is useful when you are adding or deleting many documents, you should note that while dependency updating is turned off, any uploaded documents are stored temporarily in the `_vti_shm` directory. This means they are not visible in FrontPage views or available to browsers. Furthermore, any documents containing WebBots are not expanded into the source and HTML documents are needed to use the pages.

When you turn document dependency back on, the entire Web is updated and checked for dependencies. This means documents in the `_vti_shm` directory are moved to whatever directory they should be stored in and documents containing WebBots are expanded. Because this is a blocking procedure, it is expected to pass output back to the caller, which is usually the exit status of the wizard.

## Parameters

`RecalcOn`: set to False to turn off document dependency updating and True to turn it back on.

> **NOTE**
>
> For some programming languages, you cannot use boolean values. In this case, the boolean values True and False can be expressed as integer values of 1 and 0 respectively.

## Return Value

None

## Usage

Visual C++:

```
void vtiSetWebRecalcDependencies(BOOL bRecalcOn);
```

Visual Basic:

```
vtiSetWebRecalcDependencies(RecalcOn as Integer)
```

# Using ActiveX Automation with the FrontPage Editor

You will use the FrontPage Editor's OLE interface whenever you want to access pages using the FrontPage Editor. This section highlights these commands.

## vtiBringToTop

The `vtiBringToTop` procedure brings the FrontPage Editor to the front of the display and makes it active.

## Parameters

None

## Return Value

None

## Usage

Visual C++:

```
void vtiBringToTop();
```

Visual Basic:

```
vtiBringToTop
```

# vtiNewWebPage

The `vtiNewWebPage` procedure tells the FrontPage Editor to create a new Web page.

## Parameters

*URL*: the name the FrontPage Editor will use if the user saves the file into a Web. Values for this parameter can reference subdirectories.

*WebURL*: the URL of the Web to which the file should be saved as a full hypertext reference. This means the *WebURL* includes everything from the `http://` to the subdirectory for the Web. You can use the FrontPage Explorer `vtiGetWebURL` procedure to set this parameter. Examples: `http://www.your_company.com` and `http://www.your_company.com/sampweb`.

*WebTitle*: the title of the Web to which the file should be saved. You can use the FrontPage Explorer `vtiGetWebTitle` procedure to set this parameter. Example: `Internet Resource Web`.

## Return Value

This procedure returns a pointer to the document. After you call this procedure, you should release the object to avoid problems that could arise if the user changes the environment.

## Usage

Visual C++:

```
LPDISPATCH vtiNewWebPage(LPCTSTR szURL, LPCTSTR szWebURL, LPCTSTR szWebTitle);
```

Visual Basic:

```
vtiNewWebPage(URL as String, WebURL as String, WebTitle as String) as Object
```

# vtiOpenWebPage

The vtiOpenWebPage procedure tells the FrontPage Editor to open a file on the user's file system.

> **NOTE**
>
> To open an existing page from the current Web or the Internet, use the FrontPage Explorer vtiEditWebPage procedure.

## Parameters

*FileName*: the full path to the file on the user's file system. Example: C:\FrontPage\newpage.htm.

*URL*: the name the FrontPage Editor uses if the user saves the file into a Web. Values for this parameter can reference subdirectories.

*WebURL*: the URL of the Web the file should be saved to as a full hypertext reference. This means the *WebURL* includes everything from the http:// to the subdirectory for the Web. You can use the FrontPage Explorer vtiGetWebURL procedure to set this parameter. Examples: http://www.your_company.com and http://www.your_company.com/sampweb.

*WebTitle*: the title of the Web to which the file should be saved. You can use the FrontPage Explorer vtiGetWebTitle procedure to set this parameter. Example: Internet Resource Web.

## Return Value

This procedure returns a pointer to the document. After you call this procedure, you should release the object to avoid problems that could arise if the user changes the environment.

## Usage

Visual C++:

```
LPDISPATCH vtiOpenWebPage(LPCTSTR szFileName, LPCTSTR szURL,
➥LPCTSTR szWebURL, LPCTSTR szWebTitle);
```

Visual Basic:

```
vtiOpenWebPage(FileName as String, URL as String, WebURL as String,
➥WebTitle as String) as Object
```

# vtiQueryWebPage

The vtiQueryWebPage procedure checks to see if a page is currently being edited in the FrontPage Editor.

## Parameters

*URL*: the name of the file you are querying about. Values for this parameter can reference subdirectories. Examples: `newpage.htm`, `_private\header.htm`.

*WebURL*: the URL of the Web the file came from, which is set as a full hypertext reference. This means the returned string includes everything from the `http://` to the subdirectory for the Web. You can use the FrontPage Explorer `vtiGetWebURL` procedure to set this parameter. Examples: `http://www.your_company.com` and `http://www.your_company.com/sampweb`.

## Return Value

The procedure returns the value of 1 to indicate success and the value of 0 to indicate failure.

## Usage

Visual C++:

```
long vtiQueryWebPage(LPCTSTR szURL, LPCTSTR szWebURL);
```

Visual Basic:

```
vtiQueryWebPage(URL as String, WebURL as String) as Long
```

# Using ActiveX Automation with the FrontPage To Do List

The FrontPage To Do List also has an OLE interface. You will use this interface to access and update task lists. This section highlights the commands used in the interface.

## vtiAddTask

The `vtiAddTask` procedure is used to add new tasks to the To Do List. Each task you assign must reference a particular document and have a name and priority.

## Parameters

*TaskName*: the name of the task to be performed, which can be a word or phrase. Examples: `Task 01`, `Banner Creation Reminder`, and `Pages Needs Image`.

*Priority*: the priority of the task, entered as an integer value from 1-3, where 1 is for high priority tasks, 2 is for medium priority tasks, and 3 is for low priority tasks. Example: 1.

*CreatedBy*: the name of the person or template that created the task. Example: `Internet Re-source Wizard`.

*URL*: the page or file to which the task refers. Values for this parameter can reference subdirectories. Valid subdirectories for most Webs include `cgi-bin`, `images`, and `_private`. Examples: `newpage.htm, images\banner.gif`.

*Cookie*: an additional identifier. Although this parameter is usually used for a specific bookmark within the referenced page, it can be used for other purposes if necessary. Example: `#book-mark`.

*Comment*: a description of the task to be performed, which is usually 1–2 sentences in length. Example: `Insert a banner that is appropriate for your Web`.

## Return Value

The procedure returns a value other than zero if the call succeeds, and 0 if the call does not succeed.

## Usage

Visual C++:

```
BOOL vtiAddTask(LPCTSTR TaskName, short Priority, LPCTSTR CreatedBy,
➥LPCTSTR URL, LPCTSTR Cookie, LPCTSTR Comment);
```

Visual Basic:

```
vtiAddTask(TaskName as String, Priority as Integer, CreatedBy as String,
➥URL as String, Cookie as String, Comment as String) as Integer
```

# vtiAddTaskAskUser

Like the `vtiAddTask` procedure, `vtiAddTaskAskUser` is used to add tasks to the To Do List. Unlike the `vtiAddTask` procedure, this procedure enables the user to assign the task to a different user.

## Parameters

*TaskName*: the name of the task to be performed, which can be a word or phrase. Examples: `Task 01`, `Banner Creation Reminder`, and `Pages Needs Image`.

*Priority*: the priority of the task, entered as an integer value from 1–3 where 1 is for high priority tasks, 2 is for medium priority tasks, and 3 is for low priority tasks. Example: `1`.

*CreatedBy*: the name of the person or template that created the task. Example: `Internet Resource Wizard`.

*URL*: the page or file to which the task refers. Values for this parameter can reference subdirectories. Valid subdirectories for most Webs include `cgi-bin`, `images`, and `_private`. Examples: `newpage.htm`, `images\banner.gif`.

*Cookie*: an additional identifier. Although this parameter is usually used for a specific bookmark within the referenced page, it can be used for other purposes if necessary. Example: `#bookmark`.

*Comment*: a description of the task to be performed, which is usually 1–2 sentences in length. Example: `Insert a banner that is appropriate for your Web.`

## Return Value

The procedure returns a value other than zero if the call succeeds, and 0 if the call does not succeed.

## Usage

Visual C++:

```
BOOL vtiAddTaskAskUser(LPCTSTR TaskName, short Priority, LPCTSTR CreatedBy,
LPCTSTR URL, LPCTSTR Cookie, LPCTSTR Comment);
```

Visual Basic:

```
vtiAddTaskAskUser(TaskName as String, Priority as Integer,
CreatedBy as String, URL as String, Cookie as String, Comment as String) as Integer
```

# vtiCompletedTaskByUrl

The `vtiCompletedTaskByUrl` procedure is used to remove accomplished tasks from the To Do List. This is done by marking the first task that matches a specified URL and Cookie as completed and then removing it from the list of active tasks.

## Parameters

*URL*: the page or file the accomplished task relates to, which is expressed using a relative path. Values for this parameter can reference subdirectories. Valid subdirectories for most Webs include `cgi-bin`, `images`, and `_private`. Examples: `newpage.htm`, `images\banner.gif`.

*Cookie*: an additional identifier set to remove only a task related to a specific bookmark within the referenced page. Example: `#bookmark`.

## Return Value

The procedure returns a value other than zero if the call succeeds, and 0 if the call does not succeed.

## Usage

Visual C++:

```
BOOL vtiCompletedTaskByUrl(LPCTSTR url, LPCTSTR cookie);
```

Visual Basic:

```
vtiCompletedTaskByUrl(URL as String, Cookie as String) as Integer
```

# vtiGetActiveCount

The vtiGetActiveCount procedure obtains the number of tasks currently in the To Do List.

## Parameters

None

## Return Value

The procedure returns the number of active tasks.

## Usage

Visual C++:

```
long vtiGetActiveCount();
```

Visual Basic:

```
vtiGetActiveCount as Long
```

# vtiHide

The vtiHide procedure closes the To Do List dialog box.

## Parameters

None

## Return Value

None

## Usage

Visual C++:

```
void vtiHide();
```

Visual Basic:

```
vtiHide
```

## vtiShow

The `vtiShow` procedure displays the To Do List dialog box.

## Parameters

None

## Return Value

None

## Usage

Visual C++:

```
void vtiShow();
```

Visual Basic:

```
vtiShow
```

## vtiWorkedOnTaskByUrl

The `vtiWorkedOnTaskByUrl` procedure specifies that the current user has worked on a task but has not completed it.

## Parameters

*URL*: the page or file to which the task relates, which is expressed using a relative path. Values for this parameter can reference subdirectories. Valid subdirectories for most Webs include `cgi-bin`, `images`, and `_private`. Examples: `newpage.htm`, `images\banner.gif`.

*Cookie*: an additional identifier set to reference a specific bookmark within the page. Example: `#bookmark`.

## Return Value

The procedure returns a value other than zero if the call succeeds, and 0 if the call does not succeed.

## Usage

Visual C++:

```
BOOL vtiWorkedOnTaskByUrl(LPCTSTR url, LPCTSTR cookie);
```

Visual Basic:

```
vtiWorkedOnTaskByUrl(URL as String, Cookie as String) as Integer
```

# VBScript Reference

# C

*by Sanjaya Hettihewa*

In order to write a VBScript, you need to learn the correct syntax and operators. This reference is a guide to get you on your way. This appendix is made up of three distinct sections: Operators, Control Structures, and Functions.

# VBScript Operators

VBScript supports several operators for various string, Boolean, and number-manipulation tasks. Various operators supported by VBScript are described in the following sections.

## Addition Operator

**Syntax:**

```
<operand1> + <operand2>
```

The addition operator can be used to add two operands. If both operands are numeric, the result of the addition operator is also numeric. However, if they are strings, VBScript does a string concatenation instead of a numeric addition. To avoid ambiguity, it is better to use the string concatenation operator (&) when joining strings, and use the addition operator (+) when adding numeric expressions.

## Subtraction Operator

**Syntax:**

```
<operand1> - <operand2>
```

**Syntax:**

```
-<OperandToNegate>
```

The subtraction operator is used as unary minus and the binary subtraction operator. When used as the binary subtraction operator, it subtracts <operand2> from <operand1> and returns the resulting value. When used as the unary minus, it changes the sign of the numeric operand from its current sign.

## Multiplication Operator

**Syntax:**

```
<operand1> * <operand2>
```

The multiplication operator takes two numeric operands, multiplies them, and returns the resulting value.

# Exponential Operator

**Syntax:**

```
<operand1> ^ <operand2>
```

The exponential operator returns the resulting value of <operand1> raised to the <operand2> power.

# Floating-Point Division Operator

**Syntax:**

```
<operand1> / <operand2>
```

The division operator is used to divide <operand1> by <operand2>. Both <operand1> and <operand2> have to be numeric expressions, and the resulting value is a floating-point number. You should always check for division by zero before dividing two numbers because the denominator can potentially be 0.

# Integer-Division Operator

**Syntax:**

```
<operand1> \ <operand2>
```

The integer-division operator is somewhat similar to the floating-point division operator. The integer-division operator returns an integer number after dividing <operand1> from <operand2>. The next few lines are examples of the integer division operator.

```
( 23 \ 4 ) = 5
( 4 \ 23 ) = 0
( 4 \ 2 ) = 2
( 5 \ 2 ) = 2
```

# String-Concatenation Operator

**Syntax:**

```
<operand1> & <operand2>
```

The string-concatenation operator can be used to join <operand1> and <operand2> together. The order of the join is from left to right.

# MOD Operator

**Syntax:**

```
<operand1> MOD <operand2>
```

The MOD (Modulus) operator is somewhat similar to the integer-division operator. The only difference is the fact that it returns the remainder of <operand1> divided by <operand2>. A few examples of the MOD operator are listed next.

```
( 23 MOD 4 ) = 3
( 4 MOD 23 ) = 4
( 4 MOD 2 ) = 0
( 5 MOD 2 ) = 1
```

# Boolean Operators

VBScript supports a number of Boolean operators. The best way to explain how Boolean operators work is with a truth table. Refer to Figure C.1 for truth tables of a number of useful VBScript Boolean operators.

**FIGURE C.1.**

*Truth tables of VBScript Boolean operators.*

| AND | | | | |
|---|---|---|---|---|
| TRUE | AND | TRUE | = | TRUE |
| TRUE | AND | FALSE | = | FALSE |
| FALSE | AND | TRUE | = | FALSE |
| FALSE | AND | FALSE | = | FALSE |
| OR | | | | |
| TRUE | OR | TRUE | = | TRUE |
| TRUE | OR | FALSE | = | TRUE |
| FALSE | OR | TRUE | = | TRUE |
| FALSE | OR | FALSE | = | FALSE |
| XOR | | | | |
| TRUE | XOR | TRUE | = | FALSE |
| TRUE | XOR | FALSE | = | TRUE |
| FALSE | XOR | TRUE | = | TRUE |
| FALSE | XOR | FALSE | = | FALSE |
| NOT | | | | |
| | NOT | TRUE | = | FALSE |
| | NOT | FALSE | = | TRUE |

## AND Operator

**Syntax:**

```
<operand1> AND <operand2>
```

The AND operator returns true if *both* <operand1> and <operand2> are true. If either operand is not true, it returns false. The AND operator can be used with expressions and with functions that return a Boolean value.

## OR **Operator**

**Syntax:**

```
<operand1> OR <operand2>
```

The OR operator returns true if either <operand1> or <operand2> is true. The OR operator can be used with expressions and with functions that return a Boolean value.

## NOT **Operator**

**Syntax:**

```
NOT <operand>
```

The NOT operator can be used to negate a Boolean value. The NOT operator can be used with expressions and functions that return a Boolean value.

## XOR **Operator**

**Syntax:**

```
<operand1> XOR <operand2>
```

The XOR operator is very similar to the OR operator. The only difference is the fact that in order for the XOR operator to return true, <operand1> or <operand2> has to be true. However, they both can't be true at the same time. The XOR operator can be used with expressions and functions that return a Boolean value.

# Equivalence Operator

**Syntax:**

```
<operand1> Eqv <operand2>
```

You can use the equivalence operator to determine whether <operand1> is equal to <operand2>. If either <operand1> or <operand2> is NULL, then the resulting value is also NULL. A truth table of the equivalence operator is listed next.

```
TRUE Eqv TRUE = TRUE
FALSE Eqv TRUE = FALSE
TRUE Eqv FALSE = FALSE
FALSE Eqv FALSE = TRUE
```

> **NOTE**
>
> TRUE in the preceding truth table can be replaced with binary 1, and FALSE can be replaced with binary 0.

# Object-Reference Operator

**Syntax:**

```
<operand1> IS <operand2>
```

The object-reference operator is used to compare two object reference variables. If <operand1> refers to the same object as <operand2>, the object-reference operator returns true. Otherwise, it returns false.

# Comparison Operators

VBScript supports several comparison operators. You can use these comparison operators to compare strings as well as numbers.

## Equal Operator

The equal operator (=) returns true if <operand1> and <operand2> are equal to each other. However, if either <operand1> or <operand2> is NULL, the equal operator returns NULL. Its syntax is

```
<operand1> = <operand2>
```

## Unequal Operator

**Syntax:**

```
<operand1> <> <operand2>
```

The unequal operator returns true if <operand1> and <operand2> are not equal. However, if either <operand1> or <operand2> is NULL, the unequal operator returns NULL.

## Less Than Operator

**Syntax:**

```
<operand1> < <operand2>
```

The less than operator returns true if <operand1> is less than <operand2>. However, if either <operand1> or <operand2> is NULL, the less than operator returns NULL.

## Less Than or Equal to Operator

**Syntax:**

```
<operand1> <= <operand2>
```

Returns true if <operand1> is less than or equal to <operand2>. However, if either <operand1> or <operand2> is NULL, the less than or equal to operator returns NULL.

## Greater Than Operator

**Syntax:**

```
<operand1> > <operand2>
```

Returns true if <operand1> is greater than <operand2>. However, if either <operand1> or <operand2> is NULL, the greater than operator returns NULL.

## Greater Than or Equal to Operator

**Syntax:**

```
<operand1> >= <operand2>
```

Returns true if <operand1> is greater than or equal to <operand2>. However, if either <operand1> or <operand2> is NULL, the greater than or equal to operator returns NULL.

# VBScript Control Structures

Control structures are an important part of any language. They give a language "life" by allowing programmers to add intelligence to programs with conditional and iterative statements. Various VBScript control structures are listed in the next few sections.

# Call

You can use Call to transfer program control to another VBScript subroutine. Note that when Call is used to transfer control to another subroutine, if that subroutine has any parameters, they should be enclosed in parentheses. However, if Call is omitted, subroutine arguments do not need to be enclosed in parentheses. Return values of functions are ignored when they are invoked with the Call statement.

# Dim

The Dim statement is used to declare variables, such as arrays, and to assign them storage space. When variables are declared with Dim, if they are numeric variables, they are initialized with the value zero. Otherwise, they are assigned an empty string. The Dim statement can be used to declare several types of variables. The following sections show the various types of variables that can be created with the Dim statement.

> **NOTE**
>
> An empty string is not the same as a null string. An empty string exists as a string with no characters in it, and a null string is simply null. If you concatenate "something" to an empty string, you get "something", but when concatenated to a null string, you get null.

## Declaring Variant Variables

**Syntax:**

```
Dim <VariableName1> , <VariableName2>
```

This statement can be used to declare variables of variant type. As shown here, several variables can be defined at the same time by separating them with commas.

## Multiple Variable Declarations

**Syntax:**

```
Dim <VariableName1> As Integer, <VariableName2> As Integer
```

One Dim statement can be used to declare several variables of more than one type. As in the case of the preceding Dim command, <VariableName1> is declared as an Integer variable and <VariableName2> is declared as a variant variable.

## Declaring Static Arrays

The Dim statement can be used to define arrays. In the following example, an array of 50 storage locations of type variant is created using the Dim statement.

The single dimension array syntax is

```
Dim <NameOfArray>(50)
```

If an index range is not specified for an array, VBScript will index the array starting at zero. For example, in this case, <NameOfArray> is indexed from 0 to 49.

The *index* of an array is the location of a specific value within that array and appears as a number in square brackets after the array name. For example, a 25-member alphabetical listing of favorite cars might have the string `"Aston-Martin"` at `ILoveCars[0]`, `"Jaguar"` at `ILoveCars[10]`, and `"Dodge Viper"` at `ILoveCars[24]`.

Multidimensional arrays have the following syntax:

```
Dim <NameOfArray>(5,1 To 5)
```

The `Dim` statement can also be used to declare multidimensional arrays. For example, the following statement can be used to declare a two-dimensional array by the name of `<NameOfArray>`. As shown in this example, the index range of an array can be customized by using a number range (`1 To 5`). By adding an `As <VariableType>` command to an array declaration, you can define an array of a certain data type.

## Declaring Dynamic Arrays

If you are unsure about the size of an array when it is first declared, VBScript allows the creation of dynamic arrays. Dynamic arrays can be expanded or reduced as needed. Use the following syntax to create Dynamic arrays.

```
Dim <NameOfArray>()
```

Storage space for additional elements can be allocated for a dynamic array using the `ReDim` statement, as shown next. (Simply indicate, in parentheses, the number of elements the array should have.)

```
ReDim <NameOfArray>(10)
```

As an added incentive, VBScript dynamic arrays can be expanded while preserving existing array values. As shown in the next example, do this by adding a `Preserve` statement between the `ReDim` statement and the array name.

```
ReDim Preserve <NameOfArray>(20)
```

Note that if a data type was defined for a dynamic array using the `As` statement, the array's data type cannot be changed using the `ReDim` statement. Also, if a dynamic array is reduced in size using the `ReDim` statement, any data stored in the portion of the array that was deleted is permanently lost.

# Do/While/Until Loop

The Do/Loop control structure can be used to iterate a group of statements until a certain Boolean expression becomes true. The syntax of the Do/Loop control structure appears in the following lines. As shown in this example, the Boolean expression of a Do/Loop structure can be placed either at the beginning or the end.

```
Do <condition> <BooleanExpression>
… VBScript statements …
Loop
```

As shown next, the Boolean expression of a Do/Loop structure can also be placed at the end of the control structure.

```
Do
… VBScript statements …
Loop <condition> <BooleanExpression>
```

The preceding two examples will repeatedly execute VBScript statements enclosed in the loop structure until <BooleanExpression> becomes true. In the examples, <condition> may be replaced with either While or Until.

As the name implies, if While is used, the loop iterates *while* <BooleanExpression> is true. In a similar manner, if Until is used, the loop iterates *until* <BooleanExpression> is true. Note that within a Do/Loop structure, it is possible to transfer control out of the loop using an Exit Do statement.

# Erase

**Syntax:**

```
Erase <NameOfArray>
```

The Erase statement is used to free memory used by dynamic arrays and reinitialize elements of static arrays. If the array is a dynamic array, all space taken up by the array is freed. Dynamic arrays then need to be reallocated using the ReDim statement before they can be used again. If the array is a static array, all array elements are initialized with zero if its elements are numeric or with empty strings, if they are other than numeric.

# Exit

The Exit statement causes program control to be transferred out of the control structure where it appears. The control structure can be a loop or a subroutine. The following list shows the various forms of the Exit command.

Exit Do: Exits a Do loop.
Exit: Exits a For loop.

Exit Func: Exits a function.

Exit: Exits a procedure.

# For/Next

The For/Next control structure iterates a group of VBScript statements a certain number of times. The syntax of the For/Next control structure is

```
For <LoopCount> = <BeginLoop> To <EndLoop> Step <StepCount>
… VBScript statements …
Next
```

The previous definition can be used to iterate a group of VBScript statements a certain number of times by replacing various labels (enclosed in pointed braces) of the definition, as follows:

<LoopCount>: Name of variable used to keep track of the number of iterations. It's best to make sure your VBScript statements do not alter the value of this variable because it can easily complicate your code and make it more difficult to debug.

<BeginLoop>: The first value of the iteration sequence.

<EndLoop>: The last value of the iteration sequence.

Step <StepCount>: <StepCount> can be replaced with the number by which <LoopCount> is incremented after each iteration of the loop. The Step statement is optional; by default, <LoopCount> is incremented by one.

Note that the Exit For statement can be used to exit a For loop.

# For Each/Next

The For Each/Next control structure is useful for iterating VBScript statements for each object in a *collection* or each element in an array. The following is the syntax of the For Each/Next loop:

```
For Each <LoopIndex> In <ArrayOrCollection>
… VBScript statements …
Next <LoopIndex>
```

A For Each/Next loop can be added to a VBScript program by substituting various labels of the preceding example, as follows:

<LoopIndex>: Name of variable used to traverse through the elements of an array or objects in a *collection*.

<ArrayOrCollection>: Name of an array or collection of objects.

Note that you can use the Exit For statement to exit a For Each loop. Also note that <LoopIndex> can be omitted in the Next <LoopIndex> statement. However, this is not recommended; it can complicate things and cause errors if a For Each loop is nested inside another For Each loop.

# Function

New functions can be defined using the `Function` statement. The syntax of the `Function` statement is as follows:

```
<FunctionType> Function <NameOfFunction> <ArgumentsOfFunction>
… VBScript statements …
<NameOfFunction> = <ReturnValueOfFunction>
End Function
```

A function can be created by replacing various labels of the above definition with these values:

> `<FunctionType>`: The `<FunctionType>` can be left out if it is not needed. By replacing `<FunctionType>` with `Static`, you can preserve values of local variables in between function calls. Unless you have a reason for doing so, `Static` functions usually are not suitable for recursion (a function calling itself).

> `<NameOfFunction>`: Used to specify the name of the function.

> `<ArgumentsOfFunction>`: Arguments of a function can be specified soon after `<NameOfFunction>`. By using commas, more than one argument can be specified. An argument can be passed either by value or reference. In order to make an argument *pass by value*, precede the argument name with `ByVal`; to *pass by reference*, precede the argument name with `ByRef`. When an argument is passed by value, its original value cannot be changed from within the function. However, when it is passed by reference, the variable used in the function is merely a pointer to the original variable. Therefore, any changes made to the value of a variable passed by reference are actually made to the original variable.

Note that the `Exit Function` statement can be used to exit a function. VBScript procedures created with the `Function` statement are very similar to procedures created with the `Sub` statement. The only difference is that procedures created with the `Function` statement can return values; procedures created with the `Sub` statement cannot.

# If/Then/Else

The `If/Then/Else` statement executes various VBScript statements based on Boolean expressions. The syntax of the `If/Then/Else` control structure is as follows:

```
IF <BooleanExpression> THEN
… VBScript statement …
ELSE IF <BooleanExpression> THEN
… VBScript statement …
ELSE
… VBScript statement …
END IF
```

As shown in the previous example, various VBScript statements can be made to execute using an `If/Then/Else` statement based on various Boolean expressions.

# Let

The Let command assigns values to variables. The Let command is not required to assign a value to a variable. The syntax of the Let command is as follows:

```
Let <variableName> = <ValueOfVariable>
```

# LSet

LSet copies a variable of one user-defined type to a variable of another user-defined type. When a variable is copied with the LSet command, it is *left-aligned.* The syntax of the LSet statement is listed next.

```
LSet <Variable> = <ValueOfVariable>
```

If the length of <Variable> is longer than that of <ValueOfVariable>, after copying <ValueOfVariable> to <Variable>, the remaining space is filled in with white spaces. In like manner, if the length of <Variable> is less than that of <ValueOfVariable>, <ValueOfVariable> will be truncated to fit in the space allocated for <Variable>. For example, if <Variable> can hold only four characters, and <ValueOfVariable> contains the string "ABCDEFG", after <Variable> is copied to <Variable> with the LSet command, it has the value "ABCD".

# Mid

Mid is a very handy statement for replacing one or more characters of a string with characters from another string. The syntax of the Mid statement is

```
Mid (<Variable>, <Begin>, <NumCharactersToReplace>) = <Replacement>
```

The Mid statement can be used by replacing various labels of the preceding example, as follows:

<Variable>: Name of variable containing the string to modify.

<Begin>: The position to begin replacing text. For example, if <Variable> contains the string "1234" and you would like "34" to be replaced with "67", use 3 in place of <Begin> because the sub string "34" begins at the third position.

<NumCharactersToReplace>: Lists the number of characters that should be replaced by <Replacement>. This value can be left out if you wish, in which case the entire <Replacement> string will copy over its portion of <Variable>.

<Replacement>: Contains string that will be copied over to <Variable>.

# On Error

Usually, when a runtime error occurs in a VBScript program, it halts execution of the VBScript program. Using the On Error Resume Next statement, however, you can ignore the error and continue with the program.

# Private

By preceding a variable declaration with the `Private` keyword, you limit its scope to the script it is declared in.

# Public

By preceding a variable declaration with the `Public` keyword, the scope of a variable can be extended to other scripts.

# Randomize

`Randomize` can be used to initialize the random-number generator. `Randomize` can be used either with or without a numeric argument. If it is used with a numeric argument, the numeric argument is used to seed the random-number generator. If `Randomize` is used without an argument, a number from the system clock is used to seed the random-number generator.

# Rem

The `Rem` command documents VBScript code with comments that explain your program to others. The syntax of the `Rem` command is

```
Rem This is a comment
```

Note that the apostrophe (') is equivalent in functionality to the `Rem` command. The only difference between the `Rem` statement and the apostrophe is the fact that if `Rem` is used in the same line with a VBScript statement, it needs to be separated from the VBScript statement with a colon.

# RSet

The syntax of the `RSet` command is

```
RSet <Variable> = <StringToCopy>
```

The `RSet` command is similar in functionality to the `LSet` command. The only difference is that when a variable is assigned a string using the `RSet` command, it is assigned to the variable *right-aligned.*

# Set

The `Set` command can be used to assign an object reference to a variable or property. The syntax of the `Set` command is as follows:

```
Set <ObjectVariable> = <Object>
```

When the keyword `Nothing` is assigned to `<ObjectVariable>`, system resources consumed by the object are freed when no other variables refer to the `<Object>`.

# Static

By preceding variable and procedure declarations with the keyword `Static`, it retains values of variables. When a procedure is declared as a static procedure, all variables in that procedure retain values assigned to them throughout the life of the program. Precede variable declarations of *nonstatic procedures* with the `Static` keyword to preserve their values. (Variable values of static procedures are automatically preserved.)

# Sub

The `Sub` statement creates VBScript procedures and is identical to the `Function` statement except for one difference. Procedures created with the `Function` statement can return values; procedures created with the `Sub` statement cannot. The syntax of the `Sub` statement is

```
<ProcedureType> Sub <NameOfProcedure> <ArgumentsOfProcedure>
… VBScript statements …
End Sub
```

Note that the `Exit Sub` statement can be used to transfer control out of a procedure. The syntax of the `Sub` statement is listed next.

A procedure can be created by replacing various labels of the preceding definition with these values:

> `<ProcedureType>`: The `<ProcedureType>` can be left out if it is not needed. By replacing `<ProcedureType>` with `Static`, it is possible to preserve values of local variables in between procedure calls. Unless you have a reason for doing so, `Static` functions are usually not suitable for recursion (a function calling itself).

> `<NameOfProcedure>`: Used to specify the name of the procedure.

> `<ArgumentsOfProcedure>`: Arguments of a procedure can be specified after `<NameOfProcedure>`. By using commas, more than one argument can be specified. An argument can be passed either by value or reference. In order to make an argument *pass by value*, precede the argument name with `ByVal`, and to *pass by reference*, precede the argument name with `ByRef`. When an argument is passed by value, its original value cannot be changed from within the procedure. However, when it is passed by reference, the variable used in the procedure is merely a pointer to the original variable. Therefore, any changes made to the value of a variable passed by reference are actually made to the original variable.

## While/Wend

The `While/Wend` control structure iterates a group of VBScript statements while a certain Boolean expression is true. The syntax of the `While/Wend` command is

```
While <BooleanExpression>
… VBScript statements …
Wend
```

# VBScript Functions

The next few sections describe various functions supported by VBScript. The following functions can be used to add a new level of interactivity to a Web site by creating active Web pages. Shortly, you will be shown how these functions can be used to develop various VBScript programs.

## Abs

The `Abs` function can be used to obtain the absolute value of a number; for example, `Abs(-30)` = 30 = `Abs(30)`.

## Array

The `Array` function can be used to quickly create an array because it returns a variant containing an array. For example, the following two commands create an array with three elements. After the two commands are executed, `Colors(2)` will equal `"Blue"`.

```
Dim Colors As Variant
Colors = Array ( "Red", "Blue", "Green" )
```

## Asc

`Asc` returns the ASCII character code of a character or the first character of a string. For example, `Asc ("A")` returns 65 and so does `Asc ("America")`.

## Atn

`Atn` returns the arc tangent of a number.

## CBool

`CBool` returns the Boolean value of an expression passed into the function. For example, `CBool ( A = B )` returns true if both `A` and `B` contain the same value.

# CByte

CByte converts a number passed into the function into a number of type byte and returns it. For example, if CByte is called with the number 123.678, it returns 123.

# CDate

If a valid date expression is passed into the function, it is converted into date type and returned. Before passing an expression to the CDate function, you can determine whether it can be converted by CDate into date type by using the IsDate function.

# CDbl

CDbl converts an expression passed into the function into a variant of subtype double.

# Chr

Chr returns the ASCII character of an ASCII code. For example, Chr(65) returns the character A.

# CInt

CInt converts an expression into a variant of subtype Integer. For example, CInt (1234.567) returns 1235.

# CLng

CLng returns a variant of subtype long after the expression passed into the function is converted into long. For example, CLng (12345.67) returns 12346.

# Cos

Cos returns the cosine of an angle (in radians) passed into the function.

# CSng

CSng converts a numerical expression passed into the function into a variant of subtype Single. For example, CSng (12.123456) returns 12.12346.

## CStr

CStr converts an expression passed into CStr into a string and returns it. For example, CStr(123.456) returns the value "123.456".

## CVErr

CVErr is used to return a user-specified error code. The syntax of CVErr is CVErr(ErrorNumber).

## Date

Date returns the date from the system clock. The value returned by the Date command at the time of this writing is 7/1/1996.

## DateSerial

DateSerial is a handy function that can be used to calculate various days. By using numerical expressions with the DateSerial function, you can count backward or forward from a date simply by adding and subtracting numbers. The syntax of the DateSerial function is as follows:

DateSerial (<Year>, <Month>, <Day>)

If the current date is 4/1/1996, for example, DateSerial(1996,4-2,1+28) returns the value 2/29/1996. (Of course, if the year was not a leap year, the result would have been 3/1/1996.)

## DateValue

Converts an expression passed into the function into a variant of subtype date and returns it. For example, DateValue("February 29, 1976") returns 2/29/1976. If the year is left out, it is obtained from the system clock.

## Day

The Day function returns a value between 1 and 31 and can be used to find the day of a date. For example, Day("4/1/1996") returns 1.

## Exp

Returns the value of e raised to a power. For example Exp(1) returns 2.71828182845905.

# Hex

Returns the hexadecimal (base 16) value of a numerical expression. For example, `Hex(10)` returns A.

# Hour

Returns the number of hours of a time expression. For example, `Hour("12:25:34")` returns 12.

# InputBox

The `InputBox` function is used to obtain input from the user by presenting a dialog box. The syntax of the `InputBox` command is as follows:

```
InputBox(<Prompt>,<Title>,<Default>,<X>,<Y>)
```

Various arguments of this command enclosed in pointed brackets can be replaced with the following values.

- `<Prompt>`: Dialog box prompt.
- `<Title>`: Title of dialog box.
- `<Default>`: Default input value.
- `<X>`: Horizontal position, in number of *twips*, from the left side of the screen. A twip is 1/20 of a printer's point, which is 1/1440 of an inch.
- `<Y>`: Vertical position, in number of twips, from the top of the screen.

# InStr

`InStr` returns the location of one string in another string. The syntax of `InStr` is as follows:

```
InStr (<BeginPosition>, <String1>, <String2>, <ComparisonType>
```

- `<BeginPosition>`: This argument is optional and specifies the starting position of the search.
- `<String1>`: String being searched.
- `<String2>`: String to locate.
- `<ComparisonType>`: This argument is optional. 0 is for a binary search, and 1 for case-insensitive search. The default value is 0.

# Int and Fix

Both `Int` and `Fix` convert numerical expressions into integers. The only difference is the fact that `Int` converts a negative number with a fraction into a smaller integer, and `Fix` converts a

914

negative number with a fraction into a larger integer. The following examples illustrate how
Int and Fix handle numbers with fractions.

```
Int(11.75) = 11
Fix(11.75) = 11
Int(12.45) = 12
Fix(12.45) = 12
Int(-17.75) = -18
Fix(-17.75) = -17
Int(-7.25) = -8
Fix(-7.25) = -7
```

# IsArray

Returns true if a variable is an array and false otherwise.

# IsDate

Returns true if an expression can be converted to a valid date or false otherwise.

# IsEmpty

Returns true if a variable has been initialized or false otherwise.

# IsError

Returns true if an expression is an error code or false otherwise.

# IsNull

Returns true if an expression is NULL or false otherwise.

# IsNumeric

Returns true if an expression is numeric or false otherwise.

# IsObject

Returns true if an expression references an OLE Automation Object or false otherwise.

# LBound

LBound can be used to find the minimum index of an array dimension. For example, if
ArrayVariable is a three-dimensional array declared with the statement Dim ArrayVariable(5
To 100, 10 To 200, 20 To 300), UBound(ArrayVariable,1) returns 5, LBound(ArrayVariable,2)
returns 10, and of course LBound(ArrayVariable,3) returns 20.

## LCase

Converts a string expression to lowercase and returns it.

## Left

Returns a certain number of characters from the left side of a string. For example, Left("Windows NT", 7) returns "Windows".

## Len

Returns the number of characters of a string expression.

## Log

Returns the natural logarithm of a nonnegative, numerical expression.

## LTrim, RTrim, and Trim

Eliminates spaces from a string and returns it. LTrim eliminates preceding spaces, RTrim eliminates trailing spaces, and Trim eliminates both trailing and preceding spaces. If you ask a user to input her name in an input box, you could use Trim to remove the spaces to do a search on whether that user's name is in your database as a repeat visitor.

## Mid

Returns a certain number of characters from a string; for example, Mid("Windows NT", 0, 7) returns "Windows".

## Minute

Returns the number of minutes when called with the time; for example, Minute("23:50:45") returns 50.

## Month

Returns the month when called with a date. For example, Month("4/1/1996") returns 4.

## MsgBox

A message box can be displayed using the MsgBox command. Here is the syntax of the MsgBox command:

```
MsgBox <MessageBoxPrompt>,<ButtonStyle>,<Title>
```

By replacing <ButtonStyle> with various values shown in Table C.1, you can customize a message box with various button styles. For example, you can create an OK dialog box with a warning message icon by replacing <ButtonStyle> with 48.

**Table C.1. Message box codes.**

| Button Type | Button Description |
| --- | --- |
| 0 | OK |
| 1 | OK and Cancel |
| 2 | Abort, Retry, and Ignore |
| 3 | Yes, No, and Cancel |
| 4 | Yes and No |
| 5 | Retry and Cancel |
| 16 | Critical Message icon (See Figure C.2.) |
| 32 | Warning Query icon (See Figure C.3.) |
| 48 | Warning Message icon (See Figure C.4.) |
| 64 | Information Message icon (See Figure C.5.) |
| 256 | Second button is default |
| 512 | Third button is default |
| 4096 | All applications are stopped until the user responds to the message box |

**FIGURE C.2.**
*The Critical message box.*

**FIGURE C.3.**
*The Warning Query box.*

**FIGURE C.4.**
*The Warning message box.*

**FIGURE C.5.**

*The Information message box.*

# Now

Returns the current date and time from the system clock. The return value is followed by the date and then the time. For example, the Now command returned the string 7/1/1996 23:08:31 at the time of this writing.

# Oct

Returns the octal value (base 8) of a numerical expression. For example, Oct(10) returns 12.

# Right

Returns a specified number of characters from the right side of a string. For example, Right("Windows NT", 2) returns "NT".

# Rnd

Returns a random number between 1 and 0. Be sure to seed the random number generator by calling Randomize before using the Rnd function.

# Second

Returns the number of seconds of a date expression. For example, Second("18:23:57") returns 57.

# Sgn

Returns the sign of a numerical expression. If the expression is 0, 0 is returned. If it is less than 0, -1 is returned. Otherwise, 1 is returned.

# Sin

Returns the sine of an angle. For example, Sin (Pi) returns 0.

# Sqr

Returns the square root of a nonnegative, numerical expression.

# Str

Converts a numeric expression into a string and returns it.

# StrComp

The syntax of the `StrComp` function is as follows:

```
StrComp (<String1>, <String2>, <ComparisonMethod>)
```

After `StrComp` compares both strings, it returns `0` if both strings are identical, `-1` if `<String1>` is less than `<String2>`, and `1` otherwise. The `<ComparisonMethod>` argument is optional. If it is `0`, a binary comparison is performed, and if it is `1`, a case-insensitive comparison is performed. If `<ComparisonMethod>` is left out, a binary comparison is performed.

# String

The `String` function is handy for repeating a character a certain number of times. For example `String(5,"*")` creates a string of five asterisks.

# Tan

The `Tan` function calculates the tangent of an angle. For example, `Tan (0)` returns `0`.

# Time

Returns the current time from the system clock. For example, the value `01:23:48` was returned by the `Time` function at the time of this writing.

# TimeSerial

This is a very handy function that can be used to perform various time calculations. For example, if the current time is 12:30, `TimeSerial` can be used to calculate the time 25 minutes ago. For example, `TimeSerial(12,30-25, 0)` returns `12:05:00`.

# TimeValue

Returns an expression passed into the function after converting it into a `variant` of subtype `Date`. For example, `TimeValue ("2:35:17pm")` returns `14:35:17`.

# UBound

`UBound` can be used to determine the maximum size of an array dimension. For example, if `ArrayVariable` is a three-dimensional array defined with the statement `Dim`

ArrayVariable(100,200,300), UBound(ArrayVariable,1) returns 100, UBound(ArrayVariable,2) returns 200, and, of course, UBound(ArrayVariable,3) returns 300.

# UCase

Converts strings passed into the function into uppercase and returns them. For example, UCase("Windows NT") returns "WINDOWS NT".

# Val

The Val function obtains a number contained in a string. The function scans the string until it encounters a character that is not part of a number. For example, Val(" 1234 567 in a string") returns the number 1234567.

# VarType

The type of a variable can be determined using the VarType function. For example, if IntVariable is an Integer variable, VarType(IntVariable) returns 2. The type of a variable can be determined by examining the return value of VarType according to Table C.2.

## Table C.2. Variable type codes.

| Value Returned | Type of Variable |
| --- | --- |
| 0 | Empty |
| 1 | Null |
| 2 | Integer |
| 3 | Long integer |
| 4 | Single-precision, floating-point number |
| 5 | Double-precision, floating-point number |
| 6 | Currency |
| 7 | Date |
| 8 | String |
| 9 | OLE Automation object |
| 10 | Error |
| 11 | Boolean |
| 12 | Variant |
| 13 | Non-OLE Automation object |
| 8192 | Array |

# Weekday

The Weekday function returns a number between 1 and 7. The numbers returned by the Weekday function correspond to days of the week, as shown in Table C.3.

**Table C.3. Day codes.**

| Day Code | Day of Week |
| --- | --- |
| 1 | Sunday |
| 2 | Monday |
| 3 | Tuesday |
| 4 | Wednesday |
| 5 | Thursday |
| 6 | Friday |
| 7 | Saturday |

For example, Weekday("April 2, 1996") returns 3—which is, indeed, a Tuesday.

# Year

Returns the year of the expression. For example, Year("February 29, 1976") returns 1976.

# What's on the CD?

# D

On the *Microsoft FrontPage Unleashed* CD-ROM, you will find all the sample files that have been presented in this book, along with a wealth of other applications and utilities.

> **NOTE**
>
> Please refer to the readme.wri file on the CD-ROM for the latest and most comprehensive listing of software included on this CD-ROM.

# Web Server and Administration Tools

- Microsoft's Internet Information Server
- The European Microsoft Windows NT Academic Center for Computing Services (EMWAC) HTTP Server, Gopher Server, Mail Server, and WAIS Toolkit
- FolkWeb HTTP Server
- Intranet Jazz by JSB Computer Systems Ltd.
- Post.Office SMTP/POP3 Server from Software.com, Inc.
- Purveyor WebServer for NetWare
- Purveyor WebServer for Windows 95
- Purveyor WebServer for Windows NT
- Blat 1.5 NT send mail utility program
- Cold Fusion 32-bit ODBC database interface demo
- Hedit, a Hex editor for Windows NT
- Somar Redial for NT keeps your connection while using RAS
- UltraBac for Windows NT by Barratt Edwards Intl. Corp.
- InContext Multimedia Demo

# Web Site HTML Tools

- Microsoft Internet Assistants for Access, Excel, PowerPoint, Schedule+, and Word
- Hot Dog 32-bit HTML editor
- HoTMeTaL HTML editor
- HTMLed HTML editor
- HTML Assistant for Windows
- WebEdit Pro HTML editor
- Web Weaver HTML editor

# Web Browser

- Microsoft Internet Explorer v2.0

# Graphics, Video, and Sound Applications

- Goldwave sound editor, player, and recorder
- MapThis image map utility
- MPEG2PLY MPEG viewer
- MPEGPLAY MPEG viewer
- Paint Shop Pro 3.0 graphics editor and graphic file format converter for Windows
- SnagIt screen capture utility
- ThumbsPlus image viewer and browser

# ActiveX

- Microsoft ActiveX Developer's Kit
- Sample controls

# Java

- Sun's Java Developer's Kit for Windows 95/NT version 1.02, with sample applets and scripts
- JFactory Java IDE
- JPad Java IDE by ModelWorks Software

# CGI

- CGI PerForm command language interpreter for Common Gateway Interface (CGI) application design
- Several sample CGI scripts and libraries

# Perl

- Perl Version 5 build 109 for Windows NT

# Utilities

■ Microsoft viewers for Excel, PowerPoint, and Word

■ Adobe Acrobat viewer

■ Microsoft PowerPoint Animation Player & Publisher

■ WinZip for Windows NT/95

■ WinZip Self-Extractor, a utility program that creates native Windows self-extracting ZIP files

# Electronic Books

■ *Teach Yourself Web Publishing with HTML 3.2 in 14 Days, Professional Reference Edition*

■ *Teach Yourself VBScript in 21 Days*

# About Shareware

Shareware is not free. Please read all documentation associated with a third-party product (usually contained within files named `readme.txt` or `license.txt`) and follow all guidelines.

# INDEX

A VIACOM SERVICE

# The Information SuperLibrary™

**Bookstore**

**Search**

**What's New**

**Reference**

**Software**

**Newsletter**

**Company Overviews**

**Yellow Pages**

**Internet Starter Kit**

**HTML Workshop**

**Win a Free T-Shirt!**

**Macmillan Computer Publishing**

**Site Map**

**Talk to Us**

# CHECK OUT THE BOOKS IN THIS LIBRARY.

You'll find thousands of shareware files and over 1600 computer books designed for both technowizards and technophobes. You can browse through 700 sample chapters, get the latest news on the Net, and find just about anything using our massive search directories.

*All Macmillan Computer Publishing books are available at your local bookstore.*

We're open 24-hours a day, 365 days a year.

**You don't need a card.**

We don't charge fines.

**And you can be as LOUD as you want.**

The Information SuperLibrary

http://www.mcp.com/mcp/ ftp.mcp.com

# Windows NT 4 Server Unleashed

*Jason Garms*

The Windows NT server has been gaining tremendous market share over Novell and the new upgrade—which includes a Windows 95 interface—is sure to add momentum to its market drive. *Windows NT 4 Server Unleashed* is written to appeal to that growing market. It provides information on disk and file management, integrated networking, BackOffice integration, and TCP/IP protocols.

Focuses on using Windows NT as an Internet server.

*Price: $49.99 USA/$70.95 CDN     User Level: Accomplished - Expert*
*ISBN: 0-672-30933-5     1,100 pages*

# Laura Lemay's Web Workshop: Microsoft FrontPage

*Laura Lemay & Denise Tyler*

This is a clear, hands-on guide to maintaining Web pages with Microsoft's FrontPage. Written in the clear, conversational style of Laura Lemay, it is packed with many interesting and colorful examples that demonstrate specific tasks of interest to the reader.

Teaches how to maintain Web pages with FrontPage. Includes all the templates, backgrounds, and materials needed on the CD-ROM!

*Price: $39.99 USA/$56.95 CDN     User Level: Casual - Accomplished*
*ISBN: 1-57521-149-1     400 pages*

# Teach Yourself VBScript in 21 Days

*Keith Brophy & Tim Koets*

Readers learn how to use VBScript to create living, interactive Web pages. This unique scripting language from Microsoft is taught with clarity and precision, providing the reader with the best and latest information on this popular language.

Teaches advanced OLE object techniques.

Explores VBScript's animation, interaction, and mathematical capabilities.

*Price: $39.99 USA/$56.95 CDN     User Level: New - Casual*
*ISBN: 1-57521-120-3     550 pages*

# CGI Developer's Guide

*Eugene Eric Kim*

This is one of the first books to provide comprehensive information on developing with CGI (the Common Gateway Interface). It covers many of the aspects of CGI, including interactivity, performance, portability, and security. After reading this book, you will be able to write robust, secure, and efficient CGI programs.

You will master forms, image maps, dynamic displays, database manipulation, and animation.

*Price: $45.00 USA/$63.95 CDN     User Level: Accomplished - Expert*
*ISBN: 1-57521-087-8     600 pages*

## Laura Lemay's Web Workshop: JavaScript

*Laura Lemay*

In this book, you explore various aspects of Web publishing—whether CGI scripting and interactivity, or graphics design, or Netscape Gold—in greater depth than with the *Teach Yourself* books.

Provides a clear, hands-on guide to creating sophisticated Web pages.

*Price: $39.99 USA/$56.95 CDN     User Level: Casual - Accomplished*
*ISBN: 1-57521-141-6       400 pages*

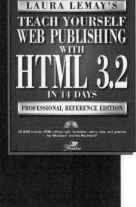

## Teach Yourself Web Publishing with HTML 3.2 in 14 Days, Professional Reference Edition

*Laura Lemay*

This is the updated edition of Lemay's previous bestseller, *Teach Yourself Web Publishing with HTML in 14 Days, Premier Edition*. In this book, you will find all the advanced topics and updates—including, adding audio, video, and animation—to Web page creation.

Explores the use of CGI scripts, tables, HTML 3.0, the Netscape and Internet Explorer extensions, Java applets and JavaScript, and VRML.

*Price: $59.99 USA/$81.95 CDN     User Level: New - Casual - Accomplished*
*ISBN: 1-57521-096-7       1,104 pages*

## Bots and Other Internet Beasties

*Joseph Williams*

Spiders, bots, and worms (software) scan the Web for information, index it, and bring it back to computer screens—saving minutes, or even hours, of search time. These intelligent agents comb the Web for new sites, or updated information on old ones, based on keywords you supply. You will learn how to develop your own agents, and how they can tap into the enormous potential that lies within the Web.

Explores ways that intelligent agents can help access information for business and home.

*Price: $49.99 USA/$67.99 CDN     User Level: Casual - Accomplished*
*ISBN: 1-57521-016-9       540 pages*

## Laura Lemay's Web Workshop:  Netscape Navigator Gold 3

*Laura Lemay & Ned Snell*

Netscape Gold and JavaScript are two powerful tools to help create and design effective Web pages. This book details not only design elements, but also how to use the Netscape Gold WYSIWYG editor. The included CD-ROM contains editors and code from the book, which will make your learning experience a quick and effective one.

Teaches how to program within Navigator Gold's rich Netscape development environment.

*Price: $39.99 USA/$53.99 CDN     User Level: Casual - Accomplished*
*ISBN: 1-57521-128-9       400 pages*

## Add to Your Sams.net Library Today
## with the Best Books for Internet Technologies

| ISBN | Quantity | Description of Item | Unit Cost | Total Cost |
|---|---|---|---|---|
| 0-672-30933-5 | | Windows NT 4 Server Unleashed (Book/CD-ROM) | $49.99 | |
| 1-57521-149-1 | | Laura Lemay's Web Workshop: Microsoft FrontPage (Book/CD-ROM) | $39.99 | |
| 1-57521-120-3 | | Teach Yourself VBScript in 21 Days (Book/CD-ROM) | $39.99 | |
| 1-57521-087-8 | | CGI Developer's Guide (Book/CD-ROM) | $45.00 | |
| 1-57521-141-6 | | Laura Lemay's Web Workshop: JavaScript (Book/CD-ROM) | $39.99 | |
| 1-57521-096-7 | | Teach Yourself Web Publishing with HTML 3.2 in 14 Days, Professional Reference Edition (Book/CD-ROM) | $59.99 | |
| 1-57521-016-9 | | Bots and Other Internet Beasties (Book/CD-ROM) | $49.99 | |
| 1-57521-128-9 | | Laura Lemay's Web Workshop: Netscape Navigator Gold 3 (Book/CD-ROM) | $39.99 | |
| | | Shipping and Handling: See information below. | | |
| | | TOTAL | | |

Shipping and Handling: $4.00 for the first book, and $1.75 for each additional book. If you need to have it NOW, we can ship product to you in 24 hours for an additional charge of approximately $18.00, and you will receive your item overnight or in two days. Overseas shipping and handling adds $2.00. Prices subject to change. Call between 9:00 a.m. and 5:00 p.m. EST for availability and pricing information on latest editions.

### 201 W. 103rd Street, Indianapolis, Indiana 46290

**1-800-428-5331 — Orders    1-800-835-3202 — FAX    1-800-858-7674 — Customer Service**

Book ISBN 1-57521-140-8

# Installing the
# CD-ROM

The companion CD-ROM contains all the source code and project files developed by the authors, plus an assortment of evaluation versions of third-party products. The installation program will create a *Microsoft FrontPage Unleashed* group in your Program Manager and place several icons within it that you can launch. To install, please follow these steps:

# Windows 95 Installation Instructions

**NOTE**

If you have the AutoPlay feature of Windows 95 enabled, the CD-ROM will install automatically. If you have disabled the AutoPlay feature, please follow the instructions below.

1. Insert the CD-ROM into your CD-ROM drive.
2. From the Windows 95 desktop, double-click on the My Computer icon.
3. Double-click on the icon representing your CD-ROM drive.
4. Double-click on the icon titled setup.exe to run the CD-ROM installation program.

# Windows NT Installation Instructions

1. Insert the CD-ROM into your CD-ROM drive.
2. From File Manager or Program Manager, choose Run from the File menu.
3. Type `<drive>\setup` and press Enter, where `<drive>` corresponds to the drive letter of your CD-ROM. For example, if your CD-ROM is drive D:, type `D:\SETUP` and press Enter.
4. Follow the on-screen instructions in the Guide to the CD-ROM program.